Foundations of Cognitive Grammar

VOLUME II

Descriptive Application

FOUNDATIONS OF COGNITIVE GRAMMAR

VOLUME II

Descriptive Application

Ronald W. Langacker

Stanford University Press Stanford, California

Stanford University Press
Stanford, California

Printed in the United States of America

CIP data appear at the end of the book

To the memory of
Margaret F. Langacker
(1937-1988)

Preface

IT WAS IN the spring of 1976 that I began developing the conception of language structure that has come to be known as **cognitive grammar**. At that time theoretical linguistics was languishing in the hard-fought but ultimately rather pointless debate between proponents of "generative" vs. "interpretive semantics," which pivoted on the still-contentious issue of whether syntax represents a distinct and autonomous component of the linguistic system. Though hardly a neutral bystander, I felt that neither camp was attacking the basic conceptual problems that needed to be resolved before that issue could be examined in a meaningful way. So one day I sat down to do just that, assuming (with the immodesty befitting a linguistic theorist) that my own efforts to formulate a natural and viable theory were unlikely to yield a product very much worse than those currently available. My strategy was to start anew by ignoring all extant theories as such, without however forgetting the factual knowledge and certain specific insights on which they were based (i.e. to raze the buildings but salvage some of the lumber). Within a few years, I had constructed a basic conceptual framework (then labelled **space grammar**) that no doubt seemed equally bizarre to linguists of all theoretical persuasions. This reaction was attributable in no small measure to superficial reasons (terminology; notation; the heavy use of diagrams), but was also due to the radical nature of the theory's central claims (the symbolic nature of grammar; the notional definability of basic grammatical classes) and the unfamiliarity of the world view it manifested. As a consequence it tended to be ignored in the busy theoretical marketplace.

The original framework has changed very little. As I and my students have probed more deeply and applied it to more languages and a vastly greater range of grammatical phenomena, it has undergone refinement and substantial elaboration, but nothing in the way of basic revision. What has changed to some degree is the prevailing intellectual context. Over the same period, many other linguists have also been responding, in their individual ways, to the imperative of their own insight and the perceived inadequacies of the generative conception. And of course, generative theory itself has both evolved (occasionally in the direction of reasonableness) and diversified into an unruly gaggle of subtheories. The present marketplace is thus a bazaar jammed with purveyors offering a kaleidoscopic array of theories. Against this backdrop, many aspects of cognitive grammar appear more obvious and less innovative than when initially formulated. Even so, the theory embodies such a fundamentally different perspective that it is still considered outlandish by many linguists—especially (I like to think) those untainted by any serious knowledge of it.

Gradually, however, the linguistic scene is starting to take on a different cast. This volume appears at a time when cognitive grammar faces a potential threat of respectability (in limited circles, to be sure). More importantly, substantial numbers of scholars whose diverse and often lonely research efforts fit comfortably under the rubrics of **cognitive** and/or **functional linguistics** are coming together to form a synergistic and self-conscious movement (which now, with the founding of the International Cognitive Linguistics Association and the journal *Cognitive Linguistics*, has a firm institutional basis). Congenial developments in related disciplines, most notable perhaps being the advent of *parallel distributed processing* (Rumelhart and McClelland 1986b; McClelland and Rumelhart 1986), have created a climate in which the cognitive-functional conception of language has a reasonable chance to flourish and establish its broad intellectual significance. Finally, the scholarship and accessible literature representing this general outlook are rapidly approaching a critical mass, as witnessed by a flood of recent books (e.g. Brugman 1989; Bybee 1985; Croft 1990; Fauconnier 1985; Givón 1989; Haiman 1985; Janda *to appear*; Johnson 1987; Kemmer *in press*; Kövecses 1990; Lakoff 1987; Lambrecht *in press*; Rudzka-Ostyn 1988; Talmy *to appear*; Vandeloise 1986; Wierzbicka 1988), not to mention an impressive catalog of articles and dissertations. The ideas are out there waiting to be applied, extended, tested, and evaluated, and the prospect of a coherent synthesis is neither distant nor unrealistic.

These two volumes represent the backbone of my own contribution to this movement. Vol. 1 (appearing in 1987) attempted to articulate a philosophy and to fashion an optimal set of tools for the characterization of linguistic structure. The present volume can be thought of as an instruction manual providing guidance and suggestions for how to use those tools. As such it does not pretend to offer a full or definitive treatment of any one of the many topics it covers (although some, e.g. the semantics of the English auxiliary, receive extended, in-depth treatment). The task of actually using the tools for large-scale construction devolves upon those with the drive and focus to pursue a single topic with fanatic devotion. That usually means graduate students. Indeed, the most extensive illustration and substantiation of cognitive grammar is afforded by a string of revelatory doctoral dissertations that I am proud to have been associated with: Lindner 1981; Tuggy 1981; Casad 1982; Hawkins 1984; Vandeloise 1984; Rice 1987a; Smith 1987; Cook 1988a; Fong 1988; Maldonado *to appear*; van Hoek *to appear*.

Out of all those who deserve acknowledgment—including the scholars I have learned from, the colleagues who have offered comments and constructive suggestions, the family and friends who have provided support during a difficult period, and the many people who have at one time or another professed to see some value in this lengthy project—I want to single out the aforementioned graduate students (and others I cannot cite individually) for their special and indispensable contributions, both personal and intellectual. Without the security of tenure, they have been willing to pursue a non-establishment vision they believe in, with full cognizance of the likely professional consequences. Regardless of theoretical orientation, I think we can all agree that such courage deserves to be admired, if not tangibly rewarded.

R. W. L.

Contents

Foundations of Cognitive Grammar

VOLUME II

Descriptive Application

Review and Introduction

THE TWO VOLUMES of *Foundations of Cognitive Grammar* introduce a new and fundamentally different conception of language structure and linguistic investigation. Despite being published several years apart, they are conceived as integral, mutually supportive facets of a single cohesive work. Their respective subtitles, *Theoretical Prerequisites* and *Descriptive Application*, reflect distinct emphases (though each has both theoretical and descriptive concerns and can perfectly well be read independently). Vol. I discussed organizing assumptions, presented the basic theoretical framework, and introduced the tools deemed necessary for the optimal description of linguistic structure. The present volume suggests how to use these tools. By systematically examining central aspects of nominal, clausal, and extraclausal structure in English, as well as selected problems in a variety of other languages, it provides tangible and appreciable illustration of the kinds of analyses the theory affords.

Though agnostic on the question of innateness, and the extent to which linguistic structure reflects special evolutionary adaptations, cognitive grammar does consider language to be indissociable from other facets of human cognition. Only arbitrarily can language be sharply delimited and distinguished from other kinds of knowledge and ability. Rather, it emerges organically from the interaction of varied inherent and experiential factors—physical, biological, behavioral, psychological, social, cultural, and communicative—each the source of constraints and formative pressures. Because many of these factors are the same or very similar for all speakers, language structure evinces considerable universality and is quite amenable to prototypic characterization. At the same time, every language represents a unique and creative adaptation to common constraints and pressures as well as to the peculiarities of its own circumstances. It thus requires a full, explicit description that is nonetheless sensitive and individually tailored.

Cognitive grammar ascribes to language an organization that is both natural and minimal granted its communicative function of allowing conceptualizations to be symbolized by phonological sequences. It claims that a linguistic system comprises just three kinds of structures: **semantic**, **phonological**, and **symbolic** (a symbolic structure residing in the relationship between a semantic and a phonological structure—its two **poles**). It further restricts allowable structures in a way that should greatly simplify and clarify the problems of language acquisition and language processing. The **content requirement** limits permitted structures to (parts of) overtly occurring expressions, to **schematizations** of permitted structures, and to **categorizing relationships** between permitted structures. Hence the only structures posited are those which are either directly apprehended (i.e. sound sequences and what they are understood to mean) or else derived from such structures by the fundamental, well-established cognitive abilities of abstraction and categorization.

A speaker's linguistic knowledge is not conceived as an algorithmic constructive device giving (all and only) well-formed expressions as "output." Instead, it is more modestly characterized as an array of **units** (i.e. thoroughly mastered structures—cognitive routines) available to the speaker for the categorization of **usage events** (actual utterances in the full richness of their phonetic detail and contextual understanding). Such units arise by a process of schematization based on the reinforcement of recurrent features; thus each embodies a commonality observable across a series of usage events. The units abstracted in this manner constitute a speaker's knowledge of linguistic convention (his "internal grammar," to use the somewhat misleading Chomskyan metaphor). Employing this knowledge, whether in a speaking or a listening capacity, implies some relationship between conventional units and usage events. Termed **coding**, this relationship involves an event's simultaneous categorization by a substantial number of units, each pertaining to a particular facet of its structure. An expression's **structural description** (its status vis-à-vis the grammar) resides in the set of categorizing relationships thus established.

Any aspect of usage events is subject to schematization, which can be carried to any degree of abstraction. As a consequence, the linguistic system subsumes units representing the same phenomenon at varying levels of detail and resolution. These form hierarchies in which a schema at a given level is **elaborated** (or **instantiated**) by subschemas, each of which conforms to its specifications but is more precise and finely specified. At the same time, the dialectic of language use—in which units must often be stretched to accommodate usage events not wholly congruent with their specifications—gives rise to new conventional units that constitute **extensions** from more basic ones. The result is that a typical linguistic category is **complex**: it is not defined by any single unit, but comprises a constellation of units that may be quite diverse despite an overall family resemblance. Cognitive grammar conceives of such a category as a **network** whose vertices (or "nodes") are semantic, phonological, or symbolic units of any size or kind. Usually clustered around a prototype, these units are linked by categorizing relationships of elaboration and extension, each unit and each relationship having some degree of cognitive salience (ease of activation).

A central tenet of the theory is that grammar reduces to symbolic relationships between semantic and phonological structures. In contrast to the generative dogma that grammar (or at least syntax) represents an "autonomous component" distinct from both semantics and lexicon, it maintains that lexicon, morphology, and syntax form a continuum of meaningful structures whose segregation into discrete components is necessarily artifactual. It claims, moreover, that this entire range of phenomena can be fully and optimally analyzed as residing in configurations of symbolic structures that conform to the content requirement. Every grammatical construct is thus attributed both conceptual and phonological import and is seen as inhering in the symbolic relationship between the two. The symbolic units of a language are heterogeneous, and differ even qualitatively owing to their position along certain parameters, notably specificity and **symbolic complexity** (analyzability into smaller symbolic elements). However, their distribution along these parameters is essentially continuous and does not offer any principled basis for dividing them into discrete components.

The symbolic units generally thought of as "lexical items" tend to be morphologically simple and quite specific in both their semantic and their phonological content. Their meanings do of course range widely along the specificity scale. And if **lexicon** comprises the fixed expressions of a language, it subsumes not only single morphemes and polymorphemic stems and words, but also thousands of multiword **conventional expressions** (clichés, idioms, standard collocations, etc.) representing usual ways of expressing oneself in a language. The units generally thought of as "grammatical" are more schematic semantically and often phonologically. So-called "grammatical morphemes" have specific phonological shapes, and though their meanings tend to be quite abstract, they are not necessarily more so than those of certain lexical items. Symbolic units highly schematic at both the semantic and the phonological poles are posited for the characterization of basic grammatical classes. Semantically, for instance, a noun is said to designate a 'thing' (in an abstract, technical sense), while phonologically it might be characterized (for a given language) as 'a sequence containing at least one vowel'. Grammatical rules take the form of **constructional schemas**, which are both schematic and symbolically complex. A constructional schema reflects the commonality observable across a set of complex expressions, hence its own organization mirrors the complexity of the expressions it schematizes.

This **symbolic alternative** to the autonomy thesis presupposes an appropriate view of linguistic meaning (Langacker 1988d). Cognitive semantics dismisses as erroneous the traditional focus on objective reality and conditions for truth. As a mentalistic theory must, it forthrightly identifies meaning with *conceptualization* (in the broadest sense), i.e. with *mental experience*, which is ultimately to be explicated in terms of cognitive processing. It further takes an **encyclopedic** approach, rejecting as both unmotivated and untenable any strict or specific demarcation between semantics and pragmatics, or linguistic and extra-linguistic knowledge (Haiman 1980). Considered inappropriate is the metaphorical folk model that portrays expressions as containers holding fixed and limited quantities of meaning (Reddy 1979). An expression is better conceived as providing access to a potentially very large array of concepts, conceptual complexes, and even whole knowledge systems, which it invokes in a flexible, open-ended manner (Moore and Carling 1982). A conception evoked as part of an expression's meaning is referred to as a **cognitive domain**, and the full complement of such conceptions as its **matrix**. Clearly, the domains of a complex matrix are not all on a par: some are central to the expression's semantic value (hence obligatorily accessed), others more peripheral. This aspect of an expression's semantic multiplicity must be distinguished from another, which is basically orthogonal to it. Specifically, an expression used with any frequency is typically **polysemous**—it has not just one meaning but a variety of related senses, each comprising a matrix with multiple domains. These senses form a complex category, in accordance with the network model.

Restricting ourselves to individual senses, the term **predication** is used for a given meaning of any expression (regardless of its size or type), and **predicate** for the meaning of a single morpheme. A fundamental notion of cognitive semantics is that a predication does not reside in conceptual content alone but necessarily incorporates a particular way of construing and portraying that content. Our capacity to construe the same content in alternate ways is referred to as **imagery**; expressions describing the same conceived situation may nonetheless be semantically quite distinct by virtue of the contrasting images they impose on it. Numerous dimensions of imagery can be discerned. One dimension is the level of specificity at which a situation is characterized (e.g. *move* vs. *run* vs. *sprint*). A second is **scope**, i.e. the array of content a predication specifically evokes for its characterization; *The door opened easily* necessarily implies an agent, for instance, whereas *The door opened* does not. A third dimension of imagery is construal relative to different background assumptions and expectations (consider *stingy* vs. *thrifty*). The fourth dimension pertains to perspective and subsumes such factors as vantage point, orientation, and **subjectivity** vs. **objectivity** (defined as the extent to which an entity functions asymmetrically as the subject vs. the object of conception). Finally, predications invoking the same content can be distinguished by the relative prominence accorded various substructures. Just two kinds of prominence will be mentioned at this juncture. First, within the **base** provided by the content that falls within its scope, every predication **profiles** (i.e. designates) some entity. For example, *hub*, *spoke*, and *rim* all invoke as their base the overall configuration of a wheel but contrast semantically by virtue of profiling different portions of it. Second, expressions that designate *relationships* accord varying degrees of prominence to the relational participants. In particular, one participant—termed the **trajector**—stands out as the *figure* within the profiled relationship. For instance, *above* and *below* apparently have the same conceptual content and profile the same spatial configuration. Their non-synonymy can only be attributed to figure/ground organization: whether the higher participant is construed as being located in relation to the lower one, or conversely.

With a properly formulated conceptualist semantics, it becomes possible to envisage a symbolic account of grammar. The lexico-grammatical resources of a language include a vast inventory of fixed expressions, both simple and symbolically complex, together with a host of schemas describing classes and constructions. An expression's grammatical class is determined by the nature of its profile. A basic distinction is drawn between **nominal** and **relational** expressions, depending on whether they profile a thing (abstractly defined) or a relationship. Nominal expressions include nouns and other noun-like elements (e.g. pronouns). Within the class of relational expressions, verbs are distinguished from such classes as adjectives, adverbs, prepositions, infinitives, and participles in virtue of designating a **process** as opposed to an **atemporal relation**. A process is characterized as a relationship followed sequentially in its evolution through conceived time, whereas an atemporal relation—whether simple (**stative**) or complex (comprising multiple component states)—views a scene holistically.

Grammar resides in patterns for combining simpler symbolic structures to form progressively more complex ones. Any such combination is referred to as a **construction**. It consists of two or more **component structures** that are **integrated** to form a **composite structure**. At each pole, integration of the component structures is effected by **correspondences** established between their substructures, and intuitively we can think of the composite structure as being derived by superimposing the corresponding entities. More technically (and more accurately), a construction is characterized as an assembly of symbolic structures linked by correspondences and categorizing relationships. This technical clarification is important because component structures are not in general describable as "building blocks" that are stacked together to form the composite expression. Often (if not typically), the composite structure displays *emergent* properties not discernible in any component taken individually: it may be more precise or inclusive in its specifications, invoke another cognitive domain, or impose an alternate image (e.g. a different profile).

Hence the component structures are best described, not as *constituting* the composite structure, but rather as *categorizing* certain facets of it and as *motivating* to some degree the form-meaning pairing it embodies.

Nevertheless, the formation of symbolically complex expressions does rely on conventional patterns of composition (it just does not rely on them *exclusively*). In cognitive grammar, a compositional "rule" assumes the form of a constructional schema: a template representing in schematic terms the common relationships among component and composite structures observable across the set of specific expressions that support its extraction. A constructional schema's semantic pole amounts to a rule of semantic composition. Such rules capture the regularities inherent in the compositional process and are thus essential to the creation and understanding of novel complex forms. Still, semantics is only partially compositional unless one makes it so as a matter of definition by imposing artificial and indefensible boundaries (e.g. between semantics and pragmatics, or literal and figurative language; Rumelhart 1979).

Standard grammatical concerns are readily addressed in this framework. Traditional classes are distinguished on the basis of their profiles (and certain other properties). The symbolic view of constructions, involving bipolar integration based on correspondences, affords a revealing account of grammatical valence. The basic **grammatical relations**, subject and direct object, are characterized not only prototypically in terms of semantic roles (agent and patient), but schematically as the primary figure (i.e. trajector) and the secondary figure at the clausal level of organization. Such notions as **head, complement**, and **modifier** are also straightforwardly defined: at a given level of constituency, the head is that component structure whose profile corresponds to the composite structure profile; the other component is a complement or a modifier depending on whether it *elaborates* a salient substructure of the head, or whether one of its salient substructures is *elaborated by* the head. For example, *above* is the head of the prepositional phrase *above the door*, since the phrase as a whole inherits its relational profile; *the door* is a complement because it elaborates a schematic participant saliently evoked by the preposition. At a higher level of constituency, *sign* is the head of *(the) sign above the door*, for the overall expression designates the sign. The prepositional phrase is a modifier at this level because the head, *sign*, elaborates its trajector.

Another fundamental concern is **distribution**: the problem of specifying which elements are allowed to occur in particular constructions, especially when the precise inventory is evidently subject to neither semantic nor phonological prediction. A natural solution is available in cognitive grammar owing to its **usage-based** (or "bottom-to-top") character, i.e. its emphasis on specific expressions and the extraction therefrom of low-level schemas as well as those representing higher levels of abstraction. A construction (or structural pattern, as the term is understood in this context) usually constitutes a complex category, a network whose nodes are constructional schemas linked by categorizing relationships of elaboration and extension. Thus a high-level schema describing a broad generalization does not exist in isolation; rather it is one node in a network that also includes subschemas corresponding to special cases of the general pattern, which may in turn have subschemas, and so on. The specification that a given element's occurrence in the construction accords with established convention is cast in the form of a constructional subschema which incorporates that specific element as one component structure. Instead of the information being specified by a contentless diacritic (such as a "rule feature"), it is provided by a structural frame that consists solely of symbolic units (both specific and schematic) and can be thought of as one, extrinsic facet of the element's characterization.

A variety of matters generally regarded as necessitating an autonomous account of grammar—including distribution, a pattern's degree of productivity, and whether an element is optional or obligatory—are viewed in cognitive grammar as consequences of a network's configuration, one dimension of which is the salience (likelihood of activation) of its individual nodes. In coding, a usage event is simultaneously categorized by many conventional units, each corresponding to a particular aspect of its structure. Each categorizing unit represents a complex category containing numerous conventional units with the potential to be selected for that purpose. Nonetheless, in a single episode of structural description some particular unit is chosen as the network's **active node** to categorize the target event; the target is then judged as well- or ill-formed (with respect to the relevant aspect of its structure) depending on whether the categorizing relationship is one of elaboration or extension. What then determines the choice of active node? As befits the complexity and variability of distributional phenomena, the competition's outcome is not necessarily consistent or preordained. Presumably it reflects the interaction of two, often antagonistic factors: a unit's intrinsic salience, and the extent of its overlap with the target. A usage event tends to activate potential categorizing units to the extent that it shares their content and organization. Other things being equal, specific structures or low-level schemas hold the advantage in this competition, because in comparison to high-level schemas, their detailed specifications provide many more points of possible overlap. On the other hand, a higher-level schema may be sufficiently salient to impose itself as the regular pattern, winning the competition in all cases (except, perhaps, when pitted against a well-entrenched specific form, e.g. an irregular past-tense verb of frequent occurrence, such as *ate*). In short, problems of distribution and productivity are best conceived in terms of activation and the relative accessibility of competing patterns. They do not in principle show what *kinds* of structures constitute these patterns, or demonstrate that grammar is autonomous in the sense of requiring something other than symbolic structures for its characterization.

Let me call attention to certain recent developments that mesh well with cognitive grammar and are far more significant than their coverage in these two volumes would tend to indicate. Of prime importance is the growing recognition that *metaphor* is a pervasive and fundamental aspect of our mental life; far from being merely decorative, it is a vehicle for understanding (even constructing) our experience that generally transcends individual linguistic expressions (Lakoff and Johnson 1980; Lakoff 1987; Turner 1987; Lakoff and Turner 1989; Sweetser 1990; Fong 1988). Its relevance here is twofold: many (if not most) of the cognitive domains invoked by predications are metaphorically structured; and at the analytical level, metaphor exerts a powerful influence on linguistic theorizing (12.1). A second development is the theory called *construction grammar* currently being formulated by Fillmore and others (Fillmore 1985, 1988; Brugman 1988; Fillmore, Kay, and O'Connor 1988). In many respects, cognitive grammar is basically congruent with construction grammar: in its usage-based nature; in its treatment of constructions as complex categories; and in its notion that part of a lexical item's characterization resides in the structural frames (constructional schemas) in which it occurs. It appears, in fact, that anything statable in construction grammar has a direct analog in cognitive grammar. The primary difference is that proponents of the former would not necessarily accept the latter's reduction of grammar to symbolic relationships—grammatical classes and other constructs are still thought of as representing a separate dimension of linguistic organization. The third development is the emergence of *parallel distributed processing* as a serious alternative to traditional processing models (Rumelhart and McClelland 1986b; McClelland and Rumelhart 1986). Its influence is observable in the idea that the units comprising a complex category compete for activation and the privilege of categorizing a usage event (cf. Elman and McClelland 1984; Elman 1985; McClelland and Elman 1986). Its broader relevance to cognitive grammar is explored in 12.3.

Let me also call attention to some major themes of the present volume. Its prime objective is of course to elucidate the symbolic alternative to autonomous theories of grammar and to demonstrate its viability. A summary discussion of this issue is offered in 12.2. A second recurrent topic is the interplay between *prototypes* and highly abstract *schemas* in the characterization of certain fundamental linguistic categories. A subject, for example, is prototypically an agent, but can always be described abstractly as the primary clause-level figure. Both prototypical and highly schematic values are similarly proposed for such notions as direct object, noun, verb, possession, motion, and substance. It is not unreasonable to suppose that basic categories like these owe their universality to rudimentary, presumably inborn cognitive abilities (e.g. to impose figure/ground organization on a scene), which are reflected in the schematic characterizations. However, these abilities emerge initially and are typically manifested through specific conceptualizations grounded in basic-level everyday experience, thus giving rise to the category prototypes (agent, patient, physical object, etc.). The other major theme of this volume is the extensive parallelism observed between nominal and clausal structure. Nouns and verbs must be recognized as the two preeminent categories at the lexical level, while nominals (i.e. "noun phrases") and finite clauses are equally universal and grammatically significant at a higher level of organization. When due allowance is made for the polar conceptual opposition between nouns and verbs, the relationship between a noun and a full nominal proves to be quite analogous to that holding between a verb and a finite clause.

This last theme motivates the organization of the present volume. Part I discusses nominal structure, and Part II deals with clause structure in a way that highlights their similarities. Considered in Part III are phenomena whose scope extends beyond the confines of a single clause, as well as a number of general theoretical issues. When taken together, Vols. 1 and 2 exhibit a comparable overall scheme, on two levels. In terms of grammatical structure, Vol. 1 began with the characterization of individual morphemes and proceeded to examine the nature of their combinatory relationships; Vol. 2 continues this progression from simpler to increasingly more complex symbolic expressions. Likewise, the ideas presented become progressively more specific. Vol. 1 started with organizing assumptions and then articulated the basic theoretical framework. Vol. 2 now applies these notions, often in painful detail, to a substantial range of representative grammatical constructions.

Part I
NOMINAL STRUCTURE

AMONG THE MOST cohesive and readily delimitable syntactic constituents are **nominals** (i.e. "noun phrases"). They are pivotal to the characterization of numerous grammatical constructions and must be posited for the cogent description of any language. Part I examines the internal organization of this fundamental and universal constituent type. In accordance with the principles of cognitive grammar, a conceptual account is offered for the basic elements of nominal structure.

Ch. 1 focuses on nouns. It describes the conceptual basis of the noun category and then extends the analysis to nominalization. Ch. 2 characterizes nominals in terms of four semantic functions: the specification of a type, the instantiation of that type, quantification, and grounding. Ch. 3 explores more carefully the notion of grounding and deals with well-known phenomena involving quantifiers. Finally, Ch. 4 examines nominals from the standpoint of their internal grammatical structure. A variety of issues and constructions are dealt with, including modifiers, classifiers, possessive constructions, and the problems of noun classes, inflection, and agreement.

CHAPTER 1

Nouns

THE DESCRIPTION OF nominals most revealingly begins with a characterization of nouns, their conceptually autonomous structural core. This chapter reviews a proposed semantic characterization of the noun class and then applies it to the analysis of nominalizations and other abstract nouns. Subsequently examined are nominal periphrasis and issues pertaining to productivity and regularity.

1.1. Conceptual Basis

A major concern of cognitive grammar is to describe the conceptual import of grammatical constructs. Numerous constructs are characterized with reference to certain "idealized cognitive models" (Lakoff 1987) that approach the status of archetypes, being grounded in everyday experience and fundamental to our conception of the world. One such model supports the characterization of both the noun and verb classes.

1.1.1. *A Cognitive Model*

We think of our world as being populated by discrete physical objects. These objects are capable of moving about through space and making contact with one another. Motion is driven by energy, which some objects draw from internal resources and others receive from the exterior. When motion results in forceful physical contact, energy is transmitted from the mover to the impacted object, which may thereby be set in motion to participate in further interactions.

Let us refer to this way of thinking about the world as the **billiard-ball model**. This archetypal folk model exerts a powerful influence on both everyday and scientific thought, and no doubt reflects fundamental aspects of cognitive organization. Our concern here is with its linguistic import, particularly its role in providing the conceptual basis for certain grammatical constructs.

Among these constructs are the universal categories **noun** and **verb**. Aspects of the billiard-ball model correspond directly to the noun and verb prototypes: discrete physical objects are clearly prototypical for the class of nouns, and their energetic interactions for the class of verbs.

Conceptually, physical objects and energetic interactions stand in polar opposition to one another. To see this, let us first consider the elemental components of the billiard-ball model. There are four such components: space, time, material substance, and energy. The essence of space and time is **extensionality**; together they provide a multidimensional setting within which the other two components are manifested. Moreover, we think of material substance as being manifested primarily in space (we can thus ask *Where is the sand?*, but hardly **When is the sand?*), whereas energy is only observable through change and thus requires time for its manifestation. I will therefore refer to space as the **domain of instantiation** for material substance, and time for change and energy.

Being composed of material substance, physical objects are instantiated in space, and we think of them as having spatial locations. An object is discrete because it incorporates a restricted quantity of substance and consequently has a limited spatial expanse—ideally, in fact, it is spatially continuous and quite compact (hence a ball or a rock comes closer to the archetypal conception than does a rope or a flock of geese). The spatial compactness of objects contrasts with their temporal expansiveness. We conceive of objects as stable entities that endure indefinitely unless subjected to destructive forces (cf. Givón 1979, pp. 320–23); limitations on their extension through time are not an inherent aspect of the billiard-ball model. Moreover, an object is autonomous, in that its spatial existence at a given moment does not intrinsically depend on any other object or on its participation in an interaction.

Interactions are maximally opposed to physical objects with respect to all these properties. An interaction does not reside in physical substance, but rather in the transfer of energy and the change thereby induced. Time and not space is thus an interaction's domain of instantiation, and the domain in which we think of it as being located. Also reversing what we observed for objects, an archetypal interaction is discrete, compact, and continuous along the temporal axis, but spatially expansive: at the very least, its spatial extension includes the locations of its various participants and the trajectories they follow through its duration. Finally, an interaction does not exist independently of its participants. Though we can perfectly well conceptualize an object separately from any interaction involving it, the conception of an interaction inherently presupposes some reference—however vague or schematic—to the entities through which it is manifested. Objects are therefore **conceptually autonomous**, and interactions **conceptually dependent**.

1.1.2. *An Abstract Characterization*

One hardly risks controversy in suggesting that physical objects and energetic interactions serve as the respective prototypes for the noun and verb categories. But what about these classes overall? Many nouns and verbs depart from the prototype, sometimes quite drastically, and it seems impossible to find any distinguishing property shared by all members of either class. It is thus a basic doctrine of modern linguistics that nouns and verbs cannot be notionally defined. Experience nonetheless teaches us to be wary of any consensus among linguistic theorists (as among economists or soothsayers). In fact, I would argue that universal categories of such fundamental grammatical significance should be expected to have a conceptual basis. Some speculative but reasonably precise proposals were presented in Part II of Vol. 1 (see also Langacker 1987b).

Any quest for a notional definition of nouns or verbs faces two daunting problems. First, since each class is extremely heterogeneous, a characterization compatible with all class members will necessarily be quite abstract. If there is any conceptual content shared by a representative set of nouns (e.g. *fork*, *blood*, *flash*, *archipelago*, *intermission*, and *insight*), it must be highly rarified. Second, the same event can often be described by either a verb or a noun (consider *It flashed* vs. *It emitted a flash*). This suggests that objective, truth-conditional factors are insufficient to distinguish the two categories—the basis for the distinction cannot reside solely in the situations being described, but must also depend on how we conceive and structure them. Though a characterization of this sort is beyond the scope of traditional, objectivist semantics, it is achievable granted a subjectivist theory of meaning based on cognitive processing. Pivotal to such a theory is our capacity for **imagery**, i.e. our ability to construe a conceived situation in alternate ways. Once this capacity is recognized, the noun and verb classes can be attributed conceptual import despite the extreme rarification of their content: their primary semantic value resides in a particular type of construal, and is thus imagic in character.

Schemas representing the semantic commonality of the noun and verb classes must be considerably more abstract than even the conceptually austere billiard-ball model. A characterization embracing the full range of nouns or verbs (not just prototypical instances) requires highly schematic constructs, with respect to which certain components of that model constitute special cases. Our initial concern is with nouns. The proposed schematic definition states that a noun **profiles** (i.e. designates) **a region in some domain**, where a **region** is defined abstractly as a **set of interconnected entities**. This schematic characterization corresponds to the billiard-ball model's conception of material substance instantiated and distributed continuously in the spatial domain. The model's notions of *material substance* and *continuity* are reflected in the schema's more abstract reference to *entities* and *interconnection*. Similarly, whereas the model invokes the conception of *physical space*, the schema simply refers to *some domain*.

Let us examine the notions that figure in the proposed schematic characterization. A nominal referent can be instantiated not just in space, but in any cognitive domain, basic or abstract (Vol. 1, Ch. 4). The noun *moment*, for instance, profiles a region in the basic domain of time, and *yellow* in color space (i.e. a range of possible color sensations). More abstractly, the calendrical cycle and the musical scale are the respective domains for *month* and *note*, while the conception of a performance is a non-basic domain supporting the instantiation of *intermission*.

I use the term **entity** in a maximally general sense. It indicates anything one might refer to for analytical purposes: objects, relationships, locations, sensations, points on a scale, distances, etc. Crucially, it is not required that an entity be discrete, individually recognized, or cognitively salient. Thus any expanse of material substance qualifies as an entity, be it an entire physical object, a recognizable part thereof, or any patch of substance (however small) selected arbitrarily from the whole. Less tangible examples of entities include a sound, a span of time, a light sensation at a certain point in the visual field, the difference in length between two lines, and the absence of material substance at a particular location.

It is not the character of individual entities that is important, but rather the fact that they are **interconnected** and thereby constitute a region. At the requisite level of abstraction, the notion of interconnection is not tied to any specific objective factors: it is a matter of construal, to be explicated in terms of cognitive processing. Two entities are said to be interconnected when those cognitive events whose occurrence constitutes their conception are coordinated as facets of an integrated, higher-order cognitive event. Consider, for example, the conceptualization of two lines, A and B, being equal in length. The conception of line A must reside in the occurrence of some cognitive event, possibly complex, that we can refer to as [e_A]. The occurrence of another event, [e_B], similarly constitutes the conception of line B. Conceptualizing the two lines as being equal in length requires not only the coactivation of [e_A] and [e_B], but also the execution of certain cognitive operations, [e_i], responsible for assessing and comparing the magnitudes of their linear expanse. The full conception therefore consists in the occurrence of the higher-order cognitive event [[e_A]-[e_i]-[e_B]], which has [e_A] and [e_B] as components. By definition, then, lines A and B collectively constitute a region. The **interconnecting operations** [e_i] establish them as a region by comparing (and thus coordinating) their constitutive cognitive events, [e_A] and [e_B].

Interconnecting operations can be of various sorts. At the extreme, the mere co-conception of two entities as part of a single mental experience is sufficient to establish them as a region.[1] The comparison of two entities also serves to interconnect them, as do cognitive operations that register their relative position in a domain (e.g. a judgment of spatial proximity). We further establish a region whenever we conceptualize a set of entities as facets of an integrated whole, for instance in imagining a group of dogs cooperating to pull a sled, or envisaging how a set of puzzle pieces fit together. Yet another sort of interconnecting operation is the recognition of entities as being instances of the same type. In addition, I assume that any conception of continuous extensionality along a parameter involves, at some level of cognitive processing, a sequence of interconnecting operations whose very occurrence constitutes that conception. The perception of a line, for example, must involve more than just the registration of visual input representing various points along its linear extension—it also requires operations that integrate these percepts so that experientially we perceive a continuous, unitary structure.

As a consequence, any physical object qualifies as a region by virtue of the continuous extensionality of its material substance: patches of substance (which need not be discrete or individually recognized) are united as a region by the very cognitive operations that mentally represent the continuity of their expanse. More abstractly, the continuously extended *absence* of material substance constitutes the region profiled by nouns like *hole*, *dent*, and *cavity*, and the absence of a certain activity for *pause*, *break*, and *intermission*. The entities comprising an *archipelago* are discrete, individually discernible, and separated by substantial stretches of water; it is not physical continuity that establishes them collectively as a region, but rather an assessment of their spatial proximity (when viewed on a certain scale), together with the recognition that all these entities instantiate the same type specification (*island*). The stars in a *constellation* may not even be spatially contiguous—what unites them as a region is their conception by observers as points in the outline of a fancied schematic image. Finally, a group of dogs can be referred to as a *team* when they are conceived as co-participants in the process of pulling a sled; the very conception of this cooperative endeavor effects their construal as a region.

The examples indicate that this abstract notion of a region is highly flexible and suggest its potential viability as a schematic characterization of nouns. Of course, not every region comes to be designated by a noun. As defined, regions are utterly ubiquitous, arising whenever entities are co-conceived. Most

[1]This may constitute the essential value of *and*, taken in its most neutral (or "logical") sense (see 11.2.1).

remain latent, however, in the sense that their status as regions is not exploited for any further cognitive processing.[2] Only a small proportion are singled out for even marginal conscious awareness, and of these, relatively few achieve sufficient cognitive salience and communicative utility to be profiled by nouns. Although one cannot predict in absolute terms whether a region will in fact receive this linguistic blessing, its chances increase to the extent that it approximates the category prototype, whose specific properties thus afford at least statistical predictions concerning class membership. The schema, by contrast, is too abstract to be predictive. Instead it specifies a type of construal that, while representing what all nouns have in common, is applicable to essentially any content.

A noun is thus claimed to profile a region in some domain, where the term region is understood abstractly, in a way that sometimes conflicts with its spatial origin. To avoid these spatial connotations, I often state more simply that a noun profiles a **thing**. The word *thing* is polysemous (often suggesting a physical object), but the sense I intend is one that can probably be identified with the noun-class schema and occurs in expressions like *another thing* and *something*. Observe that in the frame *Another thing I really like is X* one can substitute for *X* virtually any sort of noun: concrete or abstract (*your dress* vs. *your diligence*); singular or plural (*a kitten* vs. *kittens*); count or mass (*a steak* vs. *steak*). Only the names of particular places and people appear to be excluded (?*Another thing I really like is* {*Nebraska*/*Cary Grant*}), presumably because *place* and *person* are entrenched as alternatives to *thing* having greater specificity.

The fundamental distinction between count and mass nouns depends on whether the profiled region is construed as being **bounded** within the scope of predication in its domain of instantiation. For physical substances, the domain of instantiation is generally space. *Lake* is thus a count noun because it designates a limited body of water whose boundaries are specifically included in the scope of predication (i.e. they are inherent to the conception of a lake). By contrast, *water* is a mass noun. Though instantiated in space, water is not intrinsically bounded in this domain: the noun itself does not impose any limits on the quantity of the profiled substance, which can be recognized as a valid instance of the category irrespective of such limits. Water is of course bounded in the sense of being distinguished from other substances; we can say that it occupies a circumscribed portion of **quality space** (Langacker 1987b). There is nevertheless a discrepancy between the domain of bounding (quality space) and the domain of instantiation (physical space), where water lies scattered about in lakes, ponds, puddles, rivers, oceans, raindrops, and tears. It is by an assessment of qualitative uniformity reflecting their common

[2]For instance, any portion of a brick is a region (characterized by the continuous extension of material substance), but attention tends to focus on the brick as a whole.

location in quality space that these myriad and spatially discontinuous instantiations of water are tied together as an abstract region.

Bounding is one of four interdependent properties distinguishing count and mass nouns, the others being **homogeneity**, **contractibility**, and **replicability**. A region is bounded when some limit is imputed to its set of constitutive entities. A *constellation* is therefore bounded because it incorporates only a limited set of stars, and a *lake* because, in tracing through its liquid expanse in any direction, one eventually reaches an endpoint. A mass noun imputes no such limit, and further portrays its profiled region as being homogeneous; though substantial internal diversity can often be observed (consider *furniture*), this is neutralized by construing the designated mass at a sufficiently high level of abstraction. Conversely, a count noun's designatum is sometimes uniform internally (e.g. *lake*; *brick*), but its boundary—an inherent aspect of its characterization—introduces a modicum of heterogeneity. A mass noun displays contractibility in that any subpart of an instance is itself a valid instance of the category, which is generally not true of count nouns. Thus, whereas a fragment of *a brick* (count noun) is not itself a brick, both the fragment and the brick as a whole instantiate the substance *brick* (mass noun). Lastly, when one instance of a count-noun category is added to another, the result is two separate instances (e.g. *two lakes*); this is the property I call replicability. On the other hand, when two instances of a mass-noun category are combined, the result is a single, expanded instance. We therefore refer to *the water* (singular mass noun) *in those two lakes*.

1.1.3. *A Polar Opposition*

Suppose, then, that a noun is correctly described as profiling a region in some domain, i.e. a set of interconnected entities. What about verbs, the polar opposite of nouns? Along with such categories as adjectives, adverbs, and prepositions, verbs belong to a class of predications that I refer to as **relational**. The most schematic definition of a relational predication specifies merely that it **profiles interconnections** (as opposed to either the entities interconnected or the region thereby established). Interconnections therefore figure in the schematic characterization of both relational and nominal predications. What distinguishes the two types is whether the special prominence called profiling is accorded to a set of interconnecting operations per se or to the region formed by the entities they interconnect.

Consider the adjective *parallel* (as in *Lines A and B are parallel*). It presupposes the conception of two lines and profiles a set of interconnections specifying their relative positions in the spatial domain. For the sake of concreteness, we can think of these interconnections as cognitive operations that assess the spatial offset between the two lines at representative points along their expanse, and that register identity throughout in the magnitude of these offsets. Now by definition the occurrence of these interconnecting operations establishes a region having the lines as component entities. The relational predication *parallel* does not, however, profile this abstract region, but rather the operations themselves (or the relationship whose conception therein resides).

Several **levels of organization**[3] can be discerned in this example and correspond to different linguistic expressions, as diagrammed in Fig. 1.1. Recall that a line is itself a region whose constitutive entities are interconnected by

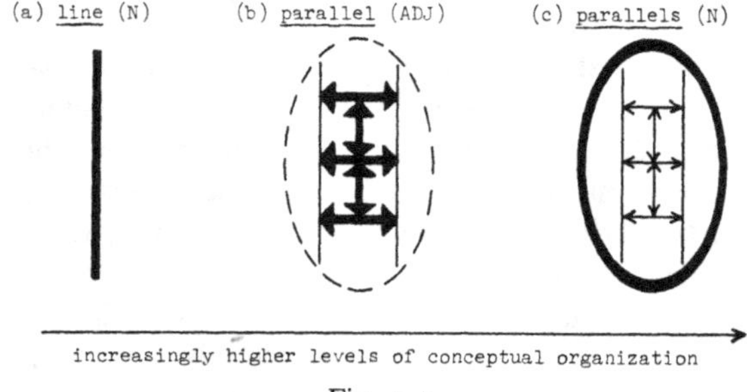

Fig. 1.1

cognitive operations representing the continuity of its linear expanse. The nominal predication *line*, depicted in 1.1(a), profiles such a region. Sketched in (b) is the semantic pole of the adjective *parallel*. This higher-order structure incorporates two instances of the line conception, which it coordinates through the interconnecting operations described in the previous paragraph. These interconnections (shown as arrows) are profiled by the adjectival expression and establish the two lines as an abstract region. Since the region may remain latent at this level of organization, it is represented by a broken-line ellipse. The region can however be recognized as such, and even profiled by a nominal predication, notably the plural noun *parallels* (e.g. *Lines A and B are parallels*). This higher-level structure is obtained by shifting the profile from the interconnections to the region they establish, as indicated in (c). Observe that the lines partake of this profiling only collectively, by virtue of their constitutive role in the designated region.

Verbs are relational predications characterized by a special kind of internal complexity (Vol. 1, Ch. 7). An adjective like *parallel* profiles a single, internally-consistent configuration, i.e. a **state**, and can thus be termed a **stative relation**. A verb inherently represents a higher level of conceptual organization because it incorporates not just one but a sequence of such relations. It is claimed, specifically, that a verb comprises a series of stative relations distrib-

[3] A conceptualization is said to represent a "higher" level of organization when it arises through cognitive operations performed on more fundamental conceptions, so that it presupposes and incorporates these "lower-level" structures.

uted continuously through conceived time, and further, that the conceptualizer scans the component states in serial fashion (**sequential scanning**) rather than simply activating them holistically as a single gestalt (**summary scanning**). A relationship meeting all these specifications is termed a **process**. Hence every verb is said to profile a process, just as every noun profiles a thing.[4]

In the simplest case, all the component states of a process are identical, i.e. the verb merely profiles the continuation through time of a stable situation. An example is *parallel* in its verbal use (e.g. *Line A parallels line B*). As a verb, *parallel* simply construes the static situation of Fig. 1.1(b) as extending through time (and scans sequentially through the component states). Such a process is said to be **imperfective**. An imperfective verb is precisely analogous to a mass noun, as it manifests homogeneity (of component states), contractibility, non-replicability, and the absence of inherent bounding in its domain of instantiation, namely time (see Langacker 1987b). On the other hand, a **perfective** verb manifests the opposite properties and is therefore directly analogous to a count noun. Because its component states are not all identical, a perfective process profiles some kind of change through time, prototypically a physical action involving the transmission of energy.

For the noun class, we described both a prototype (*physical object*) and a schema (*thing*), the import of the latter consisting mainly in a way of construing conceptual content. Certain aspects of the prototype are reflected abstractly in the schema: the notions *space, material substance*, and *continuity* have the respective schematic counterparts *domain, entity*, and *interconnection*. For the verb class we have similarly posited both a prototype (*energetic physical interaction*) and a schema (*process*) whose primary import pertains to construal. In the prototype, one physical object moves through space and makes contact with another, resulting in a transfer of energy that has some effect on the impacted object. The verb-class schema is much more abstract: what all verbs have in common is essentially limited to the profiling and sequential scanning of a relationship distributed through conceived time. As for the nature of the profiled relationship, the schema specifies only the interconnection of entities in some domain. The schematic notions *interconnection, entity*, and *domain* are abstract counterparts of the prototype's *contact, physical object*, and *space*, respectively.

We saw previously that the noun and verb prototypes (*physical object* vs. *energetic interaction*) stand in polar opposition despite their common grounding in the billiard-ball model. A maximal opposition can also be observed between the noun and verb schemas, even though they employ the same abstract constructs (*interconnection, entity*, and *domain*). The contrast resides in both profiling (an aspect of construal) and level of organizational complexity. Whereas a noun profiles a thing, a relational predication designates a

[4] Also, this schematic notion of a process constitutes the meaning of the auxiliary verb *do*, just as one sense of *thing* corresponds to the noun-class schema.

set of interconnections. A verb, moreover, is an especially complex relation, in that it profiles a series of relational configurations, and further specifies their continuous distribution through time. There is also an abstract sense in which a thing is "contractive" or "point-like" in nature: a thing is established as such to the extent that its constitutive entities lose their individual salience, being subordinated to a unitary whole and profiled only collectively. By contrast, a process is doubly "expansive," first by its profiling of interconnections, and second by its temporal extension.

Proponents of different grammatical theories have concurred that nouns and verbs are basic categories which are in some sense maximally opposed. For example, Ross (1972b) placed nouns and verbs at opposite extremes of his category spectrum, flanking such intermediate classes as adjectives and prepositions. In similar fashion, government-binding theorists commonly represent nouns by the feature complex [+N, −V], and verbs as [−N, +V] (adjectives and prepositions being [+N, +V] and [−N, −V], respectively). The present analysis is radically different from such accounts because it offers an explicit characterization of nouns and verbs in terms of their inherent conceptual import. By so doing, it explains both the fundamental nature of these categories and their polar opposition.

1.2. Nominalization

Nouns are often derived from other classes, most commonly from verbs (e.g. *printer*, *draftee*, *vacillation*, *skiing*) and secondarily from adjectives (*clarity*, *freedom*, *helplessness*). Nominalization is not only pervasive but theoretically significant: certain of its properties are frequently taken as demonstrating the autonomy of grammar and the distinction between syntax and lexicon. We must therefore consider (at least in broad outline) how nominalization is accommodated in cognitive grammar, which makes very different claims about grammatical organization.

Several issues serve as reference points for the following discussion. From the truth-conditional equivalence of pairs like *explode/explosion*, it is often concluded that nouns and verbs are purely grammatical classes that lack inherent meaning. Moreover, when the implicit arguments of a nominalization are spelled out periphrastically, as in *the army's destruction of the village*, they are accompanied by certain "meaningless" morphemes (*'s*, *of*) that appear to function as grammatical markers and nothing more. Finally, whenever a pattern of nominalization is less than fully productive, or its output semantically unpredictable, it is generally considered lexical rather than syntactic.

Things look very different from the perspective of cognitive grammar. *Explode* and *explosion* are not considered semantically equivalent: nominalization involves a conceptual reification whose character can be explicated with reference to the notional definitions proposed for the noun and verb classes.

Also, the morphemes employed for nominal periphrasis are regarded as meaningful; the semantic values attributed to them are compatible with their meanings in other uses and figure straightforwardly in determining the composite sense of the overall nominal expression. Furthermore, the question of whether nominalization belongs to the syntax or in the lexicon does not even arise in cognitive grammar, which refuses to impose such an arbitrary boundary.[5] Neither the non-productivity of nominalization patterns nor the absence of full semantic predictability is problematic in this usage-based model (Vol. 1, Ch. 11).

1.2.1. *Kinds*

There are many kinds of nominalization distinguishable on the basis of semantic, morphological, and grammatical properties. The following description is far from exhaustive, but it does elucidate the conceptual import of a representative array of nominalization patterns. Along one parameter, they vary as to which facet of the underlying relational predication is selected for reification and profiling. A second dimension of variation pertains to the internal organization of the relational predication, in particular whether it represents the conception of a process type or a specific instance of that type.

1.2.1.1. *Alternate Profiling.* The simplest type of nominalization merely shifts the profile of a verb to some nominal entity evoked as part of its inherent structure. The profiled element is most commonly the verb stem's **trajector** (i.e. its internal subject), as in *complainer*, *dancer*, *blender*, *judge*, and *cook*. Other possibilities include the **landmark** (internal object) of the verb stem (*draftee*, *advisee*, *choice*), an instrument (*rocker*, *walker*, *probe*), a product (*painting*, *bruise*, *mark*), and some kind of setting or location (*diner, lounge, bowl* (= 'bowling alley')).

The semantic pole of such a nominalization is diagrammed in Fig. 1.2 (see also Figs. 8.8 and 9.12 in Vol. 1). The verb stem (V) and nominalizer (NR) are **component structures** that are integrated to form the **composite structure** (N). The verb stem profiles a process. It follows through time (indicated by an arrow) the evolution of a relationship between two nominal participants (shown as circles), its trajector (*tr*) and its landmark (*lm*). The nominalizing morpheme depicted is equivalent semantically to the *-ee* of *inductee*, *employee*, etc. Its **base** (or cognitive domain) consists of a schematically characterized process, and its profile is the landmark of that process. The dotted line indicates that the specific process profiled by V is placed in correspondence with the schematic process of NR (i.e. the two are equated). Also, the

[5] The question "Where's morphology?" (Anderson 1982) also fails to arise in this framework, which posits a continuum of symbolic units subsuming lexicon, morphology, and syntax. Asking that question is as senseless as asking "Where's lexicon?" or "Where's syntax?"—morphology isn't *somewhere*, it just *is*.

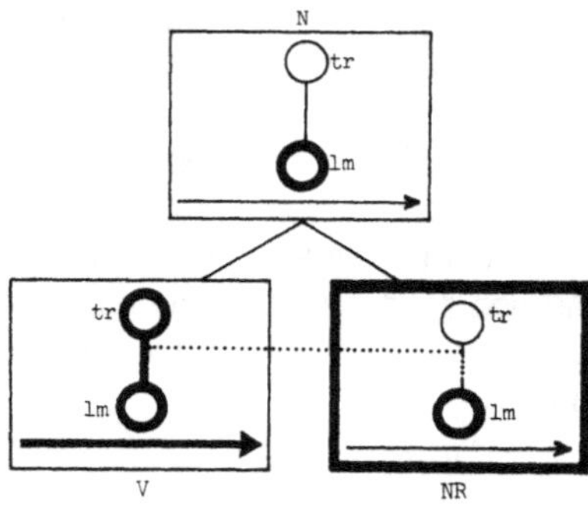

Fig. 1.2

heavy-line box identifies NR as the **profile determinant**, which means that its profile (not that of V) prevails at the composite structure level. Thus, since the composite structure inherits the content of V but the profiling of NR, the derived noun profiles the landmark of the process designated by the verb stem.

A second type of nominalization designates a single episode of the process profiled by a perfective verb: one can take a *walk*, make a *throw*, do an *imitation*, give out a *shout*, have an *argument*, witness an *explosion*, see a *flash*, perform an *operation*, receive a *nudge*, cop a *feel*, or deliver a *kick* in the pants. Granted the schematic characterizations proposed for the noun and verb classes, the analysis of episodic nominalizations is actually quite straightforward. Recall that a verb scans sequentially through a series of temporally distributed component states, each of which profiles a relation, as sketched in Fig. 1.3(a).[6] Now relations are entities (by our broad definition

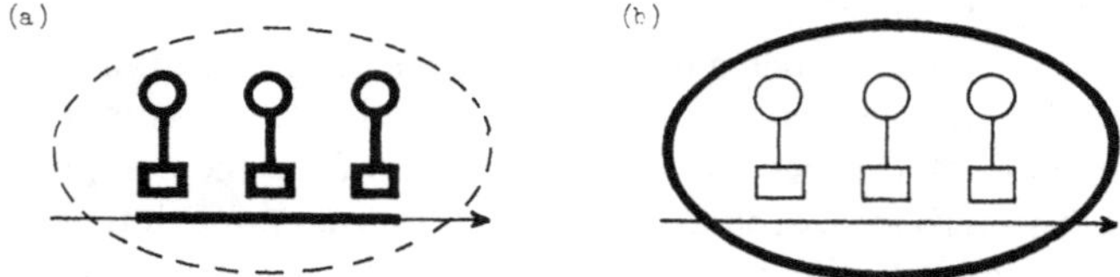

Fig. 1.3

of that term), and scanning through them sequentially is a type of interconnecting operation. Inherent in every verb, consequently, is an abstract region (i.e. a set of interconnected entities) comprising its component states. Within the verb itself this region is only latent, so it is depicted in (a) with

[6]Only three such states are shown explicitly in Fig. 1.3, but they stand for a continuous sequence. The heavy-line portion of the time arrow indicates sequential scanning, whose extension is referred to as the **temporal profile** of the process.

a broken-line ellipse. However, nothing prevents this latent region from being recognized as such, or even profiled, as shown in (b); the result is a derived noun that profiles a region whose constitutive entities are the component states of a process. This seems quite reasonable for the characterization of an episodic noun.

This account of nouns and verbs has the further advantage of explaining a striking asymmetry observable cross-linguistically in derivational patterns. It is normal for a language to display patterns of nominalization whereby virtually any verb can be nominalized with no essential modification of its conceptual content. Thus *complainer* does not add anything to the conceptual content of *complain*, nor *explosion* to that of *explode*—the semantic contribution of nominalization is limited to profiling (an aspect of construal). By contrast, the derivation of a verb from a noun is generally accompanied by the addition of conceptual content. For example, common values of denominal verbs include 'add N' (*salt*; *water*; *beautify*), 'remove N' (*weed*; *peel*; *declaw*), 'use N as an instrument' (*glue*; *pencil (a response)*; *head (a soccer ball)*), 'turn into N' (*coil*; *liquefy*; *vaporize*), and so on (cf. Clark and Clark 1979). This asymmetry reflects the intrinsic nature of nouns and verbs. A verb necessarily incorporates a series of component states that constitute a latent region, and being conceptually dependent, it makes inherent reference to its participants; a noun is thus derivable, with no effect on conceptual content, just by shifting the profile either to this region or to some participant. On the other hand, a noun is conceptually autonomous: we can normally conceptualize its designatum without conceiving of its participation in any higher-order process. Because a derived verb profiles such a process, verbalization requires the addition of conceptual content.

The fact that episodic nominalizations are count nouns follows directly from their characterization: an episodic noun profiles a region comprising the component states of a perfective process, and since such a process is inherently bounded, so is the region it forms (i.e. there is some limit to the set of constitutive entities). However, perfective verbs give rise to other nominalizations, typically derived by *-ing*, that function as mass nouns. Though verbs like *walk*, *complain*, and *sleep* are in some sense internally homogeneous, they are construed as occurring in bounded episodes, and are thus perfective, as shown by their ability to take the progressive:

(1) *Sylvester is {walking/complaining/sleeping}.*

The mass-noun status of the corresponding nominalizations is clearly demonstrated by data like the following:

(2)(a) *Walking is very good for one's health.*
(b) *McTavish always does a lot of complaining.*
(c) * *My cat does several sleepings every day.*

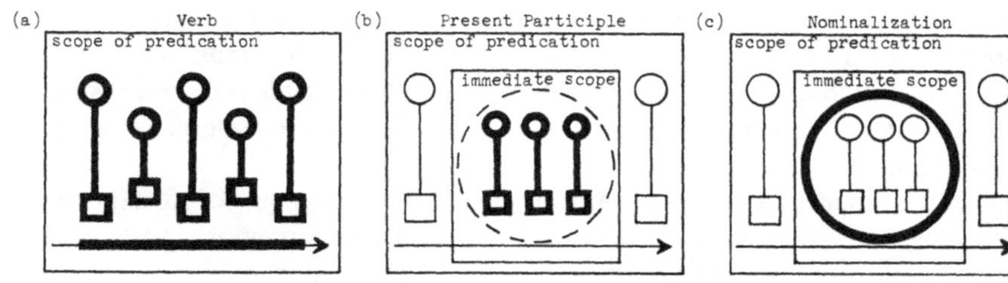

Fig. 1.4

Derived nouns like *walking*, *complaining*, *sleeping*, etc. require no determiner, take quantifiers that occur only with mass nouns (*a lot of* {*light*/ **lamp*}), and do not tolerate pluralization.

The fact that these nouns are derived by *-ing*, which also appears in the progressive construction, provides a clue to their semantic analysis. I have argued elsewhere (1987b) that the progressive *-ing* does three things to a perfective verb stem: (1) it construes the event holistically (by suspending sequential scanning); (2) it confines the profile to an immediate scope of predication consisting of an internal series of component states; and (3) it construes these states at a level of abstraction that neutralizes their differences. The impact of *-ing* is diagrammed in Fig. 1.4, where (a) represents a perfective stem, and (b) its present participle. As before, the profiled states implicitly define an abstract region. Nominalizations like *walking*, *complaining*, etc. represent a higher level of conceptual organization obtained by shifting the profile to this region, as shown in (c).

The mass-noun status of these expressions reflects the conceived homogeneity of the profiled region and the absence of bounding within the scope of predication. The constitutive entities are homogeneous by virtue of their common construal as 'representative internal states' of the process designated by the verb stem. The designated region can therefore be expanded or contracted without altering its basic character, so long as it is confined to such states; however, the endpoints of the process are necessarily excluded from the profiled region, being neither 'representative' nor 'internal'. Now by definition, the profile at a given level of organization is restricted to the scope of predication at that level, and in this construction the profile is coextensive with the immediate scope imposed by *-ing*. An expression like *walking* or *complaining* thus conforms to the characterization of a mass noun: the profiled region lacks inherent bounding within the scope of predication, since the endpoints of the process fall outside the relevant scope.[7]

The region profiled by a mass noun like *walking* or *complaining* can be

[7] The limitations imposed by the scope of predication itself are not sufficient to establish the count-noun status of a region—some kind of bounding *within* the scope of predication is required. A region coextensive with the scope is thus construed as unbounded.

regarded as an abstract "substance," for it is directly analogous to a physical substance such as *water*, *sand*, or *plastic*. Observe the following parallels, for example:

(3)(a) *We saw nothing but water anywhere we looked.*
(b) *We heard nothing but complaining all day long.*

(4)(a) *The water in those lakes is probably contaminated.*
(b) *The complaining in those gripe sessions is always bitter.*

(5)(a) *Three large buckets of water failed to douse the fire.*
(b) *Three solid hours of complaining failed to change his attitude.*

Recall that a physical substance is manifested discontinuously in its domain of instantiation (space); its myriad instantiations collectively form a region not because of spatial contiguity, but rather through an assessment of qualitative uniformity (i.e. a common location in quality space). Since a noun like *complaining* is characterized with reference to a process, its domain of instantiation is time, and the abstract substance it designates is similarly distributed discontinuously in this domain: the category is instantiated whenever somebody engages in the process *complain*. Despite their temporal (and also spatial) dispersal, these countless instantiations constitute an abstract region precisely because of their qualitative uniformity, each consisting of 'representative internal states' extracted from the same type of process.

This notion of an abstract substance permits the analysis of a large number of nominalizations and other abstract nouns, so it is important that we understand it clearly. The relationship between physical and abstract substances is analogous to that between physical objects and other sorts of regions, or between energetic interactions and other sorts of processes: though the former is in each case prototypical, one can posit a schematic characterization subsuming both it and other instances as special cases. For substances, the requisite characterization amounts to a schema for the mass-noun category, i.e. it incorporates the conception of an abstract region but specifically lacks the identifying feature of a count noun, namely inherent bounding in the domain of instantiation. Importantly, the region's constitutive entities need not exhibit continuity in this domain, and since anything qualifies as an entity (relationships, sensations, etc.), they can perfectly well be non-material.

As shown in Fig. 1.5, count and mass nouns can be regarded as inverses. The **matrix** for either type of noun (i.e. the full set of domains required for its characterization) includes both the domain of instantiation and any number of additional parameters pertaining to qualitative distinctions. A count noun is bounded and generally continuous in its domain of instantiation but need not be qualitatively uniform; whereas a *pencil*, for example, is bounded and continuous in physical space, its various subparts (the lead, the wood casing, the eraser) are composed of different substances and thus project to different

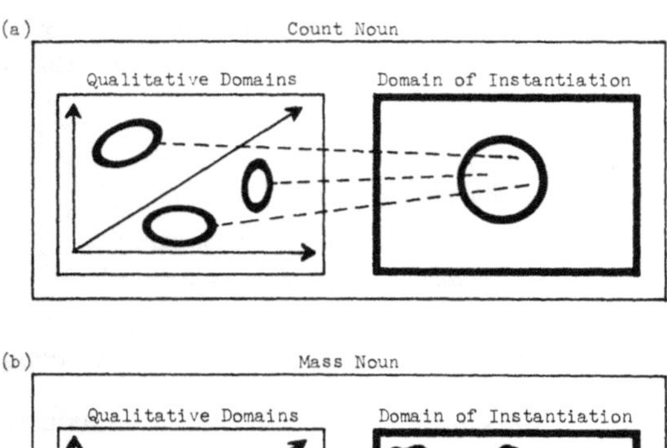

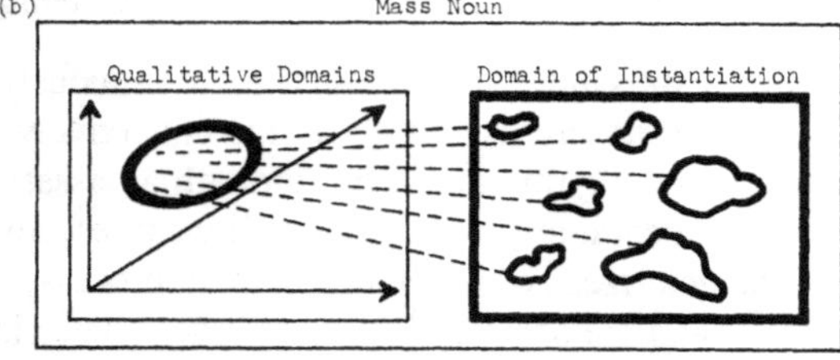

Fig. 1.5

areas of quality space. On the other hand, the hallmark of a mass noun is some kind of qualitative uniformity—its myriad instantiations all project to a common locus in quality space, and it is precisely this assessment of qualitative homogeneity that knits them together into an abstract region. Any number of separate instantiations are collectively construable as a single instance of the designated substance, and any expanse of the substance (whether continuously or discontinuously instantiated) counts as an instance even if it remains unbounded in the scope of predication.

The instantiations of a physical substance are material, and the domains invoked for its qualitative characterization pertain to such properties as color, viscosity, transparency, taste, particulateness, density, solidity, rigidity, brittleness, and so on. By contrast, the abstract substance designated by a noun like *walking* or *complaining* has no independent material existence, being manifested only through the occurrence of a process. Its constitutive entities are not patches of matter, but rather *relationships*, namely component states of the process in question. The qualitative characterization of the abstract substance resides in the very conception of this process: only through their construal as representative internal states of the process can a series of relationships be recognized as instantiating the substance.

Granted this type of analysis, there is no reason why only processes should be capable of providing the qualitative characterization of an abstract substance—an assessment of qualitative uniformity can just as well be based on a sensation or the conception of a stative relation. Consider a color term like *yellow*, which has a variety of alternate senses representing different grammatical categories:

(6)(a) *Yellow is definitely a cheerful color.*
(b) *I don't like that yellow wallpaper.*
(c) *There certainly is a lot of yellow in this painting.*

In (6)(a) *yellow* functions as a count noun, for it designates a bounded region in color space; in this type of usage, where a color is simply being described abstractly without regard to its distribution in space or the visual field, color space is both a qualitative domain and the domain of instantiation. Illustrated in (6)(b) is the adjectival sense of *yellow*, which profiles the relationship between a sensation from the *yellow* region of color space and some entity associated with that sensation. Our present concern is the usage in (6)(c), where *yellow* occurs as a mass noun that designates an abstract substance. Rather than treating the sensation in purely qualitative terms, this usage focuses on its distribution within some visual scene and thereby construes it as an abstract but quantifiable substance analogous to *water*, *steel*, or *nitrogen*. The visual scene is consequently the domain of instantiation, and the substance is neither continuous nor inherently bounded in this domain. The bounded region in color space profiled by the count-noun sense of *yellow* serves instead, in this mass-noun usage, to specify the qualitative uniformity that establishes its instantiations as an abstract region. It is instantiated at every place in the visual scene that gives rise to this type of sensation.

I suspect that nouns like *fear*, *anger*, *hope*, *anxiety*, and *joy* should be analyzed in parallel fashion. Each names an emotive sensation (just as *yellow* names a color sensation) and in uses like (7)(a) can be interpreted as designating a region in emotive space (just as *yellow*, in (6)(a), designates a region in color space):

(7)(a) *Fear is very similar to anxiety.*
(b) *I've noticed a lot of fear and anxiety around here.*

Moreover, they also have mass-noun uses, illustrated in (7)(b), that are reminiscent of the mass-noun sense of *yellow* (cf. (6)(c)).[8] When employed as a mass noun, a term like *fear*, *anxiety*, or *hope* pertains not to the quality of the emotive sensation per se, but rather to the extent of its manifestation in time and space or across participants. Hence the qualitative domain is distinct from the domain of instantiation, as is generally the case for mass nouns (Fig. 1.5(b)). An abstract substance like *fear* or *anxiety* is characterized quali-

[8] Additionally, the corresponding adjectives (*fearful, angry, hopeful, anxious, joyful*) are analogous to the adjectival sense of *yellow*, in that they profile the relationship between an emotive sensation and the individual in which it is manifested.

tatively with reference to some region in the emotive domain and is instantiated whenever some individual experiences the emotion in question. "Fragments" of such experience are the constitutive entities of the substance.

Under this type of analysis, even a noun like *freedom* can be analyzed as designating an abstract substance. Its qualitative description is provided by the stative relation *free*, which specifies the absence of restraints on its trajector. The substance has no independent material existence, but is instantiated whenever and wherever some individual finds himself in the specified circumstance. To be sure, this characterization does not exhaust the meaning of *freedom*—it does not, for example, address the additional value the word assumes in a political context. The analysis does however confront the central problem of such nominalizations by describing fairly precisely the conceptual reification they are claimed to exhibit.

Let us consider for now just one other type of nominalization, exemplified in (8):

(8)(a) *Abernathy's walk is peculiar.*
(b) *Ted Williams had a very graceful swing.*
(c) *That pitcher has a jerky delivery.*

The nouns *walk*, *swing*, and *delivery* are not functioning here as episodic nominalizations. Instead they designate a 'style' or 'manner' of carrying out the activity in question, just as *wine* and *glue* sometimes indicate a 'type' or 'brand' of the corresponding physical substance (*a dry wine; a good glue*). The analysis hinges in both instances on the claim that qualitative factors assume greater importance in these uses than spatio-temporal distribution. As a consequence, the domain of instantiation is identified with quality space itself (rather than physical space or time).

When *wine* is used as a mass noun, its instantiations project to a particular region of quality space (Fig. 1.5(b)); this region—call it Q—is specified by ranges of possible values along such parameters as taste, color, smell, viscosity, and so forth. For a given activity, like walking, we can similarly posit a set of qualitative parameters with respect to which instantiations can be situated: rate, energy level, how far forward the arms swing, the degree to which the walker sways from side to side, etc. There is once again a bounded region, Q, in this quality space such that any activity judged to be an instantiation of the category falls within it.

The qualitative sense of *wine* or *walk* (*a dry wine*; *a peculiar walk*) is diagrammed in Fig. 1.6. As noted, its domain of instantiation is identified with quality space. Additionally, region Q is adopted as the immediate scope of predication in this domain, and the profile is restricted to a limited subregion, Q′, within this scope. Because it profiles a proper subpart of Q in quality space, the resulting nominal expression has the approximate value 'brand

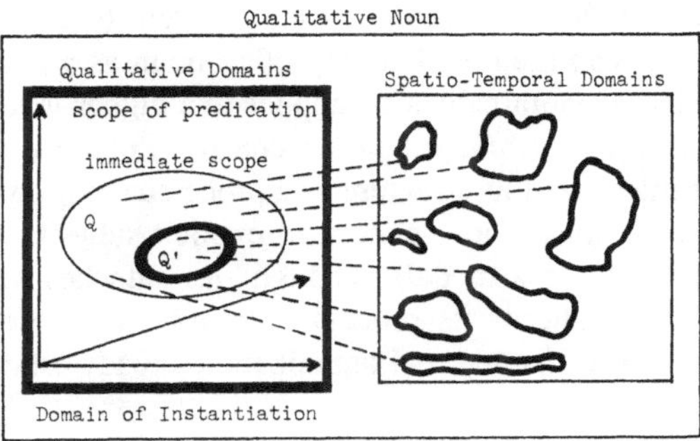

Fig. 1.6

(of wine)' or 'style (of walking)'. Moreover, its count-noun status is a direct consequence of its characterization: as a qualitative noun, *wine* or *walk* profiles a region (Q′) that is bounded within the immediate scope of predication (Q) in the domain of instantiation (quality space).

1.2.1.2. *Type vs. Instance Nominalizations.* A classic problem is the contrast between the two patterns of nominalization illustrated by *Zelda's signing of the contract* vs. *Zelda's signing the contract.* In the former, often called an "action" nominalization, the preposition *of* occurs between the nominalized verb and its notional object; in the latter, called a "factive" or "gerundive" nominalization, this *of* is absent (cf. Lees 1960; Fraser 1970; Chomsky 1970). These two kinds of nominalization are known to differ substantially in their grammatical properties. For example, an action nominalization can be modified by an adjective, does not tolerate an auxiliary verb, but does allow a definite article (with optional *by*-periphrasis):

(9)(a) *Zelda's reluctant signing of the contract*
(b) * *Zelda's having signed of the contract*
(c) *the signing of the contract (by Zelda)*

By contrast, a factive nominalization takes an adverb rather than an adjective, does occur with non-modal auxiliaries, but does not permit the definite article:

(10)(a) *Zelda's reluctantly signing the contract*
(b) *Zelda's having signed the contract*
(c) * *the signing the contract (by Zelda)*

In short, action nominalizations are parallel in structure to other nominals (compare (9)(a) to *Zelda's new friend from Detroit*), whereas factive nominalizations have the internal structure of a clause (apart from *-'s* and *-ing*).

What this suggests is that action and factive nominalizations differ with respect to the level of organization at which the nominalizing operation takes place. Action nominalization applies to a verb stem (e.g. *sign*), deriving a noun (*signing*) that can then act like any other noun as a nominal head. On the other hand, factive nominalization applies to a higher-level structure such as *sign the contract*, *reluctantly sign the contract*, or *have signed the contract*; we can characterize this structure as a processual expression that has all the ingredients of a finite clause except an explicit subject and a grounding predication (i.e. tense or a modal). Though *-ing* attaches to the verb from which this structure inherits its processual profile, it is the structure as a whole—with its clause-like internal organization already established—that is nominalized.

The terms "action" and "factive" were prompted by a semantic difference observed between the two kinds of nominalization. It was noted that only an action nominalization occurs as the subject of adjectives such as *meticulous*, which describe the manner in which the activity is carried out, whereas factive nominalizations are found in sentences that presuppose the factuality of the reified events:

(11)(a) *Sam's washing of the windows was meticulous.*
(b) **Sam's washing the windows was meticulous.*
(c) *Sam's washing the windows was a shock to everybody.*

Thus action nominalizations seem to focus on the event as a physical activity, which is consonant with the notion that only the verb stem is nominalized. The clause-like source of a factive nominalization is similarly compatible with its more abstract analysis as focusing on the fact that the designated event has indeed occurred. It should be noted, however, that these semantic characterizations are not only vague but also somewhat inaccurate. In different contexts, for example, various facets of an action nominalization can be highlighted, including the manner, the duration, the propriety, or even the factuality of the event:

(12)(a) *Harvey's taunting of the bear was merciless.*
(b) *Harvey's taunting of the bear lasted three hours.*
(c) *Harvey's taunting of the bear was ill-advised.*
(d) *Harvey's taunting of the bear came as a big surprise.*

Furthermore, "factive" nominalizations are sometimes used in contexts where it is clear that factuality is not assumed:

(13)(a) *I would definitely object to your taunting the bear (should you ever decide to do it).*
(b) *The very idea of his taunting a bear is so preposterous that I can't even contemplate it.*

Let me therefore propose an alternative analysis based on functional properties of the structure that undergoes the nominalization. A major theme unfolding in later chapters is that nominals and finite clauses show extensive parallels from the standpoint of semantic function. In particular, the semantic relationship between a simple noun and a full nominal (e.g. between *bear* and *the bear*) is held to be precisely analogous to that between a verb stem and a finite clause (e.g. *taunt* and *Harvey taunted the bear*). I argue in Ch. 2 that the semantic function of a simple noun is limited to specifying a **type**, whereas a full nominal designates a **grounded instance** of that type, i.e. an instance distinguished from others and situated with respect to speaker/hearer knowledge. Similarly, it is claimed that a verb stem merely specifies a process type, while a finite clause evokes a more elaborate conception in which the profiled process represents a grounded instance of the type. Hence *taunt* is a process type capable of being instantiated at any location in time and with any appropriate set of participants. The elements that combine with the stem to form a finite clause include the finite verb inflection (*-ed*) and the subject and object nominals (*Harvey*; *the bear*). Semantically, they anchor the type conception in time (relative to the ground) and tie it to specific participants, thereby converting it into the conception of an instance.

On the basis of semantic function, we can thus distinguish at least three levels of organization in the assembly of a finite clause: that of the verb stem, which merely provides a type specification; that of the finite clause as a whole, which profiles a grounded instance of the type; and an intermediate level which profiles an instance that is left ungrounded. Each level designates a process and gives rise to a particular sort of nominalization when the component states are construed as an abstract region and put in profile. Specifically, an action nominalization derives from a *process type*; a factive nominalization, from an *ungrounded instance* of the type; and a *that*-clause nominal from a *grounded instance*.

When only a verb stem is nominalized, the result is an action nominalization, e.g. *taunting*. Being based on a type specification (that of the verb stem *taunt*), the noun so derived itself represents the conception of a type rather than an instance, since reification per se has no instantiating function. The noun can however be employed as the head of a nominal, in which grounding and instantiation are effected by other elements; in *Harvey's taunting of the bear*, these functions are accomplished by the periphrastic specification of processual participants (see 1.2.2). The fact that various aspects of such nominals (manner, duration, etc.) can be highlighted by an appropriate context, as seen in (12), does not motivate the postulation of distinct meanings or underlying structures for the nominal or its head. Note that comparable variation is observable even with underived nouns like *party*:

(14)(a) *The party was boisterous.*
(b) *The party lasted three hours.*
(c) *The party was ill-advised.*
(d) *The party came as a big surprise.*

From the properties exhibited in (10), we concluded that "factive" nominalization applies to a structure that is like a finite clause except for the absence of an explicit subject and a predication of tense or modality. Intermediate in size between a simple verb stem and a finite clause, this structure is hypothesized to be intermediate in terms of semantic function as well: in contrast to a verb stem, the profiled process is construed as an instance rather than a type; but in contrast to a finite clause, the instance remains ungrounded. The fact that the nominalized structure incorporates a fully specified direct object supports the claim that it represents an instance and not just a type. Its ungrounded character follows from the lack of tense and modality, since these are the grounding predications for a finite clause.

This pattern of nominalization applies to an intermediate-level structure such as *cruelly taunt the bear*, a processual predication whose trajector is construed as being a specific individual but is specified only schematically. The result is a complex noun, *cruelly taunting the bear*, whose schematic trajector is then expressed through possessive periphrasis: *Harvey's cruelly taunting the bear*. The construal of the reified process as representing a particular instance renders it compatible with contexts that presuppose its factuality, as in (15)(a):

(15)(a) *Harvey's cruelly taunting the bear was a severe blow to his campaign for presidency of the S.P.C.A.*
(b) *Harvey's cruelly taunting the bear is something that could simply never happen.*

Examples like (15)(b) remind us, however, that the nominalization itself does not carry any strong supposition that the profiled event is factual. We can attribute this to the ungrounded character of the reified process. A process is grounded by being situated in time and reality relative to the speech event. In the absence of grounding, a process has no specific status in this regard—even a processual instance involving definite participants. An ungrounded instance can be conceived as occupying any position in time and as being either real or imagined.

Conceptual reification is also applicable to a full finite clause, which profiles a grounded instance of a process type. The result is a complex noun that can stand alone as a nominal and function as either the subject or the object of another clause:

(16)(a) ***That Harvey taunted the bear*** *is unfortunate.*
(b) ***That Zelda signed the contract*** *is simply false.*
(c) *Many people believe* ***that masturbation causes blindness****.*
(d) *Reagan denies* ***that he is responsible for tripling the national debt****.*

A finite clause portrays the designated process as having a particular status in regard to time and reality; for example, *Harvey taunted the bear* expresses the past reality of the profiled event, and when used alone as a full sentence it asserts that reality. The effect of reification (marked by *that*) is to "step back" from the situation—including both the event and its relation to the ground—and construe it as an abstract object or **proposition** capable of being manipulated, evaluated, and commented on. Instead of being asserted, this proposition is taken as one participant in a higher-order relationship (e.g. a relationship of belief, denial, evaluation, etc.), whence its role as a clausal subject or object.

1.2.2. *Periphrasis*

We turn now to the relationship between a finite clause and the corresponding action nominalization, e.g. between *Zelda signed the contract* and *Zelda's signing of the contract*. Despite their formal differences, the clause and the nominalization are semantically quite similar; in particular, *Zelda* is in each case understood as the subject of *sign*, and *the contract* as its object. In the generative tradition, attempts to capture this parallelism have followed either of two basic approaches. One approach, originated by Lees (1960), is to nominalize the clause by means of a syntactic transformation. The second, due to Chomsky (1970), claims that finite clauses and noun phrases are configurationally parallel in a way that permits a cross-categorial definition of the subject and object relations (cf. Jackendoff 1977). Neither approach accords a central role to *'s* and *of* or attributes them any semantic content—they are assumed to be empty markers inserted for purely grammatical purposes.

Both approaches conflict with the claims and assumptions of cognitive grammar, which does not permit syntactic derivations from underlying structures and does not define subjects and objects configurationally. Moreover, their treatment of *'s* and *of* violates a basic tenet of the framework: that so-called "grammatical markers" invariably have some kind of conceptual import, which may be quite abstract but is nonetheless essential to their function. Semantic characterizations of the nominalizing morphemes *-er*, *-ee*, and *-ing* have already been proposed (1.2.1.1). We must now examine the markings that accompany the "subject" and "object" of a nominalization, notably *'s*, *of*, and *by*. Each morpheme should be attributed a meaning that reflects its grammatical function and is naturally related to the values it assumes in other uses.

The function of these morphemes is periphrastic. When a verb is nominalized, its participants are no longer capable of being specified directly by a subject and object, as they are in a finite clause. The alternative is to specify them indirectly, as complements of a relational expression whose import, in effect, is to state explicitly that these complements represent participants of the nominalized verb. Grammatically, therefore, *Zelda* and *the contract* are not the subject and object of *sign(ing)* in *Zelda's signing of the contract* (as they are in the corresponding finite clause), but rather complements of the relational predications *'s* and *of*. The net result of these periphrastic constructions is nevertheless to identify them semantically with the appropriate participants.

To see how this works, we must first review the semantic structure of a verb and the nature of its relation to the subject and object of a clause. A verb is conceptually dependent: it profiles a set of interconnections involving one or more participants and thus makes inherent (though schematic) reference to these participants. In its construal of the scene, a verb portrays its participants with varying degrees of prominence. One is maximally salient in the sense of being selected as *figure* within the profiled relationship; this I call the trajector. If some participant other than the trajector is accorded special prominence, I refer to this as the (primary) landmark. The trajector and landmark of a verb are part of its internal semantic structure—its "inner subject and object," as Tuggy (1981) aptly describes them. Schematic reference to these entities is necessary to support the conception of the profiled interconnections.

When a verb functions as the head of a finite clause, it is generally accompanied by nominals that elaborate its trajector and landmark. These nominals are, by definition, the subject and direct object of the verb and of the finite clause. *Zelda* is therefore the subject in *Zelda signed the contract*, since it elaborates the schematic trajector of *sign(ed)*, while *the contract* elaborates its primary landmark and is thus the direct object. Semantic in nature, these elaborative relationships are not dependent on any particular constituency (which is generally variable—see Vol. 1, 8.4.2). They can even be characterized with reference to a trinary structure, as depicted abstractly in Fig. 1.7.

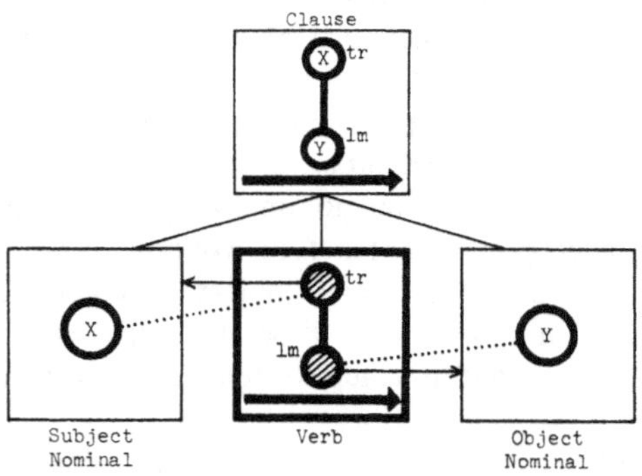

Fig. 1.7

The verb designates a process, and as profile determinant (clausal head), it lends its processual profile to the clause as a whole. The verb's schematically characterized participants serve as **elaboration sites (e-sites** for short); these are cross-hatched for ease of identification, and elaborative relationships are represented by arrows. Each such relationship is effected by a correspondence between a verbal participant and the profile of the elaborating nominal. Corresponding entities are construed as identical, and their specifications are superimposed in forming the composite structure. As a consequence, the subject's semantic specifications (abbreviated X) are inherited by the trajector at the composite structure level, whereas the object's specifications (labeled Y) are inherited by the landmark.

The structure in Fig. 1.7 can be regarded as the semantic pole of a constructional schema. That is, it specifies (in simplified fashion) the pattern of semantic integration that occurs in one basic type of finite clause and can be used as a template for assembling novel expressions of that type. According to this schema, the clausal head is processual (i.e. a verb) and profiles the interconnections that link the two elaboration sites. Nominalization thus renders a verb incapable of participating in this construction, since the derived noun is non-processual: though it incorporates the conception of a process, it represents a higher level of organization that does not profile interconnections but rather an abstract region whose constitutive entities are component states of that process (cf. Fig. 1.3). Should the speaker wish to characterize the schematic participants of the underlying process, he must therefore resort to other constructions.

Serving this purpose are periphrastic expressions with *of*, *by*, and *'s*, all of which are regularly employed in noun modifiers (e.g. *the rim of the canyon*; *a poem by Rimbaud*; *Zelda's toe*). Nominal periphrasis represents a special adaptation of these modifying constructions but does not alter their basic character—the expressions still function as noun modifiers, and the constructions conform to the general patterns established in other uses. What distinguishes the periphrastic variants is their application to a particular cognitive domain, namely the conception of a process. When this process corresponds to the profile of the nominalized verb, the conceptual import of the modifying relationship is to specify one of the verbal participants.

The preposition *of* is commonly considered meaningless, but I have argued elsewhere (1982b; Vol. 1, 6.2.2) that it designates an 'intrinsic relationship' between its trajector and landmark. Often the trajector is an inherent subpart of the landmark (*the tip of your nose*; *the back of my hand*; *a drop of water*; *most of that brandy*; *the center of the room*). In another variant, the landmark specifies the substance out of which the trajector is fashioned, or an ingredient that provides its essential character (*a bracelet of pure gold*; *a game of chance*; *a book of matches*; *several kinds of cheese*; *a moment of panic*; *a man of good taste*). *Of* is also employed with inherently relational nouns like *friend*, *father*, and *chief*, where its landmark represents the entity with respect to which the relationship is reckoned: *a friend of Tom*; *the father of the bride*; *the chief of that tribe*. Observe that when another preposition is substituted, the relationship it profiles is no longer intrinsic to the characterization of the head noun—*the father with the bride* is probably someone else's father (not the bride's), and *the chief from that tribe* may have become a chief only after leaving that tribe to join another.

We can profit from a closer look at expressions like *the father of the bride*, whose semantic pole is sketched in Fig. 1.8.[9] At the first level of constituency, *of* combines with *the bride* to form the prepositional phrase *of the bride*. The

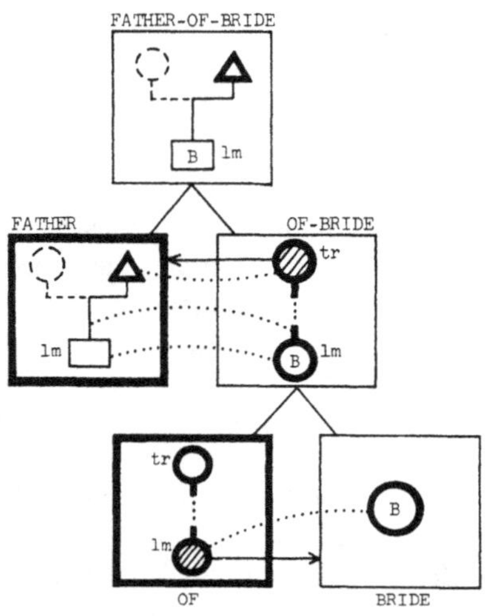

Fig. 1.8

preposition designates a stative relation that is characterized as constituting some kind of 'intrinsic relationship' but is otherwise schematic (hence the three dots in the line representing the profiled interconnections). *Of*'s landmark serves as e-site and is elaborated by *the bride*, which is thereby identified as the prepositional object. Since *of* is the head, the composite structure inherits its relational profile: *of the bride* designates an intrinsic relationship between the bride and a schematically characterized trajector.

The composite expression *of the bride* is in turn a component structure at the second level of constituency, where it combines with *father*, the head noun, as a prepositional-phrase modifier. Since one is a *father* only with reference to some other individual, this noun is inherently relational, taking for its base the conception of a parent-offspring relationship; it designates one participant in this relationship (the male parent), and the unprofiled reference individual (the offspring) can be thought of as a kind of landmark. The trajec-

[9]Definite articles are ignored, and the semantic specifications of *bride* are abbreviated as B. The fact that *bride* (like *father*) is a relational noun is not pertinent to this example.

tor of the prepositional phrase is an e-site elaborated by *father* and thus corresponds to the head noun's profile. Equally important, however, are additional correspondences that identify the parent-offspring relationship inherent in *father* with the 'intrinsic relationship' profiled by *of the bride*; because of these correspondences, the relationships are superimposed in forming the composite structure. We therefore interpret *the father of the bride* as indicating that the father's offspring is the bride in particular (not some other individual), and that the intrinsic relationship signaled by *of* is none other than their parent-child association.

Nominal periphrasis with *of* is very similar to the construction just described. The only essential difference between *the father of the bride* and *the signing of the contract* lies in the nature of their head nouns—both nouns incorporate a relational conception, but *father* profiles one participant in a stative relation, whereas *signing* reifies a process and designates the abstract region comprising its component states. The properties of a head are reflected in the e-site of its modifier, since the two are construed as specific and schematic representations of the same entity. *Of*'s use for nominal periphrasis thus induces a specialized variant in which its trajector represents the schematic conception of a reified process. This conception is diagrammed in Fig. 1.9(a).

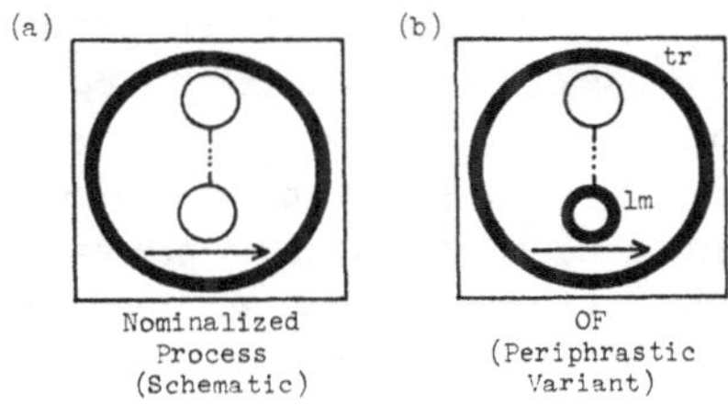

Fig. 1.9

The preposition's periphrastic variant is obtained by construing the reified process as the trajector of a higher-order stative relation whose landmark is a participant in that process, as shown in Fig. 1.9(b); in other words, *of* profiles the relationship between the reified process overall and one of its subparts (a participant). The resulting predication is fully consonant with *of*'s general value of designating an intrinsic relationship, since the conception of a process makes inherent reference to its participants (i.e. a process is conceptually dependent).

An explicit account of nominal periphrasis with *of* can now be offered. Examination of Fig. 1.10 reveals that *the signing of the contract* is structurally parallel to *the father of the bride* (Fig. 1.8), except that *of* has the special value just described. At the first level of constituency, the preposition's landmark—identified as a processual participant—is elaborated by *the contract*

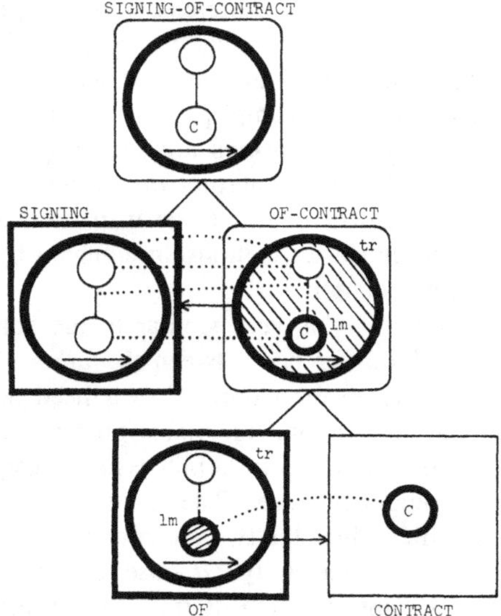

Fig. 1.10

and thus inherits its specifications (abbreviated C) in the composite structure. *Signing* elaborates the trajector of the resulting prepositional phrase, *of the contract*, at the second level of constituency; a correspondence between the trajector and the nominal profile effects this head-modifier relationship. Additional correspondences equate the specific process invoked by the head (namely *sign*) with the schematic process presupposed by the prepositional phrase, and further equate their respective participants. As a consequence, the composite expression designates an abstract region comprising the component states of the process *sign*, one of whose participants is further identified as *the contract*.

Beyond profiling the intrinsic relationship between a reified process and one of its central participants, the periphrastic *of* has very little content. *Of*-periphrasis is therefore quite flexible, as witnessed by the well-known ambiguity of expressions like *the shooting of the hunters*: either the trajector or the landmark of the verb stem can be specified by the *of*-phrase, depending on which one is selected as *of*'s landmark. Moreover, the prepositional object can be identified as the trajector of the underlying process whether its role is agentive (e.g. *the performance of the rock band*) or completely passive (*the disappearance of the money*). Also capable of nominal periphrasis are elements that are more specific in their conceptual content and hence more precise concerning the semantic role of the participant they introduce. *By*, for example, specifically identifies its object as the trajector of the nominalized verb and further suggests that its role is active to some degree. Expressions like **the disappearance by the money* are therefore peculiar (in contrast to *the performance by the rock band*), and *the shooting by the hunters* can only mean that the hunters did the shooting (not that they were shot). The *by* employed for nominal periphrasis is obviously quite similar semantically to the one that occurs in passives (cf. Langacker 1982b) or to identify the creator of an artistic work (*a film by Fellini*; *a symphony by Prokofiev*).

Nominal periphrasis with *by* is illustrated in Fig. 1.11. One conventional use of a *by*-phrase is to specify the trajector of a nominal whose landmark has already been specified through *of*-periphrasis; in the present example, *by*

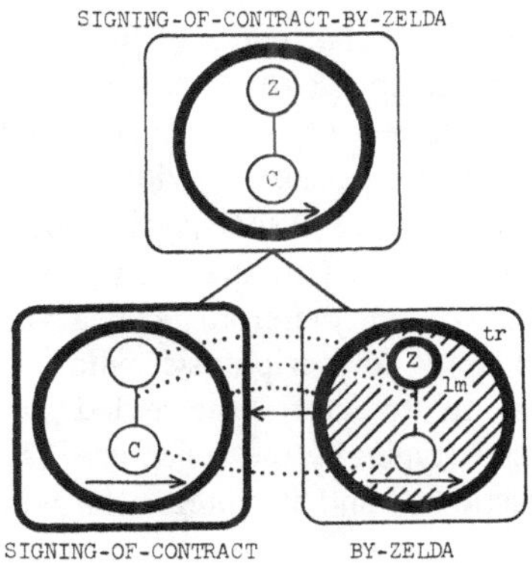

Fig. 1.11

Zelda combines with the composite structure from Fig. 1.10 to form the complex nominal expression *the signing of the contract by Zelda*. The trajector of *by* is a reified process (characterized only schematically), and its landmark—elaborated by *Zelda* at a lower level of constituency—is identified as the trajector of that process.[10] The constructional head *signing of the contract* elaborates the schematic trajector of its prepositional-phrase modifier, and correspondences equate the processes evoked by the two component structures as well as the processual participants. The resulting composite expression profiles a reified process both of whose central participants are specified.

Possessive inflection can also be employed for nominal periphrasis, most commonly to specify the trajector of the underlying process (*Zelda's signing of the contract*), but occasionally for its landmark (*Lincoln's assassination*).

[10] Like profiling, trajector/landmark assignation pertains to a particular level of conceptual organization. This sense of *by* involves three organizational levels: a process, the abstract region obtained by its reification, and a stative relationship between this region and one of the processual participants. It is neither unusual nor problematic for the same entity to function as trajector at one level and landmark at another.

Though standard, the term "possessive" is somewhat misleading, since the morpheme in question is used for the most diverse array of relationships, only some of which involve possession in the prototypical sense of 'ownership' (e.g. *my new car*; *Zelda's dog*). The morpheme also frequently marks the relationship between a whole and its parts (*your shoulder*; *the plane's propeller*), between associated individuals (*Roger's sister*; *their friends*), or between a setting and some entity situated therein (*Africa's wildlife*; *the play's central character*; *the year's major event*). Virtually any type of association is susceptible to possessive encoding. If each of us thinks of a prime number, and we then compare them, I might announce that *My prime number is larger than yours*—but obviously we do not own the numbers we have chosen.

If there is anything that all occurrences of the possessive morpheme have in common, it is that its landmark (the "possessor") is construed as some kind of **reference point** with respect to which another entity is identified. The morpheme's periphrastic use is consistent with this characterization, since it is perfectly natural to regard processual participants as reference points: a process cannot occur without its participants, and its location cannot be distinguished from theirs. We can therefore posit a variant of the possessive morpheme, specially adapted for periphrasis, whose cognitive domain is the conception of a process; its trajector is the reified process itself, whereas its landmark is a participant (typically the trajector). This variant is thus quite similar to the periphrastic *of*, and its integration with the nominal head is parallel to Figs. 1.10–11.

The periphrastic morphemes (*of*, *by*, and the possessive) have a variety of other uses, and in general they are semantically distinct. The semantic contrast is considerably attenuated in the periphrastic adaptations of these morphemes, if only because each invokes the conception of a reified process and profiles a stative relation between this process and a central participant. Hence the three are often interchangeable with only subtle differences in meaning, as in *the performance of the band* vs. *the performance by the band* vs. *the band's performance*. Despite this overlapping function, the semantic distinctions are not entirely obliterated. The notions 'reference point' and 'intrinsic relationship' still motivate the periphrastic uses of the possessive and *of*, whereas *by* underscores the active role of its object.

A final matter is the relationship between an adverbial modifier in a finite clause and the adjectival modifier that occurs in the corresponding nominalization, e.g. between *carefully* in *he drives the car carefully* and *careful* in *his careful driving of the car*. Their analysis appears to pose certain problems. By the assumptions of cognitive grammar, a difference in grammatical class implies a difference in meaning, yet the semantic contrast between *careful* and *carefully* is not self-evident (and is often denied). Moreover, the modifying relation between *careful* and *driving* seems quite parallel semantically to that between *carefully* and *drive*, despite the fact that the heads and modifiers represent different grammatical categories in the two constructions. What sort of analysis is capable of expressing both the similarities and the differences between the two constructions?

The key to the matter is the distinction drawn in cognitive grammar between conceptual content and how that content is construed (imagery). The adverb *carefully* and the adjective *careful* are perceived as being semantically equivalent because they have the same conceptual content and profile the same interconnections, as sketched in Fig. 1.12. Each invokes the conception

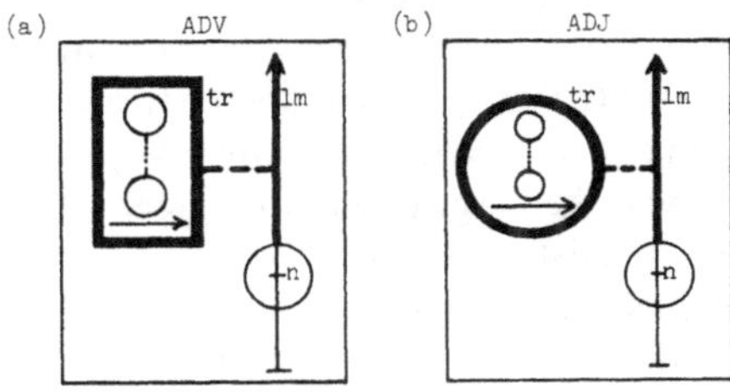

Fig. 1.12

of a comparison scale pertaining to the degree of care exercised in carrying out some activity and specifies that some process falls within that portion of the scale located beyond the neighborhood of the norm (*n*). Moreover, each predication chooses this schematically characterized process for its trajector and profiles the interconnections (specifically, the relationship of inclusion) between the process and the scalar region (a type of landmark).

The semantic distinction resides in whether the trajector is simply construed as a process, as in (a), or whether it is reified to form an abstract region, as indicated by the heavy-line circle in (b). Subtle though this contrast is, it constitutes a difference in meaning and is responsible for the difference in grammatical category. The schematic trajector in each case functions as an e-site in a modifying relationship, being elaborated by the head. Because its trajector is processual, structure (a) is adapted for the modification of a verb and is therefore categorized as an adverb. On the other hand, structure (b) is adjectival owing to the nominal character of its trajector and e-site. The modifying relationships are parallel nonetheless, for in both instances a process is situated within the landmark region of the scale, whether it retains its processual construal or undergoes reification.

1.2.3. *Predictability*

For the past two decades, theoretical discussions of nominalization (and of derivational morphology in general) have wrestled with the issue of whether this phenomenon is best accommodated "in the syntax" or "in the lexicon" (cf. Chomsky 1970; Jackendoff 1975; Aronoff 1976; Downing 1977; Levi 1978; Lieber 1981; Selkirk 1982; Bresnan 1982). On grounds of productivity and regularity, it has generally been concluded that nominalization is primarily a lexical phenomenon: whether a stem undergoes a particular pattern of nominalization cannot be predicted with any certainty, nor can the specific properties of the resulting form. Thus some kind of lexical listing is thought to be required.

The question of whether nominalization belongs "in the syntax" or "in the lexicon" presupposes the compartmentalization of linguistic structure into discrete "components." The issue is therefore meaningless from the standpoint of cognitive grammar, which posits for lexicon, morphology, and syntax an array of symbolic units that range continuously along such parameters as specificity, entrenchment, and symbolic complexity (Langacker 1988b). In many respects, however, the description of nominalization in this framework is compatible with lexicalist approaches. The very definition of a grammar (Vol. 1, Ch. 2) requires the listing of specific expressions that have achieved the status of conventional units. Since a grammar is non-constructive, the idiosyncratic properties of specific forms do not prevent their categorization by constructional schemas, whose function is thus analogous to that of lexical redundancy rules. Additionally, the "syntactic" derivation of a nominal such as *Zelda's signing of the contract* from an underlying clausal source is precluded by the highly restrictive **content requirement**.[11] Of course, these tenets of cognitive grammar hold not just for nominalization and derivational morphology, but for all facets of lexico-grammatical structure.

Any viable account of nominalization must come to grips with a number of basic observations. First, the picture offered by nominalization is not one of total chaos and idiosyncrasy—there are indeed patterns to be discerned and characterized. Thus a description cannot be limited to the listing of individual expressions. A second observation is that patterns vary in their degree of productivity, i.e. in whether they permit new formations, and whether they extend to all forms that meet their specifications. Nominalizations derived by *-er*, for example, are much more numerous and freely coinable than those formed with *-ee*. Third, many expressions that appear to instantiate a nominalizing pattern nevertheless have unpredictable semantic properties. They are often more specific than anything a rule could predict (hence an *elevator* is not just 'something that elevates') and may even conflict with the expected value (e.g. a *grinder* in yachting does not actually grind anything). As a fourth observation, note the dual function of nominalizing patterns: to characterize established expressions, and to permit the computation of novel in-

[11] The only units permitted in a grammar are (1) structures that occur overtly; (2) schematizations of such structures; and (3) categorizing relationships involving (1) and (2).

stantiations. Our conception of derivational rules must allow them to serve in both capacities. Finally, the correlations between the morphological and the semantic aspects of nominalization are inconsistent at best. A single morphological pattern may be used for multiple semantic relationships; for instance, a deverbal noun with *-er* can designate the agent, instrument, or location of the verbal process (*complainer*, *rocker*, *diner*). Conversely, the same semantic relationship may be signaled by different morphological devices, such as *-er* and zero for the processual trajector (*a flatterer* vs. *a flirt*).

These properties of nominalization are straightforwardly accommodated in cognitive grammar. To see just how, we must start with some basic ideas. A central feature of the framework is that the characterization of lexicogrammatical structure is effected solely by symbolic units, each residing in the association of semantic and phonological content. As noted, these units are variably situated with respect to three parameters: entrenchment, specificity, and symbolic complexity. Entrenchment pertains to how frequently a structure has been invoked and thus to the thoroughness of its mastery and the ease of its subsequent activation. Along the parameter of specificity, units range from particular expressions at one extreme, through schematizations at different levels of abstraction, to maximally schematic structures representing entire grammatical categories or constructions at the opposite extreme. A unit is symbolically complex if it incorporates other symbolic units as components; whereas morphemes, by definition, are symbolically basic, their successive integration gives rise to units of indefinite symbolic complexity.

These parameters provide the basis for rational definitions of some traditional notions and a coherent view of their interrelationship. One such notion is **lexicon**, which recent linguistic theory has characterized in wildly inconsistent ways.[12] To my mind, lexicon is most usefully and sensibly described as the set of *fixed expressions* in a language, irrespective of size and regularity. Thereby included as lexical items are morphemes, stems, words, compounds, phrases, and even longer expressions—provided that they are learned as established units, but regardless of whether their formation is in any way idiosyncratic. In terms of our three parameters, lexicon consists of those symbolic structures that are high in both specificity and entrenchment: they represent particular expressions (rather than schemas) that have achieved the status of conventional units. Symbolic complexity is not a factor, for lexical items can fall anywhere along this scale.

[12] Once thought of as a list of unpredictable details, lexicon is now conceived by many theorists as incorporating various kinds of rules, including rules of derivational morphology responsible for the computation of novel expressions. Other scholars (e.g. Akmajian, Demers, and Harnish 1984, p. 54) identify lexicon with the words of a language, even though expressions both larger and smaller than words have the status of lexical items, while words are often novel (and are in some languages the primary locus of grammatical structure).

For grammar, on the other hand, symbolic complexity is crucial. In fact, **grammar** can be quite simply defined as patterns for the successive integration of symbolic structures to form progressively more elaborate expressions. The traditional distinction between **morphology** and **syntax** depends on integration at the phonological pole: we speak of morphology when the composite structure falls at the word level or below with respect to the hierarchy of phonological complexity (Vol. 1, Ch. 9), and of syntax when the composite structure is larger than a word. Although we use grammatical patterns for the construction of novel expressions, these patterns are themselves established as conventional units and thus show some degree of entrenchment. They differ from lexical units in being schematic rather than specific—they do not represent particular expressions, but schematizations over sets of expressions parallel in formation.

It is claimed that all grammatical elements—morphemes, classes, and rules—are properly described in terms of schematic symbolic units. We have already characterized the meanings of representative "grammatical morphemes," such as *-ee*, *of*, and *by* (Figs. 1.2, 1.8–11); despite their semantic schematicity, they are phonologically specific and can therefore be regarded as lexical items exploited for grammatical purposes. Basic grammatical classes (noun, verb, adjective, count noun, etc.) are defined by symbolic units that are schematic at both the semantic and the phonological poles. Defining the class of nouns, for example, is the schematic unit [[THING]/[. . .]], where [THING] is understood abstractly (cf. 1.1.2) and [. . .] represents a highly schematic phonological structure (essentially, 'any segment sequence'). Grammatical rules take the form of constructional schemas, which specify the relationships among two or more component structures and the composite structure that results from their bipolar integration. Constructional schemas resemble class schemas in being schematic at both poles but differ by virtue of their inherent symbolic complexity: they schematize expressions that are symbolically complex, and serve as templates for the assembly of analogous expressions.

The notion that grammatical rules are simply schematizations of particular expressions is one of several factors I have in mind in referring to cognitive grammar as a **usage-based** approach. A second factor is its recognition that specific expressions are capable of achieving the status of conventional units even when their formation is perfectly regular; such expressions constitute lexical items (as defined above), and in the mental representation of linguistic structure they coexist with the constructional schemas they instantiate. Yet another factor is the importance attributed to low-level schemas, which embody "local" generalizations holding for limited ranges of data. Even when "global" generalizations are captured in the form of highly abstract schemas, an array of lower-level schemas may still be needed to specify which of the options they sanction are in fact conventionally exploited. It is further suggested that low-level schemas are more readily activated in the construction and evaluation of novel expressions (cf. Vol. 1, Ch. 11 and Langacker 1988c).

Let us now examine how a model of this sort accommodates the observations previously made concerning nominalization. In learning and speaking a language, one encounters a substantial variety of nominalized forms, some with sufficient frequency to be acquired as lexical items. When a pattern is discernible, i.e. when a number of expressions are parallel in formation, the speaker presumably extracts a constructional schema to represent their commonality. The existence of a schema does not affect the lexical status of the expressions that support its extraction—they are simply categorized as instances of a local or global pattern, so that their structure is to some degree motivated rather than arbitrary. As a general matter, schemas coexist in the cognitive representation of language with those instantiations that achieve the status of units.

Once established, a constructional schema may guide the formation of additional nominalizations on the same pattern. Now a grammar, in this framework, is neither generative nor constructive—it is simply a catalog of symbolic resources available to the speaker. Hence the schema's role is not to construct new expressions, any more than a set of blueprints is responsible for constructing a building. The schema does however provide a model that the speaker can employ for computing a novel expression (cf. Vol. 1, 11.3) or assessing its conventionality. In either case, the schema serves to categorize the expression, which is judged well-formed to the extent that it conforms to the schema's specifications. This categorizing relationship is precisely analogous to that holding between the schema and its lexical instantiations (indeed, with a certain amount of rehearsal the new expression will become a lexical item). The framework thus offers a unified account of the dual function of the nominalizing pattern.

The non-constructive nature of a grammar renders unproblematic the existence of nominalizations with unpredictable semantic properties. Because the meaning of *elevator* is far more specific than just 'something that elevates', a rule for the general V + *-er*/*-or* nominalizing pattern could not *construct* this expression in all its elaborate detail. However, this specificity does not prevent the noun from being *categorized* by the appropriate constructional schema; in fact, it is categorized as a valid instantiation of the pattern, since it meets the specifications of the schema and the verb stem (it simply goes beyond their specifications to incorporate additional detail). The schema can also be used for the categorization of *grinder*, which—in its yachting sense—is found to conflict with the predicted, "compositional" value (since a grinder does no actual grinding); the expression thus constitutes an extension from the pattern instead of a regular instance. Either type of judgment is possible when a schema is activated for the evaluation of a novel expression, and either type can be incorporated in the grammar as an established categorizing relationship when the expression attains the status of a lexical item.

As it pertains to nominalization, therefore, a speaker's grasp of linguistic convention resides in an array of symbolically complex structures that include both particular expressions and schemas characterized at varying levels of abstraction. Each structure has some degree of entrenchment, which reflects the frequency of its previous activation and determines the likelihood of its subsequent activation. Degree of entrenchment varies greatly, even among those structures sufficiently well entrenched to be considered established units; some lexical items, for example, are far more familiar and readily brought to mind than others. If comparable differences in degree of entrenchment are attributed to constructional schemas, they can be held responsible for the variable productivity of nominalization patterns: schemas representing the V + *-er* pattern are presumably far better entrenched than those involving *-ee*, and far more easily elicited in the formation of new expressions.

When a speaker has a notion to express, how does he choose among the symbolic resources at his disposal? The likelihood of a given structure being invoked appears to correlate positively with both entrenchment and specificity. As a consequence, a familiar lexical item is generally used in preference to a novel expression when the two are equally appropriate: the former is well-entrenched (by definition) and more specific than any schema which might be activated to construct a novel alternative. For example, because the word *elevator* is readily available, we have no reason to coin a term like *hoister* or *lifter* to name this type of object. Suppose, however, that a novel word is required. In this event a low-level schema, because of its greater specificity, is more likely to be invoked than a more abstract structure of comparable entrenchment. If the opposite were true, we might expect the attested instantiations of a pattern to be distributed randomly through the space of possibilities defined by the highest-level schema; but instead we normally find them concentrated in certain regions—among the *-ee* forms, for instance, we find a subclass based on verbs of instruction (*trainee*, *advisee*, *indoctrinee*), and another pertaining to enforced group membership (*draftee*, *inductee*, *detainee*). This is the basis for the traditional view that analogy is a major determinant of new formations. In our terms, it suggests that novel instantiations are most commonly sanctioned by subschemas representing local rather than global generalizations.

The final observation to be accounted for is the inconsistent correlation between the semantic and the morphological aspects of nominalization. This inconsistency led Jackendoff (1975) to postulate separate morphological and semantic rules, different combinations of which are manifested in particular forms. To exemplify the situation, he cites the forms *discussion*, *congregation*, *copulation*, *argument*, *government*, *establishment*, *rebuttal*, and *refusal*. His three morphological rules involve the suffixation of *-ion*, *-ment*, and *-al* to the verb stem, while his semantic rules specify the approximate values 'abstract result of Ving', 'group that Vs', and 'act of Ving'. Clearly, particular morphological rules do not correlate neatly with particular semantic rules—instead the two sets are largely cross-cutting. Thus any of the suffixes can occur on nouns meaning 'abstract result of Ving' (*discussion*, *argument*, *rebuttal*) or 'act of Ving' (*copulation*, *establishment*, *refusal*), and two of them with nouns meaning 'group that Vs' (*congregation*, *government*).

Though the distinction between 'abstract result' and 'act' bears further examination, let us accept the facts as given and see how cognitive grammar might describe them. Their description is rendered straightforward by the usage-based nature of this framework, especially its emphasis on low-level schemas that embody local generalizations. The data being considered require eight such schemas; all are presumed to be established units and to coexist in the grammar with those of their instantiations that also have unit status. Each schema represents an attested pattern of nominalization involving a derivational suffix with a particular form and a particular meaning.

These eight low-level schemas are depicted in the middle row of Fig. 1.13. Observe that [V/v] stands for the verb stem, whereas [RESULT], [GROUP], and [ACT] abbreviate the alternate meanings of the suffix. In the format

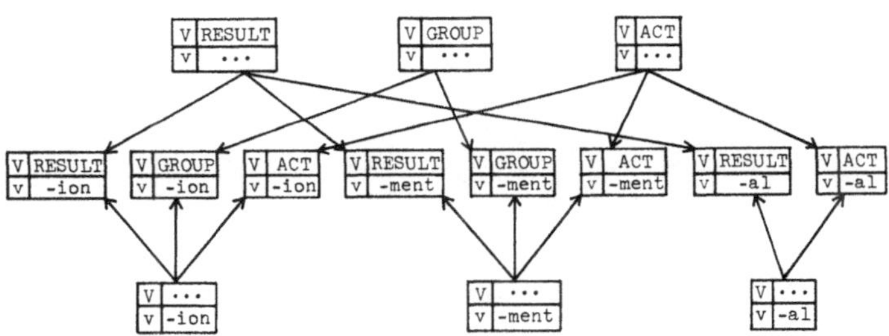

Fig. 1.13

adopted (cf. Vol. 1, Fig. 11.2), the box for each schema is divided into four sectors, the top two representing the semantic poles of the component structures, and the bottom two their phonological poles. Hence the leftmost schema, which in a linear format would be given as [[V/v]-[RESULT/-ion]], specifies the bipolar integration of the verb stem [V/v] with the nominalizing suffix [RESULT/-ion]. The composite structure (not shown) is obtained by integrating the two component structures at each pole (i.e. [V] with [RESULT], and [v] with [-ion]).

In addition to the local patterns represented by these schemas, certain broader generalizations can be captured. The three higher-level schemas in the top row correspond to Jackendoff's semantic rules: each indicates the existence of a nominalizing pattern with particular semantic characteristics but abstracts away from the varied ways in which the nominalization is marked; for example, [[V/v]-[RESULT/ . . .]] schematizes the phonologically more specific structures [[V/v]-[RESULT/-ion]], [[V/v]-[RESULT/-ment]], and [[V/v]-[RESULT/-al]]. Similarly, the higher-level schemas in the bottom row correspond to Jackendoff's morphological rules: they specify certain general ways of marking nominalization phonologically but are neutral concerning its precise semantic import. Of course, the extraction of these schemas does not imply that a given semantic pattern can be marked in any way whatever, or that a phonological pattern can be used regardless of meaning—it simply means that each type of pattern is observable in the data. Their actual distribution depends on the specific arrays of low-level schemas and lexical items that instantiate them, together with the relative entrenchment of these structures.

CHAPTER 2

Nominals: Functional Organization

NOUNS AND VERBS are the two most fundamental grammatical categories: semantically, they represent a maximal conceptual opposition rooted in the billiard-ball model; grammatically, they are pivotal to the description of every natural language. The respective counterparts of nouns and verbs at the level of sentence structure are nominals and finite clauses, whose universality and grammatical significance are also beyond dispute. A nominal or a finite clause is generally quite cohesive and readily identified as a constituent. Moreover, the statement of numerous grammatical patterns must refer in some way to these constituent types.

This chapter examines the structure of nominals and argues that semantic function (rather than constituency) is the critical factor for understanding their internal organization. The most basic difference between a simple noun and a nominal is that the former names a **type**, whereas the latter designates an **instance** of that type. When a type is conceived as having multiple instances, some specification of **quantity** is pertinent to identifying the designated entity. An additional semantic function is **grounding**, which pertains to the relation between the designatum and the speech-act participants.

2.1. Semantic Functions

What is the relation between nouns and nominals? What distinguishes forms like *cat*, *roof*, *wine*, *galaxy*, and *anxiety* from such expressions as *those three black cats*, *a leaky roof*, *the red wine in the jug on the top shelf*, *every galaxy in the universe*, and *a lot of intense anxiety stemming from marital difficulties*? The most obvious difference is that the former are single words, whereas the latter consist of multiword sequences. Size, however, can hardly be the distinguishing factor, since many nominals have only one word (e.g. *Eisenhower*, *nobody*, *I*, *Jupiter*, *everything*). Moreover, an expression of any size can be categorized as a noun and function as the head of a nominal. In the nominal of (1)(a), for instance, the head noun *site* can be replaced by a compound of indefinite length:

(1)(a) *an excellent* ***site*** *in the Midwest*
(b) *an excellent* ***convention site*** *in the Midwest*
(c) *an excellent* ***designer convention site*** *in the Midwest*
(d) *an excellent* ***toothbrush designer convention site*** *in the Midwest*

We come closer to an adequate characterization by observing that a nominal can stand alone as the subject or object of a clause, while a simple noun generally cannot. Hence the sentences in (2) are perfectly acceptable, while those in (3) are ill-formed:

(2)(a) ***Those three black cats*** *ate all the tuna.*
(b) *Their new house has* ***a leaky roof****.*

(3)(a)* ***Cat*** *ate all the tuna.*
(b)* *Their new house has* ***roof****.*

Also, a simple noun is incorporable as the first element of a compound, whereas a full nominal is excluded, as illustrated by the following contrasts:

(4)(a) *Geraldine is a dedicated* ***cat lover****.*
(b)* *Geraldine is a dedicated* ***those three black cats lover****.*

(5)(a) *This is an excellent* ***convention site****.*
(b)* *This is an excellent* ***our convention site****.*
(c)* *This is an excellent site for* ***convention****.*
(d) *This is an excellent site for* ***our convention****.*

Observe that the noun *convention* is acceptable in a compound but not as the object of a preposition, but that the converse is true of the nominal *our convention*.

Still, a revealing characterization of the difference between nouns and nominals requires something more than a list of contrasting grammatical properties. We are encouraged by the principles of cognitive grammar to seek an underlying conceptual distinction for which their differing grammatical behavior can be regarded as symptomatic. For nouns, of course, an abstract conceptual definition has already been proposed: a noun profiles a thing, i.e. a region (set of interconnected entities) in some domain. However, this definition was not intended to distinguish between simple nouns and nominals, but rather to express the commonality of nominal predications as a broadly defined class (in opposition to the equally broad class of relational predications). The definition is therefore valid for a simple noun like *site*, a compound like *convention site*, or a full nominal such as *an excellent convention site*, each of which profiles a thing and qualifies as a noun in this inclusive sense of the term. Our problem is thus to find some additional conceptual property, limited to nominals in particular, which sets them apart from nouns that are incapable of serving as clausal subject or object.

My proposal is that the **type/instance** distinction provides the requisite property. The semantic content of a simple noun like *site* amounts to nothing more than a **type specification**: it specifies the basis for identifying various entities as being representatives of the same class but is not tied to any particular instance of that class. This type specification is rendered progressively more specific in complex expressions such as *convention site*, *excellent convention site*, and *excellent convention site in the Midwest*. On the other hand, a full nominal like *the site*, *an excellent site*, or *two convention sites in the Midwest* presupposes **instantiation** of the type in question and designates one or more instances. Note that information is furnished concerning both the number of instances and their status vis-à-vis the speech-act participants (the latter through the definite/indefinite contrast).

This suggests that we can profitably examine the organization of nominals from the standpoint of semantic function, abstracting away from any details of structural implementation. The overall function of a nominal is to mention a thing and thus to make it a momentary focus of attention (generally for purposes of indicating its participation in an event or some other kind of relationship). This is no simple matter, for our mental world contains indefinitely many entities with the potential to be construed as things, any of which we might conceivably wish to talk about. How, then, is it possible to single out any one of these things for specific mention to the exclusion of others? A set of proper names providing each of these entities with its own unique label is clearly out of the question; indeed, though proper names are sometimes taken as paradigmatic for the class of nominal expressions, they are actually quite atypical. For the most part nominals employ a different strategy, based on type specifications, to accomplish their referential function.

A type specification makes an initial delimitation among the potential objects of thought, confining attention to a set of things regarded as equivalent in certain respects. We have seen that the lexical and grammatical resources of a language permit a type to be characterized with any desired degree of precision. The conforming entities may nevertheless constitute an open-ended class, so if a nominal is to serve its function of singling out particular instances of the specified type, it must supply additional information. This is of two sorts. First, a nominal provides some indication of **quantity**, either in absolute terms (e.g. *three cats*) or proportionally (*most cats*). Second, a nominal effects the **grounding** of the designated instances, i.e. it indicates how they relate to the speech event and its participants (the **ground**). Grounding pertains primarily to whether, within some frame of reference, an instance of the type (or a set of instances) is uniquely apparent to both the speaker and hearer. It is therefore not the case that every instance receives a distinct label—the same expression (e.g. *the cat*) refers to different entities on different occasions. This arrangement does however afford the speech-act participants a communicatively useful way of alluding to any member of a class.

These semantic functions tend to be reflected iconically in a nominal's structure. Its type specification is normally provided by the head noun along with any adjectives or other modifiers that render it more precise. Together these form a kind of nucleus, which resists disruption by extrinsic elements. Thus a quantifier is generally added as a separate layer external to the nucleus, e.g. *three black cats* (but not **black three cats*). Moreover, a grounding expression is usually appended as the outermost layer, reflecting its status as the predication most extrinsic to the characterization of the designated entity (cf. Vol. 1, 4.2.2). Hence *those three black cats* manifests an ordering that is not unusual among the world's languages, whereas we seldom if ever encounter expressions like **three those black cats*, **three black those cats*, or **black three those cats*.

Although this layered organization is certainly canonical (and informs the X-bar conception of nominal structure—cf. Jackendoff 1977), it is important to observe that many nominals fail to display it, and that the semantic functions in question are not uniquely associated with distinct levels of constituency. For example, there are many nominals that lack a head noun (e.g. *she*; *those who disagree*; *each one*; *for Sarah to resign* [*would be foolish*]; *that he is unhappy* [*is obvious*]). Demonstratives and quantifiers can occur as full nominals without a type specification, either individually (*these*; *some*; *several*; *three*) or in combination (*all three*; *those two*). Also, expressions of quantity do not form a well-defined structural level. Observe that in *those three black cats* number is indicated not only by the quantifier *three* but also by the grounding predication (*those*) and the head noun. In fact, certain quantifiers, including *some*, *most*, *each*, *all*, and *every*, are themselves grounding predications, which is why they do not take a preceding article or demonstrative: **a some dog*; **those all ostriches*; **the every hangman* (cf. *those two ostriches*; *the many hangmen* [*that I have known*]; *this one honest banker*).

Owing to the structural diversity of nominals, a universally valid schematic characterization must be couched in terms of meaning and semantic function rather than formal properties such as constituency. Specifically, I propose that **every nominal profiles a thing construed as an instance of some type and further incorporates some specification of quantity and grounding**. Type, quantity, and grounding are often represented by separate words or phrases, and a language tends to develop specific, iconically motivated patterns of composition and constituency for expressions of this sort. Invariably, however, there are nominals that depart from these prototypical patterns while conforming to the schematic definition. It may be that multiple semantic functions are subsumed by a single word; for example, a proper noun like

Iraq makes inherent specifications of type (nation), quantity (singular), and grounding (definiteness) and therefore stands alone as a full nominal. A specification can also be left implicit, especially when it assumes its default-case value; thus *two hotdogs* is understood as indefinite despite the absence of an overt grounding expression. Moreover, when a nominal's type specification is fully schematic (i.e. equivalent to the *thing* of *something*), it may lack a head noun (e.g. *this*; *several*; *each*; *those two*).

This chapter examines nominal structure from the standpoint of these semantic functions. We will first consider the type/instance distinction and seek to clarify the notion of instantiation. Subsequently discussed are expressions of quantity and various quantifier constructions. A final section explicates the special nature of grounding predications and serves as preface to the more detailed analysis of Ch. 3.

2.2. Instantiation

The basic difference between a simple noun like *spoon* and a nominal such as *the spoon* is that the former constitutes a type specification whereas the latter singles out an instance of that type. The instantiation of a type is thus essential to the structure of a nominal and prerequisite to both quantification and grounding, yet its nature is less than self-evident. We must therefore investigate both the conceptual basis of the type/instance distinction and some of its linguistic manifestations.

2.2.1. *Type vs. Instance*

The type/instance distinction is reminiscent of that in logic between **intension** and **extension** (or the related distinction between **sense** and **reference**). The extension of a term is the set of objects in a given world that are appropriately labeled by it; the extension of *cat*, for instance, is the set of cats. A term's intension is described as a function from worlds to extensions, i.e. some kind of *characterization* that, for an arbitrary world, picks out precisely those objects which constitute the term's extension in that world. If intensions are regarded as psychological entities, the intension of *cat* can be identified with the concept [CAT] (doubtless to the horror of many logicians).

However, the type/instance distinction required for cognitive grammar differs in important respects from both intension vs. extension and sense vs. reference. Though it is hardly standard in logic to interpret intensions as concepts, the type specifications of cognitive grammar have to be attributed a conceptual basis. Moreover, since this framework is not specifically concerned with truth or reality, but only with how conceived situations are linguistically portrayed, instances are also dealt with as conceptual entities. The instance designated by *the cat* is therefore equivalent neither to the reference of this nominal, which is generally taken to be an object in the world (a particular cat), nor to the extension of *cat* (the set of all such objects). Instead, the semantic pole of the nominal is a conceptualization one of whose substructures—the profile—is construed as instantiating the type specification provided by the noun. On this view it is perfectly coherent to describe a nominal as designating an instance of the appropriate type even when it is non-specific or non-referential, as in (6):

(6) *He desperately needed* ***a job****, but* ***no job*** *was available.*

A nominal of this sort both evokes and profiles the conception of an instance, albeit an instance whose referential status is negated by the grounding predication or the overall context.

Our task is thus to elucidate the contrast between a **type conception** and an **instance conception**, either of which can function as the semantic pole of a linguistic predication. For example, how can we describe the conceptual distinction between *cat* on the one hand and *a cat* or *the cat* on the other? It is not a matter of definiteness or of any specific relation to the speech-act participants, since nominals disagree in these respects. Nor can the difference be attributed to profiling, which might seem a likely candidate because some entity within the base is singled out as the designatum. As understood in cognitive grammar, the notion of designation is applicable to both type and instance conceptions, being essential to the semantic value of every linguistic predication. Observe that both the noun *arc* and a nominal such as *this arc* evoke the conception of a circle, and each profiles some segment thereof (cf. Vol. 1, Fig. 5.1). Without this profiling, neither the type predication nor the instance predication would succeed in characterizing an arc (as opposed to just a circle).

A notion discussed in Ch. 1, namely domain of instantiation, proves necessary to a proper understanding of the type/instance distinction. We can describe this notion intuitively as the domain in which an entity is thought of as residing or having its primary manifestation; time is thus the domain of instantiation for events, and space for material substance. It can further be described as the domain that determines the basic "aspect" of a noun or verb, which depends on whether the profiled entity is bounded within the scope of predication. In the case of verbs, time is always the relevant domain: the presence vs. the absence of temporal bounding determines the categorization of a verb as perfective or imperfective. Though nouns are more variable in this regard, bounding in space is generally the determining factor for entities in the physical realm. *Lake* is thus a count noun, since a spatial boundary is intrinsic to its characterization, whereas *water* is a mass noun because it occupies physical space but is not inherently bounded in this domain.

Directly relevant to the problem at hand is a third way of describing the domain of instantiation: as the domain in which the location of an entity is sufficient to establish it as an instance of a category distinct from other potential instances. For example, temporal location is sufficient to distinguish one event from another; if two identical events occur at different points in time, they can be construed as distinct instances of the same event type, but hardly as the same instance. In similar fashion, spatial location is distinctive for physical objects. Two objects at different locations at a given moment cannot be regarded as the same object, though they can of course be perceived as instances of the same object type. Objects viewed on different occasions can however be recognized as the same, even if they are not precisely identical.

It seems apparent, then, that domain of instantiation is a critical notion for explicating the type/instance distinction. How can we use it? Could we say, for example, that a type conception makes no inherent reference to the domain of instantiation (i.e. that this domain is absent from its matrix)? An instance conception would then be derived by evoking the domain of instantiation together with the type specification. This proposal proves unworkable, for the simple reason that specifications pertaining to the domain of instantiation are crucial to the characterization of a type. Evolution through time is fundamental to the conception of a process, either as a type or as an instance. Similarly, the type description for a class of physical objects can hardly omit a shape specification invoking the spatial domain; the characteristic shape of a *spoon*, *cat*, or *bicycle* is central to the type conception of the category and is as readily called to mind by the noun as by a nominal.

Type and instance conceptions thus share the property of profiling some entity in the domain of instantiation. For example, both *cat* and *a cat* evoke and profile the conception of a furry creature that occupies physical space and has a certain configuration in this domain (i.e. a shape). We must therefore ask what additional factor might be responsible for the type/instance distinction. My suggestion is quite simple: **that an instance (but not a type) is thought of as having a particular location in the domain of instantiation**. That is, a type specification merely uses the domain of instantiation to describe some property of the designated entity, such as shape or temporal extension. An instance conception goes beyond this by conceiving the domain as having sufficient expanse to support the simultaneous manifestation of multiple entities and by regarding the profiled entity as being situated within this expanse at a specific location in contrast to other possible locations. It may be helpful to imagine a type specification as floating about unattached through the domain of instantiation, with the potential to be manifested anywhere within it. This potential is realized, and an instance conception obtained, when the specification is anchored at a particular spot, as sketched in Fig. 2.1.

This description recalls an explicit reference-tracking device employed in American Sign Language (the primary language used by the deaf in the United States). To establish a referent, the ASL signer simply points to some

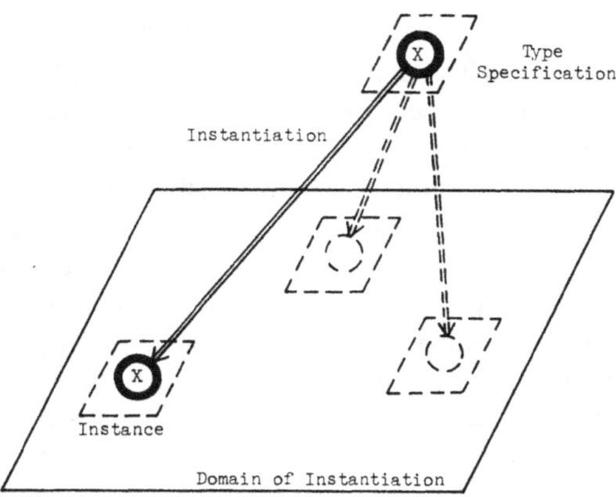

Fig. 2.1

location in signing space. The location is arbitrary, but once it is selected, the signer can refer back to the individual in question simply by returning to that point. Multiple referents are simultaneously maintained and distinguished in this fashion, each anchored at a particular point in signing space. I suggest that instantiation be regarded as a conceptual analog of this device. The location of an instance within the domain of instantiation is arbitrary—the speaker's knowledge of this location may be limited to its anchoring function—but the very fact of being anchored at some location is what establishes an instance distinct from other possible instances. It should however be emphasized that instantiation is not equated with either reference or grounding. A grounding predication (e.g. a specification of definiteness or indefiniteness) presupposes that an instance has been established and gives some indication concerning its relation to the speech-act participants; instantiation per se provides no such indication. Moreover, the effect of the grounding predication may be to deny the referential status of the profiled instance, as we saw in regard to (6).

2.2.2. *Proper Names*

The type/instance distinction is independent of any particular structural configuration. Nominals such as *this spoon*, in which the type specification and the notion of instantiation are respectively indicated by the head noun and the accompanying grounding predication, can probably be regarded as prototypical. We have seen, however, that the head can itself be a structure of indefinite complexity (cf. (1)). Moreover, any number of modifiers can be appended, each of them adding certain refinements and thus deriving a higher-order type specification of greater precision: *spoon* introduces a general type, *slender spoon* a more specific type, *long slender spoon* a type that is more specific still, and so on. On the other hand, an element that appears to be a modifier in structural terms may have no impact on the type specification, representing instead an editorial comment by the speaker (*this damn spoon*; *a so-called expert*; *those fuckin' chickens*). Nor is a type specification the exclusive province of a head noun and its modifiers. A grounding predication can itself be analyzed as having a type specification that is maximally schematic; for example, the demonstrative *this* embodies a type specification essentially equivalent to [THING] (the semantic pole of the noun-class schema). Normally this schematic specification is elaborated by the remaining nominal elements (e.g. by *long slender spoon* in *this long slender spoon*), but even a nominal consisting of a demonstrative standing alone can be thought of as specifying a minimally restrictive type.

Proper names represent another kind of departure from the prototypical pattern. A standard proper name, e.g. *Stan Smith*, furnishes a variety of information. For one thing, it incorporates a type specification; convention tells us that the individual designated by *Stan Smith* is a male human (cf. Haiman 1980). Since the name is taken as characteristic of a specific person, it further presupposes instantiation and makes an implicit specification of quantity. Grounding is subsumed as well, for the nominal is definite and portrays the profiled individual as being uniquely apparent to the speaker and hearer on the basis of this name alone. Hence type, instantiation, quantity, and grounding are conflated in a single expression whose component parts fail to correlate with these semantic functions.[1] Precisely because these functions are fulfilled, the expression qualifies as a nominal despite its non-canonical structure.

Now it happens that I have known (or known of) no less than three separate people named Stan Smith. Thus, if more than one of them should fall within the potential scope of discourse (so that the name alone would be confusing), I would have to distinguish them by means of descriptive expressions like *the Stan Smith who used to play professional tennis* or *the Stan Smith who married my sister-in-law*. Grammatically, *Stan Smith* is acting as a common rather than a proper noun in these locutions, for it occurs with a definite article and takes a restrictive relative clause. I would argue that it acts as a common noun grammatically because it is so treated semantically, i.e. the grammatical behavior is symptomatic of its meaning. When used as a proper noun, *Stan Smith* incorporates the supposition that there is only one individual with that name in the universe of discourse. When functioning as a common noun, it lacks that supposition and is construed instead as a higher-order type specification with the approximate value 'person named *Stan Smith*'.

[1]That is, the functions are associated with the name as a whole—it is not the case, for instance, that *Stan* expresses the type specification exclusively, and *Smith* the other three functions.

This phenomenon has often been observed; of interest here is its naturalness from the standpoint of cognitive grammar and the specific manner in which it is described. Pertinent features of the framework include the encyclopedic view of linguistic semantics and the ready accommodation of self-referential aspects of language. According to the encyclopedic view, the matrix for an expression comprises an open-ended set of domains, whose specifications differ in centrality and in how intrinsic they are to the designated entity. The potential for linguistic self-reference follows from the fact that any type of conception can be a domain, even the knowledge of linguistic convention and symbolic relationships. How a notion is symbolized linguistically is therefore one aspect—albeit extrinsic and peripheral—of the symbolizing expression's semantic value. That is, phonological space can be thought of as one domain in the matrix of an expression, and symbolization by its phonological pole as one of its semantic specifications.[2]

We can now be more precise about the meaning of *Stan Smith*. In its basic use as a proper noun, *Stan Smith* profiles a thing characterized as a human male and thus evokes the various domains required for these specifications. It further evokes an idealized cognitive model reflecting the cultural practice of giving every person a name supposedly unique to that person and hence sufficient as a means of identification; with respect to this domain, it specifies that *Stan Smith* in particular (its phonological pole) is the name of the designated individual. The uniqueness of the name assures the definiteness of this nominal expression—provided, that is, that the world conforms to the cognitive model. When it does not, i.e. when the same name is borne by more than one person, the conditions are present for using it as a common noun. *Stan Smith* becomes a common noun when the idealized model is supplanted in its matrix by the conception of a world in which multiple individuals are so named. In reference to this domain, the properties of being human, male, and called *Stan Smith* are not sufficient to identify a unique entity; rather they amount to a type specification capable of being instantiated by numerous individuals. The status of *Stan Smith* as a simple common noun (as opposed to a full nominal) is an automatic consequence of this construal.

2.2.3. *Type Hierarchies*

Speakers of every language sort the objects of their experience into distinctly-labeled classes. The taxonomy reflected in a linguistic system invariably shows some degree of hierarchical arrangement, so that a particular object simultaneously instantiates a number of different types representing different levels of abstraction; my cat Metathesis, for example, is not only a

[2] See Vol. 1, 2.2.1. Linguistic symbolization is not at all peripheral to the meaning of certain expressions. Central to the meaning of *Tuesday*, for instance, is the very fact that the day is known by that term (and also that it follows a day named *Monday* and precedes one named *Wednesday*).

cat, but also (*inter alia*) a *mammal*, an *animal*, and a *thing*. The categories in question form an ordered sequence that we can refer to as a **type hierarchy**, e.g. *thing* > *animal* > *mammal* > *cat*. The ordering in such a hierarchy can be established on the basis of either meaning or extension: in terms of meaning, each type specification is schematic for the one that follows; as for extension, the members of each category include those of the next as a proper subset.

An issue worth raising is whether a specific class member should be incorporated as the lowest level in a type hierarchy. For example, should *thing* > *animal* > *mammal* > *cat* be expanded to *thing* > *animal* > *mammal* > *cat* > *Metathesis*? A negative answer is generally assumed. It is customary to distinguish between a **type/subtype** relationship on the one hand, and a **type/instance** (or **type/token**) relationship on the other. The relation between a type and a subtype (e.g. between *mammal* and *cat*) reduces to precision of specification; extreme diversity may be observable among the subtypes of a type (consider *cat*, *human*, *whale*, and *okapi* as subtypes of *mammal*), and each subtype represents a category with an open-ended set of members. By contrast, an instance need not be characterized with substantially greater precision than a type (consider *dog* and *Fido*). Moreover, the instances of a type represent distinct individuals rather than open-ended classes, and they are generally more similar to one another than are an array of subtypes (e.g. Fido and Rover are likely to have more in common than a dog and a whale).

To the extent that one wishes to maintain the distinction, the term **elaboration** can be applied to the relation between a type and a subtype, and **instantiation** reserved for that between a (sub)type and an instance. I would argue, however, that the distinction is not absolute, and that instantiation is best considered a special case of elaboration. For one thing, the construal of an entity as having a particular location in the domain of instantiation constitutes a semantic specification (as defined in this framework); this property alone renders an instance conception somewhat more precise than the corresponding type conception (which lacks it). Furthermore, there are instance expressions that are far more specific and semantically elaborate than the type expressions they instantiate, even if we confine our attention to knowledge that is sufficiently widespread to be regarded as conventional (Vol. 1, 2.1.3). For example, the semantic value of *New York* is not limited to its being a particular instance of *city* but also includes more precise specifications concerning relative size, geographical location, commercial importance, and so on. In cases like this, instantiation is only one of the many respects in which the instance conception elaborates the type conception.

Let us assume, then, that the lowest level in a type hierarchy consists of specific instances distinguished by their position in the domain of instantiation. A partial hierarchy such as *mammal* > *cat* > *Metathesis* can thus be represented as in Fig. 2.2, which treats the relationship of instantiation be-

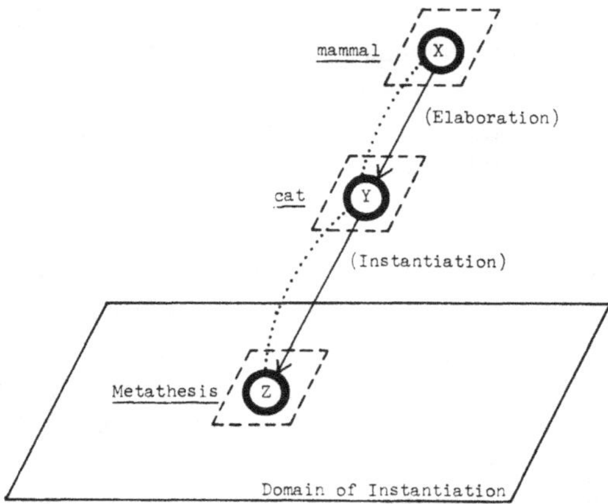

Fig. 2.2

tween *cat* and *Metathesis* as parallel to the elaborative relationship between *mammal* and *cat*. Each relationship is resolvable into two factors. One factor, represented by a dotted line, is a correspondence between the profiles of the two predications; for example, *mammal* and *cat* are schematic and more specific characterizations of what is taken as the same entity for purposes of comparison and categorization.[3] This relation of schematicity between the characterizations at adjacent levels constitutes the second factor and is represented as usual by a solid arrow. Thus X is schematic for Y, and Y for Z, where X, Y, and Z stand for the respective semantic specifications of *mammal*, *cat*, and *Metathesis*.

Symbolic relationships hold at particular levels in a type hierarchy, though a term defined at one level is applicable to lower levels as well (notably to instances). For example, the semantic pole of *mammal* is an abstract type conception, and that of *cat* a less schematic type conception, yet both terms are appropriately used in referring to Metathesis or to any other instance of these categories. This is possible because a type conception is **immanent** in the conception of an instance, i.e. those cognitive events required for the former are subsumed by the more elaborate set of events responsible for the latter. Hence the conception of Metathesis inherently activates those events which constitute the semantic pole of *cat*, so that this symbolic unit as a whole has some tendency to be elicited. A proper name like *Metathesis* can be seen as a limiting case, in which the symbolic relationship holds at the lowest level in the type hierarchy. Because there is no distinction between type and instance at this level, a proper name is degenerate—its semantic pole is a type

[3]Correspondences are inherent in every categorizing relationship, for the result of comparing two structures depends on which substructures are matched against one another to determine their degree of congruence (cf. Vol. 1, 2.3.2). The global correspondence between the profiled entities is only one of the many correspondences that would figure in an exhaustive description.

conception that is also an instance conception (i.e. it is a type with only one instance).

Further supporting the incorporation of instances as the lowest level in type hierarchies, as well as the non-distinctness of elaboration and instantiation, are expressions in which types are themselves construed as instances. Consider the following sentences:

(7)(a) *The okapi and the wombat are two mammals seldom found in zoos.*
(b) *Orange and blue are my two favorite colors.*
(c) *Squash and lima beans are two vegetables that David will never eat.*
(d) *F-sharp and B-flat are two notes that are hard for me to hit.*
(e) *March and October are generally the two wettest months of the year.*

The subject nominals receive a generic interpretation. In (7)(a), for example, one is not concerned with a particular, spatially-instantiated okapi or wombat, but rather with the okapi and the wombat as types. At the same time, however, these types appear to be construed as distinct instantiations of a higher-order type (*mammal*); as such they are subject to quantification and eligible for labeling by the higher-order term: the okapi is *one mammal*, the wombat is *another mammal*, and collectively we can refer to them as *two mammals*. Grammatically, this usage is precisely analogous to using *my two cats* in reference to Alice and Metathesis, or *two cities* for New York and Madrid.

In the present framework, the description of this usage is fairly straightforward. Consider first the normal situation, in which instantiations constitute the lowest level in a type hierarchy. Fig. 2.3(a) depicts this situation using a

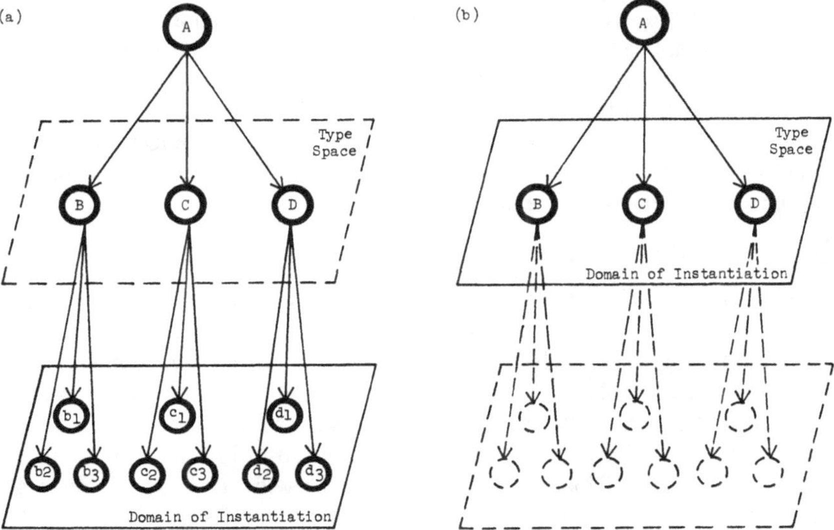

Fig. 2.3

simplified format (in particular, correspondence lines are omitted for sake of diagrammatic clarity). Structure A represents a type, while B, C, and D are three of its subtypes, each with multiple instantiations; for example, if A is the type specification for *mammal*, C could be that of *cat*, with c_2 and c_3 being Alice and Metathesis. As previously explained, labels project to lower levels—thus Alice and Metathesis can each be referred to as a *cat* (or even as a *mammal*). Quantification is possible because they occupy different locations in the domain of instantiation and thus constitute distinct instances of the category. We can therefore describe Alice and Metathesis collectively as *two cats* (or *two mammals*).

For a given type, A, let us refer to the range of possible subtypes as the **type space** of A. The type space of *mammal*, for example, includes the notions *cat*, *human*, *whale*, *okapi*, *wombat*, and countless other subtypes, both actual and potential. Type space is akin to quality space, which figured prominently in our discussion of mass nouns in Ch. 1. Recall that a substance such as *wine* occupies a bounded region, Q, in quality space but is neither continuous nor inherently bounded in its domain of instantiation (physical space). There is however a count-noun use, illustrated by *a dry wine*, in which quality space itself functions as the domain of instantiation; Q then defines the immediate scope of predication, and the count-noun sense of *wine* profiles a bounded subregion Q′ properly included within it (cf. Fig. 1.6). I analyze sentences like (7) as involving a comparable departure from the default-case domain of instantiation. When I speak of the okapi and the wombat being *two mammals*, the pertinent domain of instantiation is no longer physical space, but rather the type space for *mammal*, as shown in Fig. 2.3(b). With respect to this abstract domain of instantiation, the type specifications for *okapi* and *wombat* are not just subtypes of *mammal* but actual, quantifiable instantiations of this category. We can therefore refer to them as *two mammals* for precisely the same reason that we can refer to Alice and Metathesis as *two cats*. Observe, however, that our ability to capture this generalization depends on the inclusion of types and instances in a single hierarchy and the essential equivalence of elaboration and instantiation.

2.2.4. *Predicate Nominative Constructions*

The sentence *Alice caught a mouse* contains a finite verb and two nominals, one of which (*Alice*) elaborates its trajector, and the other its landmark. This description applies as well to *Alice is a mouser*, yet the two sentences are structurally quite different. The former is transitive, *a mouse* serving as the direct object of *catch*. By contrast, *a mouser* is not a direct object in the latter, nor is *be* a transitive verb—it is generally referred to instead as a "copula" or "linking verb." This copular verb combines with *a mouser* to form an intransitive clausal "predicate." A nominal that functions in this way as the essential part of the clausal predicate is known as a **predicate nominative**.

The first step in analyzing the predicate nominative construction is to describe the meaning of *be*. Here there are two main traditions, each of them erroneous. According to one tradition, *be* is a meaningless element inserted for purely grammatical purposes in specifiable environments (cf. Bach 1967); naturally, such an analysis runs counter to the principles of cognitive grammar. A more standard approach is to regard *be* as itself expressing a relationship of identity or class inclusion. One difficulty with this analysis is that a comparable semantic relationship is found in various constructions in which *be* fails to occur:

(8)(a) *Tom is the person most likely to succeed.*
(b) *They voted Tom the person most likely to succeed.*

(9)(a) *Tom is a necrophiliac.*
(b) *Tom a necrophiliac? You must be joking.*

This suggests that the identity or inclusion relation is independent of *be*.

In a variety of publications (e.g. 1981, 1982a, 1982b, 1987b), I have argued that *be* is a meaningful element whose primary function is temporal and aspectual. *Be* is schematic for the class of imperfective processes: it profiles the continuation through time of a stable situation characterized only as a stative relation; it is a true verb, all of whose component states are construed as being identical, but apart from their being relational it is maximally unspecific concerning their nature. The schematic relationship followed through time by *be* can serve as elaboration site in a grammatical construction, where it is rendered specific by the addition of a stative predication such as an adjective or a prepositional phrase (e.g. *be hungry*; *be on the counter*). Since *be* is the profile determinant, the composite expression inherits its processual character—it profiles the continuation through time of the specific relationship indicated by the stative complement. This "temporalization" of a stative relation allows it to occur as the profiled relationship in a finite clause, which would otherwise be precluded (since a finite clause always designates a process).

The most attractive analysis of the "copular" *be* in predicate nominative constructions would be one that makes it exactly parallel to these other uses. That is, one would like to analyze *Alice is a mouser* as being directly analogous to *Alice is hungry* and *Alice is on the counter*, as suggested by their formal similarity. Such an analysis is possible, however, only if the predicate nominative is treated as a stative relation. But is this reasonable? Can we plausibly say that a nominal such as *a mouser*, when it occurs in certain constructions, is construed as a stative relation parallel to an adjective or a prepositional phrase? I see little reason to doubt it. English is replete with zero derivations from one grammatical class to another (hence the noun *salt* is used as a verb, the verb *cook* as a noun, the preposition *near* as a verb, and so on). The shift in class may be confined to a particular construction; *pig*, for example, functions as a verb only in the verb-particle combination *pig out* (cf. *flip out*, *pass out*, *clear out*, etc.). Moreover, zero-marked shifts in class are not inherently limited to "lexical" elements such as simple nouns and verbs. Many speakers tolerate expressions like the following, where an entire prepositional phrase is construed as a nominal employed as clausal subject:

(10)(a) *By the fire is much warmer.*
(b) *Behind the dresser is all dusty.*

It seems evident on intuitive grounds that what the subject phrase designates in (10) is a spatial location (not a locative relationship).

I thus consider it plausible to analyze a predicate nominative as being relational despite its nominal form. We can posit for English a derivational pattern whereby a nominal is incorporated as part of a more elaborate conception and thereby comes to designate a stative relation at a higher level of conceptual organization. The semantic pole of this derivation is sketched in Fig. 2.4. The box on the left stands for the meaning of the nominal; it profiles

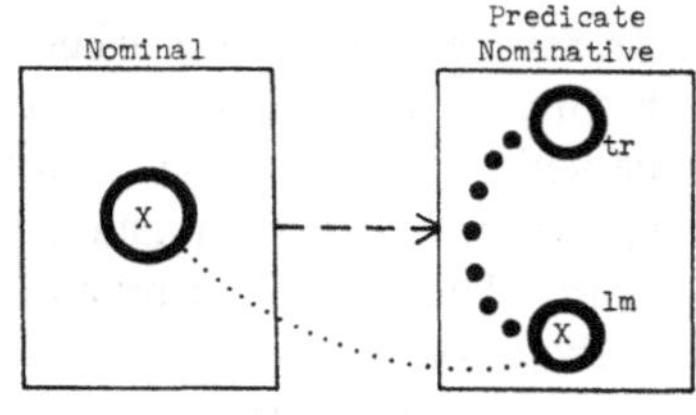

Fig. 2.4

a thing whose semantic specifications are abbreviated as X. Depicted on the right is the semantic value of the same expression under its relational construal as a predicate nominative. Observe that the entity profiled by the nominal is retained as the relational landmark, while the trajector is a thing specified only schematically. The profiled relationship between the trajector and landmark, one of identity, is conveniently represented by a dotted correspondence line. Most of the relational predication's conceptual content resides in its landmark: the trajector is highly schematic, and the profiled identity relation is conceptually minimal. Because so little content is added to that of the underlying nominal, it is not unnatural that the derivation should be marked by zero.[4]

We must next explore what it means to say that the trajector and landmark

[4]There are several options for thinking about this derivational pattern: as a productive pattern of semantic extension; as a construction involving a phonologically-zero derivational morpheme; or as a defective construction having only one, non-head component structure. In the formalism of cognitive grammar, these alternatives prove to be exactly equivalent, i.e. different ways of describing the same structural configuration (see 12.2.2 and Figs. 12.6–8 in Vol. 1).

are identical. On first examination, there appear to be two basic sorts of identity relations expressed by predicate nominative constructions: "referential" identity vs. class inclusion. These are illustrated in (11)(a) and (b), respectively:

(11)(a) *Alice is the cat that stole the liver.*
(b) *Alice is a thief.*

In (a), the subject and predicate nominative separately describe specific individuals, and the construction specifies that these two individuals happen to be the same. In (b), on the other hand, the predicate nominative names a class, and the subject is identified as a member of that class.

The problem with this more-or-less standard account is that the predicate nominative in (11)(b) does not have the form we would expect if it merely named a class. It is not just a noun but a full nominal, so presumably it does not represent a type specification but rather an instance of that type. An analysis along these lines is in fact quite feasible in view of our overall approach. Recall that instantiation is regarded as distinct from such factors as definiteness, specificity, and referentiality. Though not a definite description, the predicate nominative in (11)(b) can thus be taken as designating an instance of the *thief* category. In both types of sentences, consequently, the predicate nominative construction specifies the identity of two instances, i.e. their coincidence in the domain of instantiation.

The relationship profiled by this kind of predicate nominative construction is diagrammed in Fig. 2.5(a).[5] A correspondence line specifies identity between the trajector and landmark. The semantic characterization of the trajector (abbreviated as A) is furnished by the clausal subject; in the case of (11), the subject is a proper name (*Alice*) that designates a particular individual supposedly apparent to both the speaker and the hearer. The landmark is characterized with reference to a type specification, T, which for (11)(a) is *cat that stole the liver*, and for (11)(b), *thief*. In each sentence, the landmark designates an instance, t_i, of the type in question, and as usual the description for the type (*cat that stole the liver* or *thief*) projects downward to its instantiation.

Up to this point, (11)(a) and (b) are equivalent in all essential respects. The crucial difference between them becomes evident when we consider the nature of the grounding predication for the landmark nominal. In (11)(a), *the* indicates that the landmark is definite, i.e. its contextual uniqueness is evident to both speech-act participants. The profiled relationship of identity thus holds between two specific, separately characterized individuals. On the other hand, the article *a* in (11)(b) is interpreted as both indefinite and non-specific: the

[5] Ignored is the semantic contribution of *be*, which provides the profiled relation with temporal extension.

landmark is identified as an instance of the *thief* category, but not as one that is unique, previously evident to the speaker and hearer, or singled out by virtue of participating in any relation other than the identity relation itself. The landmark is thus an **arbitrary** member of the *thief* class (just as the object of *find* is an arbitrary member of the *job* class in *Jason would like to find a job*). It is arbitrary in the sense that this instance conception is "conjured up" by the speaker and hearer solely for purposes of making a type attribution, and has no status outside the confines of this predicate nominative construction. In effect, the speaker says: "Imagine an instance of the *thief* category—Alice can be equated with such an entity." The inclusion of Alice in the *thief* class is therefore specified indirectly, via her identification with an arbitrary member. We see, then, that (11)(b) *implies* a class-inclusion relationship but *profiles* a relationship of identity. The former holds between the *thief* class and the non-specific instance t_i, and the latter between t_i and *Alice*.

Fig. 2.5(a) shows the trajector and landmark at different (arbitrary) locations in the domain of instantiation, but of course the import of the identity relationship is that their positions actually coincide. Fig. 2.5(b) provides an

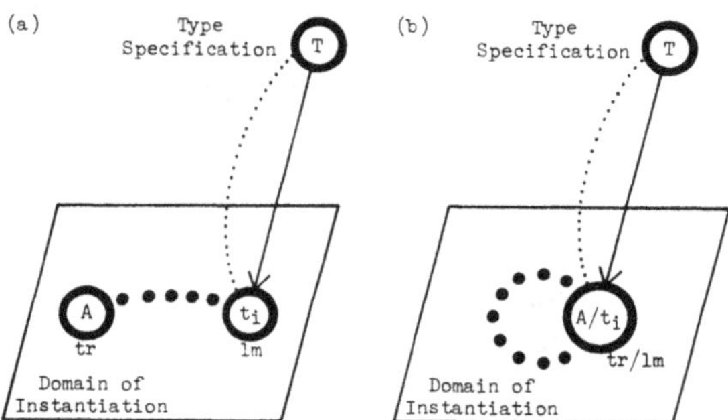

Fig. 2.5

alternate notation which shows the trajector/landmark identity more directly. With either notation, the profiled correspondence holds within the domain of instantiation, i.e. the trajector and landmark nominals each provide instance descriptions which happen to apply to the same entity. A correspondence within the domain of instantiation is not precisely equivalent to one holding between a type specification and an instance (or more specifically, between the profiles of the type conception and an instance conception). A "vertical" correspondence of this sort merely indicates what structures are being compared for purposes of categorization. A single type specification corresponds in this fashion to indefinitely many distinct instances, which, however, are not thereby identified with one another (except as being members of the same category). The special character of vertical type/instance correspondences is a consequence of the fact that a type conception per se lacks instantiation and therefore cannot participate in a "same instance" relationship or even mediate one.

Like a "horizontal" correspondence between two instances, a vertical correspondence is however capable of being profiled in a predicate nominative construction. This is the analysis I propose for sentences like those in (12), from French:

(12)(a) *Alain est professeur.* 'Alan is (a) teacher.'
(b) *Pierre est médecin.* 'Peter is (a) doctor.'

Note that the predicate nominative in these expressions is a simple noun rather than a full nominal (in particular, there is no article or any other grounding predication). I therefore posit the structure in Fig. 2.6, in which the profiled

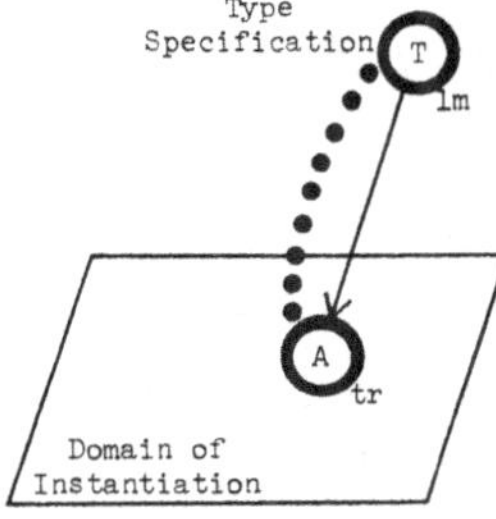

Fig. 2.6

relationship is a correspondence between the type specification provided by the predicate noun and the instance described by the subject nominal. No new constructs need be invoked; indeed, the possibility of such a structure is suggested by our previously-assembled descriptive apparatus. Moreover, the analysis both respects the overt form of the expressions and reveals how they differ semantically from their English counterparts while being functionally equivalent.

Let us conclude by considering the use of a predicate nominative construction for generic statements. The sentences in (13) appear to be parallel except that the subject has an indefinite article in (a) and a definite article in (b):

(13)(a) *A wombat is a mammal.*
(b) *The okapi is a mammal.*

Nevertheless, previous discussion should make it evident that their semantic contrast is fairly substantial. In particular, I analyze both statements as predicating identity between two instances, but they differ as to which level in the type hierarchy is taken as the domain of instantiation for this purpose. In

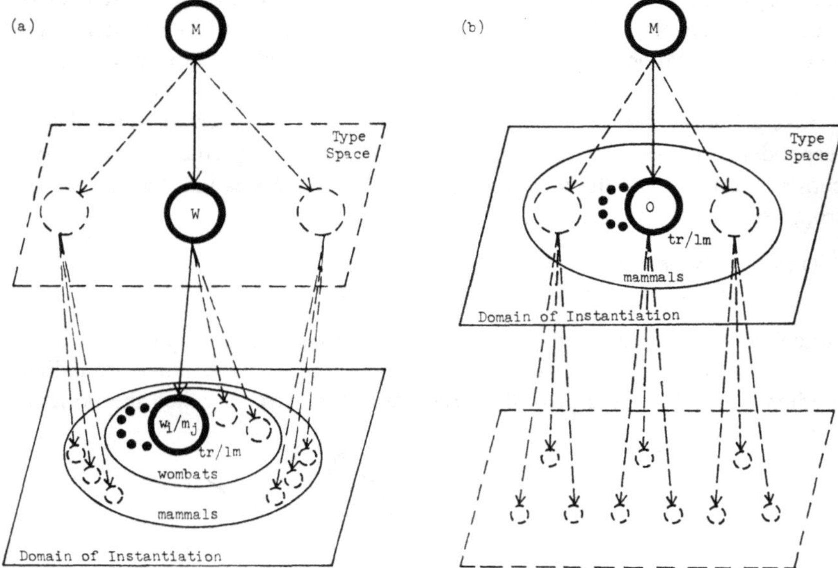

Fig. 2.7

(13)(a), the domain of instantiation is physical space (the default-case option), whereas in (13)(b) the relevant domain is the type space associated with *mammal* (cf. Fig. 2.3).

The identity relation of (13)(a) is diagrammed in Fig. 2.7(a). The type specifications of *mammal* and *wombat* are given by M and W, respectively; each projects to a set of instances in the domain of instantiation, that of *mammal* properly including that of *wombat*. The profiled relationship is one of identity between an arbitrary instance of the wombat category, w_i, serving as trajector, and an arbitrary instance of the mammal category, m_j, serving as landmark. The form of the subject and the predicate nominative is regularly determined: each takes the article *a*, since it is both indefinite and nonspecific, and for its head noun each inherits the name of its type description. Because wombats are a proper subset of mammals, an arbitrarily chosen instance of the wombat category always bears an identity relation to some mammal. In similar fashion, an arbitrarily chosen set of wombats is always identical to some set of mammals; the sentence *Wombats are mammals* results when sets rather than individuals are selected for designation by the subject and predicate nominative.[6]

[6]Though not our immediate concern, the trajector/landmark asymmetry is crucial to these examples. The trajector (relational figure) is the entity being located or characterized. So long as one or a set of wombats is selected for this purpose, it will be found to coincide with some instance(s) of the mammal class; the converse does not hold, of course.

Depicted in Fig. 2.7(b) is the identity relation profiled in (13)(b). The type specification for *okapi*, represented as O, is only one of the many specifications constituting the type space of *mammal*. The distinctive property of (13)(b) is that this type space is construed as the domain of instantiation, with the consequence that type specifications count as instances of the *mammal* category. The identity relation holds between two such types: its trajector is the specific type *okapi*, which has its own name and can take the definite article because it is contextually unique (i.e. there is only one instance of the type *okapi* in this type space); its landmark is an arbitrary instance in type space of the *mammal* category, which inherits the name of the superordinate type and takes the article *a* because it is non-unique, indefinite, and non-specific.

Finally, we can now be more precise about the analysis of sentences like those in (7), e.g. *The okapi and the wombat are two mammals*. The profiled relationship is directly analogous to that in Fig. 2.7(b) except that the trajector and landmark represent sets of type specifications instead of single types. The trajector consists of the two types *okapi* and *wombat*, each definite by virtue of being unique. The landmark comprises two arbitrary instances of the *mammal* category, which turn out to be subtypes because the type space of *mammal* functions as the domain of instantiation. Granted that type space functions in this way, the predicate nominative construction is once more seen as designating a relationship of identity between (sets of) instances.

2.2.5. *Role Specifications*

Pope Paul VI died in 1978. His successor, Pope John Paul I, died just a few weeks later. At that point it was appropriate to say the following: *The pope died again*. The import of the sentence was not that either person died once, was resurrected from the dead, and then died a second time. What it meant instead was that, for the second time in the recent past, a person had died while holding the office of pope—a different person on each occasion.

To accommodate such phenomena, Fauconnier (1985) invokes the notion of a **role** that can assume distinct **values** in different conceived worlds ("mental spaces"). The role of pope, for example, is in some sense constant regardless of who might happen to fill it. The value of this role is the person who holds the office at a given moment, and different points in time define distinct worlds (spaces) across which the value can vary. Fauconnier observes that an expression like *the pope* applies to the role itself or to any of its values. For instance, in (14)(a) it is used to describe the papal role, but in (14)(b) it refers to a particular individual:

(14)(a) *The pope is elected by the College of Cardinals.*
(b) *The pope just scratched his nose.*

A complete description of Fauconnier's sophisticated analysis cannot be attempted here. We can however raise the question of how roles and values relate to notions previously introduced.

The answer, in brief, is that the role/value distinction reduces to the type/instance distinction but involves a special application of it. Specifically, a role is characterized with respect to a **world type**, and a value is the correspondent of that role in a particular **world instance**. In the case of *the pope*, for example, the real world in its current state counts as one world instance, and so does the world as it was constituted in 1975, in 1943, or in 1375. Other instances include the world as it will appear at any given point in the future, as well as imagined worlds that diverge in various ways from past or present reality, provided that the institution of the papacy remains an active part of them. The world type with respect to which the role is characterized represents a schematization of all these instances. Although it may be quite limited in scope, this type conception must at least retain from relevant world instances a schematic description of those factors that figure directly and centrally in the characterization of the role: general notions pertaining to human society and the practice of religion; the institution of the Roman Catholic Church; the hierarchical structure of this organization, with a single individual selected as its leader by the College of Cardinals; the kinds of activities in which this leader engages; and so forth.

Hence the role of *pope* is characterized with respect to an abstract world type that is schematic for an open-ended set of world instances which manifest its essential properties. The type conception functions as a cognitive domain, and *pope* profiles a person identified by his position within it (i.e. his participation in the various relationships just described). Each compatible world instance includes a person who occupies an analogous position and thereby instantiates the role. The term *pope* is applicable to this person for the same reason that *cat* is applicable to Metathesis (2.2.3): the type specification (role) is immanent in the instance conception (value), so that activation of the latter inherently activates those cognitive events constituting the semantic pole of *pope* (as defined at the type level). The definite article is appropriate for either the type or any single instantiation, since uniqueness is specified as part of the role characterization and assumed for a given world instance. Of course, if we expand the scope of predication to include multiple world instances, the role no longer has a unique instantiation. We can therefore speak, for example, of the *two popes* who died in 1978 (each representing a different world instance and a different instantiation of the role).

The role/value distinction is therefore not fundamentally different from the basic type/instance distinction. If we compare prototypical examples of each, e.g. *pope* and *cat*, we find two main points of divergence. First, extrinsic properties (participation in relationships with other entities) figure far more saliently in the characterization of *pope* than of *cat*. As a consequence, *pope* invokes considerably more context for central aspects of its type specification; the requisite context amounts to a schematic conception of the world (and in particular, of society and certain religious institutions). On the other hand, the context needed for central specifications of *cat* is essentially restricted to a scope of predication in space and other domains sufficient to support a description of a cat's physical properties; but substantial though it is, the difference between this limited scope and a schematic world type is actually only one of degree. A second point of divergence is that the type description for *pope* implies uniqueness in a particular world. Reference to multiple world instances is thus required for multiple instantiations of *pope*, whereas multiple instantiations of *cat* are possible and expected in a single world.

The type/instance distinction consequently subsumes the role/value distinction as a special case, and any type specification can be regarded as a role specification of sorts. Also subsumed by the type/instance distinction is the contrast noted by Donnellan (1966) between the **attributive** and the **referential** use of a definite description (cf. Fauconnier 1985, pp. 159–61). A standard example of this contrast is the sentence *Smith's murderer is insane*. Under the attributive interpretation, *Smith's murderer* refers to whoever it might be that murdered Smith—the speaker presumably has no idea as to the identity of the killer but concludes that anyone capable of such a vile deed must be insane. Under the referential interpretation, the speaker knows who murdered Smith and simply chooses to refer to this individual by means of a definite description rather than a proper name. Clearly, the attributive sense of *Smith's murderer* amounts to a role specification of a limited sort: the role is characterized as that of the perpetrator of one specific event, the murder of Smith. Now there are any number of people who may have knocked off Smith, i.e. there are many possible versions of reality distinguished by the identity of the assassin. Each such version represents a distinct world instance, and the world type with respect to which the role is defined is simply the schematization of these various instances, in which the killer's identity is left unspecified. When used referentially, *Smith's murderer* pertains to one particular world instance and designates a specific person rather than a type. As usual, the instantiation inherits the description of its type specification.

2.3. Quantity

Instantiation presupposes some notion of a type (however vague), for an instance conception arises when a type specification is anchored in the domain of instantiation and thought of as having a particular location in that domain. Quantification in turn presupposes instantiation, since quantity does not pertain to an unanchored type conception but rather to instances of a type. Languages primarily employ two sorts of devices to indicate quantity within a nominal. Many languages have a category of **number** (e.g. singular vs. plural), which tends to be marked on the head noun. Beyond this, all languages have a variety of **quantifiers** (e.g. *one*, *three*, *several*, *few*, *most*) that make possible a finer-grained indication of quantity.

2.3.1. *Number*

The English-type system in which nouns are marked for a two-way contrast between singular and plural is very common cross-linguistically but by no means universal. Some languages do without number marking on nouns altogether, or for all but a certain class of nouns (e.g. humans or animates); it is therefore left implicit whether one instance of the category is involved or more than one, unless this information is provided by some other element, such as the verb or a quantifier. Other languages make a three-way distinction among singular, dual, and plural, in which case plural has the value 'more than two' (instead of 'more than one'). Other numbers, specifically trial 'three' and paucal 'a few', have been attested but are rare by comparison.

For the issues that concern us, it is sufficient to examine the two-way opposition singular vs. plural. There are two basic patterns for marking this opposition. The typical pattern is for the singular to be unmarked, with plural explicitly indicated through affixation or some other morphological device. English of course exemplifies this pattern: *spoon/spoons*; *top/tops*; *church/churches*; *knife/knives*; *goose/geese*; etc. The other possibility is for singular and plural both to be overtly marked, as illustrated by the Swahili noun-class prefixes: *ki-su* 'knife'/*vi-su* 'knives'; *ki-tabu* 'book'/*vi-tabu* 'books'; *m-toto* 'child'/*wa-toto* 'children'; *m-zee* 'old man'/*wa-zee* 'old men'; *m-kono* 'arm'/*mi-kono* 'arms'; and so forth.

It is natural that in the first kind of system it should be the singular that is left unmarked. This relationship between the singular and plural forms is iconic to their semantic relationship in two respects: first, the conception of a single instance is simpler than one encompassing multiple instances; second, and more significantly, the conception of a single instance is the basis for constructing the more complex notion, which is obtained by replicating this instance conception an indefinite number of times.[7] Indeed, many languages carry this form/meaning iconicity a step farther and derive the plural by reduplicating all or part of the singular stem (e.g. Hopi *saaqa* 'ladder'/*saa-saqa* 'ladders'; *kiihɨ* 'house'/*kii-kihɨ* 'houses').

However, there is also a sense in which the Swahili-type system is semantically revealing. When the singular and plural are each marked by some

[7] We will soon find reason to qualify this statement. It is more accurate to say that the conception of multiple instances involves replication of the type specification (whose content is essentially equivalent to that of an instance) without specifically invoking the notion of singularity.

modification of the stem, a formal distinction is made between a type specification (given by the stem alone) and the conception of a single instance (stem plus singular marking). This distinction remains covert in an English-type system where the stem itself is used as the singular form. Despite their formal identity, a noun that occurs alone (e.g. *cat*) or incorporated as the first element of a compound (*cat lover*) is not equivalent semantically to a singular noun that functions as a nominal head (*the cat*). The former represents the conception of a type per se, and since it lacks the notion of instantiation, the question of quantity does not arise (hence the number of cats subjected to the affection of a *cat lover* is completely indeterminate—certainly more than one can be involved). By contrast, a singular head noun comprises a type conception construed as being anchored at a particular location in the domain of instantiation and specifically limits the profile to this single instance. Though subtle, the distinction is linguistically significant. It is diagrammed in Fig. 2.8, where T abbreviates the semantic specifications that characterize

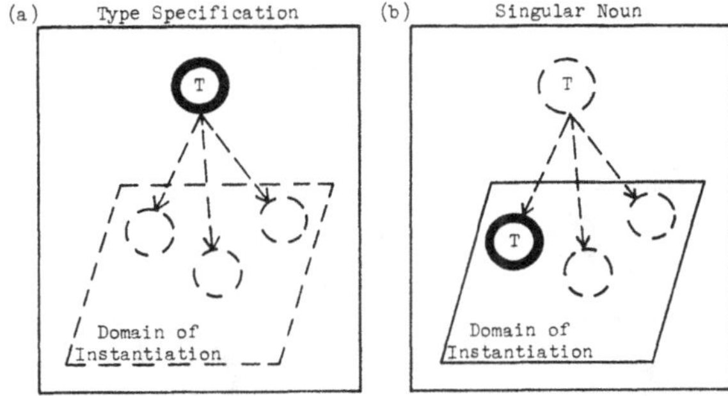

Fig. 2.8

a type. Because a type specification and a singular noun differ so minimally in their conceptual content, it is hardly surprising that they are often not distinguished morphologically. For an English-type system, we can posit a pattern of zero derivation (or equivalently, of semantic extension—see fn. 4) whereby any noun stem can be construed as designating a single instance of the category.

What about plurals? Now that we have distinguished between a noun stem that merely labels a type and a formally identical stem that is specifically singular, the question arises as to which of these a plural is derived from. It is far more plausible, I suggest, to derive it from the former. We have no reason to assume that the construction of a plural conception from a type specification involves as an intermediate step the specific conception of a single instance. Separately deriving both singulars and plurals directly from a numberless stem has the further advantage of making the English-

and Swahili-type systems more similar: their essential difference reduces to whether the singular derivation is marked overtly or by zero. Furthermore, if plurals did derive from stems that were specifically singular, we would predict that both the singular and the plural markings should generally occur on a plural noun—so that in Swahili, for example, we would expect **vi-ki-su* 'knives', **vi-ki-tabu* 'books', **wa-m-toto* 'children', etc.—but this is either non-existent or exceedingly rare.

Let us assume, then, that a plural noun is formed directly on a numberless stem whose meaning is restricted to a type specification. The semantic pole of a plural-noun construction will therefore be as diagrammed in Fig. 2.9.[8]

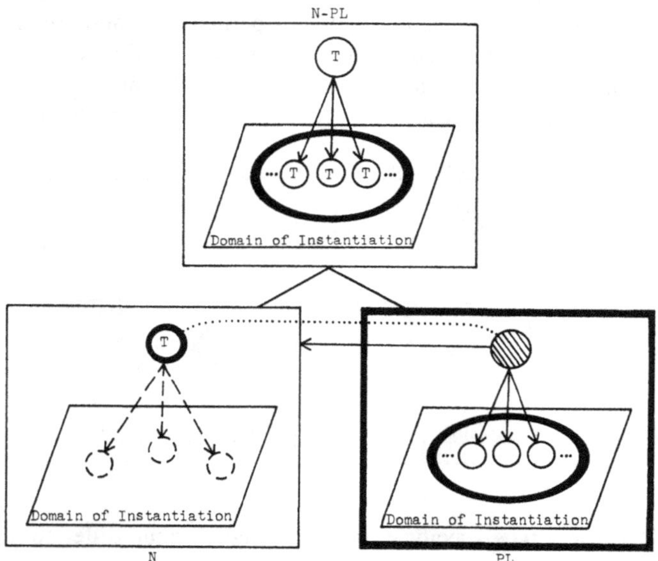

Fig. 2.9

The component structure on the left is the noun stem, which profiles a bounded region and may be characterized in any amount of detail, but nonetheless remains an uninstantiated type. The component on the right is the plural morpheme, which amounts to a schema for the class of plural nouns. Since plurals are a subclass of mass nouns, the profile of the plural predication is a region that is unbounded within its scope in the domain of instantiation. This abstract region comprises an open-ended set of things (only three of which are shown explicitly) that constitute a region precisely because they all

[8]This diagram is a refinement of Fig. 8.7 in Vol. 1, which was formulated without any reference to the type/instance distinction. Note that the horizontal correspondence line equates two types (not two instances, as in Fig. 2.5).

instantiate the same type specification. Their type specification is of course highly schematic within the plural morpheme itself—it is the noun stem that renders it specific. Hence the schematic type specification of PL serves as e-site and is elaborated by the semantically richer type specification of N. Because PL is the profile determinant, the composite structure (the plural noun) designates a mass (unbounded region) consisting of indefinitely many instances of the type (T) supplied by the noun stem.

I will mention only in passing the fact that not every noun which is plural in form can be taken as representing the pattern in Fig. 2.9, though it is clearly prototypical. Many "plural" nouns have a referent that is not divisible into clearly discrete components each capable of being labeled individually by the corresponding singular stem (if, indeed, there is such a stem): *oats*, *guts*, *bowels*, *binoculars*, *pants*, *scissors*, *pliers*, *bleachers*, *catacombs*, *Pyrenees*, *Alps*, *woods*, etc. In these expressions, the plural inflection assumes slightly different values that constitute semantic extensions from its prototypical meaning. Roughly, it highlights the internal complexity of a unitary entity whose subparts are in some sense functionally equivalent but can either be delimited only arbitrarily or else do not occur (or serve any useful purpose) independently.[9]

Though plurals can only be formed on count nouns, plurals themselves fall under the mass-noun category. One symptom of their mass-noun status is the fact that a plural noun is not susceptible to further pluralization. Beyond this, plurals and other mass nouns behave alike in numerous respects. Each can occur as a full nominal without a quantifier or an overt grounding predication: *They're looking for {diamonds/gold}*. Both occur with the definite article, but neither tolerates the indefinite article: *the {diamonds/gold}*; **a {diamonds/gold}*. Moreover, both appear with a variety of quantifiers not permitted with count nouns: *most {diamonds/gold/*diamond}*; *all {diamonds/gold/*diamond}*; *a lot of {diamonds/gold/*diamond}*.[10] To be sure, plurals have certain properties that set them apart as a special subclass within the mass-noun category. In particular, they are countable, take the plural demonstratives, and also occur with a number of special quantifiers: *eight diamonds* vs. **eight gold*; *these diamonds* vs. *this gold*; *many diamonds* vs. *much gold*; *few diamonds* vs. *little gold*; *several diamonds* vs. **several gold*; etc.

Evidently, the basis for this contrast is the salience in plurals of the notion that the designated mass is constituted of an indeterminate number of discrete entities all of the same type (each of which can be named by the corresponding singular stem). By its very nature, a plural is special because it profiles a mass that we can think of as being formed by replicating indefinitely many

[9] For additional discussion and insightful analysis, see McCawley 1975 and Wierzbicka 1985.

[10] Naturally, these expressions are acceptable if *diamond* is construed as a mass, i.e. as the name of a substance rather than a discrete object.

times a discrete entity that we are accustomed to dealing with individually—I thus refer to it as a **replicate** mass. Hence a plural inherently tends to heighten the individuation of the mass it designates, whereas a non-plural mass noun has the opposite proclivity. Although a non-replicate mass may be perceived as particulate to one degree or another (consider *sand*, *corn*, *gravel*, *lumber*), its portrayal by a non-plural noun de-emphasizes this aspect of its composition and focuses instead on the sense in which it can be regarded as continuous. As evidence for this difference in construal, observe the greater naturalness of referring to three-dozen pebbles as *gravel* when they are piled together in a heap than when they are spread out several yards apart on a gymnasium floor; there is no difficulty using *pebbles* in the latter case. Similarly, if I am holding just two smallish slabs of wood, one in each hand, the term *boards* comes more readily to mind than *lumber*, which evokes the image of a large number of boards stacked together.

Common nouns are thus divisible into three basic classes with contrasting semantic properties, as reflected in their occurrence with different sets of quantifiers and grounding predications. Where necessary, they can be distinguished by the abbreviatory notations in Fig. 2.10 (though I will also continue

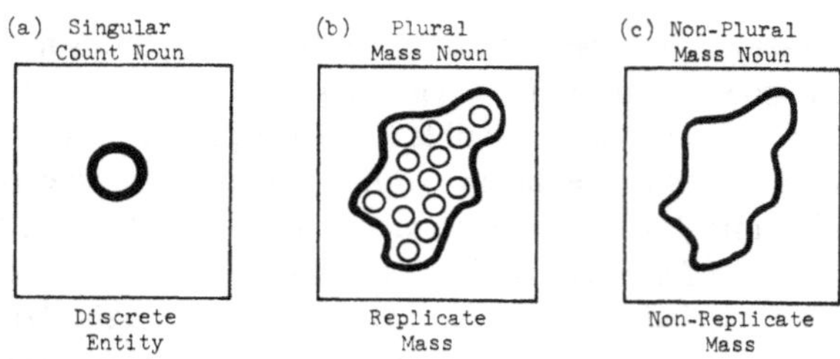

Fig. 2.10

to use a circle for nouns in general). A singular count noun, such as *pebble*, designates one discrete entity (a bounded region). At the other extreme, a non-plural mass noun, e.g. *gravel*, profiles a mass (unbounded region) that may be particulate but is nevertheless construed so as to highlight its internal uniformity. Combining their properties is a plural noun like *pebbles*: it is classed with other mass nouns on the basis of its profile, but its formation assures that considerable prominence is accorded to the discrete entities out of which the mass is constituted.

For the following account of quantification and grounding, it is essential to realize that **a singular noun and its corresponding plural represent distinct categories** and that what counts as an instance is consequently very different in the two cases. A single small stone qualifies as a valid instance of the *pebble* category, but not of *pebbles*: only a set consisting of two or more stones counts as an instance of the latter. The two nouns embody separate type specifications lying at different levels of conceptual organization. The type description of *pebble* profiles a discrete object and is conceptually simpler. At the higher level of organization, *pebbles* designates a mass comprising indefinitely many instances of *pebble*, hence it presupposes the multiple instantiation of this lower-order category. The instantiation of *pebble* must be distinguished from that of *pebbles*, however. To effect the latter requires a still more elaborate conception in which a non-unit set of constituent entities is anchored in the domain of instantiation and thereby distinguished from other such sets. This distinction between a plural noun construed as a type specification and as an instance of that type is diagrammed in Fig. 2.11. The

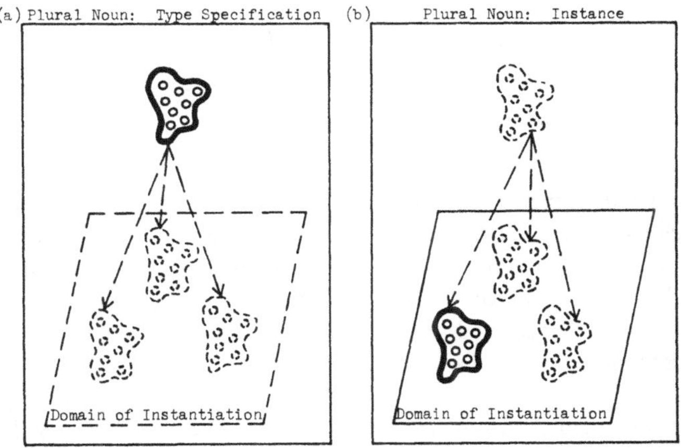

Fig. 2.11

instantiation of a plural noun is implied by its occurrence as a quantified, grounded nominal head (e.g. in *those four pebbles*, or even just *pebbles* when used as a full nominal) but is not signalled by any difference in form. We can assume that a plural stem, like a numberless stem, undergoes the pattern of zero derivation noted above whereby a noun is construed as designating a single instance of the type it specifies. Therefore, just as *pebble* has either of the values sketched in Fig. 2.8, so can *pebbles* have either of those shown in 2.11.

Except for the contrast between replicate and non-replicate masses, the instantiation of plurals is exactly the same as that of other mass nouns. The type specification for a mass incorporates both a qualitative characterization and the conception of the designated substance having an indefinite expanse. Instantiation occurs when some expanse of substance is anchored, or thought of as having a particular location, in the domain of instantiation. The properties of homogeneity and contractibility ensure that any expanse, however

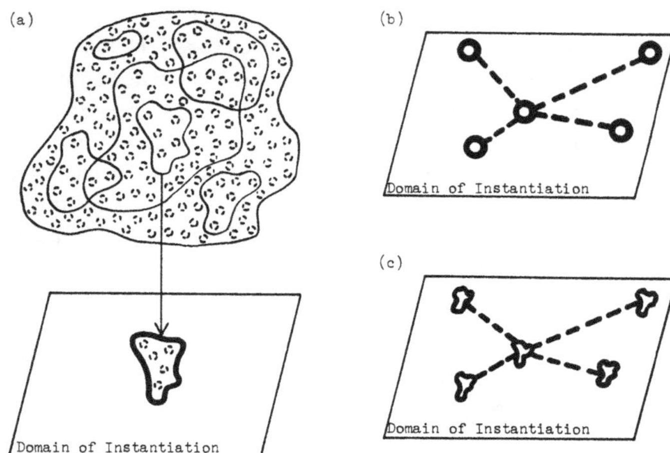

Fig. 2.12

large or small, represents a possible instance of the mass-noun category.[11] The various solid-line curves in Fig. 2.12(a) indicate just a few of the countless options, only one of which is shown as having been selected. Note that the small circles stand for the discrete entities that constitute a replicate mass; the import of using dashed lines is that these entities are optional, i.e. a precisely analogous range of options is available for plurals and for other mass nouns.

One refinement is necessary. Recall that an instance of a mass is not necessarily continuous in the domain of instantiation—instead of contiguity in this domain, it is qualitative uniformity that establishes the constitutive entities as a region. What counts as a single instance of a mass-noun category may therefore be scattered about the domain of instantiation, as respectively shown for a replicate and a non-replicate mass in Figs. 2.12(b) and (c). For example, *those five quarterbacks* may refer to the ones who currently lead the NFL in passing statistics; collectively they constitute a single instance of the *quarterbacks* category even if they have never been assembled in one place. Similarly, *the water in the five saltiest lakes in the world* designates one instance of the *water* category, even though the patches of water in question are spatially discontinuous. In cases like these, the profiled instance does not have a *unitary* location in the domain of instantiation, but rather a *complex* location

[11] There is, to be sure, a lower limit, as the sample must be large enough to permit the identification of the mass. For physical substances, no less than a molecule will suffice, even for purely technical definitions (see McCawley 1975 for more detailed discussion). In the case of a plural (which designates an abstract substance), the bare minimum is a set consisting of two component entities.

which reduces to those of its components, be they discrete objects or patches of substance. It has a location nonetheless and is thereby distinguished from other instances.

The proposed analysis not only fully captures the parallelism between plurals and other mass nouns but also achieves a semantic description that is maximally congruent with the grammatical structure of nominals. In particular, a nominal always designates a *single instance* of the pertinent category (cf. Löbner 1985), and when this category is specified (i.e. when it is not left implicit or schematic, as in *this* or *those three in the back*), it is always determined by the head as a whole (together with possible modifiers). Consider *the pebble*, *the pebbles*, and *the gravel*, whose heads—which I take to be the second word in each case—correspond to the three noun classes diagrammed in Fig. 2.10. The claim is that *the pebbles* designates one instance of the *pebbles* category, just as *the pebble* and *the gravel* respectively designate one instance of the *pebble* and *gravel* categories. The same is true even when a quantifier is added, e.g. *the seven pebbles*. The analysis holds that this nominal profiles one instance of *pebbles*, not seven instances of *pebble*; hence the role of the quantifier is not to specify the number of instances, but rather the *cardinality* of the single profiled instance. The two descriptions are of course extensionally equivalent, but the one adopted here seems better motivated in terms of linguistic structure.

2.3.2. *Quantifiers*

A pivotal claim of the analysis being pursued is that every nominal profiles a single instance of some type, which is generally provided by the head noun together with its number specification. The role of a quantifier is therefore not to specify the *number* of instances (which is always just one) but rather to indicate the *size* of the profiled instance. For a plural, of course, the size of the instance will be given by the number of its component entities, but collectively these entities constitute just one instance of the plural-noun type. It should also be remembered that grounding represents a distinct parameter that is superimposed on the structures of present concern at a higher level of conceptual organization. As a consequence, the assertion that a nominal such as *no dog*, *any dog*, or *every dog* designates a single instance of the *dog* category is perfectly coherent. For example, *No dog likes cabbage* does incorporate the conception of a single canine; however, the effect of the grounding predication *no* is to deny the existence (in a particular mental world) of a cabbage-liking relationship in which an instance of *dog* participates.

For our purposes, it is important to distinguish between expressions that merely specify the size of the profiled instance and those with the exclusive or additional function of grounding that instance. The traditional usage of

quantifier subsumes both classes and is too well entrenched to be jettisoned, but I will also use the term narrowly for the first class in particular, so that it stands in opposition to **grounding predication**. *One* is thus a quantifier in the narrow construal of the term, whereas the article *a* is a grounding predication because it renders a nominal indefinite. In fact, all the favorite "quantifiers" of logicians—*some*, *any*, *each*, *all*, *no*, *every*—constitute grounding expressions rather than quantifiers by this definition (note that, like *a*, they only form indefinites). Once these are excluded, the remaining quantifiers show a higher degree of semantic coherence. There is a clear sense, for example, in which *three*, *seven*, *much*, *many*, *several*, *few*, *little*, and *numerous* all specify the size of some mass. *One* can be thought of as a limiting case in this regard, as it specifies the size of a degenerate replicate mass comprising only a single component entity.

On the basis of a concomitant semantic property, we can refer to the "true" quantifiers and those with a grounding function as **absolute** and **relative quantifiers**, respectively. A relative quantifier is so called because it specifies a quantity in relation to a **reference mass**; in the default-case interpretation, this reference mass consists of the maximal instantiation of the pertinent category (i.e. its full extension in all conceivable worlds). The clearest examples are *all* and *most*: *all dogs* profiles a replicate mass that bears a relationship of identity to the reference mass (the maximal extension of *dogs*), while the mass profiled by *most dogs* is characterized as a proper subpart of the reference mass that comes reasonably close to exhausting it. Although the other grounding quantifiers are less straightforward in this regard, I will argue that in some fashion they too invoke a reference mass. On the other hand, an absolute quantifier specifies the size of the profiled instance without referring to the maximal extension of the relevant category. If I speak of *many dogs*, *several dogs*, or *seven dogs*, I am saying something vague or precise about the number of dogs involved independently of any estimate as to how this total stacks up in relation to the set of all dogs. We can thus explain the fact that, in response to the question *How many California condors still exist?*, an absolute quantifier such as *few*, *several*, or *nineteen* is perfectly acceptable, whereas those relative quantifiers that most saliently and crucially invoke a reference mass—*all*, *most*, *every*, and *each*—are impermissible. The reason is that the question itself asks for the size of a reference mass (as determined by present reality), so that a felicitous answer cannot be expressed as a proportion of that mass.

Drawn on semantic grounds, the distinction between relative and absolute quantifiers also proves to have structural significance. If the former are indeed grounding expressions, it makes sense that they do not occur with one another, nor with the most obvious instances of grounding predications, namely articles and demonstratives: **the some dogs*; **that every dog*; **an any dog*;

those most dogs*; **the all dogs*; etc.[12] The absolute quantifiers do however occur with demonstratives and the definite article, and sometimes even with relative quantifiers: *those three dogs*; *the many cats I have owned*; *these few statesmen*; *the little hope he retains*; *all seven hummingbirds*; *any three ballerinas*.[13] Their failure to take the indefinite article is readily explained. *One* would be redundant with this article: **a one dog*. On the other hand, those quantifiers that go on mass nouns conflict with *a* semantically, either because they imply a higher cardinality (a three dogs*; **a several balloons*), or else because the two have opposite values in regard to discreteness: **a much sadness*. (In *a little*, *a few*, *a lot*, etc., *a* is part of the quantifier; such expressions are considered below.)

Another structural difference is that only absolute quantifiers occur as the lexical head of a clause:

(15)(a) *The problems we have to deal with are {three/few/many/several/numerous}.*

(b) **The politicians who sacrifice their principles for sake of election are {all/most/some/any/every}.*

Though hardly colloquial, the construction in (15)(a) is familiar and readily understood; the corresponding construction with a relative quantifier is neither, as we see in (15)(b). It is significant that *be* can only be followed by a relational complement (e.g. an adjective, prepositional phrase, participle, or predicate nominative), which strongly suggests that absolute quantifiers are also relational (or have relational variants). By contrast, the non-occurrence of relative quantifiers with *be* leaves open the possibility (to be supported later on principled grounds) that they are always nominal.

In short, there is ample motivation for making a fundamental distinction between absolute and relative quantifiers (cf. Jackendoff 1977, ch. 5). The former are "true" quantifiers that offer a direct description of magnitude and confine themselves to that role. The latter are best regarded as grounding predications that fulfill this function through a quantitative assessment made relative to a reference mass. Our immediate task is thus to provide a characterization of absolute quantifiers. Though an exhaustive description cannot be

[12] There are some apparent exceptions, but they all have special properties that put them outside the intended scope of the generalization. Conjunction figures in *each and every dog*. *The most dogs* involves the superlative sense of *most* (it does not quantify over the set of dogs as a whole). *All those dogs* represents a variant of the pattern displayed by *all of those dogs*, *most of these trees*, *some of the spaghetti*, etc.; *all* is the head, and *those dogs* functions as a nominal complement (see Langacker 1982b for discussion and analysis). The *most* in *most any dog*, *most every dog*, and *most all dogs* is an adverbial modifier of the following word (cf. *almost*).

[13] When *much* is used in a positive sense, it is marginal at best in such expressions: ?*the much sadness I have known*; ?**the much milk she drank*. This sense is in any case disappearing in the face of competition from *a lot of*.

attempted here, we can at least survey the most common exemplars and establish their basic nature.

One approach is to classify these quantifiers according to the type of nouns they occur with. Restricting our attention to simple quantifiers of frequent occurrence, it is striking that each occurs with just one basic type and that plural nouns have by far the greatest selection. The only "core" quantifier that goes with singular nouns is *one*, which is hardly surprising in view of their limited quantitative possibilities.[14] For non-plural mass nouns, the options are also quite limited: *much*, *little*, and *a little* exhaust the list. Plurals offer a richer variety: in addition to *many*, *few*, and *a few* (the replicate counterparts of *much*, *little*, and *a little*), we find *several* and the somewhat more peripheral *numerous*, not to mention an open-ended set of numbers.

Semantically, the mass-noun quantifiers (*much* and *(a) little*) presuppose a continuous scale of magnitude, whereas all the others are characterized with respect to the counting numbers. The latter include both specific and schematic expressions: basic number terms (*one*, *two*, *three*, . . .) peg a quantity to a particular step along the counting scale, but *many*, *several*, *numerous*, and *(a) few* merely place the value within a vaguely-delimited range. The range for *several* begins with three, and although it has no precise upper limit, its use becomes tenuous if there are more component entities than one can simultaneously hold in mind as individuals (roughly seven plus-or-minus two—see Miller 1956). *Numerous* is less specific still; perhaps one can say that its range begins where that of *several* leaves off. The remaining forms make reference to some norm or baseline value and constitute a neatly-structured system. *Many*, *few*, and *a few* match up perfectly with their non-replicate analogs *much*, *little*, and *a little*. The values for *many* and *much* lie beyond the implicit norm, and those of *few* and *little* fall below it. What about *a few* and *a little*? In terms of actual quantity, these may be the same as *few* and *little*. What distinguishes the pairs is that *a few* and *a little* are reckoned from a baseline of zero and indicate a modest positive departure therefrom, while *few* and *little* are negative, indicating a value below some expectation.

Suppose, then, that each absolute quantifier has for its base the conception of an appropriate scale (continuous or discrete, with or without a norm). Each quantifier also has a landmark, identified as the range to which its possible values are confined; in the case of a number, for instance, the landmark is a particular point on the counting scale. A quantifier must further incorporate the conception of a mass (degenerate in the case of *one*) whose magnitude is

[14] I will not consider such "non-core" alternatives as *single*, *sole*, *unique*, and *only* (which have special properties and are semantically more complex) or "partitive" expressions like *half*, *partial*, and *full*. Comparable exclusions are made for the other classes. This is primarily a matter of convenience: no special status is necessarily attributed to the "core" quantifiers, nor is a clear-cut dichotomy assumed. The division does however appear to have some intuitive basis.

being assessed with respect to the scale. Crucial as well are interconnections, i.e. the particular way in which the mass is conceived as being matched against the scale for purposes of making the assessment. For a replicate mass, we can think of these interconnections as establishing a correspondence between each successive point on the scale and some component of the mass until the mass is exhausted. All these elements figure in the conceptual content of a quantifier. They are diagrammed in Fig. 2.13(a) for the specific example *three*.

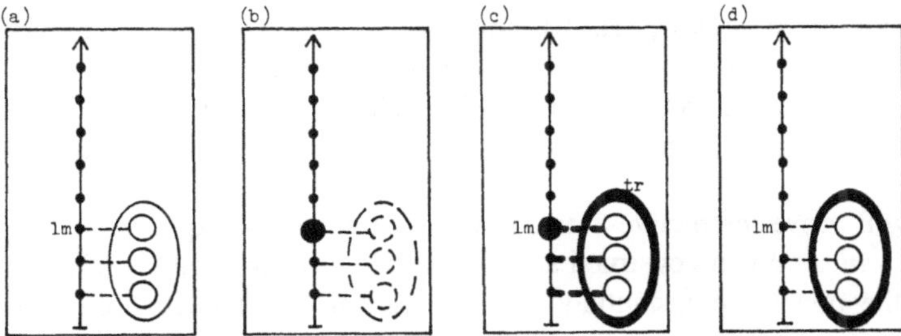

Fig. 2.13

What profiling is imposed on this content? That depends on how the expression is used, and in the case of numbers there are three distinct possibilities, exemplified in (16).

(16)(a) *Three is the number between two and four.*
(b) *Three tables ought to be sufficient.*
(c) *I could only find three.*

First, a number term can be used as such, i.e. as the name of a number rather than as a quantifier. In this event it merely designates a point along the numerical scale, as shown in Fig. 2.13(b); the notion of a mass mapped onto this scale is latent or absent altogether. The use of *three* as a simple quantifier is illustrated in (16)(b) and diagrammed in Fig. 2.13(c). We noted previously (in regard to (15)(a)) that a quantifier is relational when employed as clausal head, and presumably it has this value when it combines directly with a noun.[15] The relational sense of *three* profiles the interconnections between the mass and the scale, choosing the former as trajector (relational figure). Except for *numerous*, all the forms being considered also have the nominal sense shown in diagram (d), in which the mass alone is profiled. When used with this meaning, as in (16)(c), they are traditionally regarded as pronouns.

[15] This is not a necessary assumption: valence principles permit the integration of a quantifier and a noun even if the former has the nominal profile of Fig. 2.13(d) (see Vol. 1, Ch. 8 and Langacker 1988a). Such an analysis can be suggested for languages where quantifiers behave as nouns morphologically.

We see, then, that alternate senses of a quantifier are revealingly described as resulting from contrasting profiles being imposed on essentially the same base. The description accounts for both the similarities and the differences among the semantic variants, which are related through zero-derivational patterns of considerable generality (observe that these patterns can apply to any number term). The choice of profile determines the expression's grammatical class as well as the constructions in which it occurs. In (16)(a) and Fig. 2.13(b), *three* profiles a specific point along the number scale and is thus a noun (actually a proper name, since the type has only one instance). With the profiling of (15)(a), (16)(b), and Fig. 2.13(c), *three* is a stative relation and can be regarded as a special sort of adjective. The region profiled in Fig. 2.13(d) is characterized only schematically, so with this value *three* is a kind of pronoun; when grounded, it can stand alone as a full nominal, as in (16)(c).

It will prove instructive at this point to compare the expressions *three* and *three tables*. When construed as a full nominal, as in (16)(b)–(c), each profiles the quantified instantiation of a type and grounds it through a zero-marked predication of indefiniteness. What concerns us is the contrasting ways in which this conception of a quantified instance comes about. In the case of *three*, it is provided directly by the pronominal variant of this quantifier (Fig. 2.13(d)). *Three* itself incorporates a type specification, albeit a highly schematic one—its type is simply 'replicate mass' (and is thus equivalent to the semantic pole of the plural morpheme).[16] Moreover, since *three* is a quantifier, it necessarily portrays the type as being instantiated. The resulting instance is put in profile and is quantified in terms of its projection along the number scale.

In the case of *three tables*, the conception of a quantified instance is built up compositionally. The type description is furnished by the plural noun *tables*, whose assembly conforms to the constructional schema sketched in Fig. 2.9. *Tables* can further be construed as designating a particular instance of this type in accordance with a pattern of zero derivation previously discussed (2.3.1). The quantification of this instance is then contributed by the adjectival variant of *three*, as diagrammed in Fig. 2.14. The integration of *three* and *tables* is effected by a correspondence between the former's trajector (an e-site) and the latter's profile. Observe that *tables* makes no inherent specification concerning the cardinality of the mass it designates (except, of course, that it must be more than one), and since any quantity of a substance counts as a valid instance of the category (contractibility), the instance profiled by the noun can always be made to match the size specified by the

[16] In context, of course, the type in question is identified more precisely, but *three* does not itself provide this information (hence its pronominal character).

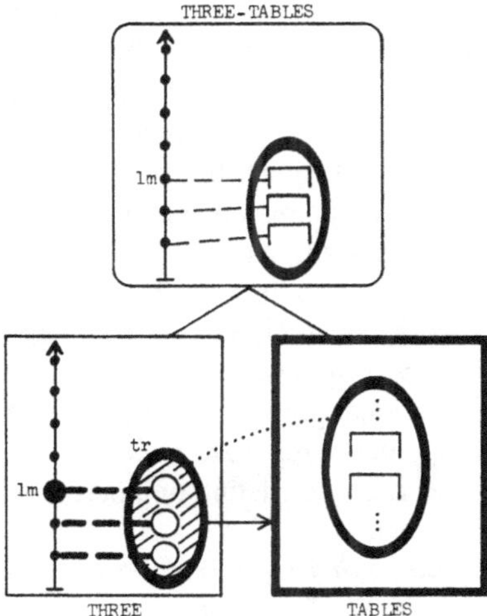

Fig. 2.14

quantifier. Hence *three* and *tables* are precise concerning number and type respectively, while the composite structure is precise in both regards because it inherits their specifications. Also, the composite expression is categorized as a noun (not an adjective) because *tables* is the profile determinant.

As a final matter, we must consider more complex expressions, particularly those in which a quantifier is followed by a prepositional phrase with *of*: *three of the tables*; *many of our friends*; *much of the difficulty*; etc. In the early days of transformational grammar, it was common for everything before the final noun to be described as a complex determiner: $[[\textit{three of the}]_{\text{DET}}$ $[\textit{tables}]_{\text{N}}]$. Demonstrating the obvious unworkability of this analysis (which nevertheless persisted at least through Chomsky 1970) is left as an exercise for the reader.[17] A later proposal, also now abandoned (see Jackendoff 1968; 1977, pp. 112–13), correctly recognized the *of*-phrase as some type of complement to the head but erroneously attempted to derive the simple quantifier expressions from the complex ones by deletion: *many of the men* ===> *many men*. Something closer to sanity now prevails, although it is still common for *of* to be treated as a meaningless formative that is inserted and/or deleted transformationally (e.g. Chomsky 1970 and Jackendoff 1977, ch. 5; see Langacker 1982b for arguments against this approach).

The account I propose is more straightforward and conforms quite closely to what is overtly present. *Three tables* and *three of the tables* are separate and parallel expressions, each assembled in just the way its form suggests.

[17] Hint: Can it really be maintained that *our friends* is not a constituent in *many of our friends*? If *cats* is the head noun in *one of those cats*, how can number agreement correctly apply?

The former employs the adjectival variant of *three* to modify the head noun *tables*, as shown in Fig. 2.14. Occurring in the latter, on the other hand, is the pronominal *three* (Fig. 2.13(d)), which functions as the nominal head. *Of* is a true, meaningful preposition that profiles an intrinsic relationship between its trajector and landmark; in this quantifier construction, its trajector is characterized more specifically as being an inherent subpart of the landmark, which is elaborated by the prepositional object. Hence *of the tables* designates an inherent part/whole relationship between a schematic trajector and a landmark identified as a specific set of tables. The integration of *three* with *of the tables* is effected by a correspondence between the profile of the head and the trajector of the prepositional phrase (cf. Fig. 1.8). As a consequence, the composite structure designates a replicate mass that has just three members and is drawn from a larger mass consisting of a particular set of tables evident to the speech-act participants.

Similar in many respects to *three of the tables* are expressions like *a bunch of carrots*, *a bucket of water*, and *a lot of sharks*. These represent a vast and varied family of constructions that merit far more attention than we can give them here. Observe that the nouns which appear as heads constitute a diverse and open-ended class: *mess*, *pile*, *heap*, *loaf*, *sprig*, *head*, *stack*, *group*, *array*, *pinch*, *tad*, *bit*, *barrel*, *crate*, *jar*, *tub*, *vat*, *keg*, *box*, *ton*, *pound*, *yard*, *foot*, *flock*, *herd*, *pride*, *school*, *bevy*, *gallon*, *pint*, *liter*, *cup*, *spoonful*, *pocketful*, *mouthful*, *closetful*, *truckload*, *shipload*, etc. We must limit ourselves to a few brief comments concerning their interpretation.

First, some of these nouns still have an interpretation in which they designate a physical, spatially-continuous entity that either serves as the container for some portion of a mass (*bucket*, *cup*, *barrel*, *crate*, *jar*, *tub*, *vat*, *keg*, *box*) or else is constituted of some such portion (*bunch*, *pile*, *heap*, *loaf*, *sprig*, *head*, *stack*, *flock*, *herd*). Thus *a bucket of water* may in fact be a physical bucket that is filled with water, and *a bunch of carrots* may actually be a lump-like object formed by tying a number of carrots together into a bunch. For each such object, there is conception of its typical size, which is part of its encyclopedic characterization. However, the size specification is secondary to the profile's status as a physical object; the domain of instantiation ranks above the size scale in the noun's complex matrix.

To one extent or another, most such nouns have taken on a different sense in which size becomes the most salient specification. For instance, a bathtub may contain *a bucket of water* without there being any bucket in it—it is only implied that the water would fill a bucket were it placed in one. Similarly, *a bunch of carrots* may refer to a certain number of carrots irrespective of their physical distribution. A noun interpreted in this fashion can be regarded as a quantifier. The notion of a discrete physical object has faded, leaving behind the conception of a schematically characterized mass (the mass that, in the original sense, either fills or constitutes the object) whose projection on the scale of magnitude then provides its primary semantic content. So construed, *a bucket* or *a bunch* is directly analogous to the pronominal sense of *three* (Fig. 2.13(d)), and *a bucket of water* or *a bunch of carrots* is parallel in construction to *three of the tables*.[18]

A further step in this evolutionary sequence would be for the second noun to be reanalyzed as the head, leaving the remainder as a complex quantifier: $[[$*a lot of*$]_{QNT}$ $[$*sharks*$]_N]_{NML}$. I leave open the question of whether this reanalysis has actually occurred, for *a lot of* or any other quantifying expression (cf. Selkirk 1977). But suppose it has, so that *a lot of tables* displays the same grammatical organization as *three tables* (apart from the morphological complexity of the quantifier). In this case *a lot of* must be adjectival at the composite structure level, i.e. roughly comparable to the adjectival sense of *three* (Fig. 2.13(c)), regardless of whether this value arises compositionally from the meanings of its parts. The integration of *a lot of* with the following noun will also then be similar to that of *three* (Fig. 2.14).

2.4. Epistemic Predications

Every nominal profiles a thing construed as a grounded, quantified instance of some type. We have so far dealt with the instantiation of types and the quantification of instances. The structures thereby assembled represent a level of organization intermediate between a simple noun and a full nominal. Each profiles a single instance that is either a discrete entity, a replicate mass, or a non-replicate mass (Fig. 2.10). The size of the profiled instance can either be left implicit (and thus characterized only schematically) or specified with greater or lesser precision with respect to a scale of quantity. The quantification observed at this level is absolute, in the sense that only the inherent expanse of the instance is considered in assessing its magnitude.

By contrast, a grounding predication relates the profiled instance to some external point of reference. For those predications whose value pertains primarily to quantity, this reference point is a more inclusive entity (reference mass) that contains the instance as a subpart. For those pertaining primarily to (in)definiteness, the reference point is identified with the speaker and hearer, who are responsible for the conceptualization serving as the semantic pole of the nominal, and who—for purposes of linguistic expression

[18] As a quantifier, *bunch* is not limited to things like carrots and radishes that are tied together in bundles (note *That has happened in a whole bunch of cities*), nor to masses of that particular size: *Fred bought a (whole) bunch of carrots* might in fact be used when Fred bought seven physical bunches (the import is that he bought *a whole lot* of them). The shift in meaning is also predictably accompanied by a change in verb agreement (e.g. from *is* to *are* in *A bunch of carrots* ____ *in the sink*). Agreement reflects the shift in profile from a discrete physical object that contains or constitutes a mass (for *bunch*, a replicate mass) to the quantified mass itself.

and successful communication—confront the challenge of directing their attention to the same instance. We can reasonably think of grounding predications as the loci through which the speech-act participants establish contact with the conceived situation and relate it to their own knowledge and circumstances. They do so by means of relationships between themselves and the most prominent entities within the situation, notably the thing profiled by a nominal and the process profiled by a finite clause. Since these relationships pertain to their knowledge of instances and their ability to single them out, grounding predications are said to be **epistemic**.

Consider a finite clause in which the verb stem *hate* is the clausal head, and where *boy* and *cats* are the respective heads of the subject and object nominals. From these lexical and grammatical specifications, we are able to construct a fairly detailed conception: we know that the clause evokes and profiles an instance of the process type *boy hate cats*. Substantial though it is, however, this conception is insufficient to serve as the meaning of a finite clause. Lacking is anything that specifically connects the *boy hate cats* instance to the speech-act participants or allows them to determine just how it is supposed to fit into their mental universe. This is the role of epistemic predications, which for clauses pertain primarily to the location of the profiled process in time and reality relative to the ground. Obviously, the import of a *boy hate cats* instance for the speaker and hearer varies enormously depending on how it is grounded by predications of tense, modality, and negation. There are numerous options (*hates*, *hated*, *will hate*, *should hate*, *may not hate*, etc.), but they are all alike in one essential respect: they extend the scope of predication to include the speech event and the associated notion of present-time reality (by definition, the locus of the speech event) and use this as a reference point to situate the designated process (see Ch. 6 and Langacker 1978).

Suppose we locate the process in present reality. There remain a wide range of options, involving alternate ways of grounding the subject and object, that differ vastly in their import: *The boy hates cats*; *Every boy hates cats*; *A boy hates these cats*; *This boy hates most cats*; *No boy hates all cats*; *That boy hates some cats*; etc. The conception of a hating relationship between an instance of *boy* and an instance of *cats* is claimed to figure in the meaning of each expression. The semantic contrasts reside in how this conception is embedded in a more inclusive configuration—specifically, in the status attributed to the *boy* and *cats* instances vis-à-vis the reference points employed for the grounding of nominals. Given the inherent constraints of the communicative situation, these reference points provide a natural basis for fulfilling the purpose of a nominal.

The objective of a speaker in using a nominal is to mention some instance of a type in such a way that the hearer can determine his intended reference.

For a given type T, there is commonly an open-ended set of instances $\{t_1, t_2, t_3, \ldots\}$; these do not have separate names—indeed, the name for the type (e.g. *boy*, *cats*, *milk*) can be applied to any one of them. How, then, can the speaker direct the hearer's attention to the instance he has in mind? One way is by providing a description (*boy who lives next door*; *black cats*; *milk on the verge of going sour*), but that merely pushes the problem back one step, for the description itself constitutes a higher-order type specification that potentially has an open-ended set of instantiations. Inherent in the situation, however, are two natural reference points that the speaker can always count on: the ground itself (the speech-act participants and their immediate circumstances) and a reference mass, R_T, from which every instance of T is drawn. R_T can be defined as the union of all instances within the realm of discourse. For a count noun like *boy*, which designates a discrete entity, R_T is equivalent to the set of all instances, i.e. $R_T = \{t_1, t_2, t_3, \ldots\}$. The instances of a mass like *cats* or *milk* are non-discrete and overlapping (Fig. 2.12(a)); any subpart of R_T (including the whole) counts as a valid instance of T.

Hence the speaker (S) and hearer (H), who jointly form the ground (G), face the task of coordinating their mental reference to some instance t_i of type T drawn from the reference mass R_T. Both G and R_T are available to serve as reference points for this purpose. The basis for using G as reference point is the psychologically defined notion of **mental contact**: a person makes mental contact with t_i when, in his current psychological state, t_i is singled out for individual conscious awareness. When both S and H make mental contact with t_i, full coordination of reference is achieved. This situation is sketched in Fig. 2.15, where the solid arrows represent instantiation and the dashed arrows indicate mental contact.[19] In one way or another, a grounding predication invokes this ideal situation—a crucial ingredient of definiteness—if only to indicate that this goal has not yet been achieved. That it has *not* been achieved is one aspect of the meaning of relative quantifiers, which are thus inherently indefinite. What distinguishes such a quantifier from a simple indefinite article is a further semantic specification that takes R_T as a reference point. In the case of *all*, for example, t_i is equated with R_T, while *most* specifies that t_i comes close to exhausting R_T.

Grounding predications have special properties that set them apart as a grammatically significant class. However, their privileged status appears on first examination to be without a conceptual basis, since seeming paraphrases exhibit very different grammatical behavior. Consider *this*, which we can ana-

[19] Although instantiation is a special case of elaboration (for which solid arrows are regularly employed), there is no connection between this use of dashed arrows and their normal function of marking relationships of partial schematicity (i.e. extension). See Chafe 1974 for broader discussion of the relevance of consciousness to linguistic structure, and Givón 1978 for typological and diachronic perspectives on matters related to definiteness and referentiality.

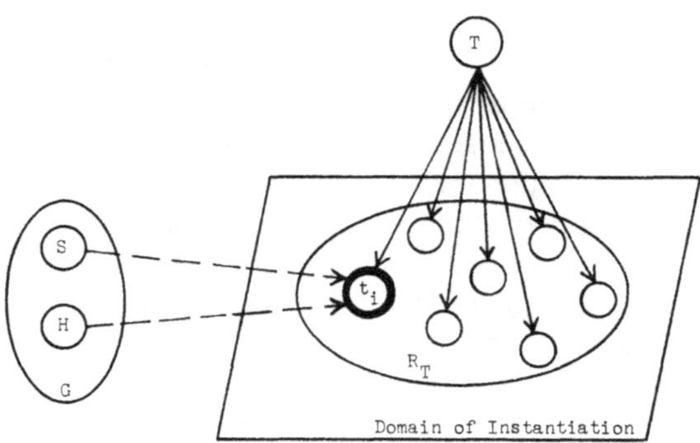

Fig. 2.15

lyze as being roughly equivalent semantically to the conjunction of *near S* and *(uniquely) apparent to S and H*. These latter expressions are stative relations, and like *this*, they are able to combine with a noun: *this boy*; *the boy near me*; *the boy apparent to you and me*. There are nonetheless a series of contrasting properties that need to be accounted for.

First, and most obviously, *this* can stand alone as a full nominal, whereas its apparent equivalents cannot, either singly or when conjoined:

(17)(a) *I like this.*
(b) **I like near me and apparent to you and me.*

Second, the demonstrative cannot be used as clausal head (except—irrelevantly—as a predicate nominative):

(18)(a) **The boy is this.* [with the meaning of (b)]
(b) *The boy is near me and apparent to both of us.*

Third, *near* and *apparent to* occur with nominals that elaborate their landmarks; there is explicit reference to these landmarks, even when they are identified with the speech-act participants (*near me*; *apparent to you and me*). By contrast, it is obligatory with *this* that the reference point remain implicit—there is no way for *me*, *you*, or *us* to be introduced as a direct complement of the demonstrative: **this (to) {me/us} boy*; *(*{the/a}*) *boy this (to) {me/us}*. Finally, except in certain literary styles the reference point for *this* can only be the speaker and hearer, even when it appears in a clause representing someone else's conception. Hence the house referred to in (19)(a) must be taken as proximate to the speaker (and evident to both S and H), despite the fact that it is Janice whose belief is reported by the subordinate clause:

(19)(a) *Janice believes that this house is haunted.*
(b) *Janice believes that a nearby house is haunted.*

In (19)(b), on the other hand, the house is readily interpretable as lying in proximity to Janice.

These properties are not peculiar to *this*—by and large, comparable observations can be made for the other grounding predications.[20] I have suggested elsewhere (1985) that the notion of **subjectivity** affords a unified explanation for their special behavior. Subjectivity pertains to the inherent asymmetry between the two roles that constitute the **construal relationship**: the role of the conceptualizer (C) and that of the conceptualization he entertains. This asymmetry is maximized when C is totally absorbed in his conception, so that he loses awareness of himself and even of the fact that he is engaging in conceptualization, i.e. when all his attention is directed outward, toward the "object" of conception (O), and none at all inward, toward his own activity as the "subject" of conception. When the relationship is maximally asymmetrical in this fashion, the role of C is said to be fully **subjective**, and that of O, fully **objective** (Vol. 1, 3.3.2.4).

For language, the relevant conceptualizers are the speech-act participants, and the relevant conceptualizations are the meanings of linguistic expressions. The role of the speaker and hearer is thus fully subjective with respect to an expression when they themselves do not figure in its meaning in any way, i.e. when the ground is excluded from its scope of predication. This is clearly impossible for deictics, which refer to the ground by definition. Still, ground elements have varying degrees of salience in deictic predications, and their subjectivity correlates inversely with their prominence. A pronoun like *I* or *you* falls at one extreme of this continuum, for it profiles a speech-act participant and thus puts it "onstage" as the focal point within the immediate scope of predication; S or H is thereby rendered maximally salient and minimally subjective. The prominence of S and H is only slightly diminished in phrases such as *near me* and *apparent to you and me*, where they function as central participants in a profiled relation. They are considerably less prominent—and hence more subjective—in the deictic construal of an expression like *across the street* (= 'across the street from here'): though included in the scope of predication, the ground remains implicit, serving only as an "offstage" point of reference.

My proposal is that epistemic predications lie at the opposite extreme of this continuum from the first- and second-person pronouns. In other words, the characteristic feature of a grounding predication is that **S and H are maximally subjective, consistent with their inclusion in the scope of predication**. This is illustrated in Fig. 2.16, where a box indicates the overall scope

[20] Recall, for example, that relative quantifiers do not occur as clausal heads, as illustrated in (15). One qualification is that not every grounding predication stands alone as a full nominal. In the case of the articles, there is probably a phonological explanation based on the semi-clitic status of *the* and *a*. I cannot explain the failure of *every* and *no* to occur independently.

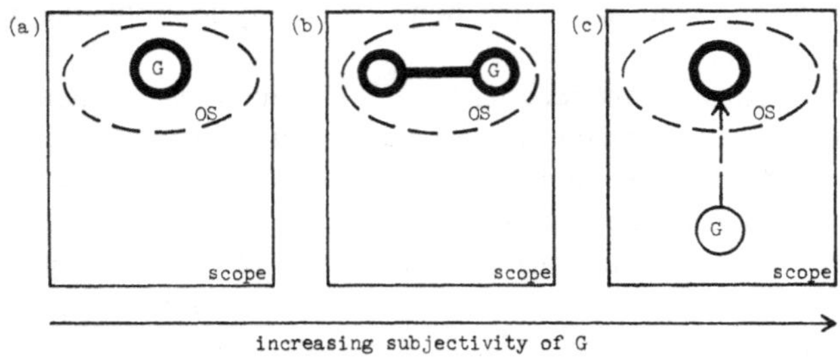

Fig. 2.16

of predication and a dashed-line ellipse delimits the immediate scope, also referred to as the onstage region or the **objective scene** (OS); this region is describable as the general locus of attention within the overall scope, and by definition the profile is confined to it. The structure in Fig. 2.16(a) profiles an element of the ground, thus making it the focal point within the objective scene (as in *I* or *you*). The ground element is still objectively construed in 2.16(b), which profiles a relation that has it for a central participant (e.g. *near me*). However, the ground is subjective in diagram (c), which represents an epistemic predication (e.g. *this*). Like (b), (c) incorporates a relation that takes some facet of the ground as a major participant. The distinctive property of (c) is that both the ground and this grounding relationship are subjectively construed. Despite its importance to the predication, G remains offstage and non-salient, so by definition it cannot be profiled. The same is true of the grounding relationship (which is shown as a dashed arrow because its pivotal component is mental contact). In short, a crucial feature of an epistemic predication is that it does not profile the grounding relationship, but rather the entity that is grounded by this relationship (namely, t_i).

This analysis not only captures the semantic distinction between *this* and its seeming paraphrase (*near me and uniquely apparent to you and me*) but provides an immediate explanation for their contrasting grammatical behavior. First, *this* can stand alone as a full nominal because it is nominal rather than relational in character, i.e. it profiles a thing (and also supplies its grounding). Second, for just this reason *this* cannot be used as clausal head, since a clause always profiles a relation (and *be* requires a relation for its non-subject complement). Third, the reference point for *this* cannot be spelled out explicitly because the overt mention of an entity enhances its salience and thus reduces its subjectivity, whereas the defining feature of an epistemic predication is the maximal subjectivity of the ground. Finally, the reference point for *this* is always identified as the speaker and hearer because they are specifically accorded that role as an inherent aspect of its semantic characterization (by contrast, the landmarks of *near* and *apparent to* are specified only schematically).

To summarize, an epistemic predication always profiles the entity that it grounds, not the grounding relation itself (which is nonetheless an essential part of its base, and thus of its meaning). For nominals, the profiled entity is of course a thing: it is a single, quantified instance t_i of type T and is drawn from the reference mass R_T. The grounding predication invokes the speaker and hearer as reference points and makes some specification concerning whether they have established mental contact with t_i. Further specifications are possible, especially pertaining to the relationship between t_i and R_T.

CHAPTER 3

Nominals: Grounding and Quantification

THE NOTION OF **grounding** must be sharply distinguished from both **designation** and **instantiation**. Designation (i.e. profiling) is the selection of some substructure as a kind of focal point within a predication; the imposition of a profile on a base is central to the value of every predication, even at the level of a type specification. The conception of an instance arises when a type is "anchored" in the domain of instantiation, i.e. when the profiled entity is thought of as occupying a particular location in that domain and thus distinguished from other instances. Grounding presupposes instantiation, for it involves the relationship between an instance and the speech-act participants. Grounding predications for nominals divide into two basic sets. Those which focus on degree of definiteness take the ground (G) as their primary reference point. Relative quantifiers also serve as grounding predications and identify an instance with reference to a more inclusive class (R_T). In this chapter we will survey the predications of each type, turning subsequently to quantifier scope and related phenomena.

3.1. Definiteness

Grounding predications for which G is the most prominent reference point include both articles and demonstratives, together with the unstressed *some* (*sŏme cats*; *sŏme milk*) and the "zero determiner" (*Cats drink milk*). It is convenient to begin with the definite article, which is the only member of the set that occurs with all three basic noun classes (*the boy*; *the cats*; *the milk*). Previous work, notably Hawkins 1978, has made it evident that the various uses of *the* are susceptible to a unified description. Our objective here is limited to providing the conceptual framework required for its statement in cognitive grammar.

3.1.1. *The Definite Article*

Fauconnier (1985) has demonstrated the importance of **mental spaces** for problems of discourse and nominal reference. A mental space is a conceived situation of any degree of complexity, comprising a set of elements and relations holding among them. Through discourse, mental spaces are evoked, created, and modified by the addition of new elements and relations. Crucially, one space can be included in another, and correspondences are established between the elements of different spaces. A person distinguishes and manipulates any number of mental spaces, which vary considerably in their cognitive (and logical) status. They include the conception of present reality and of reality as it stood at any previous time. Also included is any vision a person might have of the future or of those aspects of the present or past he has no knowledge of. The alternative reality of a story, film, play, or dream constitutes a mental space, as does any imagined world or situation. Importantly, a person knows that any other person also has a conception of reality and manipulates an array of mental spaces comparable to his own. Person A's conception of person B's view of reality (or some other mental space available to B) can be regarded as a subspace within A's own reality conception.

To characterize the definite article, we need a construct that we can call the **current discourse space**. This mental space comprises those elements and relations construed as being shared by the speaker and hearer as a basis for communication at a given moment in the flow of discourse. More specifically, the entities that constitute the discourse space fall within what is understood to be the realm of current discussion and are immediately available to both S and H, either figuring directly in their conscious awareness or being readily elicited (e.g. through association or simple inference). The discourse space may subsume all or portions of other, previously existing spaces, or a new space may be created by the discourse itself, as in (1):

(1) *Once upon a time, there was a beautiful princess who lived with an ugly frog in a castle overlooking a championship golf course . . .*

In the absence of special indications, a cognitively salient domain such as present reality or the immediate physical context may be adopted as the discourse space by default. Naturally, the content of the current discourse space continually changes. As the discourse unfolds, new specifications are constantly added and others slowly fade from awareness.

Another pivotal notion is mental contact, which we have defined in terms of an entity being singled out for individual conscious awareness in the conceptualizer's current psychological state. Mental contact is easily achieved, for the entity involved need not be real or referential (it can inhabit any mental space) and nothing specific need be known about it (mere awareness of it—however induced—is sufficient). Thus (1) brings the listener into mental contact with a princess, a frog, a castle, and a golf course, despite their sketchy description and the presumption that they are imaginary. Similarly, (2) establishes mental contact between the hearer and a fish, even on the non-specific reading, where the fish exists only in the space representing David's desire:

(2) *David wants to catch a fish.*

On the specific reading, where David has a particular fish in mind, it is not presumed that the speech-act participants know anything about the fish other than that David wants to catch it.

We can now attempt to characterize the meaning of the definite article: **use of the definite article with type description T in a nominal implies that (1) the designated instance t_i of T is unique and maximal in relation to the current discourse space; (2) S has mental contact with t_i; and (3) either H has mental contact with t_i or the nominal alone is sufficient to establish it**. The basic import of *the* is that the speaker and hearer, just by using the nominal it grounds, establish mental contact with the same instance t_i; at that point coordination of reference has been achieved, as depicted in Fig. 2.15. It should further be noted that the article itself profiles t_i and that the grounding relationship (the mental contact of S and H with t_i) is an unprofiled facet of the base—this is the hallmark of an epistemic predication (recall Fig. 2.16(c)).

Though it is no doubt an oversimplification, for present purposes we can assume that the current discourse space is updated on a clause-by-clause basis. The information provided by one clause is thus incorporated in the discourse space relative to which the following clause is interpreted. By the foregoing definition, then, nothing in the clause containing a *the*-marked nominal is required for establishing coordinated mental contact with t_i other than that nominal itself. Consider (3):

(3) *I bought a shirt and a belt, but the shirt was too small.*

The use of *the* is proper in the second clause because the first clause has already brought a specific instance of *shirt* into the discourse and established it in the current awareness of S and H; reference to the size of the shirt plays no role in its identification. On the other hand, I could hardly use (4) to start a conversation with a perfect stranger:

(4) *I just found the quarter.*

Assuming that the quarter is in my pocket out of sight, I have no reason to believe that any instance of *quarter* (let alone the one I intend) figures in the present awareness of the addressee. It is true, of course, that the utterance itself evokes such awareness, and even puts H in mental contact with a uniquely identified instance—namely, the quarter I just found. However, *the* implies that the nominal alone (independently of the clause containing it) is sufficient for such contact. From *the quarter* alone, H lacks the basis for directing his attention to any particular instance.

Although *the* is commonly used when H already has mental contact with t_i, as in (3), prior contact is not specifically required. Often H's awareness of t_i is fully prefigured and thus a matter of imminent potential, awaiting only S's utterance of the nominal for its **actualization** (Vol. 1, p. 437). Examples like the following are unexceptionable and easily multiplied:

(5)(a) *I ought to sell my car; the engine is almost shot.*
(b) *I saw a great film last night; I really admire the director.*
(c) *Our soccer team is in last place because the goalie is utterly incompetent.*

The speaker cannot assume that mentioning a car, a film, or a soccer team will necessarily evoke in the hearer the conception of an engine, a director, or a goalie; H can perfectly well conceive of the former in generalized fashion and thus fail to single out the latter for individual conscious awareness. Still, the notions *engine*, *director*, and *goalie* are fairly central to the encyclopedic characterizations of *car*, *film*, and *soccer team*, and mention of a *car*, for example, pushes the concept *engine* to the brink of consciousness (psychologists would speak of a **priming** effect based on the mental association of *car* with *engine*). Moreover, just one engine figures in the normal conception of a car (and similarly for the other examples). The first clause in (5)(a) thus introduces into the discourse space a uniquely identified instance of *engine*, namely the instance inherently associated with *my car*. Though it may remain latent as the first clause is processed, the conception of this instance is actualized by the occurrence of *the engine* in the second clause and mental contact is thereby established.

The degree to which H's awareness of t_i is prefigured by the current discourse space is quite variable. When the discourse space furnishes only an indirect basis for such awareness, or no basis at all, the status of t_i as an element of this space is tenuous or non-existent. Use of the definite article is nevertheless appropriate and in conformity with the proposed definition provided that the nominal itself puts H in mental contact with t_i and that t_i is unique when construed in relation to the discourse space. For some nominals, the very content of the type description implies that there is only one instance, so uniqueness is ensured regardless of the discourse state:

(6)(a) *the last day of 1987*
(b) *the only person to have hit a golf ball on the moon*

(c) *the letter between P and R in the alphabet*
(d) *the tip of Fred's nose*

That the type has just one instance is specified directly by *last* and *only* in (6)(a)–(b), whereas in (c) and (d) it follows from our knowledge of the alphabet and human physiognomy. It can also happen that H has no grounds for suspecting the existence or the uniqueness of t_i other than the fact that S employs the definite article. I can therefore utter (7)(a) to warn an unsuspecting hiker of imminent danger, or (7)(b) to inform someone learning to drive that the vintage car we are using has an archaic feature called a *choke* (and moreover, that it has just one of them):

(7)(a) *Watch out for the snake behind you!*
(b) *This is the choke.*

In cases like these, the nominal is solely responsible for introducing and establishing mental contact with t_i. The current discourse space does not include t_i, for H has no awareness of this entity prior to the utterance, not even a latent awareness actualizable through a simple cognitive process such as association or direct inference. Such uses stretch the limits of *the*'s applicability. They might well be analyzed as representing a communicative strategy wherein S acts as though the definite article were appropriate despite his knowledge that it actually is not.

It remains to clarify the import of the specification that t_i is unique and maximal in relation to the current discourse space. The uniqueness requirement is illustrated in (8).

(8)(a) *I have a cat and a dog. The cat is very lazy.*
(b) **I have a gray cat and a calico cat. The cat is very lazy.*

In (8)(a), the first clause creates a discourse space containing just one instance of *cat*; hence the intended reference is unambiguous when, in the second clause, *the cat* is construed in relation to this space. By contrast, the discourse space holds two instances of *cat* in (8)(b), so t_i is non-unique and *the* is inappropriate. The requirement of maximality pertains to mass nouns and specifies that t_i can only be identified as the most inclusive instance in the discourse space. Consider (9):

(9)(a) *I have seven cats. The cats are very lazy.*
(b) *Tom bought seven gallons of milk. The milk turned sour.*

The initial sentences in these examples introduce an instance of *cats* with a cardinality of seven and an instance of *milk* with a volume of seven gallons. These are the maximal instances in the discourse space, and *the cats* and *the milk* refer to them felicitously. Recall, however, that any subpart of a mass-noun instance is also a valid instance of the category. Therefore the discourse space in (9)(a) contains not only the maximal instance of *cats* (of cardinality seven) but also various less inclusive instances (with cardinality ranging from two to six). Similarly, the discourse space in (9)(b) includes indefinitely many instances of *milk* less than seven gallons in volume. The maximality requirement accounts for the fact that *the cats* in (a) can only refer to all seven, and *the milk* in (b) to the full seven gallons. Moreover, with the understanding that only the maximal instance of a mass is eligible for consideration, t_i is in each case unique in the discourse space.[1]

One question that immediately arises is why *the* cannot occur with mass nouns when they are construed generically as designating the maximal extension of the specified substance (i.e. when $t_i = R_T$). Thus (10)(a) cannot be interpreted to mean that the boy hates all cats, nor (10)(b) to mean that the girl loves all cheese—to achieve these construals, the definite article must be omitted.

(10)(a) *The boy hates the cats.*
(b) *The girl loves the cheese.*

This is probably not due to semantic incompatibility (observe that the definite article occurs with such generics in French: *les chats*; *le fromage*). I attribute it instead to the fact that the reference mass, R_T, is inherently ambivalent as to definiteness, and assume that English (in contrast to French) has simply conventionalized the indefinite construal. If full generic reference is intended, then R_T is necessarily the maximal instance of T in the relevant discourse space, and also unique, so it could be considered definite. At the same time, however, generic reference can be thought of as arising by default when nothing is done to single out any portion of R_T. And because the singling out of some instance for individual awareness is the crucial ingredient of definiteness, there is also a rationale—which English apparently seizes upon—for construing a generic mass as indefinite. Generic masses are thus assimilated to the general pattern whereby a zero-marked indefinite such as *cats* or *cheese* is applicable to a mass of any size (including R_T as a limiting case).

The definite article would also be semantically compatible with proper names but generally cannot occur with them in English (**the Stan Smith*). Here the motivation is evidently the avoidance of redundancy, for a proper name conveys the essential content of *the* as part of its own semantic structure. A name incorporates the idealized cognitive model which specifies that

[1]Hawkins (1978) elegantly accommodates both uniqueness and maximality by stating that a *the*-marked nominal refers "inclusively" within the relevant pragmatic set. With a singular noun, this implies uniqueness, for if there were more than one potential referent, a plural would be needed.

it is borne by, and suffices to identify, just one individual. As a consequence, mention of the name itself is presumed capable of establishing mental contact with the unique instance of the type. Of course, languages do not invariably shy away from redundancy, so it is hardly astonishing that definite articles do sometimes occur with proper nouns (e.g. *la France*). An article's range of application in a given language is obviously subject to conventional determination, involving varied rationales and countless subtleties that we cannot explore here.

Most closely related to the definite article are the demonstratives, which also are definite and imply that both S and H make mental contact with t_i (Fig. 2.15). The four English demonstratives are distinguished by two binary oppositions: *these* and *those* ground replicate masses (*these cats*; *those boys*), whereas *this* and *that* are used for both discrete entities and non-replicate masses (*this cat*; *that milk*); within each set there is a further distinction often referred to as **proximal** vs. **distal** (*this/these* vs. *that/those*). Though many languages lack articles, every language has a demonstrative system, and some kind of "proximity" distinction is typical if not universal.

The analysis of demonstratives poses many interesting problems (for various perspectives, see Lakoff 1974; Hawkins 1978; Kirsner 1979a, 1987), but we will focus on how they differ from the definite article. It is not unreasonable to regard the article as neutralizing the distinctions made by the demonstratives, and thus as being schematic for the class. Against this, Hawkins has correctly pointed out that demonstratives contrast with the article by lacking the supposition of uniqueness. Whereas *the* is infelicitous if more than one instance of T is in the current discourse space, a demonstrative is perfectly comfortable in that situation:

(11)(a) **The cat is friendlier than the cat.*
(b) *This cat is friendlier than that cat.*

However, this difference correlates with the greater semantic specificity of demonstratives and their use when the speaker is actively engaged in pointing out the intended referent. This pointing function may actually be carried out by a physical gesture, as is likely in (11)(b); in cognitive grammar, this gesture is unproblematically considered an aspect of the demonstrative's form, and its import an aspect of its meaning (Vol. 1, 2.1.2 and 2.2.1). In the absence of a gesture, the specification for proximity (or in other languages, for visibility, animacy, etc.) accomplishes this demonstrative function more abstractly.

Now unless there is more than one candidate, pointing to the intended referent—either physically or abstractly—is not really necessary to identify it (though it may still be done for emphatic or affective purposes). There is consequently a natural correlation between the pointing function of a demonstrative and its tolerance of multiple instances of T in the current discourse space; the definite article lacks such tolerance precisely because it is more schematic semantically and cannot be used for pointing. Observe, however, that once the gestural components of a demonstrative (physical or abstract) are taken into account, the intended referent t_i is uniquely determined. Hence a demonstrative is fully compatible with the proposed characterization of the definite article, since the nominal itself enables H to establish mental contact with the appropriate instance. We can therefore analyze a demonstrative as incorporating the meaning of *the* together with certain gestural components, which permit the selection of the intended referent from multiple instances of T. Lacking such components, the definite article can only select the proper referent if there is just one candidate to begin with.

3.1.2. *The Indefinite Article*

The remaining grounding predications taking G as primary reference point are all indefinite and specifically suggest that the nominals they ground are insufficient to put H in mental contact with a uniquely determined instance of T. There is a clear division of function: the indefinite article occurs only with singular count nouns, while the other two predications—symbolized by the unstressed *some* and zero (Ø)—occur with both sorts of mass nouns.[2] The contrast between *sŏme* and Ø pertains to quantity. *Sŏme* indicates that the designated instance is quite limited, but with Ø it can be of any size, even exhaustive of the reference mass. Thus either *sŏme* or Ø can be used in (12), where the content of the clause makes it evident that only a restricted quantity is involved:

(12)(a) *Alice drank (sŏme) milk.*
(b) *(Sŏme) rats got into the storeroom.*

(13)(a) *The formula for (*sŏme) water is* H_2O.
(b) *(*Sŏme) dogs are mammals.*

On the other hand, (13) demonstrates that only Ø tolerates a full generic construal (where $t_i = R_T$).

With the indefinite article, it is customary to distinguish between a **specific** and a **non-specific** interpretation (Baker 1966). Either is possible in (14):

(14) *Ollie hopes to marry a blonde.*

[2]Remember that an epistemic predication profiles the entity it grounds, not the grounding relationship (Fig. 2.16(c)). Hence *a* profiles a schematically characterized bounded region (equivalent to the semantic pole of the count-noun schema), whereas *sŏme* and Ø profile an unbounded region (equivalent to the semantic pole of the mass-noun schema, apart from *sŏme*'s quantity specification). Similarly, the profile of *these/those* is a schematic replicate mass.

Under the specific interpretation, Ollie has a particular blonde in mind that he wishes to marry; on the non-specific reading, he does not—any blonde might do. Note that *certain* forces the specific reading: if I say that Ollie hopes to marry *a certain blonde*, he must have a particular person in mind. Another manifestation of this contrast is that (supposedly) only a specific use creates a "discourse referent" that can be referred to anaphorically in a subsequent sentence. Thus, if I continue the discourse in (14) by saying *She is tall, rich, and beautiful*, referring back to *a blonde* with the pronoun *she*, the former must be interpreted as specific.

The analysis I propose represents a slight refinement of this standard account: a single meaning accommodates both the specific and the non-specific uses of the indefinite article, and either use is capable of establishing a discourse referent. I am essentially paraphrasing Hawkins (1978) in stating that the indefinite article contrasts with the definite in regard to uniqueness: the former implies that the nominal alone is *not* sufficient to put the hearer in mental contact with a uniquely determined instance of the category. Thus, if you and I are working on a car and there are several wrenches lying about, I can perfectly well say *Hand me a wrench!*—but hardly *Hand me the wrench!*—because there are multiple instances of *wrench* in the current discourse space defined by our immediate physical circumstances. The opposite would of course be true if there were only one wrench at our disposal.

The basic analysis, then, is that *a* profiles a discrete thing (a schematically characterized bounded region) and indicates that, while the nominal it grounds does establish mental contact between H and an instance t_i of T, the nominal itself does not render the choice of t_i unique in relation to the current discourse space. As for specificity, I suggest that the property of establishing a discourse referent should be put aside as a red herring. The proper definition of specificity pertains to whether the speaker (S), or some **surrogate speaker** (S′) whose conscious awareness is being described, has some pre-existing or independent mental contact with t_i. If so, the *a*-marked nominal is specific. It is non-specific when t_i represents an arbitrary instance of T, i.e. when it is "conjured up" for a particular immediate purpose and has no status outside the special mental space thereby created.

The special feature of examples like (14) is that the indefinite occurs in an **opaque** context.[3] In Fauconnier's theory of mental spaces, the structure that appears in an opaque context constitutes a mental space distinct from its "parent" space; the parent space in (14), for instance, is present reality (the space

[3] A context is opaque when the substitution of one expression by another expression of identical reference does not necessarily preserve truth value. For example, if the specific blonde in question happens to be the Princess of Eastern Herzegovina, the truth of (14) does not entail that of *Ollie hopes to marry the Princess of Eastern Herzegovina* (e.g. he might not know that the blonde is a princess, and he hates princesses).

in which Ollie entertains his hopes), while the conception of his marrying a blonde is a separate, subordinate space representing the situation Ollie envisages and desires. Let us call the parent space R, and the subordinate space R′. Space R resides in the mind of the speaker, S, whereas R′ resides in the mind of a surrogate speaker, S′, identified as the subject of *hope* (i.e. Ollie); we can represent these host-space relationships as S(R) and S′(R′). Of course, S′(R′) is itself one component of R, so that, indirectly, R includes R′ as a subspace.

The non-specific reading of (14) can now be characterized as one in which the blonde inhabits R′ (the space representing Ollie's hope) but has no other, independent connection with either S′ (Ollie) or S (the speaker). That is, the blonde resides only in the world of Ollie's desire and is accessible to S and S′ only as an element of that space. The specific reading (forced by *certain*) is that in which there *is* some other connection: S′ necessarily has pre-existing mental contact with the blonde (i.e. she is not merely a figment of his hope and thus has some existence outside R′)—this is what it means to say that S′ has a particular individual in mind. In the case of S, such prior contact is possible but not implied. S may know who Ollie has in mind (and thus have access to her other than via S′(R′)), but it is also possible that S knows nothing about the blonde besides the fact that Ollie hopes to marry her.

Observe that this characterization of specificity is independent of whether a discourse referent is established. If a specific interpretation is intended, there is of course no problem in following (14) with *She is tall, rich, and beautiful*, where *she* refers back to *a blonde*. But consider the non-specific interpretation and the anomaly of continuing in this fashion if Ollie has no particular blonde in mind. I would argue that the reason for the infelicity is not that the non-specific occurrence of *a blonde* fails to establish a discourse referent, but rather that the following sentence locates this referent in the wrong mental space. Under the non-specific interpretation, the blonde only inhabits R′; she is accessible to other spaces only via the relation S′(R′). Yet the continuation *She is tall, rich, and beautiful* places her directly in reality (R) by virtue of its present tense and the absence of a modal (see Ch. 6 and Langacker 1978). When some adjustment is made to indicate that the subsequent discourse still pertains to R′, the anaphoric pronoun is perfectly acceptable. For example:

(15) *Ollie hopes to marry a blonde—but she must be tall, rich, and beautiful.*

Here the continuation embellishes on the mental space R′ created in (14), and the imagined blonde is spared the schizophrenia of simultaneously having to be part of present reality.

We have now found several applications for the notion of an arbitrary instance. We have used it here to explicate the non-specificity of a nominal that occurs in an opaque context. In 2.2.4 we used it to describe the value of the indefinite article that appears in the predicate-nominative construction (e.g. *Alice is a thief*). Another use involves generic sentences such as *A wombat is a mammal* (Fig. 2.7), or the following well-known example:

(16) *A beaver builds dams.*

All of these can be regarded as cases of non-specificity in which a conceived instance t_i of T is invoked for a particular limited purpose and has no standing except in that context.

Clearly, these sentences do not imply that either S or H has any pre-existing mental contact with the instance designated by the *a*-marked nominal. The instance is conjured up just for purposes of making the generic statement and as such is thought of as a representative instance of the category rather than a particular instance known on independent grounds. I suggest, in fact, that the full generic relationship (*a wombat be a mammal*; *a beaver build dams*) is situated in a special mental space—call it R′ once more—that is distinguished from present reality (R), though it is related to R, and though it, like R, is hosted by S. This special space, R′, represents a fragment of the speaker's conception of **how the world is structured**. It does not correspond to any particular event that involves specific participants and unfolds at the time of speaking, but rather to a canonical (and perhaps necessary) relationship inherent in the fabric of the world as it is presently constituted.

By postulating spaces of this sort, we can account for the so-called "habitual" interpretation of the English present tense. As (17) demonstrates, this construal is not restricted to clauses with generic participants:

(17) *Fred walks his dog in the afternoon.*

The present tense clearly does not imply that an instance of Fred walking his dog occurs at the moment of speaking—the sentence could perfectly well be uttered in the morning or evening. Instead, I would analyze (17) in the following way (cf. Langacker 1987b; Goldsmith and Woisetschlaeger 1982; Johnson-Laird 1983). The relationship *Fred walk his dog in the afternoon* is construed as constituting a mental space R′. Now R′ is not contemplated in isolation, but is thought of as representing a fragment of how the world is structured; in other words, R′ participates in a relationship whereby it figures as an inherent aspect of the world as it is presently institutionalized. It is this higher-order relationship involving R′ that is taken as extending through the time of speaking in a sentence like (17). It is not the specific process *Fred walk his dog in the afternoon* that coincides with the speech event, but rather the status of that process as a canonical, institutionalized occurrence.

The same sort of analysis is proposed for generic sentences involving non-specific participants, e.g. (16). The generic relationship *a beaver build dams* is part of a mental space R′ representing what is thought of as canonical beaver behavior, and the present tense marks the current reality (at the time of the speech event) of the higher-order relationship in which R′ is construed as an inherent component of how the world is structured. For immediate purposes, the important point is that the profiled instance of *beaver*—and also of *dams*—is an element of R′ only, and that the speech-act participants have no pre-existing mental contact with it, nor any access to it except as an element of R′. Hence *a beaver* and *dams* are non-specific in much the same way that *a blonde* is in *Ollie hopes to marry a blonde*. Neither one allows subsequent pronominal reference that implies its location in R:

(18)(a) **A beaver builds dams—it finished one last night.*
(b) **A beaver builds dams, but they may be swept away by this evening.*

However, pronominal reference is possible provided that the subsequent discourse is still describing R′:

(19)(a) *A beaver builds dams—it normally needs three weeks to finish one.*
(b) *A beaver builds dams, and they last for years.*

Anaphoric reference is even possible (though marginal) with the subject in a predicate nominative construction:

(20) *A wombat is a mammal—of course, it is only a mammal if it is a real wombat, not a wombat doll.*

Anaphoric reference appears not to be possible with the predicate nominative itself, perhaps because it is part of the intransitive clausal predicate rather than a clausal participant.

3.2. Relative Quantifiers

The relative quantifiers are indefinite and make a further specification involving a reference mass, R_T, which is generally fully inclusive for type T (representing its maximal extension in relevant worlds). These quantifiers divide into two groups: *all*, *most*, *some*, and *no* profile a mass characterized as a proportion of R_T, while *every*, *each*, and *any* are conceptually more complex.

3.2.1. *Proportional Quantifiers*

The first group involves some kind of comparison of the profiled mass (P) and the reference mass with respect to their magnitudes. Of course, neither mass is continuously distributed in the domain of instantiation, and R_T, at least, is not inherently bounded in that domain. Still, it is possible—and I think likely—that these quantifiers are understood metaphorically in terms of the comparison of discrete, continuous physical entities, where one entity is physically superimposed on the other to see how close their boundaries come to coinciding. We actually become fairly adept at performing this operation mentally, even if one of the objects has to be supplied by imagining it. I have often estimated the length of a desk or table (with tolerable accuracy) by imagining that I was laying a ruler along its surface and "seeing" how many ruler lengths were needed to exhaust its expanse.

It is not implausible that *all* and *most* involve a similar kind of mental operation. As a preliminary step, P and R_T must undergo a type of reification, being conceptualized (for sake of comparison) as spatially continuous entities with boundaries.[4] This accomplished, P is mentally superimposed on R_T and matched against it to see how close their boundaries come to coinciding, as sketched in Fig. 3.1. For any "slice" through P and R_T (note the dashed-line

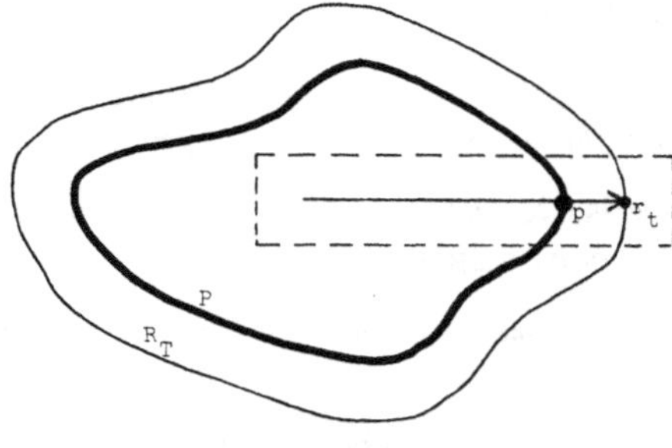

Fig. 3.1

box), one can estimate the distance between the boundary points, p and r_t, of P and R_T, respectively. The meanings of *all* and *most* are then describable in terms of two **basic conceptual relations** that are ubiquitous and fundamental to the characterization of countless predications (Vol. 1, 6.2). In its strictest sense, *all* specifies the coincidence (or identity) of p and r_t (it can of course be construed more loosely). On the other hand, *most* situates p in the "neighborhood" of r_t, i.e. the relation between them is one of association or proximity.[5]

Let us pause to consider the valence relation between a quantifier like *most*

[4]There is nothing extraordinary about this kind of mental transformation. We do something quite analogous, for instance, when we divide the integers on an odd/even basis and portray them as belonging to two container-like subsets: {1, 3, 5, 7, 9, . . .}; {2, 4, 6, 8, 10, . . .}.

[5]An alternative (or complementary) description might emphasize the likelihood of S or H encountering an instance of T with the property specified in the clause when some element of R_T is selected at random. For example, *All swans are white* implies that choosing a swan at random *must* yield a white one; similarly, with *most* random selection *should* produce a white swan, and with *some* it *may* do so. This way of looking at things reveals an interesting parallelism between relative quantifiers and modals, which function respectively as epistemic predications for nominals and finite clauses.

and the predication that it grounds, as in *most children*. First of all, the quantifier is itself nominal as opposed to relational, in accordance with the general principle that an epistemic predication profiles the grounded entity rather than the grounding relationship. The profile in Fig. 3.1 is thus the region P itself and not the relation borne by P to either G or R_T (crucial though these are). Since they designate things and inherently serve to ground them, these quantifiers are able to stand alone as full nominals:

(21) *Some are cute and most are well-behaved, but all appear to have boundless energy.*

The type specification supplied by the quantifier is highly schematic, but through context or syntagmatic combination it is rendered more specific. An expression like *most children* involves an elaborative relationship between P and the mass profiled by *children* (cf. Fig. 2.14). Without the quantifier, *children*'s profile can represent any proportion of the reference mass for the category. The construction, however, has the effect of equating the quantifier's reference mass R_T with that of the noun. As a consequence, *most children* designates a set of children, P, that is neither arbitrary in size nor exhaustive of the reference mass—P is specifically characterized as a proper subset of the reference mass for *children* that nevertheless approximates the boundaries of that mass.

We turn now to *some*, and in particular to uses where it bears a certain amount of stress (i.e. *sóme* or *sòme*, not *sŏme*). The key to *some* is its opposition to *most* and *all*, which place the boundaries of P in proximity or contact with those of R_T. In normal usage—that is, in the speech of people other than logicians—*some* indicates that P's boundaries are not within the neighborhood of R_T's. While a logician would insist on the truth and well-formedness of (22), naive intuition urges the replacement of *some* by *all*:

(22) *Some even numbers are divisible by two.*

Hence the prototypical value of *some* specifies that p lies outside the vicinity of r_t, though it is otherwise quite vague about its position. *Some* does however mean that P is not empty; if the arrow in Fig. 3.1 is regarded as a scale of magnitude, the boundary point p must be located beyond its origin.

The contrast with *most* and *all* is important to *some*'s semantic value. Thus (23) suggests quite strongly that there are children (and not just a few) who do *not* need paddling, or at least that the speaker only has information about a restricted subset:

(23) *Some children ought to be paddled.*

This notion of a limited portion of R_T standing in opposition to the remainder is much weaker or absent altogether with the unstressed *some*, which merely indicates a small positive departure from a quantity of zero and does not saliently invoke the reference mass. Hence (24) indicates the existence of children at the door (in limited quantity) without in any way underscoring the existence of a complementary set who are absent:

(24) *There are sŏme children at the door.*

This description explains why the continuation *but certainly not all* is felicitous with (23) and odd with (24), and why (25) is unambiguous and can only be read with stress on *some*.

(25) *Some children came to see me—but certainly not all.*

Note that the reference mass in (25) would be a contextually determined set of children rather than the maximal extension of the category (its default-case value).

Whereas the unstressed *some* only occurs with mass nouns (**sŏme key*), the stressed *some* is also used with singular count nouns:

(26)(a) *There's some man at the door to see you.*
(b) *Some cat must have been digging in the garden.*

It functions as a somewhat emphatic alternative to the indefinite article. Because the cardinality of a singular noun is fixed at one, *some* cannot contrast directly with *most* or *all* in this use. There is however a contrast with *no*:

(27) *You say you let no cat in the house? Well, some cat must have eaten the shrimp!*

Such contrast is one aspect of how this meaning of *some* is related to its meaning with mass nouns. Additionally, its count-noun sense can be analyzed as invoking a reference mass and quantity scale, as in Fig. 3.1, and as indicating a small positive departure from the origin of that scale.

The contrast between *some* and *no* suggests that the latter might also be characterized with reference to R_T and the associated quantity scale. Supporting this approach is the ability of both *some* and *no* to occur with all three classes of nouns: *some cat/no cat*; *some children/no children*; *some music/no music*). It is thus proposed that *no*, like the other proportional quantifiers, profiles one instance of the type in question but represents the limiting case in which the magnitude of the instance is zero (i.e. P is confined to the origin of the quantity scale—it is a point in the Euclidean sense of lacking extension).[6] The effect of a sentence like (28)(a) is thus to evoke the conception of

[6]This may seem problematic, since a mass of zero magnitude is too small to be identified as an instance of the designated substance, and since a cardinality of zero conflicts with the number specification of a singular noun. I think the problem is only apparent. Negation is conceptually dependent, i.e. it invokes the conception of the entity negated (cf. Givón 1979, ch. 3). Hence the notion of an instance figures in a predication like *no cat* or *no music* (as its profile in fact) even though *no* has the effect of cancelling its import in constructing a mental representation of the situation being described.

the cousin liking an instance of music but to undermine this conception by specifying that the instance has zero magnitude.[7]

(28)(a) *My cousin likes no music.*
(b) *My cousin doesn't like any music.*

In (28)(b), on the other hand, the conception of the cousin liking an arbitrary (non-zero) instance of music is portrayed as being inapplicable to present reality. Whereas the classic generative analysis of such pairs treats them as transformationally related (Klima 1964), they are seen in cognitive grammar as being independent and conceptually distinct (though logically equivalent). We will return to this issue in 3.3.3.

3.2.2. *Other Universal Quantifiers*

English has more than its fair share of universal quantifiers. No less than six distinct constructions are available for a universal statement:

(29)(a) *All nations have economic difficulties.*
(b) *Nations have economic difficulties.*
(c) *A nation has economic difficulties.*
(d) *Every nation has economic difficulties.*
(e) *Each nation has economic difficulties.*
(f) *Any nation has economic difficulties.*

In (29)(a), *all* profiles a mass (P) which is specified to coincide with the reference mass (R_T), normally identified as the maximal extension of the type (T). For a mass noun like *nations*, any proportion of R_T counts as a valid instance, including R_T as a whole, and the zero epistemic predication places no restrictions on its magnitude; consequently, (29)(b) also has a universal interpretation. Sentence (c) has a generic construal, whereby an arbitrary instance of *nation* (as defined in 3.1.2) is seen as participating in the relation *nation have economic difficulties* and this relation, at a higher level of conceptual organization, is regarded as inherent in the structure of the world as presently constituted (i.e. it is one facet of "what the world is like"). Our attention now shifts to *every*, *each*, and *any*, as exemplified in (d)–(f). They are quite complex conceptually, but I will try to show that the notions required for their description are all independently motivated.

Let us begin with *every*. One notion figuring in its characterization is that of an arbitrary instance, which is situated in a special mental space and enjoys no pre-existing mental contact by the speaker, the hearer, or any surrogate speaker—it is simply conjured up for a special purpose and has no status independent of that purpose. We have previously used this notion to explicate the non-specific reading of *a blonde* in *Ollie hopes to marry a blonde*, the

[7] If this seems implausible, consider the sentence *His talent is non-existent*, which effects a similar cancellation at the clausal level.

predicate nominative in sentences such as *Alice is a thief*, and also the generic interpretation of sentences like (29)(c), as just described. In the case of *every*, this notion helps account for a striking fact: even though a sentence like (29)(d) applies to all instances of *nation* in R_T, the nominal marked by *every* is singular (as witnessed by the form of the noun and by verb agreement). I will claim, in essence, that the instance t_i profiled by an *every*-marked nominal is construed as a representative instance of T, so that the property ascribed to it holds for all members.

The property ascribed to the profiled instance is furnished by the clause in which the nominal appears; in (29)(d), it is the property of having economic difficulties. Intuitively, *every* evokes the conception of such a property quite strongly—it is hard to imagine *every* being used except for indicating the universality among class members of participation in some relationship. Thus, although *every* designates a thing, t_i, its base incorporates the conception of an unprofiled and schematic relationship in which t_i somehow participates. In this respect *every* is quite comparable to a nominalizing predication like *-er* or *-ee* (Fig. 1.2), except that t_i plays no particular role in the base relation.

A notion not previously introduced is that of a **replicate process**, which is the processual equivalent of the replicate mass profiled by a plural noun. A replicate process is a complex relationship consisting of indefinitely many instances of a process type. Thus, if the simplified notation of Fig. 3.2(a) is

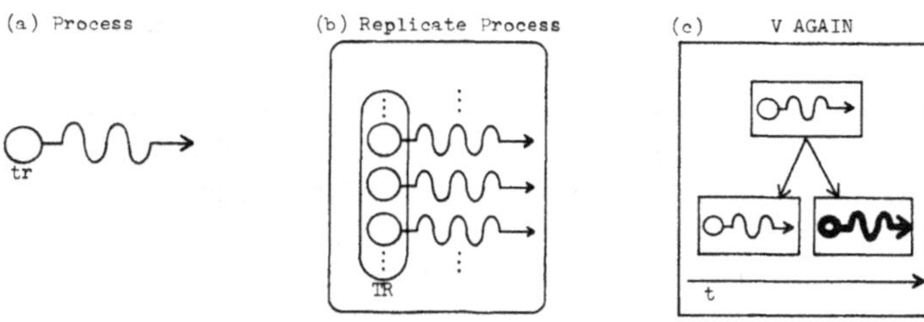

Fig. 3.2

used for a unitary process (the squiggly arrow standing for the evolution of a situation through time), a replicate process can be represented in the manner of 3.2(b). Moreover, the trajector of a replicate process (TR) can be characterized as the replicate mass comprising the trajectors of the component process instances; a comparable definition can be offered for the landmark of the replicate process or any other role within it. Although some languages overtly mark the formation of a replicate process through reduplication or some other morphological device, English allows any verb stem to be construed as a replicate process by zero-derivation. The conception of a replicate process figures in the meaning of most clauses with plural participants. An example is *The bombs exploded*: the verb profiles a complex event involving numerous instances of the process type *explode*, and *the bombs* elaborates the trajector (TR) of this complex process.

Just two more notions are needed. One is the conception of a mass coinciding with a reference mass; this, of course, is central to the meaning of *all*. The other notion is the construal of a single, profiled instance in relation to other, unprofiled instances. This can be exemplified by an expression of the form *V again* (as in *The pope died again*), sketched in Fig. 3.2(c). The overall expression designates one instantiation of a process type and portrays it as being subsequent to another instantiation along the temporal axis. Note that *again* itself does not specify any particular process—its reference to a process type and process instances is schematic; the type is rendered specific in construction with a verb.

Putting the pieces together, the semantic structure of *every* is diagrammed in Fig. 3.3. *Every* profiles a thing identified as an arbitrary instance t_i of type T. The profiled instance is further identified as participating in some process,

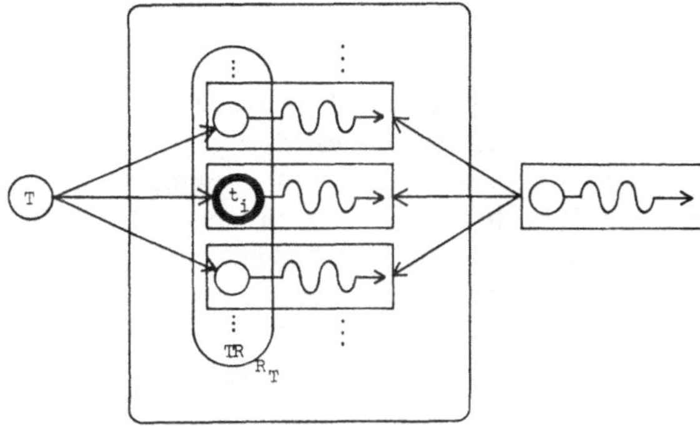

Fig. 3.3

whether as the trajector (as shown in 3.3) or in some other role. Crucially, t_i is not just an arbitrary but a **representative** instance of T with respect to participating in the process. That is, t_i is specifically construed in relation to other instances, which are seen as equivalent from the standpoint of their processual role: participation in the process is not idiosyncratic to t_i but rather characteristic of T's instantiations (which are specifically evoked in this regard). *Every* thus incorporates (as an unprofiled aspect of its base) the conception of a replicate process whose components all instantiate the same process type, and collectively the trajectors of these components—including t_i—constitute the trajector (TR) of the replicate process. It follows from the status of t_i as a representative instance of T that TR and R_T coincide, i.e. the same mass functions simultaneously as trajector of the replicate process and as reference mass for T. Hence, in this somewhat roundabout way, *every* specifies that participation in processual instances of the same type is universal to instances of T, even though only t_i is singled out for profiling.

Every is very similar to *each*, yet additional properties render the latter semantically distinct. The most obvious difference is apparent from (30):

(30)(a) *Every tiger has stripes.*
(b) *Each tiger has stripes.*

The first sentence is a straightforward universal statement of generic import. By contrast, (30)(b) could hardly be used to attribute stripedness to the set of all tigers (i.e. the maximal extension of the category)—rather it implies that some particular, restricted set of tigers has been examined (e.g. those in the San Diego Zoo) and that stripedness is universal within that subset. Thus one special property of *each* is that the reference mass R_T, while still equated with the trajector of the replicate process (or some other processual participant), does not represent the maximal extension of T but rather a limited, contextually identified portion thereof. Assuming this restrictive interpretation of R_T, which is possible for *every* but virtually obligatory for *each*, Fig. 3.3 is still appropriate.

Appeal to a contextually determined reference mass not exhaustive of a category is of course independently attested, e.g. in a sentence like *All passengers are now aboard*, where the set of passengers exhausted by *all* is limited to those scheduled for conveyance on a particular vehicle on a single occasion. Two other notions, also independently motivated, combine to account for the other special property of *each*. The first is simply the concept of sequential ordering, as manifested, say, in expressions such as *in turn* or *one after the other*. The second is the idea of **subjective motion** (see Vol. 1, 4.3.2 and Langacker 1986a), which is illustrated by semantic contrasts like the following:

(31)(a) *Her property extends from the road back to the river.*
(b) *Her property extends from the river out to the road.*

Clearly, these sentences incorporate a sense of directionality, which is oppositely aligned in the two and hence responsible for their difference in meaning. However, the scene described is a static one—objectively, nothing moves. Where, then, does the sense of directionality come from? The proposal is that the speaker scans mentally through the scene in one direction or the other (or more precisely, that he proceeds in one direction or the other in building up his conceptualization of it). This motion by the speaker is subjective because it is part of the conceptualization process: it is carried out by the subject of conception and is not itself an object of conception (i.e. S merely constructs a conception of the scene—he does not think of himself as moving through it).

There is reason to suspect that the meaning of *each* involves not only the structure in Fig. 3.3 (with the limitation on R_T described above), but also a conception that the various instances in TR/R_T are in some sense being examined in sequence rather than simultaneously. To some degree, this sequential examination may be imputed to an objectively construed entity, such as the subject in (32):

(32) *The teacher carefully scrutinized each boy's face.*

This use of *each* is very natural, for it is hardly possible to carefully scrutinize more than one face at a time. My own judgment is that the sentence is rendered slightly less natural when *every* is substituted for *each*. It is not that *every* is wrong, just that the contextually demanded notion of sequential access is merely consistent with *every*, whereas *each* actually tends to elicit it. The contrast in (33) (due to George Lakoff) is more striking:

(33)(a) *Tonight you can see each star in the Milky Way.*
(b) *Tonight you can see every star in the Milky Way.*

Speakers readily volunteer that (33)(a) evokes the image of the viewer shifting his gaze from star to star, while (b) suggests their simultaneous visibility.

However, the sequentiality cannot always be objective. For instance, there is nothing objectively sequential in (29)(e) *Each nation has economic difficulties* (as applied, say, to the nations of Central America), and there is nothing improper about using (34) in a situation where all the students finished simultaneously:

(34) *Each student finished the exam with time to spare.*

Intuitively, though, I still sense sequentiality in such examples, just as I sense directionality in (31). The same solution may be in order: the sequentiality is subjective, reflecting the speaker's mental access to the various instances of T that constitute TR/R_T. The speaker, in building up his conception of the complex situation, makes mental contact with a number of instances in succession and thus construes the profiled instance t_i as being just one in the sequence. This is fully consistent with the objective sequentiality of (32)–(33), for when S conceives of some other individual examining entities in sequence, objectively, S makes sequential mental contact with these same entities, subjectively, as an inherent aspect of the process of conceptualizing the objective sequence. The suggestion, then, is that *each* invokes this subjective sequentiality even when there is no conception of objective sequencing to support (and mask) it. If one takes this view, there is a possible explanation for why *each* is only applicable to restricted reference masses: it is hard to imagine the members of an open-ended set being subjected to examination that is both exhaustive and sequential.

We come at last to *any*, whose use as a universal quantifier is illustrated in (29)(f), *Any nation has economic difficulties*, and in (35):

(35) *Tonight you can see any star in the Milky Way.*

The contrast with (33) is very clear—(35) does not convey that all the stars in the Milky Way are seen, individually or sequentially, but rather that a single, arbitrarily chosen star can be seen should one wish to look at it. *Any* thus shares with *every* and *each* the property of designating an arbitrary instance of T construed as participating in an unprofiled relationship. However, rather than portraying t_i as a **representative** instance (thus invoking the notion of a replicate mass), *any* portrays it as a **randomly selected** instance: whichever instance you happen to choose, that instance will have the property in question. In effect, S makes mental contact only with t_i instead of with all elements of R_T, so the issue of simultaneity vs. sequentiality does not even arise.

Because *any* saliently evokes just a single instance, it is similar to the indefinite article on its non-specific interpretation. *Any*'s distinctive character stems primarily from the conception of S making mental contact with t_i through unconstrained random selection, a notion that renders R_T more prominent (as the region to which the choice is confined) and adds a nuance of exhaustiveness (the selection of t_i is not just *arbitrary* but *explicitly unrestricted* within R_T). Indeed, although *any* can also appear with mass nouns, and *a* can also be specific, in their region of overlap—when each is non-specific and combines with a singular count noun—they display a parallel range of functions. Both are found in the mental space representing a hope or desire, and in fact, *any* can co-occur with *a* to force its non-specific interpretation:

(36) *Ollie hopes to marry a blonde—any blonde.*

Moreover, both are subject to generic construal, where the relationship in which the arbitrary instance t_i participates is considered part of the structure of the world:

(37) *A beaver builds dams—any beaver does.*

Again, we see that *any* can be used to force the non-specific interpretation of *a* by reinforcing the notion of arbitrariness.

Finally, both *a* and *any* occur in a negative context:

(38) *Ollie doesn't have a girlfriend—any girlfriend.*

Here the notion of an arbitrary instance interacts with the phenomenon of implicational scales (Fauconnier 1975, 1977) to account for the fact that the non-existence of the relation *Ollie have girlfriend* extends to all members of the *girlfriend* class. If a particular instance of *girlfriend* were involved, then Ollie not having that girlfriend would leave it open whether he had some other. If the instance is arbitrary, on the other hand, then there is nothing special about t_i in regard to not being a girlfriend of Ollie. Moreover, once it is clear that quantity is the relevant consideration (as opposed to specific identities), the notion of a scale is operative: if more than one instance of T participates in the relation, it is also true that one instance does; hence the denial of the relationship for a single (arbitrary) instance implies its non-existence for any larger quantity.

Even from these brief descriptions, it should be evident that the analyses proposed for the various universal quantifiers go a long way toward explaining their differential behavior. Most obviously, *every* and *each* occur with singular count nouns because they profile a single discrete entity construed as representative of its class (Fig. 3.3), whereas *all* occurs with either sort of mass noun because it profiles a mass (Fig. 3.1). Unlike *every* and *each*, *any* does not depend on the conception of a replicate mass (the trajector of a replicate process) to achieve its universal import, but relies instead on the notion of random selection; since random choice is applicable to either discrete or mass-like entities, it is not surprising that *any* can occur with all three classes of nouns: *any cat*; *any children*; *any difficulty*.

Data like the following can also be explicated:

(39)(a) *All cats are alike.*
(b) ?*Every cat is alike.*
(c) *{*Each/any*} *cat is alike.*

Alike presupposes comparison and hence the simultaneous consideration of multiple entities. It is therefore maximally compatible with *all*, for in construction with a plural noun *all* profiles a replicate mass comprising multiple entities belonging to the same category. *Every* is acceptable with *alike* but less natural; although it incorporates the conception of a replicate mass, and is consistent with the simultaneous construal of its components, only a single instance is profiled. On the other hand, *each* and *any* are incompatible with *alike*, the former because the entities in TR/R_T are scanned in sequential rather than simultaneous fashion, and the latter because only a single instance is saliently evoked. Now consider (40):

(40)(a) *She examined* {*each/every*} *one in turn.*
(b) ?*She examined all in turn.*
(c) **She examined any in turn.*

In contrast to *alike*, *in turn* implies sequential examination. *Each* reinforces this notion of sequentiality and *every* is at least compatible with it. With *all*, there is a measure of conflict, for its profiling encourages a collective construal of the entities involved. Once again, *any* is not allowed, and for the same reason as in (39): it only evokes a single instance, while the context demands multiple instances.

3.3. Quantificational Interactions

A simple clause like *The boy lifted the chair* poses little difficulty from the standpoint of quantification. It profiles a relationship involving two discrete and unitary participants, and if there is no indication to the contrary, it is construed as designating just a single instance of the process type *lift*. An event of this sort represents an "atomic" transitive interaction—in terms of the billiard-ball model, it corresponds to one ball colliding with another and causing it to move. The minimality of this assembly leaves no uncertainty as to how its component elements (the boy, the chair, and the action) are connected.

However, each of the major clausal components (subject, object, and verb) potentially represents a complex entity comprising a multiplicity of simpler ones, as in *Three boys repeatedly lifted two chairs*, where the subject and object are plural and the verb repetitive. In a clause of this sort, there is considerable uncertainty as to how the constitutive entities are connected and even how many there are. Do the boys cooperate to lift each chair or lift them individually? Are the chairs lifted separately or in a stack? Does each boy lift the same set of chairs? Is each chair lifted by the same set of boys? How many repetitions are there? Are the same boys involved each time? Are the same chairs involved each time? It is evident that the clause can code an open-ended class of situations representing distinct configurations of atomic elements and interactions.

This section examines various phenomena observable when one or more of the major clausal components are complex instead of unitary. Some, including "Quantifier Float" (exemplified by the relation between *All the boys arrived* and *The boys all arrived*), arise even in clauses where just a single participant is multiplex. Problems of "scope" pertain to the interaction between two quantifiers (or other "logical" elements) in the same expression.

3.3.1. *Replicate Processes and Participants*

For English nouns, the multiple instantiation of a type to form a replicate mass is for the most part morphologically marked, resulting in a special plural stem. There is, however, no distinct marking for the multiple instantiation of a process type. By productive patterns of zero derivation, a verb stem like *slip* can be extended to designate not just one instance of slipping, as in (41)(a), but a replicate process consisting of multiple instances distributed through time, across participants, or both, as respectively illustrated in (b)–(d):

(41)(a) *Peter slipped on the icy sidewalk.*
(b) *Peter repeatedly slipped on the icy sidewalk.*
(c) *The shoppers slipped on the icy sidewalk.*
(d) *The shoppers repeatedly slipped on the icy sidewalk.*

In contrast to many languages, a verb stem in English is formally invariant whether one or multiple instances of the process type are profiled, and regardless of their temporal distribution and the number of participants involved.[8]

For a given verb stem, we must therefore recognize a number of semantic variants, some of them well-entrenched units and others spawned as needed in accordance with general patterns. The prototypical variant is normally the conception of a single, atomic instance of the process type (e.g. one slip on the part of one person). A repetitive construal, as in (41)(b), or a replicate process involving multiple participants, as in (c), may well gain the status of a unit for a particular stem. The most schematic variant merely specifies the occurrence of some number of atomic instances, abstracting away from the difference between a simple and a replicate process and from the various ways in which the atomic instances are distributed over time and participants. Of course, the replicate construal of any process defines a higher-order process type analogous to a plural noun; collectively, any assembly of atomic instances constitutes a single instance of the higher-order type, and its trajector (or its landmark, etc.) is the replicate mass comprising the trajectors (landmarks, etc.) of the atomic instances (Fig. 3.2(b)).

Consider, then, some possible interpretations of a clause with a plural subject and singular object, e.g. *The boys lifted the chair*. One construal, sketched in Fig. 3.4(a), involves just a single instance of chair-lifting but requires the collaborative efforts of a number of boys (the chair is too heavy for any one of them to lift it individually); this comes close to being an atomic instance of *lift*, but it is somewhat removed from the prototype owing to the complexity of the trajector. A second interpretation (not diagrammed) consists of multiple, temporally distinct occurrences of the configuration in 3.4(a), i.e. a set of boys collaborate on repeated occasions to lift the same chair. More likely is the construal shown in 3.4(b), where each boy individually lifts the chair. The clause thus profiles a replicate process, and each component of the higher-order trajector (TR) anchors one atomic instance of *lift*. Naturally, configuration (b) can also be repetitive—in fact, the repetition can be introduced at two different levels of conceptual organization, as exemplified in (42):

(42)(a) *In turn, the boys each lifted the chair again and again.*
(b) *Again and again, the boys each lifted the chair in turn.*

[8] Number agreement with the subject (e.g. *is* vs. *are*) is analyzed as one aspect of the grounding predication for a finite clause, not as part of the stem at the level of organization we are presently concerned with.

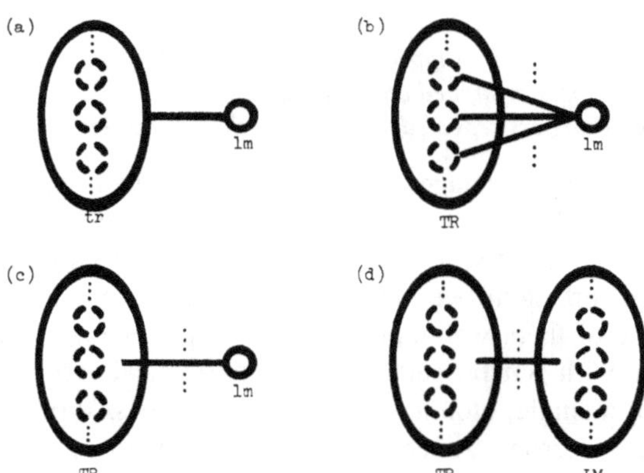

Fig. 3.4

In (42)(a), an atomic instance of *lift* is made repetitive, and at a higher level of organization the entire repetitive act is then replicated by being attributed to each member of a set of boys (acting in turn). On the other hand, in (42)(b) an atomic instance is distributed over the set of boys, deriving configuration 3.4(b), and that whole configuration is then repeated over time. The complex conceptualizations that result are structurally (hence logically) distinct. The contrast between them reflects the different orders in which two principles of extension (or zero derivation) apply in building up the complex notion from the conception of an atomic instance: whether repetition through time creates the input for replication across trajectors, or conversely.

Though a particular interpretation may be forced by context or by adverbials, as in (42), the necessary import of *The boys lifted the chair* per se is highly schematic, as indicated in Fig. 3.4(c). This conception is neutral as to whether it comprises one atomic instance of chair-lifting or more than one, and also whether such an instance is anchored by TR as a whole (*the boys*, as in 3.4(a)) or by one of its components (a single boy, as in (b)). To be sure, a person who uses the sentence will almost certainly impose a more specific construal—the point, however, is simply that conventional patterns of English permit all the configurations noted (and others besides) to be coded by a verb stem such as *lift* with no morphological indication of the differences. Moreover, comparable variation is observable for the landmark; *The boy lifted the chairs* may mean that the chairs collectively underwent a single instance of lifting (e.g. while stacked together) or else that they were lifted individually, and a repetitive construal is possible with either interpretation. A sentence like *The boys lifted the chairs* consequently has more conceivable interpretations than I would care to enumerate (hence this is left as an exercise for the reader). What they share is the schematic configuration diagrammed in Fig.

3.4(d): a set of boys (TR) and a set of chairs (LM) are somehow linked by one or more atomic instances of *lift*.

In addition to adverbs, at least two grammatical devices are available that help to reduce the uncertainty in the construal of such sentences. The first device, illustrated in (43), is the inclusion of a quantifier in the verb group:

(43)(a) *The boys all lifted the chair.*
(b) *The boys each lifted the chair.*

In English, the quantifiers permitted in this construction are limited to *all*, *each*, and *both* (the dual counterpart of *all*), and the quantification always pertains to the clausal subject. These restrictions are not untypical, though details vary from language to language (for representative examples, see Kayne 1975, Munro 1984, and Cook 1987, 1988a).

The standard generative analysis derives expressions like (43) by a rule called Quantifier Float from underlying structures in which the quantifier is part of the subject nominal: *All the boys lifted the chair* ===> *The boys all lifted the chair*. One problem with this movement-rule account is its failure to generalize to expressions like (44), where a full nominal (not just a quantifier) occurs in the verb group:

(44)(a) *The children are all of them doing their best.*
(b) *We have each of us noticed the difficulty.*

Moreover, a simple movement rule could not derive (43)(b), since the putative source is ill-formed: **Each the boys lifted the chair*. The facts thus suggest an alternative analysis in which the quantifier, rather than being "floated" from the subject, is treated as a pronominal element serving to specify certain quantificational properties of the trajector with respect to the verb. Subsequently, at the clausal level of organization, the trajector is specified in greater detail by a full subject nominal.

In this construction, *all* and *each* indicate explicitly that participation in the clausal process extends to the full set of entities profiled by the subject, and *each* has the further import that these entities function individually as trajectors with respect to separate instances of the process type in question. These meanings diverge only slightly from those the quantifiers have as grounding predications in nominals. Both *all* and *each* invoke a reference mass (R_T) as part of their normal value, and they do so here as well, with the difference that the members of R_T need not all instantiate the same type:

(45) *The dog, the cat, and the rabbit all sniffed at the food.*

Also, R_T is specifically equated with a processual trajector, whereas with nominals it can have any role in a process.

The integration of *each* with a verb is sketched in Fig. 3.5. The diagram

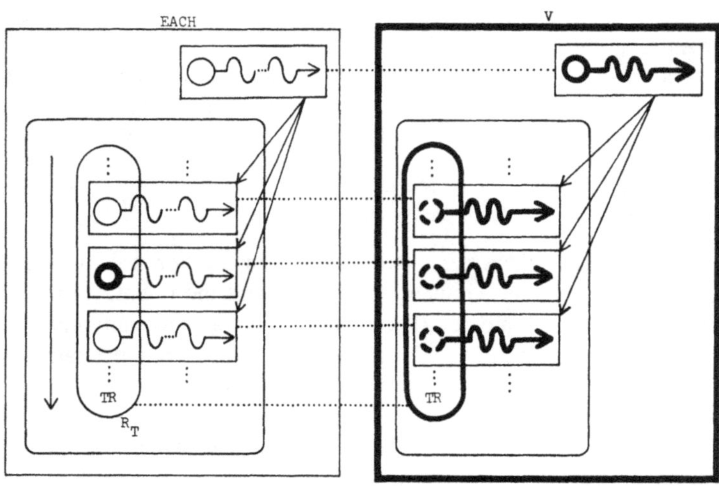

Fig. 3.5

for *each* is a minor variant of that offered earlier for *each* and *every* (Fig. 3.3). The base is a replicate process comprising multiple instances of a schematically characterized process type. TR, the higher-order trajector of this replicate process, is specified as coinciding with a reference mass R_T. I have also added a vertical arrow to make explicit a semantic nuance of *each*, namely that the speaker establishes mental contact with the components of TR/R_T sequentially in building up his conception of the scene (3.2.2). To be compatible with *each*, the verb must be construed as profiling a replicate process. Integration is then straightforward: the specific process profiled by V is put in correspondence (at both the type and instance levels) with the schematic process evoked by *each*, and the higher-order trajector of V corresponds to TR/R_T. *Each* contributes nothing substantial to the characterization of V's trajector—only the notion of subjective sequentiality and the specification that TR coincides with a reference mass; the composite structure (not separately shown) is equivalent to V except for these enhancements. The real semantic contribution of *each* is that it forces the selection of a replicate variant of V, which would otherwise represent just one option.

The construction with *all* is parallel but less elaborate, since *all* is conceptually simpler than *each*. As in Fig. 3.5, *all* incorporates a higher-order trajector TR and equates it with R_T, but unlike *each* it profiles TR as a whole and lacks the notions of individuation and sequentiality. *All* is consequently neutral as to whether the process corresponding to V is simple (as in Fig. 3.4(a)) or replicate, so a sentence like (43)(a) can be interpreted in either fashion. The semantic effect of *all* is merely to underscore that the trajector of V is exhaustive of the mass designated by the subject.

We turn now to a second grammatical device that sometimes reduces the uncertainty in how to construe a clause involving complex participants. Imagine that there are three boys and three chairs, and that each boy, individually, lifts exactly one chair (different in each instance). There are many ways of describing this complex event, including the following:

(46)(a) *Three boys lifted chairs.*
(b) *Three boys lifted a chair.*

Both sentences are of course compatible with many situations besides the one in question; (46)(a), for instance, could mean that each boy lifted more than one chair, and (b) could be used when all three boys lifted the same chair (individually or collectively). For present purposes, however, it is only relevant that both sentences are applicable to the situation described, and moreover, that certain interpretations of (a) are impossible for (b). In particular, (b) limits each boy's lifting to a single chair (barring a repetitive construal). It is still vague in certain respects (e.g. individual vs. collective activity, and whether each boy lifted the same chair). Nevertheless, making the object singular imposes a significant constraint on possible interpretations.

What is striking is that a singular object is appropriate even when three separate chairs are involved. How can this be? It is not generally possible in English to use a singular to designate a multiplex entity—we cannot use *The boy lifted a chair* to mean that he lifted more than one. Why, then, is (46)(b) a permissible coding of the situation in which three separate chairs are lifted (one by each boy)? And how can we characterize the requisite grammatical construction?

Under the stipulated interpretation of (46)(b), *lift a chair* constitutes the description of a process type, and each individual subsumed by the subject is construed as trajector with respect to an instance of that type. On this interpretation (46)(b) does not mean that three boys were engaged in lifting the same chair (though this is also a possible reading) but rather that participation in an instance of the process type *lift a chair* is a property attributed to each boy. Hence the direct object does not refer to a specific chair. Instead it represents an arbitrary instance of the *chair* category conjured up solely for purposes of describing a process type and confined to the mental space which constitutes that type description. The speaker and hearer thus have no preexisting or independent mental contact with this instance of *chair*, and when the process type is construed as having multiple instantiations, there is no basis for assuming that any two instances involve the same chair.

The requisite grammatical construction, diagrammed in Fig. 3.6, requires no constructs that have not already been introduced and independently motivated. The verb is construed as profiling a replicate process comprising multiple instances of the same process type. Their trajectors are specifically recognized as constituting an abstract region, TR, which is accorded the status

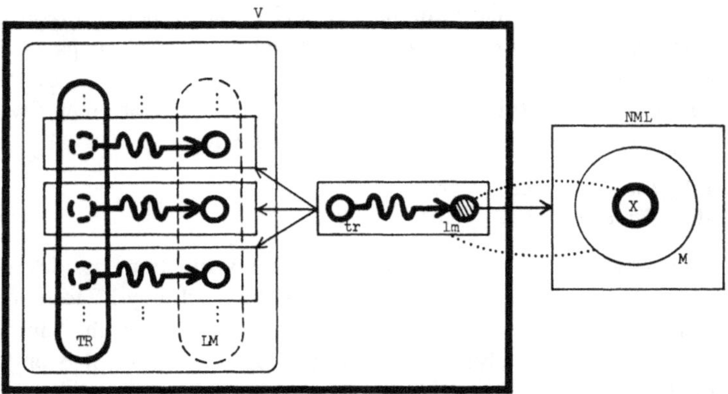

Fig. 3.6

of relational figure, to be elaborated by the clausal subject. At the present level of organization, the verb is elaborated by the direct-object nominal. Now the direct-object construction, like any other, is a complex category consisting of numerous constructional variants linked by categorizing relationships (of extension, schematicity, etc.) to form a network. The variant depicted here is one subtype of the construction as it applies to replicate processes. In this particular variant, the higher-order landmark LM remains latent.[9] Chosen instead as e-site is the landmark internal to the processual type specification. This landmark is put in correspondence with the nominal's profile, whose semantic specifications are abbreviated as X. Recall that the direct-object nominal is non-specific, an arbitrary instance of its category existing only in a special mental space, M, created to characterize a process type. There is consequently a correspondence between M and the type specification of the verb.

The phenomenon of elaborating the type specification immanent to all the members of a replicate structure actually has considerable generality. We observed it previously in the formation of a plural noun from a numberless stem (Fig. 2.9). At the clause level, it is by no means confined to direct objects. With some effort, it can be made to happen with subjects; thus the second clause of the discourse in (47) can be interpreted to mean that each chair has the property of having been lifted by some boy (different in each case).

(47) *Was only one of those chairs lifted by a boy?*
No, a boy lifted THREE of those chairs.

It also occurs with prepositional objects, possessed nouns, and even whole clauses:

[9]By contrast, in (46)(a) LM is specifically evoked as part of the relational profile and serves as elaboration site for the object.

(48)(a) *Three boys lost coins in a chair.* [different chairs]
(b) *Three boys raised their hand.* [each his own hand]
(c) *A boy repeatedly lifted a chair.* [an event of that type recurred, involving different boys and different chairs each time]

Although the full extent of the phenomenon has not yet been explored, in English or for other languages, its description in cognitive grammar appears to pose no problems in principle.

3.3.2. *Quantifier Scope*

Problems pertaining to quantifiers and their scope have long preoccupied logicians and formal semanticists. Even a skeletal survey of the data, issues, and competing analyses would constitute a massive project in its own right (see McCawley 1981a for one attempted synthesis). We will therefore consider just a few representative examples and focus on a single, pivotal theoretical issue: the relation between quantifier scope and grammatical structure. The objective is merely to indicate programmatically how one might approach the phenomena from the standpoint of cognitive grammar.

Problems of scope arise when a single expression contains two or more "logical" elements, such as quantifiers,[10] negation, and the linguistic counterparts of logical connectives (e.g. *and, or, if . . . then*). It is well known, for example, that a sentence like (49) is ambiguous:

(49) *Every athlete here excels at three sports.*

It may simply mean that all the athletes are multi-talented, i.e. that the property of excelling at three sports (but not necessarily the same sports) is attributed to each of them. Under this interpretation, *three* is said to be "in the scope of" *every*, since the quantification effected by *three* is part of the notion that *every* replicates and associates with each of the athletes in question. On the other hand, (49) may mean that there are three specific sports (e.g. football, squash, and curling) such that every athlete here excels at them. Under this second interpretation, *every* is in the scope of *three* because the quantification effected by *every* is part of the notion which characterizes the set of sports that *three* quantifies. A sentence like (50) also has two readings reflecting alternate scope relations:

(50) *Sean didn't notice many mistakes.*

The more likely interpretation puts *many* in the scope of negation: that the mistakes noticed by Sean were many is part of what is being denied. In context, however, or with extra stress on *many*, the scope relation is reversible:

(51) *Sean didn't notice this mistake, nor this one. . . . In fact, Sean didn't notice MANY mistakes.*

[10] Both grounding predications and quantifiers in the narrow sense (2.3.2) are included.

It is apparent in (51) that *many* quantifies the set of mistakes characterized by the property of Sean not noticing them—in other words, *many* has the negation in its scope.

In formal logic, scope relations are represented by the hierarchical organization inherent in complex logical formulas.[11] For example, the ambiguity of *Someone likes everyone* is captured by the formulas in (52), where ∃ is the "existential" quantifier (*some*), ∀ the "universal" quantifier (*every*), and L the predicate *like*:

(52)(a) $\exists x[\forall y[Lx,y]]$ *(b)* $\forall y[\exists x[Lx,y]]$

Formula (a) can be read 'There exists an individual x such that, for every individual y, x likes y' (i.e. there is someone who dislikes nobody), whereas (b) means that 'For every individual y, there exists some individual x such that x likes y' (i.e. everyone has at least one person who likes him). A logical element is said to have "wide" or "narrow" scope depending on whether it lies outside or inside a pair of brackets relative to another. Thus *some* has wide scope in (a) and narrow scope in (b), while the reverse holds for *every*.

The bracketing in a logical formula is reminiscent of that used for syntactic constituency, so it is natural to raise the question of how the two might be related. The standard view is that they are basically independent, and on the face of it this appears to be correct: there is no direct or consistent correlation between the hierarchical structure representing semantic scope relations on the one hand and that representing grammatical constituency on the other. Thus *Someone likes everyone* appears to have the constituent structure shown in (53) regardless of which quantifier is taken as having wider scope:

(53) [*someone* [*likes everyone*]]

Moreover, quantifiers occur as parts of nominals, often at a low level of constituency (corresponding to inner brackets), even when their scope is maximal. It is uncontroversial, for example, that under either interpretation of (49), *three* is one constituent of a nominal that in turn is one constituent of a prepositional phrase serving as a complement of the verb. This apparent independence of logical and grammatical form is commonly taken as an argument for the autonomy of syntax.

Still, the generative notion of "deep" or underlying structure permits grammatical analyses that fly in the face of "surface" facts, and in generative semantics an attempt was made to reconcile logical and grammatical constituency at the deep-structure level (see Lakoff 1969). Quantifiers, negation, and other elements participating in semantic scope relations were analyzed as verb-like predicates defining separate propositions (clauses) in underlying

[11] This hierarchical structure is understood even when the bracketing in formulas like (52) is suppressed for the sake of notational convenience.

structure, and one such element was shown to be in the scope of another through the syntactic relationship of subordination. The ambiguity of a sentence like (54)(a) was thus captured by deriving it from underlying representations analogous to either (b) or (c), where square brackets indicate subordinate clauses:

(54)(a) *Few men read many books.*
(b) *the men [the books [men read books] are many] are few]*
(c) *the books [the men [men read books] are few] are many]*

That is, on one interpretation (54)(a) is roughly paraphrased by 'Few are the men such that many are the books such that the men read the books', and on the other, by 'Many are the books such that few are the men such that the men read the books'. The analysis requires a globally constrained rule of Quantifier Lowering that moves a quantifier into a subordinate clause and attaches it to the appropriate noun, thereby eliminating the higher clause in which it originates. By dual application of this rule, structures (b) and (c) both yield (a) as their surface form.

Deriving a surface form from a radically different underlying structure is of course precluded in cognitive grammar by the content requirement (Vol. 1, 1.2.6.2). The analysis is also known to be inadequate on empirical grounds. The problem is that a sentence like (54)(a) has a third interpretation, one in which neither quantifier is in the scope of the other, but the analysis as it stands permits multiple quantifiers only by subordinating one to the other. There is consequently no way of deriving (54)(a) when it means that a complex relationship of reading obtains between a set of men and a set of books, such that the total number of men involved is small, and the total number of books, large.[12] In short, there are more meanings than the proposed underlying representations are able to distinguish. It should be noted, however, that standard logical formulas like (52) manifest the same deficiency if their style of representation is extended to all natural language quantifiers.

I therefore agree with the standard view that grammatical constituency and hierarchical relationships of quantifier scope are distinct and basically independent. However, this position does not entail the autonomy of grammar, nor does it imply that algebraic formulas like (52) are adequate or appropriate to represent the meanings of logical elements or the sentences containing them.

I maintain that only symbolic units, each with conceptual import, are required for the description of grammatical structure. Grammatical constituency reflects the order in which symbolic structures are successively integrated, at

[12] This third reading is more perspicuous with an example such as *Never have so many owed so much to so few*. Similarly, *Three hunters shot two deer* may mean that a party of three hunters set out for deer and returned with a total of two.

both the semantic and the phonological poles, to form structures that represent progressively higher levels of organization and are more and more complex internally. Crucially, the hierarchy embodied by this compositional path must be distinguished from the internal structure of the conceptualization functioning as the semantic pole at any hierarchical level. At any level of composition (i.e. at any level of grammatical constituency) the composite semantic structure is an integrated conceptualization, and any hierarchical arrangement it might display internally does not necessarily dovetail with that constituting the history of its assembly. A relationship of quantifier scope is inherent in the structure of a complex conceptualization (which a linear string of algebraic symbols, such as a logical formula, can hardly characterize adequately). It resides in a conceptual configuration that need not be isomorphic to the compositional path one follows in arriving at it.

Consider the three interpretations of (54)(a), *Few men read many books*. Each resides in a conceptualization that includes a complex relationship of reading, a set of men characterized as being few in number, and a set of books characterized as being numerous; *read*, *few men*, and *many books* are the respective symbolizations of these conceived entities. On all three interpretations, the men are identified in some fashion with the trajector of *read*, and the books with its landmark. These relationships are the semantic basis for the bipolar integration giving rise to grammatical constituency. Let us assume the canonical constituency in which *read* is first integrated with *many books* to derive the symbolic structure *read many books*, which then combines with *few men* to yield *Few men read many books*. This order of assembly defines the hierarchically structured compositional path depicted in Fig. 3.7, which

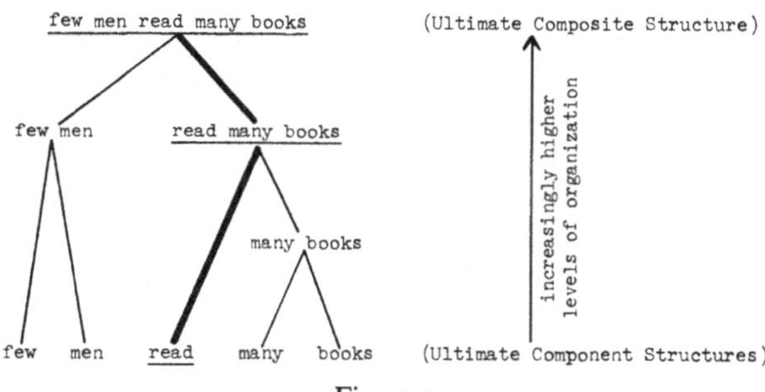

Fig. 3.7

is compatible with all three interpretations. Note in particular the highlighted subpath *read* > *read many books* > *few men read many books*, along which the complex process of reading is specified in progressively greater detail. It is precisely because the path contains the intermediate-level structure *read many books*, in which the landmark is specific while the trajector remains schematic, that *read* and *many books* are said to form a grammatical constituent.

The three interpretations of *Few men read many books* differ with respect to a property that is independent of the compositional path's hierarchical organization. The differences do involve hierarchical structure, but that structure is internal to the conceptualizations that function as the semantic pole at certain stations along the path. In particular, each structure in the subpath *read* > *read many books* > *few men read many books* profiles a complex process comprising numerous atomic instances of the process type *read*. Various arrangements are possible for how these atomic instances cluster into larger assemblies. Given other notions already introduced and motivated, quantifier scope can be explicated with reference to hierarchical relationships inherent in these assemblies.

The simplest type of assembly corresponds to the interpretation where neither quantifier has the other in its scope, i.e. where it is specified with respect to the *men read books* relationship that the total number of men involved is small while the total number of books is large. The profiled assembly is simply a replicate process, based on *read*, that comprises a multiplicity of atomic instances. Selected as the most prominent participants—and thus included in the relational profile—are the higher-order trajector (TR) and landmark (LM) of the replicate process (consisting respectively of the trajectors and landmarks of the atomic instances), as sketched in Fig. 3.8(a). In accordance with general patterns noted earlier, this entire assembly can be symbolized by the verb stem *read* (cf. Fig. 3.4(d)). The construction of the sentence is then quite regular: *few men* elaborates the trajector (TR) of the profiled relationship, which makes it the clausal subject, and *many books* is the direct object by virtue of elaborating its landmark (LM). It should be evident that the same composite structure results regardless of the order in which these elaborations are effected (Vol. 1, 8.4.2). The absence of a scope relationship between *few* and *many* reflects the internal structure of the complex process, which is independent of such ordering (and thus of grammatical constituency).

In a replicate process, the trajectors of the component instances are generally distinct, as are their landmarks; this is the situation depicted in Fig. 3.8(a). As a special case, however, it is possible for all the component instances to have the same trajector, as in 3.8(b), or the same landmark, as in (c). Configurations of this sort are pivotal to sentences in which one quantifier is interpreted as having another in its scope. A scopal interpretation comes about when configuration (b) or (c), as a whole, is construed as a type specification having multiple instantiations to form a replicate process at a higher level of conceptual organization. When configuration (b) is replicated, the result is the higher-order process diagrammed in (b′): each component of the

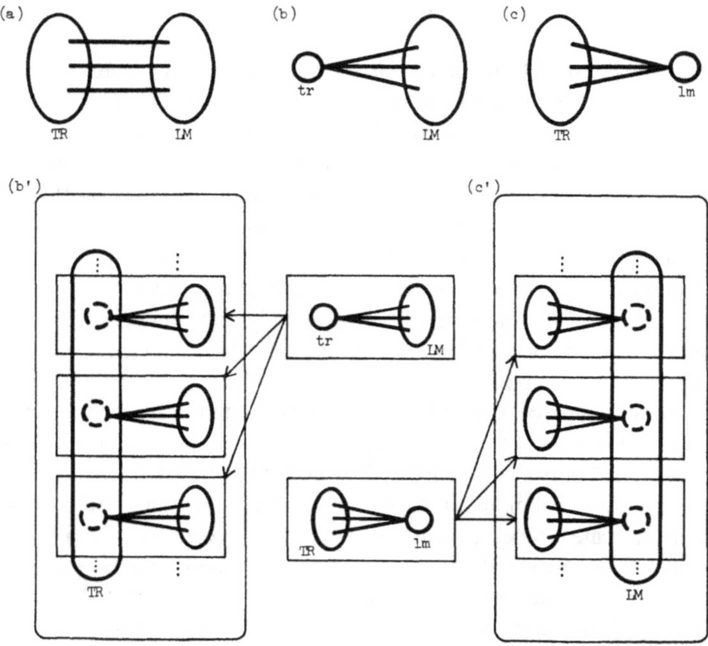

Fig. 3.8

replicate process is itself an instance of the complex process type (b), and collectively the trajectors of these instances constitute a higher-order trajector TR. Similarly, replication of the complex process type (c) yields the higher-order process sketched in (c′), whose overall landmark LM comprises those of its component instances. The complicated appearance of these diagrams should not be allowed to obscure the straightforward character of what they represent: it is simply a matter of the same well-established phenomenon (multiple instantiation of a process type to form a replicate process) occurring at two successive levels of conceptual organization. Moreover, both (b′) and (c′) instantiate the schema of Fig. 3.4(d), which sanctions their symbolization by a simple verb stem such as *read*.

Structure (b′) corresponds to the interpretation of (54)(a) in which *few* has wide scope ('the men who read many books are few'). The verb stem *read* symbolizes this entire assembly, involving the replication of a process type at two separate levels of organization. With the verb construed in this complex yet regular fashion, the construction of the full sentence is also quite regular. *Few men* elaborates TR and is thus the clausal subject. As for the object, *many books*, we must identify its e-site with the landmark (LM) of the type specification, just as we did earlier (Fig. 3.6) for sentences such as *Three boys lifted a chair*; an independently established variant of the direct-object construction is thus employed. The import of choosing this e-site is that *many books* represents an arbitrary instance of the *books* category conjured up just for purposes of characterizing a type and hence confined to the mental space which defines it. Consequently, the property of reading many books is attributed to each of a set of men quantified by *few*; no particular books are involved, and the inventory is presumably different for each man. This conception is hierarchically structured, in that the multiplicity of LM (quantified by *many*) is part of the characterization that is replicated and distributed across the members of TR (which *few* quantifies). However, this hierarchy is an aspect of how the verb is construed that is independent of grammatical constituency. Provided that the same e-sites are chosen for the subject and object nominals, the same composite structure results regardless of whether Fig. 3.7 or some other order of composition is followed.

Structure (c′) in Fig. 3.8 corresponds to the remaining interpretation, where *many* has wide scope ('the books that few men read are many'). It is precisely analogous to (b′) except that replication at the first level of organization creates a complex trajector (TR), so that the property of undergoing a process with such a trajector is replicated at the second level and attributed to each member of the set of entities that collectively constitute LM. *Many books* elaborates LM in accordance with a standard variant of the direct-object construction, while the subject's e-site is identified with the TR of the type specification.[13] The relationship of quantifier scope resides once more in the hierarchical arrangement inherent in the complex conceptualization (and is independent of grammatical constituency). Specifically, the multiplicity of TR (quantified by *few*) is part of the characterization that is replicated and attributed to each member of LM (quantified by *many*).

Quantifier scope is thus explicated with reference to the intrinsic organization of a complex conceptualization and is only incidentally related to how the symbolic structure having this conceptualization for its semantic pole is progressively assembled from smaller symbolic elements (recall the discussion of **unipolar** vs. **bipolar componentiality** in Vol. 1, 2.3.1.2). It is a matter of one quantifier being part of a type description whose multiple instantiations are distributed across the members of a set quantified by another. This latter quantifier has "wide scope" in the sense that the associated members are directly accessed and can be taken as specific individuals. By contrast, the "narrow-scope" quantifier pertains to non-specific entities confined to the mental space of the type specification. These entities achieve specific reference only in relation to a particular individual who, by anchoring an

[13] Again, this choice of e-site requires no special apparatus: we have seen previously that the phenomenon of elaborating only the type specification immanent to all instances of a replicate structure is quite general (recall (47)–(48)).

instantiation of that type, serves as a kind of **reference point** through which the speech-act participants gain access to them and determine their place in the current discourse space. Naturally, prominent entities have the best chance of being selected as reference points for this purpose. It is no accident, therefore, that a quantifier on the subject (the most prominent clausal participant) is generally interpreted as having wide scope. It also stands to reason that other sorts of prominence—e.g. that associated with heavy stress or "new information"—are capable of overriding this inherent bias and elevating a non-subject to the status of reference point. Consequently, the quantifier on the direct object is taken as having wide scope in examples like (47) and (51).

3.3.3. *Scope of Negation*

A relationship of semantic scope is analyzed in cognitive grammar as residing in the structure of a complex conceptualization. It reflects the correspondences established between two predications and the nature of their integration within some composite conceptualization that subsumes them both. One expression, Q_2, is said to be in the scope of another, Q_1, when Q_2 is identified with a substructure of Q_1 and thereby functions as part of the configuration affected by Q_1's central semantic specifications; Q_2 thus falls within Q_1's scope of predication (i.e. its base), while Q_1 determines the overall organization of the composite conception. We have seen how this works in the case of quantifiers: the quantification effected by Q_2 is confined to a type description within Q_1, where it helps to characterize a property ascribed to all elements of the set or mass that Q_1 quantifies. Let us conclude by applying the description to negation, whose interaction with quantifiers is a classic concern.

How can we describe the meaning of *not*, or of negation (NEG) more generally? Though it is sometimes regarded as a semantic primitive, I believe that NEG in fact has conceptual import that can be analyzed and characterized with reference to other notions. Previous work offers clues about the nature of a possible description. Givón (1979, ch. 3) has established that negation is the marked member of the positive/negative opposition—we are primarily concerned with what *is*, and we say that something *is not* only in response to some evocation (perhaps implicit) of the positive situation (e.g. I would hardly announce *We're not having pizza for supper* unless there were some expectation that we were). In the terminology of cognitive grammar, NEG is conceptually dependent, for it makes salient (though schematic) internal reference to the situation whose existence it denies. Also relevant is the dictum that *existence* is always *existence in some location*, which suggests the corollary that *non-existence* is always *non-existence in some location*. In its positive form, this notion has been used insightfully by Bolinger (1977, ch. 5) and Lakoff (1987, case study 3) to describe the existential *there*-construction (e.g. *There's dissension on the team*); both interpret *there* as referring to the conscious awareness of the speech-act participants, and Lakoff further identifies its referent as a mental space in the sense of Fauconnier 1985. If the *there*-construction introduces some entity into a mental space, perhaps the function of negation is to specify its absence from such a space (e.g. from present reality).[14]

How do we conceive of something being absent from a mental space? Clearly, we do not just envisage the space without it—the conception of a space per se is not equivalent to that of something being missing from it. Indeed, since negation makes inherent reference to the situation being denied, our conception must include the absent entity in its expected position within the space. But is that not contradictory? How can a notion be consistent if it incorporates the conception of a mental space both containing and not containing the same entity? The problem is only apparent. Cognitive grammar does not assume that an expression's meaning necessarily reduces to a single, consistent configuration. It claims that our ability to construe one conceived situation in relation to another, regardless of their degree of compatibility, is fundamental to linguistic semantics. Hence the meaning of a complex expression is defined as including not only its composite semantic structure but also the compositional path through which that structure is assembled (see Vol. 1: 8.2.2; Ch. 12). As a further example, recognizing the metaphorical nature of an expression like *take the bull by the horns* requires the co-construal of two very different conceptions, its literal sense and its figurative value.

Internally, many predications have the character of a **complex scene**, in which one conception is construed against the background of another from which it diverges in some respect (cf. Vol. 1: 3.4.2; 9.2.2). Their relationship manifests the inherent asymmetry of a categorizing relationship: the background conception serves as a standard of comparison, while the foregrounded target of categorization is the **active** structure, i.e. the one employed for purposes of coding or higher-level composition. For example, *toward* evokes the conception of a trajector moving along a full path that reaches some goal, but against the backdrop of this *potential* path, it portrays as *actual* (and profiles) only the trajector's motion along a restricted initial portion. Similarly, the notion of identity (as in *Alice is the thief*) presents as actual a situation in which there is just one individual, but construes it in relation to a background conception involving two separate individuals. This identity relation is depicted in Fig. 3.9(a), where the dashed-line box encloses the background conception. The mutual correspondence of two conceived

[14] This approach enables us to understand how an expression like *without* could come to have negative value. Briefly, one sense of *with* expresses possession, i.e. location within a region anchored by a reference point, while *out* indicates departure from a region. If negation is absence from a space, *without* amounts to the negation of a possessive relationship. Hence *a boy without a dog* is roughly equivalent to *a boy who has no dog*.

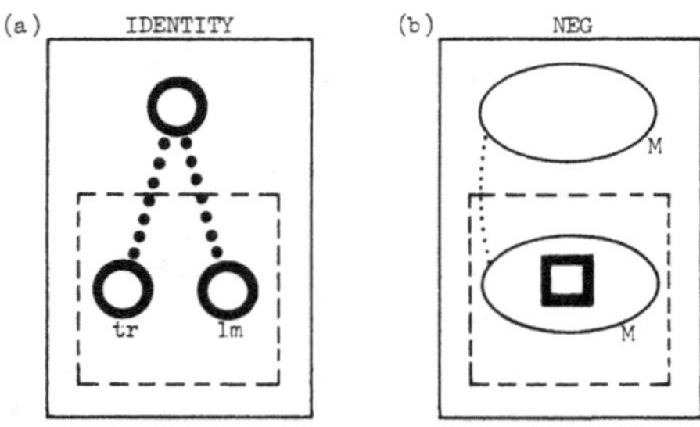

Fig. 3.9

individuals to what is in actuality the same individual constitutes the profiled relationship.[15]

Negation can thus be characterized, at least roughly, as shown in Fig. 3.9(b). With respect to a background conception in which some entity occupies a mental space, M, it portrays as actual a situation in which that entity fails to appear in M. The missing entity is a process in the case of clausal negation, but that is not the only possibility; for example, when *no* is used to ground a nominal (as in *no cat* or *no luck*), the entity absent from M is a thing. By the analysis adopted here, NEG profiles the missing entity, as opposed to the relationship it bears to M. The result of combining *no* with *cat* is therefore a nominal, not a stative relation (such as *absent* or *missing*), and the processual nature of a finite clause is unaltered by *not*. This suggests that NEG should be considered an epistemic predication, or at least a close cousin—recall that the hallmark of such a predication is that it profiles the grounded entity rather than the grounding relationship (2.4).[16]

A distinction is customarily made between "internal" and "external" negation, as illustrated by the following contrast:

(55)(a) *The King of France didn't lose any hair.*
(b) *The King of France DIDN'T lose some hair.*

The negation in (55)(a) is an integral facet of the clause's semantic and grammatical organization. It requires no special linguistic context and simply specifies the absence from past reality of the profiled relationship (that of the

[15] By making provision for a background conception, we conflate in a single diagram the two facets of an identity relation depicted separately in Figs. 2.5(a) and (b). The two styles of representation should be regarded as notational variants.

[16] Negation alone is insufficient to ground a clause and render it finite—after all, *not* occurs with infinitives, participles, and nominalizations. Still, its close association with the grounding predication of a finite clause is witnessed by their phonological proximity (*didn't, isn't, shouldn't*, etc.), and semantically they both situate the profiled process with respect to a mental space. I suspect that clausal *not* becomes epistemic when M is put in correspondence with the mental space (e.g. present or past reality) that is introduced by the inherently epistemic tense/modality predication.

King of France losing hair). Observe that internal negation induces *any* on the direct object (in lieu of *some*) and has no effect on clausal presuppositions (that there was a King of France, and that he had some hair to lose). On the other hand, (55)(b) would hardly occur except in response to a previous utterance of the specific words *The King of France lost some hair*, or at least a close approximation. The negation has a metalinguistic function: it indicates that the utterance it responds to, and recapitulates in negative form, is inappropriate in some respect. It may be inappropriate due to the failure of a presupposition:

(56) *The King of France DIDN'T lose some hair . . .*
 (a) *. . . he had no hair to begin with.*
 (b) *. . . there is no King of France.*

The problem may be that the description of some entity is inaccurate:

(57) *The KING OF FRANCE didn't lose some hair . . . it was the Princess of Eastern Herzegovina.*

External negation can even be used to indicate that some word has been mispronounced:

(58) *It wasn't a NUCULAR warhead . . . it was a NUCLEAR warhead.*

Of course, the utterance may have been inappropriate simply because the profiled process did not in fact occur, in which case external and internal negation are effectively equivalent.

External negation implies the construction sketched in Fig. 3.10. In line with its metalinguistic nature, it identifies M not with present or past reality, but with the conception of a well-formed discourse in which each utterance is contextually and linguistically appropriate (correspondence with reality being just one aspect of appropriateness). The entity excluded from this space—as

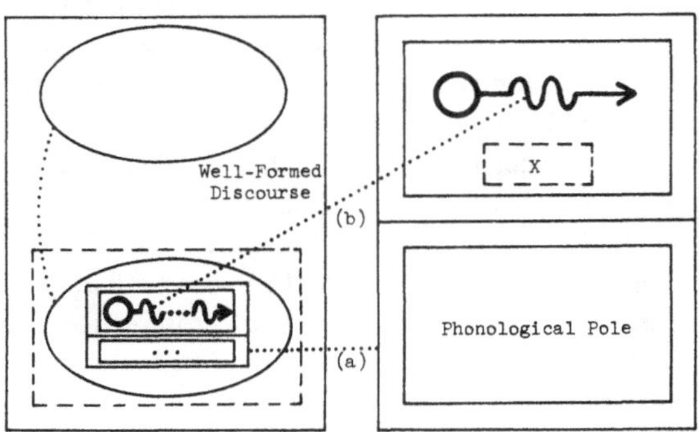

Fig. 3.10

being contextually or linguistically inappropriate in some fashion—is a bipolar structure representing the speaker's rendition of the utterance he is responding to. Schematic reference to this entity is made by NEG, the component structure shown at the left. The component structure on the right presents in specific terms the speaker's recapitulation of the inappropriate utterance: semantically, it includes not only the profiled process but also the full array of presuppositions and other background assumptions (abbreviated X) with respect to which this process is construed and characterized; phonologically, it includes as much phonetic detail as the speaker deems relevant (given that the inappropriateness may lie with nuances of the pronunciation itself). The correspondence labeled (a) effects the global identification of this bipolar structure with the absent entity. Subsumed by (a) are a number of local correspondences, including (b), which equates their processual profiles. It is the analog of correspondence (b) that is pivotal to internal negation at the clause level.

Internal negation identifies M with some conception of reality and specifies the absence from M of the process designated by the clause in which it appears. The absent entity is characterized in unipolar terms—no reference is made to the form of a previous utterance, and the processual profile (as opposed to background assumptions) is the focal point in determining inadmissibility to M. Within these limitations, differences in scope can still be observed, particularly with respect to quantifiers. Consider the ambiguity of *Everyone didn't understand*: either *every* can be interpreted as having wide scope (the property of not understanding was characteristic of everyone), or else NEG can (the property of understanding did not extend to everyone). The contrast is independent of grammatical constituency, which we may assume to be [*everyone* [*didn't understand*]] under either interpretation.

Our problem, then, is to specify the integration of *everyone* with *didn't understand* in such a way that either of two distinct conceptions, embodying alternate scope relations, can be derived as the composite structure. We can accomplish this by positing two variants of the same basic construction; these are represented in the grammar as elaborations (subschemas) of the same constructional schema (which in turn is a special case of the schema describing the integration of a subject nominal with the remainder of a finite clause). Note that our present concern is limited to characterizing the two variants. We will not consider the factors that determine the possibility or the likelihood of a particular variant being chosen, except to observe that an element's having wide scope is facilitated by various sorts of prominence, including linear precedence, heavy stress, and occurrence as part of the clausal subject (relational figure).

The integration of *everyone* and *didn't understand* in accordance with these constructional subschemas is depicted in Fig. 3.11. *Everyone* is semantically

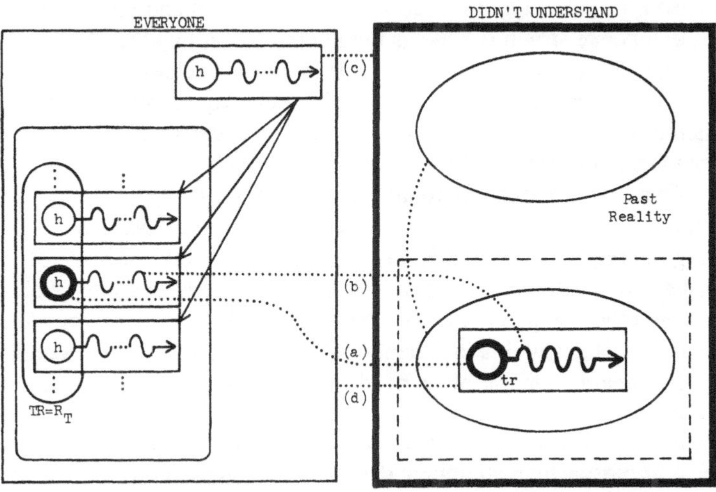

Fig. 3.11

equivalent to *every* (Fig. 3.3) except that its type specification is 'human' (h) rather than being fully schematic. It invokes the conception of a replicate process, consisting of multiple instances of a schematic process type, whose higher-order trajector (TR) coincides with a reference mass (R_T). Within this base, *everyone* profiles one element of TR, considered a representative element from the standpoint of participating in a process of the type in question. The other component, *didn't understand*, reflects the prior integration of *do*, NEG, *understand*, and the past-tense predication at lower levels of constituency. It profiles an instance of the process type *understand* and specifies its absence from past reality. The trajector of *didn't understand* is characterized only schematically and is elaborated in this construction by the subject nominal.

Under either interpretation, the trajector of *didn't understand* is identified with the profile of *everyone* by the correspondence labeled (a). Moreover, the process designated by *didn't understand* is equated, via correspondence (b), with the process that the profile of *everyone* participates in. What distinguishes the two constructional variants is a third correspondence, either (c) or (d)—the choice between them determines the overall organization of the composite structure. The interpretation in which *every* has wide scope results from choosing correspondence (c). The import of (c) is that the full characterization of *didn't understand*, including the absence of the designated process from past reality, is taken as defining the process type distributed by *everyone* to all members of TR/R_T. That is, the relationship that each member of TR/R_T takes part in is not simply one of understanding, as implied by (a) and (b) alone, but more precisely one in which the understanding is specified as being absent from past reality. When correspondence (d) is chosen instead, the resulting composite structure reflects the interpretation in which NEG has wide scope. The effect of (d) is to identify the structure excluded from past reality as being the entire configuration evoked by *everyone*. What is absent from this mental space is not the profiled instance of understanding taken in isolation, but rather the more elaborate situation in which that instance is representative of a property extending to all members of TR/R_T.

A final matter to consider is the interaction between NEG and *any*. The meaning of *any* is often regarded as problematic because in some of its uses it translates most straightforwardly into formal logic with a universal quantifier, and in others with an existential quantifier. For instance, *Any child likes ice cream* translates with a universal quantifier: 'For all x, if x is a child, then x likes ice cream'. On the other hand, an existential quantifier figures in the most obvious translation of *I don't see any wrench*: 'There does not exist an x such that x is a wrench and I see x'. The analysis pursued here is more in the spirit of those which attempt to derive all instances of *any* from a universal quantifier (cf. LeGrand 1974; McCawley 1981a, pp. 263–64). However, the meaning proposed for it does not correspond to any standard interpretation of the universal quantifier.

Evidence was given in 3.2.2 that *any* designates an instance t_i of T that is both *arbitrary* (non-specific) and conceived as being *randomly selected*. Let me now suggest that *any* assumes a similar but slightly attenuated value in those contexts where it is conceptually subordinated to a negation: when interpreted with "narrow scope," *any* still designates an *arbitrary* instance t_i of T, but the notion of random choice and unrestricted selection within R_T is considerably less salient (perhaps to the point of being absent altogether). To the extent that this is so, *any* becomes quite comparable to the indefinite article, except that its interpretation is necessarily non-specific. That is, t_i can only be an arbitrary instance conjured up just to specify a type of process whose occurrence is being negated. With the indefinite article, on the other hand, this interpretation is possible but not necessary. Hence *I don't see a wrench* can be disambiguated as either *I don't see any wrench* (arbitrary/non-specific) or *I don't see a certain wrench* (specific).

Unless it grounds a subject, *any* has the same potential as other quantifiers for ambiguity based on semantic scope when it co-occurs with NEG.[17] Thus (28)(b), *My cousin doesn't like any music*, may be interpreted with NEG in

[17] When it occurs on the subject, *any* necessarily has wide scope over clausal negation: *Any child doesn't like spinach* can only mean that the property of not liking spinach will prove applicable to any child one might randomly choose for examination. This limitation may reflect a conflict between the semantic attenuation characteristic of *any*'s "narrow-scope" value and the inherent salience of a subject. (Stress may also be a factor. Accenting the *any* in *I don't see any wrench* reinforces the notion of random selection that otherwise tends to fade away. Observe that the "wide-scope" *any* which grounds a subject nominal normally bears substantial stress.)

the scope of *any*, in line with the following rough paraphrase: 'If an instance of *music* is randomly selected for examination, it will prove to have the property that my cousin doesn't like it'. More likely, of course, is the interpretation having *any* in the scope of NEG. The conceptual import of (28)(b) is then something like this: 'An examination of present reality will fail to reveal a situation of the type *my cousin like* [*any*] *music*', where the brackets around *any* indicate the attenuated value just described. I regard these as substantially different conceptualizations, even though the two interpretations have the same truth conditions and are therefore logically equivalent.

The integration of *doesn't like* with *any music* is diagrammed in Fig. 3.12, which is quite analogous to Fig. 3.11 except that the quantifier is *any* instead of *every* and grounds the direct object rather than the subject. *Any music*

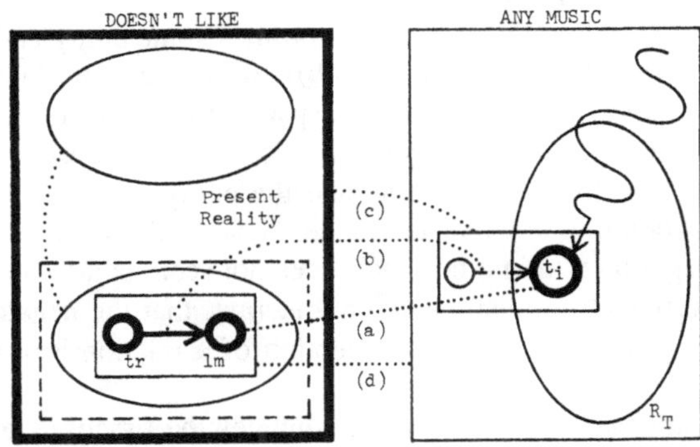

Fig. 3.12

profiles a single, arbitrary instance of the *music* category and further portrays it (with varying degrees of salience) as being randomly chosen from the reference mass R_T. By virtue of t_i's random selection (indicated by the squiggly arrow), the speaker and hearer have no prior mental contact with it: t_i exists only within the mental space representing the schematic conception of a process type and is conjured up just for purposes of constructing that type conception. The effect of correspondences (a) and (b) is to identify that type with *like* in particular and t_i with its landmark; *any music* is thus the direct object of *doesn't like*. As before, the difference in scope depends on whether (c) or (d) is established as an additional correspondence. Opting for (c) implies that the property attributed to the randomly selected t_i encompasses the entire configuration evoked by *doesn't like*—the relationship with respect to which t_i functions as landmark is not simply the process of liking, but rather the higher-order relationship in which that process is construed as being absent from present reality. On the other hand, opting for (d) implies that the exclusion of liking from present reality holds for an arbitrary instance of *music* (i.e. one conjured up just to specify the process type in question). The extent to which this arbitrariness is conceived in terms of random selection depends on stress (fn. 17) and other factors.

What about (28)(a), *My cousin likes no music*? It is commonly regarded as equivalent to (28)(b), *My cousin doesn't like any music*, on the interpretation where NEG has wide scope; indeed, a classic transformational analysis derives it from that source (Klima 1964). The principles of cognitive grammar demand an alternative analysis that conforms more closely to the surface evidence. The fact that *no* is part of the object nominal in (28)(a) suggests that the negation it expresses applies to the content of that nominal, not to the process designated by the clause containing it. Though negation is generally thought of as being applicable only to clause-like entities (propositions), no such limitation is intrinsic to the approach adopted here. Our schematic characterization of NEG merely states that it profiles some entity and specifies its absence from a mental space (Fig. 3.9(b)). In the case of clausal negation, the profiled entity is a process and the space in question is normally some conception of reality. However, we have also considered external negation, where M is a well-formed discourse and the entity excluded from it is the speaker's rendition of a previous utterance. Hence a third variant, specifically tailored for negation within a nominal, does not seem at all implausible. The specific properties of nominal negation are, first, that the negated entity is a thing, and second, that M is the conception of a relationship in which that thing participates.

The determiner *no*, as in *no music*, conflates the functions of grounding, negation, and quantification. As a grounding predication, it profiles a thing and indicates that the profiled instance t_i is both indefinite and non-specific. In its quantificational aspect, *no* can be grouped with *all, most*, and *some*; these proportional quantifiers give the size of t_i by matching its extension against that of a reference mass, R_T. Though it was not depicted in Fig. 3.1, these quantifiers evoke the conception of a property or relationship and specify what proportion of R_T participates in it. *No* represents the limiting case: the extension of t_i is zero, so all of R_T is excluded from participating. The status of *no* as a kind of negation becomes apparent when the relationship is regarded as a mental space, and when it is recognized that the conceptualization of zero extension incorporates that of positive extension as a background notion. Hence *no* is like other sorts of negation in that its meaning resides in a complex scene. The conception it evokes as background is equivalent to *some*: t_i (with positive extension) is conceived as participating in the relationship. Against this backdrop, *no* portrays as actual the situation in which t_i fails to participate (i.e. it is absent from the mental space).

What, then, do we say about (28)(a), *My cousin likes no music*? It does profile a relationship of liking on the part of my cousin and equates its landmark with an instance of *music*. However, *no* specifies that this instance has zero extension, with the consequence that the profiled relationship is rendered degenerate. But is a degenerate relationship still a relationship of the type in question? Can we speak of liking when the magnitude of its object is zero? We can if we choose to view it in that manner, just as we can see the rationale for regarding a point as the degenerate instance of a circle (a circle with zero radius). Logically, liking only a zero instance of *music* is equivalent to not liking any music, but linguistically and conceptually the situations are distinct.

CHAPTER 4

Nominal Constructions

PREVIOUS CHAPTERS have offered a definition of nominals in terms of meaning and semantic function: every nominal profiles a thing which is further identified as a grounded, quantified instance of some type. This characterization is independent of any particular structural configuration, and indeed, there are no significant structural features that all nominals share without exception. Nominal structure now becomes our focus. We will first examine how functional organization is manifested by the nominal structures of English. There follows a discussion of how a system employing only symbolic units is capable of representing the necessary patterns and restrictions. Considered next are alternate ways of implementing the same semantic functions, including possessive and classifier constructions. The final section deals with inflection, agreement, and related issues.

4.1. Structural Organization

Viewed in terms of traditional categories, there is no structural element or configuration displayed by every nominal in English, let alone for all languages. Not even the presence of a head noun is a universal structural feature, as attested by examples like the following: *this*; *six more*; *several*; *those on the table*; *the brave*; *that there are too many lawyers*.[1] Nominals do, however, display certain structural tendencies, and particular configurations can be regarded as prototypical, both within a language and cross-linguistically. Such configurations reflect the functional organization of nominals and are thus a natural place to begin our exposition of their structure.

4.1.1. *Canonical Structure*

Certain types of nominals are clearly more prototypical than others. For example, the patterns instantiated by such expressions as *this cup*, *some milk*,

[1] Since the technical definition of a noun in cognitive grammar is quite broad (an expression which profiles a thing—see Vol. 1, p. 242), every nominal does contain a noun (in fact, every nominal *is* a noun). Often, though, the element in question is not traditionally recognized as a noun or as the nominal head.

a big house, *the two sisters*, *those three black cats*, and *every student in the class* will be central to any reasonable description of English nominal structure. By contrast, nominals like *three from Toledo*, *the poor*, and *for Harold to resign* represent secondary constructions that occur less frequently or only in special grammatical circumstances. It is significant that the nominals regarded as prototypical can be identified as those whose structure most directly mirrors semantic function. Most obviously, a prototypical nominal incorporates, as distinct and overt elements, both a head noun (*cup*, *milk*, *house*, *sisters*, *cats*, *student*) and a "determiner" (*this*, *some*, *a*, *the*, *those*, *every*). Each fulfills a major semantic function: the head specifies a type, and the determiner grounds an instance of that type. Furthermore, the head noun and determiner comprise, respectively, the innermost and outermost layers of grammatical constituency: (*those* (*three* (*black* (*cats*)))). This formal relationship can be seen as iconic for their relationship in terms of meaning and semantic function.

This form-meaning iconicity has a number of facets. For one thing, the semantic functions of a nominal exhibit a layering that is quite analogous to its grammatical constituency: grounding and quantification presuppose instantiation, which in turn presupposes the conception of a type. A type specification is thus the innermost functional layer and has the potential to occur autonomously (e.g. *cat* represents a type, but not an instance, in the compound *cat lover*). A second facet of the iconicity is a comparable **A/D asymmetry** (Vol. 1: 8.3; Ch. 9) between the meanings of the head noun and the determiner. Generally the head is conceptually autonomous vis-à-vis the determiner, i.e. its characterization of the profiled entity does not refer in any way to the ground. On the other hand, the grounding predication is conceptually dependent, making reference to a thing as a salient portion of its internal structure—indeed, as its profile (Fig. 2.16(c)). A further aspect of the form-meaning iconicity is that inner layers of structure describe more intrinsic properties of the entity designated by the nominal. Observe that the head noun and determiner stand maximally opposed in this regard: the type specification is fully intrinsic to the characterization of the designated entity, whereas its grounding is wholly extrinsic, pertaining not to properties inherent in the entity itself, but rather to whether the speech-act participants have established mental contact with it. Finally, the head noun represents an open-ended class and typically supplies a vast amount of detailed conceptual content. Once again, determiners lie at the opposite extreme, being limited in number and highly schematic in their content.

Let us examine more carefully the layered structure of canonical English nominals. The innermost layer consists of what is traditionally known as the **head noun**. Although the structural significance of this element is universally acknowledged, standard notions provide no satisfactory way to characterize it. The terms **head** and **noun** are appropriate but insufficient, for both are equally applicable to a variety of other constituents representing distinct levels of organization within a nominal. In *those three black cats*, for example, *cats* is not the only expression that profiles a thing and is thereby categorized as a noun: the same is true of *black cats*, *three black cats*, and the nominal as a whole. This cannot be rectified by defining the head as the smallest expression categorized as a noun, for then *cat* rather than *cats* would be identified as the head in *those three black cats*, and *truth* (or even *-ness*) rather than *truthfulness* in *Abernathy's truthfulness*. Further requiring that the head not be smaller than a word still fails to yield the proper results, for *site* (rather than *convention site*) will be singled out as the head noun of *an excellent convention site in the Midwest*.

The term head is similarly applicable to multiple constituents within a nominal. Though definitions vary (cf. Williams 1981; Zwicky 1985; Hudson 1987; Langacker 1986b), I maintain that a head is properly described as the profile determinant at a given level of constituency (Vol. 1, pp. 309–10). *Cats* is thus the head with respect to *black cats*, but *-s* is also the head at a lower level of organization (within *cats*), and so is *black cats* at a higher level (within *three black cats*). In *an excellent convention site in the Midwest*, the heads at various levels include *site*, *convention site*, and *excellent convention site*. The problem, then, is to specify the level of organization at which the notion head noun, as traditionally understood, is applicable.

With their customary terminological imprecision, linguists often refer to the element in question as the "lexical head." This term reflects the fact that the head noun usually has the rich, detailed semantic content characteristic of "lexical items," as opposed to the limited, schematic content of "grammatical" morphemes. However, invoking the notion **lexicon** serves only to muddy the waters. For one thing, the putative semantic contrast between lexical and grammatical units is actually just a matter of degree (cf. Langacker 1988b); it will not, in any case, distinguish among *cat*, *cats*, and *black cats*, nor among *site*, *convention site*, and *excellent convention site*. The only way to define the notion lexicon that is useful, avoids arbitrary divisions, and approximates traditional usage is to identify it with the set of fixed expressions in a language (i.e. those enjoying the status of conventional units). But by that criterion, the lexicon has to incorporate both "lexical" and "grammatical" expressions (as does a dictionary). Also counting as lexical items by that definition will be many expressions both more and less inclusive than the head noun, while the head itself will often fail to qualify: we saw in 2.1 that the head can be a newly created expression of great complexity, e.g. *toothbrush designer convention site*.

To escape this morass, I suggest that we consider the problem from the standpoint of semantic function. My specific proposal pertains to instantiation, which is intimately associated with number. In fact, number can be thought of as effecting the instantiation of a type. In 2.3.1, we saw that a numberless count-noun stem (e.g. *cat*) can either be used as such (*cat lover*) or else subjected to one of two derivational processes. The first is pluralization, which effects both instantiation and replication to yield the conception of a mass comprising indefinitely many instances of the designated type (thus defining a higher-order type specification). The second is a zero derivation whereby any noun that specifies a type can also be construed as designating a single instance of that type. When applied to a stem like *cat*, this second process derives a noun that is formally unchanged but specifically construed as singular (rather than numberless). The same process is also applicable to both underived mass nouns (*milk*) and the replicate mass derived by pluralization (*cats*); although the resulting expressions are not customarily thought of as being singular, they too designate a single instance of the specified type. In all three cases, the derived form can then be grounded and serve as a nominal head (*the cat*; *the milk*; *the cats*).

It is therefore suggestive that overt number marking in English (i.e. pluralization) occurs at the level of the head noun. The head noun *cats*, for example, is marked plural whether it stands alone as the grounded structure (*the cats*) or is expanded by a series of modifiers (*the three black cats under the ladder*). Moreover, number marking applies to the head noun as a whole, not to elements at lower levels of constituency. We thus encounter *truths* in the role of head noun (*these eternal truths*) but not as an inner constituent of the head (**Abernathy's truthsfulness*). With heads formed by compounding, the matter is not so clear-cut, but an analysis conforming to the generalization is both possible and intuitively reasonable. Note first that non-final members of a compound cannot in general be pluralized: **feetball*; **cats lover*; **conventions site*.[2] Superficially, the final member of a compound does appear to pluralize (*footballs*; *cat lovers*; *convention sites*). However, nothing prevents an analysis of such expressions whereby the compound as a whole undergoes the pluralization. It is not uncommon for a predication that applies to a complex structure to be realized morphologically on its final element (see Vol. 1, 9.3.2).

Prototypical English nominals are thus susceptible to an analysis in which the head noun constitutes a structurally significant level characterized in terms of meaning and semantic function. The most basic requirement is that the head be a constituent whose profile is inherited by the nominal as a whole. There may of course be a number of such constituents (e.g. *cats*, *black cats*,

[2] With multiword compounds, pluralization of a non-final member occurs as a secondary pattern (*arms deal*; *parts catalog*; *civil rights lawyer*). The plural noun cannot be the head, because the replicate mass it designates is not the profile at higher levels: a compound's profile is determined by its final member, and the compound as a whole serves as nominal head (*an* ***arms deal***; *this new* ***parts catalog***; *every* ***civil rights lawyer*** *in Florida*).

three black cats; or *site*, *convention site*, *excellent convention site*). The one traditionally recognized as the head noun is describable as the immediate result of instantiation, i.e. the minimal structure that not only specifies a type but is further construed as designating a single instance of that type. If the step-by-step assembly of a nominal from its component morphemes is thought of as defining a **compositional path** (Vol. 1, 8.2.2), the head noun is the first structure encountered that incorporates a number specification and profiles the same instance as the nominal overall. So identified, the head represents a structurally significant level of organization in that English noun-modifier constructions apply only at that level and above.

The canonical structure of English nominals can now be summarized. The pivotal element is the head, obtained when some noun undergoes instantiation and thereby comes to designate a single instance of the specified type. The noun in question can be supplied in various ways. It may be an underived count- or mass-noun stem, such as *cat* or *milk*, or a mass noun formed by pluralization (e.g. *cats*). It may arise through morphological derivation (*designer*) or by compounding (*toothbrush*). The combined and repeated application of these derivational processes makes available an open-ended set of potential nominal heads, both fixed and novel (e.g. *truthfulness*; *football player*; *arms dealers*; *catnip mouse purchaser*; *toothbrush designer convention sites*; *fire alarm assembly plant site selection committee chairmen*).

Once the head is created by instantiation, further composition takes on a different character. Phonologically, it is no longer effected by morphological devices or compounding, but rather via the grouping of full words or phrases into higher-order phrases (*black / cats*; *convention site / in the Midwest*). Semantically, in contrast to the head-internal complement relationships characteristic of morphological derivation, higher-level integration relies almost exclusively on modifier relationships.[3] Any number of modifiers can be added at successive levels of composition: *cats* > *black cats* > *ugly black cats* > *big ugly black cats* > *big ugly black cats with long whiskers*. Although the addition of each modifier results in a higher-order type specification, the profile remains unchanged and is simply construed as instantiating a particular subtype of the basic type specified by the head noun. Among the possible modifiers is an absolute quantifier indicating the magnitude of the designated instance; it can be analyzed as occurring externally to all the other modifiers (*three big ugly black cats with long whiskers*). Finally, a full-fledged nominal is obtained by appending a grounding predication at the highest level of constituency (*those three big ugly black cats with long whiskers*).

[3]Consider *black cats*. In the composition of the head noun, *cat* is a complement because it elaborates a substructure of the plural predication, which functions as profile determinant (Fig. 2.9). At the higher level, *black* is a modifier because the profile determinant, *cats*, elaborates its schematic trajector. (See Vol. 1, 8.3.4.)

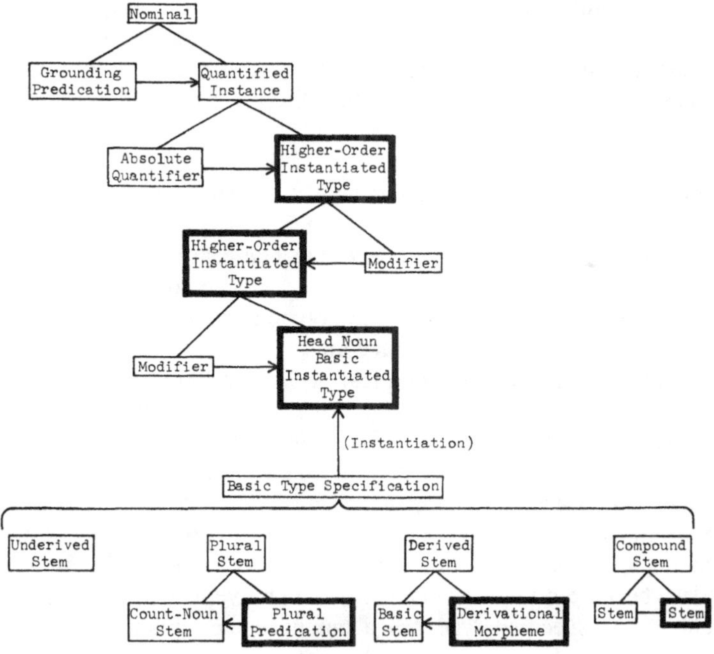

Fig. 4.1

The prototypical organization of English nominals is sketched in Fig. 4.1, which ought to be self-explanatory. With a plural noun chosen as head, the specific structure depicted corresponds to a nominal such as *the three black cats under the ladder*. Observe that numerous elements function as heads in one or another sense of that term. *Cats* qualifies as the "global" head within the nominal, i.e. the element traditionally identified as the head noun, in accordance with the foregoing characterization. The term head can also be applied to the profile determinant at any level of constituency. So defined, *-s* is the "local" head within *cats*; *cats* within *black cats*; *black cats* within *black cats under the ladder*; and *black cats under the ladder* within *three black cats under the ladder*.

A special situation arises at the highest level of constituency. Remember that an epistemic predication profiles the grounded entity, not the grounding relationship (2.4). Consequently, the profile of the grounding predication corresponds to that of the structure it combines with; in our example, *the* and *three black cats under the ladder* designate the same conceived entity, the former providing a schematic characterization which the latter serves to elaborate. The two components have equal claim to the status of local head, since both their profiles correspond to the composite-structure profile (that of the nominal as a whole). To the extent that *the* is regarded as the head, the other component—which elaborates the head—is a complement. To the extent that the elaborating structure is regarded as the head, *the* constitutes a modifier. Both views have precedent in grammatical theory.

4.1.2. *Other Configurations*

Without attempting an exhaustive inventory, let us now consider some nominal structures of English that deviate from the canonical organization outlined above. The patterns that concern us conform to the schematic characterization of a nominal as designating a grounded, quantified instance of some type. Their departure from the prototype pertains only to the structural implementation of these semantic functions.

Some nominals are non-prototypical because the semantic functions are associated with the nominal as a whole (which may in fact be unanalyzable) and thus fail to receive individual symbolization. Three kinds of examples are worth mentioning: a proper name, a personal pronoun, and a nominalized finite clause. A proper name (e.g. *Joyce Jones*; *Fido*; *Norway*) carries with it a type specification ('human female'; 'pet dog'; 'nation') and is construed as designating a single instance of that type. Moreover, a name is definite (hence grounded) because it invokes an idealized cognitive model wherein every individual of the specified type has a unique name sufficient to identify it (2.2.2). A personal pronoun similarly profiles a single instance of a schematically specified type: 'human' in the case of *I*; 'human female' for *she*; 'replicate mass' for *they*; etc. The distinguishing property of such a pronoun is that it evokes the speech event as its cognitive domain and indicates the status of its profile with respect to the roles of speaker and addressee. Because our conception of the ground presumes that the speaker and hearer are in mental contact with themselves and one another, the first- and second-person pronouns are inherently definite. The third-person pronouns are also definite and identify the designatum as a specific entity distinct from the speech-act participants.

The nominalization of a finite clause produces a structure that, despite its internal complexity, must be categorized as a noun: it profiles the abstract region comprising the component states of the clausal process (1.2.1.2). Like a proper name or personal pronoun, this complex noun itself constitutes a nominal, as witnessed by its ability to occur alone as subject or direct object:

(1)(a) ***That prices will continue to rise*** *is obvious.*
(b) *I realize* ***that the firm has filed for bankruptcy.***

The proposition conveyed by the nominalized clause can be regarded as a detailed type specification for the resulting noun. Moreover, since the entire finite clause undergoes the nominalization, including its grounding of the profiled process, the unique circumstances of the grounding relationship are incorporated in that proposition; an inherent aspect of the noun's type characterization is thus the location of the reified process with respect to the specific time and participants of the speech event. The specified type therefore has only a single instance, with the consequence that the derived noun is inherently definite (i.e. the noun itself puts the speaker and hearer in mental contact with the profiled instance—see 3.1.1). Hence no separate grounding predication is required: conceptual reification alone converts a finite clause into a nominal.

A second class of departures from the prototype consists of complex nominals formed by the apposition of component structures each of which is itself a nominal. The integration of the component nominals is effected by a correspondence between their profiles, and since each of these corresponds to the composite structure profile (which is thus a doubly-characterized, doubly-grounded thing), the two components have equal claim to the status of profile determinant and nominal head. Among these appositional constructions, one subclass takes a nominalized finite clause as its second element: *the fact that whales are mammals*; *the very idea that she might be unfaithful*; *your idiotic claim that celery causes warts*. Another subclass (discussed and analyzed in Langacker 1982b) has for its first member either *all* or its dual form *both*: *all those kittens*; *both the starting defensive tackles*. Expressions such as *Jack the Ripper*, *my daughter the lawyer*, and *we the people* illustrate other subtypes.

Nominals like *milk*, *three cats*, and *happy children* appear to deviate from the prototype because they lack a grounding predication. However, following the tradition that posits a "zero determiner," I will assume that these nominals are grounded by a predicate which has no effect on their phonological manifestation (Vol. 1, p. 345). We observed in 3.1.2 that *a*, *sŏme*, and ø form a contrastive set of indefinite determiners: *a* occurs with count nouns, the others with both kinds of mass nouns; *sŏme* indicates that the designated mass is quite limited, whereas ø allows it to be of any size and even to exhaust the reference mass. It is of course common for one member of a contrastive set to be symbolized by zero, and here the choice is iconic, for ø is almost as transparent semantically as it is phonologically. With respect to all three parameters of its meaning—indefiniteness, the unboundedness of a mass, and unspecificity in regard to size—ø's value can be described as one of diffuseness and the absence of precise delimitation.

Even though not every nominal contains an overt quantifier, some aspect of quantification is always present. One such aspect is the construal of a nominal as designating a single instance of the specified type. Inherent in plurals is a second aspect of quantification, namely the multiple instantiation of a lower-order type to form a replicate mass. Those elements traditionally recognized as quantifiers pertain to the magnitude of the profiled instance. Some of them (e.g. *three*, *many*, *little*) specify its magnitude in absolute terms; others (*all*, *most*, *some*) compare its extension to that of the reference mass and are analyzed as grounding predications. In the absence of either sort of quantifier, the magnitude of the designated instance is characterized only schematically.

A nominal's type specification can also be left schematic. In the canonical situation, a detailed type characterization is provided by the head noun, but often this noun has little specificity or is absent altogether. Nouns of course range in value from the highly specific to the maximally schematic, e.g. *toothbrush* > *brush* > *implement* > *object* > *thing*. Those at the extremity of this scale approximate the noun-class schema in their degree of abstraction and can thus be regarded as pronouns of a sort. Unlike personal pronouns, which are inherently grounded and stand alone as nominals, forms such as *thing*, *place*, *time*, *body*, and *one* provide only a minimal type specification and thus require the support of an epistemic predication; combined with *some*, they form what are traditionally known as indefinite pronouns: *something*, *someplace*, *sometime*, *somebody*, *someone*.[4] *One* is specifically human as part of *someone*, but it occurs more generally as a pro-form, in which case its meaning is equivalent to the count-noun schema. It is well known that *one* can refer anaphorically to the head noun together with any number of modifiers:

(2)(a) *That ugly black* ***cat*** *dislikes this pretty white* ***one***.
(b) *That ugly* ***black cat*** *dislikes this pretty* ***one***.
(c) *That* ***ugly black cat*** *dislikes this* ***one***.

Not surprisingly, *ones* is likewise schematic for the class of plural nouns and can also be used anaphorically:

(3)(a) *Those ugly black* ***cats*** *resemble the pretty white* ***ones*** *I used to own.*
(b) *Those ugly* ***black cats*** *resemble the pretty* ***ones*** *I used to own.*
(c) *Those* ***ugly black cats*** *resemble the* ***ones*** *I used to own.*

In a nominal such as *this one* or *the pretty ones I used to own*, *one*(*s*) is simply a head noun that makes a schematic type specification. Its anaphoric relationship to the basic or higher-order type description of another nominal involves an overarching grammatical construction representing a higher level of structural organization (hence it is beyond the scope of present discussion).

When a grounding expression occurs by itself as a full nominal (e.g. *that*, *these*, *some*, *any*, *all*, *each*), it incorporates a type specification despite the

[4] *One* also has a nominal use (e.g. *One never knows*) in which it is non-specific and generic for the class of humans (cf. 3.1.2). Some speakers achieve the same effect by combining the *body* of *somebody* with the indefinite article: *A body never knows*.

absence of a head noun. The type is specified by the grounding predication itself, which profiles the grounded entity and thus provides a schematic characterization of this entity as part of its internal structure: *all* identifies its designatum as a mass, *these* as a replicate mass, *each* as a discrete entity, etc. Whereas in prototypical nominals this schematic profile serves as e-site for a structure comprising the head together with its modifiers, an appropriate linguistic or situational context allows such elaboration to be dispensed with. Observe that a form like *one*, *place*, or *thing* is a pro-*noun* because it merely supplies an abstract type description (only in combination with *some* does it constitute a nominal). By contrast, an epistemic predication is a pro-*nominal* because, in addition to specifying a type, it inherently grounds the profiled instance.

At first blush, it appears that absolute quantifiers (which we have not analyzed as epistemic predications) are also pro-*nominal*: ***Few*** *had anything to say*; *I need* ***three***; ***Several*** *were lost in transit*. Because these nominals are indefinite, however, they are more revealingly analyzed as incorporating the zero determiner. For example, just as *three cats* consists of ø *three cats* (with ø an indefinite grounding predication), so *three* consists of ø *three*, which in turn is parallel to such expressions as *those three*, *all three*, and *any three*. By this analysis, then, the pronominal sense of *three* (diagrammed in Fig. 2.13(d)) represents the composite structure obtained when its adjectival variant (Fig. 2.13(c)) combines with ø; their integration involves a correspondence between *three*'s trajector and the schematic mass designated by ø, which functions as profile determinant. Comparable analyses hold for ø *few*, ø *several*, ø *much*, etc., and also for such expressions as *those three*, *all three*, and *any three*: the first element is in each case modified by the second, and since it both grounds and profiles a schematically characterized thing, the resulting expression is pro-*nominal*.

These constructions exemplify a broader class of departures from the canonical organization of English nominals. Prototypically, modifiers attach to the head noun, and the complex structure so derived elaborates the schematic profile of the grounding predication (Fig. 4.1). But since this latter profiles a thing, it is capable in principle of being modified directly by an adjectival expression, and English has conventionalized a variety of such constructions for nominals that lack a head noun. Expressions like *you three* and *we two* are parallel to those just considered, since the personal pronouns are actually grounding predications; although they normally stand alone as nominals, *we* and *you* are occasionally elaborated by a head noun: *we linguists*; *you bastard!* (cf. Postal 1969). Though the pattern is very limited, nominals such as *the poor*, *the brave*, *the good*, and *the less fortunate* should perhaps be analyzed in comparable fashion. More productive are patterns involving modifiers that normally follow the head noun, i.e. prepositional phrases, participial phrases, and relative clauses. They occur most freely with demonstratives, but not exclusively: *those with families*; *some without handles*; *the three sitting by the door*; *that chosen by the majority of experts*; *all I want*; *we who know better*. All these cases can be analyzed as constructions in which the schematic thing profiled by the grounding predication (the local head) corresponds directly to the entity that normally serves as the modifier's e-site.

4.2. Patterns and Restrictions

How can the various patterns and restrictions of English nominal structure be stated in a cognitive grammar? As conceived in this framework, a speaker's knowledge of grammatical convention resides in a **structured inventory of symbolic units**—structured in the sense that some units function as components of other, more complex units. A symbolic unit is complex when it consists of either a categorizing relationship (in which one unit serves as standard for the categorization of another) or a relationship of composition (where a composite structure is construed in relation to two or more component structures). There is no inherent limit to the size or complexity of the structural configurations that can arise through multiple compositional and categorizing relationships and coalesce as units with varying degrees of entrenchment.

4.2.1. *Class Schemas*

Regularities are expressed by schematic symbolic units extracted to embody the commonality observable across a set of specific expressions, which they thereby categorize. These categorizing schemas vary in regard to **symbolic complexity**, i.e. their decomposability into smaller symbolic units. A schema that is symbolically minimal (having no symbolic components) defines a grammatical class; for example, the class of nouns (broadly construed) is defined by the schema [THING/ . . .], which is instantiated by any symbolic structure whose semantic pole profiles a thing (a region in some domain). Schemas that are symbolically complex characterize grammatical constructions. A constructional schema is structurally parallel to the complex expressions it categorizes, consisting of component and composite structures linked by horizontal and vertical correspondences at each pole. Since one constructional schema can be incorporated as part of another, structural patterns of indefinite complexity are capable of being established as conventional units.

Class schemas that may be extracted and referred to in the characterization of nominal structure are numerous and diverse. Within the class of nouns, for instance, subclasses such as count vs. mass, human vs. non-human, animate vs. inanimate, etc. are definable by means of subschemas that make the appropriate specifications at their semantic pole. Orthogonal to these distinctions is categorization on the basis of semantic function; in principle, schematic reference is possible to nouns that represent an uninstantiated type specification, to nouns that designate an unquantified instance of a type, to nouns that designate an instance which is quantified but ungrounded, and so on. A nominal is characterized schematically as an expression that not only profiles a thing but also grounds it in some fashion. Schematic descriptions based on intrinsic semantic properties are also achievable for such classes as absolute quantifiers, personal pronouns, and proper names.

For the characterization of certain other classes, reference to both intrinsic and extrinsic properties is required. For example, meaning alone is insufficient to distinguish adjectives and prepositions in English: both classes profile atemporal relations; their conceptual content may be quite similar (cf. *nearby* vs. *near*); and an adjective often resembles a preposition in having a landmark construable as a thing (e.g. a region along some scale). The reason why certain atemporal relations are singled out as prepositions is their participation in the prepositional-phrase construction, wherein a nominal elaborates the primary landmark of the relational predication and follows it directly in the phonological sequence. Similarly, grounding expressions such as articles, demonstratives, and relative quantifiers satisfy the schematic definition of a nominal (they both profile a thing and ground it). The basis for grouping them into a special class of "determiners" is twofold: the schematicity with which they characterize the profiled thing; and more importantly, their combination with an ungrounded noun (possibly complex) that elaborates this schematic profile to derive a higher-order nominal of greater specificity. I assume that both intrinsic and extrinsic factors can figure in the commonality leading to co-classification (Vol. 1, 11.1.3.2), so occurrence in a particular construction is indeed a possible basis for categorization.[5] I further assume that the structures so categorized can be identified as class members even outside the defining construction (just as a person can be a *Midwesterner* even while living in California). Although such characterizations are less straightforward than those based solely on intrinsic properties, they nonetheless make reference only to symbolic structures and relationships.

Consider the categorization of *near* as a preposition. We have noted that the characterization of prepositions makes inherent reference to their participation in the prepositional-phrase construction. The schema describing this construction, shown on the left in Fig. 4.2, comprises two component structures and the composite structure effected by their bipolar integration. On the basis of intrinsic properties, the component structure representing the preposition is characterized semantically as an atemporal relation, and phonologi-

[5]This follows from other principles of cognitive grammar: the encyclopedic characterization of symbolic units (whereby even highly extrinsic specifications are included); and the fact that linguistic structures can themselves function as cognitive domains.

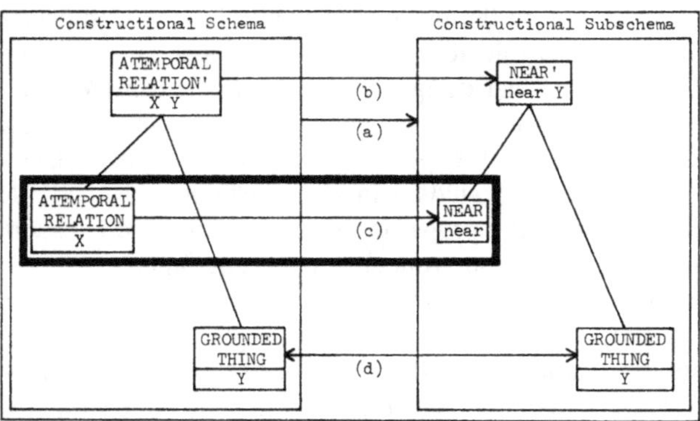

Fig. 4.2

cally as a word or phrase (abbreviated X): [ATEMPORAL RELATION/X]. The other component structure can be identified as the schema for the class of nominals; semantically it profiles and grounds a thing, and phonologically it consists of a word or word sequence (abbreviated Y): [GROUNDED THING/Y]. A more elaborate diagram would also show the correspondences responsible for their integration; at the semantic pole, for instance, the nominal profile is placed in correspondence with the atemporal relation's primary landmark. The composite structure is obtained by superimposing the specifications of corresponding entities. The resulting semantic structure, given as [ATEMPORAL RELATION′], is equivalent to the preposition except that its landmark inherits the specifications of the nominal. Phonological integration gives rise to the temporally ordered sequence [X Y].

The preposition class is characterized schematically by the occurrence of the unit [ATEMPORAL RELATION/X] in the context specified by this constructional schema. That is, the basis for categorization (the **scope** of the categorizing relationship) includes not only inherent aspects of the element being categorized but also the extrinsic property of appearing in this construction. Hence the categorization of *near* as a preposition implies the full configuration of Fig. 4.2, in which the constructional schema is instantiated by a subschema that situates [NEAR/near] in the requisite context. The heavy-line box indicates that the categorizing relationship labeled (c) is in focus (i.e. that *near* is the element being categorized), but the scope of the categorization is the construction as a whole. Observe that multiple categorizations may be possible with respect to the same scope. For example, by shifting the focus to relationship (b), we obtain the classification of [NEAR′/near Y] as one type of prepositional phrase, described schematically by the intrinsic characterization [ATEMPORAL RELATION′/X Y] and by the extrinsic property of occurring in this construction as its composite structure. Similarly, relationship

(a) (for which scope and focus coincide) represents the full structural description of *near* + NOMINAL expressions as instances of the prepositional-phrase construction.

If Fig. 4.2 seems unduly complex for the simple categorization of *near* as a preposition, that is merely because the diagram is explicit about how prepositions might actually be *characterized* (not just *labeled*). One should further bear in mind that a structure of great internal complexity is effectively simple in terms of cognitive processing once it achieves the status of a unit (Vol. 1, 2.1.1), and also that schemas are **immanent** in their instantiations, not distinct and autonomous elements, despite their separate depiction for analytical purposes (Vol. 1, 12.1.3). Still, diagrams like Fig. 4.2 are too unwieldy for general use, especially when numerous patterns need to be described. Let us therefore adopt a series of abbreviatory conventions that will convert such diagrams into formulaic representations of the sort that linguists are more accustomed to. It is crucial, however, that we not lose sight of the underlying complexity concealed by these formulas or the symbolic character of the structures they abbreviate.

These conventions are listed in Fig. 4.3, where ">>" indicates an abbreviatory relationship. The import of convention (a) is that some arbitrary symbol, Q, can be adopted to stand for a structural configuration, however

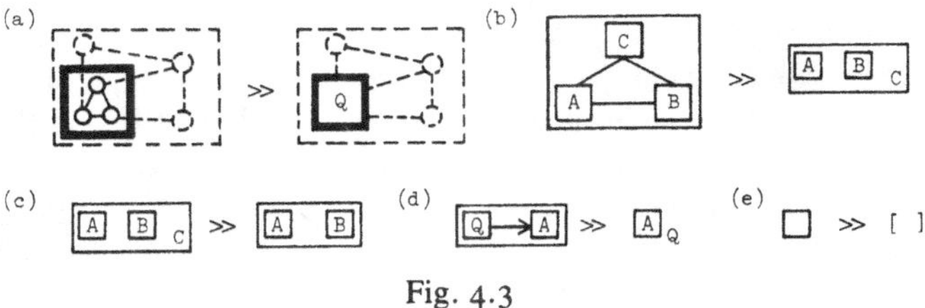

Fig. 4.3

complex it might be; the heavy-line box encloses the configuration thus symbolized, and the outer box (in dashed lines) delimits any context that might be required for Q's characterization. Convention (b) allows one to represent a construction without depicting its composite structure, C, as a separate box; in effect, the component structures, A and B, are shown iconically as subparts of C. Going one step further, convention (c) permits the suppression of any explicit reference to C—the construction is represented by its component structures alone, the composite structure remaining implicit. Convention (d) provides a compact notation for a categorizing relationship, whereby the label for the categorizing schema is given as a subscript to the box enclosing the categorized element. Finally, our practice of using square brackets in lieu of a box is sanctioned by convention (e).

The effect of these abbreviatory conventions is illustrated in Fig. 4.4. The

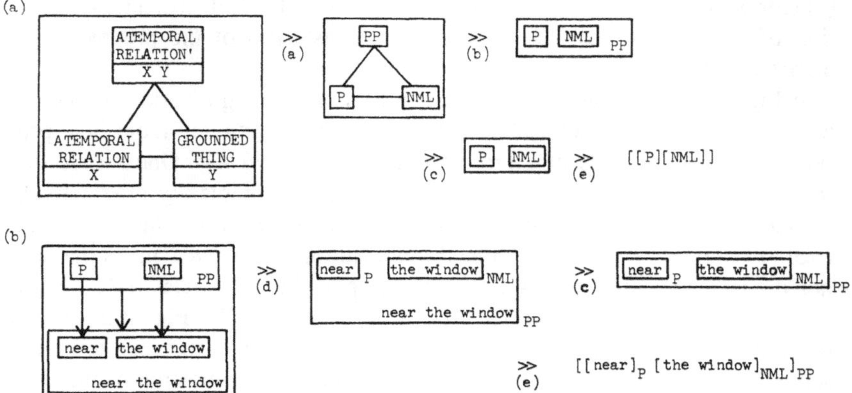

Fig. 4.4

top diagram shows their application to the constructional schema for prepositional phrases. By convention (a), the symbol P is adopted for the symbolic structure [ATEMPORAL RELATION/X] when it occurs in the context of this construction; PP is similarly adopted for the composite structure [ATEMPORAL RELATION'/X Y] in the context of the construction; and NML abbreviates [GROUNDED THING/Y] (the schema for nominals). The resulting representation is then further compacted in accordance with conventions (b), (c), and (e), which yield [[P][NML]]. Moreover, by suppressing internal brackets we can obtain an even simpler formula: [[P][NML]] >> [P NML].

Depicted in the bottom diagram is the structural description of the specific prepositional phrase *near the window*, which consists in its categorization by the constructional schema. The initial structure in the sequence reflects the previous application of conventions (a) and (b) to both the schema and the categorized expression; for the latter, observe that orthographic representations abbreviate symbolic structures: [NEAR/near] >> [near], etc. The next structure in the sequence is obtained by three applications of convention (d), one to each categorizing relationship (e.g. [[P]→[near]] >> $[\text{near}]_P$). Conventions (c) and (e) then derive a labeled bracketing (which is equivalent to a phrase tree): $[[\text{near}]_P\ [\text{the window}]_{NML}]_{PP}$. This last format is standard and dear to the heart of every syntactic theorist. In the present framework, however, such formulas have the status of abbreviatory notations and nothing more. The actual characterization of grammatical structure resides in the complex symbolic configurations that they stand for.

4.2.2. *Constructional Schemas*

A speaker's full, detailed knowledge of English nominal structure comprises an immense inventory of constructional schemas grouped into larger assemblies through relationships of categorization and composition. Several factors contribute to the vastness of this inventory: the need to accommodate both canonically organized nominals and various departures from the canon; the coexistence of high-level schemas, describing constructions in maximally general terms, with arrays of subschemas that specify (at different levels of abstraction) their conventionally established subpatterns; and the incorporation of constructional schemas into higher-order schemas of greater symbolic complexity. For the sake of manageability, let us confine our attention here to central patterns reflecting canonical organization. We will further concentrate on nominal structure above the level of the head noun, assuming for illustrative purposes the constituency of Fig. 4.1.

Each level of constituency in Fig. 4.1 represents a grammatical construction describable by means of an abstract constructional schema. At the lowest level, an adjective and head noun combine to form a higher-order noun (e.g. *black cats*). The following, given formulaically, is a first approximation to the requisite schema: $[[ADJ][N]_N]$.[6] Represented at the second level of constituency is the modification of a noun by a prepositional phrase (*black cats under the ladder*), again resulting in a higher-order noun: $[[N][PP]_N]$. At the third level, the constructional schema $[[QNT][N]_N]$ sanctions the modification of a noun by an absolute quantifier (*three black cats under the ladder*). Finally, a full nominal (such as *the three black cats under the ladder*) is formed by the addition of a grounding predication at the highest level of organization: $[[G][N]_{NML}]$.

These constructional schemas embrace the full range of expressions we are presently concerned with. As formulated, however, they are also consistent with many types of expressions that the conventions of English grammar do not allow. How can the proper restrictions be imposed? The apparatus deployable for this purpose is severely constrained by the assumptions of cognitive grammar: only symbolic units are permitted in the description, and these are further limited (by the content requirement) to units that occur overtly, schematizations of such units, and categorizing relationships. Nevertheless, an adequate account is in principle achievable.

Even as initially formulated, the constructional schemas do rule out many possibilities. For example, a prepositional phrase must follow, not precede, the noun it modifies (*the cats under the ladder*; **the under the ladder cats*). This restriction is imposed merely by including the schema $[[N][PP]_N]$ among the conventional units of the grammar, where it is available as a template for

[6]Observe that [ADJ] and [N], the two component structures, are superimposed on $[\ _N]$, the composite structure, in accordance with abbreviatory convention (b) of Fig. 4.3. These formulas employ the further convention of representing temporal ordering by the left-to-right sequencing of components (in actuality, temporal ordering is specified at the composite structure's phonological pole).

the construction and evaluation of specific expressions, and by not gratuitously positing a schema that would sanction expressions with the contrary ordering (i.e. $[[PP][N]_{N}]$). In similar fashion, the limitation of grounding predications and quantifiers to pre-head position (*the three cats*; **the cats three*; **three cats the*) is captured by the inclusion of $[[G][N]_{NML}]$ and $[[QNT][N]_{N}]$ among the conventional units of English, together with the non-inclusion of counterparts with the opposite temporal ordering. Other restrictions follow automatically from the proper characterization of component structures. For instance, certain grounding predications inherently specify the basic class of the grounded element: the indefinite article grounds a discrete entity; *all* grounds a mass; *these*, a replicate mass; and so forth. Hence a consistent composite structure emerges only when the grounded element is elaborated by a compatible noun (*a desk*; *all cheese*; *these pencils*). If it is not, the resulting nominal is semantically anomalous (**all desk*; **these cheese*; **a pencils*).

Other restrictions demand a refinement in our statement of the constructional schemas. As presently formulated, for example, schemas $[[ADJ][N]_{N}]$ and $[[QNT][N]_{N}]$ fail to distinguish between conventionally sanctioned expressions such as *three black cats* and *many fine books* on the one hand, and impermissible expressions like **black three cats* and **fine many books* on the other. The problem arises because our reference to nouns has not yet taken semantic function into account. We have seen that nominal structure reflects a conceptual layering, wherein grounding and quantification presuppose instantiation, which in turn presupposes a type specification. Since a nominal construction pertains to a particular level of functional organization, a noun that serves as its component or composite structure can be characterized accordingly.

Let us therefore distinguish nouns on the basis of semantic function. By means of superscripts, we can refer as needed to a noun that represents the instantiation of a type (N^{i}), to a quantified instance (N^{i+q}), to an instance that remains ungrounded (N^{i-g}), and so on.[7] Recall, now, that the head noun is characterized in terms of instantiation (4.1.1), and that our sole concern at present is with structures above that level; every reference to N in our constructional schemas can thus be replaced by N^{i}, as a minimal specification. Suppose we further specify that an adjective or prepositional phrase can only modify an unquantified instance: $[[ADJ][N^{i-q}]_{N^{i-q}}]$; $[[N^{i-q}][PP]_{N^{i-q}}]$. An absolute quantifier also modifies an unquantified instance, but the resulting composite structure is of course quantified: $[[QNT][N^{i-q}]_{N^{i+q}}]$. Clearly, the

[7]These superscripts are shorthand notations for structures having certain conceptual properties. Adopted for expository convenience, they are not per se attributed to the linguistic system and thus do not run afoul of the content requirement (which precludes the postulation of contentless diacritics).

effect of these refinements is to limit a quantifier to the outermost layer among the modifiers of a noun. This accounts for the contrast between such pairs as *three black cats* vs. **black three cats*, and also for the non-occurrence of doubly-quantified nouns (**several three cats*). Finally, at the highest level of constituency a grounding predication combines with a noun that may be quantified but is ungrounded: [[G][N^{i-g}]$_{NML}$].

4.2.3. *Larger Configurations*

Nominal restrictions can also arise from larger structural assemblies, including complex constructional schemas. Consider the schema [[QNT] [[ADJ][N]$_{N}$]$_{N}$] (where [[ADJ][N]$_{N}$] instantiates the second component structure of [[QNT][N]$_{N}$]). Extracted from countless expressions on the pattern of *three black cats*, *many good ideas*, etc., this complex schema specifies the conventional order QNT ADJ N, and presumably it is well-enough entrenched to be activated for the construction and evaluation of novel expressions. Consequently, in the absence of a schema to sanction the non-conventional ordering ADJ QNT N, an expression such as **black three cats* will be categorized as a deviant manifestation of [[QNT] [[ADJ][N]$_{N}$]$_{N}$]. Even if [[QNT][N]$_{N}$] and [[ADJ][N]$_{N}$] made no reference to semantic function, and thus permitted such expressions, the complex schema would still provide the basis for judging them ill-formed. We see, then, that distributional restrictions reflect the interaction of local and global patterns. More generally, an expression's well-formedness is assessed through its simultaneous categorization by many conventional units, each pertaining to a particular kind of content and having a certain scope.

Normally, a grammatical construction must be analyzed as a complex category: its full description requires not just one constructional schema, but a family of such schemas linked by categorizing relationships to form a network. The configuration of this network determines the distributional import of individual schemas, i.e. how their specifications translate into restrictions on permissible expressions. For a given scope, just one node in a network is assumed to be responsible for the primary categorization of an expression—only this **active node** participates directly in constructing the expression or assessing its well-formedness (though other nodes are activated secondarily). The likelihood of a particular schema being chosen as the active node is hypothesized to be a function of two potentially antagonistic factors: its specificity, and its degree of entrenchment or cognitive salience (see Vol. I, 11.2.2). Thus, if two schemas with the same scope are comparably well entrenched, the more specific is selected and provides the basis for judgments of conventionality.

For an example, let us consider not only simple adjectives that precede the head noun, but also complex adjectives that incorporate an infinitival complement and necessarily follow the head: *a prisoner anxious to escape*; *those students able to answer*; *any passenger ready to depart*. The schema [[ADJ][N] $_N$] was posited for simple adjectives and obviously fails to accommodate these other expressions. They require a separate constructional schema which specifies the opposite temporal order, and which identifies the modifier as a complex adjective consisting of a simple adjective followed by an infinitive: [[N] [[ADJ][INF] $_{ADJ}$] $_N$]. We can reasonably assume that [[ADJ][N] $_N$] is prototypical and thus more deeply entrenched, but the other schema is considerably more specific in its characterization of the modifier. Suppose, then, that a speaker has reason for using a complex adjective to modify a noun. In assembling this complex modifier (e.g. *anxious to escape*), he must activate the constructional schema [[ADJ][INF] $_{ADJ}$], whose detailed overlap with [[N] [[ADJ][INF]] $_{ADJ}$] $_N$] ensures that this latter will be activated for constructing and evaluating the adjective-noun combination. By virtue of greater entrenchment, however, [[ADJ][N] $_N$] represents the default-case option and is selected as the active node when a noun is modified by a simple adjective.

These two constructional schemas are just a small part of the network describing conventional patterns for the modification of nouns by adjectives. Presumably they both instantiate a higher-level schema which specifies that the head noun elaborates the adjectival trajector, but which is neutral as to temporal ordering and whether the adjective is simple or complex. The two schemas are themselves instantiated by subschemas describing arrays of conventionally established subpatterns. Instantiating [[ADJ][N] $_N$], for example, is the complex schema representing the special case in which [N] itself consists of a noun modified by an adjective: [[ADJ] [[ADJ][N] $_N$] $_N$]. This in turn is instantiated by lower-level subschemas referring to particular kinds of adjectives; e.g. [[SIZE] [[COLOR][N] $_N$] $_N$] embodies the well-entrenched pattern of English wherein adjectives of size precede adjectives of color (*long red pencil*; *tiny black dot*; *big green bullfrog*; *tall gray building*). Now although a schema at any level describes some regularity, its precise distributional import is determined by the array of established subschemas, for these take precedence in the sanction of new expressions. Consider a form like **orange gigantic balloon*, which is judged to be incorrect despite its adherence to the [[ADJ] [[ADJ][N] $_N$] $_N$] schema. When a noun is modified by both a size and a color adjective, the more specific pattern [[SIZE] [[COLOR][N] $_N$] $_N$] is chosen as the active node and assumes responsibility for primary categorization. **Orange gigantic balloon* is perceived as deviant because it violates the temporal ordering stipulated by this subschema.

There are many linguistic patterns (sometimes called "minor rules") that seem too obvious to be ignored and yet cannot be extended to new instances. One such pattern is the marking of past tense by the substitution of [ɔt] for everything after the initial consonant (or *Cr* cluster) of the verb stem: *taught*, *sought*, *caught*, *fought*, *brought*, etc. Although this pattern would have to be mentioned in any comprehensive description of English morphology, it is limited to a fixed set of stems, being applicable neither to additional stems already in the language (e.g. **traught* as the past tense of *trounce*) nor to stems that are newly created (if I invent the verb *flump*, meaning 'hit with a pillow', its past tense must be *flumped*, not **flaught*). To handle such patterns, we can reasonably suggest that only schemas with a certain degree of entrenchment or cognitive salience are capable of being evoked for the sanction of new expressions, and that some constructional schemas simply fall below the threshold.

A pattern of this sort in the domain of nominal structure is the use of personal pronouns as determiners. Though restricted in certain ways that need not concern us here, the construction permits an open-ended set of expressions involving the pronouns *we* and *you*, the latter in both its singular and plural variants (*we Midwesterners*; *you stupid sonovabitch!*; *you misguided linguists*). We must therefore posit, for each of these pronouns, a constructional schema that is capable of being invoked for the sanction of novel exemplars: [[we][N] $_{NML}$]; [[you SG][N] $_{NML}$]; [[you PL][N] $_{NML}$]. These schemas are clearly parallel in central respects, and if speakers represent their commonality, it takes the form of the higher-order schema [[PRON][N] $_{NML}$]. However, the mere existence of this schema does not ensure its ability to license new expressions—forms like **I Midwesterner*, **he sonovabitch!*, **she doctor*, and **they physicists* meet its specifications but are unacceptable nonetheless. Because [[PRON][N] $_{NML}$] is extracted from schemas that are themselves somewhat marginal, we can plausibly suppose that it is insufficiently salient to sanction novel expressions.

A final distributional problem is the failure of certain grounding predications to stand alone as full nominals. Although the limitation may in certain instances be phonologically motivated (*the*, *a*, *sŏme*, *ø*), in the case of *no* and *every* it appears to have neither a semantic nor a phonological basis. Why, for example, should *each* but not *every* occur as a nominal (*Each arrived*; **Every arrived*) when the two have such similar meanings? Even should some rationale be found, it is unlikely to be strongly predictive (i.e. the facts of English could in principle have been otherwise). I assume, then, that the restriction must somehow be listed in the grammar as a matter of linguistic convention. How can this be done?

One possibility is for the grammar to incorporate an explicit prohibition on the occurrence of *every* (also *no*, *the*, etc.) in particular grammatical constructions. For example, the network of schemas defining the prepositional-object construction might include the subschema *[[P][every] $_{PP}$], which specifies the ill-formedness of a prepositional phrase whose object nominal consists of *every* and nothing more. Similar "filters" would prevent the appearance of *every* as a clausal subject, as a direct object, and so on. The postulation of filters hardly lacks precedent in linguistic theory (e.g. Perlmutter 1971; Chomsky and Lasnik 1977), but on grounds of naturalness and learnability I consider it desirable that only positive statements of what *does* occur be permitted in a linguistic description (hence the content requirement). Though the matter has yet to be thoroughly investigated, the avoidance of explicit prohibitions is thus adopted in cognitive grammar as a working strategy.

Let me briefly outline three mutually compatible options that conform to this strategy; conceivably each has some role in maintaining the restriction. The first involves the availability of well-entrenched alternatives. For example, since demonstratives subsume the meaning of *the* and are thoroughly established as full nominals, they tend strongly to pre-empt the definite article on any occasion when it might be so employed. In like manner, the use of *a*, *no*, and *every* as full nominals may be forestalled by the ready availability of *one*, *none*, and *every one*. This type of account does, I believe, have some validity, but by itself it is hardly sufficient. While the entrenchment of one locution may to some degree inhibit the adoption of a functionally equivalent alternative, this influence is certainly limited (note, for instance, that *each* and *each one* both occur as full nominals).

A second option is suggested by an obvious but significant fact: that a linguistic unit often occurs only as one component of a specific higher-order structure (or a small number of such structures). The normally imperfective verb *be*, for instance, has a semantic variant that is neutral as to perfectivity, but that particular variant occurs only in the context of the passive construction (Langacker 1982b). Likewise, we must posit the verb stem *aggress* as the basis for *aggressor*, *aggressive*, and *aggression*, but for many speakers it cannot occur except in these forms (cf. Lakoff 1970). We must therefore assume that a component unit is sometimes so tightly linked to a higher-order structure (or a small set of mutually inhibitory higher-order structures) that activation of the former necessarily leads to (one of) the latter being activated.[8] The failure of *every* to occur as a full nominal can then be attributed to such a link between *every* itself and the constructional schema [[every][N^{i-g}]$_{NML}$]. Under this analysis, *every*'s use as a nominal is not specifically prohibited—rather, its combination with a noun to derive a higher-order nominal is rendered obligatory.

The final option is far more speculative. It exploits the idea that symbolic units are categorizable on the basis of both intrinsic and extrinsic properties (Fig. 4.2). Suppose we distinguish between two characterizations of a nominal: one that only refers to inherent semantic properties (i.e. the designation and grounding of a thing); and one that also makes reference to occurrence in

[8] Otherwise phrased, the **transition** between the component and the higher-order structure is deeply entrenched and easily elicited. (See Vol. 1: 4.3.4; 11.3.1).

a certain array of structural frames (as clausal subject, clausal direct object, prepositional object, and so on).[9] It is clearly possible for an expression to satisfy the first of these characterizations but not the second. Hence a grounding predication, though it qualifies as a nominal semantically, does not automatically belong to the class of nominals defined in both semantic and distributional terms. A speaker's knowledge that a particular kind of structure is conventionally established as a nominal in this second sense resides in a specific categorizing unit: [[NML]→[DEM]] makes the generalization that demonstratives function in this capacity; [[NML]→[each]] indicates that *each* does; and so on. The failure of *every* to stand alone as a nominal is then reflected in the grammar by the absence of [[NML]→[every]] from the inventory of conventional units. Moreover, the distributional facts are not necessarily altered if a schema is extracted to embody the regularity observable in [[NML]→[DEM]], [[NML]→[each]], etc. This schematic categorizing relationship, [[NML]→[G]], expresses the conventional pattern in which a grounding predication occurs by itself as a full nominal. However, not every schematic unit is well enough entrenched to license novel instances; we need only assume that [[NML]→[G]] is insufficiently salient to serve as an active node for this purpose.

Distributional restrictions raise complex descriptive and theoretical issues that have only begun to be addressed in the framework of cognitive grammar. How a particular phenomenon should be accommodated is not yet always clear, at least at the level of specific detail. There are nonetheless grounds for believing that the necessary restrictions can in principle be implemented in a system that conforms to the content requirement and posits only symbolic units for the description of grammatical structure. Although the theory is stringent from the standpoint of ruling out arbitrary constructs, the permitted apparatus is potentially quite powerful, in ways that seem both natural and cognitively realistic.

4.3. Functional Alternatives

The canonical structure of English nominals displays an iconicity between grammatical form and semantic function (4.1.1). Despite the felicity of this arrangement, the structural implementation of these functions is also achieved in other ways, some of which are common across languages or even universal. We will focus here on two important kinds of constructions: those involving

[9]That is, speakers may be capable of seizing upon this distributional property as an abstract similarity employed for purposes of categorization, and then—through a kind of "bootstrapping"—referring to this category in their representation of the constructions on which it is based. It is a matter of no consequence that the class of nominals, so defined, is partly "grammatical" (and no longer purely "semantic"), for the theory explicitly acknowledges the existence of grammatical structures and classes defined with reference to them. The contrast with "autonomous" theories of grammar lies instead in the claim that all the structures concerned are symbolic in nature.

noun classifiers, which represent a different way of introducing type specifications; and possessive constructions, which provide an alternative means of grounding.

4.3.1. *Noun Classifiers*

A prominent feature of many languages is a set of **classifiers** that occur with nouns under certain grammatical conditions. The most common use of a classifier is for modification by a numeral, though it may also be required by other elements, such as demonstratives or possessives. Typical is its use in Mandarin Chinese with numerals and demonstratives:[10]

(4)(a)	*wǒ xǐhuān kàn*	*shū*		'I like to read books.'	
	I like read	book			
(b)	*wǒ kàn-le*	*yī-běn*	*shū*	'I've read a book.'	
	I read-PERF	one-CLSF	book		
(c)	*wǒ kàn-le*	*zhè-běn*	*shū*	'I've read this book.'	
	I read-PERF	this-CLSF	book		

In (4)(a), *shū* 'book' appears without a classifier because it is indefinite and no particular quantity is indicated. However, a number or demonstrative demands a classifier and attaches to it rather than to the noun, as (b) and (c) illustrate.

The classifiers of a language can range in number from a handful to many dozens. Though a wide variety of semantic categories are represented in classifier systems—pertaining to animacy, consistency, quantity, social status, etc.—shape specifications can perhaps be considered prototypical. A noun tends to be conventionally associated with a particular classifier, e.g. Mandarin *shū* 'book' with *běn* 'book-like object'. Often, however, various options are permitted, each portraying the noun's referent in a different fashion. For example, the Mandarin classifiers *tiáo* 'long, thin object', *juǎn* 'roll', and *duàn* 'segment' can all occur with *shéngzi* 'rope': *yī-tiáo shéngzi* 'one rope'; *yī-juǎn shéngzi* 'one coil of rope'; *liǎng-duàn shéngzi* 'two pieces of rope'. While the nouns that take a given classifier may form a coherent class largely predictable from its meaning, they can also be quite heterogeneous. This latter situation arises when a classifier is extended by virtue of cultural association or metaphor to entities that do not satisfy its original or narrowest semantic characterization (see Lakoff 1987, ch. 6, for examples and extensive discussion).

There are different opinions concerning the *raison d'être* of classifiers. Allan (1977) emphasizes their perceptual basis. Denny (1976) argues that the classes they define relate primarily to human interaction with the environment. Lee (1987) attempts a synthesis of these positions and discusses the

[10] My information on Mandarin was furnished by Tony Hung and Steve Poteet. PERF stands for perfect aspect, and CLSF for a classifier. The superscripts are indications of tone.

origin of classifiers with reference to the psychological notion of basic-level categories. In her comprehensive study of Japanese classifiers, Downing (1984) finds it useful to distinguish between "kind" classifiers (e.g. *ken* 'building'), whose members share numerous physical and functional traits, and "quality" classifiers (e.g. *hon* 'long, thin object'), which are based on just one or two salient properties. She also investigates the discourse function of classifiers, particularly their use in referring anaphorically to a previously mentioned noun.

Our focus here, though, is on the internal structure of nominals containing classifiers. It is not particularly controversial to claim that noun classifiers are themselves nouns. This is evident from a variety of factors: their noun-like meanings; their occurrence with numerals, demonstratives, and possessives; and the fact that they derive historically from nouns (indeed, the same form is often used as both a noun and a classifier). I thus regard classifiers as schematic for potentially open-ended classes of nouns, in much the same way that *be* and *do* are schematic for classes of verbs. There is also good reason for regarding a classifier as the head of the nominal, at least in the sense of being central to its structure, whereas the accompanying "lexical" noun is more peripheral. One indication of this is the attachment of grounding predications (notably demonstratives) to the classifier, as shown in (4)(c). Another indication is that the lexical noun can sometimes be omitted, so that the grounded classifier assumes a kind of pronominal function. Moreover, in view of the close association between head nouns and number marking (4.1.1), it is highly suggestive that a classifier is the primary locus for specifications of quantity.

In regard to the structural implementation of semantic function, substantial differences can thus be observed between a typical English nominal, such as *two ropes*, and its counterpart in a classifier language, e.g. Mandarin *liǎng-tiáo shéngzi*. One difference is that number (i.e. plurality) and cardinality ('two') are separately marked in the English expression, whereas *liǎng* 'two' is the only indication of quantity in its Chinese equivalent. A second point of divergence is that the English head noun has a dual role from the standpoint of semantic function: *ropes* supplies a detailed type specification and also represents the minimal structure construed as designating an instance of that type (cf. Fig. 4.1). By contrast, different nouns serve these functions in the Mandarin example. The classifier *tiáo* undergoes instantiation and quantification but makes only a highly schematic type description ('long, thin object'). On the other hand, *shéngzi* 'rope' provides a far more specific type characterization, which elaborates that of *tiáo*, but it is not itself instantiated or quantified.

We can see this more clearly by examining the step-by-step assembly of *liǎng-tiáo shéngzi* 'two ropes', as diagrammed in Fig. 4.5. The components *liǎng* 'two' and *tiáo* 'long, thin object' are integrated at the first level of

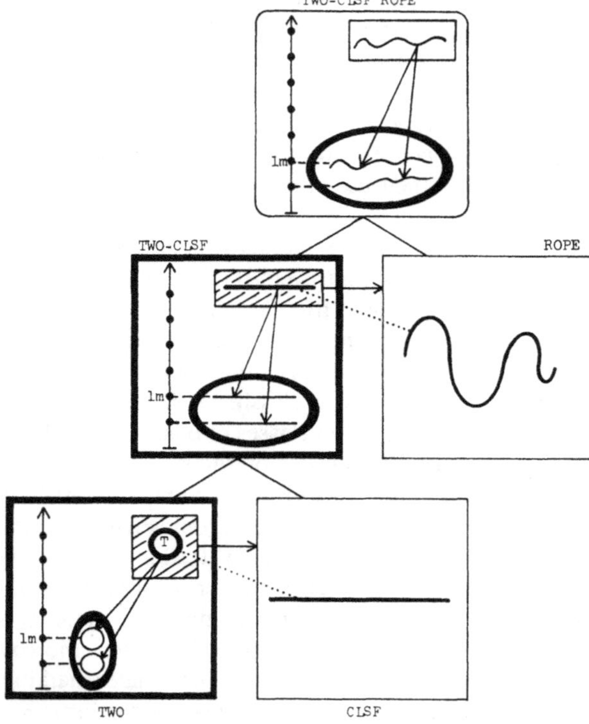

Fig. 4.5

constituency to form the quantified but still schematic noun *liǎng-tiáo* 'two long, thin objects'. Though other analyses are conceivable, I will assume that *tiáo* is a numberless stem, with *liǎng* combining the functions performed separately in English by plural marking and the numeral (cf. Figs. 2.9 and 2.14). *Liǎng* resembles the plural in that it profiles a replicate mass comprising multiple discrete entities all of which instantiate some type (T); as a numeral, it specifies the cardinality of the profiled mass, thus presupposing its construal as an instance of the mass-noun category. Integration is effected by *tiáo* elaborating *liǎng*'s schematic type specification. Hence the composite structure *liǎng-tiáo* designates a replicate mass consisting of two discrete entities that instantiate the schematic type 'long, thin object'. This type description is then further elaborated by *shéngzi* 'rope' at the second level of constituency, which is structurally parallel to the first.

Under this analysis, an expression like *liǎng-tiáo shéngzi* has no constituent that is precisely equivalent to a head noun in English. Structurally, *liǎng-tiáo* and *ropes* do play analogous roles, each representing the innermost constituent of its nominal: ((*liǎng-tiáo) shéngzi*); (*two* (*rope-s*)). They contrast, however, in that *ropes* is specific in type but schematic in regard to quantity, whereas *liǎng-tiáo* displays the opposite arrangement. At a higher level of constituency, the property left schematic in this structural core is spelled out more precisely by a separate predication; thus *two* specifies the quantity of *ropes*, and *shéngzi* elaborates *liǎng-tiáo*'s type description. We see, then, that the two languages have alternate structural means for implementing the same semantic functions.

There are many classifiers that seem on first examination to be rather different from those considered so far. Used primarily with nouns whose referents have no inherent shape, they name some kind of container or discrete unit representing the physical manifestation of a limited quantity of substance. Typical examples from Mandarin are *yī-bēi chá* 'one cup (of) tea', *yī-dī shuǐ* 'one drop (of) water', and *liǎng-duī tǔ* 'two piles (of) dirt'. The supposed contrast with cases like *liǎng-tiáo shéngzi* lies in the fact that, while *tiáo* 'long, thin object' is clearly schematic for *shéngzi* 'rope', *bēi* 'cup' does not appear to be schematic for *chá* 'tea', or *duī* 'pile' for *tǔ* 'dirt'. A rope is certainly one kind of long, thin object, but we can hardly say that tea is one kind of cup.

I suspect, however, that this contrast is only apparent, and that virtually the same analysis holds for both sorts of quantifiers. It was noted previously (2.3.2) that an English expression like *cup of tea* or *bucket of water* is ambiguous. Though *cup* or *bucket* normally designates a physical container, in this construction it can also be interpreted as referring to a schematically characterized mass whose volume is such that it would just fit in such a container. It is not implausible that classifiers such as *bēi* 'cup', *dī* 'drop', and *duī* 'pile' might undergo a similar semantic shift, so that instead of designating a physical unit or container, they are construed as profiling a mass that constitutes or fills it. If so, the analysis of Fig. 4.5 can be maintained with just minor adjustments, since the classifier—when it profiles a mass—is indeed schematic for the noun that elaborates it. The construction then works as before, provided that the entities comprising the numeral's designatum are construed as patches of substance having a certain shape or magnitude (not as discrete objects in the usual sense).

4.3.2. *Possessive Constructions*

Every language has some means of indicating possession, both at the clause level (*The boy has a dog*) and within a nominal (*the boy's dog*). In nominal possessives (our present focus), the thing possessed is represented by the head noun, while generally the possessor is itself a full nominal. The possessive relationship can be marked in various ways. The simplest is by mere juxtaposition, in which case the possessor nominal usually precedes the head, as in Mandarin *tā lǎoshī* (he teacher) 'his teacher'. Often the possessor bears some overt marking, such as English *-'s*, or functions as the object of a preposition (e.g. *a friend of Tom*). When the possessor is pronominal, it frequently attaches to the head, as it does in Luiseño: *po-kii* 'his house'. A non-pronominal possessor may then be accommodated by combining this construction with the appropriate nominal, e.g. *yaʔaš po-kii* (man his-house) 'the man's house'.[11]

There is some indication that possessives function as grounding predications. For one thing, a possessor often precludes any other explicit grounding: we can say either *the hat* or *Tom's hat*, but hardly **the Tom's hat*.[12] Moreover, a nominal such as *Tom's hat* is considered definite, and only the possessor is present to contribute that value. Yet the notion that possessives might be inherently definite grounding predications meets with certain difficulties. A grounding predication must establish some relationship between the designated entity and the speech-act participants, but it is not obvious that a third-person possessive (e.g. *Tom's*) accomplishes this. Also, possessive modifiers and grounding predications do sometimes co-occur:

(5) *ny alika-ko* 'my dog' [Malagasy]
the dog-my

(6) *tā nèi-běn shū* 'that book of his' [Mandarin]
he that-CLSF book

Furthermore, a possessed noun is not invariably definite; the object in (7) can be interpreted as indefinite and non-specific:

(7) *I want* ***some teenager's car*** *to enter in a demolition derby.*

The speaker need not have any particular car in mind, nor any specific teenager—he may simply want a beat-up old jalopy to enter in the race, and he knows that the car of any teenager is liable to qualify.

The issue of whether possessives should be analyzed as grounding predications is therefore not clear-cut. We learn nothing definitive from their occurrence or non-occurrence with other such predications, since the overt manifestation of grounding relationships is subject to considerable variation: some languages allow them to remain implicit, while others may mark them redundantly. The semantic facts are inconclusive as well, for grounding predications can specify either definiteness or indefiniteness. They also differ in the prominence accorded to these and other relations between the designatum

[11] Luiseño is a Uto-Aztecan language of southern California. See Smith 1964, Katz and Postal 1964 (pp. 137–38), and Langacker 1968 for early analyses of possessives in generative grammar. For various modern perspectives, see Seiler 1983, Nichols 1986, Deane 1987, and Langacker 1988a.

[12] In expressions like *the boy's dog*, the article is part of the possessor nominal, i.e. it does not ground *dog* but rather *boy*.

and the speech-act participants; such relations are pivotal to the meaning of demonstratives, for example, but far less salient in proportional quantifiers, whose primary value resides in the comparison of the profiled mass to a reference mass. In short, grounding predications constitute a heterogeneous class, and possessives are ambivalent in regard to their possible membership. This ambivalence undoubtedly reflects the meaning of possessives, so to clarify their status we must first attempt a semantic characterization of the possessive relationship.

4.3.2.1. *Abstract Possession.* It is widely appreciated that the linguistic category of possession does not reduce to any single, familiar value, such as ownership. A moment's thought reveals the extraordinary variety of the relationships coded by possessive constructions. With respect to the possessor, the thing possessed may constitute: a part (*my elbow*); a more inclusive assembly (*her team*); a relative (*your cousin*); some other associated individual (*their friend*); something owned (*his watch*); an unowned possession (*the baby's crib*); something manipulated (*my rook*); something at one's disposal (*her office*); something hosted (*the cat's fleas*); a physical quality (*his health*); a mental quality (*your patience*); a transient location (*my spot*); a permanent location (*their home*); a situation (*her predicament*); an action carried out (*his departure*); an action undergone (*Lincoln's assassination*); something selected (*my horse* [i.e. the one I bet on]); something that fulfills a particular function (*your bus*); someone serving in an official capacity (*our mayor*); and so on indefinitely. Though certain kinds of relationships can be regarded as prototypical for possessive constructions—including part/whole, kinship, and ownership relations—it is doubtful that all the others are motivated solely as metaphorical extensions from these. We might also ask what part/whole, kinship, and ownership relations have in common—why should these particular relations (as opposed to others) cluster as prototypical values of the same construction? Both considerations encourage us to seek a more abstract characterization of possession.

One proposal is that any kind of association counts as a possible possessive relationship. On this account, the schematic import of possession is merely that two entities figure in the same cognitive domain—any conception whatever can function as the domain, and either relational participant can have any role within it. This analysis is clearly abstract enough to handle all the data, but it is probably too extreme. In particular, it offers no basis for the asymmetries observable in possessive relations. For example, it fails to explain why the whole is generally construed as the possessor of a part, rather than conversely (e.g. *the girl's neck* vs. **the neck's girl*), or why, in the association between an object and its owner, possessor status is virtually always conferred on the latter (*the boy's knife* vs. **the knife's boy*). We find these asymmetries both in constructions that take the possessor as a landmark (*the roof of the house* vs. **the house of the roof*) and in those that make it the trajector (*The house has a roof* vs. **The roof has a house*). The possessor/possessed asymmetry is consequently independent of trajector/landmark alignment.

I propose that possessives are susceptible to schematic characterization intermediate in abstractness between such notions as ownership and part/whole relations on the one hand, and mere association on the other. Possessive constructions evoke an idealized cognitive model that is comparable to the billiard-ball model (1.1.1) in terms of being abstract, ubiquitous in its applicability to everyday experience, and fundamental to how we conceptualize the world. The essence of this model is simply that some entities are most easily located with reference to others. The world is conceived as being populated by countless objects of diverse character. These objects vary greatly in their salience to a given observer; like stars in the nighttime sky, some are immediately apparent to the viewer, whereas others become apparent only if special effort is devoted to seeking them out. Salient objects serve as **reference points** for this purpose: if the viewer knows that a non-salient object lies near a salient one, he can find it by directing his attention to the latter and searching in its vicinity.

Let us refer to this idealized conception as the **reference-point model**. Its essentials are diagrammed in Fig. 4.6, where W stands for the world, V for the viewer, and T for the **target**, i.e. the object that the viewer seeks to locate.

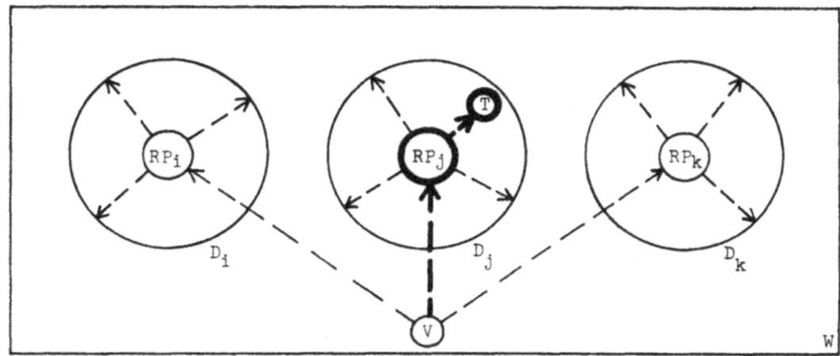

Fig. 4.6

The world contains many salient objects with the potential to serve as reference points (RP), although just three are shown explicitly. Each reference point anchors a region that will be called its **dominion** (D). Depending on one's purpose, the dominion of a reference point can be characterized in either of two ways: as its neighborhood in W; or as the set of objects that it can be used to locate. The viewer locates an object when he establishes mental contact with it (singles it out for individual conscious awareness). The dashed arrows represent various paths through which such contact can be achieved (cf. Fig. 2.15); heavy lines indicate the specific path through which V makes contact with T.

With respect to this model, we can define a notion of **abstract possession** that represents what all possessive expressions supposedly share. Abstract possession is simply the relationship profiled in Fig. 4.6, in which the conceptualizer traces a mental path through the reference point to the target; the reference point constitutes the possessor, and the target, the entity possessed. Of course, a particular expression will generally invoke a more specific relationship, which may involve some **objective** path leading from the possessor to the possessed—objective in the sense of having some basis in the structure of the conceived situation (2.4). For example, the possessor may apply some force to the object possessed for purposes of manipulating or controlling it. An objective path of this sort is analogous to the conceptualizer's **subjective** path and hence *motivates* a particular choice of possessor/possessed alignment. Objective factors do not invariably furnish such motivation, however, and they are sometimes overridden. If all possessive expressions have a common denominator, it is limited to the subjective construal of Fig. 4.6.[13]

This analysis accounts for the broad range of relationships coded by possessive constructions and for the asymmetries noted previously. Virtually any sort of conceptual content affords the possibility of construing one entity as a reference point for locating another. Such construal is almost inevitable in the case of part/whole and kinship relationships, which are prototypical values of possession; it is therefore natural that nouns for body parts and kinship relations obligatorily take possessives in many languages. Moreover, since a reference point is chosen on the basis of salience, empirically observed asymmetries in possessor/possessed alignment are predictable from universal cognitive principles. These principles include the following: a whole is more salient than its parts; a physical object is more salient than an abstract entity; and a person has maximal cognitive salience.[14]

A whole is thus the possessor of its parts, rather than conversely, because its greater prominence makes it the obvious choice as reference point (*the girl's neck* vs. **the neck's girl*). Owners are possessors because people are more likely to be recognized individually than are their inanimate possessions (*the boy's knife* vs. **the knife's boy*). We construe a cat as the possessor of its fleas (*the cat's fleas*) because the cat is far more salient perceptually, and is also accorded greater empathy; resorting to the opposite alignment (*the fleas'*

[13]The relation between abstract possession and prototypical possession (such as ownership) is analogous to that between abstract vs. spatial regions (1.1.2), abstract vs. physical substances (1.2.1.1), or abstract vs. spatial motion (Vol. 1, 4.3). In each case, the abstract notion is primarily a matter of construal and is independent of any specific conceptual content. It is only at this level of abstraction that universally valid characterizations of basic grammatical categories are possible (e.g. every noun profiles an abstract region).

[14]These same factors are crucial in **active zone** phenomena (Langacker 1984; Vol. 1, 7.3.4). In special circumstances, they can of course be outweighed by other considerations.

cat) would suggest that the speaker is concerned with the welfare of the fleas and views the situation from their standpoint. Further explained by the analysis is the periphrastic use of possessives with nominalization, as in *his departure* and *Lincoln's assassination* (1.2.2). The derived noun itself represents the reification of a process and is therefore quite abstract. By contrast, the possessor corresponds to a participant in the reified process and is generally a person or some other physical entity, which makes it a natural reference point. It is additionally worth noting that the location of a process is always determined by that of its participants.

4.3.2.2. *Basic Constructions.* Various sorts of predications and constructions are characterized with respect to the basic possessive configuration of Fig. 4.6. One such predication is a possessive verb like *have*, which typically displays a wide spectrum of specific values:

(8)(a) *Watch out—he has a knife!*
(b) *Maurice has very broad shoulders.*
(c) *Do you have any pets?*
(d) *I have another serious complaint.*
(e) *She has an amazing lack of talent.*

A possessive verb usually derives historically from one expressing physical control (e.g. 'hold', 'keep', 'guard'), so it may retain a vestige of the objective asymmetry wherein the possessor exerts some force directed at the possessed. Even a maximally general verb like *have* reflects its origin by choosing the possessor as its trajector, and the possessed as its primary landmark. Also, since *have* is imperfective, the profiled relationship (in which the trajector serves as reference point for the target) is construed as being stable—it continues through conceived time without essential modification and is scanned sequentially. *Have*'s structure is thus as depicted in Fig. 4.7(a).

Possession is also expressed by non-verbal elements such as prepositions,

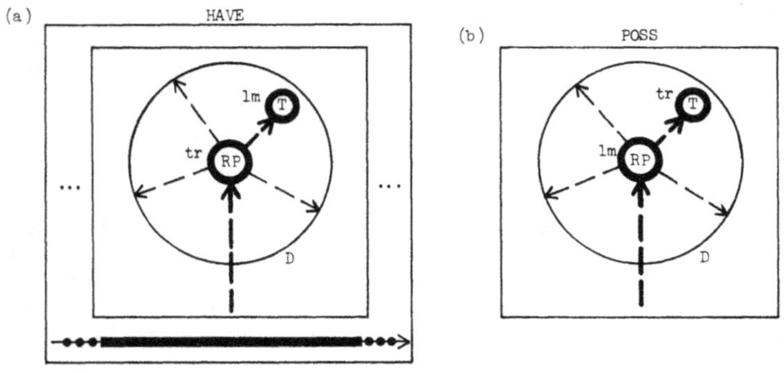

Fig. 4.7

postpositions, and nominal inflections, which can all be analyzed as stative relations. In its original or prototypical sense, an adposition usually situates a mobile trajector with respect to some spatial landmark. Its extension to possessive use may then be based on spatial metaphor, or may simply stem from the fact that spatial proximity is a usual concomitant of possession. But in either case, the objective, spatial relationship becomes less and less important as the adposition evolves into a generalized possessive marker, with the eventual result that the subjective relationship of abstract possession remains as its primary value. The figure/ground alignment of the possessive predication is a consequence of this origin: the target and reference point correspond respectively to the spatial trajector and landmark. Hence the configuration of Fig. 4.7(b) is typical for stative possessives.[15]

Though it is not an adposition, I will assume that the possessive inflection of English also has this structure. Because it forms a modifier, this predicate (labeled POSS) must be atemporal, as are all non-finite modifiers (Langacker 1987b). Moreover, the typical behavior of such modifiers supports the trajector/landmark alignment imputed to POSS. It is almost invariably the trajector of a non-finite modifier that corresponds to the head (i.e. to the profile of the modified structure). The trajector of POSS is probably its target, therefore, since the modified noun represents the thing possessed, not the possessor.

Illustrating this construction is a nominal such as *the boy's knife*, whose semantic composition is sketched in Fig. 4.8. The possessor is specified by a full nominal, *the boy*, which elaborates the landmark of POSS at the first level of constituency. Note that B abbreviates the semantic specifications of *boy*, G stands for the ground, and the line from B to G represents the unprofiled grounding relation (in this case one of definiteness). Now it happens that each component structure makes reference to mental contact: in the nominal, the mental contact that the speech-act participants establish with the profile is pivotal to its grounding; as for POSS, mental contact with the landmark—and then, via the landmark, with the trajector—constitutes the profiled relationship. The import of the lower correspondence line is that these instances of mental contact are equated: the contact inherent in the grounding relation is assimilated to that established with the landmark of POSS. Thus, although

[15] Let me re-emphasize that the possessor/possessed asymmetry is independent of trajector/landmark alignment, as the two pertain to different levels of conceptual organization. The former is characterized with respect to the pivotal roles (reference point and target) of an idealized cognitive model considered fundamental to our mental experience—not primarily or uniquely linguistic, this model reflects the omnipresent experience of invoking one conceived entity in the process of establishing mental contact with another. The latter reduces to the imposition of figure/ground alignment on this common conceptual base for purposes of linguistic coding. Since trajector and landmark are characterized schematically in terms of prominence rather than content (specifically, as primary and secondary relational figure—see Ch. 7), it is unproblematic that possessive structures assign these levels of prominence to the reference point and target in alternate ways. Variability in profiling can also be observed (4.3.2.3).

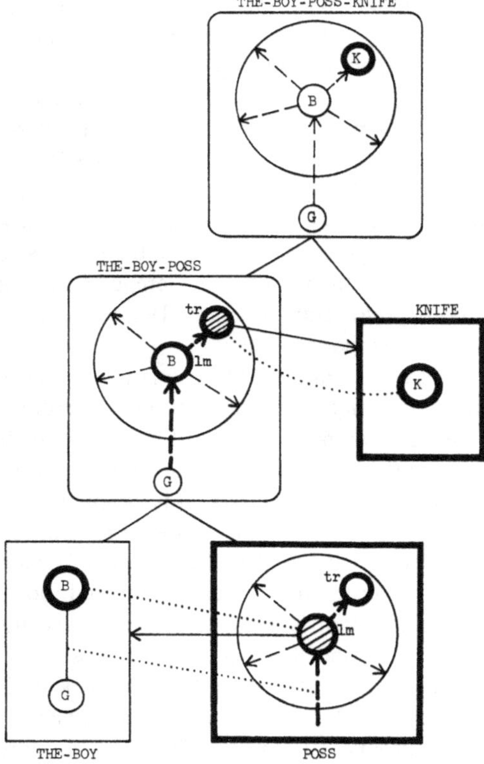

Fig. 4.8

POSS itself does not specify who it is that traces the profiled mental path, the speaker and hearer are identified as the relevant conceptualizers in the resulting composite structure.

This first-level composite structure, i.e. *the boy's*, inherits its profile from POSS. Hence it, like POSS, profiles a relationship of abstract possession in which a target falls within the dominion of a reference point. This landmark, of course, is now specific: it is characterized as a boy with whom the speech-act participants have established mental contact (as detailed in 3.1.1). However, the target is still schematic. It is elaborated by *knife* (whose semantic specifications are abbreviated as K) at the second level of constituency. *Knife* is the head, for its profile corresponds to that of the composite expression, *the boy's knife*. And since its trajector is elaborated by the head, *the boy's* functions as a possessive modifier.

We can now return to the question posed at the outset, namely whether a possessive modifier constitutes a grounding predication. The answer, in brief, is that it has the potential to do so, and that it should probably be so analyzed in the English construction just described. The essence of a grounding predication is an unprofiled epistemic relationship between the speech-act participants and the nominal profile. A glance at the topmost composite structure in Fig. 4.8 reveals that such a relationship can indeed be discerned—*the boy's knife* invokes an unprofiled relationship in which the speaker and hearer establish mental contact with a specific instance of *knife*, which is profiled by the nominal as a whole. The special feature of this construction—what distinguishes it from other, more straightforward cases of grounding—is its indirectness. The speech-act participants have mental access to the profiled instance only with reference to the boy, who is grounded directly. Their knowledge of the profile may be limited to its occurrence within the dominion of this reference point.

The ambivalent status of possessive modifiers no longer seems problematic. They can indeed serve as grounding predications, but the indirectness of the grounding relationship renders them atypical members of that category. There is consequently no assurance that languages will invariably interpret them as fulfilling this function. Many possessives appear in fact to be simple modifiers and co-occur with predications whose grounding role is undisputed (e.g. *a friend of Tom*). Even when construed as a grounding predication, a possessive is not inherently incompatible with another predication that grounds the designatum more directly; for example, in (6) *tā nèi-běn shū* (he that-CLSF book) 'that book of his', it is conceivable that the possessive and the demonstrative function simultaneously and independently in a grounding capacity. Finally, a possessive's grounding potential is not strictly dependent on the possessor being definite, since the notion of mental contact also figures in a specification of indefiniteness (it is simply not pre-established contact with a unique instance of the category). Grounding through an indefinite possessor, as in (7), *I want some teenager's car to enter in a demolition derby*, is therefore possible, albeit far from optimal.

4.3.2.3. *Other Constructions.* Let us conclude by discussing, in the briefest possible terms, some additional possessive constructions and related phenomena. It should first be noted that English possessive inflection is not limited to prenominal modifiers (e.g. *Tom's hat*); nominals bearing this inflection also occur following *be* (*The hat is Tom's*) and as the object of a modifying preposition (*a friend of Tom's*). When the possessor is a pronoun, there are certain morphological differences between the prenominal form and the other two: ***my*** *hat* vs. *The hat is* ***mine*** and *a friend of* ***mine***; ***her*** *hat* vs. *The hat is* ***hers*** and *a friend of* ***hers***; etc. However, the morphological facts appear not to be grammatically revelatory in this instance. An alternate grouping, wherein ***my*** *hat* and *The hat is* ***mine*** stand together in opposition to *a friend of* ***mine***, is better motivated by semantic and grammatical considerations.

From non-possessive constructions, we know that a noun modifier is generally an atemporal relation, and that a complement following *be* also has this character (2.2.4). We can therefore analyze *Tom's* as a stative relation in both *Tom's hat* and *The hat is Tom's*, with possessive inflection in each instance being attributed the value POSS (Fig. 4.7(b)). On the other hand, only nominals function as the objects of prepositions in English, so presumably *Tom's* is a nominal, not a stative relation, in *a friend of Tom's*. What, then, is the profile of this nominal? I take it to be the possessor's *dominion*. That is, *Tom's* designates the dominion having Tom for its reference point, and *a friend of Tom's* is an individual situated within that dominion (i.e. one of the objects that the reference point—Tom—can be used to locate). An implication of this analysis is that possessive inflection assumes a special value in the context of this construction. Diagrammed in Fig. 4.9, this value (POSS′) diverges from

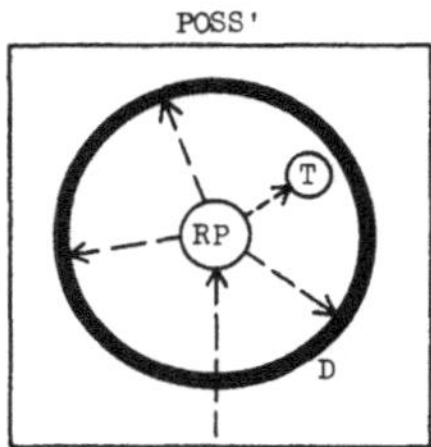

Fig. 4.9

POSS only in its choice of profile, but the profile is what determines its grammatical category: POSS′ is a noun (rather than a stative relation) because it designates an abstract region. When a nominal such as *Tom* elaborates its schematic reference point, the result is a higher-order nominal (*Tom's*) that names the dominion of a specific individual. This nominal functions as object of the preposition *of*, which profiles the intrinsic part/whole relationship between its trajector—elaborated by *friend*—and its landmark (the dominion).

But is this analysis viable? Can it plausibly be maintained that an abstractly defined entity like a dominion is capable of being profiled and playing a significant role in grammatical structure? The answer is clearly affirmative. For one thing, a dominion is hardly more abstract than the regions profiled by many nominalizations (1.2.1). Furthermore, the semantic extension from POSS to POSS′ is directly analogous to one noted earlier (2.2.4) involving locative predications:

(9)(a) *Under the bed needs dusting.*
(b) *By the window is much brighter.*
(c) *Near the fire is almost too hot for comfort.*

The subjects in (9) have the form of prepositional phrases, but semantically they are nominals that profile regions in space. Their nominal variants derive by a pattern of semantic extension whereby the profile shifts from a locative relationship to the associated **search domain**, defined as the region to which a locative predication confines its trajector (i.e. the set of points such that the specifications of the locative are satisfied if the trajector occupies that point). A dominion is simply the search domain of a possessive predication: the set of points that the target can occupy (or more abstractly, the set of possible targets). Indeed, if Figs. 4.7(b) and 4.9 are given a spatial interpretation, the relation between them effectively depicts the pattern of semantic extension exemplified in (9).

It can further be shown that the notion search domain is grammatically significant. Consider its role in the "nested-locative" construction:

(10) *Your camera is downstairs in the bedroom in the dresser in the bottom drawer under the pile of socks.*

The special property of this construction is that each locative expression in the sequence narrows down the possible location of the subject, confining it to just a portion of the region specified by the preceding locative. Stated formally, the construction specifies a correspondence between the *search domain* of one locative and the *scope of predication* of the locative that directly follows (Vol. 1, Fig. 8.3). We see, then, that grammatical constructions can indeed refer to abstract constructs of this sort and even establish correspondences between them. An additional feature of nested locatives is that, at any point in the sequence, the scope (which equals the prior search domain) functions as the current discourse space for purposes of determining whether the definite article is used (3.1.1). In (10), for instance, there may be several dressers in the house but only one in the downstairs bedroom; *dresser* then takes *the* rather than *a* because there is a unique instance of the category in the relevant discourse space.

These phenomena suggest a possible analysis for the possessive pattern of Mandarin illustrated in (6): *tā nèi-běn shū* (he that-CLSF book) 'that book of his'. Both *tā*, the third-person singular pronoun, and *nèi-běn shū* 'that book' have the potential to stand alone as independent nominals. In this construction, they are simply juxtaposed to form a higher-order nominal, without any overt marking to signal the possessor status of *tā*.[16] It was noted earlier that when possession is marked by simple juxtaposition, the possessor usually precedes the possessed. We can explain this fact by treating the possessor as a kind of **topic**, since initial position is usual for topics and essentially obligatory for topics that are otherwise unmarked. The proposal, then, is that the possessor in a construction of this sort be analyzed as a **local topic**, i.e. a

[16]There can be such a marking, namely the particle *de* regularly used with a variety of modifiers: *tā de nèi-běn shū* 'that book of his'. However, our present concern is limited to the zero construction.

topic at the nominal (as opposed to the clausal) level. The thing possessed is located with reference to this nominal topic in just the same way that a proposition is situated with reference to a clausal topic.

Possessive constructions of this general type are characterized schematically in Fig. 4.10. A and B abbreviate the respective semantic specifications of the possessor and the possessed, which are full nominals in the Mandarin

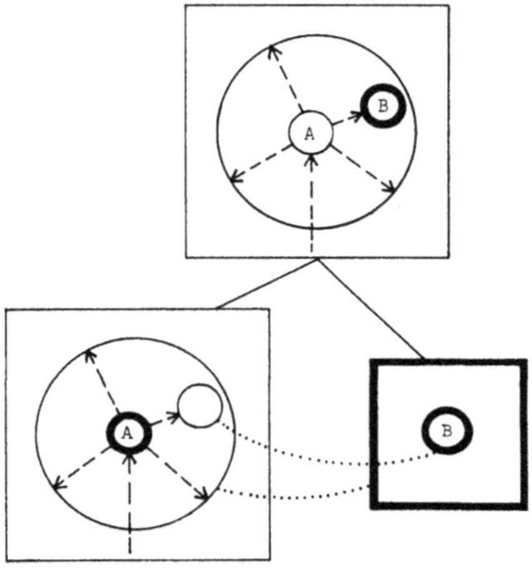

Fig. 4.10

example, but can sometimes be simple nouns. It need not be the case that either component structure is intrinsically possessive—each may simply profile a thing whose description, ordinarily, fails to saliently evoke any notion of possession. Still, any thing has the potential to be construed as a reference point, and for some things (most notably, for a person) that potential is very real indeed. Because the function of this construction is precisely to indicate a possessive relationship, the role of A as reference point is a prominent specification of the constructional schema, with the consequence that this latent role is activated in any specific expression that instantiates the schema. The possessor status of A then affords the basis for integrating the two component structures. The upper correspondence line equates B with one of the entities in A's dominion. The lower correspondence identifies A's dominion with the second component structure's scope of predication in the domain of instantiation. What this means is that, for purposes of determining what instance of B is profiled by the nominal as a whole, A's dominion delimits the region of search.

In (6), *tā nèi-běn shū* 'that book of his', the possessor probably owns the book. Ownership, however, is just a special case of abstract possession, which is what this construction is based on. The essence of abstract possession is the ability of a conceptualizer (in particular, a speech-act participant) to use the conception of one entity as a reference point to establish mental contact with another. Actually, that is not unreasonable as a first approximation to a definition of the notion topic, and I will assume that something along those lines is in fact correct. Hence the suggestion that the possessor in this construction be regarded as a local topic is not entirely vacuous—it achieves the status of a substantive proposal to the extent that we have succeeded in describing the conceptual import of abstract possession.

Such notions are applicable to a wide array of grammatical phenomena. Let me mention just two in conclusion. The first is a well-known construction of French in which a direct object occurs without a possessive and yet is understood as being possessed by the subject:

(11)(a) *Il ouvre la bouche.* 'He opens his mouth.'
(b) *Il enlève le chapeau.* 'He takes off his hat.'

The distinctive property of this construction is that the subject and object, in addition to elaborating the trajector and landmark of the verb, participate in a relationship analogous to Fig. 4.10; that is, the object lies within the subject's dominion, which defines the object's scope of predication in the domain of instantiation. Possession need not be marked on the object because the possessive relationship is inherent in the construction. Moreover, the object takes the definite article because the subject's dominion serves as its scope of predication, and the uniqueness of a mouth or a hat within such a scope is conventionally assumed.[17]

The other phenomenon, which goes by the name of "sloppy identity," is exemplified in (12).

(12) *Ted scratched his nose, and so did Jimmy.*

At issue is the favored interpretation of (12), in which Ted and Jimmy each scratches his own nose. Thus, even though two different noses are involved, there is an anaphoric relationship such that *scratched his nose* in the first clause is taken as the antecedent of the schematic expression *so did* in the second. A full analysis will not be attempted here. We can however observe that the subject in each clause is construed as the reference point for the object (which is overt in one case, implied in the other). Also, there is no presumption that the speaker and hearer have established mental contact with either nose independently of the relation it bears to that reference point—for discourse purposes, each nose resides only in the mental space definable as the dominion of its reference point.[18] The two clauses thus instantiate the same

[17] This analysis is a refinement of the one sketched in Vol. 1, Fig. 8.4.

[18] Note that in a sentence like *Ted scratched that nose, and so did Jimmy*, the same nose is scratched in each clause.

process type, which specifies, roughly, that some individual scratched the nose located within the dominion of that individual. It is this common type specification that supports the anaphoric relationship.

4.4. Inflection and Agreement

An important aspect of nominal structure is the marking of certain categories commonly regarded as "purely grammatical," including gender, number, and case. Though sometimes marked by separate words or particles, these categories are generally manifested through nominal inflections. Often such inflections display a pattern of "agreement," appearing not only on the head noun but also on its modifiers. Involving as they do the proliferation of markings supposedly devoid of semantic content, nominal inflection and agreement are frequently cited as demonstrating the autonomy of grammatical structure. We must therefore attempt to show—at least in principle—how a system employing only symbolic units can handle these phenomena. The discussion will focus on gender-type categories and on patterns of agreement.[19]

4.4.1. *Noun Classes*

The gender categories familiar from Indo-European languages represent a special case of a phenomenon that in cross-linguistic terms is considerably more variegated (cf. Allan 1977; Greenberg 1978; Craig 1986). Stated most generally, it involves the nouns of a language being partitioned into classes such that the class membership of a noun determines which marking (out of a set of alternatives) occurs with it in an expression, either on the noun itself or elsewhere. By this broad definition, even the categorization of nouns on the basis of what classifier they take counts as an instance of the phenomenon (4.3.1). The number of classes in the system can therefore be substantial, and gender is only one of the many semantic properties in terms of which the categories might be organized. Gender-based systems are nevertheless sufficient for illustrative purposes.

Usually the classes in question appear to have a semantic basis. Thus we traditionally speak of a "gender" system in French, and refer to the two noun classes as "masculine" and "feminine," rather than adopting arbitrary labels such as "class A" and "class B." However, it is easily demonstrated that the semantic characterizations are non-predictive, and that in actuality the classes are established on grounds of common grammatical behavior. Linguists fre-

[19] The discussion of case is better deferred until Part II, because its semantic value pertains primarily to clause-level relationships. Number markings will not be considered since their meaningfulness is reasonably apparent, and since they pose no descriptive problems that do not also arise for gender. (The analysis of examples like *scissors, pants, binoculars, guts, bleachers*, etc. was briefly sketched in 2.3.1.)

quently cite this finding to illustrate the superiority of their scientific approach to the informal methods of traditional grammar; it is a rare introductory textbook that does not include such examples as French *la sentinelle* 'the sentinel' [feminine] and German *das Mädchen* 'the girl' [neuter], which show the need to distinguish between natural (or "semantic") gender on the one hand, and linguistic (or "grammatical") gender on the other. According to the strictest view, even the terms masculine, feminine, and gender constitute an ill-advised throwback to the pre-scientific era: for the grammatical categories, labels such as "class A" and "class B" are considered more appropriate.

Each type of nomenclature has some motivation, for the membership of a noun class is typically intermediate between the extreme possibilities of full semantic predictability and total arbitrariness. Normally, semantic properties largely determine class membership for a substantial set of cases, but not across the vocabulary as a whole. In French, for example, masculine and feminine gender correlate quite closely with natural gender wherever that notion is applicable (roughly, for animate nouns), and in many instances linguistic gender clearly signals a difference in sex (e.g. *le chat* 'the [male] cat' vs. *la chatte* 'the [female] cat'). Hence the terms masculine and feminine are semantically appropriate and reveal an undeniably important aspect of these linguistic classes. At the same time, sporadic exceptions do occur (*la sentinelle*), and the formal distinction extends beyond the set of nouns for which natural gender is relevant—all nouns are classed as either masculine or feminine, even inanimates. Consequently, over a large portion of the lexicon the classification is semantically opaque and must simply be learned as a matter of grammatical convention.[20]

A typical noun-class system therefore shows a kind of prototype organization. Each class has central members that instantiate a prototypical semantic value and are clearly included in the class precisely for that reason. However, also associated with each class are nouns whose membership, from the standpoint of meaning, is arbitrary for all intents and purposes. Such a system can be regarded as a mixture of two ideal types: one that is fully transparent semantically, and one that is fully opaque. We will see that a description employing only symbolic units can be devised for an ideal system of either sort. It should then be quite apparent that a mixed system can also be so described.

The basis for a gender-type system is some marking that is sensitive to the class of a co-occurring noun. In a fully transparent system, there is a perfect correlation between markings and semantic properties of the noun: whenever the noun has a certain property, a particular marking is chosen; whenever the noun has a contrasting property, another marking occurs instead. The marking

[20] There is actually far more systematicity than one might think. See, for example, Zubin and Köpcke 1986.

is thus predictable from the noun's semantic characterization. For the sake of concreteness, let us assume that the marking in question resides in the choice of definite article, and that the determining semantic property is natural gender. We can use a familiar language like Spanish for convenient illustration, provided that we confine our attention to that fragment of the vocabulary for which gender is semantically transparent. We are thus concerned with contrasting sets of expressions like those in (13).

(13)(a) *el hombre* 'the man'; *el hijo* 'the son'; *el perro* 'the [male] dog'
(b) *la mujer* 'the woman'; *la hija* 'the daughter'; *la perra* 'the [female] dog'

If these data were representative of the language as a whole, how would it be analyzed? We must first describe the articles. Suppose we represent the semantic pole of a simple definite article as [DEFINITE THING], where THING is the schematic characterization of its profile and DEFINITE stands for the unprofiled grounding relationship. This, however, is not quite sufficient for the articles in our hypothesized ideal system—*el* and *la* further indicate the sex of the designated individual, and since they do so with full regularity, that specification must be regarded as an inherent aspect of their meaning. The full bipolar representations of these articles are thus [DEFINITE MALE/el] and [DEFINITE FEMALE/la], where the more specific characterizations MALE and FEMALE occur in lieu of THING. We must further posit constructional schemas for the article-noun combinations. Because the nouns in each class are homogeneous in regard to natural gender, they conform to schemas that we can give as [MALE/ . . .] and [FEMALE/ . . .]. The required constructional schemas are then [[DEFINITE MALE/ el][MALE/ . . .]] and [[DEFINITE FEMALE/la][FEMALE/ . . .]]. Despite the abbreviatory notations, it should be apparent that only symbolic units figure in this description.

Swinging now to the other extreme, consider a language where nouns similarly divide into classes on the basis of which article they take, but where the classes have no semantic rationale whatever. We can once again use Spanish as an illustration, this time confining our attention to those portions of the vocabulary for which gender is fully opaque. Data like those in (14) are thus representative:

(14)(a) *el palo* 'the stick'; *el sudor* 'the sweat'; *el cerro* 'the hill'
(b) *la mesa* 'the table'; *la puerta* 'the door'; *la mano* 'the hand'

Here, of course, we have no reason for analyzing *el* and *la* as anything more than simple definite articles: [DEFINITE THING/el]; [DEFINITE THING/ la]. Also, since neither article is limited to nouns of any particular type, the constructional schemas describing article-noun combinations can only refer to the noun in generalized fashion: [[DEFINITE THING/el][THING/ . . .]];

[[DEFINITE THING/la][THING/ . . .]]. We thus face the problem of specifying which nouns participate in each construction. How can this be done using only symbolic units?

By assumption, these classes are grammatically rather than semantically defined. The behavior of a noun cannot be predicted from its meaning—speakers must learn specifically, for each individual noun, which article it occurs with. What form does this knowledge take? Little psychological plausibility attaches to the usual descriptive practice in such cases, which is to tag each noun with a contentless diacritic (or "syntactic feature") and to state that only nouns with the proper diacritic are allowed in a given construction. This practice is in any event illegal in cognitive grammar, even among consenting linguists, because the content requirement proscribes the use of artificial devices (i.e. those with no inherent semantic or phonological content). Fortunately, there is a simple and natural alternative. To say that a speaker specifically learns that *palo* 'stick' takes *el*, that *mesa* 'table' takes *la*, etc. is equivalent to saying that the complex expressions *el palo*, *la mesa*, etc. have the status of conventional units. By definition, conventional units are part of the grammar of a language, even those which constitute regular instantiations of other, more schematic units. Hence specific units such as [[DEFINITE THING/el][STICK/palo]] and [[DEFINITE THING/la][TABLE/mesa]] coexist in the grammar with the constructional schemas they instantiate, namely [[DEFINITE THING/el][THING/ . . .]] and [[DEFINITE THING/la] [THING/ . . .]], respectively. In short, the availability of the required information—in the form of symbolic units—follows automatically from the assumptions and definitions of the theory.

Having examined the two extremes, let us now return to the actual facts of a mixed system like that of Spanish. The required analysis must accommodate both semantically transparent examples, such as the ones in (13), and also those that are semantically opaque, as in (14). The most obvious description is simply the sum of the units posited for the two ideal types considered individually; the following array of symbolic units is thus imputed to the grammar of Spanish. First, it has a large inventory of specific nouns: [MAN/hombre]; [WOMAN/mujer]; [STICK/palo]; [TABLE/mesa]; etc. Coexisting with these nouns are schemas of varying abstractness, including [THING/ . . .] (the overall noun-class schema) as well as the subschemas [MALE/ . . .] and [FEMALE/ . . .]. Additionally, these units participate in categorizing relationships, e.g. [[MALE/ . . .]→[MAN/hombre]]. Second, the grammar includes units representing the definite articles. *El* and *la* each has at least two semantic variants: one in which the grounded entity is characterized as male or female, and one which merely identifies it as a thing. We can further posit a schema for these articles, i.e. [[DEFINITE THING/ . . . l . . .]], together with categorizing relationships linking these units to form a network. Finally, the grammar contains the various constructional schemas listed previously, which form a network that also incorporates a high-level schema describing the article-noun construction with maximal generality: [[DEFINITE THING/ . . . l . . .][THING/ . . .]]. At the other extreme of specificity, the lower-level constructional schemas are instantiated by a large set of expressions with unit status: *el hombre, la mesa*, etc.

Such an analysis appears both reasonable and workable, for it states the available generalizations, imposes the proper restrictions, and defines the appropriate classes. The patterns observable at different levels of abstraction are captured by a hierarchy of constructional schemas. In particular, the major regularity—that the choice of *el* vs. *la* is determined by natural gender whenever that notion is applicable—is expressed by the intermediate-level constructional schemas [[DEFINITE MALE/el][MALE/ . . .]] and [[DEFINITE FEMALE/la][FEMALE/ . . .]]. Observe that these schemas are more specific than their counterparts formulated for inanimate nouns (i.e. [[DEFINITE THING/el][THING/ . . .]] and [[DEFINITE THING/la][THING/ . . .]]), which ensures their activation for the primary categorization of expressions involving animates. Suppose, for example, that a male duck is under discussion. Because of its greater specificity, [[DEFINITE MALE/el][MALE/ . . .]] is selected as the active node in preference to [[DEFINITE THING/la][THING/ . . .]], with the consequence that *el pato* (not **la pato*) is judged to be correct. In the case of inanimates, unit expressions such as [[DEFINITE THING/la][TABLE/mesa]] (i.e. *la mesa*) dictate the proper form; they are too specific not to be chosen as active nodes.

We have seen that classes are definable on the basis of extrinsic properties, including occurrence in a particular grammatical construction (Fig. 4.2). Such is the nature of gender classes established for the vocabulary as a whole ("grammatical gender"). How, then, might we characterize a masculine noun in Spanish? A partial answer is that it instantiates the second component structure of the constructional schema [[DEFINITE THING/el][THING/ . . .]] (or more simply, that it follows *el*). The class of grammatically feminine nouns is similarly characterized with reference to [[DEFINITE THING/la][THING/ . . .]]. Of course, choice of definite article is just one illustrative property. A gender-type class may well be defined with respect to an array of distinct constructions, in each of which the categorized element has a particular structural role; collectively, these constructions provide a complex structural frame that functions as the scope of categorization.[21]

[21] A characterization of this sort is essentially equivalent to traditional definitions based on distribution. The validity of such definitions is not at issue, only their theoretical interpretation: the existence of grammatically defined classes does not prove that grammar is an autonomous realm of structure distinct from semantics, because the defining constructions comprise only symbolic units.

4.4.2. *Gender Inflections*

To one degree or another, the members of a noun class may also display some similarity in their form. If all members have a certain formal property, e.g. if they share a common tone pattern or take the same prefix, that property is incorporated in the structural frame that constitutes the schematic characterization of the class. More typical is the situation in Spanish, where the respective endings *-o* and *-a* correlate quite strongly with the classes of masculine and feminine nouns, but are far from universal in these categories. While *-o* and *-a* must clearly be analyzed as gender-marking suffixes, certain questions immediately arise. What is the meaning of a suffix that signals membership in a grammatically defined class? And what do we say about class members that fail to display this marking?

Like most common expressions, *-o* and *-a* are polysemous. Their prototypical values, manifested over a substantial range of vocabulary, are 'male' for *-o* and 'female' for *-a*: *hermano* 'brother' vs. *hermana* 'sister'; *suegro* 'father-in-law' vs. *suegra* 'mother-in-law'; *oso* 'male bear' vs. *osa* 'female bear'; *alumno* 'male student' vs. *alumna* 'female student'; *gato* 'male cat' vs. *gata* 'female cat'; *muchacho* 'boy' vs. *muchacha* 'girl'; etc. Examples like these conform to the classic notion of morphemic analysis. Both phonologically and semantically, each expression is a regular compositional function of two component morphemes: a stem that is neutral in regard to gender (e.g. *muchach* 'child'), and a derivational suffix that specifies either 'male' or 'female'. The composite expressions instantiate productive morphological patterns represented in the grammar as constructional schemas.

As analyzed in cognitive grammar, a derivational morpheme is generally schematic for the class it derives. Thus *-o* and *-a* are viewed as schematic nouns that identify their profile only as a male or female creature, whose type is elaborated by the genderless stem. With that in mind, let us turn now to examples where sex is irrelevant, i.e. inanimate nouns like *cerro* 'hill' and *mesa* 'table'. Here the endings *-o* and *-a* cannot mean 'male' and 'female', so they seem to be problematic for the claim that all grammatical units are meaningful. However, cognitive grammar recognizes meanings that are highly abstract, and further acknowledges the meaningfulness of a unit whose semantic value is totally overlapped by that of a co-occurring element.[22] I therefore propose that *-o* and *-a* simply mean 'thing' when they occur as gender markers on inanimate nouns, i.e. their semantic value is that of the noun-class schema. In the context of the theory, this is not only reasonable but well motivated, since *-o* and *-a* are noun-forming suffixes.

[22] For example, the auxiliary verb *do* is semantically equivalent to the verb-class schema, so its meaning is fully subsumed by that of a co-occurring verb (Vol. 1, pp. 354–55).

Nouns like *cerro* 'hill' and *mesa* 'table' are problematic in another way from the standpoint of traditional morphemic analysis. Because the endings *-o* and *-a* occur with such frequency on masculine and feminine nouns, they have to be considered class-marking morphemes. Yet they are not obviously segmentable, since the residue may not occur separately or have the appropriate meaning independently—by itself, for instance, *mes* can only mean 'month'. The source of the difficulty is that the traditional view embraces the **building-block metaphor**; this all-pervasive metaphor portrays a composite structure as being assembled out of its component morphemes, which contribute all of its content in the form of discrete chunks. Though helpful up to a point (and unavoidable for expository purposes), the building-block metaphor is far from adequate as a serious model for natural-language composition. Cognitive grammar makes the alternative assumption of partial rather than full compositionality, and regards component structures as categorizing (hence motivating) certain facets of the composite structure, not as being stacked together to constitute it (Vol. 1, Ch. 12). This approach straightforwardly allows the segmentation of a morpheme even when the residue is not itself a recognizable unit. A noun like *mesa*, for example, is analyzed as having a composite structure, [TABLE/mesa], and just one component morpheme, namely [THING/-a].

Nouns like *muchacha* 'girl' and those like *mesa* 'table' thus differ in two respects: whether the initial portion is identifiable as a morpheme, and whether the ending is [FEMALE/-a] or simply [THING/-a]. It is important, however, that both variants of *-a* are analyzed as schematic nouns, differing only in their level of abstraction. Of course, what makes a noun grammatically feminine is not this ending per se, but rather the fact that it occurs in particular structural frames (e.g. it takes *la* as the definite article). As a consequence, a form like *mano* 'hand' can perfectly well be feminine even though it lacks the suffix (it is unanalyzable, and the final *o* is part of the stem). There is nevertheless a regular correlation, in that every noun taking either variant of the suffix is classed as feminine for grammatical purposes. We can express this generalization by positing, for each relevant frame (or the complex frame that they collectively constitute), a prominent subschema that specifically identifies the noun as ending in *-a*. For example, associated with [[DEFINITE THING/la][THING/ . . .]], the constructional schema describing the combination of a noun and the feminine definite article, is the salient subschema [[DEFINITE THING/la][THING/ . . . -a]], which is instantiated by expressions such as *la muchacha* 'the girl' and *la mesa* 'the table'.

4.4.3. *Agreement Patterns*

One more topic must be discussed, namely the marking of gender on noun modifiers. This is generally treated as a matter of "agreement" with the head, mechanically induced and devoid of semantic content. Thus, in expressions such as *gato blanco* 'white male cat' vs. *gata blanca* 'white female cat', the endings occurring on the nouns and on the adjectives are analyzed differently. It is recognized that the *-o*/*-a* contrast is meaningful on the nouns, distinguishing *gato* 'male cat' from *gata* 'female cat'. However, the same contrast on the adjective contributes nothing to the meaning of the expressions, adjectival *-o* and *-a* being semantically empty grammatical markers.

Needless to say, I reject this type of analysis, which rests on certain assumptions that are both gratuitous and erroneous. One such assumption is that an element is meaningless unless it contributes information not specified elsewhere in the same expression. By now, however, it should be apparent that all grammatical constructions involve a certain amount of semantic overlap, and that full overlap—where the meaning of one element is fully subsumed by that of another—is just an expected limiting case. Redundancy must therefore be distinguished from meaninglessness. Another assumption is that a marking cannot be meaningful if its occurrence is obligatory, i.e. a matter of grammatical rule rather than speaker choice. Now if an element is obligatory, there is certainly a sense in which its occurrence is uninformative, but that is very different from saying that it has no semantic content. Grammatical convention can perfectly well demand the appearance of a specific meaningful element in particular circumstances. I therefore analyze "agreement" as the multiple specification of some property. Apart from being required by grammatical convention, it is not fundamentally different from other sorts of expressive redundancy.

For simple illustration, let us consider the agreement in gender between an adjective and a noun in Spanish. An initial problem is to determine what meaning a gender marking has when it occurs on an adjective. The most desirable solution would be to attribute it the same meaning it has with a noun, especially since it is often the same in form on a noun and on an adjective. By this account, the adjectival *-o* has the value MALE whenever appropriate (i.e. when the modified noun is animate), and THING otherwise; similarly, *-a* means either FEMALE or THING, depending on the noun. The analysis does prove workable, so we will provisionally adopt it, at least for sake of exposition.[23]

The next task is to describe the combination of these endings with an adjectival stem, e.g. *blanc* 'white'. The endings are analyzed as schematic nouns, each with two semantic variants: [MALE/-o]; [THING/-o]; [FEMALE/-a]; [THING/-a]. Because the stem designates a stative relation, as does the composite structure (*blanco* or *blanca*), it is the stem that functions as profile determinant. The adjective and suffix are integrated at the semantic pole by a correspondence between the former's schematic trajector and the

[23] A viable alternative is to analyze *-o* and *-a* as schematic adjectives whose trajector is characterized either as MALE/FEMALE or simply as THING. This makes the ending a derivational suffix (i.e. it is schematic for the class it derives).

latter's profile (which may be equally schematic); phonologically, the adjectival stem elaborates the schematic stem implied by the suffixal status of *-o* or *-a*. Suppose we adopt the notation [RELATION (THING)] for the semantic pole of an adjective, where RELATION indicates its relational profile, and (THING) stands for the characterization of its trajector. The bipolar representation of *blanc* is then [WHITE (THING)/blanc]. When this stem is inflected by *-o* or *-a*, the resulting composite structure is one of the following: [WHITE (MALE)/blanco]; [WHITE (THING)/blanco]; [WHITE (FEMALE)/blanca]; [WHITE (THING)/blanca].

We must now examine how such an adjective combines with a noun, as in *gata blanca* 'white female cat'. Since the noun and adjective each incorporate a gender specification, we can represent them as [FEMALE CAT/gata] and [WHITE (FEMALE)/blanca], respectively. At the phonological pole, the constructional schema specifies the contiguity of these structures and a particular temporal sequence. This phonological integration symbolizes their semantic relationship, wherein the noun elaborates the schematic trajector of the adjective (i.e. FEMALE→FEMALE CAT) and also acts as the profile determinant; hence the composite expression designates a female cat with the further, unprofiled specification of being white: [WHITE FEMALE CAT/gata blanca]. We see, then, that the construction is a straightforward instance of a modifying relationship between an adjective and a head noun. Though gender is doubly specified, this much semantic overlap is hardly out of the ordinary.

The patterns (or "rules") of agreement reside in the constructional schemas serving as templates for the assembly of such expressions. These rules are obligatory to the extent that they constitute the only schemas available for that purpose, or are sufficiently well-entrenched to ensure their activation for the primary categorization of expressions with certain properties. For example, *gata blanca* instantiates a constructional schema that specifies the agreement of an adjective with a semantically feminine noun. More precisely, it describes the modification of a noun that designates a female by an adjective whose trajector is also female, where the gender of each component structure is signalled phonologically by the ending *-a*: [[FEMALE/ . . . -a][RELATION (FEMALE)/ . . . -a]]. Coexisting with this prototype are constructional variants making other phonological specifications. For instance, an expression like *mujer hermosa* 'beautiful woman' is sanctioned by a slightly more abstract constructional schema that does not require the noun to end in *-a*: [[FEMALE/ . . .][RELATION (FEMALE)/ . . . -a]]. Agreement with semantically masculine nouns, as in *gato blanco* 'white cat', is described by a parallel array of schemas centered on the prototypical pattern [[MALE/ . . . -o][RELATION (MALE)/ . . . -o]]. We can further envisage high-level schemas expressing broader generalizations (e.g. a superschema which indicates that the noun and the adjectival trajector have the same gender specification, but is neutral as to which gender it is and also as to how it is manifested phonologically).

Of course, agreement is not confined to natural gender. Patterns established for central cases, where the markings have specific meaning, can be extended to other nouns where the semantic motivation is less apparent, or to the vocabulary as a whole. Thus the central pattern [[FEMALE/ . . .][RELATION (FEMALE)/ . . . -a]] gives rise by abstraction to [[THING/ . . .][RELATION (THING)/ . . . -a]], the constructional schema which sanctions such expressions as *pared blanca* 'white wall'. In like fashion, *papel blanco* 'white paper' instantiates the constructional schema [[THING/ . . .][RELATION (THING)/ . . . -o]], which represents a parallel extension from the central pattern [[MALE/ . . .][RELATION (MALE)/ . . . -o]].

How does one know which pattern to use for a given inanimate noun? In the worst case, one simply has to learn this as an idiosyncratic property of each noun.[24] But the problem is directly analogous to that of choosing the proper definite article, and the same solution is available. Indeed, both [[DEFINITE THING/la][THING/ . . .]] and [[THING/ . . .][RELATION (THING)/ . . . -a]] can be taken as components of the complex structural frame that functions as the scope of categorization for defining the class of grammatically feminine nouns. That is, the properties of taking *la* as the definite article, and of being modified by adjectives inflected with *-a*, may very well count as a single specification in the cognitive representation of class membership; grammatically feminine nouns presumably constitute a unitary class, albeit one characterized extrinsically with reference to a structural frame having multiple parameters.

Quite clearly, the foregoing discussion is both fragmentary and exploratory. It offers neither a full solution to the descriptive problems posed by gender-type classes and nominal agreement, nor a thorough exposition of the theoretical issues they raise. However, by sketching a way of approaching such phenomena in the context of cognitive grammar, it does suggest that they are not inherently intractable for a symbolic account of grammatical structure. Contrary to what is commonly assumed, their mere existence is insufficient to prove that grammar constitutes an autonomous domain or level of linguistic organization.

[24] It is doubtful that this worst case actually ever obtains. Careful examination of gender-like classes invariably reveals numerous "local" patterns, in which most or all nouns with a given semantic or phonological property belong to the same class. For example, van Hoek (*in press*) has determined that nouns for large sharp objects are regularly feminine in Yiddish, as are nouns ending in final unstressed *e*. Redundancies such as these are readily expressed in cognitive grammar by means of constructional subschemas.

Part II
CLAUSE STRUCTURE

AS WE LEAVE Part I and enter Part II, our focus shifts from one basic aspect of conceptual and grammatical structure to another: conceptually, from *things* to *relations*; grammatically, from *nouns* to *verbs*; and in terms of the billiard-ball model, from *discrete physical objects* to their *energetic interactions*. These are maximal oppositions whose universality suggests that they are rooted in fundamental yet contrasting modes of cognitive processing. At the same time, however, the linguistic structures headed by nouns and by verbs are parallel in significant respects.

The relation between a simple noun and a nominal is directly analogous to that between a simple verb and a finite clause. Like a noun, a verb makes a type specification; and like a nominal, a finite clause profiles a grounded instance of that type. The same semantic functions are operative in the nominal and clausal realms, and in each realm these functions tend to be reflected iconically in grammatical organization. Nevertheless, the contrast between a nominal and a processual profile has extensive grammatical ramifications. Since time (rather than space) is the primary domain of instantiation for a process, temporal location and distribution are pivotal to its grounding and quantification. Moreover, a process is conceptually dependent, i.e. it cannot be conceived without some reference to its participants. The specification of these participants and their role within the designated process is thus a major facet of clausal structure.

The organization of Part II reflects these special concerns. Semantic function is dealt with in Chs. 5 and 6, which analyze the system of English verbal auxiliaries. The next three chapters concentrate on phenomena pertaining to clausal participants: Ch. 7 discusses transitivity and basic grammatical relations, notably subject and direct object; Ch. 8 examines constructions (such as the passive) representing departures from the canonical way of coding events; and Ch. 9 describes case marking as well as the distinction between *accusativity* and *ergativity*.

CHAPTER 5

The Auxiliary: Clausal Head

THE ESSENTIAL COMPONENT of a sentence is a finite clause, and within a clause, the pivotal element is a verb. A clause, however, is often not content with a single verb or verb-like element. Though it may indeed have just one, as in *She **washed** the car*, a clause is equally likely to contain a **verb group** having two or more members: *She **is washing** the car*; *She **had washed** the car*; *She **will be washing** the car*; *She **should have been washing** the car*; *The car **has been washed***; *The car **should have been being washed***. The semantically specific member of such a group (e.g. *wash*) is traditionally referred to as the **main verb**, whereas the more schematic members (*will*, *be*, *have*, etc.) are known as **auxiliary verbs**.

Some kind of verb group or auxiliary system can be found in every language, substantial differences in structure and grammatical function notwithstanding (cf. Steele 1973, 1978; Steele *et al.* 1981). The auxiliary system of English is therefore not fully representative of this important linguistic phenomenon, nor exhaustive of its structural possibilities. The English auxiliary is nevertheless elaborate and poses a significant descriptive challenge to any grammatical theory—indeed, since Chomsky 1957 it has been a focal point of theoretical discussion (e.g. Ross 1969a; Pullum and Wilson 1977; Langacker 1978; Akmajian, Steele, and Wasow 1979; Gazdar, Pullum, and Sag 1982). A cognitive grammar analysis of the English system is thus an appropriate way to begin our investigation of clause structure. In this chapter, we will examine the overall organization of the auxiliary, describe those elements that pertain to voice and aspect, and discuss them from the standpoint of grammatical structure and behavior. The following chapter deals with auxiliary elements that function as grounding predications.

5.1. Function and Organization

With respect to their profiles, nominals and finite clauses are polar opposites. Prototypically, a nominal designates a physical object, whereas a finite clause profiles an energetic interaction. Schematically, a nominal always profiles a thing (set of interconnected entities), while every finite clause designates a process, i.e. a series of relations (each a complex set of interconnections) scanned sequentially through conceived time. Significant parallels are nonetheless discernible in the global organization of these basic grammatical constituents, notably in regard to semantic function and its structural implementation. Whether the designated entity is a thing or a process, it instantiates some type, is subject to various sorts of quantification, and is grounded with reference to the speech event. Moreover, the inherent conceptual layering of these semantic functions tends in each case to be reflected iconically in grammatical constituency (4.1.1).

Finite clauses are inherently more complex than nominals due to the nature of their profiles. A nominal is conceptually autonomous, in that we can generally conceive of the thing it designates without essential reference to any process in which it might participate. A clause, on the other hand, is conceptually dependent. A process cannot ordinarily be conceptualized without evoking some conception of the entities related by the profiled interconnections. This semantic asymmetry engenders a corresponding asymmetry in grammatical structure: it is normal for clauses to have nominal complements, but not conversely. The greater structural complexity of clauses stems in large measure from their incorporation of nominals to identify participants in the designated process.

Three facets of nominal structure are usefully distinguished: the internal structure of the head noun; modifiers at different levels of organization; and the grounding predication (see Fig. 4.1). Direct analogs of all three are also found in a finite clause, together with nominal complements, which constitute a fourth. Our attention here is confined to those facets of clause structure encompassed by the verb group, namely grounding and the clausal counterpart of a head noun. Modifiers and nominal complements are dealt with elsewhere.

Unfortunately, the traditional distinction between main and auxiliary verbs does not coincide with the one between grounding predication and clausal head. Consider a maximal verb group, e.g. *should have been being washed*. The traditional account treats *washed* (or *wash*) as the main verb, with *should*, *have*, *been*, and *being* analyzed as auxiliaries. What motivates this division is that *wash* is a "lexical" verb with detailed semantic content, in contrast to the others, which supposedly belong to grammar rather than lexicon, and whose meanings are quite abstract. The auxiliary verbs also have distinctive grammatical properties, such as their ability to precede the subject in a question (*Should he?*; *Has he?*; *Was he?*; but not **Washed he?*). Auxiliaries must therefore be accorded some special status, even if any strict dichotomy between lexicon and grammar is regarded as untenable.

However, semantic function suggests an alternate division, in which *should* is identified as the grounding predication, and the entire sequence *have been being washed* is recognized as the functional equivalent of a head noun. By this analysis, auxiliary verbs do not serve a single semantic function, nor does "the auxiliary"—i.e. the sequence *should have been being*—constitute a grammatical constituent. The segmentation of *should* (or more generally, tense and modality) from the remainder of the verb group is further supported by structural evidence. For example, an infinitive (marked by *to*) can be formed on a main verb together with any combination of auxiliaries, with the exception that tense and modality are necessarily excluded: *to wash*; *to be washing*; *to have washed*; *to have been washed*; *to have been being washed*; but not **to washed*; **to should wash*; **to should be washing*; **to had been washed*; or **to should have been being washed*. Hence the recognition of auxiliaries as a class cannot be accomplished by grouping them as a constituent. Grammatically, the fundamental division appears to fall instead between tense-modality and the remainder of the verb group.[1]

The proposal, then, is that the specification of tense and modality be analyzed as the grounding predication, with the remainder of the verb group (other auxiliaries and the main verb) regarded as a complex **clausal head** analogous to a head noun. Because a finite clause is grounded by definition, the obligatory nature of tense-modality supports its analysis as a grounding predication; every finite clause provides some indication of tense-modality (even when marked by zero), whereas the other auxiliary elements are optional. If the function of tense-modality is to ground a clause and thereby make it finite, its exclusion from *to*-phrases (**to should wash*, etc.) follows from their characterization as non-finite forms (hence the term **infinitive**). Moreover, the analysis has a firm semantic basis. Tense and modality are the only auxiliary elements that specifically invoke the ground as a reference point: tense locates the designated process with reference to the time of the speech event, while the presence vs. the absence of a modal indicates whether the speech-act participants accept the profiled relationship as a matter of established reality.

Though initially less obvious, the functional equivalence between the remainder of the verb group and a head noun is actually well supported. Let us first review the analysis of a head noun. It is relevant that the head can incorporate an overt number predication, such as the plural *-s* in English *chairs*. There are several respects in which the plural morpheme contrasts with the structure it attaches to: (1) semantically, *-s* is quite schematic, while *chair* is

[1] With its construct INFL ("inflection"), government-binding theory also recognizes the special status of tense-modality. Steele (1973) first established its import in cross-linguistic terms. Observe that the arguments for auxiliaries being a special grammatical class do not support the claim that the full auxiliary sequence is a constituent; for instance, only the *first* auxiliary appears before the subject in a question: *Has she been washing the car?*; **Has been she washing the car?*.

specific; (2) in terms of semantic function, *chair* simply provides an initial type specification, whereas *-s* represents an aspect of quantification (and further derives a higher-order type); and (3) the entity profiled by *-s* is the one that is grounded and profiled by the nominal as a whole. In short, *chair* furnishes most of the semantic content, and *-s* imposes a particular image on this content. We can thus refer to *chair* as the **content structure** within the head noun, and to *-s* (in view of property (3)) as the **grounded structure**. Note that the content structure may be internally complex; we have seen that in English it can be an expression of any size: *cat*; *lover*; *cat lover*; *cat lover debate*; *cat lover debate moderator*; etc. The plural morpheme is analyzed as combining with the content structure as a whole, regardless of its size, e.g. ((*cat lover debate moderator*)*s*).

Consider now the parallelism between a head noun and the head of a finite clause (i.e. the verb group exclusive of tense-modality). If the head noun is singular, e.g. *chair*, there is no distinction between the content structure and the grounded structure (the content structure is itself grounded). This is analogous to a clausal head consisting of a main verb alone, with no auxiliaries, as in *She may* ***wash*** *the car*. A plural head noun is divisible into a portion that supplies specific conceptual content (*chair*) and a schematic portion that construes this content in a certain way (*-s*). I take this as being parallel to a clausal head in which the main verb is accompanied by one or more auxiliaries. In *She may* ***have been washing*** *the car*, for example, *wash* provides the essential semantic content, and the schematic auxiliary sequence *have been . . . -ing* imposes a particular construal on it. What is traditionally known as the main verb can thus be identified with the content structure of the clausal head; let us then call it the **content verb**.[2] Like the content structure of a head noun, a content verb can be quite complex internally (*babysit*; *unzip*; *reconceptualize*; *look up*; *take advantage of*; etc.), but regardless of complexity it can be analyzed as combining as a whole with the auxiliary sequence.

The entire auxiliary sequence (exclusive of tense-modality) is thus considered functionally equivalent to number inflection on a head noun. The elements that may be included are *have* and . . . *-ed*, which together mark perfect aspect; *be* and . . . *-ing*, which mark progressive aspect; plus *be* and . . . *-ed*, which signal passive voice. These three pairs of elements can occur singly or in any combination: *be being . . . -ed*; *have been . . . -ing*; *have been . . . -ed*; *have been being . . . -ed*. As it turns out, the leftmost verb in the sequence—*be*, *have*, or the content verb if it stands alone—contributes its profile to the clause as a whole and can thus be characterized as the grounded structure within the clausal head; let us then call it the

[2]This term is more descriptive than main verb, which has the further disadvantage of being ambiguous: a main verb can either be a non-auxiliary verb or one that occurs in a main (i.e. non-subordinate) clause.

grounded verb. In the absence of a modal, the grounded verb is further identifiable as the one inflected for tense and agreement: *She* ***is*** *washing the car*; *She* ***had*** *been washing the car*; *The car* ***was*** *washed*; *The car* ***has*** *been being washed*.

Despite its greater complexity, the auxiliary sequence has the same properties cited above for the plural morpheme: (1) all of its elements are schematic; (2) they pertain to quantity and derive higher-order type specifications; and (3) as one facet of their imagery, they determine which entity is grounded and profiled by the clause as a whole. The aspectual markers are quantificational in the sense that they indicate, with respect to some temporal reference point, whether the process designated by the content verb has been completed or is still in progress (hence only partially accomplished). Passive marking overrides the content verb with respect to one dimension of imagery, namely which processual participant assumes the status of trajector (relational figure). Moreover, each auxiliary element imposes its profile on the structure it combines with, thereby deriving a distinct higher-order type specification. When multiple auxiliaries occur, the one added at the highest level of constituency functions as profile determinant for the entire clausal head, so its profile (not that of the content verb or any intermediate-level structure) is grounded and designated by the full clause. Within a complex clausal head, the grounded verb is thus the profile determinant at the highest level of constituency.

It may be helpful to compare this analysis to the classic account of Chomsky 1957. With minor adjustments, Chomsky's well-known formula is presented in (1).[3]

(1) *AUX* → *TNS* (*MDL*) (*have -ed*) (*be -ing*) (*be -ed*)

This is a phrase-structure rule detailing the contents of the verbal auxiliary (AUX), which Chomsky analyzed as a constituent separate from the main verb. Parentheses bracket optional elements; thus tense is the only auxiliary element that is obligatorily present. There are also three sets of dependencies: *have* and *-ed* occur as a pair, as do *be* and *-ing*, as well as *be* and *-ed*. Accompanying this rule is a transformation—which has come to be called "Affix Hopping"—that moves a verbal affix (i.e. TNS, *-ed*, or *-ing*) one step to the right, attaching it as a suffix to whatever verbal element happens to follow (a modal, *have*, *be*, or the main verb). It is readily seen that this description economically generates the proper combinations of elements.

Still, the hindsight of three decades enables us to detect certain shortcom-

[3]TNS (for "tense") and MDL (for "modal") replace Chomsky's C and M. I have also used *-ed* rather than *-en* to represent the past participial morpheme, which of course has varied morphological realizations. For expository convenience, I have further included the markings for passive voice in the formula, even though Chomsky's analysis introduced them as part of the passive transformation.

ings. First, since Chomsky's sole concern was with syntactic patterns and their independence from meaning, the analysis provides no semantic characterization of auxiliary elements. Second, the postulated constituent structure is incorrect. There is no reason to believe that the auxiliary elements form a constituent, nor is constituency assigned to the sequences that behave as such. Third, generating elements in the wrong order, only to realign them with a special rule, is inherently suspicious. Except for *-ing*, it is in any case an oversimplification to speak of affixes and describe them as uniformly following the verbal element they combine with; the inflections are hardly suffixal in forms like *is*, *were*, *might*, *would*, *sat*, *broke*, *kept*, *ate*, *stood*, *went*, *caught*, *cut*, *frozen*, etc. (cf. Vol. 1, 9.1.2). Fourth, the analysis merely stipulates that *have* co-occurs with *-ed*, and *be* with either *-ing* or *-ed*. No explanation is offered for why these elements should occur in pairs. Fifth, the stipulated pairing is actually not always observed. In particular, *-ing* and *-ed* occur without the paired auxiliary verb in adjectival uses: *the man working over there*; *a basket filled with kittens*. (In early transformational accounts, such expressions were obtained by deletion, e.g. *the man who is working over there* = = => *the man working over there*.)

An analysis that overcomes these difficulties is presented in the remainder of this chapter. Naturally, all the auxiliary elements are claimed to be meaningful; section 5.2 describes their meanings in fairly precise detail. The auxiliary is not analyzed as a grammatical constituent: tense and modality comprise a grounding predication, whereas the content verb and the remaining auxiliary elements constitute the clausal head, whose organization is summarized in (2).

(2) (*have* ($PERF_4$ (be_1 (*-ing* (be_2 ($PERF_3$ (V)))))))

In this formula, V represents the content verb, and PERF is the past or perfect participial morpheme (*-ed* is only one of its phonological manifestations). The subscripts indicate that different senses of *be* are involved in the progressive and passive constructions, and that PERF has different senses in the passive and perfect constructions. Here the parentheses do not stand for optionality (as they do in (1)), but rather for constituency, or at least—since constituency may be flexible (Vol. 1, 8.4.2)—for a certain kind of semantic and grammatical relationship. Specifically, in each configuration of the form (B (A)), A is a complement of B (i.e. A is the conceptually autonomous member of the pair and elaborates a salient substructure of B, which imposes its profile on the composite expression).

Linear order is not significant in (2), which merely summarizes an assembly of grammatical constructions. For each individual construction, e.g. ($PERF_3$ (V)), the appropriate temporal ordering is specified by the constructional schema as one facet of how the component structures are integrated at the phonological pole. There may of course be subschemas that specify different patterns of phonological integration, of which temporal sequencing is only one type; the varied manifestations of the participial morpheme (*watched, frozen, gone, caught, cut*, etc.) are thus unproblematic. Formula (2) represents a maximal clausal head, in which all the possible elements are simultaneously present. With one exception, however, each conceptually autonomous structure—i.e. each structure enclosed in a set of parentheses—can stand alone as either a clausal head or a noun modifier. Working from the core (V) outwards, the expressions in (3) exemplify these respective possibilities:

(3)(a) *She may **climb** that tree.*
(b) *a **questioned** suspect*
(c) *The project will definitely **be finished**.*
(d) *any woman **being followed***
(e) *That case should **be being investigated**.*
(f) ---
(g) *I may very well **have been being followed**.*

The exception (for which a functional explanation is proposed in 5.3.2) is that PERF_4 only occurs together with *have*, hence the gap in (f).

There is considerable regularity in this pattern. Moving from V outwards, the morphemes successively encountered alternate between being phonologically dependent (i.e. affixal or inflectional) and phonologically autonomous (stems). Semantically, the affixal/inflectional morpheme is in each case an atemporal relation, whereas the stem designates a process and is consequently a schematic verb. Each morpheme in the sequence is the profile determinant at its own level of organization. Thus, as one moves along the path from V outwards, the progressively more elaborate composite expressions thereby created display the same alternating pattern: V is a verb; (PERF_3 (V)) is an atemporal relation; (be_2 (PERF_3 (V))) is a verb; (*-ing* (be_2 (PERF_3 (V)))) is an atemporal relation; etc. Whether an expression is atemporal or processual determines how it can be used. In particular, only a process can function as clausal head, and only an atemporal relation can modify a noun (leaving aside finite relative clauses). The examples in (3) thus alternate between clausal and nominal use.

We now have an explanation for why the auxiliary elements of the clausal head occur in pairs: *have* with PERF_4; be_1 with *-ing*; and be_2 with PERF_3. Each pair represents two successive levels in the formation of a complex clausal head from its autonomous core (V). The affixal/inflectional member in each case combines with a verb and derives an atemporal relation, which is suitable as a noun modifier but cannot per se be used as clausal head. The associated schematic verb (*have* or *be*) is then available to impose its own processual profile on the atemporal relation, creating another verb at a higher level of conceptual organization. Hence each pair defines one possible derivational cycle leading from a verb to an atemporal relation to another verb. Since there are three pairs, up to three such cycles can occur in the formation of an English clausal head, as in (3)(g); all the pairs are optional, however, and any combination of options is permissible. Although the pairs are not grammatical constituents, the members of a given pair must co-occur if the resulting expression is to be processual and thus able to serve as clausal head. The grounded verb is the one that imposes its processual profile in the final cycle (at the highest level of organization). Either *have* or *be* functions as the grounded verb, depending on which pairs of auxiliary elements are chosen. If none is chosen, the grounded verb and content verb (V) are the same.

5.2. Voice and Aspect

The auxiliary elements of the English clausal head will now be systematically examined. They form three layered pairs, each consisting of a phonologically dependent morpheme that profiles an atemporal relation, together with a schematic verb stem that re-establishes the processual character of the composite expression. The innermost pair, PERF_3 and be_2, is the essential portion of the **passive** construction. The other two pairs are aspectual: *-ing* and be_1 constitute the **progressive** construction, while PERF_4 and *have* define the **perfect** construction.

5.2.1. *The Passive Construction*

Since Chomsky 1957, the relationship between an active clause and its corresponding passive has been a pivotal issue in grammatical theory. Chomsky's analysis was simply to derive the passive from the active by means of a transformation, which interchanged the subject and object nominals and inserted *be*, *-ed*, and *by* as (presumably meaningless) grammatical markers. A sentence like (4)(b) was thus attributed the same (active) underlying structure as (4)(a):

(4)(a) *The cat chased the rat.*
(b) *The rat was chased by the cat.*

Though subsequent treatments are far too numerous and diverse for even a cursory survey to be attempted here, the general trend has been toward stating the active/passive relationship at the verb (or "lexical") level rather than the clause level (at least for English). This agrees with one central claim of the cognitive grammar analysis, which was first detailed in Langacker 1982b. Its other basic claim—that *be*, *-ed*, and *by* are meaningful, and that the organization of a passive clause is a straightforward consequence of their meanings—has apparently been considered too preposterous for widespread acknowledgment or acceptance.

A brief summary of the analysis runs as follows. Each "grammatical" morpheme takes on a special sense in the passive construction, but one that constitutes a straightforward extension from the meanings it has in other uses. The crucial feature of a passive, namely that the subject (trajector) is identified with a processual participant that would otherwise be the direct object (primary landmark), is attributed to the meaning of $PERF_3$, i.e. the passive variant of the past-participial morpheme (*-ed*). Hence a passive participle, such as *chased*, itself displays the trajector/landmark alignment characteristic of passives independently of its occurrence in a clause. Because the passive participle is atemporal, to function as clausal head it requires the support of *be*$_2$, the passive variant of *be*, which imposes its processual profile on the composite expression, e.g. *be chased*. The trajector of *be chased* (which corresponds to the landmark of *chase*) is then elaborated by the clausal subject in the normal way. The other participant (i.e. the trajector of *chase*) may either be left implicit or specified periphrastically with a *by*-phrase, as previously described for nominalizations (1.2.2).

Our sole interest here is the passive clausal head, i.e. (*be*$_2$ ($PERF_3$ (V))). Either a perfective or an imperfective can function as the content verb (V). The process it designates must however incorporate two nominal participants, one construed as its trajector, and the other as its primary landmark; were V to stand alone as clausal head, a nominal would elaborate this landmark in accordance with the regular direct-object construction. The joint effect of $PERF_3$ and *be*$_2$, however, is to derive from V a complex clausal head that is intransitive (for reasons discussed in Chs. 7 and 8) and whose trajector corresponds to the landmark of V.

The semantic pole of $PERF_3$, diagrammed in Fig. 5.1, is a **dependent predication** (Vol. 1, 9.2.2). Reflecting schematically the derivation it performs, it consists of two substructures: the **standard**, which functions as elaboration site for V, and the **target**, which determines the organization of

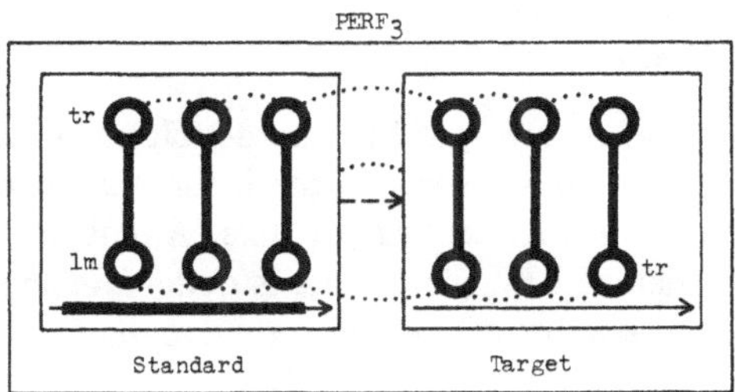

Fig. 5.1

the composite expression. Using different metaphors, we can say that the standard is mapped onto the target, that the standard categorizes the target, or simply that the target is characterized with reference to the standard.[4] The standard of $PERF_3$ is a schematic process whose trajector and primary landmark are both things. The target diverges from this standard in just two respects: it chooses as trajector (relational figure) the participant that corresponds to the standard's landmark; and it lacks a **temporal profile** (i.e. it employs summary rather than sequential scanning), so that the profiled relationship is not a process but a complex atemporal relation. The effect of $PERF_3$ is thus to convert a process (specified by the content verb) into an atemporal relation with a contrasting figure/ground organization (see Vol. 1, Fig. 9.11).

The perfect participial morpheme has several other semantic variants that join with $PERF_3$ to form a network of related senses. The variant that occurs in the perfect construction ($PERF_4$) will be discussed in 5.2.3. $PERF_1$ and $PERF_2$ derive what are known as **stative** (or "adjectival") participles. $PERF_1$ is formed on intransitives:

(5)(a) *The windshield is* ***cracked***.
(b) *Our cash reserves are almost* ***gone***.
(c) *Your jaw is rather* ***swollen***.

Typically the verb it combines with profiles a process whose single participant undergoes an internal change of state. The standard of $PERF_1$ is thus a schematic process of this sort, as shown on the left in Fig. 5.2(a); a circle indicates the participant, and the change of state is represented by squiggly arrows. Comparison with the target reveals that $PERF_1$ derives a stative relation by restricting the profile to the final, resultant state of the process. Because there is only one participant, the trajector remains the same.

By contrast, $PERF_2$ applies to transitive verbs and does cause a shift in trajector:

(6)(a) *A tornado left the town totally* ***devastated***.
(b) *After the game, the field was all* ***torn up***.
(c) *This car is undoubtedly* ***stolen***.

$PERF_2$ is diagrammed in Fig. 5.2(b). The double arrows indicate that the standard's trajector transmits energy to the landmark (or affects it in some other way), thereby inducing a change of state. Although $PERF_2$ has a more complex standard than $PERF_1$, their effect is quite comparable: each derives a stative relation by confining the target's profile to the final, resultant state of

[4] A dependent predication is directly analogous to a phonologically dependent morpheme. For instance, one variant of the past participial morpheme (occurring in *swum, begun, sung, swung*, etc.) can be represented as follows: [[. . .ɪN]---->[. . . ʌN]]. That is, it maps the standard [. . . ɪN] (where N is a nasal) onto the target [. . . ʌN].

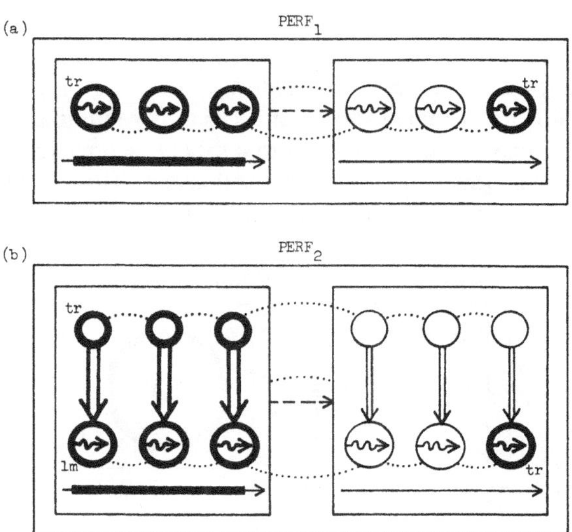

Fig. 5.2

the process that constitutes the standard. Observe that the profiled relationship is limited to the resulting condition of the entity undergoing the change of state. As the only profiled participant, that entity assumes the status of trajector.[5]

The family resemblance among $PERF_1$, $PERF_2$, and $PERF_3$ is quite apparent. All three convert a process into an atemporal relation. Beyond this, $PERF_1$ and $PERF_2$ are alike in restricting the profile to a single state that results from a participant undergoing a change, while $PERF_2$ and $PERF_3$ are alike in elevating to trajector status the participant corresponding to the standard's primary landmark. An additional similarity is that all three variants enhance the salience of a "downstream" element (cf. DeLancey's notion of "terminal viewpoint" (1981)). In the case of $PERF_1$ and $PERF_2$, this element is the final state, which is downstream from the others with respect to the flow of time, and surpasses them in salience by virtue of being profiled. With $PERF_2$ and $PERF_3$, the element in question is a "terminal participant," i.e. one that lies downstream from another with respect to the flow of energy (or some analog thereof), and it is prominent by virtue of being made the relational figure (trajector).

The participial morpheme has one variant, $PERF_n$, that combines with nouns instead of verbs. The basic pattern is illustrated by expressions like the following: *bearded professor*; *freckled nose*; *hooded sweatshirt*; *domed sta-*

[5]This analysis of $PERF_2$ has benefitted from discussion with Ken Cook. See Langacker 1982b for evidence that $PERF_3$ profiles all the component states of the base process (i.e. the standard), whereas $PERF_1$ and $PERF_2$ profile only the final state.

dium; *red-headed woodpecker*; *blue-eyed boy*; *high-ceilinged room*; *kind-hearted prostitute*; etc. From a noun (*beard*, *freckle*, *hood*, . . .), $PERF_n$ derives a stative relation (*bearded*, *freckled*, *hooded*, . . .) that is used as an adjectival modifier.[6] The noun $PERF_n$ attaches to is **relational**, i.e. its designatum bears an unprofiled relationship to a salient landmark; for the present range of examples, this is a part/whole relationship. The standard of $PERF_n$ is a schematic noun of this sort, as shown on the left in Fig. 5.3. Its target,

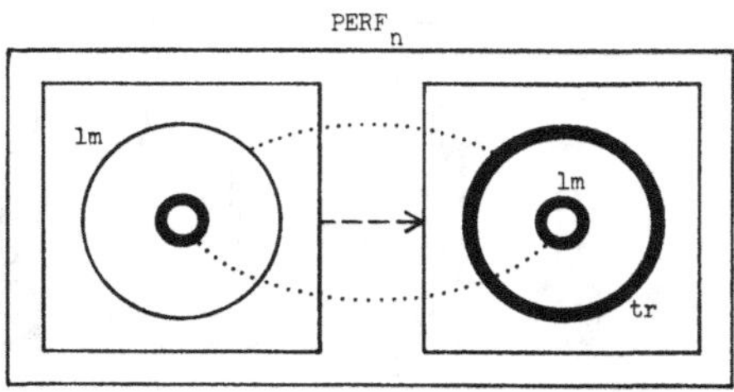

Fig. 5.3

of course, is a stative relation—in fact, it designates the same part/whole relationship that is saliently evoked (though unprofiled) by the standard. Moreover, the landmark of the relational noun is selected as the trajector of the stative relation (e.g. the trajector of *bearded* is the person who wears the beard).[7] We can thus discern two respects in which $PERF_n$ is similar to the other variants. First, it derives a stative relation (albeit from a noun rather than a verb). Second, it resembles $PERF_2$ and $PERF_3$ in elevating a participant of only secondary salience (a nominal landmark) to the status of trajector.

The upshot is that essential relationships are missed if $PERF_3$ is treated as a meaningless grammatical marker or inserted as part of a transformation deriving passive clauses from underlying actives. To be regarded as natural and revealing, an analysis must recognize the place of $PERF_3$ in a network of distinct but related meanings assumed by the participial inflection in different grammatical constructions. $PERF_3$'s specific value is a function of both its **syntagmatic** and its **systemic context** (Vol. 1, 10.4): syntagmatically, it is shaped by the special exigencies of the passive construction; systemically, it is linked by categorizing relationships to other senses of the participial morpheme, whose semantic variants display an obvious family resemblance.

Comparable remarks hold for the other passive markers, namely *by* and *be*. Only the latter concerns us at this juncture. In most of its uses, *be* is describ-

[6]The first elements of these modifiers (*red-*, *high-*, etc.) pose interesting descriptive problems, but their examination would lead us too far afield (cf. Hirtle 1970).

[7]How do we know? Because it is virtually always the trajector of a non-finite modifier that corresponds to the profile of the modified noun. In the case of *bearded professor*, it must therefore be the wearer of the beard that functions as the adjectival trajector. (Note also the predicative use of the participles: *The professor is bearded*, etc.)

able as a maximally schematic imperfective process. It is processual because it scans sequentially through a series of profiled relationships distributed continuously over a span of conceived time. The process is imperfective because each of these relationships (i.e. each component state) is construed as being identical to all the others—a single configuration extends through time without essential change and thus lacks inherent bounding within the temporal scope of predication. The process is schematic because the profiled configuration has no specific content: it is simply characterized as a stative relation.

This basic variant of *be*, labeled be_1, is too abstract to be useful by itself as a clausal head (unless it is interpreted anaphorically). Its role instead is to *derive* a clausal head from an atemporal relation, which could not otherwise serve in that capacity due to its non-processual character. Be_1 performs this function with adjectives, prepositional phrases, and predicate nominatives: whereas *tall*, *under the table*, and *a teacher* (with the construal of Fig. 2.5) are stative relations, *be tall*, *be under the table*, and *be a teacher* are imperfective processes capable of heading a finite clause. Be_1 also derives imperfective processes from the stative expressions formed by $PERF_1$ and $PERF_2$: *be swollen*; *be devastated*. From the standpoint of constructing a viable clausal head, be_1 and the stative predication it combines with make complementary semantic contributions, the former providing the requisite processual profile, and the latter supplying its specific conceptual content. The grammatical construction is straightforward: be_1 is the profile determinant, and the stative predication merely elaborates the schematic relationship it follows through conceived time (see Vol. 1, Fig. 8.12).

The related meanings of *be* cannot be fully appreciated unless those of *do* are also taken into account. *Do* occurs as both an auxiliary verb and a content verb. As an auxiliary, *do* is employed when no other auxiliary verb is present but one is required for grammatical purposes. It co-occurs with the content verb, which can either be perfective or imperfective: *Did she say that?*; *Does she know that?*. Because it also functions as the pro-form for the class of verbs (e.g. *Did she?*; *She does*), the auxiliary *do* is best analyzed as designating a maximally schematic process—it neutralizes even the perfective/imperfective distinction. Be_1 and the auxiliary *do* are thus semantically quite similar, except that the former is specifically imperfective. They contrast grammatically in that *do* occurs *in addition to* a content verb, whereas be_1 serves to *derive* a content verb from a stative predication. Note that *do* and the verb V that it is in construction with are both processual, depicting the same process in schematic and specific terms; hence V elaborates all the component states of *do* when they co-occur (so that *do* as a whole is the e-site), as sketched in Fig. 5.4(a). On the other hand, an elaborating stative predication corresponds to just a single component state of be_1, as shown in Fig. 5.4(b). However, since be_1's component states are construed as identical, in effect they are all elaborated simultaneously.

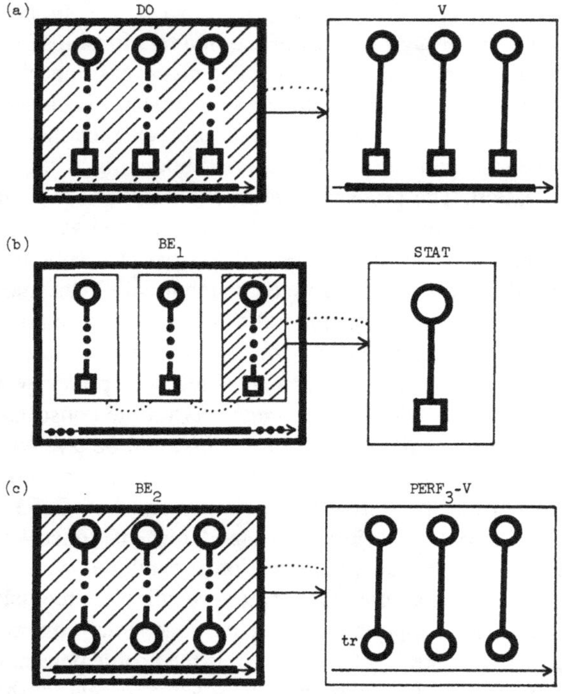

Fig. 5.4

We can now examine be_2, the variant that occurs in passives. It is of course tailored semantically to fit the special needs of this construction. Be_2 combines with a complex atemporal relation, specifically a passive participle derived by $PERF_3$; its function is to reimpose sequential scanning, thus deriving a processual expression that can serve as a passive clausal head. Hence the base of be_2 is a schematic passive participle, and on this base it imposes a processual profile by scanning sequentially through its component states. In the derivational construction, be_2's schematic base is elaborated by a specific passive participle, as depicted in Fig. 5.4(c).[8]

If we now compare the diagrams in Fig. 5.4, an interesting fact emerges: be_2 is actually more similar to the auxiliary *do* than it is to be_1. Grammatically, it resembles *do* in being elaborated by a complex rather than a simple (stative) relation, so that the e-site comprises all its component states. Be_2 is

[8] Although the normal convention is for the upper participant in such diagrams to be taken as the trajector, here the lower participant is so labeled; this is a reminder of the trajector/landmark inversion effected by $PERF_3$ in deriving the passive participle. For the sake of comparison, be_2 is represented in a compacted format. In the exploded format of Figs. 5.1–3, the schematic participle would be separately shown as the standard and e-site, and the profiled process would constitute the target.

like *do* semantically, and unlike be_1, in that it neutralizes the perfective/imperfective contrast.[9] Observe that be_2 is elaborated by a passive participle formed on either a perfective or an imperfective stem: *be examined*; *be liked*. Moreover, the stem determines whether the composite expression is perfective or imperfective, as shown by the usual tests, such as occurrence in the progressive and the simple present (Vol. 1, 7.2):

(7)(a) *He is being examined by a doctor.*
(b) **He is examined by a doctor.*
(c) **He is being liked by everybody.*
(d) *He is liked by everybody.*

Hence $PERF_3$ and be_2 are transparent to the perfective/imperfective aspect of the stem: their schematicity extends to being non-committal as to whether all their component states are identical, with the consequence that the aspect of the stem is simply inherited by the passive participle and clausal head.

A further parallel between *be* and *do* is that each has an "active" variant in which the trajector exercises volitional control in carrying out some activity. *Do* has this value when used as a content verb (see Ross 1972a; Langacker 1975, 1981). It takes a direct object that refers to the activity (e.g. *He did something terrible*), and like any other content verb, it co-occurs with the auxiliary *do* (*What did he do?*). In its active sense, *be* means something like 'act in a certain way' and takes an adjectival complement: *Don't be silly!*; *Tom is being mean again!*. The active *do* and *be* are both perfective, but despite their rough similarity they occupy different positions in their respective semantic networks. The active *do* is a central variant; indeed, the auxiliary *do* is plausibly regarded as an extension from it. By contrast, the active *be* is quite marginal and constitutes an extension from be_1, the category prototype.

5.2.2. *The Progressive Construction*

A verb's ability to take the progressive is widely and correctly acknowledged as a diagnostic for its perfectivity. Essentially any perfective verb is able to occur in the progressive, whereas verbs that are clearly imperfective cannot; the examples in (8) are typical:

(8)(a) *He is {learning/writing/studying/reciting/copying} the poem.*
(b) **He is {knowing/liking/understanding/seeing/having} the poem.*

It is manifestly reasonable that only perfectives should take the progressive, since the function of this construction is to derive an imperfective clausal

[9] Despite these similarities, be_2 and the auxiliary *do* are not identical, if only because be_2—specially tailored for the passive construction—necessarily designates a process involving two nominal participants.

head. The vacuity of imperfectivizing a verb that is already imperfective is sensibly avoided by the collective wisdom of conventional English usage.

When examined in detail, the perfective-progressive correlation raises subtle issues and descriptive problems that can be mentioned here only in passing (for extensive discussion, see Langacker 1987b and Vol. 1, 7.2). For example, many verbs are ambivalent, their categorization as perfective or imperfective being determined by the nature of their nominal complements (*I admire her courage* vs. *I'm admiring her dress*); by the perspective taken on a scene (*This road winds through the mountains* vs. *This road is winding through the mountains*); or by other factors. A verb that is normally imperfective because it profiles a stable situation (e.g. *I like this*) can sometimes receive a perfective construal, either because the situation is conceived as changing in some way (*I'm liking this more and more*), or because the period of stability is regarded as a bounded episode rather than something expected to continue indefinitely (*At least for now, I'm liking this*). Conversely, any perfective verb may be construed as generic or habitual and thus rendered imperfective (*A beaver builds dams*; *Ralph always votes Republican*).

What does the progressive do, exactly? What is the semantic contrast between a simple perfective and its progressive counterpart (e.g. between *She will wash the car* and *She will be washing the car*)? On intuitive grounds, the progressive is often described as taking an "internal perspective" on an event, as if one is watching it unfold rather than viewing it holistically as a unitary entity. I accept the essential correctness of this characterization and will try to make it precise. There is, however, a class of perfectives that appear problematic, namely **punctual** verbs like *blink*, *sneeze*, *flash*, *cough*, *wink*, *burp*, and *pop*. Under normal circumstances, an "internal perspective" hardly seems possible for the point-like events they designate, and indeed, in the progressive they generally receive a **repetitive** construal—*She is blinking* refers to a series of blinks (not one blink in the process of unfolding). Must we then recognize repetitive aspect as an alternate meaning of the progressive?

Although constructional polysemy is certainly possible, I think a different analysis is warranted here. It relies on two patterns of zero derivation that are independently attested for English. First, any verb can be interpreted as designating a replicate process comprising multiple instances of the process type it names (3.2.2). Repetitive aspect is just a special case, involving replication through time with the same participants. Even without the progressive, therefore, a clause such as *The light flashed* may be construed as repetitive (note the possible response *How many times?*). Second, the process designated by an imperfective verb may be limited to a bounded episode (as we saw above for *like*), and the bounding makes it perfective. Thus, despite its mass-like character, a process formed by replication is nevertheless perfective if the repetitions are construed as constituting a limited episode. This appears in fact to be what distinguishes repetitives from habituals in English; whereas the imperfective *He kicks his dog* describes a habitual practice, the repetitive action of *He is kicking his dog* may represent a unique occurrence. I therefore analyze the progressive in such expressions as having its normal value, i.e. it takes an internal perspective on a perfective process—this just happens to be a bounded repetitive process. With punctual verbs like *blink* and *flash*, the repetitive construal is the only one for which an internal perspective is conceptually plausible.

I will assume, then, that the progressive construction always views a perfective process from an internal perspective and thereby renders it imperfective. How, precisely, does it accomplish this? Using the constructs of cognitive grammar, we can readily characterize this special construal. Viewing a process from an internal perspective is a matter of restricting its profile to a series of component states that does not include the initial and final states. The profiled relationship is rendered imperfective if the component states are construed at a level of schematicity that neutralizes their differences; I conjecture that they are regarded as identical by virtue of a highly abstract property, namely their common status as "representative states" of the perfective process (the initiation and completion of the process are thus excluded as being non-representative). Both these factors—profile restriction and "homogenization" of profiled states—are attributable to *-ing* and largely constitute its semantic value. In addition, *-ing* suspends sequential scanning, since the form it derives is not a verb but an atemporal relation (the present participle).

The meaning of *-ing* was previously described (1.2.1.1) and also diagrammed: Figs. 1.4(a) and 1.4(b) represent its standard and target, respectively, provided that the structures depicted are interpreted as schematic rather than specific. These figures are repeated in Fig. 5.5, but in a simpler format.

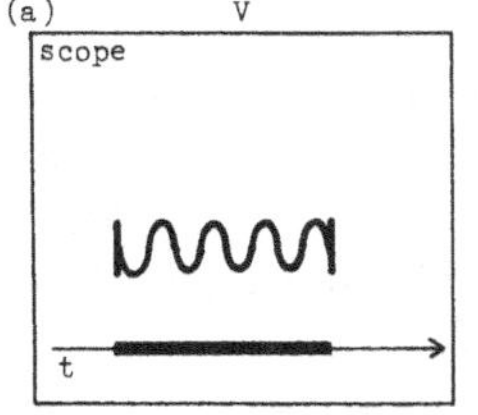

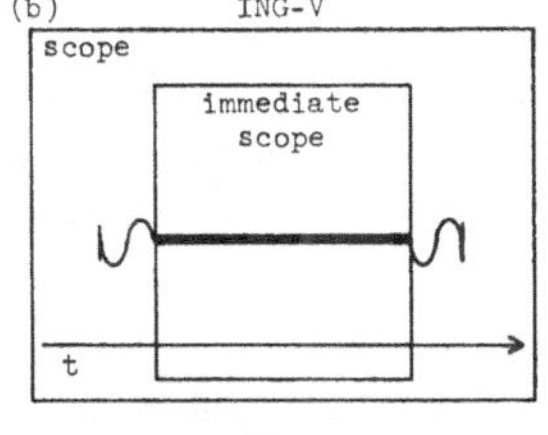

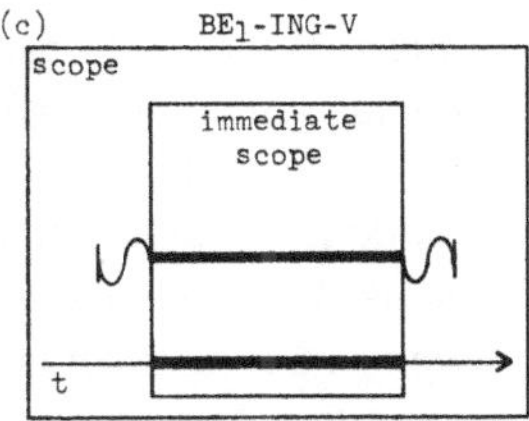

Fig. 5.5

Once again, diagrams (a) and (b) represent either the standard and target of *-ing*, or else a content verb and the present participle that *-ing* derives from it, depending on whether the structures depicted are considered schematic or specific.[10] The crucial notational convention is that the sequence of component states comprising a process is shown as a line; a wavy line indicates change through time, and a straight line, the absence of change. Fig. 5.5(a) thus stands for a perfective process: it profiles a changing relationship, including its endpoints, and scans them sequentially (note the heavy-line portion of the time arrow).

Hence the contrast between Figs. 5.5(a) and 5.5(b) represents the meaning of *-ing*. To review, the three points of difference are as follows: (1) *-ing* suspends sequential scanning, which makes the derived expression atemporal; (2) with respect to the overall scope of predication provided by V, *-ing* imposes a restricted immediate scope of predication that excludes the endpoints of the base process—by definition, the immediate scope delimits the expanse of the profile; and (3) the profiled states are construed at a level of schematicity which renders them equivalent.

As an atemporal relation, the expression derived by *-ing* can be used to modify a noun. The specifics of the modifying construction will not concern us here, except for two brief observations. First, the structure on which the present participle is formed may be quite complex, including far more than just a verb stem (though *-ing* attaches phonologically to the verb stem that functions as its head). A variety of subpatterns can be distinguished and described by means of constructional subschemas, and depending on the nature of the participialized structure, the modifier can either precede or follow the noun: *complaining customers*; *egg-laying mammal*; *anyone being followed*; *nude descending a staircase*; *children playing in the rain*; etc. Second, when the participle modifies a noun rather than combining with *be* to derive a progressive clausal head, it can be formed on an imperfective verb as well as a perfective one: *anyone knowing his whereabouts*; *students having difficulty with their homework*; *people still believing that the earth is flat*. This difference between the progressive and modifying uses is easily explained. As noted earlier, the progressive construction derives an *imperfective verb*, so using it with a verb that is already imperfective would be superfluous; hence *-ing* is limited to perfectives in the context of that construction. However, *-ing* by itself derives an *atemporal relation*, which is what the modification of a noun requires. Neither a perfective nor an imperfective verb can modify a noun directly, so a verb of either sort needs the atemporalization effected by *-ing* to be usable for that purpose.

Finally, we must consider the integration of *be* with the present participle to complete the progressive construction. The effect of adding *be* is simply to retemporalize the expression (i.e. to reimpose sequential scanning), thereby

[10] Recall that the internal structure of a dependent predication reflects schematically the derivation it performs (i.e. the relation between the autonomous structure it combines with and the composite structure that results from their integration).

deriving an imperfective process, as shown in Fig. 5.5(c). Because the profiled states are all construed as identical and remain so at the composite structure level, we can identify the progressive variant of *be* as be_1. However, its integration with the participle is not that of Fig. 5.4(b), since the participle is a complex atemporal relation rather than a simple (or stative) relation. Instead the integration is analogous to that between be_2 and the passive participle in Fig. 5.4(c): be_1's e-site is not just a single state but its entire sequence of profiled states, which are elaborated by those of the participle. Of course, in the passive these component states are not necessarily identical, as they are in the progressive.

5.2.3. *The Perfect Construction*

Of the auxiliary elements in the English clausal head, the perfect construction is the most difficult to describe semantically. Both *have* and the perfect participial morpheme take on values in this construction whose relation to their other senses is less than obvious. Moreover, the subtle but important notion of subjectivity—which is easy neither to grasp nor to elucidate—is crucial to the auxiliary *have*'s meaning. Granted this and certain other descriptive constructs, however, the construction proves susceptible to revealing characterization.

5.2.3.1. *Current Relevance.* There are two facets to the meaning of the English perfect construction. First, it specifies the temporal location of a process, though in a manner quite different from tense. The English tenses (PRESENT and PAST) are grounding predications and directly situate the profiled process with respect to the time of the speech event. By contrast, the perfect construction is non-epistemic and does not itself refer to the ground. Instead it invokes a temporal reference point, which we will symbolize RP (though R is customary), and indicates that the process designated by the content verb is prior to that reference point (Reichenbach 1947). Where this process is located in relation to the speech event thus depends on where RP itself is located, and RP's position is specified by the grounding of *have*. When *have* is in the present tense (i.e. in the **present perfect**), RP is equated with the time of speaking. When *have* is marked for past tense (the **past perfect**), RP may be any time that precedes the speech event; a particular time is often apparent from the context or specified by an adverbial expression (e.g. *They had already left when the vice squad arrived*).

The second facet of the perfect construction's meaning is observable from the contrast between the present perfect and the simple past. For example, *I have broken my leg* is not the same as *I broke my leg*—the former suggests that I am still incapacitated, whereas the latter may refer to a childhood injury long since recovered from. Use of the perfect conveys that the event is not simply over and done with but continues to have some "current relevance", in this case because its results remain in force. This current relevance can be manifested in a variety of other ways (cf. Huddleston 1969; McCawley 1971, 1981b). The event may be currently relevant in the sense that it might happen again; one would therefore use (9)(a) in speaking of a boxer still active, and (9)(b) in describing a completed career.

(9)(a) *His nose has been broken seven times.*
(b) *His nose was broken seven times.*

(10)(a) *Have you seen the pandas at the zoo?*
(b) *Did you see the pandas at the zoo?*

(11)(a) *She has believed in reincarnation for several years.*
(b) *She believed in reincarnation for several years.*

In (10), the relevance is a matter of the event still being possible; (10)(a) is inappropriate if the pandas have already been sent back to China. Another form of current relevance is illustrated in (11): with an imperfective content verb (and a suitable adverbial), the perfect intimates that the designated situation continues through the reference time, while the non-perfect form portrays it as a finished episode.

We will attempt neither to list exhaustively the varieties of current relevance nor to discuss them in any detail; our objective is rather to achieve a unified understanding of the phenomenon. The problem is reminiscent of the one we faced previously in regard to possession, where we also encountered an array of values difficult to distinguish or list exhaustively, but where the notion of abstract possession based on the reference-point model afforded a unified analysis (4.3.2). It is therefore quite suggestive that a temporal reference point is pivotal to the meaning of the perfect construction, and that one of its components, the auxiliary verb *have*, is clearly related to the basic verb of possession. To ascertain the meaning of the auxiliary *have*, we might profitably begin by examining that of the corresponding content verb.

As a content verb (diagrammed in Fig. 4.7(a)), *have* accords trajector status to the possessor and displays the full range of values subsumed by abstract possession. What all these values share is the subjective property of the trajector being used as a reference point for establishing mental contact with the landmark. To varying degrees, this subjective path from the trajector to the landmark may be overlaid and motivated by a comparable objective path, often involving the (potential) exertion of either physical or abstract force on the landmark for purposes of controlling or manipulating it. There is a wide spectrum of possibilities:

(12)(a) *The duchess had the gardener trim the hedges.*
(b) *The robber had a gun in his hand.*
(c) *Brygida has a new chainsaw.*

(d) *Sally has a dog.*
(e) *We have a lot of skunks around here.*

We see from (12)(a) that one sense of *have* is active, perfective, and volitional (as is the case for *be* and *do*—see 5.2.1). Specifically, it designates an act of causation that is effected through the exertion of social (as opposed to physical) force and results in the occurrence of the desired process within the trajector's dominion. More central to the category are the meanings of *have* represented in (12)(b)-(d). In (b), the robber exerts physical force to control the position of the gun (and its possible operation). The focus in (c) is more on ownership, but the notion of direct physical control remains salient; for an object like a chainsaw, availability for purposes of physical manipulation is a major concomitant of ownership. In (d), the conception of physical force may still be present to some extent, but ownership, care, and authority assume greater prominence; these relationships are abstract, but their asymmetry nonetheless provides an objective basis for the subjective directionality.

In the present context, the most interesting example is (12)(e). Any objective basis for its trajector/landmark alignment is somewhat fanciful—there is no energetic interaction (either physical or abstract), and nothing traverses a subject-to-object path. The essential import of the construction is rather that the subject functions as a spatial reference point for locating the object. What determines the choice of trajector, consequently, is not the structure of the situation described, but a subjective factor based on cognitive salience: we are far more likely to know where people are than skunks, so people are better suited as locative reference points for skunks than conversely. That this *have*-construction construes its subject primarily as a spatial entity (not as an actor) is supported by several observations. First, the subject *we* in (12)(e) refers collectively to the people who inhabit some area, not to specific individuals; hence (13) could not be employed to indicate that skunks are prevalent in San Diego County (it would mean instead that we keep them around the house).

(13) *Peggy and I have a lot of skunks around here.*

Also occurring as the subject in this construction are the pronouns *you* and *they*, which can likewise refer to "people in general":

(14)(a) *Do you have skunks where you live?*
(b) *They have armadillos in Texas.*

Note further that the locative adverb is virtually obligatory in (12)(e) and (14) unless some other meaning is intended (e.g. ownership). If the construction expresses abstract possession in the spatial domain, this adverb can be analyzed as specifying the dominion of the locative reference point.

Thus, *have*'s meaning in this construction is almost reducible to the subject's functioning as a spatial reference point for establishing mental contact with the object. But not quite. There remains at least a shadow of the idea that the subject and object might interact by virtue of their spatial propinquity, i.e. that the occurrence of the object within the subject's dominion is potentially *relevant* to the subject in some fashion. No specific kind of interaction is implied; the form it might take depends on our encyclopedic knowledge of the entities concerned. For example, (12)(e) could suggest the possibility of our occasionally encountering a skunk, of smelling it at night, or of finding its carcass on the highway—but one way or another, skunks are portrayed as an actual or potential part of our lives. This notion of potential relevance is only applicable to sentient creatures and is predictably absent in other constructions that take an abstract or locative subject:

(15)(a) *There are a lot of skunks around here.*
(b) *San Diego County has a lot of skunks.*

Potential relevance is the last remaining vestige of the more specific objective interactions that *have* evokes (with varying degrees of salience) in certain of its other uses as a content verb.

It should now be apparent why we have focused on this special sense of *have*. The two facets of this meaning—spatial reference point and potential relevance—are strikingly similar to those that characterize *have* as an auxiliary verb. It can therefore be suggested that the auxiliary *have* arises from this sense (or a similar one) via the well-worn path of semantic extension leading from the spatial to the temporal domain. Thus a spatial reference point becomes a reference point in time, and potential relevance comes to be construed temporally as *current* relevance.

Though presumably correct so far as it goes, this account leaves unexplained certain discrepancies between the auxiliary *have* and its apparent source. Most obviously, the trajector and landmark of the content verb are both things, whereas the auxiliary's landmark is an atemporal relation derived by $PERF_4$, a variant of the past-participial morpheme. A subtler yet more substantial discrepancy pertains to the reference point. With the content verb, the trajector is the reference point with respect to both facets of its meaning: it is used to locate the object spatially, and it is the entity to whom the occurrence of the landmark within its dominion is potentially relevant. By contrast, the reference point invoked by the auxiliary *have* cannot be identified with its trajector. In (16), for example, it is clear that the entity designated by the subject is neither RP, i.e. the point in time prior to which the participialized process occurred, nor the individuals to whom it is currently relevant:

(16)(a) *The water main has broken!*
(b) *There had been several robberies in the neighborhood.*
(c) *Tabs have been kept for several years on suspected cognitive grammarians.*

In the present perfect, RP is equated with the time of speaking, and the event bears current relevance to the speech-act participants (or some more inclusive group). When the perfect construction occurs in another tense, as in (16)(b), the reference time and concerned individuals need not be specified (at least within the clause); in particular, the subject does not serve to identify them.

This discrepancy between the content- and auxiliary-verb senses of *have* proves not to be an isolated phenomenon. It is a direct consequence of **subjectification**, a type of semantic shift that appears to be quite common (if not ubiquitous) in the evolution of "grammatical" morphemes from their "lexical" progenitors. A clear understanding of subjectification is therefore essential, for both present and later purposes.

5.2.3.2. *Subjectification.* The notions subjectivity and objectivity pertain to the **construal relation** between a conceptualizer and the conception he entertains, i.e. between the **subject** and **object of conception** (Langacker 1985; Vol. 1, 3.3.2.4). With respect to this relation, an entity is said to be construed **subjectively** to the extent that its participation is confined to the subject role, and **objectively** when it is limited to the object role. A subjectively construed entity is therefore part of the conceptualizing process or apparatus itself but excluded from the content of the conceptualization. To take a perceptual example (*per*ception being one aspect of *con*ception), the glasses I am wearing are construed subjectively: they are part of my perceptual apparatus and help determine what I see, but I do not see the glasses themselves and am generally not aware of them. Naturally, the opposite is true for an objectively construed entity. I construe my glasses objectively when I take them off and look at them, so that they no longer figure in the perceptual process except as the object of perception. The distinction between subjective and objective construal is clearly a matter of degree. For instance, while wearing my glasses I am sometimes conscious of them and can vaguely see certain portions of them.

Subjectification (discussed more fully in Langacker 1990b) is a semantic shift or extension in which an entity originally construed objectively comes to receive a more subjective construal. Our present interest lies with two types (or degrees) of subjectification affecting relational predications. Consider first a relationship whose construal is wholly objective, as diagrammed in Fig. 5.6(a). Full objectivity implies that a conception makes no reference to the conceptualizer, and since the relevant conceptualizers are the speech-act participants, the ground (G) is shown outside the box representing the scope of predication. The dashed arrow stands for the construal relation, while the dashed ellipse delimits the immediate scope of predication (i.e. the locus of attention within the overall scope), also known as the objective scene or onstage region (OS). X and Y are used here as labels for certain facets of the profiled relation, each consisting of interconnections involving the trajector

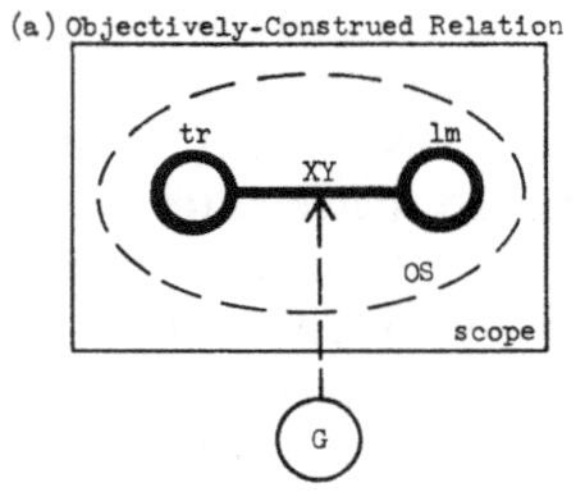

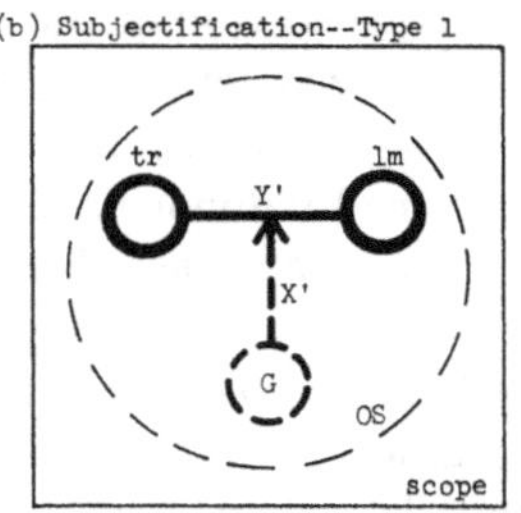

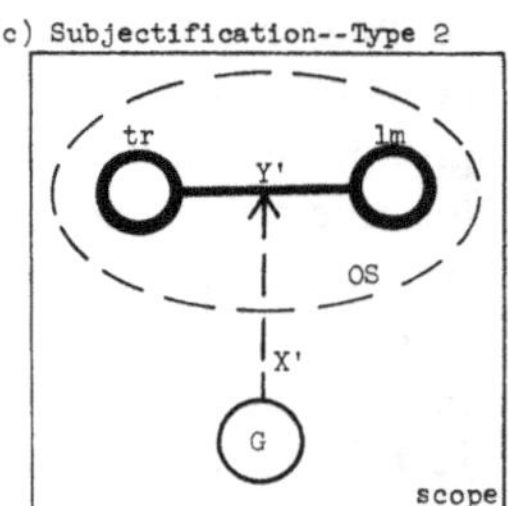

Fig. 5.6

and landmark. Relationship XY runs along the **objective axis**; that is, it holds within the objective scene (making no reference to the ground) and associates two objectively construed participants. Orthogonal to the objective axis is the **subjective axis** defined by the construal relation, which leads from G to the focal point in OS, namely the designatum.

The first type of subjectification occurs when some facet of the profiled relationship is reoriented from the objective axis to the subjective axis, as depicted in Fig. 5.6(b). More precisely, some set of interconnections (X) holding objectively between the trajector and landmark is supplanted by a comparable set (X′) that holds instead between G and the rest of the original profile (Y′). Or to put it another way, part of the profiled relationship loses its objective manifestation, but some vestige of it is preserved subjectively as one aspect of how the remaining situation is construed. This reorientation eliminates the polar opposition of Fig. 5.6(a) between the objective profile and the subjective construal relation. Because G now anchors one facet of the designated relationship, it is necessarily included in the scope of predication, and to some extent it is brought onstage as a profiled participant; hence the extension renders G more objective (cf. Fig. 2.16). At the same time, X is subjectified: objective in origin, it is realigned to coincide with the subjective axis, becoming part of the conceptualization process itself.

In the second type, the subjectification of X is carried one step further by a diminution in the salience of X′. As shown in Fig. 5.6(c), X′ recedes into the base, leaving Y′ to stand alone as the profiled relationship. The resulting configuration is equivalent to that of a grounding predication (Fig. 2.16(c)): although both G and the relationship it bears to the designatum are essential to the expression's meaning, and thus included in the scope of predication, they remain offstage and unprofiled. There is reason to believe that epistemic predications can indeed arise in this fashion, and that the full progression (a) > (b) > (c) of Fig. 5.6 represents a possible course of historical evolution. Importantly, these developments do not entail any change in trajector/landmark assignation—the same objectively construed participants can retain these roles at all three stages.

When applied to specific examples, these notions become intuitively accessible. The first type of subjectification is exemplified by the contrast between two senses of *across*:

(17)(a) *Harvey crawled across the table.*
(b) *A famous movie star is sitting across the table.*

In (17)(a), the trajector of *across* successively occupies all the points along a path leading from one side of its landmark to the other. The profiled relationship, sketched in Fig. 5.7(a), is purely objective and makes no reference to

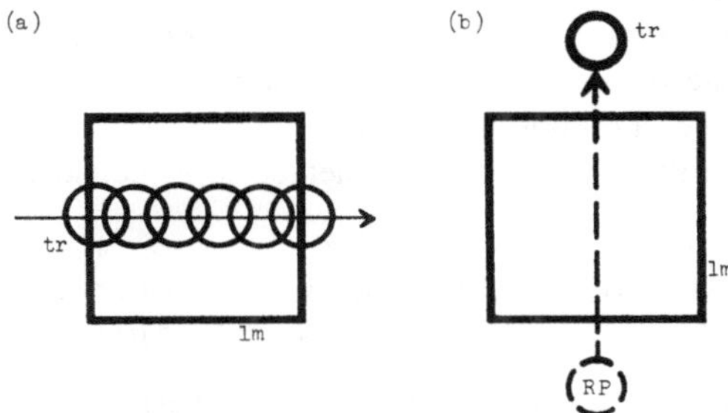

Fig. 5.7

the ground. In line with the summary scanning of this complex atemporal relation, its component states are superimposed in a single diagram, which shows the trajector at various positions it assumes with the passage of time, as indicated by the arrow.

Diagrammed in Fig. 5.7(b) is the meaning displayed by *across* in (17)(b). This is a simple rather than a complex atemporal relation: the trajector does not move, but occupies a single, static position with respect to the landmark. There is, however, a sense of directionality and the notion of a path. To specify the trajector's location vis-à-vis the landmark, a reference point is invoked that is generally equated with the ground (unless otherwise indicated). In particular, the trajector lies at the endpoint of a path that originates at the reference point and traverses the landmark in just the same way that the moving trajector does in (17)(a). Here, though, nothing moves objectively. It is the conceptualizer who traces along the path to compute the trajector's fixed location, but he does so only mentally, as one aspect of his construal of the scene (cf. Vol. 1, 4.3.2). Hence the objective motion figuring in the first meaning of *across* is replaced in the second by a kind of subjective motion inherent in the construal relation. The subjective path is an essential part of the profiled relationship, for it determines its configuration.

This example shares certain properties with other instances of subjectification, including those of the second type. Note first that **objective physical motion by the trajector** is converted under subjectification to **abstract sub-**

jective motion by the conceptualizer. Moreover, as a consequence of motion being reoriented from the objective to the subjective axis (so that objective change through conceived time is replaced by subjective scanning through processing time), the remaining objective relationship is simple rather than complex, i.e. it reduces to a single configuration. In the case of *across*, subjectification converts a complex atemporal relation into a simple (stative) relation. With a verb, it may instead derive an imperfective process from a perfective one.

However, the *across* of (17)(b) and Fig. 5.7(b) displays additional properties that do not carry over to other, more radical examples of subjectification. First, its reference point is not always identified with the ground, even though this represents the default-case value. Second, there is a conventionalized grammatical device (a prepositional phrase with *from*) for specifying the reference point overtly, regardless of whether it is equated with a ground element:

(18)(a) *A famous movie star is sitting across the table from me.*
(b) *A famous movie star is sitting across the table from Sylvester.*

Third, the subjectified relationship is pivotal to determining the configuration of the objective relationship. All three properties are lacking in the next example, which exemplifies a second type of subjectification.

The verb *rise* exhibits contrasting senses in the following expressions (for detailed analysis, see Vol. 1, 7.2.3):

(19)(a) *The balloon rose slowly.*
(b) *The hill gently rises from the bank of the river.*

In (19)(a), *rise* designates a perfective process in which the trajector moves objectively through physical space. On the other hand, its meaning in (19)(b) clearly reflects the reorientation of motion from the objective to the subjective axis. The configuration is stable through time, which renders the process imperfective. It is the conceptualizer who moves subjectively through the scene, mentally tracing an upward path along the hill's expanse, thus imposing a notion of directionality on the static situation. Observe, however, that the objective configuration is established independently of the subjective movement: the hill bears the same spatial relationship to the river regardless of whether the conceptualizer scans upward or downward along its expanse in building up his conception of the scene. The subjective directionality might therefore be analyzed as an unprofiled facet of the base, a nuance of construal added to flavor the objective profile; if so, it corresponds to X′ in Fig. 5.6(c). As further indication of a high degree of subjectification, note that the mover can only be identified with the conceptualizer, and that there is no conventional device for expressing it overtly.

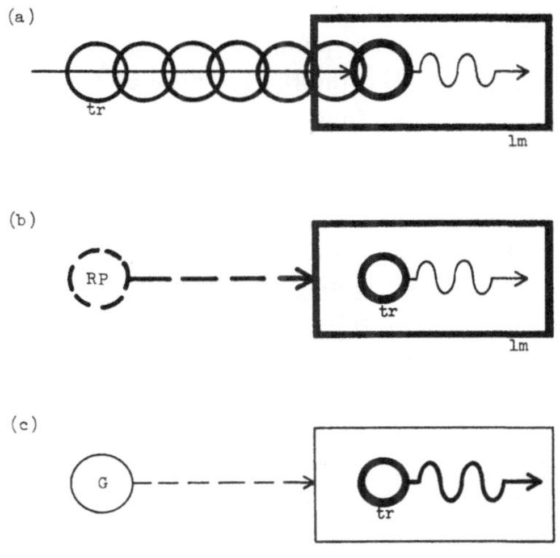

Fig. 5.8

Let us look at just one more case. It is well known that verbs meaning 'go' often evolve historically into markers of futurity (cf. Givón 1973). This is illustrated by both the French example in (20) and its English translation:

(20) *Il va ouvrir la porte.* 'He is going to open the door.'

The sentence is ambiguous in both languages. On the objective reading, diagrammed in Fig. 5.8(a), it means that the subject is following a spatial path at the end of which he will initiate the process of opening the door. Observe that the trajector of 'go' is also the trajector of the resulting process, which is construed atemporally (because it is not in profile at the clause level) and is elaborated by the infinitival complement.

In both languages, (20) can also mean that the subject will open the door in the imminent future. This interpretation is purely temporal—no spatial movement is implied, either objective or subjective. The semantic extension giving rise to the future sense of 'go' therefore involves not only subjectification but also a shift in domain, from space to time (for detailed discussion, see Langacker 1986a). The resulting predication is diagrammed in Fig. 5.8(b). Replacing the trajector's objective spatial path is a subjective temporal path traversed by the conceptualizer. This path is anchored by a temporal reference point, which is equated with the time of speaking when 'go' is in the present tense, as in (20), but can also take some other value:

(21) *Il allait ouvrir la porte.* 'He was going to open the door.'

Starting from this reference point, the conceptualizer traces downstream through time to the landmark process, which is thus situated at a time subsequent to the reference time. For a limited period, this relationship of temporal precedence between the reference point and the landmark represents an essentially stable configuration. The future 'go' profiles the continuation of this relationship through conceived time and thus constitutes an imperfective process.[11] Observe that the trajector of this overall imperfective process is the same as that of the atemporalized downstream process specified by the infinitival complement.

The future 'go' of English or French is periphrastic, for it functions as a clausal head that specifically profiles the relationship of futurity (as opposed to profiling the future event itself, which is expressed instead by the non-finite complement). It is not a grounding predication, since its reference point is not necessarily identified with the ground, and since it can itself be grounded in different ways, as in (20)-(21). Both languages do however mark future tense with a grounding predication, which in French is expressed by verbal inflection, and in English by a modal:

(22) *Il ouvrira la porte.* 'He will open the door.'

The contrast between a periphrastic future and a true future tense corresponds exactly to the difference between the two kinds of subjectification depicted in Figs. 5.6, i.e. it comes down to whether the relationship of futurity is profiled or whether it is construed more subjectively as an unprofiled facet of the base. From a periphrastic future as diagrammed in Fig. 5.8(b), a future tense with the status of a grounding predication may well evolve through further subjectification. Fig. 5.8(c) shows the outcome: the reference point is identified as the ground in particular, and the profile is restricted to the downstream process (which is given a processual construal). This conforms to the characterization of a grounding predication as profiling the grounded entity rather than the grounding relationship.

5.2.3.3. *Synthesis.* Let us first review the basic organization of the perfect construction. Semantically, it describes a process as occurring prior to a temporal reference point, RP, at which time it nevertheless retains some current relevance. The process is construed atemporally and expressed by a perfect participle (derived by $PERF_4$, one variant of the past-participial morpheme). Combining with the participle to form a processual clausal head is the auxiliary verb *have*. Since *have* is the grounded verb, its profile is inherited by the clause as a whole; it is the temporal location of this profiled process that constitutes the reference time. Through the grounding of *have*, RP is situated with respect to the time of speaking (and so, indirectly, is the participialized

[11] *Aller* 'go' is inherently imperfective in French, while the English construction is imperfective because it incorporates the progressive. I am ignoring this difference in order to simplify the exposition.

process). *Have*'s trajector is elaborated by the clausal subject and is further equated with the trajector of the participle—however, it is not identified as the individual(s) to whom the event is currently relevant at RP. Thus in (16)(a), *The water main has broken!*, the water main is understood as the trajector of *broken*, but the event is currently relevant to the speech-act participants (or some wider group of contemporaneous individuals).

To describe this construction adequately, we must give precise semantic characterizations of $PERF_4$ and *have*, relate these meanings to those assumed by the same forms in other constructions, and show how their integration yields a clausal head with the appropriate properties. I will analyze $PERF_4$ as being responsible for the notion of temporal anteriority. Although *have* situates an event within the dominion of a temporal reference point, it may itself be neutral as to whether this event lies upstream or downstream in time from RP. Observe the following contrast: *She has left* vs. *She has to leave*. Only the choice of $PERF_4$ vs. *to* signals the difference between the current relevance of a prior event and that of a future event.[12] $PERF_4$ will thus be characterized as having two effects on the content verb it combines with: it construes the profiled event atemporally, by means of summary scanning; and it specifies that the event is prior to a temporal reference point.

Hence $PERF_4$ is like $PERF_3$ (the passive variant) in that all the component states of the underlying process remain in profile, and like $PERF_1$ in that it makes no change in trajector/landmark alignment. Of course, it resembles $PERF_1$, $PERF_2$, and $PERF_3$ because all four variants suspend the sequential scanning of a process to derive an atemporal relation. A more tenuous similarity uniting this gang of four is that all of them in some way enhance the salience of a "terminal" element (cf. 5.2.1; DeLancey 1981). $PERF_1$ and $PERF_2$ restrict the profile to the final, resultant state of the process. $PERF_2$ and $PERF_3$ confer trajector status on the "downstream" participant that would otherwise be manifested as the direct object. Although $PERF_4$ does neither, at least a hint of terminal prominence is associated with the notion of anteriority. There is a real sense in which the profiled event is viewed from the vantage point of RP (by those to whom it is currently relevant). Because the event precedes RP, its termination is temporally closest to RP (just as the initiation is closest in the case of a subsequent event), so from the viewer's perspective, the event's completion is foregrounded and to some degree rendered more prominent.

Turning now to *have*, we noted in 5.2.3.1 a semantic variant of the content

[12] The current relevance of a future event is a major ingredient of the obligation expressed by *have to*, which is a periphrastic modal. It is true that only the perfect *have* functions as an auxiliary (*Has she left?* vs. ?**Has she to leave?*), so that different senses may be involved, but the contrast with *have to* is suggestive nonetheless. Whether the auxiliary *have* is neutral or whether it also indicates temporal anteriority may be indeterminate and is not a matter of any great import—the analysis is easily formulated either way.

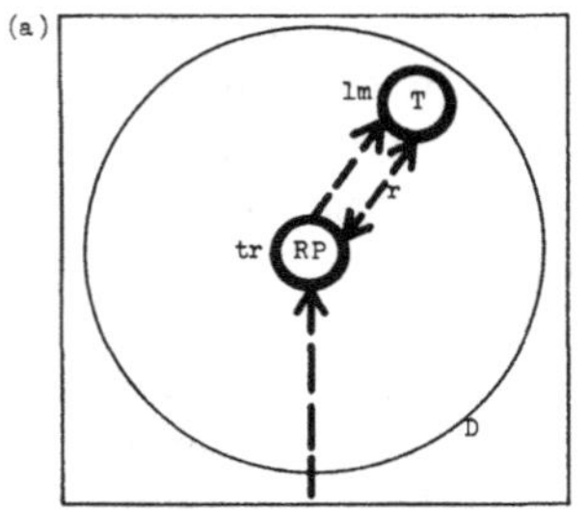

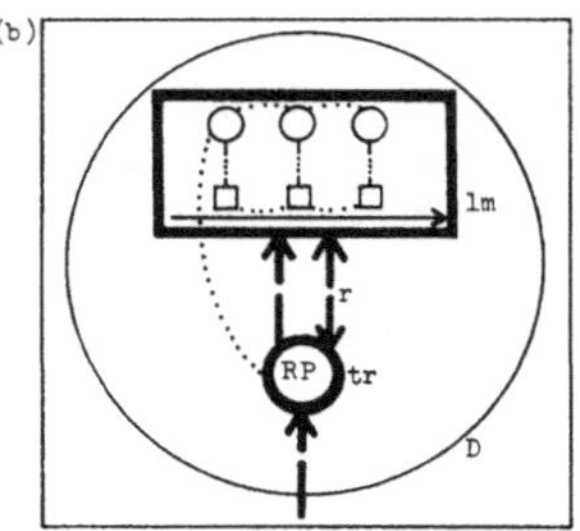

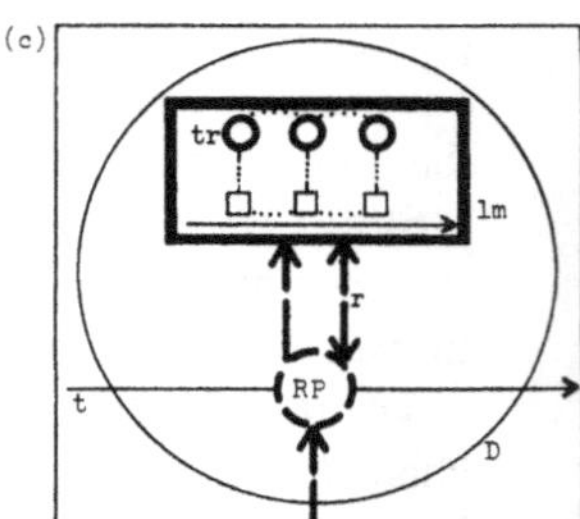

Fig. 5.9

verb that is rather similar to what is required for the auxiliary. In a sentence like (12)(e), *We have a lot of skunks around here*, the subject functions as a spatial reference point for locating the object, and moreover, the occurrence of the object within the subject's dominion is conceived as being of potential relevance to the subject. The essential components of this situation are diagrammed in Fig. 5.9(a). Most of the notations pertain to abstract possession (4.3.2): RP, D, and T stand respectively for the reference point, the dominion associated with that reference point, and the target (i.e. the entity located within RP's dominion); and the single-headed arrows indicate the path through which the conceptualizer establishes mental contact with T. Observe that this aspect of the profiled relationship is *subjective*, a matter of how the conceptualizer makes use of the entities concerned in construing the scene. On the other hand, the double-headed arrow represents an *objective* relationship, namely the relationship of potential relevance (labeled *r*) that T bears to RP. With RP chosen as trajector and T as primary landmark, this entire configuration constitutes one component state of *have*, which portrays it as continuing through conceived time to form an imperfective process (cf. Fig. 4.7).

The auxiliary *have* differs from this content verb in three respects. First, its landmark is not a thing but an atemporal relation (elaborated by the perfect participle). This adjustment is made in Fig. 5.9(b). Included is a correspondence line which indicates that the overall trajector is also the trajector of the relational landmark. This is an inherent property of many verbs taking relational complements, for instance *try* (*He tried to get up*) and the motion sense of 'go' in sentences like (20), *Il va ouvrir la porte* 'He is going to open the door', as diagrammed in Fig. 5.8(a). It is the source of an important feature of the perfect construction, namely that the clausal subject is understood as the trajector of the participle.

The other two differences between the content verb *have* and the auxiliary verb turn out to be exactly the same as those between the motion and future senses of 'go' in (20). Relating these two senses are (1) transfer from the spatial to the temporal domain, and (2) subjectification to the first degree, as shown diagrammatically by the contrast between (a) and (b) in Figs. 5.6–8. In this type of subjectification, some facet of the profiled relationship is reoriented from the objective to the subjective axis, though it remains in profile. Now the figure within the scene is necessarily construed objectively and is thus limited to the objective axis. Reorienting a relation to the subjective axis therefore has the result of detaching it from the trajector, whose role within it is replaced by a subjectively construed reference point.

The effect of applying these operations to Fig. 5.9(b) is depicted in 5.9(c). RP is identified as a point along the temporal axis (*t*). It is *r*, the relation of potential relevance, that undergoes reorientation from the objective to the subjective axis (the relation based on mental contact is already subjective). What is the conceptual import of this realignment? That the event's current relevance no longer pertains to its own trajector (as implied by the correspondence line in diagram (b)), but rather to RP (or to those individuals who view the event from this vantage point). The result is that both facets of the profiled relationship are subjective: the landmark event is currently relevant to RP, and RP is used to establish mental contact with it. Moreover, the trajector and the reference point are now distinct, respectively occupying the objective and the subjective axes. Observe that *tr* is simultaneously the trajector of the overall predication and that of the landmark event.

Fig. 5.9(c) represents one component state of the auxiliary verb *have*, which functions as the profile determinant in Fig. 5.10. In accordance with the usual notational convention for imperfective processes, only one component state is explicitly diagrammed, but it is understood as continuing unchanged over a span of conceived time (through which it is scanned sequentially). Because conceived time is also the domain of the profiled relationship, the reference point for each component state of *have* is identified with one of the points in its temporal profile, as indicated by a correspondence line.[13] *Have*'s landmark is a schematic atemporal relation. Though situated with reference to RP, it is depicted above the time arrow on the assumption that *have* itself is neutral as to whether it precedes or follows RP. That information is in any case provided by the perfect participle, the component structure given on the right. Derived by $PERF_4$, this structure designates a specific atemporal relation and further specifies its temporal anteriority to a reference point. The participle elaborates the schematic landmark of *have*, their integration being

[13] Conceived time is shown twice because of its dual role: the role it has in any process as the dimension along which the profiled relationship evolves, and its special role as the domain with respect to which the relationship happens in this instance to be characterized. Distinguished for analytical purposes, the two temporal axes are nonetheless identical, hence the correspondence. It is by virtue of this identity that *have*'s temporal profile constitutes the reference point (thus it is actually a span of time, not a point in the narrow sense).

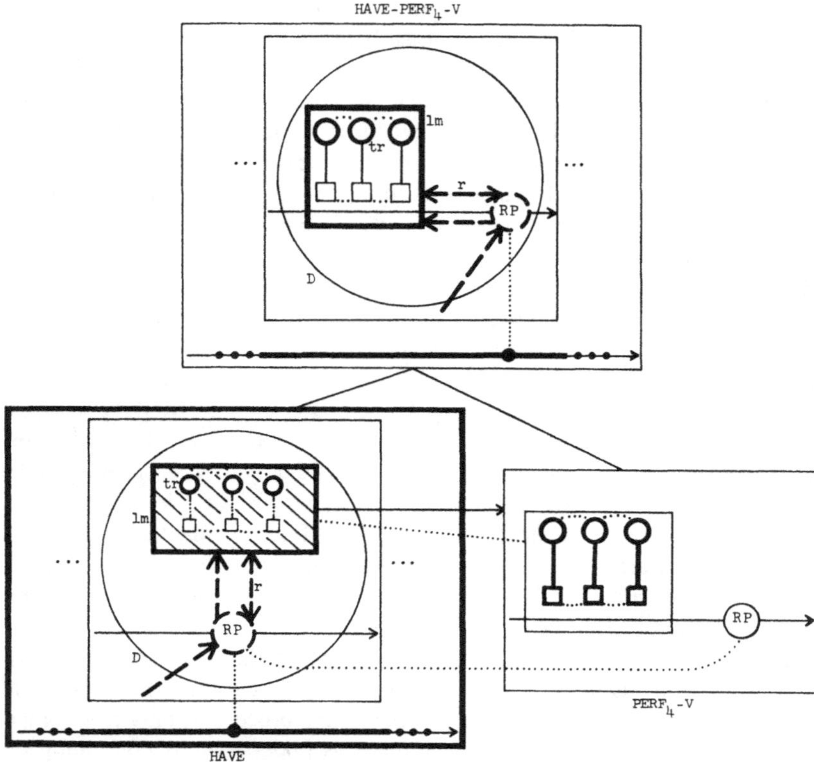

Fig. 5.10

effected by correspondences between the two atemporal relations and between the two reference points. The composite expression (e.g. *have broken*) profiles the continuation, through the reference time, of a stable relationship in which a specific process has previously occurred but remains of current relevance.

The perfect construction provides a periphrastic means of indicating past time (with respect to RP) with the added nuance that the completed event continues to be relevant. It is well known that in certain other languages, such as French, Spanish, and German, a formally parallel construction has largely lost this nuance of current relevance and come to be used (in the present tense) as a neutral, even the usual way of referring to past-time events. Consider, for example, the French *passé composé*: *Il a travaillé* is more adequately translated by *He worked* than by *He has worked*, even though it is formed with the auxiliary verb *avoir* 'have' and the past participle. The change from a true perfect (like the English construction) to a simple periphrastic past (such as the *passé composé*) is very easily described in terms of our analysis and notational conventions: from the perfect construction as diagrammed in Fig. 5.10, one need only eliminate the arrow labeled *r*—everything else remains the same and requires no augmentation.

The French *passé composé* is still periphrastic, for it specifically profiles the relationship of temporal anteriority. Hence it is not a grounding predication, and indeed, the auxiliary verb *avoir* itself takes finite-verb inflections. What would be needed for such a construction to develop into a true past-tense marking with the status of a grounding predication? This further development would only require the additional degree of subjectification represented by the contrast between (b) and (c) in Fig. 5.6 (or 5.8). That is, it would simply be a matter of the processual profile shifting from the relationship of temporal anteriority to the target event (i.e. the previous landmark), and the reference point being identified obligatorily (not just as the unmarked option) with the time of speaking.

5.3. Patterns and Structure

We have now examined each auxiliary element of the English clausal head and ascribed to it a precisely characterized meaning closely related to the senses it has in other uses. For each element, we have also described the grammatical construction through which it combines with a conceptually autonomous complement, e.g. *have* with a perfect participle (Fig. 5.10). This portion of the auxiliary will now be considered from the standpoint of grammatical behavior and its representation as a structured system.

5.3.1. *The Basic System*

We must first ask how the conventional units of the grammar specify the proper combinations of elements. A standard of comparison in this regard is Chomsky's original phrase-structure rule (previously stated in (1)); together with Affix Hopping, it economically generates just the right set of strings. One might argue that the seeming elegance of this formulation is outweighed by its glaring deficiencies.[14] And cognitive grammar, as a usage-based framework, is more concerned with realistically describing the mental representation of linguistic structure, in all its likely complexity, than with reducing the description to a single formula containing the fewest possible symbols (Langacker 1988c; Vol. 1, 1.2.3). Still, a viable alternative to Chomsky's classic account must at least get the pieces in the right places and express any valid generalizations.

[14] Among others, these include its failure to deal with meaning; the fact that it merely stipulates the orderings and dependencies; the incorrectness of the constituent structure it assigns; and its inability to directly generate the auxiliary sequences found in noun modifiers.

Chomsky's rule (1) specifies a linear sequence and does not posit any constituency groupings within the auxiliary. Formula (2), which summarizes the present analysis, does essentially the opposite: the parentheses indicate constituency, which was motivated in 5.1, while the formula's left-to-right order is only mnemonic. The description must of course state the sequencing of auxiliary elements. However, cognitive grammar does not treat temporal order as a dimension of constituent structure (as does transformational grammar), but rather as one dimension of phonological space; hence the proper temporal sequencing is prescribed at the phonological pole of each constructional schema involving an auxiliary element. The problem, then, is to ensure that each such element takes the proper set of complements. We will concentrate on the clausal head, as sketched in (2), leaving tense and modality for Ch. 6. Observe, however, that the status of tense-modality as a grounding predication is responsible both for its being obligatory in a finite clause and also for its constituting the outermost layer within the verb group (i.e. it takes the entire clausal head as its complement).

Unlike (1), formula (2) is simply a convenient summary of structural relationships and does not per se constitute the grammatical description of the phenomena covered. The actual characterization of the clausal head resides in an inventory of symbolic units of varying degrees of complexity, some of which function as components of others. The simplest units are the individual morphemes: [have], [$PERF_4$], [be_1], etc. These notations are of course abbreviatory—each represents a bipolar structure that is internally complex at each pole. Also, it is somewhat arbitrary to impose a strict dichotomy between the internal structure of a morpheme and the set of structural frames in which it conventionally appears; to regard these as different facets of a symbolic unit subsuming both intrinsic and extrinsic specifications is more in keeping with our overall approach (cf. Vol. 1: 9.3.1, 10.4.2).

Another group of units consists of constructional schemas describing how each auxiliary morpheme combines with its complement. In discussing them, we will continue using the format of (2). It employs the following abbreviatory convention, where D and A represent the conceptually dependent and autonomous component structures, and C the composite structure resulting from their integration: [[D][A] $_C$] >> [D [A]]. That is, explicit reference to the composite structure is omitted, and A is included within the brackets enclosing D to indicate that A elaborates a substructure of D. The constructional schema for passive participles is therefore abbreviated from [[$PERF_3$][V_t] $_{PRTC}$] to [$PERF_3$ [V_t]], which indicates that a transitive content verb elaborates a substructure of the participial morpheme. This notation is both simpler and has the advantage of showing A/D alignment.

Let us briefly survey the basic constructional schemas, working outward from the content verb. $PERF_3$ requires that its complement be transitive, so the schema for passive participles specifically mentions a verb of that sort (abbreviated V_t).[15] *Be_2* also requires a specific kind of complement, namely a passive participle, for it is a special variant that only occurs in passives; the constructional schema therefore incorporates, as the autonomous (elaborating) structure, the schema for such participles: [be_2 [$PERF_3$ [V_t]]]. By contrast, *-ing* allows essentially any verb as its complement, whether simple or complex (e.g. *breaking* vs. *being broken*), perfective or imperfective (the latter in noun modifiers). A maximally general formulation is therefore possible, i.e. [-ing [V]], but our main concern here is with the progressive and hence with the subschema that specifies a perfective verb: [-ing [V_p]]. This subschema represents the complement of *be_1* in the progressive construction: [be_1 [-ing [V_p]]]. Alternatively, in a slightly different construction, *be_1* combines with a stative relation (such as an adjective, prepositional phrase, or predicate nominative). Finally, $PERF_4$ takes any kind of verb for its complement, permitting the general statement [$PERF_4$ [V]], while a complement of the auxiliary *have* can only be a participle of that sort: [have [$PERF_4$ [V]]].

These structures are nothing more than schematized expressions. They represent a speaker's thorough mastery of the minimal locutionary patterns *Ved*, *be Ved*, *Ving*, *be Ving*, and *have Ved*. Moreover, in view of their frequency, we have little reason to doubt that more elaborate patterns—such as *be being Ved*, *have been Ved*, *have been Ving*, perhaps even *have been being Ved*—also achieve the status of well-entrenched units. With respect to the basic constructional schemas just described, these units constitute subschemas in which V is instantiated by a specific complex structure. Thus *be being Ved*, given formulaically as [be_1 [-ing [be_2 [$PERF_3$ [V_p]]]]], is a special case of [be_1 [-ing [V_p]]], that in which [V_p] consists in particular of a passive structure, i.e. [be_2 [$PERF_3$ [V_p]]].[16] Similarly, *have been Ved* and *have been Ving* reflect established subschemas of the perfect construction, [have [$PERF_4$ [V]]]. In the former, [V] is instantiated by the general passive schema [be_2 [$PERF_3$ [V_t]]], resulting in [have [$PERF_4$ [be_2 [$PERF_3$ [V_t]]]]]. In the latter, [V] is instead instantiated by the progressive schema [be_1 [-ing [V_p]]], yielding [have [$PERF_4$ [be_1 [-ing [V_p]]]]]. If the full pattern *have been being Ved* is indeed a unit, it constitutes a special case of this last subschema, that where [V_p] is passive. The constructional subschema for this maximal pattern is equivalent to formula (2): [have [$PERF_4$ [be_1 [-ing [be_2 [$PERF_3$ [V_p]]]]]]].

[15] A conceptual characterization of transitivity is offered in Ch. 7. There are of course other constructional schemas, involving other variants of the past participial morpheme, that make different specifications (e.g. $PERF_1$ takes intransitive complements). An additional restriction—which holds for all the constructions under discussion—is that the verb must be ungrounded.

[16] Because it functions as the perfective verb in the progressive construction, this passive structure must itself be perfective, which comes about when the passive participle is formed on a perfective stem (recall that the aspect of the stem determines that of *be Ved* as a whole). This specification correctly rules out such expressions as **be being known*.

The presumption, then, is that the mental representation of the auxiliary system does not reside in a single compact formula from which the speaker computes whatever combination of elements is needed on a given occasion, but rather comprises a substantial number of constructional schemas reflecting the mastery and automatization of particular expression types (e.g. *be Ving*, *have Ved*, *have been Ving*). These schemas should not be thought of as separate, unrelated entities—on the contrary, they constitute a highly structured assembly, in which the successive combination of simpler units gives rise to schemas of progressively greater complexity, and the same units (even some that are fairly complex) function simultaneously as components of multiple higher-level schemas, which therefore show a great deal of overlap. If there is a single schema that incorporates all the component morphemes and describes the maximal pattern for a clausal head, it is nevertheless embedded in this larger assembly of interlocking structures, representing different facets of a speaker's grasp of established convention.[17]

5.3.2. *Restrictions*

All the valid generalizations are captured and expressed by constructional schemas. For example, [be_1 [-ing [V_p]]] constitutes a fully general characterization of the progressive construction, while [$PERF_4$ [V]] indicates that a perfect participle can be formed on any kind of verb. It is easily seen, moreover, that the schemas sanction all the occurring sequences. The remaining question is whether the description is sufficiently restrictive or whether it also sanctions impermissible sequences. The issue is familiar—it was raised in the generative tradition by analyses claiming that auxiliaries are really main verbs; since the rules generating sequences of successively embedded verbs would, if unrestricted, allow any combination whatever, attempts were made to show that semantic factors or other independent constraints would rule out all sequences other than the occurring ones (e.g. McCawley 1971; Pullum and Wilson 1977). Although our discussion will parallel these attempts to some degree, several important differences should be noted. First, our analysis does *not* claim that auxiliaries are "main verbs"; within the verb class, auxiliaries are distinguished from content verbs on the basis of meaning, semantic function, and grammatical behavior. Second, our analysis treats $PERF_4$, *-ing*, and $PERF_3$ as meaningful elements, not as markings that a verb mechanically induces on its complement. Third, we do not posit a general syntactic rule that, left to its own devices, would generate every possible verb

[17]It is irrelevant that a description of this sort appears more complicated than Chomsky's generative rules, for the two analyses are incommensurate. They attempt to account for different ranges of phenomena and reflect distinct ways of interpreting general principles of scientific methodology (e.g. the principle of economy) and applying them to the specific problems of linguistic analysis (Langacker 1988c; Vol. 1, 1.2).

sequence; our starting point is rather an assembly of fairly specific constructional schemas abstracted directly from sets of overtly occurring expressions.

Certain fundamental restrictions follow immediately from the schemas as already formulated. For one thing, they preclude the direct combination either of two verbs or of two non-verbal auxiliary elements. Because *have*, for instance, is only introduced as part of [have [$PERF_4$ [V]]] and its subschemas—which stipulate that its complement is a perfect participle—there is nothing to sanction such expressions as **have see*, **have be working*, or **have be criticized*. Similarly, $PERF_4$ appears only in [$PERF_4$ [V]] and its subschemas, and since these require that its complement be a verb, its attachment to a participle is unsanctioned and non-conventional: **workinged*; **criticizeded*. It is also clear that the schemas associate each auxiliary verb with the proper type of atemporal complement. By virtue of [have [$PERF_4$ [V]]] and [be_1 [-ing [V]]], for example, *have* and be_1 respectively occur with perfect and present participles, but nothing enables *have* to combine with a present participle: **have working*; **have being criticized*.

What remains to be determined is whether the constructional schemas let just the right auxiliary verbs occur as complements to the atemporalizing predications. The schemas do, of course, specifically sanction certain combinations. For example, [have [$PERF_4$ [be_2 [$PERF_3$ [V_t]]]]] directly states that $PERF_4$ combines with be_2 to derive a perfect participle from a passive (e.g. *have been criticized*). But are there other combinations, not individually mentioned by a schema, that conform to its specifications and are nonetheless impermissible? It is certainly true that not all combinations are allowed. Especially finnicky is the passive participial $PERF_3$, which does not take any auxiliary complement: neither a perfect with *have* (**be had criticized*), nor a progressive with be_1 (**be been criticizing*), nor another passive with be_2 (**be been criticized*). However, it is not obvious that our present schema, [$PERF_3$ [V_t]], imposes the necessary restrictions.

Several factors are plausibly taken as ruling out some or all of the impermissible combinations. Let us first suppose (as will be argued in 5.3.4) that auxiliary verbs are semantically distinguishable from content verbs. If so, the constructional schema for passive participles is easily adjusted to reflect the systematic exclusion of auxiliaries. We need only fine-tune its characterization of the complement, so that instead of just any ungrounded verb, it mentions a content verb in particular: [$PERF_3$ [V_c]]. There is then no schema capable of sanctioning the derivation of a passive participle from an auxiliary.

Such expressions are also precluded on independent grounds. In the case of passives formed with be_2, it is a matter of transitivity: $PERF_3$ inherently requires a transitive verb for its complement (Fig. 5.1). Although a verb like *criticize* is transitive, the passive *be criticized* is uncontroversially intransitive (it takes a subject but not a direct object), hence it cannot undergo another cycle of passivization (*be been criticized*). The same explanation is not obviously available for the perfect or the progressive, since these are regarded as transitive when formed on a transitive stem (*have criticized NML*; *be criticizing NML*). It may however be significant that *have* and be_1 are not themselves transitive—it is the content verb that licenses the direct object. If we identify a predicate's primary landmark as the non-trajector substructure elaborated by a complement, then the primary landmarks of *have* and be_1 (in fact, of all the auxiliary verbs) are relational rather than nominal, which renders these verbs intransitive. Conceivably $PERF_3$ requires transitivity of the verb it attaches to directly, not just the overall complement.

Be that as it may, the passivization of a perfect or a progressive would probably be prevented by yet another factor. The converse arrangement, i.e. the formation of a perfect or a progressive on a passive, is thoroughly familiar and conventional. In cognitive terms, the patterns *have been Ved* and *be being Ved* are represented by constructional schemas that are deeply entrenched and easily elicited: [have [$PERF_4$ [be_2 [$PERF_3$ [V_t]]]]]; [be_1 [-ing [be_2 [$PERF_3$ [V_t]]]]]. Thus, if both the passive construction and either the perfect or the progressive are used in the same clausal head, one of these schemas is bound to be selected as the active node for purposes of constructing or evaluating the expression—they are far more specific than the passive schema, [be_2 [$PERF_3$ [V_t]]], which is the only established schema that might conceivably sanction a passivized perfect or progressive. As a consequence, an expression such as **be had criticized* or **be been criticizing* will not be interpreted as a well-formed instantiation of the passive schema, but rather as a distorted manifestation of the perfect-passive or progressive-passive construction.

Consider next the complements of *-ing*, for which we have posited both a general schema, [-ing [V]], and a subschema that specifies a perfective complement and occurs as one component of the progressive construction: [be_1 [-ing [V_p]]]. With *-ing*, there is clearly no blanket prohibition of auxiliary-verb complements, as witnessed by progressive passives; the passive complement must however be perfective, as determined by the content verb (e.g. *be being criticized*, but not **be being known*). Since McCawley 1971, it has been observed that this restriction of the progressive to perfective complements prevents it from occurring with the auxiliary *have*, which is imperfective (**be having worked*). Furthermore, because the progressive is an imperfectivizing construction, the progressive cannot itself undergo another round of progressivization (**be being working*). Hence the requirement of perfectivity correctly limits the progressive *-ing* to certain instances of the passive be_2 (among the auxiliary verbs).

McCawley's explanation has been rejected by Akmajian, Steele, and Wasow (1979, p. 19) on the grounds that, while imperfectives may appear in the progressive given the right context, the auxiliary *have* may not:

(23)(a) *He is liking his job more and more.*
(b) **He is having slept longer every day.*

However, this argument is fallacious and illustrates the danger of relying on distributional evidence without a thorough understanding of all the semantic factors that may be involved. The analysis of (23)(a) is fairly straightforward: though *like his job* would normally be imperfective, the adverb *more and more* implies a change through time and thus induces a perfective construal, so the progressive is warranted. We may grant that in (23)(b) the comparative adverbial *-er every day* likewise implies a change through time, yet the infelicity of the progressive suggests that *have slept longer every day* remains imperfective. How can this be? The answer is apparent when we consider the meaning of the perfect construction and its interaction with the adverb's meaning. The perfect construction profiles the continuation through time of a stable relationship of anteriority and current relevance that a process—construed atemporally and expressed by the perfect participle—bears to a temporal reference point (see the composite structure in Fig. 5.10). Now in the expression *have slept longer every day*, what precisely is it that changes from one day to the next? It is not the relationship of temporal anteriority and current relevance, but rather the period of sleeping. Hence the effect of the adverb is confined to the internal structure of the participialized process, which constitutes a landmark of *have*, not its profile. The construction remains imperfective, and thus resists the progressive, because the profiled relation is unaffected.

The restriction of *-ing* to perfectives holds only in the context of the progressive construction, [be_1 [-ing [V_p]]]. Outside that context, for instance in the formation of noun modifiers, *-ing* attaches to both perfectives and imperfectives (*those men working over there*; *those students knowing the answer*). Having posited the general schema [-ing [V]] to accommodate these possibilities, we must now ask whether it is sufficiently restrictive. Are all the structures it sanctions actually used? In particular, can any auxiliary verb occur as its complement? It turns out that all the options are not in fact conventionally exploited, and the actual distribution holds a certain amount of interest. Briefly, *-ing* forms modifiers from perfective passives but not from imperfectives: *a portrait being done by an expert*; **any answer being known by all the students*. It does occur with the auxiliary *have*, which is unsurprising in the present analysis, though quite unanticipated in terms of Chomsky's original formula: *those patients having eaten before noon*; *anyone having known her for at least two years*. However, *-ing* does not take progressive complements: **those men being working over there*.

There are two separate issues to address. First, why do we encounter this particular distribution? Is it arbitrary, or can it somehow be motivated? Second, how can the necessary restrictions be implemented? With respect to the first matter, it is not difficult to find a functional motivation for the distribution. In a nutshell, the non-occurring combinations are those for which simpler alternatives are available that do essentially the same job, i.e. they provide effectively equivalent information without creating potentially awkward ambiguities. Thus the progressive is superfluous in noun modifiers because a present participle formed on the content verb alone describes precisely the same situation—given the availability of *those men working over there*, a speaker has no reason to resort to the more complex **those men being working over there*.[18] Similarly, a present participle formed on an imperfective passive is more complex than the unadorned passive participle, without making any significant semantic contribution by way of compensation: **any answer being known by all the students* vs. *any answer known by all the students*. With a perfective passive, on the other hand, the added complexity serves some purpose: *a portrait being done by an expert* specifically indicates that the portrait is under way but not completed, whereas *a portrait done by an expert* would more likely be interpreted as designating a finished work. Ambiguity is also forestalled by the derivation of modifying participles from the full perfect construction with *have*; the semantic distinction between *those patients having eaten before noon* and *those patients eaten before noon* is hardly trivial.

In short, the distribution is anything but arbitrary. It is a fine example of how linguistic structure is shaped by ecological pressures and thereby achieves a delicate balance of expressive richness and communicative efficiency. Nevertheless, functional motivation is not the same as explicit description—however well we understand the reason for the facts being as they are, we still face the problem of characterizing the linguistic system they reflect. It seems quite evident, therefore, that the high-level schema [-ing [V]] is insufficient as a characterization of present participles that modify nouns in English. Although it is reasonable to postulate such a schema, the actual distribution must be spelled out by a set of subschemas that are more specific and hence more likely to be activated for the construction and evaluation of novel expressions. These include: [-ing [V_c]] (whereby *-ing* attaches to a content verb, regardless of perfectivity); [-ing [be_2 [$PERF_3$ [V_p]]]] (for modifiers based on perfective passives); and [-ing [have [$PERF_4$ [V]]]] (for present participles derived from the perfect construction). Presumably [-ing [V]] itself

[18]One might attempt instead to explain this restriction in terms of the constraint adduced by Ross (1972c) against two successive verbs bearing *-ing* (e.g. *It is continuing to rain* vs. **It is continuing raining*). However, that does not account for the non-conventionality of noun modifiers formed by *-ing* from be_1 plus a stative relation: **the balloon being red*; **the bookcase being in the study*. The proposed analysis affords a unified account—these latter expressions are not conventionally employed because simpler alternatives are readily available (*the red balloon*; *the bookcase in the study*).

lacks the salience to be selected as an active node capable of sanctioning participial modifiers representing other conceivable subpatterns.

Finally, we must consider the complements of $PERF_4$, the perfect participial morpheme. We have thus far posited only the maximally general schema [$PERF_4$ [V]], which is presumed to obligatorily activate the more elaborate structure [have [$PERF_4$ [V]]] (i.e. the perfect participle is limited to the context of the full perfect construction with *have*). In accordance with this general formulation, both perfective and imperfective content verbs give rise to perfect participles (*have worked*; *have known*). Perfect participles can also be formed on both passive and progressive structures (*have been criticized*; *have been criticizing*). The one restriction is that a perfect participle cannot be derived from another perfect: **have had worked*. It is tempting to argue that such expressions are avoided because their meanings are unlikely to have much communicative utility (they would convey the current relevance of an event's current relevance to a previous reference point), but once again, a functional explanation is not equivalent to a description.[19] We must therefore suppose that [$PERF_4$ [V]] is not itself well enough entrenched to sanction novel expressions on its own. Its actual distributional import is specified by subschemas reflecting those particular patterns that have been established in conventional usage. At the present level of delicacy, just two are sufficient: [$PERF_4$ [V_c]] sanctions the participialization of a content verb (*have criticized*; *have known*); and [$PERF_4$ [be [. . .]]]—where *be* is schematic for be_1 and be_2—handles the other cases (*have been working*; *have been criticized*; *have been ready*).

The conclusion to be drawn from this survey is that an analysis of the sort envisaged is workable and capable in principle of imposing the proper restrictions. The fact that particular patterns are conventionalized to the exclusion of others, and that the permissible patterns have to be listed as such in the grammar (not being subject to absolute predictability on semantic or functional grounds), does not entail the autonomy of grammatical structure. Both the patterns and their limitations are describable by means of constructional schemas comprising symbolic units and nothing more.

5.3.3. *Componentiality*

The English auxiliary provides a striking example of the interplay between **unipolar** and **bipolar componentiality** (Vol. 1, 2.3.1.2). Unipolar compo-

[19] A seemingly plausible suggestion is that subjectification of the sort embodied in the perfect construction cannot apply to an already subjectified conception. That, however, is precisely what happens in such expressions as the following: *I have been going to do that for ages* (cf. Figs. 5.8(b) and 5.10). To be sure, double subjectification is highly marked (note that the future 'go' in French or Spanish cannot be cast in the perfect—there is no direct translation of the English example just cited).

nentiality pertains to the natural hierarchy of semantic or phonological structures examined independently. At the phonological pole, we observe such componentiality in the organization of segments into syllables, syllables into words, words into phonological phrases, and so on. Such units and their constituency are established without regard to semantic considerations. On the other hand, bipolar units are postulated and delimited precisely because semantic and phonological structures stand in symbolic relationships. Bipolar componentiality comprises the hierarchical organization of symbolic structures, i.e. the combination of simpler ones to form symbolic structures of progressively greater complexity.

In this symbolic theory of grammar, bipolar componentiality is the same as grammatical constituency (both morphological and syntactic). It is therefore bipolar componentiality that is indicated in our formulas for auxiliary constructions, e.g. [have [$PERF_4$ [be_1 [-ing [V_p]]]]]. Because unipolar and bipolar hierarchies represent separate dimensions of organization and are shaped by different factors, their constituents do not necessarily coincide; in particular, the phonological manifestation of a grammatical constituent is not invariably a constituent with respect to the natural (unipolar) phonological hierarchy. Consider a clausal head such as *have been working*. Grammatically, we have recognized *be working* as a constituent (i.e. [be_1 [-ing [V_p]]]). Phonologically, however, the individual words of *have been working* are natural constituents. *Be working* is not a constituent in terms of the unipolar hierarchy, but rather a discontinuous sequence that cuts across word boundaries.

Such discrepancies between the two hierarchies can be seen as reflecting a kind of communicative efficiency. Suppose a symbolic unit, e.g. $PERF_4$, is added to an already assembled constituent of some complexity, such as *be working*. If the symbolization of this unit were to respect the natural phonological hierarchy, it would have to be a separate word standing as a co-constituent of *be working* in a phonological phrase. The discrepancy arises because $PERF_4$ is actually symbolized more simply, without even adding to the number of syllables: ***been** working*. Moreover, $PERF_4$ is manifested phonologically on the head of the structure it combines with, i.e. on *be_1*, which contributes its processual profile to *be working* as a whole and thereby creates the semantic configuration that $PERF_4$ requires. There is clearly some sense in which it is optimal for a predication to show up phonologically on the element that most directly motivates its occurrence. For "grammatical" notions to be marked specifically on the head of a complex structure is in fact a ubiquitous phenomenon, and one whose description in cognitive grammar is singularly unproblematic (Vol. 1: 9.1.3; 9.3.2).

Let us examine *have been working* in slightly more detail. Its formulaic representation, [have [$PERF_4$ [be_1 [-ing [work]]]]], abbreviates a complex structure that is shown more fully in Fig. 5.11, which employs the constitu-

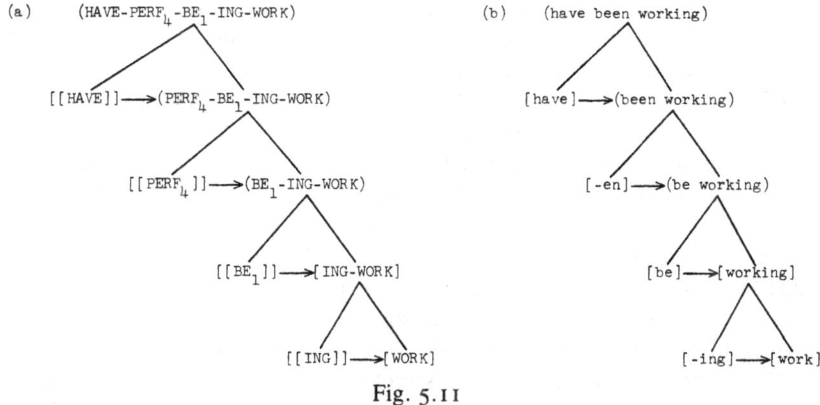

Fig. 5.11

ency-tree format (Vol. 1, 8.4.1). The semantic and phonological poles are diagrammed in (a) and (b), respectively, with the choice of brackets vs. parentheses signalling whether or not the structure they enclose is presumed to be a familiar unit. The arrows stand for elaborative relationships (though e-sites are not indicated), and the double brackets in (a) identify the head (profile determinant) for each level of constituency at the semantic pole. Naturally, corresponding elements at the two poles are linked by symbolic relationships. Participating in such relationships, at each level of constituency, are (1) the two component structures; (2) the way in which these component structures are integrated; and (3) the composite structure that results.

It is bipolar componentiality, i.e. grammatical constituency, that is depicted by the configuration of these tree diagrams. Together with the structure it dominates, each node defines a grammatical constituent, and as one traces an upward path through the tree, each node encountered represents a constituent of the one that follows. For example, one such path at the phonological pole is *work* > *working* > *be working* > *been working* > *have been working*. Thus, with respect to bipolar organization, *work* is a constituent of *working*, which is in turn a constituent of *be working*, etc. The two *grammatical* constituents of *been working* are therefore *be working* and *-en*. On the other hand, its two *phonological* constituents are *been* and *working*. Although this format is not designed to show it, each node in diagrams (a) and (b) is a complex semantic or phonological structure that is internally coherent and hierarchically organized in unipolar terms. *Been working*, for instance, is a phonological phrase having two words as constituents; each word has one or two syllables, and each syllable comprises a number of segments. We see, then, that unipolar constituency pertains to the internal structure of individual nodes, whereas bipolar constituency resides in configurations of nodes.

In the step-by-step assembly of a complex clausal head, each successive composite structure conforms to the phonotactic patterns of the language and manifests a particular unipolar constituency. For example, each structure along the compositional path *work* > *working* > *be working* > *been working* > *have been working* has the potential to be pronounced independently as a well-formed word or phonological phrase. From one step to the next, however, the organization may change to accommodate the additional phonological material contributed by the newly appended morpheme; reorganization occurs whenever—in unipolar terms—the new material is somehow incorporated into the previous structure rather than being adjoined to it as a co-constituent (grammatically, of course, it *is* a co-constituent). For instance, *be working* consists of two words and in some cases retains this organization in more complex expressions (e.g. *to be working*; *may be working*). Appending $PERF_4$ results in another two-word structure, *been working*, but one that is differently organized: *be* is no longer a word, only part of a word consisting of a different type of syllable (and in most American dialects even the vowel is distinct). Such realignment is hardly surprising—it simply means that regular phonological patterns are brought into play at every step along a compositional path. In the present framework, these patterns are expressed as phonological schemas and viewed as freely available resources exploited by constructions in their characterization of the composite phonological structure.

Let us focus here on the phonological incorporation that triggers such reorganization. An initial comment is that incorporation is more the rule than the exception. Although linguists are accustomed to thinking in terms of one component structure being juxtaposed or adjoined to another, this conception is more a reflection of the building-block metaphor than of linguistic reality. The phonological integration of two structures virtually always results in realignment at some level of unipolar organization; for instance, the suffixation of *-ing* to *work* induces a resyllabification, wherein the *k* shifts from being syllable-final to syllable-initial (or at least ambisyllabic). It appears, moreover, that *-ing*, $PERF_3$, and $PERF_4$ must be analyzed as combining with a potentially complex structure, within which they attach to the head in particular. If we were only dealing with expressions like *been working*, it might be possible to maintain that the grammatical constituency matches the phonological constituency (i.e. that $PERF_4$ and *be_1* form a grammatical constituent, rather than $PERF_4$ combining with [be_1 [-ing [work]]] as a whole). However, other cases suggest that these morphemes must in fact "look for" the head in a complex structure.[20] For example, when *-ing* combines with what is clearly

[20] They are parallel in this respect to the English plural morpheme, which is manifested on the second element of a compound (its profile determinant) even though it applies to the type specification provided by the compound as a whole: *cameramen*, but not **camerasman* or **cameramans*. (See 4.1.1.)

a complex verb, such as *pick up*, it can only suffix to the verbal head: *picking up*, not **pick upping*. Cases where the participialized stem is modified by an adverb (e.g. *be quietly working*) point to the same conclusion.

With its notion of dependent morphemes (Vol. 1, 9.1.3), cognitive grammar handles such constructions unproblematically. The phonological characterization of a dependent morpheme is precisely analogous to that of a dependent predication: it resides in the mapping between a standard, which serves as e-site, and a target, which determines the organization of the composite expression (cf. Fig. 5.1). Thus, if *-ing* always combined with a structure consisting phonologically of just a single stem, its phonological pole would be as follows: [[. . .]---->[. . . ing]]. That is, the stem (given schematically as [. . .]) is mapped onto a structure consisting of the same phonological sequence augmented by *ing*. However, because this morpheme in fact combines with larger structures, within which it attaches specifically to the stem representing the semantic head, its actual description is more elaborate: [[. . . $(. . .)_H$ . . .]---->[. . . (. . . $ing)_H$ . . .]]. Of course, $(. . .)_H$ is simply a convenient abbreviation for the appropriate stem, which is easily characterized in terms of constructs available within the theory. It is identifiable with reference to a particular configuration of semantic structures and symbolic relationships: the semantic head is the profile determinant, i.e. the component structure whose profile corresponds to the composite structure profile, and $(. . .)_H$ is the profile determinant's phonological pole.

In sum, unipolar and bipolar constituency represent independent and often cross-cutting dimensions of hierarchical structure that are simultaneously valid and inherently accommodated in the basic organizational scheme of cognitive grammar. The point is general, but it is particularly important in the case of the English auxiliary: without referring to words, much of the auxiliary's grammatical behavior cannot be described succinctly. Pullum and Wilson have rightly pointed out (1977, p. 747) that a number of well-known rules, which were stated rather awkwardly in early transformational analyses, are more easily formulated if allowed to mention "the first word of the auxiliary." For example, the first word of the auxiliary occurs before the subject in certain questions (***Have** they been examined?*; *When **will** he be exercising?*), and *not* appears after the first word when used for normal clausal negation (*That **was** not being discussed*; *I **did** not object*). Furthermore, various sorts of ellipsis allow a portion of the verb group to remain unexpressed, but the overt portion is always measured in words, not fragments thereof:

(24)(a) *Phil **has been interviewed**, and Merv **has been** too.*
(b) *Phil **has been interviewed**, and Merv **has** too.*

(25)(a) *She **will have been working** longer than I **will have been**.*
(b) *She **will have been working** longer than I **will have**.*
(c) *She **will have been working** longer than I **will**.*

Although we will not now attempt to describe these constructions, it seems apparent that both unipolar and bipolar constituents must figure in an overall account of auxiliary structure.

5.3.4. *Auxiliary Verbs*

A final issue is whether it is indeed possible, as suggested earlier, to provide a semantic characterization of auxiliary verbs in English. Though it might not be essential (given other options available in the theory), such a characterization would afford a straightforward way of referring to auxiliaries as a class and would thus facilitate the statement of certain grammatical patterns. The verbs in question are *be*$_1$, *be*$_2$, the perfect *have*, the auxiliary *do*, and a limited set of modals (including *can*, *may*, *will*, *shall*, *must*, and maybe others). From a functional standpoint, this is not a homogeneous group: the modals are grounding predications, whereas *be* and *have* belong to the clausal head; and while *do* is also analyzed as part of the clausal head, it only appears in the absence of any other auxiliary when one is needed for grammatical purposes. Yet these verbs do behave alike in various ways, as noted above.

An auxiliary verb can be characterized (at least for English) as **a verb whose conceptual content in the objective axis is limited to a fully schematic process**. On the other hand, a content verb is one that represents the designated process with at least a minimal degree of specificity. Though its meaning may be tenuous or hard to describe, even the most abstract content verb provides some information about the profile beyond its processual character. Consider *do*, for example. When it functions as a content verb, *do* is extraordinarily vague about the nature of the process it refers to—it is even used in questions and anaphoric expressions:

(26)(a) *What should I do?*
(b) *Laverne apologized, and Shirley did so too.*

Still, despite a certain amount of variability, *do* always conveys some notion of activity or some kind of volitionality or control on the part of the subject. Its use is odd when these are totally absent:

(27)(a) **Laverne likes spinach, and Shirley does so too.*
(b) **God exists, and Nietzsche does so too.*

By contrast, the auxiliary *do* occurs with any content verb and refers to any sort of process (*Does Laverne exist?*; *Does Nietzsche like spinach?*).

Assuming its basic plausibility, we must spell out more explicitly the intended import of the definition. Each auxiliary verb of English is analyzed as having the following properties: (1) it is in fact a verb, i.e. it profiles a process; (2) its objectively construed content is essentially limited to the conception of a process; and (3) this conception has virtually no content beyond that implied by the very notion of a process—it is maximally schematic in regard to both the nature of the relationship and the domain in which it is manifested. Observe that the processes referred to in (1) and (2) are usually but not necessarily the same (for *have* we need to distinguish them). Also, because the schematicity demanded by (3) applies only to relationships along the objective axis, this definition does not prevent auxiliary verbs from contrasting semantically and even having substantial conceptual content.

The auxiliary verb *do* is the best exemplar of this category, for it profiles a fully schematic process and has no additional conceptual content. To be sure, a certain amount of content is inherent in the notion of a process: it invokes the domain of conceived time, together with whatever content is required to support the notion of a relation (as opposed to a thing). However, *do* supplies nothing beyond this bare minimum; it does not specify the domain with respect to which the component states are characterized, nor even whether the profiled relationship is stable or changes through time. A comparable level of abstraction is displayed by the two variants of *be* that function as auxiliary verbs. Be_1 differs from *do* by indicating that the profiled relationship is constant through time, but it provides no specific information about the nature of this relation. Be_2 is neutral in regard to perfectivity; although, as the passive variant, it indicates that the process has two nominal participants, any further content it might have is extremely rarified.

The modals, to be discussed in Ch. 6, clearly have substantial conceptual content. However, they are analyzed as reflecting the second degree of subjectification (Fig. 5.6(c)), so this content is aligned along the subjective axis. The objectively construed content is limited to a fully schematic process, which is elaborated by the clausal head. This process functions as the profile: since modals are grounding predications, they profile the grounded entity rather than the grounding relationship. The meaning of *have* also hinges on a relationship in the subjective axis; it designates a subjectively construed relation of anteriority and current relevance to a temporal reference point (Fig. 5.10). In the objective axis, it does invoke the conception of a fully schematic process, which represents the anterior, currently relevant event. What distinguishes *have* from the other auxiliaries is that this process is not in profile—it is instead a relational landmark, construed atemporally and elaborated by a perfect participle. Thus, if *do* is the prototypical auxiliary verb, *have* is a peripheral (or at least non-central) member of the category.

CHAPTER 6

The Auxiliary: Grounding

THE ENGLISH AUXILIARY is not a grammatical constituent. Rather, it comprises a series of predications that fulfill a particular semantic function: collectively, they convert the initial process type specified by a content verb into the grounded process instance profiled by a finite clause. Examined in Ch. 5 were the auxiliary elements of the clausal head (functionally equivalent to a head noun); from the type specification provided by the content verb, these predications of voice and aspect derive a higher-order type, an instance of which is grounded and designated by the clause as a whole. Traditionally, the elements that effect this grounding are recognized as part of the auxiliary and described semantically as indicating **tense** and **modality**. In this chapter, we will first consider the grounding predications as a coherent system. Tense and the modals will then be separately discussed in more detail.

6.1. Epistemic Distance

Among the auxiliary elements, tense and the modals stand out as being special in various ways. Tense was the only element specified as obligatory in Chomsky's original description of the auxiliary (1957). And while modals clearly function as auxiliary verbs (in regard to question formation, the placement of *not*, and so on), they differ from *have*, *be*, and *do* in several respects. For one thing, modals do not show agreement with the subject: *I have* vs. *he has*; *I am* vs. *he is*; *I do* vs. *he does*; but *I will/he will*, *I may/he may*, *I must/he must*, etc. Indeed, they are often considered morphologically defective—a modal has only a "present-tense" and a "past-tense" form (e.g. *may* vs. *might*) and cannot be rendered as a past participle (**mayen*), a present participle (**maying*), or an infinitive (**to may*). Modals are further different from *have* and *be* in that they cannot occur after another auxiliary (**have mayen*; **be maying*), and also in that the following verb is uninflected: *must criticize* (cf. *have criticiz**ed***; *be criticiz**ed***; *be criticiz**ing***).

Naturally, attempts have been made to explain such peculiarities. For example, both McCawley (1971) and Pullum and Wilson (1977) have argued that the inability of modals to follow another auxiliary is a consequence of their defective morphology: *have* and *be* require that the following verb be inflected as a past or present participle, but a modal has no participial form. A mechanical explanation of this sort is clearly unsatisfactory. Why should modals be defective in the first place? And could the fact that *all* of them are defective be nothing more than a grand coincidence? I find it far more plausible to suppose that semantic factors are responsible. Indeed, I will argue that the special properties of tense and the modals are readily accounted for once their meaning and semantic function are properly understood.

An initial view of the tense-modality system (roughly that of Chomsky 1957) can be outlined as follows. (1) There are two tenses: present (PRES) and past (PAST). (2) There are five basic modals: *may*, *can*, *shall*, *will*, and *must*. (3) Tense is obligatory in a finite clause, but the presence of a modal is optional. (4) When a modal is chosen, it is marked for tense; otherwise, tense is borne by the first auxiliary verb (if there is one) or the main verb. (5) Present tense is marked by either zero or *-s*, depending on person (*I work*; *she works*); past tense is marked in a variety of ways. (6) The modals take zero for the present tense (e.g. *may + PRES = may*), regardless of person (*I may*; *she may*). (7) In the past tense, the modals have special forms: *may + PAST = might*; *can + PAST = could*; *shall + PAST = should*; *will + PAST = would*; *must + PAST = must*.

While this account provides the right set of forms, it is problematic in certain respects. One issue is whether English does indeed have a present-tense morpheme, since *-s* can be analyzed as marking third-person singular, while in other persons the bare stem is used for the present. We must also ask whether *must* is invariable because its past tense is marked by zero, or whether it simply has no past-tense form. More seriously, the account is known to be inadequate from the standpoint of meaning. For one thing, to speak of "tense" (i.e. location in time relative to the ground) is an oversimplification. It is a truism that the "present tense" has uses where the situation described is not located at the time of speaking; it may, for example, be employed for future events (*The tournament starts tomorrow*) or in "timeless" statements (*Energy equals mass times the square of the speed of light*). With modals, the "past tense" does not in general indicate past time: the contrast between *I may be interested* and *I might be interested* pertains to degree of likelihood rather than temporal location. Furthermore, modals are polysemous (e.g. *may* signals either permission or possibility), and the meanings of their "past-tense" forms appear not to be derivable in any regular fashion—note, for instance, that even though *shall* and *will* are often interchangeable, *should* and *would* are quite different.

A more adequate analysis of the grounding predications will have to be

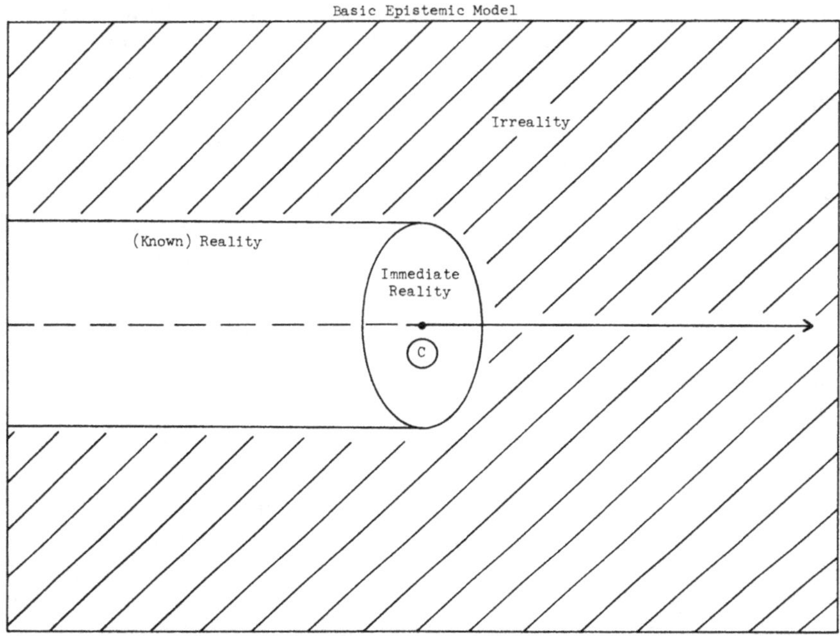

Fig. 6.1

based on a clear understanding of their conceptual import. This in turn requires the description of certain idealized cognitive models, which function as the cognitive domains in terms of which these meanings are characterized. The models underlying basic predications of tense-modality are naturally quite abstract, involving fundamental notions of the world and our place within it. At this juncture, three such models are relevant. Although they may in fact represent indissociable aspects of a single elaborate conception, for analytical purposes it is convenient to discuss them individually.

The first, labeled the **basic epistemic model**, is sketched in Fig. 6.1. Its essential notion is that certain situations (or "states of affairs") are accepted by a particular conceptualizer (C) as being real, whereas others are not. Collectively, the situations accorded that status constitute C's conception of **known reality** (which for now I will simply refer to as **reality** unless there is some need to make a distinction).[1] Reality is neither simple nor static, but an ever-evolving entity whose evolution continuously augments the complexity of the structure already defined by its previous history; the cylinder depicting

[1] One is reminded of the opening line of Wittgenstein's *Tractatus* (1922): "The world is everything that is the case." An important difference, however, is that the basic epistemic model pertains not to absolute truth, but rather to what a particular person knows (or thinks he knows). Also, I will understand the term "world" more concretely (6.2.3.1).

it should thus be imagined as "growing" along the axis indicated by the arrow. The leading edge of this expanding structure (i.e. the face of the cylinder) is termed **immediate reality**. It is from this vantage point—from reality at the latest stage of its evolution—that C views things, and he has direct perceptual access only to portions of this region. **Irreality** comprises everything other than (known) reality. It is important to bear in mind that a situation does not belong to reality or irreality on the basis of how the world has actually evolved, but depends instead on whether the conceptualizer knows and accepts it as being part of that evolutionary sequence.

Starting from this basic conception, distinct (though compatible) elaborations yield the other two models. The first of these, depicted in Fig. 6.2(a), will be called the **elaborated epistemic model**. To the basic epistemic model, it adds the conceptualizer's realization that reality as he knows it is not exhaustive of the world and its evolutionary history. The core of known reality is thus surrounded by a much larger region of **unknown reality**. Included in this region are situations of at least two sorts: those whose reality C suspects or contemplates but does not accept as having been established; and those of which he is entirely ignorant. Observe that unknown reality is part of irreality, of which the remainder constitutes **non-reality**.

The other elaboration of the basic epistemic model, dubbed the **time-line model** and diagrammed in Fig. 6.2(b), incorporates two additional notions. One is time (t), specifically conceived as the axis along which reality evolves.[2] Additionally, the time-line model invokes the conception of the ground (G), i.e. the speech event and its circumstances. The locus of a speech event is immediate reality, and from that vantage point the speaker and hearer conceptualize an expression's meaning. It is linguistically significant that an act of speech is not punctual but has a brief temporal duration, as indicated by the squiggly line. A certain time depth must therefore be attributed to both the ground and the immediate reality associated with a speech event, and on this basis time is segmentable into past, present, and future. On the strictest construal, the present coincides exactly with the time of speaking.

These cognitive models enable us to start making sense of the tense-modality system. They bear in particular on the oft-raised issue of whether, in the case of English, it is proper to speak of "tense" at all, since futurity is expressed by a modal, the "past-tense" inflection does not invariably indicate past time, and the "present" is both semantically heterogeneous and marked by zero. On the other hand, the past-present-future division seems intuitively compelling (I would hazard a guess that few linguists have investigated tense without at some point drawing a time line). An analysis will be proposed that succeeds in reconciling these apparently conflicting observations. It employs

[2] To what extent our conception of time is independent of (or derives from) our experience of changing reality is an interesting question that fortunately lies outside our purview.

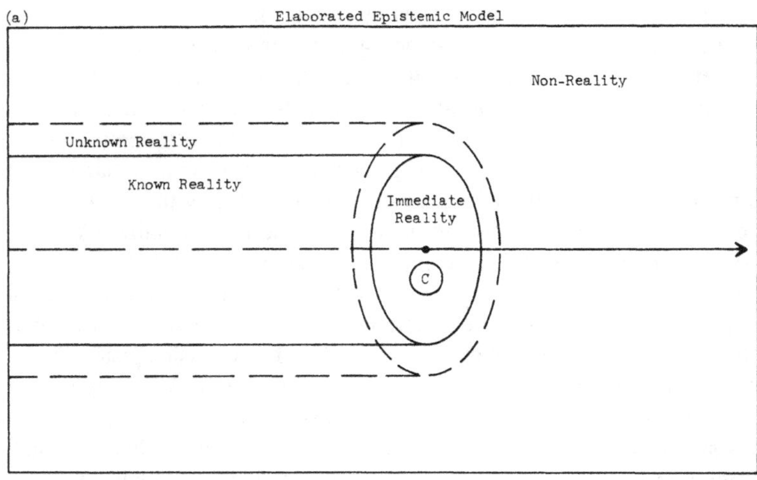

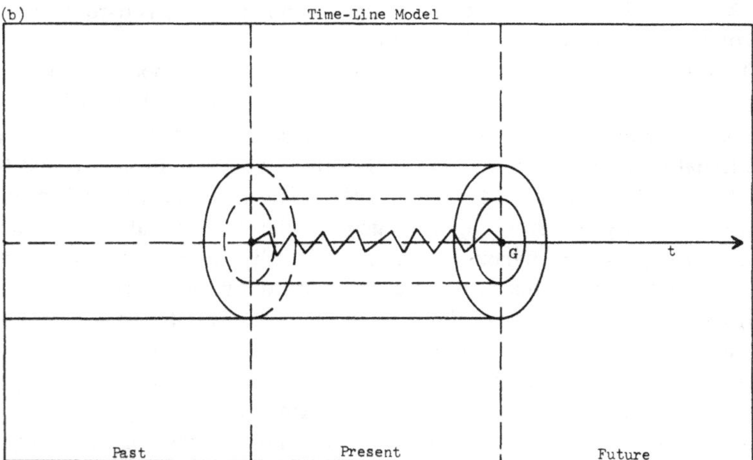

Fig. 6.2

the basic epistemic model, where time per se is not a factor, for the *schematic* characterization of all the grounding elements; at the schematic level, the system is purely one of modality. However, some of these elements also have more specific, *prototypical* values that evoke the time-line model and can thus be regarded as tense predications. As for the elaborated epistemic model, we will see that it plays a central role in characterizing certain uses of the modals.

Every finite clause is grounded, by definition. In English, the requisite grounding is effected by the tense-modal complex, which—though analyzable to some degree—counts as a single predication from the standpoint of fulfilling that semantic function.[3] Because an epistemic predication profiles the grounded entity (not the subjectively construed grounding relationship), the tense-modal complex designates a schematic process, which it locates vis-à-vis the ground in an "epistemic" domain. This schematic process serves as e-site, being elaborated by the clausal head. Grounding is thereby imposed on the specific process designated by the head, and the verb from which the head inherits this profile (i.e. its own head, or profile determinant) is referred to as the grounded verb (5.1).

At the schematic level, all the grounding elements are characterized with reference to the basic epistemic model (Fig. 6.1), with the speaker identified as the conceptualizer. The core system is simple and elegant. Formally, there are two oppositions: the presence vs. the absence of a modal, and the presence vs. the absence of the "past-tense" morpheme (the "present" being marked by zero). Each formal opposition signals a conceptual opposition, and does so iconically, in that zero represents the default-case option in which the designated process is directly accessible to the speaker, while the overt element marks some kind of separation. In the case of modals, the contrast pertains to speaker knowledge: the zero option indicates that the speaker accepts the designated process as part of known reality, whereas a modal specifically places it in the realm of irreality. The other opposition is based on an abstract notion of proximity, so instead of "present" vs. "past" we can speak more generally of a **proximal/distal** constrast in the epistemic sphere. The import of the unmarked (zero) member is that the designated process is **immediate** to the speaker. Its overtly-marked counterpart—what we can now call the distal morpheme—conveys some sort of non-immediacy. The intersection of these two oppositions yields four basic types of grounding predications. Each situates the designated process in a particular epistemic region: *immediate reality*, *non-immediate reality*, *immediate irreality*, or *non-immediate irreality*.

Both conceptually and formally, the predication of immediate reality represents the unmarked option. It is unmarked conceptually because the speaker, in tracing a mental path to specify the location of a process, takes his own position in immediate reality as the origin. Moreover, since reality is signalled by the absence of a modal, and immediacy by the absence of the distal morpheme, it is formally zero as well. The zero-marked grounding predication is therefore analyzed as deriving its primary value from a pair of oppositions characterized with reference to the basic epistemic model—it is not, fundamentally, a tense predication. Nevertheless, immediate reality co-

[3] In this regard it is quite analogous to an English demonstrative. Indeed, definiteness (presupposed mental contact with a referent) is very similar to the acceptance of a situation as part of known reality, and the proximal/distal contrast in demonstratives corresponds to the PRES/PAST opposition.

incides temporally with the time of speaking, so to the extent that the notion of time is specifically invoked, present time is conceived as one facet of immediate reality. Because the basic epistemic model is elaborated in cognitively salient fashion by the time-line model, the predication of immediate reality can be interpreted more concretely as one of present time.

In precisely analogous fashion, the predication of non-immediate reality is equivalent to one of past time. Formally, it is signalled by the absence of a modal and the presence of the distal morpheme, which respectively indicate that the profiled process is part of known reality, but that it is not immediate to the speaker. These notions are basically epistemic, i.e. they do not refer specifically to time, yet they have an obvious interpretation with reference to the time-line model: since reality subsumes the past and present (but not the future), and immediate reality constitutes the present, the temporal projection of non-immediate reality can only be the past. Presumably, then, the distal morpheme has a prototypical value that invokes the time-line model and is reasonably considered a past-tense predication. That, however, is only one manifestation of its basic epistemic import.

A modal places the designated process in the region of irreality. As a very rough first approximation, the modals can be described as contrasting with one another because they situate the process at varying distances from the speaker's position at immediate known reality.[4] *Must*, for example, places it very close to known reality—the speaker has deduced that accepting it as real seems warranted (though he has not yet taken that final step)—whereas *may* implies only that he regards the situation as compatible with what he knows. The alternate forms of the modals (*may/might*; *will/would*; *shall/should*; *can/could*) are analyzed as reflecting the presence vs. the absence of the distal morpheme (e.g. *may* + *DIST* = *might*); the invariant *must* is claimed not to have a distal form. Importantly, DIST signals non-immediacy rather than past time (which does, however, count as one possible type of non-immediacy). It is evident that the distal form of the modal does in each case indicate a greater epistemic distance than the zero form; *might*, for instance, suggests a more tenuous possibility than *may*. That the distal meanings are to some degree variable and idiosyncratic is unproblematic in cognitive grammar, where partial compositionality is taken as the norm (Vol. 1, Ch. 12), and where established expressions are expected to have a number of related senses.

Hence the zero and distal forms of the modals respectively locate the designated process in *immediate* and *non-immediate irreality*. These terms are

[4]Cf. Langacker 1978. For the moment we will confine our attention to the **epistemic** values of the modals, i.e. those pertaining solely to degree of likelihood. The **root** values (involving obligation, permission, etc.) are considered in 6.3, which offers a more elaborate semantic analysis based on force dynamics.

not quite self-explanatory, so let us be clear about their intended import. The terms should *not* be taken as suggesting that, on the basis of epistemic distance, irreality is divisible in any absolute or consistent way into two discrete zones; observe, for instance, that the distal form *should* expresses greater likelihood (lesser epistemic distance) than the zero form *may*. The notion of non-immediacy must instead be assessed with respect to the distance implied by each individual modal. More precisely, the distal predication indicates that the modal's epistemic distance is not computed directly from immediate reality, but rather from a point that is somehow removed from it. For example, if *Jeff will finish on time* conveys that Jeff's finishing on time is predictable with some confidence on the basis of present reality, then *Jeff would finish on time* makes a comparable extrapolation with reference to some hypothetical situation (e.g. . . . *if he had more help*). Granted an analysis along these lines, a functional explanation can be offered for *must* not having a distal form: *must* has a special place in the system, representing the minimum possible epistemic distance consistent with modal status; though it could in principle have a distal form, there is a sense in which any increase in epistemic distance would run directly counter to its *raison d'être*.

Several brief points will conclude this initial statement of the analysis. First, a grounding predication is posited for a finite clause even when it has no overt manifestation (e.g. *They like her*). Thus, among the grounding elements is one that is phonologically zero (i.e. [[. . .]---->[. . .]]) and locates the profiled process in immediate reality. Second, what is traditionally known as "subject-verb agreement" is analyzed as being part of the grounding predication. A sentence such as *He likes her* is grounded by *-s*, which not only situates the designated process in immediate reality but also specifies that the trajector of that process is non-plural and third-person (i.e. distinct from the speech-act participants). Finally, it must be realized that the grounded clausal head represents a particular level of conceptual organization whose import is not absolute but may be overridden at higher levels. Standing alone as an assertion, *He likes her* indeed implies that the speaker accepts the profiled situation as part of immediate reality (11.4.1). However, in larger expressions such as *Perhaps he likes her*, *It is doubtful that he likes her*, or *The nurse believes that he likes her*, the conception of the situation being located in immediate reality is embedded as part of a larger conception which assesses its validity or confines it to a particular mental space.

Having outlined the analysis in preliminary fashion, let us now consider how the special properties of the tense-modality elements follow as direct consequences of their meaning and semantic function. The first such property is that tense appears to be the only auxiliary element that is obligatory. A more accurate statement, we can now observe, is that grounding is part of the very definition of a finite clause, so every such clause has some sort of grounding predication. The basic options—each of which carries a particular meaning—are the presence vs. the absence of a modal, and the presence vs. the absence of the distal predication. In this respect, tense (i.e. the proximal/distal contrast) and modality are exactly on a par. The only reason that tense is usually regarded as the sole obligatory element is that the zero form is erroneously taken as marking tense exclusively, its modal function being ignored.

Next, modals function as auxiliary verbs with respect to those grammatical constructions sensitive to "the first word of the auxiliary" (5.3.3). They do so because they are in fact auxiliary verbs by the definition of 5.3.4 and do have the status of words phonologically (note that the zero and distal predications meet the semantic definition but are not words). When present, a modal is the first word of the auxiliary because it takes the entire clausal head as its complement; it is a global regularity of English auxiliary constructions that an auxiliary verb precedes the structure that elaborates it. The fact that a modal has the entire clausal head for its complement is determined by its semantic function as a grounding predication and explains its inability to occur *inside* the clausal head as a complement of *have* or *be*.

Why is a modal morphologically defective? It cannot be rendered as a participle or an infinitive (**mayen*, **maying*, **to may*) because that would be inconsistent with its grounding function. *To* and the participial morphemes derive atemporal relations, but the grounding predication for a finite clause cannot be atemporalized—it must itself profile a schematic process. The fact that a modal does not agree with the subject (**She mays like it*) follows from our characterization of *-s*: it is itself a full grounding predication that situates the profiled process in immediate reality and specifies that its trajector is third-person singular; hence it does not occur with a modal, which places the designated process in the region of irreality.

Finally, the verb which follows a modal is uninflected (*She may like it*). This is due to the inherent restriction that a grounding predication and its head must represent the same grammatical class (as determined by their profiles); for clauses, each must be processual. Thus, because an infinitive or participle is atemporal, the complement of a modal must be a simple verb. Why is the following verb not inflected for tense or subject agreement? That is, why can we not say **She may likes it* or **She may liked it*? The reason is that the grounding elements constitute a single complex predication which combines as a whole with the clausal head, and more specifically with the immediately following verb (the grounded verb). When there is no modal, the grounded verb is inflected morphologically, since the non-modal grounding predications are phonologically dependent (*She {likes/liked} it*). However, the predications of irreality are phonologically autonomous, i.e. independent words, so their integration with the grounded verb results in a two-word sequence in which that verb is morphologically unchanged (*may like*).

6.2. Tense

In large measure, we have sustained the standard view that English has two tenses, present and past (future being marked by a modal). We have indeed posited two opposing predications, even though, phonologically, one of them is generally zero. And while their fundamental semantic characterization pertains to epistemic distance, they are prototypically construed with reference to the time-line model, where—for situations accepted as real—immediacy vs. non-immediacy translate into present vs. past time. Thus, to the extent that we confine our attention to such uses, it is quite reasonable to follow tradition and speak of a present-tense/past-tense contrast.

However, it is also traditionally observed that the tense morphemes do not invariably signal present and past time, even when they occur without a modal. Present-tense verbs appear to describe not only situations that obtain at the time of speaking, but past, future, hypothetical, and even timeless situations as well:

(1)(a) *The mop is in the garage.*
(b) *This scruffy-looking student comes into my office yesterday and says he wants a loan.*
(c) *The train leaves in seven minutes.*
(d) *If he is really intelligent, he does a good job of hiding it.*
(e) *2 is the only even prime number.*

Furthermore, some instances of the past-tense morpheme have been analyzed as the present tense in disguise. For example, if Zelda utters (2)(a), using the present tense, her statement can later be reported as in (2)(b), with a past-tense verb in the subordinate clause:

(2)(a) *I am pregnant.*
(b) *Zelda said that she was pregnant.*

The tense marking on the lower verb is often attributed to a "sequence-of-tenses" rule, which supposedly makes the verb of a subordinate clause agree in tense with that of the main clause under certain conditions. By this analysis, the past-tense marking is grammatically induced and does not indicate past time.

There may, however, be better ways of describing these constructions. Indeed, I suspect that what seems to be the most naive view of present and past tense—namely, that they consistently mark present and past time—is probably correct. I therefore propose that we take this idea seriously and see how far we can push it.

6.2.1. *A Naive Characterization*

In the absence of a modal, grounding predications locate the profiled process within the realm of reality, where the proximal and distal morphemes are susceptible to a temporal construal. They can therefore be regarded as tense morphemes, and in many uses, they clearly indicate that the designated process occurs in the present or in the past with reference to the time of speaking. The issue before us is how consistently they assume these values, and how narrowly the notions 'present' and 'past' can be interpreted. If it is viable, one would like to maintain the strongest possible claim, to the effect that the tense morphemes *always* mean 'present' and 'past' in a very narrow sense. The following characterization is thus proposed for all non-modal uses: **PRES indicates the occurrence of a full instantiation of the profiled process that precisely coincides with the time of speaking; PAST indicates the occurrence of a full instantiation of the profiled process prior to the time of speaking.** Our strategy will be to adopt this description as a working hypothesis and see where it leads us.

With canonical examples, this strict definition works unproblematically and lets us explain the interaction between tense and perfectivity (cf. Langacker 1982a, 1987b; Vol. 1, 7.2). The first observation to be accounted for is that any perfective or imperfective verb can occur in the past tense with its usual interpretation, i.e. it profiles a single instance of the process type in question. Although this may seem obvious, it is important to understand precisely why it should be so.

Consider first a past-tense perfective (e.g. *He learned it*), as diagrammed in Fig. 6.3(a). The squiggly line labeled G is the speech event, the heavy-line squiggle represents the profiled perfective process, and the ellipse indicates the objective scene (OS) or immediate scope of predication (recall that the objective scene is the general locus of viewing attention, and that the profile is confined to OS and constitutes its focal point). In a simple past-tense predication, OS is identified as some portion of known reality whose temporal projection precedes the time of speaking. Because there are no inherent constraints on the size of OS, it can always be construed as having sufficient temporal expanse to encompass a full instance of a perfective process, including its endpoints; for this reason perfective verbs freely occur in the simple past tense. A past-tense imperfective (e.g. *He knew it*) is similarly always possible. Represented by a straight line in Fig. 6.3(b), an imperfective process involves the continuation through time of a stable situation and has in-

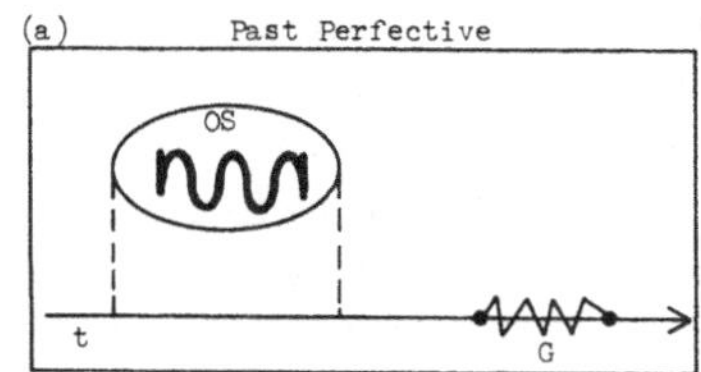

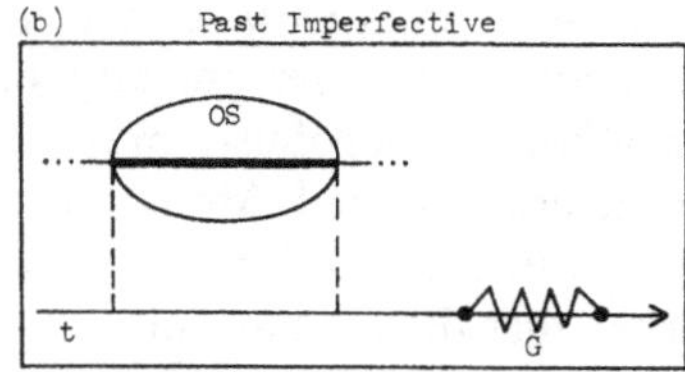

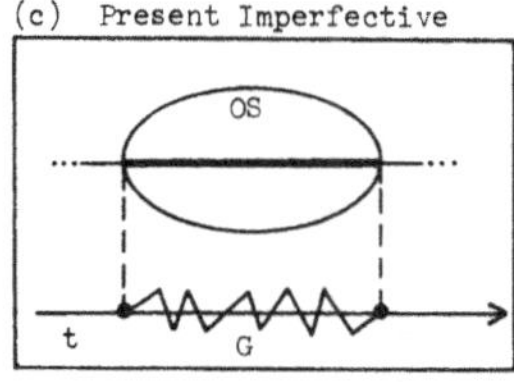

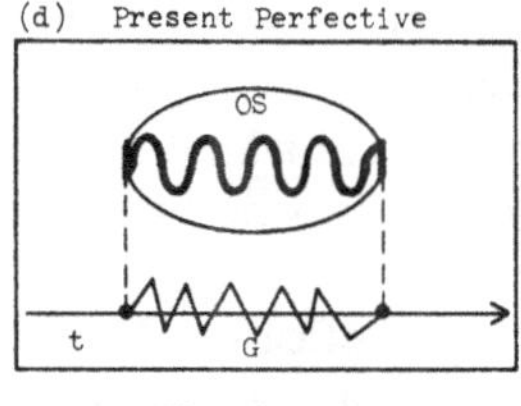

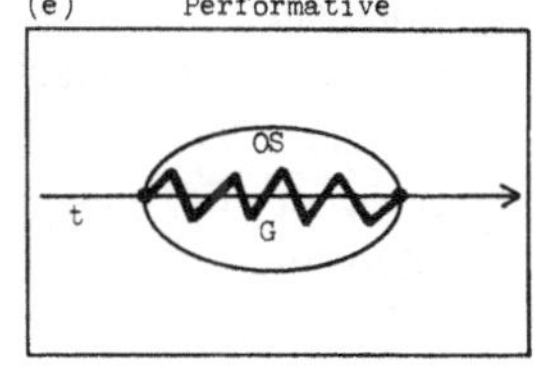

Fig. 6.3

definite temporal extension. Its crucial property is contractibility (1.1.3), whereby any sequence of component states constitutes a valid instance of the category. Suppose, then, that an imperfective process is not limited to the past but continues right through the time of speaking (e.g. *He knew the answer, and he still does*). In that case only part of the overall process is profiled by virtue of falling within the OS imposed by the past-tense predication, yet that part is sufficient to count as a category instance. A full instantiation of the process type thus occurs prior to G.

In the present tense, OS is some portion of immediate reality whose temporal extension is coincident with the speech event, as indicated in Fig. 6.3(c). Being thus tied to G, the duration of OS is not freely variable (as it is in the past), yet a present-tense imperfective is always possible (e.g. *He knows it*). The contractibility of an imperfective is once more responsible: for any such process that extends through the time of speaking, those component states which fall within OS constitute a full instantiation of the process type; and since OS delimits the profile, the designated process coincides exactly with the speech act. Of course, it is not implied that the situation tracked through time comes into existence with the onset of speaking and disappears once the utterance is completed—it is simply a matter of limiting the profile to that segment of its duration which coincides with the speech event, the situation being portrayed as stable for that period.

What about a present-tense perfective? By the strictest definition, a verb of this sort would profile a bounded process precisely coincident with the time of speaking, as diagrammed in Fig. 6.3(d). However, though this configuration is internally coherent, there are reasons why it generally cannot arise: the duration of an event is seldom equal to that of an utterance describing it, and perfectives lack the property of contractibility (hence the entire event—including its endpoints—must be profiled for it to count as a full instantiation of the process type). Moreover, even for an event that happens to be the right length, to describe it in the present tense (under the narrowest construal) requires that the speaker initiate his utterance simultaneously with the event's onset, before he has a chance to observe and identify it. A true present-tense perfective is therefore possible only under very special circumstances. A sentence such as *He learns it*, which appears to be an example, is actually interpreted in some other manner, e.g. as habitual (*He learns it every January and forgets it by March*) or perhaps as a kind of future (*He learns it by tomorrow or he doesn't get the job*). It does not receive the 'one instance right now' interpretation of Fig. 6.3(d).

There is, however, one class of cases where the coincidence of a perfective process with the time of speaking is not only possible but holds as a matter of definition. This is the class of **performative** sentences (Austin 1962). A performative is a sentence whose main verb names a type of speech act, and whose very utterance accomplishes that speech act (if all appropriate conditions are met):

(3)(a) *I **promise** to be home on time.*
(b) *I **order** you to desist immediately!*
(c) *I hereby **sentence** you to six months at hard labor.*

Performatives represent the special situation in which the speech event itself is objectified and goes onstage as the process profiled by a finite clause, as sketched in Fig. 6.3(e); they are processual counterparts to the pronouns *I* and *you*, which put a speech-event participant onstage as the designated entity (cf. Fig. 2.16(a)). Here their interest lies in the fact that they constitute a systematic exception to the generalization that perfectives do not occur in the simple present. In terms of our analysis, the exceptionality of performatives is predictable: when the speech event and profile are identical, the proposed definition of present tense is automatically satisfied.[5]

In summary, our naive characterization of PRES and PAST provides a natural explanation for the observed interaction between tense and perfectivity. Perhaps it is not so naive after all. To show its viability, however, we must deal with the apparently problematic cases cited at the outset. Let us first examine the sequence-of-tenses phenomenon, turning subsequently to special uses of the present.

[5]Observe that the performative use of a perfective verb actually renders it non-perfective, since perfectivity requires that the endpoints fall *within* the immediate scope of predication (OS), and not simply coincide with its boundaries (Vol. 1, 7.2.2). However, because grounding represents the final step in assembling the verb group, this has no structural consequences.

6.2.2. *Sequence of Tenses*

A sequence-of-tenses rule of the sort described earlier would be inconsistent with the principles of cognitive grammar. We must reject a rule that mechanically changes one verb to agree in tense with another, so that an overt marking for past or present tense is interpreted semantically as meaningless or as having the opposite value. There may well be grammatical constructions which specify the occurrence of one tense rather than the other, or even a particular combination of tenses, but such constructions must treat the tenses as meaningful elements. Each occurrence of a tense marking is presumed to be semantically motivated in some fashion.

6.2.2.1. *Indirect Speech.* Why might one posit a sequence-of-tenses rule? An apparent basis is the observation that a past-tense form can be used to report the content of a previous present-tense utterance, as in (2)(b) *Zelda said that she was pregnant* (when Zelda's exact words were *I am pregnant*). However, to claim that a subordinate-clause verb in English mechanically agrees in tense with the main verb would clearly be untenable, if only because all possible combinations of tenses occur:

(4)(a) *Jeff says he is tired.* [PRES,PRES]
(b) *Jeff says he was tired.* [PRES,PAST]
(c) *Jeff said he is tired.* [PAST,PRES]
(d) *Jeff said he was tired.* [PAST,PAST]

More significantly, each combination produces a different meaning. Examples (4)(a) and (b) describe Jeff's present contention about being tired, a situation he ascribes to the present and the past, respectively. In (c) and (d), Jeff's statement occurred in the past, and in both instances Jeff probably used the present tense and said *I am tired*. By choosing (c), the speaker implies that Jeff was describing a condition that he envisaged as lasting for some time, long enough to encompass the time of the speaker's own utterance. There is no such implication in (d), which indicates only that Jeff's statement pertained to the situation in effect at the time he made it.

For sentences like these, which describe another speech event, it is important to distinguish between the actual speaker (S), who is responsible for the sentence as a whole, and the **surrogate speaker** (S′)—Jeff in this instance—whose speech is being reported and who is responsible only for the essential content of the subordinate clause. The actual speaker has a certain conception of reality (R), which includes himself and the actual ground (G). The surrogate speaker is similarly part of a **surrogate ground** (G′), i.e. the supposed circumstances of the speech event being described, and is attributed his own conception of reality (R′). To indicate that S and S′ entertain their respective reality conceptions, we will employ the notations S(R) and S′(R′) (cf. 3.1.2).

Both R and R′ are mental spaces, and an essential property of sentences like (4) is that one such space is embedded in another.[6] One facet of what the speaker (S) portrays in (4) as his own conception of reality (R) is that S′ describes a situation of tiredness (T) as being part of R′. Abstracting away from certain details, we thus have the following configuration: $S(_R \ldots S'(_{R'} \ldots T \ldots _{R'}) \ldots _R)$. It is situation T that represents the essential content of the subordinate clause. Crucially, S and S′ have different perspectives on this situation and describe it accordingly. Let us see how this works for the specific examples of sentences (c) and (d).

In his original statement, S′ (i.e. Jeff) views situation T from the vantage point of G′ (which for him, of course, constitutes the actual ground rather than the surrogate ground). He may regard T as a situation of some duration, or it may be just momentary, but provided that it is stable through a period that temporally subsumes G′, he describes it by means of a present-tense imperfective (*I am tired*). The profile thus comprises the portion of T's existence delimited by OS′, which coincides with the time of speaking (cf. Fig. 6.3(c)). At a later moment, the actual speaker, S, reports Jeff's statement from the perspective of G. From that vantage point, Jeff's utterance appears as a discrete event situated in past reality, so S describes it using a past-tense perfective (*Jeff said*). S must also convey the import of Jeff's utterance, and for this purpose he employs a finite subordinate clause. But how, exactly, is the form of that clause determined?

One option permitted by English is a direct quotation, in which S is obliged to echo the exact words of S′ (*Jeff said "I am tired"*). However, the expressions that concern us invoke the construction for "indirect speech," in which the original statement is not quoted but simply reported. The subordinate clause in this construction represents a recapitulation by S of what S′ said—but in his own words, and from his own vantage point at G. S′ has put forth a certain conception of situation T and its epistemic status, and while S must be reasonably faithful to that conception from the standpoint of its essential content, the description reflects his own construal with respect to imagic factors such as profiling and deictic reference point. In referring to Jeff, for example, S does not use the pronoun *I*, but rather *he*; with G as the vantage point, person is computed with reference to S, from whose perspective S′ is third-person (i.e. neither speaker nor hearer).

The tense of the subordinate clause must also be computed with reference to G. Let us first consider (4)(d), *Jeff said he was tired*, which is diagrammed in Fig. 6.4(a). In Jeff's original present-tense utterance, the ground was G′,

[6] Naturally, reported speech is not alone in having this property; Fauconnier 1985 affords some appreciation of its ubiquity.

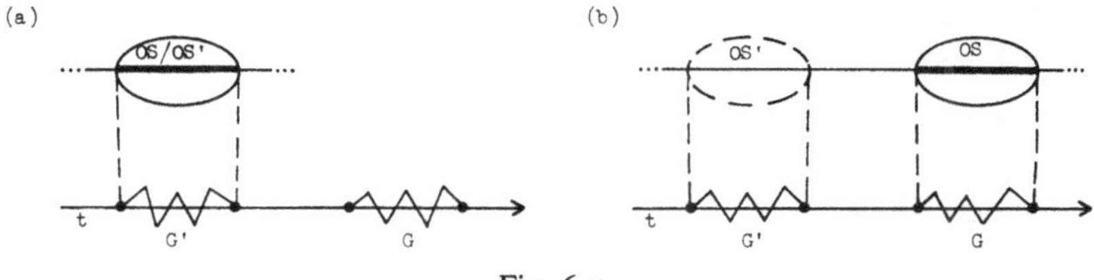

Fig. 6.4

the objective scene OS′ was temporally coincident with G′, and the profile was that portion of T delimited by OS′. Sentence (4)(d) reports this utterance with the smallest possible adjustment: the vantage point is shifted from G′ to G, but no change is made in either the locus of viewing attention (hence OS = OS′) or the profile. Although the profiled segment of T is part of immediate reality with respect to G′, from the perspective of G it belongs to past reality, and the past-tense form of the verb is used as a consequence. Observe that S is not himself asserting the existence of T at that location in past reality—he is merely reporting what S′ said. He does so by describing T as if it has the epistemic status that S′ imputes to it, but as it appears from G rather than G′.

With (4)(c), *Jeff said he is tired*, there is a slightly greater disparity between the original utterance and its later description. As shown in Fig. 6.4(b), S interprets S′ as having attributed to situation T a temporal duration sufficient to extend through the actual speech event (G), even though the expression specifically profiled only that portion of T coincident with G′ (i.e. immediate reality at the time of speaking). The subordinate clause in (4)(c) not only shifts the vantage point from G′ to G but also adjusts OS and hence the profile as well: the focus is placed on T's manifestation in current reality, at G, whereas S′ was more concerned with G′. But this change in emphasis is a matter of imagery, not of content, so it is permissible provided that S is correct in his assessment of what S′ intended.

That tense is determined in this manner follows from a broader generalization concerning epistemic predications in English: in ordinary speech (i.e. ignoring direct quotation and certain literary styles), a grounding predication always takes the actual ground (G) for its deictic reference point, never a surrogate ground (G′). Even when S employs a subordinate clause to describe the mental world of another individual S′ (his thoughts, beliefs, statements, feelings, etc.), a grounding predication in that clause reflects the vantage point of S rather than S′. Hence the demonstrative in (5)(a) can only be interpreted as meaning that the window is close to the actual speaker (not to Sarah), and the present tense of *is* indicates that the situation of the window being stuck continues through the current speech event (not just the time of Sarah's statement).

(5)(a) *Sarah said that* ***this*** *window* ***is*** *stuck.*
(b) *Sam felt that he should* ***immediately*** *go* ***upstairs****.*

By contrast, the non-epistemic deictics *immediately* and *upstairs* in (5)(b) take as their respective reference points the time at which Sam experienced his feeling and his spatial location at that time.

6.2.2.2. *Reported Modals.* Often (if not always), the historical evolution of a grounding predication involves abstraction and subjectification. True epistemic predications display both properties that result from subjectification of the second type (Fig. 5.6(c)): G is obligatorily taken as a reference point; yet the relationship involving G remains "offstage" and unprofiled (hence the construal of G is maximally subjective, given that it has a crucial role in the predication). It is for this reason that a grounding predication profiles the grounded entity rather than the grounding relationship; a demonstrative, for example, profiles a thing and constitutes a schematic nominal, while a tense predication designates a process and is thus a schematic finite clause. On the other hand, a non-epistemic deictic such as *immediately* or *upstairs* need not take G for its reference point, and the relationship anchored by that reference point is profiled (the predication is therefore a stative relation). One also finds intermediate cases, i.e. deictic expressions that obligatorily take G as a reference point but profile the relation in which it figures. *Yesterday* and *tomorrow* have this character:

(6)(a) *Jill said that she would finish* ***yesterday****.*
(b) *Jill said she might help us* ***tomorrow****.*

Even when construed as part of the subordinate clause, these adverbs situate the finishing or the helping with respect to G, not to G′ (thus, if Jill spoke on Monday and today is Friday, the finishing was projected for Thursday, and the helping for Saturday). However, they are not grounding predications, for rather than profiling a schematic process, they designate the relationship that such a process bears to G. Hence they too are stative relations (cf. *The game was yesterday; The concert is tomorrow*).

Sentences like those in (6) have also been analyzed as showing the application of a sequence-of-tenses rule. We can suppose that Jill's actual words were *I will finish Thursday* and *I may help you Saturday*, but in the subordinate clause describing her statement, *will* is reported as *would*, and *may* as *might*. The sequence-of-tenses rule would achieve this result by changing the modal from its present- to its past-tense form to agree with *said* in the main clause. Indeed, this behavior provides the main evidence that modals such as *would* and *might* are still analyzable as being related to *will* and *may*, and that the distinction is one of tense.

The implausibility of this agreement-rule approach should now be evident. If the discrepancy between the form of the original utterance and that of a subordinate clause reporting it is to be handled by syntactic derivation, then it is not enough to posit such a rule for tense: additional rules are needed to change the form of pronouns (from *I* to *she*, and from *you* to *us*), and to convert one adverb into another, e.g. *Thursday* into *yesterday* (provided that the overall speech event is on Friday—other syntactic rules would be in effect on other days of the week). Apart from being unworkable, mechanical rules of this sort would miss the unifying generalization that the reporting clause has just the form one expects if its essential content is described from the vantage point of G rather than G′. And though we must indeed postulate a synchronic relationship between the members of each modal pair (*will/would*, *may/might*, etc.), I will argue that even in examples like (6) it is best regarded as a proximal/distal contrast, not one of tense.

The agreement-rule analysis is undermined once more by the fact that any combination of proximal/distal predications can occur in the main and subordinate clauses, each combination resulting in a different meaning:

(7)(a) *Jill says she may help us.* [PROX,PROX]
(b) *Jill says she might help us.* [PROX,DIST]
(c) *Jill said she may help us.* [DIST,PROX]
(d) *Jill said she might help us.* [DIST,DIST]

According to the first two sentences, Jill subscribes at present to the possibility of her helping us. The choice of *might* instead of *may* signals that in (7)(b) the likelihood of this occurring is considered more tenuous (its epistemic distance greater) than in (7)(a). In effect, the distal predication indicates that the conceptualizer is not quite ready to describe the event as having the degree of probability that the zero form *may* would suggest—the circumstance in which he would do so is somewhat removed from his actual situation, hence the use of DIST to mark its non-immediacy. But who is the conceptualizer? As before, it is the speaker (S), even though the modal appears in a subordinate clause reporting someone else's statement. Responsibility for assessing the event's likelihood falls with S′ (Jill), but both the event and its epistemic status (as assessed by S′) are described by S from his own vantage point. With regard to time, observe that there is no essential difference between G and G′, both of which precede the envisaged act of helping.[7]

In (7)(c)-(d), the past-tense marking on *say* does of course imply a difference in time between G and G′, and this temporal discrepancy makes it easier

[7] G and G′ can be temporally coincident in (7)(a)–(b) (also in (4)(a)–(b)) because *say* is used as an imperfective: rather than designating a single act of speech, it means that the subject, having expressed a certain view, holds to it over a period of time. We will interpret *say* perfectively in (c) and (d).

to determine which vantage point is being assumed. Examples like (7)(c) provide clear evidence that the subordinate-clause modal is reckoned from the vantage point of G, and not G′. A modal situates the designated process in the realm of irreality, and when that process is perfective, its temporal location must be subsequent to the reference point. In the case of (7)(c), it is intuitively apparent that the event of helping is construed as lying in the future with respect to the actual time of speaking, i.e. at G its occurrence remains a matter of future potentiality. Depicting this configuration is Fig. 6.5(a), where the dashed arrow from G to OS indicates that the event is located with reference to G in accordance with the semantic value of *may*. Now it is also true that the event was a matter of future potentiality at the time of Jill's utterance (G′). How, then, do we know that *may* is being reckoned from G rather than G′? Because if G is the only possible vantage point, the judgments in (8) are correctly predicted:

(8)(a) *Jill said she may help us tomorrow.*
(b) **Jill said she may help us yesterday.*

Assuming that *yesterday* modifies *help* (the only relevant interpretation), the ill-formedness of (8)(b) follows from two independently established facts: that *yesterday* can only take G as its reference point; and that a perfective event must be future relative to the reference point of a modal that grounds it. Suppose, however, that G′ were a possible vantage point. One would then incorrectly predict the well-formedness of (8)(b), since an event can be future with respect to G′ and yet occur *yesterday* (as viewed from G).

Turning now to (7)(d), *Jill said she might help us*, we find that the sentence has two very different interpretations. On one reading, depicted in Fig. 6.5(b), it is directly analogous to (7)(c), except that the event of helping is portrayed as having a somewhat diminished likelihood (Jill's actual words could have been *I might help you*). The distal predication indicates that there is some disparity between the actual situation, G, and the imagined situation—labeled Q—with respect to which the speaker would feel justified in using *may* to locate the profiled process. With a modal, the import of DIST is that the epistemic distance implied by the base form is computed from a reference point (Q) that is in some way removed from G.

The other interpretation of (7)(d) is the one that the sequence-of-tenses analysis is meant to account for: Jill says *I may help you*, and S later reports this with the subordinate-clause paraphrase *she might help us*. With this reading, it is not necessary that the event of helping be subsequent to the actual speech event—it can precede, follow, or even coincide with G:

(9)(a) *Jill said she might help us yesterday, but she didn't.*
(b) *Jill said she might help us, and she is actually doing so.*
(c) *Jill said she might help us tomorrow, and she very well may.*

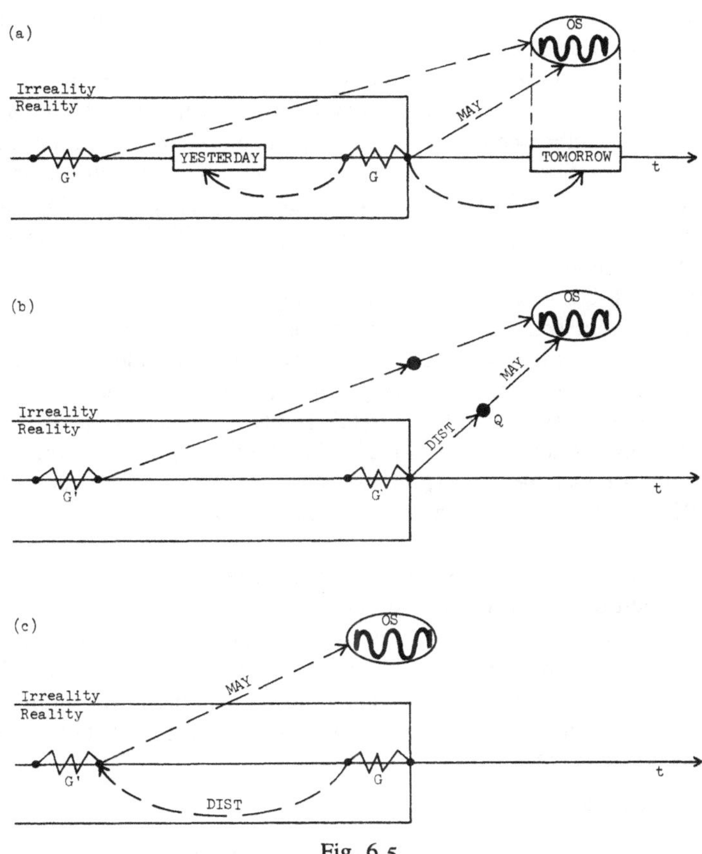

Fig. 6.5

It is however required that the event come after G′:

(10) **Jill said this morning that she might help us yesterday.*

One might argue on this basis that the modal in the subordinate clause is reckoned from G′ instead of G. This is indeed true if, by "modal," one means the modal component of the grounding predication (i.e. the *may* component of *might*, exclusive of DIST). But it is not true if by "modal" we mean the grounding predication as a whole, which in this case is the full word *might* (*may* + DIST). On the reading in question, it is *may* rather than *might* that properly expresses the epistemic distance from the vantage point of G′ (*may* is the word that Jill herself is presumed to have used).

Our claim is that G is always the vantage point for the grounding predication *taken as a whole*. Thus, when Jill says *I may help you* and this is subsequently reported as (7)(d), the word *might* specifies the location of the helping event with respect to G in particular. The way in which it does so is diagrammed in Fig. 6.5(c). In a complex modal such as *might*, the import of DIST is that the epistemic distance associated with the base form (*may*) is computed with reference to a point, Q, that is somehow dissociated from G. This characterization is schematic and places no inherent restrictions on Q. Though Q in general falls within the region of irreality, as in Fig. 6.5(b), nothing precludes the special case in which Q is identified with some point in reality that is non-immediate to G. This is so in diagram (c), where Q is identified with G′, which is removed from G not only temporally, but also in the sense of representing the vantage point of another conceptualizer (S′). What this means is that S reckons the location of the profiled event in terms of a two-step path that takes the perspective of S′ into account: *may* specifies the position of the event in relation to G′, and DIST indicates the dissociation of G′ from G. Although DIST could be interpreted here as marking the past time of the original speech act, the two-step nature of the path connecting G with OC constitutes its primary value, just as in diagram (b).

6.2.2.3. *Additional Matters.* Having established this alternative to the sequence-of-tenses-rule analysis, we can now return to a previous issue and resolve it in a principled manner. The issue is whether *must* is truly defective in the sense of not having a distal form, as suggested earlier, or whether its proximal and distal forms simply happen to be phonologically indistiguishable. Given our analysis, the two claims make different predictions concerning sentences like (11):

(11) *Zelda said that we must come see her.*

If *must* is always proximal, it should only have a reading analogous to that of (7)(c), diagrammed in Fig. 6.5(a). The judgments in (12) are thus predicted (cf. (8)):

(12)(a) *Zelda said that we must come see her tomorrow.*
(b) **Zelda said that we must come see her yesterday.*

On the other hand, if *must* can also be distal, it should have interpretations corresponding to both readings of (7)(d). In particular, one should be able to construe it in the fashion of Fig. 6.5(c), where DIST reflects the temporal anteriority of G′ and the profiled event is situated with respect to G′ in the same way that the proximal variant situates it with respect to G. On this construal, there are no inherent restrictions on the temporal location of the event in relation to G (cf. (9))—it need only follow G′. It is therefore predicted that (12)(b) should be well-formed, but it is not (except, irrelevantly, when *yesterday* modifies the main-clause verb). We can thus conclude that *must* does not have a distal variant.[8]

Two further observations ought to be made concerning the temporal implications of modal predications. First, the English modals always situate the designated process in the present or in the future with respect to their reference point, never in the past. For example, *She may be angry* can be interpreted as meaning that she will possibly be angry at some future time, or else that she is possibly angry now (without my knowing it), but it cannot indicate the possibility that she was angry at some previous time. To convey that meaning, we must resort to the perfect construction: *She may have been angry*. Note that *have* functions as the grounded verb in this expression, so it is the process profiled by *have*—not that of being angry—which *may* situates with respect to G. That process, involving the continuation through time of a relationship of temporal anteriority and current relevance (Fig. 5.10), is indeed construed as coincident with the time of speaking in *She may have been angry*, which thus conforms to the generalization. Hence the English modals are "future oriented" in the sense that they themselves can only locate the grounded process in present or future irreality.[9] However, when the perfect *have* is grounded by a modal and given a present-time construal, its periphrastic specification of temporal anteriority has the effect of situating in past irreality the atemporalized process expressed by its participial complement.

The other observation is that modals are aspectually transparent, which has certain consequences for the temporal construal of the grounded process. Since a modal profiles the grounded process (rather than the grounding relationship), and characterizes that process with maximal schematicity, it has no effect on the perfectivity of the clausal head it combines with: like *jump*, *may jump* is perfective; and like *be angry*, *may be angry* is imperfective. Consider, then, the temporal interpretation of *She may jump*.[10] Due to the future-oriented nature of a modal, the envisaged jump cannot be situated in the past. Location in the present (coincident with the time of speaking) is precluded for the same reason that true present-tense perfectives are normally infelicitous: it cannot be presumed that a perfective event has exactly the same duration as a speech event describing it. Hence *She may jump* is only taken as indicating the pos-

[8] There may be dialectal variation on this point (see Palmer 1979, p. 98). In the dialect described here, necessity with respect to a reference point in the past is expressed by the periphrastic modal *have to* (which is not a grounding predication): *Zelda said that we had to come see her yesterday*.

[9] The construal diagrammed in Fig. 6.5(c) shows that this is specifically a property of the modal base (not of the grounding predication as a whole), and that the pertinent reference point is Q.

[10] Bear in mind that the proximal predication (the selection of *may* instead of *might*) does not per se have any temporal implication—with a modal it merely indicates that the base form's epistemic distance is reckoned from G (i.e. G = Q).

sibility of a jump occurring in the future. By contrast, an imperfective such as *She may be angry* is also susceptible to a present construal. This is for the same reason that present-tense imperfectives are freely permitted: any subpart of an imperfective process counts as a valid instance of the processual category, so that portion which precisely coincides with the speech event can be profiled as a present-time instantiation (cf. Fig. 6.3(c)).

It is worth noting that, in terms of the elaborated epistemic model (Fig. 6.2(a)), the two interpretations of *She may be angry* differ somewhat in the epistemic status attributed to the anger. Although both interpretations locate the profiled situation in the realm of irreality, the future construal necessarily puts it in the region of non-reality, whereas the import of a present construal is that it may be part of unknown reality. We will return to this matter in 6.3, when we discuss the modals in fuller detail.

6.2.3. *Present Tense*

In 6.2.1 we considered a naive characterization of the present tense in English: that it consistently indicates the occurrence of a full instantiation of the profiled process that precisely coincides with the time of speaking. We saw that this simple and natural definition neatly accounts for some basic distributional facts, namely that an imperfective can always occur in the present tense, whereas a perfective never can, with the predictable exception of performatives. Yet it is not at all obvious that this analysis can be maintained, elegant and appealing though it may be. We must now confront the well-known difficulties that it faces, with the objective of determining what one must do to overcome them. The tentative conclusion will be that the moves one is thereby forced to make are not unreasonable.

In formal terms, perfectives do of course occur in the present tense. The actual restriction is semantic in nature: a present-tense perfective is always interpreted in some "special" manner, i.e. it does not have the 'one instance right now' meaning of a true present. Such an expression can in fact be construed in many different ways, each of which is thought to represent a distinct meaning of the inflectional category (for which the label "present tense" is thus regarded as a misnomer). For example, the simple clause *he buries it* is susceptible to any one of a number of special interpretations:

(13)(a) *Whenever I give Fido a bone, he buries it.*
(b) *What does a paranoid miser do with his money? He buries it.*
(c) *Yorick walks to center stage. He picks up a skull. He examines it. He buries it.*
(d) *The king is sad because his favorite dog has just died. He buries it tomorrow at a state funeral.*
(e) *I'm sitting on the porch yesterday and this suspicious-looking guy comes*

into my yard carrying a sack. He buries it. Then he looks up and sees I'm watching.
(f) *McHale passes to Bird. Bird moves out to 3-point range. He shoots. He buries it!*
(g) *If he buries it, he will never find it again.*

In the proper context, *he buries it* may be construed as (a) habitual; (b) generic; (c) a stage direction; (d) an event scheduled for some time in the future; (e) the "historical present"; (f) part of a play-by-play account; or (g) a hypothetical occurrence.

These examples are representative of the many purposes for which present-tense inflection is conventionally employed. However, the special semantic properties of these expressions do not necessarily oblige us to posit distinct meanings for the present-tense morpheme—they might be attributable to other factors. The problematic usages fall into two broad classes, for which different explanations will be proposed. For the first class, it is argued that even though the verb is normally perfective, the designated process actually receives an imperfective construal. Hypothesized for the second class is some kind of mental transfer, whereby the speaker assumes a non-standard vantage point as part of a special mode of discourse or to characterize a particular mental space. Once these factors are properly taken into account, we can describe the present-tense morpheme itself as consistently meaning 'one instance right now'.

6.2.3.1. *A Structured World.* Let us start with habituals, which typify the first class of uses. A simple yet crucial observation is that a perfective may be construed as habitual not only in the present but also in the past and future, and even as an infinitival complement:

(14)(a) *Zelda drinks her whisky straight.*
(b) *When Zelda was young, she drank her whisky straight.*
(c) *When Zelda grows up, she will drink her whisky straight.*
(d) *Zelda wants to drink her whisky straight, but after many years of trying she still can't stand the taste.*

This argues quite strongly that habituality is independent of grounding and should not be postulated as a meaning of the present-tense inflection. Another crucial point is that a clause interpreted as habitual does not profile any particular instance of the perfective process its verb ordinarily designates. Thus (14)(a) does not imply that Zelda is drinking whisky at this moment, nor does it pertain to any single act of whisky-drinking on her part. The import is rather that drinking whisky straight represents her normal practice—that is how she does things whenever the occasion arises. For this reason I suggest that what the clause actually designates is the status of this activity as part of the normal course of events. That is, the profiled relationship is not the perfective process per se, but rather the higher-order, imperfective process consisting of the continuation through time of the stable configuration in which events of this type constitute a regular, expected occurrence. And because the designated process is imperfective, a present-tense use is unproblematic.

Though standard, the term habitual is a bit misleading; (14)(a) does not imply that Zelda has a drinking habit, or even that she is *in the habit* of drinking straight whisky (cf. *Zelda drinks her whisky straight, but she hasn't touched a drop for several years*). Closer to the mark is a distinction made by Goldsmith and Woisetschlaeger (1982) between "structural" and "phenomenal" knowledge, the former pertaining to "the structure of the world" or "how the world is made," and the latter to the things that happen within that framework.[11] I interpret this contrast as reflecting an idealized cognitive model of fundamental significance; let us call it the **structured world model**. According to this basic conception, the world is structured in a particular way, so that certain kinds of events are capable of occurring while others are impossible. Within the realm of possibility, events differ in their status. Some are *incidental*, arising in ad hoc fashion from particular circumstances; though compatible with the structure of the world, they are not specifically anticipated or predicted in terms of it. On the other hand, certain events are direct manifestations of the world's structure—they are in some sense regular or predictable, and are thus expected to occur whenever the appropriate preconditions are satisfied. It is in reference to such occurrences that we speak of the *normal course of events*.

The proposal, then, is that the structured world model figures in the so-called "habitual" construal of perfectives. Posited as a conventional unit of English is a productive pattern of zero derivation whose semantic pole is sketched in Fig. 6.6. This rule is applicable to a processual predication having any degree of internal complexity (e.g. in (14) it applies to *(Zelda) drink her whisky straight*).[12] Its effect is to embed this processual notion as part of a more elaborate configuration functioning as the component state of a higher-order imperfective process. In that configuration, the original process is con-

[11] Goldsmith and Woisetschlaeger associate phenomenal knowledge with the *be . . . -ing* progressive construction, but I have argued (1987b) that the relationship is indirect: phenomenal status implies temporal bounding, and this perfectivity makes the progressive applicable (and necessary for speaking of the present).

[12] Rules such as this—productive patterns of zero derivation (semantic extension) applicable to structures of any size—are straightforward given the basic constructs of cognitive grammar and appear to be fairly common. Other examples include the construal of nominals as stative relations in the predicate nominative construction (2.2.4), and the use of a path expression to designate the locative relationship constituting the final configuration of that path (e.g. *They marched over the bridge, across the field, and through the woods* vs. *Their camp is over the bridge, across the field, and through the woods*).

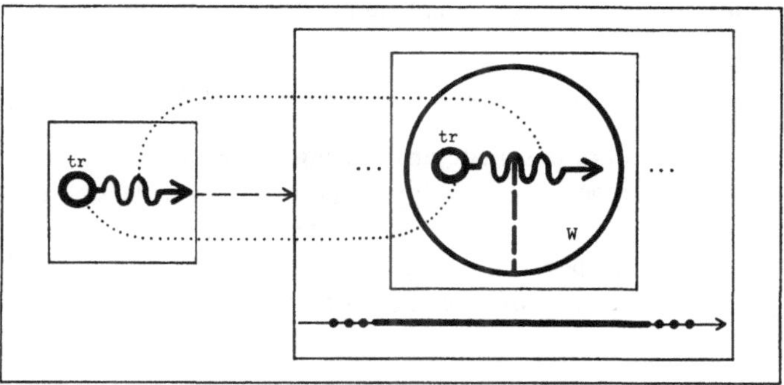

Fig. 6.6

ceived as being one facet of the structure of the world, as it is currently constituted; the circle labeled W represents that structure, and the dashed line makes explicit its inclusion of the lower-order process. Observe that this part/whole relationship is central to the higher-order processual profile: the derived predication designates the continuation through time of the stable situation in which the process type in question is part of the world's structure (so that instances of that type are expected to occur under the appropriate conditions).

The structured world model is interpreted relative to human experience. What counts as "the world" is therefore quite variable, ranging from the laws of physics at one extreme to expectations concerning particular individuals at the other. The world is subject to change as well: though $E = mc^2$ may always be true, and 2 is unlikely ever to be joined by another even prime number, the world's structure also comprises more modest regularities that have no pretensions as to permanence. Thus, despite its fairly minor role in the evolution of the universe, Zelda's practice of drinking whisky straight is construed in (14) as an integral part of how the world is constituted during a particular span of time. It is neither expected nor required that this situation will continue indefinitely, even within Zelda's lifetime—it is merely portrayed as stable within the temporal limits of the scope of predication.

Once we recognize how flexibly the structured world model is interpreted, habitual, generic, and timeless statements can all be seen as special cases of the same phenomenon: an expression is generic when the property in question is somehow ascribed to all members of a class rather than a specific individual (e.g. *Beavers build dams*); it is timeless when the property is regarded as immutable, hence constant throughout any temporal scope of predication (*The area of a circle equals pi times the square of its radius*). Though less obviously, we can also invoke the structured world model to explicate other conventional uses of the present tense. One aspect of the world's structure is that there is a proper way of doing things in order to achieve a certain result.

Present-tense forms can thus be employed in the instructions for running some machine:

(15) *To turn off the dishwasher, you move the lever all the way to the left.*

This sentence does not designate any specific instance of moving the lever, but indicates that an action of this type is part of the normal course of events constituting the canonical way of operating the device. Similarly, by using the present tense in a recipe or in giving directions, one is portraying the world as being so structured that the specified sequence of events regularly leads to the desired outcome:

(16)(a) *First you get a big mixing bowl. Next you put in two cups of flour and the whites of three eggs.*

(b) *You go down to that light and turn left. Then you drive about six miles and look for a big water tower.*

Stage directions (as in (13)(c)) can be regarded as a recipe for the proper performance of a play.

What about the present tense used for a scheduled future event (e.g. *The game starts at 8 PM*)? We must remember here that the world is viewed in terms of human experience. Plans, schedules, and intentions determine the expected course of human activity in much the same way that physical forces and properties determine the normal behavior of physical objects. Thus, the import of describing a future event in the present tense is that plans have been made, the machinery set in motion for its occurrence, which will eventuate unless unforeseen factors should intervene and prevent things from running their course. As in all these examples, it is not the event per se that is profiled by the clause, but rather the imperfective process defined by its stable role as part of the "script" of how the world is expected to work. More precisely, the clause designates that portion of the imperfective process that coincides with the time of speaking: the verbal inflection represents a true present tense.

6.2.3.2. *A Shifted Deictic Center*. The second class of problematic present-tense usages can be accommodated in terms of our capacity for conceiving a situation as it appears from different perspectives. Crucially, it is how we conceptualize a situation, not objective reality, that determines the meaning of a linguistic expression describing it. While riding on a train, for instance, I might very well utter (17), intending it as a straightforward description of what I actually see.

(17) *The telephone poles are rushing past at 60 miles per hour.*

I am aware that the poles are really stationary and that I am the one who is moving, but that is not what the sentence means. What I have done is to imagine myself as being stationary and to interpret my visual experience within that frame of reference; the resulting conceptualization functions as the cognitive domain with respect to which the expression's composite semantic structure is characterized.

Comparable shifts in perspective are presupposed by certain modes of discourse that are conventionally established in English and frequently employed despite their special character. One such mode, illustrated in (13)(e), is commonly referred to as the "historical present." Intuitively, it is fairly clear what this mode of speech involves: the speaker describes a previous sequence of events as if they were unfolding right now, before his very eyes; he takes the hearer through them step by step, achieving a sort of "vividness" by portraying them as immediate. Analytically, we must posit a radical mental transfer pertaining to the **deictic center**, i.e. the vantage point assumed for deictic expressions, including grounding predications. The speaker **decouples** the deictic center from the here-and-now of the actual speech event and shifts it to another location, which in the case of the historical present is specifically identified with the time and place of the events being reported.[13] For descriptive purposes, the speaker is in effect pretending that these events are indeed occurring 'right here, right now', and by so presenting them, he enables the addressee to view them with the same immediacy.

Analyzing the historical present as a special meaning of the present-tense morpheme is regarded as inappropriate, since the shift in deictic center is not peculiar to tense, as that analysis would imply, but is also presupposed by other deictic elements (e.g. *this* and *come* in (13)(e)). It is claimed instead that the historical present represents a special mode of discourse in which the speaker assumes a remembered or imagined spatio-temporal vantage point with respect to which the reported events are seen as immediate. From the perspective of this shifted deictic center, each event is construed as coinciding with the time of the speech event describing it, so that the present-tense morpheme is used with its normal meaning. But how is this possible? It was argued previously that perfectives do not have a true present-tense interpretation because the profiled event does not in general have the same length as the speech event, and also because the speaker would have to be prescient in order to begin describing an event at the exact instant of its onset. However, these problems evaporate in the special circumstances of the historical present, for although an event is described as if it were happening at the moment of speaking, in actuality it is being imagined or recalled. Hence the speaker knows from the outset what event he intends to describe, and because what counts

[13] This notion of decoupling is due to Leonard Talmy, who has explored it more systematically in work that is yet unpublished. Observe that some deictics (e.g. *yesterday* in (13)(e)) presuppose the original deictic center; I have not explored the interesting question of what determines the choice.

as its present occurrence is actually a mental "replay," he can scan through it as quickly or slowly as necessary to make it coincide with the speech act.

Exemplified in (13)(f), the familiar play-by-play mode of speech might be thought of as a special adaptation of the historical present, in which an event reported as simultaneous with the time of speaking actually precedes it, but only at a very short interval. An announcer cannot time his statements to coincide exactly with the actions they describe—however stereotypical these may be—but he does shadow them closely, anticipate their outcome once initiated, and report them with the shortest possible time-lag. We must of course distinguish between what the announcer is really doing and what we conceive him as doing; I suspect that this mode of discourse rests on the conventional fiction that simultaneous reporting can indeed occur. There is at least a conventional agreement that any time-lag is insignificant and thus to be ignored.[14]

Particularly interesting are examples like the following, observed in the speech of many announcers (and some real people):

(18) *He catches that pass and the game is tied.*

The context is crucial: in this usage, (18) occurs immediately after the pass has been dropped, so in fact the pass was not caught and the game is not tied. Must we therefore posit a semantic variant of the present-tense morpheme having some kind of negative or counterfactual value? I think not. Instead I believe that the speaker tacitly constructs a mental space representing what the situation would have been had events taken a different course. He then decouples the deictic center from the here-and-now of his actual circumstances and shifts it into that mental space for purposes of describing its contents; viewed from that vantage point, the profiled relationships are a matter of immediate reality and thus described in the present tense.[15] Of course, the speaker and hearer both realize that the assumed vantage point is not the actual one and that the situation is really counterfactual, just as they know in (17) that the telephone poles are not really moving by at 60 miles per hour.

If we have the capacity to shift the deictic center to a special mental space created without explicit marking, it stands to reason that we can also shift it to a space whose creation is signalled overtly. Consider in this regard the common observation that the present tense occurs "with future meaning"

[14] The play-by-play mode must be abandoned to describe an event that falls outside the expected range of occurrences for the type of activity in question (e.g. one would not say *The scoreboard explodes!*, but rather *The scoreboard just exploded!*). This recalls the use of the present tense for recipes, stage directions, etc. and suggests a possible connection with the structured world model.

[15] This usage is analogous to the historical present, except that the deictic center is shifted to a location in non-reality rather than past reality (Fig. 6.2). It may also fall within the future-time region of non-reality: *You miss this field goal and you lose your job.*

in clauses introduced by certain space-creating subordinators, including *if*, *when*, *before*, and *after*:

(19) {*If/when/before/after*} *the guests all leave, we'll open a bottle of champagne.*

Pending detailed investigation, we might hypothesize that these constructions require the contents of the mental space established by the subordinator to be described from a shifted deictic center located within that space, with the consequence that the subordinate-clause verb occurs in the present tense. While this proposal is only speculative, it would surely be premature to conclude from examples like (19) that the present-tense morpheme means 'future' when it occurs in these types of subordinate clauses.

6.3. Modals

English modals have been studied by many scholars from a variety of theoretical perspectives (e.g. Antinucci and Parisi 1971; Boyd and Thorne 1969; Coates 1983; Joos 1968; Palmer 1977, 1979; Perkins 1982; Turewicz 1986). We will not attempt here either to survey the vast body of previous research or to describe the full range of meanings and uses displayed by each individual modal. We must limit our concern to establishing the basic character of the English modals and sketching one promising approach to their analysis.

6.3.1. *Historical Development*

It is uncontroversial that concrete meanings often give rise to more abstract ones, and that this kind of semantic change generally accompanies the historical evolution of lexical items into grammatical markers. Of course, the lexical/grammatical distinction is seen in cognitive grammar as a matter of degree, with the English modals representing an intermediate case. Although I am not prepared to discuss their history in any detail, a certain amount of diachronic perspective should greatly clarify the synchronic analysis to be proposed.

The historical antecedents of the modern English modals were main verbs (i.e. content verbs) in Old English and even later. *Will*, for example, derives from a verb that meant 'want'. Similarly, *can* originally indicated that its subject had the knowledge or mental ability to do something, and *may*, that it had the necessary strength or physical ability. For our purposes, it is sufficient to observe that these original senses share certain properties which provide the basis for their subsequent evolution into modals. These common organizational features are roughly diagrammed in Fig. 6.7(a).

First, each original verb evokes the conception of an associated activity. One does not simply want, know how, or have a physical capacity in the abstract—rather, one wants, knows how, or has the capacity *to do something*.

Thus each verb makes schematic reference to another process, which serves as a landmark and as the e-site for a relational complement. Second, the overall trajector and that of the relational landmark are equated (note the correspondence line). The source expressions are comparable in this regard to such modern English locutions as {*want/know how/be able*} *to swim*, where the overall subject is necessarily construed as the trajector of *swim*. Third, the subject is the locus of some kind of **potency** directed at the landmark process, i.e. a physical or mental force that, when unleashed, tends to bring about an occurrence of that process. This potency is represented diagrammatically by the double arrow, which is drawn with dashed lines to indicate that the unleashing of this force and the consequent realization of the landmark process are *potential* rather than *actual*. The latency of this event constitutes the fourth property of the original expressions: {*want/know how/be able*} *to swim* does not imply that an act of swimming takes place, but simply that the world (specifically, the trajector) is so structured that it can be expected to happen under the appropriate circumstances.

Inherent in the configuration of Fig. 6.7(a) are the essential ingredients of the modern English modals: reference to a schematically characterized process; the occurrence of this process being potential rather than actual; and the

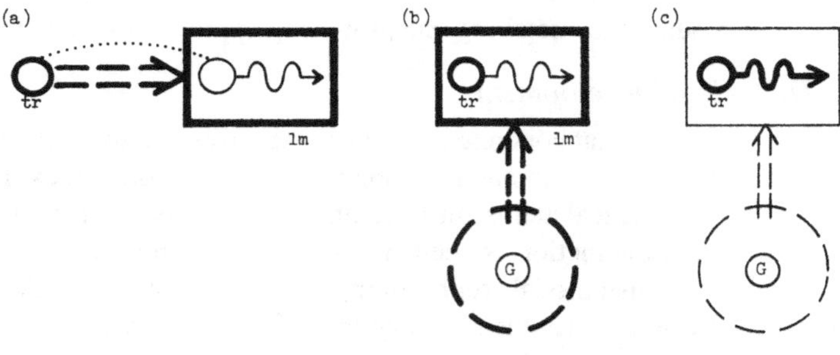

Fig. 6.7

notion of a force directed toward its realization. In fact, if we abstract away from the idiosyncrasies of individual forms and consider the modals as a class, the semantic contrast between the original content verbs and the contemporary grounding predications can be summarized in a single word: *subjectification*. Recall that subjectification involves some facet of the profiled relationship being reoriented from the objective axis to the subjective axis, so that it is no longer anchored by an objective participant (the subject), but rather by a reference point construed more subjectively (the default case being G itself). There are two basic degrees of subjectification, distinguished by whether the reoriented relationship remains in profile or is pulled offstage to become an unprofiled facet of the base (Fig. 5.6). Thus, starting from Fig. 6.7(a), the result of subjectification is the structure of either 6.7(b) or 6.7(c), depending on which type occurs.

The relationship that undergoes realignment from the objective to the subjective axis is the notion of potency directed toward realization of the landmark process. The locus of that potency is therefore no longer the trajector of the process, but rather the ground or another entity with which G is somehow associated (e.g. in *It must be finished by noon!*, the speaker either imposes the obligation himself or reports the obligation imposed by another source). In terms of conceptual content, there is no inherent contrast between structures (b) and (c): the essential difference is whether it is the potency relationship that is put in profile, or the process at which this potency is directed. Though seemingly minor, this distinction is quite significant grammatically, for configuration (c) is characteristic of a grounding predication (it profiles the grounded entity instead of the grounding relationship), whereas (b) represents a periphrastic modal (a likely intermediate stage in the evolution of a content verb into a modal capable of grounding a finite clause).[16]

The English modals are grounding predications and are therefore attributed the structure of Fig. 6.7(c). By contrast, the semantically similar German modals have the structure of Fig. 6.7(b), for they are definitely periphrastic (i.e. the modal relationship is put onstage and profiled). That the German modals are not grounding predications is shown by several differences between their grammatical behavior and that of their English counterparts. For one thing, they all have infinitival forms, which is inconsistent with the function of grounding a finite clause: *wollen* 'to want to'; *sollen* 'to be supposed to'; *müssen* 'to have to'; *mögen* 'to like to'; *dürfen* 'to be allowed to'; *können* 'to be able to'. They also form past participles that occur in the perfect construction as complements to the auxiliary verb 'have', e.g. *Ich habe es gemusst* 'I have had to do it'. Furthermore, the German modals agree in person with the subject: *ich darf* 'I may', *du darfst* 'you may', *wir dürfen* 'we may', etc. In 6.1, we analyzed the person inflection of English as a grounding element that is manifested on the grounded verb.

It is important that this distinction between a periphrastic modal and one that functions as a grounding predication not be confused with a second basic contrast, namely that between **root** (or **deontic**) modals on the one hand, and **epistemic** modals on the other. The two distinctions are independent: either a periphrastic or a grounding modal can have both a root and an epistemic

[16]The contrast between (b) and (c) is thus analogous to that between a periphrastic future based on 'go' and a true future-tense marking (e.g. French *Il va finir* 'He is going to finish' vs. *Il finira* 'He will finish'—cf. Fig. 5.8), or between a periphrastic past derived from a perfect and a true past-tense inflection (Spanish *Ha llegado* 'He (has) arrived' vs. *Llegó* 'He arrived').

value. The English modals can all be used in either fashion. Some typical examples of root and epistemic modal senses are exemplified in (20) and (21), respectively:

(20)(a) *This noise must cease immediately!*
(b) *You may leave the table now.*
(c) *She really should phone her mother more often.*
(d) *He absolutely will not agree to it.*
(e) *Could you please pass the carrots?*

(21)(a) *It must be lonely there at night.*
(b) *There may be some snow by tomorrow evening.*
(c) *That should be enough.*
(d) *Umbrage will certainly be taken at those remarks.*
(e) *Could she actually be older than my aunt?*

A modal is regarded as epistemic when its sole import is to indicate the likelihood of the designated process. In a root modal, there is additionally some conception of potency directed toward the realization of that process, i.e. some notion of obligation, permission, desire, ability, etc.

The distinction between root and epistemic modals is not always easy to maintain. Nor is it always possible, with a root modal, to determine with precision either the locus or the nature of the potency directed at the profiled process. Thus (20)(d) suggests volition and resolve, but a simple future interpretation is more likely if the adverb *absolutely* is omitted, and is marginally possible even when it is present. In (20)(a), the source of the authority is probably the speaker, but it could be that the speaker is only reporting the obligation imposed by someone else (e.g. the landlord), or even by some aspect of the physical world (*This noise must cease immediately or there will be an avalanche!*). Should we identify the locus of the obligation in (20)(c) with the subject (who bears that obligation), with the speaker (who assesses it), or with the social standards that support the judgment? In (20)(e), does *could* refer to physical ability, to willingness, or to social obligation?

This indeterminacy suggests that an analysis of the modals ought to focus more on the existence and strength of the directed potency than on pinning it down to a specific source and type (although each modal does have a certain range of conventional values and tends to be used in certain kinds of circumstances). Indeed, the historical evolution of modals—leading from main verbs, through root modals of various sorts, to epistemic modals—is revealingly described as a matter of the locus of this potency becoming progressively less salient and well-defined. At the main-verb stage (Fig. 6.7(a)), the locus of potency is the subject, an objectively construed participant accorded maximal salience. Since objectivity is one aspect of salience, the two degrees of subjectification (Figs. 6.7(b)–(c)) render the locus of potency successively less prominent, even if it is well-defined in the sense of being identified with the speaker. We have seen, however, that this represents only one possible construal of a root modal. The locus can also be some other individual, whose identity may or may not be clear from context. Or it might be interpreted even more vaguely, as some unspecified facet of the physical or social world.[17]

Epistemic modals are naturally regarded as the endpoint of this developmental process. They lie at the opposite extreme from the main-verb expressions in regard to how the locus of potency is conceived and characterized: with a main verb the locus is salient and well-delineated (usually a particular person), whereas an epistemic modal represents the limiting case in which it is not identified with any individual or any specifiable facet of the world. Conceived with maximal vagueness and minimal restrictiveness, the locus of potency is in effect equated with the world and its evolution, construed inclusively as an undifferentiated whole. Impetus toward realization of the designated process is not provided by any specific force, but rather by the generalized force consisting in the fact that the world has a certain structure and reality is unfolding in a particular way. An epistemic modal offers an assessment of whether this evolutionary "momentum" will carry reality far enough along the appropriate path to "reach" the process in question.

This analysis is intended as a refinement of the one presented by Sweetser (1982, 1984), which greatly expanded on Talmy's original insight (1985, 1988a) that the English modals are best analyzed in terms of force dynamics. Sweetser's basic proposal is that the modals have force-dynamic values applicable either to the domain of social interaction or to the domain of reasoning, and that this difference in domain accounts for the contrast between the root and epistemic senses. These force-dynamic values can be exemplified by *may* 'absence of a potentially present barrier', *must* 'compelling, irresistible force', *can* 'positive ability', and *will* 'completed path to a goal' (whose force-dynamic status Sweetser regards as problematic (1984, p. 67)). The root and epistemic values thus attributed to *may* and *must* are as follows:

(22)(a) *You may leave.* [ROOT; SOCIAL DOMAIN]
'You are not barred by (my or some other) authority from leaving.'
(b) *She may be tired.* [EPISTEMIC; DOMAIN OF REASONING]
'I am not barred by my premises from the conclusion that she is tired.'

(23)(a) *You must leave.* [ROOT; SOCIAL DOMAIN]
'The direct force of (someone's) authority compels you to leave.'
(b) *She must be tired.* [EPISTEMIC; DOMAIN OF REASONING]
'The available (direct) evidence compels me to the conclusion that she is tired.'

The glosses, taken essentially verbatim from Sweetser 1984 (p. 76), are obviously not intended as serious paraphrases, if only because they profile the

[17] The locus may still be the subject, particularly in the case of *can* (e.g. *Can she lift it?*). This is just one option, however—at the main-verb stage it was the only option.

force-dynamic relationship, whereas a modal leaves it offstage and unprofiled (Fig. 6.7(c)). But if we interpret her characterizations in this latter fashion, Sweetser's analysis is very much in the same spirit as the one proposed here: both are force-dynamic accounts, and their descriptions of the basic modal values (e.g. *may* as the absence of a barrier) are essentially compatible. The one noteworthy difference pertains to the specific way in which force is claimed to figure in the epistemic meanings. In Sweetser's account, an epistemic modal invokes the metaphorically structured domain of reasoning and portrays the speaker as being subjected to the force of evidence, which tends to push him along a path of deduction to a certain conclusion. The proposed alternative (spelled out more fully in the following section) invokes other cognitive models. It does not refer to the force of evidence, but rather to the momentum of reality evolving in the context of a structured world. And instead of viewing the speaker as being driven metaphorically along a deductive path, it is reality that is seen as being carried in the direction of a particular outcome.

These analyses are not so different as they might at first appear, nor are they incompatible. The speaker is involved in any case as the primary conceptualizer and the person responsible for assessing the likelihood of reality evolving in a certain way. When the speaker conceives of how the world is structured and how reality is currently developing, his activity can be thought of as the weighing of evidence. And when he uses that conception as a basis for extrapolation, projecting as best he can the future evolution of reality, the mental path he thereby traces can be thought of as a deductive path leading from the evidence toward a possible conclusion. Thus, modal senses based on the notion of evolutionary momentum might well engender the conception of the speaker being carried by the force of evidence along a deductive path—this latter conception arises to the extent that the speaker's role in construing the evolution of reality becomes an object of conceptualization in its own right. It is not implausible that these two ways of understanding things might coexist as complementary aspects of the modal meanings. If so, the only issue is their relative cognitive salience.

I have several reasons for thinking that the account based on evolutionary momentum tells at least part of the story. First, it follows naturally from our overall description of how the modals have developed historically and the cognitive models that appear to be relevant for grounding predications in English. Second, it straightforwardly allows a force-dynamic analysis of *will* (6.3.2), which is problematic at best with Sweetser's approach. Third, it conforms to the general pattern of the speaker being construed with maximal subjectivity in a grounding predication, whereas the notion of the speaker being forced along a deductive path implies a more objective construal, even if left unprofiled. Finally, it affords a natural way to characterize the conceptual distinction between two types of epistemic modals.

What is this distinction? Simply that some modal uses pertain to the future, and others to present situations that are not yet part of known reality. With an imperfective process, both options are viable. For instance, *She may be tired* can either mean that she will possibly be tired at some future time, or else that she may be tired right now (without the speaker knowing it). With a perfective process, on the other hand, the construal is necessarily future (owing to the aspectual transparency of modals, together with the problem posed by present-time perfectives); *She may wake up* can only refer to a future event, not one that occurs at the moment of speaking. As an indication that this contrast is linguistically significant, observe that *must* is limited to a present-time construal when used with epistemic value.[18] In reference to the present, *She must be there* is interpreted epistemically, but *must* can only be a root modal (conveying the notion of obligation) if the process is situated in the future.

We have outlined a developmental sequence—leading from main verbs, through root modals of various sorts, to epistemic modals—whose organizing property is that the locus of potency is construed with progressively greater subjectivity at each step along the path. If the future-time epistemic modals are characterized in terms of evolutionary momentum, we can see the origin of the present-time interpretations as constituting one last step in this sequence. Of course, a future-time modal is already quite subjective in its construal of directed potency, but it is still concerned with what might happen in the world, i.e. with reality evolving in one way rather than another. By contrast, a present-time modal pertains to a situation whose status as part of reality or non-reality has already been determined—it is just that the speaker does not yet know where it falls. Hence it is not *reality*, but rather *the speaker's knowledge of present reality*, whose continued evolution must be assessed and projected into the future. The notion of evolutionary momentum therefore receives a more subjective construal, because it is now attributed to known reality, which lies within the province of the conceptualizer.[19]

6.3.2. *The Dynamic Evolutionary Model*

We are now ready to attempt a unified discussion of the epistemic modals. The key to this account is an idealized cognitive model that incorporates certain others previously introduced and embodies fundamental aspects of how we think about the world. One of its components is the structured world model

[18] This restriction reflects the special place of *must* in the modal system: *must* implies the minimum epistemic distance compatible with modal status (see 6.1). The lack of a distal form is another manifestation of this immediacy.

[19] This is similar to Sweetser's description of the speaker being impelled along a deductive path, but there is still a distinction to be made between *force being applied to the speaker* on the one hand, and *momentum inhering in the evolution of speaker knowledge*, on the other. Once again, I do not rule out the possibility that these might be coexisting facets of the modal meanings.

(6.2.3.1), which holds that the world is structured in a particular way, so that certain events and situations are possible, while others are precluded. A second component is the elaborated epistemic model (Fig. 6.2(a)), pertaining to the evolution of reality and the fact that only a limited portion of reality is known to a given conceptualizer. Also included are certain force-dynamic concepts, which yield the notion of evolutionary momentum when applied metaphorically to these models. The elaborate conception that subsumes and integrates these elements will be referred to as the **dynamic evolutionary model**.

Inspired by the contrast drawn by Goldsmith and Woisetschlaeger (1982) between "structural" and "phenomenal" knowledge, I have been distinguishing between "the world" and what happens within it. We conceive of the world as the stable framework within which situations arise and events unfold. What counts as the world depends on one's outlook and concerns. Primarily, of course, we identify it with the physical universe, but we also think in terms of a social world, a mental world, a spiritual world, and so on. Although the world does change (some facets more quickly or readily than others), over a certain period and within a certain scope of interest it can be regarded as fixed and constant for all intents and purposes.

But to describe the world as a stable framework is not to imply that it is merely a static configuration of elements. There is an essential force-dynamic aspect to our conception of its structure, which we see as constraining and influencing the events that unfold within it. Part of what it means for the world to have a particular structure is that it is biased toward the occurrence of certain events and event sequences as opposed to others. Some are inherently disposed to occur whenever appropriate circumstances arise, and will do so unless energy is somehow exerted to counteract this tendency; these represent the "normal course of events." Others encounter resistance and can only take place if sufficient energy is expended to overcome it. Of course, some things cannot happen at all because they are flatly inconsistent with how the world is structured.

We have understood the term "reality" as referring to the history of what has happened in the world.[20] At any given moment, present reality is the particular configuration then obtaining among the entities in the world (out of the countless configurations possible in the sense of being compatible with its structure). But reality never holds still. It relentlessly evolves through time, "growing" toward the future as each instantiation of present reality gives rise to the next and thus becomes part of the past. This evolution exhibits a kind of organic continuity: successive instantiations of reality cannot represent totally distinct and unrelated conceptions. Instead, one instantiation bequeathes most of its organization to its successor, which diverges from it only in limited ways, and only as permitted by the world's structure.

[20] We are now concerned with reality overall, not just known reality.

Given how the world is structured, therefore, the present state of reality severely constrains the possible course of its future evolution (at least in the short term). Many evolutionary paths are foreclosed by virtue of requiring an impermissibly sharp discontinuity between one stage of reality and the next. Among those paths that future reality could conceivably follow, some are favored because present circumstances include those under which the world is biased toward the occurrence of particular sequences of events. The term "evolutionary momentum" refers to this tendency for reality, having evolved to its present state, to continue its evolution along certain paths in preference to others. This evolution can thus be likened to a sled gliding down a snow-covered hill. The motion of the sled is continuous, in that it keeps on going (rather than stopping and starting) and makes a smooth track (instead of jumping from place to place). The motion is also irreversible: once the sled has descended to a certain point, it cannot go back up or descend by an alternate route. Moreover, the sled's position and downward momentum strongly constrain and influence its subsequent path. There are places farther down where it simply cannot go (because they would require too sharp a turn), and places where the contour of the slope is almost certain to take it (unless enough energy should be exerted to deflect it onto another course).

Fig. 6.8 diagrams some important aspects of the dynamic evolutionary model. As before, reality is depicted by a cylinder (to be envisaged as growing along the temporal axis), and C is the conceptualizer (identified as the speaker). The dashed arrow represents reality's evolutionary momentum, which tends to carry it along certain future paths and keeps it from following others. Those paths it is not precluded from following are collectively referred

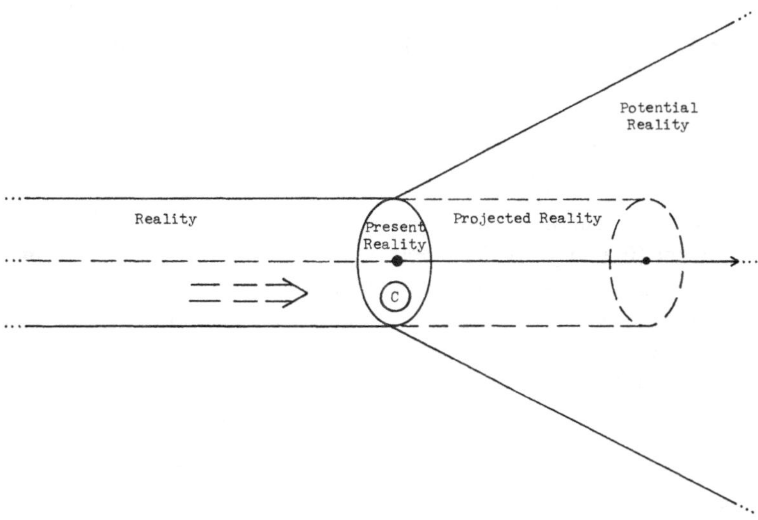

Fig. 6.8

to as **potential reality**. Often, evolutionary momentum is conceived as being strong enough that the future course of reality can be projected with considerable confidence (i.e. an extraordinary or wholly unanticipated input of energy would be required to push it out of this predetermined path). For such cases we will use the term **projected reality**.

With respect to this model, a basic characterization of future-time epistemic senses of the English modals is quite straightforward. The system is fairly limited, especially for the simple forms: *must* has no future-time epistemic use; for *can* (more readily construed as a root modal) this use is only marginal; and many speakers hardly use *shall* at all (and then just with a root-modal sense). That leaves only *may* and *will* (as in *She {may/will} quit*). *May* is very simply described as situating the designated process in the realm of potential reality. That is, nothing in the speaker's present conception of reality is seen as barring it from evolving along a path leading to the occurrence of that process (there is no insurmountable energy barrier to overcome). In similar fashion, *will* places the designated process in the realm of projected reality. *Will* is thus a force-dynamic expression: if not rerouted by an unforeseen input of energy, reality is compelled by its evolutionary momentum to pursue a course such that the process does take place.[21]

The distal forms employ these same concepts but invoke a reference point (Q) that is somehow removed from G. Consider *might*. As envisaged by the speaker, the circumstances at Q are such that, given the evolutionary momentum of reality (reality at Q, that is), the designated process falls within the realm of potential reality. Where is Q itself situated? There are various possibilities. In a sentence like (24)(a), Q resides in potential reality (as reckoned from G); the import of *might* is that reality has the potential of evolving to a situation in which *may* would be appropriate to convey the status of the profiled process (cf. Fig. 6.5(b)).

(24)(a) *She might accept our offer.*
(b) *She said she might finish yesterday.*
(c) *If you weren't so stupid, you might learn something.*

In (24)(b), Q is identified with the surrogate ground established by a prior speech event (Fig. 6.5(c)). Yet another option is for Q to occupy a mental space representing a hypothetical or counterfactual state of affairs; (24)(c) is a commonplace example (the sentence is frequently heard in scientific discussions between linguists of different theoretical persuasions).

In view of the similar meanings of *will* and *shall*, it is hardly surprising that both *would* and *should* locate the designated process in *projected* reality

[21] It may be that the notion of evolutionary momentum figures in the meaning of *will* with varying degrees of prominence. To the extent that it fades from the picture, what remains is a simple future-tense predication based on the time-line model (Fig. 6.2(b)).

with respect to some point Q that is non-immediate to G. They are distinguished primarily by their characterization of Q. In the case of *would*, Q is generally either a surrogate ground, as in (25)(a), or a hypothetical/counterfactual situation, as in (25)(b).

(25)(a) *She said she would finish yesterday.*
(b) *If you weren't so stupid, you would learn something.*

A comparison of these sentences with (24)(b)-(c) clearly reveals that the *might/would* contrast is one of potential vs. projected reality (with reference to Q). However, changing *might* to *would* in (24)(a) does not merely effect a shift from potential to projected reality, but also suggests that Q is counterfactual; *She would accept our offer* feels elliptic by itself and leads us to anticipate a continuation such as . . . *if she could*. It is *should*, not *would*, that is minimally distinct from *might* in sentences like (24)(a). If *should* is interpreted epistemically (not as meaning 'ought'), *She should accept our offer* indicates the imminent potentiality of a situation in which her acceptance would be seen as a matter of projected reality. Hence the overall import is that the event is quite likely—just a bit more assurance would enable the speaker to project its future reality.

Actually, in the case of both *might* and *should*, the potentiality of Q need not involve the future evolution of reality itself. An alternative construal is that the profiled relationship might be seen as located in potential or projected reality if the speaker had fuller information about the present—in terms of the elaborated epistemic model (Fig. 6.2(a)), Q may lie in the unknown portion of present reality. An interpretation of this sort is intermediate between a future-time epistemic sense and a present-time sense in which both Q (if distinct from G) and the designated process itself are located in unknown present reality (e.g. *They might be there by now*). Recall that the present-time epistemic meanings arise when the focus shifts from the evolution of reality to that of the speaker's conception of reality, so that the relevant evolutionary momentum inheres in the speaker's own thought processes. The notions of potential and projected reality remain coherent under this construal, although they no longer pertain to what might *happen*, but rather to what might *prove to be the case*. Indeed, Fig. 6.8 is appropriate for the present-time epistemic senses provided that "reality" is read throughout as "known reality."

Once this adjustment is made, the present-time epistemic meanings are by and large quite comparable to the basic future-time senses. For example, *They should be there by now* indicates real likelihood (it is one step removed from an actual projection), and the potentiality of *They may be there by now* is rendered more tenuous when *may* is replaced by *might*. One noteworthy difference is that *must* is part of the present-time system. For some speakers, *must* is essentially the present-time counterpart of *will*, situating the designated process in the realm of projected known reality. For other speakers, there is a subtle contrast: *That will be Jack* (said when the doorbell rings) is not quite the same as *That must be Jack*. Our overall analysis leads to the natural proposal that *must* conveys immediacy, whereas *will* suggests a certain epistemic distance. Although the profiled process is in each case a projection from known reality, *will* implies that confirmation requires a non-negligible expansion of present knowledge (so that new information might alter the prediction), whereas *must* (on the strictest interpretation) indicates that confirmation is regarded as virtually inevitable. The judgments in (26) are thus predicted:

(26)(a) *They {will/*must} quite possibly be there by now.*
(b) *Since you saw it with your own eyes, it {must/*will} exist.*

One last problem is to characterize the meaning of *will* in sentences like the following:

(27)(a) *Water will boil when heated to 100 degrees centigrade.*
(b) *With double-clutching, a condor will lay two eggs a year.*
(c) *He will get rather petulant whenever he's had too much to drink.*
(d) *It will only rain here during the winter.*

Will does not have its future-time epistemic value in these examples, since it does not pertain exclusively to future events. Nor is its meaning quite that of a present-time epistemic, for the sentences clearly purport to be descriptions of *known* reality. They are actually quite similar to "habitual" expressions, for rather than designating a single instance of the event in question, they indicate that an event of that type is in some sense a regular or expected occurrence. Indeed, present-tense habituals offer fairly close paraphrases:

(28)(a) *Water boils when heated to 100 degrees centigrade.*
(b) *With double-clutching, a condor lays two eggs a year.*
(c) *He gets rather petulant whenever he's had too much to drink.*
(d) *It only rains here during the winter.*

Impressionistically, the sentences in (28) describe the regularities matter-of-factly, while those in (27) are in some way "predictive" and seem more "energetic."

An analysis based on the structured world model was advanced in 6.2.3.1 for habitual, generic, and timeless expressions like those in (28). It was claimed that these do not profile a single instance of the perfective process named, but rather a higher-order, imperfective process consisting of the continuation through time of the relationship wherein that process type is part of the world's structure (Fig. 6.6). Let me now propose that the same analysis holds for the sentences in (27), except that *will* renders their meanings slightly more elaborate. What does *will* contribute, precisely? I suggest that it highlights the force-dynamic aspects of the structured world model. In (28), the inclusion of the process type in the structure of the world is portrayed in rather static terms, essentially as a part/whole relation. The effect of *will* is to invoke the full dynamic evolutionary model, which brings to the fore the force-dynamic implications of this relationship.

The crux of this model is the notion that the world predisposes the occurrence of particular event sequences under certain kinds of circumstances. Hence the configuration of reality at a given point, Q, has substantial influence on the direction of its subsequent evolution—it is as though reality were striving to evolve along a particular path. When Q is equated with present reality, we are sometimes able to project its future course on the basis of this evolutionary momentum; *will* (in its basic epistemic sense) indicates that the designated process is so projected. The meaning displayed by *will* in (27) results when Q is not equated with present reality or identified in any way. With Q unanchored in time and reality, *will* is no longer deictic but amounts instead to a type specification, and the relationship it invokes (as elaborated by the clausal head) can thus be interpreted generically as a facet of how the world is structured. Since Q is the reference point from which the occurrence of the designated process is projected, the overall effect is to specify that evolutionary momentum leading to the occurrence of that process is present *whenever its antecedent circumstances might arise*. In other words, the force-dynamic relationship evoked by *will* is now viewed in generalized fashion as an aspect of the world's structure (instead of being construed specifically with reference to present reality). This same conception is latent in the construction exemplified in (28), perhaps even active to some degree, but *will* brings it into the foreground.

CHAPTER 7

Transitivity and Grammatical Relations

MY CENTRAL THEORETICAL claim is that grammatical structure is inherently symbolic and that all valid grammatical constructs have some kind of conceptual import. This chapter initiates the investigation of a closely related set of topics—including transitivity, grammatical relations, voice, and case—that have long resisted convincing semantic description. In fact, the lack of notional definitions for the subject and object relations, the apparent synonymy of actives and their corresponding passives, and the semantic unpredictability of case markings are often taken as prime evidence for the autonomy of grammar.

In recent years, intensive research on many fronts has changed this picture considerably. Functional, typological, and discourse studies have added a fundamentally important new dimension to our understanding of these grammatical constructs. Moreover, with the advent of cognitive semantics we can approach the question of their meaningfulness from a radically different perspective: granted the prototype theory of categorization, the characterization of meanings with respect to idealized cognitive models, and the centrality of imagery (construal) to semantic structure, a viable semantic description of these constructs can realistically be envisaged. The present chapter applies these notions to the description of transitivity and grammatical relations.

7.1. The Conception of Events

Meanings are characterized relative to cognitive domains, many of which are idealized cognitive models in the sense of Lakoff 1987. Cognitive models fundamental to our experience and our conception of the world are claimed to underlie the prototypical values of certain grammatical constructs pertaining to clause structure. Grammatically significant as well is the structure of events—or more precisely, the structure of our *conception* of events—in terms of conceptual autonomy and dependence. Clausal organization is in large measure shaped by the interaction of these factors.

7.1.1. *Models and Archetypes*

It was argued earlier (1.1) that the universality of nouns and verbs and their centrality to grammatical structure stem directly from the archetypal status of the billiard-ball model. The elements of this model are space, time, material substance, and energy.[1] These elements are conceived as constituting a world in which discrete objects move around in space, make contact with one another, and participate in energetic interactions. Conceptually, objects and interactions present a maximal contrast, having opposite values for such properties as domain of instantiation (space vs. time), essential constituent (substance vs. energy transfer), and the possibility of conceptualizing one independently of the other (autonomous vs. dependent). Physical objects and energetic interactions provide the respective prototypes for the noun and verb categories, which likewise represent a polar opposition among the basic grammatical classes.

The billiard-ball model also figures in the characterization of a prototypical finite clause, which inherits its profile from a content verb designating an energetic interaction. A useful construct for describing many aspects of clause structure is the notion of an **action chain**, diagrammed in Fig. 7.1. An action

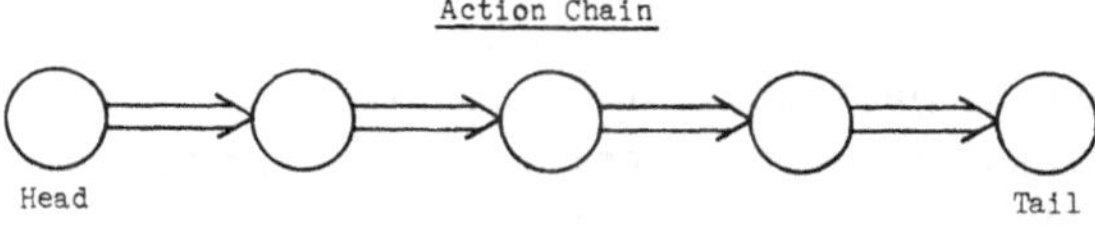

Fig. 7.1

chain arises when one object (shown as a circle) makes forceful contact with another, resulting in a transfer of energy (depicted by a double arrow); this second object is thereby driven into contact with a third, again resulting in the transmission of energy; and so on indefinitely, until the energy is exhausted or no further contact is made. The initial object in such a chain will be referred to as its **head**, and the final object, as its **tail**. Naturally, the simplest non-degenerate action chain is one in which the head and tail interact without intermediaries, so that there are only two participating objects.[2]

A second basic model pertains to perceptual experience. Let us call it the

[1] Is it fanciful to see a connection with the four elements posited by Greek philosophers? In three instances the equation is straightforward: *earth* = *material substance*; *air* = *space*; *fire* = *energy*. But can *water* be equated with *time*? I will simply note that the passage of time is very naturally understood metaphorically in terms of a flowing river.

[2] I am certainly not the first to entertain a conception of this sort. The closest explicitly formulated parallel is by Croft (1986, 1990), whose treatment of clause structure shows many similarities to that presented here and is basically compatible with it. Both analyses owe much to Talmy 1985, a seminal work that first revealed the prevalence of force-dynamic notions and their critical relevance to many facets of linguistic structure (cf. 6.3).

stage model, for the role of perceiver is in many ways analogous to that of someone watching a play.[3] An observer's gaze is generally directed outward, toward other objects. At any one moment his field of vision subtends only a limited portion of his surroundings, within which his attention is focused on a particular region, just as a theater-goer focuses his attention on the stage.[4] Now a stage is stable and inclusive, a fixed platform for the actors who move about and handle various props; in similar fashion, a viewer tends to organize the scene he observes into an inclusive **setting** populated by interacting **participants**, who are small and mobile by comparison. There is further organization along the temporal axis, where clusters of contiguous interactions (particularly those involving the same participants) are perceived as forming discrete **events**. In summary, the stage model idealizes a fundamental aspect of our moment-to-moment experience: the observation of external events, each comprising the interactions of participants within a setting.

Additional cognitive models reside in our conception of basic semantic roles, such as agent, patient, instrument, and experiencer. The linguistic importance of such roles was first made apparent by Gruber (1965) and Fillmore (1968). They are commonly referred to these days as "thematic relations" (or "theta roles"), and most contemporary theories make some use of them for semantic, lexical, and/or grammatical description. It is generally assumed that a rigorous linguistic theory has to provide a definitive list of these roles, and that some element from that inventory should correctly describe each participant's involvement in any verbal or clausal relationship; the failure to devise a satisfactory list has been a continuing source of concern. I do not believe, however, that a list of this sort is either necessary or achievable. An inventory of semantic roles can always be refined and articulated into more specific types on the basis of further data or a finer-grained analysis—at the extreme, every verb defines a distinct set of participant roles that reflect its own unique semantic properties (e.g. the subject of *bite* is a slightly different kind of agent from the subject of *chew*). Conversely, a role conception is arrived at by abstracting away from the peculiarities of individual examples. Since any kind of commonality provides the basis for a possible schema, and since schematization can be carried to any degree, we should not expect a fixed and limited inventory to accommodate all phenomena in every language.

I do not believe that semantic roles are first and foremost linguistic con-

[3] Metaphorical terms are adopted to facilitate description of the cognitive models, but it is not claimed that the models themselves are metaphorical. The stage and billiard-ball models are presumably universal and cognitively more fundamental than the culture-specific notions of theater and billiards.

[4] The perceptual distinction between the overall field of vision and the locus of viewing attention is parallel to the linguistic distinction between the overall scope of predication and the immediate scope, which is thus referred to as the *onstage region*. (Cf. Langacker 1985 and Vol. 1, p. 130.)

structs, but rather pre-linguistic conceptions grounded in everyday experience. Like any other conceptualization, they can however be invoked as part of the meaning of linguistic expressions or the characterization of linguistic elements, and certain role conceptions are so basic and experientially ubiquitous that their manifestation in language is for all intents and purposes inevitable. In order to call attention to their primal status and non-linguistic origin, I refer to these as **role archetypes**. Recognition of these archetypes does not imply that they are the only semantic roles of any linguistic significance; moreover, the cognitive salience of these and other roles is a matter of degree, and their construal for linguistic purposes is flexible and subject to a certain amount of variation. Role archetypes are not like a row of statues in an art museum, but are instead analogous to the highest peaks in a mountain range.

These archetypes reflect our experience as mobile and sentient creatures and as manipulators of physical objects. The archetypal **agent** is a person who volitionally initiates physical activity resulting, through physical contact, in the transfer of energy to an external object. Its polar opposite is an archetypal **patient**, an inanimate object that absorbs the energy transmitted via externally initiated physical contact and thereby undergoes an internal change of state. An **instrument** is a physical object manipulated by an agent to affect a patient; it serves as an intermediary in the transmission of energy. I will use the term **experiencer** for a person engaged in mental activity (be it intellectual, perceptual, or emotive), and **mover** for an entity that undergoes a change of location. This roster is hardly surprising, nor are the characterizations original. The important thing is to realize the non-linguistic origin of these roles, and that they do not form an exclusive club. Finer distinctions can be made (e.g. among the types and degrees of agency—cf. DeLancey 1984, 1985, and Croft 1986, pp. 146–48), and other roles (such as animate patient or non-human agent) may become both cognitively prominent and linguistically relevant.

By combining certain of the models described above, we obtain the complex conceptualization sketched in Fig. 7.2, which might be termed the

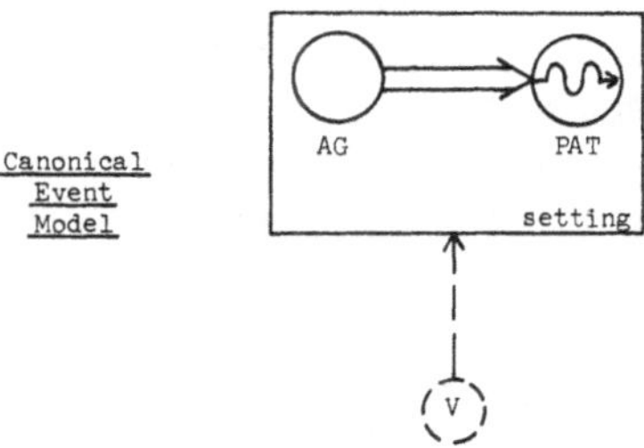

Fig. 7.2

canonical event model. The stage model contributes the notion of an event occurring within a setting and a viewer (V) observing it from an external vantage point. Inherited from the billiard-ball model is the minimal conception of an action chain, in which one discrete object transmits energy to another through forceful physical contact. Moreover, the action-chain head is characterized as an agent, and its tail as a patient that undergoes a resultant change of state (indicated by the squiggly arrow). In sum, the canonical event model represents **the normal observation of a prototypical action**. Its relevance to clause structure should be quite apparent and will be dealt with in 7.2.

7.1.2. *Conceptual Autonomy*

The distinction between autonomous and dependent elements is an essential feature of language design. A/D asymmetry is observable for both semantic and phonological structures, and for structures defined in both unipolar and bipolar terms (Vol. 1, Chs. 8–9). A vowel, for example, is autonomous with respect to its tautosyllabic consonants, and a root or stem with respect to an affix that it bears. Here our interest lies with semantic structures defined in unipolar terms. Specifically, the A/D alignment inherent in the conception of events is a major factor in the shaping of clause structure.

An event is conceptually dependent vis-à-vis its participants. For instance, one cannot conceptualize an act of slapping without making some kind of mental reference to the entity doing the slapping and the one receiving it—however vaguely these entities might be portrayed, if they are absent altogether the conception is incoherent. The verb *slap* is thus described as referring schematically to these participants as salient facets of its semantic structure. By contrast, a person or a physical object can be conceptualized independently of any event in which it might participate; although it is part of what we know about such entities that they do function as event participants, our conception of them is coherent even if this knowledge remains latent. They are, in short, conceptually autonomous.

Event conceptions display A/D asymmetry along a second axis as well. Most events are complex, in the sense that they are divisible into component subevents or constitutive relationships. Conceptually, for example, the bursting of a balloon can be analyzed as involving the release of pent-up pressure, the emission of a popping sound, and a sudden, drastic change in the shape and spatial distribution of the rubber membrane comprising it. A wink is decomposable into the motion of the eyelid to cover the surface of the eyeball, the muscular contractions that induce this motion, and the volitional control exerted by the winker (not to mention the perception of the wink by the person to whom it is directed, together with the various components of the social interaction in which the wink is embedded). Now it may be possible to conceptualize certain event components independently of the others, which makes them conceptually autonomous. For instance, we can imagine a popping sound without envisaging a change in the spatial properties of a rubber membrane, and conversely; though closely associated in our experience, these subevents do not presuppose one another for the very possibility of their conception.

Often, however, one event component is conceptually dependent on another. For example, the exertion of volitional control presupposes some conception of the activity being carried out—one does not exert control *tout court*, in the abstract. An instance of perception similarly presupposes some notion of the entity perceived. In an event of winking, therefore, both the exertion of volitional control by the winker and the perception of the act by the person winked at are conceptually dependent with respect to the motion of the eyelid. On the other hand, the eyelid's motion is conceptually autonomous, for it can easily be conceived as occurring in the absence of volition or perception (cf. *blink*). Such A/D asymmetry among the components of a complex event is both common and linguistically significant. In particular, it is a usual feature of events involving causation, as illustrated in (1).

(1)(a) *The wind caused the tree to fall over.*
(b) *The tree fell over.*
(c) **The wind caused.*

In (1)(a), the wind is described as having supplied the energy that resulted in the tree's change of position. We can also readily conceptualize this change as occurring autonomously, i.e. in the absence of any external force (apart from gravity); (1)(b) portrays it in this fashion. But (1)(c) is peculiar, for causation is conceptually dependent—the very notion makes inherent (albeit schematic) reference to the change induced.

Thus, to some significant extent the conception of an event exhibits A/D layering analogous to the layering of phonological segments within a syllable (Vol. 1, Fig. 9.1) or the morphological layering of a complex word. We must therefore ask what constitutes the innermost layer of such a conception—i.e. what is the functional analog of the syllabic nucleus or the morphological root? I take it to be a comparatively simple, conceptually autonomous relationship involving just a single participant.[5] Let us call this a **thematic relationship** and refer to the participant as a **theme**. The theme may represent any one of several role archetypes, and on this basis some fundamental kinds of thematic relationships can be distinguished. It is not claimed that these

[5] Autonomy/dependence is a relative matter, and while a relationship is dependent with respect to its participants, it may nevertheless be autonomous with respect to another relationship. Also, there is nothing anomalous about a relationship involving just one participant: a relation is defined in terms of interconnections, which may hold between subparts of a single participant or between a participant and some facet of a domain or setting.

types afford an exhaustive classification, or that a given thematic relationship will always straightforwardly instantiate a single type. Like the role archetypes they incorporate, these basic thematic relationships are comparable to the highest peaks in a mountain range.

The most elemental kind of thematic relationship is one in which the participant merely occupies some location or exhibits some static property. *Exist*, *round*, and *red* are good examples of expressions that profile such relationships. The semantic role of the participant will be referred to as **zero**, for conceptually it is minimal and non-distinctive. In fact, the zero role is inherent in the others (e.g. something has to be in a place in order to move, or have a property in order to change) and can be thought of as representing the degenerate case to which all of them collapse when a static view precludes the manifestation of their distinctive characteristics. Importantly, the zero role per se is unaltered if the description of a location or property should happen to be complex or incorporate a nominal. Consider *Alice is under the bed*. At the clause level, there is only one participant—Alice—and the thematic relationship is one of being in a certain location. The bed is invoked merely to specify that location; it is not a clausal *participant* (though it could be in other expressions), but rather part of the *setting*. Similarly, there is just one clause-level participant in *Alice is smarter than Metathesis*. Unlike *Alice chased Metathesis*, which describes a two-participant *interaction*, it mentions Metathesis only to characterize the property ascribed to Alice.

Fig. 7.3 gives the abbreviations adopted for the basic thematic roles. A participant in the zero role is represented quite naturally by an unadorned circle. Because the other roles can only be manifested with the passage of

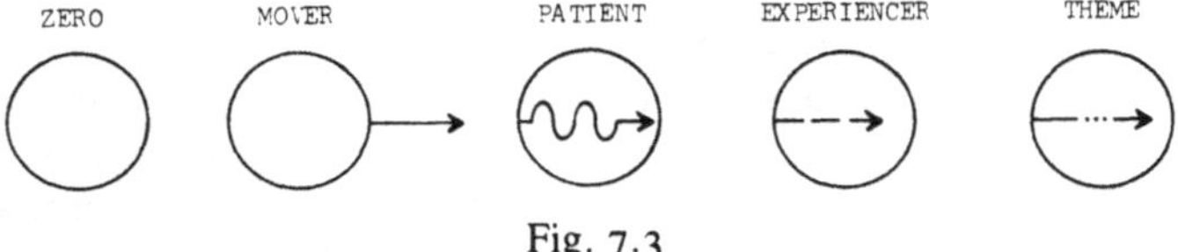

Fig. 7.3

time, various kinds of arrows are employed to distinguish them notationally. As noted previously, a mover changes position with respect to its surroundings, a patient is characterized as undergoing an internal change of state (i.e. some change in its own constitution), and an experiencer is the locus of a mental process (emotion, perception, ideation, etc.). I am using the term *theme* schematically for the participant in a thematic relationship; it thus subsumes the foregoing notions as special cases, as well as any other role associated with the autonomous core of an event conception.[6]

[6]Terminology in this area varies considerably. *Patient* is often understood more broadly (as something akin to *theme*), and *theme* more narrowly (as *mover* in a generalized sense). And

Strictly speaking, a thematic relationship involving a mover, experiencer, or patient is limited to the motion, mental experience, or change of state itself, exclusive of the forces that bring it about. A pure thematic relationship of motion, for example, consists of nothing more than a continuous series of locative configurations distributed over a span of conceived time; even if we believe that all motion involves energy in some way, it is nonetheless true that a non-energetic conception of motion is internally coherent. We can likewise imagine a person simply having a certain mental experience (feeling an itch, being joyful, etc.) without evoking any conception of its cause. Many changes of state are readily conceptualized with no essential reference to force dynamics: hair growing longer, the fading of a color, the solidification of a liquid, and so on. Even for events that are saliently energetic, it is often possible to factor out the force-dynamic component and conceive of the change of state autonomously. We can, for example, envisage the bursting of a balloon as merely the rapid spatial deformation of a rubber membrane, abstracting away from such notions as inflation and the release of pent-up pressure.

Yet, achieving this non-energetic construal is decidedly effortful, a feat of mental gymnastics. This difficulty suggests the need to distinguish two ways of defining conceptual autonomy (and hence thematic relationships), one reflecting the intrinsic organization of event conceptions, and the other having an experiential basis. **Intrinsic** A/D alignment pertains to whether one conceptual component presupposes another for its coherent manifestation, i.e. whether—given the nature of our cognitive abilities—it is possible *in principle* for the former to occur independently. By contrast, **experiential** A/D alignment is a matter of whether a conceptual component does in fact occur independently, or only as part of a larger configuration; that is, it takes into account the actual clusterings of event components that are encountered in experience and coalesce to form established concepts. The spatial deformation characteristic of a bursting balloon is intrinsically but not experientially autonomous, for in our experience it is always associated with the release of pressure and a popping noise. It is analogous to a morphological root such as *nat*, which does not occur as a separate word but is nonetheless the autonomous core of words like *native*, *nation*, *natal*, and *nature*; or to a phonologically autonomous vocalic nucleus in a language where a vowel never stands alone as a full syllable.

Because lexical units represent established concepts, experiential rather than intrinsic A/D alignment is more directly relevant for most linguistic purposes. The expressions conventionally used for the sudden, destructive defor-

whereas *thematic relation* is commonly used for any basic semantic role (including agent and instrument), I am distinguishing between thematic *relationships*—conceptually autonomous event components—and the thematic *roles* instantiated by their participants (which do not include agent or instrument).

mation of a balloon—*burst*, *break*, and *pop*—all portray the event as energetic in some fashion; we have no standard way of describing it autonomously as a purely spatial phenomenon. Hence the spatial deformation and the energy most immediately involved in its occurrence are facets of a single gestalt at the **level of initial lexicalization** (Vol. 1, p. 89); the event components are **sublexical** and can only be arrived at through conceptual analysis. On the other hand, an overt structural contrast marks the distinction between an event of that sort and a more elaborate event in which it is triggered by external forces:

(2)(a) *My balloon {burst/broke/popped}.*
(b) *Jason {burst/broke/popped} my balloon.*

From the standpoint of intrinsic A/D alignment, the intransitive verb stems in (2)(a) incorporate both a change-of-state thematic relationship and a conception of the energy most immediately responsible for it. Experientially, however, the events in (2)(a) are minimal (being dissociable into components only through intellectual effort) and conceptually autonomous. From this perspective they can themselves be regarded as thematic relationships, with the transitive stems in (2)(b) then arising when the conception is expanded to include an input of energy that induces the change of state.

Similarly, the event described in (1)(b), *The tree fell over*, can be analyzed as incorporating an autonomous thematic relationship wherein the tree changes orientation and position with respect to the ground, together with the conceptually dependent notion of gravitational force acting to bring this about. Experientially, of course, these two event components are packaged in a single gestalt that is lexicalized by *fall over* and constitutes a thematic relationship functioning as the autonomous core of a sentence like (1)(a), *The wind caused the tree to fall over*. But while the experientially-based analysis is the one reflected overtly in linguistic structure, in this case there is direct evidence that the finer-grained analysis in terms of intrinsic A/D alignment also has cognitive validity. For one thing, we are familiar in this space age with the behavior of objects in gravity-free environments and can readily envisage a spatial reorientation occurring independently of gravitational force. Furthermore, certain metaphorical extensions of *fall* into non-spatial domains preserve the notion of movement along some axis, whereas the conception of force, if present at all, is quite non-salient:

(3) *{The temperature/their level of concentration/his batting average} is gradually falling.*

We can likewise tease apart the various conceptual components of *walk*, even though experientially they form a tightly-bound package. Normally, as in (4)(a), the components of volitionality, muscular exertion, motion of the legs, force-dynamic interaction with the ground, and resultant change of location are all associated with a single participant:

(4)(a) *A balding waiter walked across the patio.*
(b) *Fred walked the semi-conscious drunk across the street.*
(c) *Sharon walked the ladder across the room.*

In (4)(b), volitionality is factored out, being attributed only to Fred, while the remaining components all involve the drunk. A different factoring is observed in (4)(c), where Sharon is the source of all control and exertion, and the ladder's role is purely that of a mover. Although it is hard in (4)(a) to separate the thematic relationship of spatial motion from the remaining components of the experiential gestalt, it is clearly isolated in (4)(c) by virtue of being assigned to a distinct participant.

Both intrinsic and experiential A/D alignment must therefore be recognized, each being relevant for certain linguistic phenomena. Under either sort of analysis, an event conception is generally describable as having a conceptually autonomous core consisting of a single-participant thematic relationship. When this autonomous thematic relationship occurs independently as the full conception evoked by a verb or a clause, I will say that its construal is **absolute**. This is to be contrasted with cases where the thematic relationship is embedded in a more elaborate conception that also makes reference to the energy that drives or sustains it; that energy may be supplied by the theme itself, as in (4)(a), or by some external source. Thus, with respect to experiential A/D alignment, the falling of the tree receives an absolute construal in (1)(b), *The tree fell over*, whereas (1)(a), *The wind caused the tree to fall over*, portrays it in force-dynamic terms.

7.1.3. *Starting Points*

The preceding sections have introduced two distinct ways of describing the structure of event conceptions. The first is the concept of an action chain (Fig. 7.1), which derives from the billiard-ball model and traces the propagation of force from one participant to the next in a series of energetic interactions. The second, pertaining to A/D layering, is the notion that an event conception is based on a conceptually autonomous thematic relationship, which can either stand alone or serve as the core of a more complex conception, typically one that portrays it as resulting from certain forces. It should by now be evident that both force dynamics and A/D organization have great cognitive significance and that their linguistic manifestations are varied and pervasive. In particular, a revealing account of clause structure must take both of them into account.

Each notion affords an important perspective on the conception of a complex event. Consider the examples in (5), which typify the linguistic coding of energetic events; analogous sets of data (though perhaps not the full paradigm) can be found in almost any language:

(5)(a) *The ice cracked.*
(b) *A rock cracked the ice.*
(c) *A waiter cracked the ice with a rock.*
(d) *The manager made a waiter crack the ice with a rock.*
(e) *The owner had the manager make a waiter crack the ice with a rock.*

Sentence (5)(a) describes a thematic relationship in which a patient (the ice) undergoes a change of state. Starting from this conceptually autonomous nucleus, each successive example expands the event description by adding a conceptually dependent layer of causation, in which an additional participant is portrayed as inducing the previously characterized event by supplying either a physical or an abstract force. Thus, if T represents a thematic relationship, and E the input of energy responsible for the occurrence of a process, the progressive assembly of the complex event conception in (5)(e) can be represented as follows: $(T) > (E_1(T)) > (E_2(E_1(T))) > (E_3(E_2(E_1(T)))) > (E_4(E_3(E_2(E_1(T)))))$. The parentheses indicate A/D organization, but if one ignores them and reads each formula linearly, it is equivalent to an action chain (the initial formula, T, represents the degenerate case of an action chain with a tail but no head).

There is an intrinsic tension between these two perspectives. An action chain traces the flow of energy from the initial *energy source* to the ultimate *energy sink* (i.e. the theme). It thus embodies the directionality inherent in cause-effect relationships, which for the most part coincides with temporal sequencing and clearly has substantial cognitive salience. At the level of conscious awareness, the most natural conceptualization of an action chain finds the conceptualizer following a mental path that mirrors the conceived energy flow from participant to participant. The A/D organization of an event conception also implies directionality, but one that runs directly counter to the flow of energy. Working outward from the nucleus, as in (5), the step-by-step assembly of a complex conception implies a mental path that starts with the theme and—in terms of energy flow—moves "upstream" from participant to participant until it reaches the action-chain head. We do not follow this second path at the level of conscious awareness, for it reflects an abstract organizational property and does not per se belong to the content of a conception.[7] Nevertheless, this outward movement from core to periphery represents one kind of cognitively natural ordering, in which each step produces a coherent and potentially independent conception.[8]

[7] In this respect it is comparable to (and partially correlated with) constituency, which reduces to a *compositional path* in the present framework.

[8] The A/D layering of an action chain, e.g. $(E_2(E_1(T)))$, is comparable to that of a syllable with a pre-nuclear consonant cluster: $(C_2(C_1(V)))$. With respect to the flow of speech time, C_2 initiates a linear path that is readily accessible to conscious awareness. Yet C_2 is not self-con-

A complex structure such as a clause has numerous levels or dimensions of organization, for each of which a particular ordering of elements may have a valid claim to being cognitively natural. Let us refer to such an ordering as a **natural path**, and to the origin of the path (i.e. the initial element in the sequence) as a **starting point**. Examples of the natural paths definable with respect to clause structure are (1) the flow of energy along an action chain; (2) the temporal sequencing of events or event components; (3) the temporal order of words at the phonological pole; (4) the core-to-periphery sequence of event components based on A/D alignment; and (5) the relative prominence of clausal participants in terms of figure/ground organization. The respective starting points of these paths are (1) the energy source (action-chain head); (2) the initial event (or event component); (3) the first word of the clause; (4) the thematic relationship; and (5) the clausal trajector. Although each path has its own rationale, they show a notable tendency to co-align with one another and for their starting points to coincide. Their failure to "harmonize" often results in marked expressions with special properties (cf. MacWhinney 1977; DeLancey 1981; Tai 1985).

Full harmonization is not in general possible, however. We have noted in particular the inherent tension between paths (1) and (4)—in a typical clause describing an energetic interaction, the starting point with respect to energy flow is the action-chain head (an agent), whereas the initial participant with respect to A/D organization is the action-chain tail (a theme). Because starting-point status entails a certain measure of cognitive salience, the conflicting directionality of these two natural paths tends to induce a contrast between two salient participants lying at their opposite extremes. In prototypical examples, these participants instantiate the archetypal roles of agent and patient, whose polar opposition reinforces that contrast. We see, then, that fundamental aspects of event conception promote the emergence of an agent (or energy source) and a patient (or theme) as especially prominent participants. For this reason they represent the unmarked choices for the basic grammatical relations of clausal subject and direct object.

7.2. The Coding of Events

The previous section dealt primarily with pre-linguistic notions. Even were language not considered, such constructs as role archetypes, the stage and billiard-ball models, action chains, and A/D alignment might well be posited

tained, being shaped in anticipation of the following autonomous structure, C_1V, which supports its implementation; C_1 similarly anticipates V and presupposes V for its full implementation. Anticipation or presupposition implies some sort of prior evocation; though not in terms of actual articulation, there must be some sense in which V is activated before C_1, and C_1V before C_2. Presumably this anteriority is reflected in the sequencing of neural events at some level of processing.

strictly on the basis of conceptual analysis. Linguistic structure does however make them visible to the analyst, and their utility for describing linguistic phenomena lends support to their validity. The interface between linguistic and conceptual structure now becomes our explicit concern. The initial topic is **coding**, i.e. the relationship between a conceptualization one wishes to express and the linguistic structures activated for that purpose.

7.2.1. *Coding and Construal*

Coding and construal are closely interdependent. How a situation is construed determines whether a particular linguistic structure is appropriate to code it. Conversely, a linguistic structure embodies conventional imagery and thus imposes a certain construal on the situation it codes. For example, the more agent-like a participant is conceived as being, the more likely it is to be coded as a subject, for which the agent role constitutes the prototypical value. And by coding a certain participant as the subject, the speaker can portray its role as approximating that of an agent. This explains why, when two cars collide, each driver says of the other: *He ran into me*.

Flexibility in regard to both coding and construal is a major reason why grammar appears arbitrary if one approaches it with the assumptions of objectivist semantics and the expectation of absolute predictability. There would be little question that grammatical constructs had conceptual import if all sentences, like *Jason broke my balloon* and *A waiter cracked the ice*, described canonical actions in which the subject and direct object conform quite well to the agent and patient archetypes—in that case the subject and object relations would simply mean 'agent' and 'patient', and the canonical event model (Fig. 7.2) would constitute the semantic characterization of transitive clauses. But in actuality, matters are far more complex on both sides of the coding gap. Conceptually, there are countless ways of construing a given event, and a particular event conception might deviate from the canon in any manner or to any degree. Linguistically, a variety of grammatical devices, each with multiple values clustered around a prototype, are usually available as alternate means of coding a given conception. An event's objective properties are consequently insufficient to predict the grammatical structure of a clause describing it.

Nevertheless, when analyzed in fine-grained detail the picture is not one of chaos, but rather of ordered complexity quite amenable to a cognitive grammar description. The very foundation of cognitive semantics is the recognition of our ability to construe a situation in alternate ways. It further recognizes that certain recurrent and sharply differentiated aspects of our experience emerge as archetypes, which we normally use to structure our conceptions insofar as possible. Since language is the means by which we describe our experience, it is natural that such archetypes should be seized upon as the prototypical values of basic linguistic constructs. Extensions from the prototype occur for the same reasons that they do with lexical items: because of our proclivity for interpreting the new or less familiar with reference to what is already well established; and from the pressure of adapting a limited inventory of conventional units to the unending, ever-varying parade of situations requiring linguistic expression. The specific set of extensions is not strictly *predictable* (one must simply learn, for example, whether the subject relation is extended from the agent to the instrument role in a particular language), but each extension is *motivated* in some fashion, and a construct has some semantic value in every one of its uses. Moreover, it is precisely because of their conceptual import—the contrasting images they impose—that alternate grammatical devices are commonly available to code the same situation.

We can best appreciate the complexity and non-deterministic nature of the relationship between an event and a clause that describes it by considering a single example in some detail. Suppose someone utters the simple, no doubt novel sentence *Floyd broke the glass*. Now there are innumerable kinds of situations for which this utterance would be appropriate: Floyd may have been dropped from a helicopter and fallen through a skylight; he may have just sounded a fire alarm; he may have inadvertently hit a drinking glass with his elbow and knocked it to the floor; he may have shattered it by singing a very high note; he may have hit a baseball through a picture window; and so on. But let us put that issue aside and assume that the utterance straightforwardly describes a particular event known in full detail—specifically, Floyd picked up a hammer, swung it at a drinking glass, made solid contact, and thereby smashed the glass to bits. Our interest lies in the options available to the speaker in the coding process. Given his intention to report the event, what construal and coding decisions does he make in arriving at the specific sentence *Floyd broke the glass*?[9]

The speaker must first decide what sorts of entities will be construed as event participants. Though we typically organize our conceptions around discrete physical objects readily perceived as such in the normal course of human experience—objects such as people, hammers, and glasses—these by no means represent the only option. The speaker could, for instance, opt to portray the event in terms of nerve impulses, muscular contractions, aerodynamics, and the propagation of discontinuities through a crystalline substance. Or, as exemplified in (6), he might select as participants entities that are either abstract (*hammer-blow*, *force*, *action*, *strength*, *structural integrity*) or function as parts rather than wholes (*sides*, *shards*, *fragments*, *arm*, *head of the hammer*):

[9]These are not necessarily conscious or effortful decisions (some represent default-case options), and the sequentiality of the following description is only for expository convenience. Obviously, we cannot yet characterize the actual cognitive processing responsible for coding—our goal is merely to elucidate some relevant factors.

(6)(a) *Floyd's hammer-blow shattered the sides of the glass.*
(b) *The force of the hammer hitting the glass caused shards to fly in all directions.*
(c) *Floyd's action generated fragments of glass.*
(d) *Floyd's arm brought the head of the hammer into contact with the glass.*
(e) *Floyd's strength overcame the structural integrity of the glass.*

That such choices are atypical, and even strike us as odd, is attributable to the special cognitive salience that attaches to a whole (relative to its parts), to the physical (as opposed to the abstract), and to entities that are directly perceivable (cf. Langacker 1984). Of course, any of these factors can be overridden in particular circumstances.

Assuming that these factors work their influence, so that the participants chosen are ordinary ones like people and manipulable physical objects, their construal still manifests a certain amount of flexibility. In particular, there may be alternate ways of grouping discernible objects into coherent assemblies that count as single participants. Our example offers at least three such possibilities, each implying a distinct action-chain configuration. *Floyd broke the glass with a hammer* codes the most natural construal of the event, wherein three participants are linked to form an action chain by a pair of two-participant interactions: *(Floyd)= = =>(hammer)= = =>(glass)*. The second grouping results from a tendency to view an instrument as an extension of the body, a construal that has a clear experiential basis.[10] When the hammer is downgraded from participant status and thought of as a mere appendage of Floyd, the action chain is effectively reduced to a single inter-participant linkage: *(Floyd-hammer)= = =>(glass)*. This is one likely motivation for the omission of explicit reference to the instrument in *Floyd broke the glass*, and also explains why Floyd would be considered disingenuous if he said *I never touched the glass!* (meaning that only the hammer came into direct physical contact with it). The third grouping is represented in the sentence *Floyd swung his arm and the hammer shattered the glass*. It reflects our ability to construe a body part as an object in its own right that can be acted on like any other object. Depending on whether the body part in question is identified as the arm alone or the arm-cum-hammer complex, the resulting action chain is either *(Floyd)= = =>(arm)= = =>(hammer)= = =>(glass)* or else *(Floyd)= = =>(arm-hammer)= = =>(glass)*.

When the speaker has selected a set of participants, and thus imposed a particular organization on the scene, he still faces an elaborate series of coding decisions. One group of choices pertains to the level of specificity at

[10] Perceptually, an instrument and its user form a spatially continuous unit and move together in a coordinated manner. Also, with enough proficiency at using an instrument we lose the sensation of wielding a foreign object; in effect it becomes a body part that we control in largely automatic fashion to "feel" and handle other objects.

which various facets of the event are to be characterized. The speaker may opt to be quite vague concerning the participants (*Someone broke something*), the action (*Floyd did something to the glass*), both the action and the participants (*Someone affected something*), or the event overall (*Something happened*). He may choose instead to be highly specific: *Floyd completely shattered Susan's favorite drinking glass by hitting it solidly with a brand new wooden-handled claw hammer*. In *Floyd broke the glass*, aspects of the event are described with varying degrees of precision. The subject is maximally precise in the sense that it names a specific person. At the other extreme, the instrument is not even mentioned—the characterization is vague not only as to its properties, but even in regard to whether one was used. The remaining elements are intermediate in specificity. *Break* and *glass* represent **basic-level categories**, a level of special cognitive significance at which we tend to operate unless there is some reason to resort to either a more specific or a more schematic notion (see Rosch 1977, 1978; Lakoff 1987).

Another matter to be resolved is the scope of the predication, i.e. how much of the overall situation the speaker selects as the intended coverage of the expression. The scope of *Floyd broke the glass* encompasses the action chain leading from Floyd (or Floyd-cum-hammer) to the glass, for it indicates that Floyd is the source of the energy by which the glass loses its structural integrity. Excluded from its scope are such matters as the color of Floyd's eyes, his effort in picking the hammer up, the spraying of the room with shards of glass, and any injury the flying shards might have caused. Of course, other expressions can be devised whose scope subsumes some or all of these elements: *His blue eyes blazing, Floyd picked up the hammer and smashed the glass to smithereens, thereby injuring several spectators with the flying shards*. By the same token, the scope of predication may include only a portion of the action chain, as in *Floyd picked up the hammer and swung it*.

The scope of predication delimits the basic conceptual content to be conveyed, and essential aspects of this content are rendered explicit by an appropriate choice of lexical items. It remains for the speaker to make a series of grammatical decisions by way of assembling the lexical items into a coherent expression that portrays this content in a particular fashion. In the case of clause structure, those decisions result in the imposition of a processual profile and a particular trajector/landmark alignment. A given scope of predication may permit a number of profiling options. For example, if the scope subsumes the Floyd-hammer-glass action chain, three different profiles are possible: *Floyd broke the glass* profiles the entire chain; *The hammer broke the glass* designates only the hammer-glass interaction; and *The glass broke easily*, though it invokes the efforts of an agent as part of its base, confines its profile to the thematic change-of-state process undergone by the glass. A given profile may likewise permit multiple choices of trajector, most notably by virtue of the active/passive alternation: *The glass was broken by Floyd* and *The glass was broken by the hammer* have the same profiles as their active counterparts, but it is the patient (rather than the agent or instrument) that functions as relational figure.

7.2.2. *Unmarked Coding*

Physical objects and energetic interactions are maximally distinct conceptual archetypes grounded in the billiard-ball model. Their polar opposition is reflected linguistically in the maximal contrast between the universal noun and verb categories, for which these archetypes constitute the prototypical values. We can thus expect a physical object to be coded by a noun, and an energetic interaction by a verb, unless special circumstances should motivate some departure from this pattern. The term **unmarked coding** will refer to this natural sort of arrangement, in which a notion approximating an archetypal conception is coded linguistically by a category taking that conception as its prototype. There are two basic sources of **marked coding**, in which this optimal arrangement does not obtain. For one thing, a linguistic structure may code a conception that deviates substantially from the corresponding archetype. This results in extension from the prototype and the growth of a complex category (Vol. 1, Ch. 10). Alternatively, a conception that does approximate an archetype may fail to be coded by the corresponding structure. An example is an action that conforms to the prototype for an active transitive clause but is coded instead by a passive (e.g. *The glass was broken by Floyd*); discourse considerations motivate this departure from unmarked coding (van Oosten 1986).

Marked clause structure is dealt with in Ch. 8. Our immediate concern is unmarked coding, and the natural place to begin is with a finite transitive clause describing an action. Such a clause has special status: both conceptually, because it corresponds to the archetype of an energetic interaction; and structurally, because it manifests the fullest array of properties that are specifically clausal (as opposed to nominal). My central claim is that the prototypical values of certain basic grammatical constructs—the values they assume in clauses of this sort—are characterized with reference to the canonical event model (Fig. 7.2). Recall that this model represents the normal observation of a prototypical action: from an external vantage point, a viewer observes an energetic interaction between an agent and a patient that occurs within an inclusive setting and constitutes a single event. The constructs that invoke this conception for the characterization of their prototypes include such notions as *subject*, *direct object*, *transitivity*, *central participant*, *clause-level adverb*, and *finite clause* itself.

The characterization of a prototypical finite clause invokes the canonical event model in its entirety. It further specifies that the agent and patient function respectively as the trajector and primary landmark, that their interaction constitutes the processual profile, and that the designated process is grounded epistemically. Because it satisfies all these specifications, a clause such as *Jason broke my balloon* is both prototypical and an instance of unmarked coding. It should be noted that the external vantage point referred to by the model corresponds linguistically to the subject and object being third person; the event involves participants other than the speaker and hearer, whose conceptualization of it is the linguistic analog of the viewing relationship. Also, the single event referred to by the model is identified specifically with the clausal profile, even if this is just one component of a more elaborate relationship within the scope of predication. As a consequence, *Jason broke my balloon* and *Jason caused my balloon to break* are not strictly synonymous. The former profiles—and portrays as a single event—the complex process designated by the grounded verb *break*, which subsumes both causation and the thematic relationship of breaking. By contrast, since the latter has *cause* for its grounded verb, it is only the act of causation—one component of the overall occurrence—that is put in profile and receives a one-event construal.[11]

Already we can see emerging an extensive parallelism between the canonical event model and the structure of a finite clause. Not only does a prototypical clause reflect the model overall, but various clausal elements correspond to particular facets of it: the speaker and hearer correspond to the viewer; their construal of the scene, to the viewing relationship; and the grounded verb, to the energetic interaction. Other grammatical constructs pertain to the participants in the interaction or to the setting. As idealized by the model, these notions are sharply distinct—the setting is stable and inclusive, whereas the participants are mobile, discrete, and small by comparison. Moreover, participants *interact* with one another but merely *occupy* the setting. An archetypal participant-participant relationship is therefore *energetic*, while the construal of a participant-setting relationship is *absolute*.

Rough grammatical correlates of the setting/participant opposition include the distinction drawn by Tesnière (1959) between "circumstantials" and "actants," and the contrast between certain adverbial expressions and the nominal complements ("arguments") of a verb. The unmarked device for coding the setting is a clause-level adverb, i.e. one whose trajector is identified with the remainder of the clause in which it appears. A form-meaning iconicity is thus discernible in the fact that such an adverb usually lies at the periphery of the clause (so that the remainder constitutes an uninterrupted sequence):

[11] An indication that the causation and the breaking may be construed as distinct (though related) events is the possibility of modifying the finite verb and its infinitival complement with separate time adverbials: ***At noon,*** *Jason caused my balloon to break* ***some time later*** *by setting it on the hot sand under the blazing sun*. See Fodor 1970; Wierzbicka 1975; Lakoff and Johnson 1980, p. 131.

(7)(a) ***In Louisiana,*** *a hurricane destroyed several small towns.*
(b) *She saw many interesting people* ***at the beach.***

(8)(a) ***In July,*** *a major hurricane struck Louisiana.*
(b) *We have made a number of important discoveries* ***during the last two years.***

We see from (7)-(8) that both spatial and temporal expanses lend themselves to construal as the setting, which is global and wholly includes the event. By contrast, a **location**—which we can characterize as a *fragment* of the setting—may be the site of just a single participant at a certain moment. Though a setting can always be left implicit, some verbs require that a location be overtly specified; an example is *put*, as shown in (9).

(9)(a) *She put the knife* ***in a drawer.***
(b) **She put the knife.*

(10)(a) *I chopped the onions* ***on the counter*** *with a cleaver.*
(b) ??*I chopped the onions with a cleaver* ***on the counter.***
(c) ?***On the counter,*** *I chopped the onions with a cleaver.*

(11)(a) ***On the counter,*** *a horde of ants was attacking a moldy crust of bread.*
(b) *A demented cook marred* ***the counter*** *with his cleaver.*

In (10), we observe another difference between a location and a setting, namely that an expression describing the former is sometimes most naturally situated in the middle of a clause instead of at its periphery. The sentences in (11) are meant to show that the status of an entity as a setting, a location, or a participant is not an inherent or immutable property but a matter of construal. While the counter functions as a location in (10), the smaller scale of (11)(a) causes it to be construed as the setting for the ants and their activity. In (11)(b), the counter achieves participant status by virtue of its interaction with the cook and cleaver. Louisiana is likewise the setting in (7)(a) but a participant in (8)(a).

Clausal participants are commonly apportioned into those with a "central" role in the profiled event—the subject and direct object primarily—and those whose role is considered secondary or peripheral. Such a distinction is well-motivated on linguistic grounds. For example, a verb may specifically require a subject and direct object, but the inclusion of such participants as an instrument or a beneficiary is almost always optional. It is common for verbs to agree with their subjects and/or objects, but not with other participants. And while the subject and object are often marked by zero, the role of other participants is virtually always signaled morphologically by means of case inflection or an adposition (i.e. a preposition or postposition). Clearly, then, the subject and object have special standing. But in what sense can we say that their role is *central*? Observe that in a canonical transitive clause like *Floyd broke the glass with a hammer* it is the instrument (not the subject or object) that is central in terms of both spatial location and the flow of energy along the action chain: (*Floyd*) = = = >(*hammer*) = = = >(*glass*). The only workable interpretation is that the subject and object are central in the more abstract sense of being the most important or *prominent* participants.

If we accept this characterization, the subject and object are more aptly referred to as **focal participants**. It is well known that neither the subject nor the object relation is consistently or uniquely associated with any single role archetype (such as agent, patient, or mover—any one of which can be coded by a subject). I suggest that they represent instead a separate dimension of organization, wherein certain participants are singled out for special prominence irrespective of their semantic role. Choosing a participant to be the subject or object is very much akin to focusing a spotlight on it; by making these selections, the speaker directs attention to the focused participants (as well as to the interconnections that involve them directly) and thereby imposes a particular image on the scene. Still, the choice of subject and object is non-arbitrary and shows a partial correlation with semantic roles. The action-chain head and the theme have a measure of intrinsic salience because they serve as starting points with respect to energy flow and A/D alignment (7.1.3), and this facilitates their selection. In canonical events, moreover, the head and theme coincide with the agent and patient archetypes (Fig. 7.2), whose cognitive salience is beyond dispute. These factors conspire to make agent and patient the prototypical values of the subject and object relations.

A clause that has both a subject and a direct object is said to be transitive. In recent years, the traditional notion of transitivity has been investigated in considerable depth and has proved to be both subtle and complex (Hopper and Thompson 1980, 1982; Rice 1987a, 1987b). There are cases where a verb is arguably transitive despite the lack of an overt object (e.g. *Roger always aims to* ***please***; *Peter washed the dishes and Marsha* ***dried***). More seriously, the occurrence of a nominal in direct-object position does not invariably render a clause transitive, as determined by such traits (depending on the language) as case marking, agreement, passivizability, and special verb morphology characteristic of transitives. For example, although the sentences in (12) have post-verbal nominals that appear to be direct objects (on the basis of position and the absence of a preposition), the infelicity of the corresponding passives in (13) calls their transitivity into question.

(12)(a) *After his divorce, Jason became a new person.*
(b) *That little boy resembles my nephew.*
(c) *Tuesday witnessed yet another gang-related slaying.*
(d) *The reactor's cooling system burst a pipe.*
(e) *The former emperor died a peaceful death.*

(13)(a) **After his divorce, a new person was become by Jason.*
(b) **My nephew is resembled by that little boy.*
(c) **Yet another gang-related slaying was witnessed by Tuesday.*

(d) **A pipe was burst by the reactor's cooling system.*
(e) **A peaceful death was died by the former emperor.*

Such considerations have made it increasingly apparent that transitivity is not definable just in terms of nominals occurring in a particular structural configuration. It is instead a matter of degree and depends on the meaning of the clause as a whole.

Works such as Hopper and Thompson 1980, Hopper 1985, and Rice 1987a have shown that a substantial number of conceptual factors contribute to transitivity. Among the properties characteristic of a prototypical transitive clause are the following: (1) it has two participants expressed by overt nominals that function as subject and object; (2) it describes an event (as opposed to a static situation); (3) the event is energetic, relatively brief, and has a well-defined endpoint; (4) the subject and object represent discrete, highly individuated physical entities; (5) these entities already exist when the event occurs (i.e. they are not products of the event); (6) the subject and object are fully distinct and participate in a strongly asymmetrical relationship; (7) the subject's participation is volitional, while that of the object is non-volitional; (8) the subject is the source of the energy, and the object is its target; (9) the object is totally affected by the action. This is not a random list. As pointed out by Rice, all these factors can be identified as facets of the canonical event model—it is this model that ties them together and provides a coherent basis for the prototypical notion of transitivity. The sentences in (12) are quite low in transitivity because they deviate from the prototype in regard to multiple factors.

From the foregoing observations, it is evident that the organization of a finite transitive clause reflects the canonical event model in numerous respects, and that aspects of this model support the characterization of certain basic grammatical constructs. Not every clause is transitive, however, nor is the model the only processual conception with a claim to archetypal status. There are other clause types that are comparably related to other conceptual archetypes, whose cognitive salience approaches that of the canonical event model (like major peaks in a mountain range that are not quite the highest); for these too we can speak of unmarked coding when a canonical conception is coded by a clause of the proper sort. For example, corresponding to the archetypal notion of an object moving along a spatial path is an intransitive clause in which the subject designates the mover, the verb describes the motion, and the path is specified by a prepositional phrase. The sentences in (14) are thus instances of unmarked coding.

(14)(a) *Rocky drove to the beach.*
(b) *An attractive woman walked into the store.*
(c) *A rock rolled down the hill.*

(15)(a) *This tree is very tall.*
(b) *Her truck was in the back yard.*

Exemplified in (15) is unmarked coding with respect to another clause type, which corresponds to the archetypal conception of a static situation in which an entity manifests an inherent property or finds itself in a certain location.

We thus expect a language to exhibit a number of basic clause types, each associated with a conceptual archetype that constitutes its prototypical value. To the extent that a notion approximates one of these archetypes, the corresponding clause type presents itself as the obvious way of coding it linguistically, possibly foreclosing other options. A conception that does not closely match any of the archetypes may be susceptible to alternate codings, each reflecting a different construal. For example, propelling oneself from the bottom of a mountain to the top is not a prototypical instance of moving along a path, for the difficulty of the task encourages us to construe the mountain as an adversary with which the climber interacts energetically. By the same token, the action deviates from the transitive-clause prototype because the mountain is inherently more like a setting than a participant and is not affected in any significant way. It is therefore unsurprising that this notion can be coded by either a transitive clause or by an intransitive clause with a path-specifying prepositional phrase:

(16)(a) *McMurtry climbed the mountain in seven hours.*
(b) *McMurtry climbed up the mountain in seven hours.*

The two sentences impose contrasting images on the scene: (16)(a) highlights the mountain's adversarial nature, while (16)(b) features its role as the landmark for defining a spatial path. They instantiate well-established patterns representing non-prototypical values of the two clause types.

A language does not necessarily have a separate clause type for every processual archetype. Consider verbs like *see*, *want*, *love*, *fear*, and *understand*, which describe the relationship between an experiencer—the locus of perception, emotion, or cognition—and some entity with which that experiencer establishes mental contact. Engaging in such relationships is certainly a fundamental aspect of our mental life, and a language may provide a special type of clause for coding them.[12] These notions are nevertheless abstract in a certain sense, and in line with our general tendency to structure abstract conceptions with reference to more concrete ones, they are commonly coded by a clause type whose prototypical value pertains to physical processes. English employs a transitive clause for this purpose:

(17) *I {see/want/love/fear/understand} it.*

[12] I am thinking in particular of dative-subject constructions (see Ch. 9).

This represents an extension from the transitive-clause prototype, since there is no transmission of energy from the subject to the object, which is totally unaffected by the relationship (i.e. the object's semantic role is zero). The extension is presumably grounded metaphorically, either through specific metaphors such as SEEING IS TOUCHING, or more generally, through the shared path-like nature attributed to such phenomena as energy flow, gaze, and directed attention (cf. Lakoff and Johnson 1980; Lakoff 1987, ch. 16; Johnson 1987).

However, directing one's attention to a particular entity can also be understood as analogous to moving along a physical path to a goal. Cook (1988a) has shown that this latter construal prevails for the corresponding verbs in Samoan, as (18) illustrates for the specific case of *see*.[13]

(18)(a)	*Na*	*tipi*	*e*	*le*	*tama*	*le*	*ufi.*	'The boy cut the yam.'
	PAST	cut	ERG	the	boy	the	yam	
(b)	*Na*	*alu*	*le*	*tama*	*'i*	*le*	*fale'oloa.*	'The boy went to the store.'
	PAST	go	the	boy	to	the	store	
(c)	*Na*	*va'ai*	*le*	*tama*	*'i*	*le*	*va'a.*	'The boy saw the ship.'
	PAST	see	the	boy	to	the	ship	

Simple perceptual contact is not coded by a transitive clause, like that in (18)(a), but rather by an intransitive clause of the sort used for physical motion—structurally, sentences (b) and (c) are precisely parallel. Hence (c) and its English translation are not equivalent semantically. Even if we assume that their conceptual content is identical, they contrast imagically if only because the event is coded by different clause types, each representing an extension from a different prototype.

7.3. Basic Grammatical Relations

The grammatical relations **subject**, **direct object**, and **indirect object** are of prime importance to the description of clause structure. Every syntactic theory has to provide some account of these notions, and as a consequence they have been the target of countless books and articles, which I will not attempt to survey systematically. Suffice it to say that the target has been elusive, and that there is no consensus regarding even the most basic issues. For example, some theorists deny that subject and object represent universal categories (Foley and Van Valin 1977, 1984), whereas others regard them as cornerstones of universal grammar. Those who accept such categories do not agree on whether they should be characterized in terms of meaning, grammar,

[13] ERG (for **ergative**) is the case marking associated with a transitive subject. The apostrophes stand for glottal stops.

discourse function, or some combination thereof. Theorists who view these relations as purely grammatical disagree as to whether they are primitive, as claimed in relational grammar (Perlmutter 1983; Perlmutter and Rosen 1984), or definable with reference to more basic constructs, such as phrase-structure configuration (Chomsky 1965a).

The following discussion does not purport to offer a complete and definitive resolution of these issues, if only because the relevant phenomena are so complex and interrelated, and the relevant cross-linguistic data so extensive. The goal is merely to sketch an account that coheres internally, is consistent with the principles of cognitive grammar, and holds some promise of proving empirically adequate. In accordance with the theory, an attempt is made to characterize the subject and object relations in terms of their conceptual import, which provides the basis for explicating both their discourse function and their grammatical behavior. Semantically, each relation represents a complex category that includes both a prototypical and a schematic value with reasonable claims to universal validity. However, the full network of values differs from one language to the next, and their manifestation in grammatical structure varies considerably. Both the universal and the language-specific aspects of these relations are thus accommodated.

7.3.1. *Subject*

It is grammatical behavior that alerts us to the special status of certain nominals within a clause and leads us to posit the subject and object relations. In a given language, the subject or object may be marked explicitly by such devices as word order, case inflection, or "agreement" registered on the verb or elsewhere. Moreover, the subject can usually be distinguished by its exclusive or preferential participation in certain grammatical constructions (Keenan 1976). It may, for example, be the only possible antecedent of a reflexive pronoun or some other anaphoric element. It may be the only nominal capable of "floating" a quantifier (3.3.1). The subject is also commonly pivotal in clause-linkage phenomena. For instance, a modifying-clause construction may require of the subject in particular that it be coreferential to the modified noun. Or a clause may contain a special marker to indicate whether or not its subject is the same as in the previous clause.

But despite its utility for the *identification* of subjects, grammatical behavior is unpromising as the basis for a universally valid *characterization* of the notion. For one thing, it is doubtful that any behavioral property (or set of properties) can be found that is both unique to subjects and characteristic of subjects in all languages. What we find instead is that certain behaviors are typical of subjects to one degree or another but are not associated with them either universally or exclusively. A more basic problem is that a simple list of behavioral properties would not per se be highly revelatory. Grammar is not an end in itself (except, perhaps, for certain linguists); rather, it is shaped and motivated by other, more fundamental considerations. The subject's tendency to assume a pivotal role in grammatical structure is most reasonably regarded as *symptomatic* of some special cognitive salience that makes it particularly accessible—a grammatical lightning rod, if you will.

7.3.1.1. *Topicality.* Of course, to characterize subjects in terms of cognitive salience is largely vacuous unless we can say more precisely what *kind* of salience is supposedly involved. A likely candidate is **topicality**, which—among those who study language from a functional perspective—is widely recognized as being closely related to subjecthood.[14] The notion of topicality is due to Givón; in numerous works (e.g. 1976, 1978, 1979, 1983, 1984) he has documented its grammatical significance. Sometimes described as "topicworthiness" (i.e. suitability for acting as a topic), topicality receives a straightforward interpretation in cognitive grammar. It is resolvable into several factors that pertain to different aspects of the conception of clausal participants. Each factor defines a natural path whose starting point has a certain measure of cognitive salience by virtue of being the initial element in an ordered sequence (7.1.3). A prototypical subject is the starting point with respect to all of these paths and therefore has maximal topicality and a high degree of prominence.

We can rank the topicality factors by their degree of objectivity, in the sense of being intrinsic to the event described (not just a matter of how it is construed). The most objective factor is an entity's semantic role, i.e. the nature of its participation in the event. Prototypically, the subject is an agent and hence the starting point with respect to energy flow along the action chain. If the profiled relationship includes a participant whose role is clearly agentive, its choice as subject represents the default-case option; choosing any other participant (as in a passive) requires special motivation and falls under the rubric of marked coding.

The second factor is a participant's location within what I will refer to as the **empathy hierarchy**.[15] This hierarchy reflects an egocentric assessment of

[14] While accepting this view, I reject the common assumption that topicality falls outside of semantics proper, belonging instead to the separate realm of pragmatics and discourse. Though traditional, such distinctions are aprioristic, unmotivated, and misleading—semantics, pragmatics, and discourse form a seamless whole. Reference to the speech event is central to the meaning of many linguistic units, and previous discourse (like any other conception) constitutes a cognitive domain with respect to which meanings are characterized.

[15] First introduced by Silverstein (1976), this well-known hierarchy goes by many names; I have chosen the one that best reflects the aspect I wish to emphasize. While the factors of *empathy* and *definiteness* are conflated in most formulations, I am treating them separately because they involve distinct natural paths based on parameters that are largely orthogonal. Deane 1987 offers a detailed description of the hierarchy and examines its relevance for English possessives. The notion of empathy is explored in Kuno and Kaburaki 1977.

the various sorts of entities that populate the world. It ranks them according to their potential to attract our empathy, i.e. on the basis of such matters as likeness and common concerns. Now the highest degree of empathy is of course with oneself—one is exactly like oneself, and shares precisely the same concerns. The starting point for the empathy hierarchy is therefore the speaker:

(19) *speaker > hearer > human > animal > physical object > abstract entity*

Ranked directly after the speaker is the hearer, for their co-participation in the speech event is an immediate common concern that can hardly be ignored. Continuing along this natural path, we next encounter a person other than the speaker and addressee, then an animal other than a human, and so on. Although empathy is for the most part less potent than agentivity as a determinant of grammatical structure, it nevertheless exerts an influence, as shown by data like the following:

(20)(a) *The dog chased me.* (a′) *I was chased by the dog.*
(b) *I chased the dog.* (b′) ??*The dog was chased by me.*

The active sentences (a) and (b) are both quite natural, for in each case the more agentive participant is chosen as subject. Yet their corresponding passives are not equally felicitous. The difference is that the subject choice in (a′) at least conforms to the empathy hierarchy, whereas in (b′) the subject ranks considerably lower than the other participant in addition to being less agentive. There are languages in which the object is not allowed to outrank the subject, or in which the verb is specially marked if it does so (cf. Hockett 1966; Hale 1973; Witherspoon 1980; Jelinek and Demers 1983).[16]

While empathy per se is a subjective notion, a participant's location on the empathy hierarchy is for the most part objectively determinable: whether an entity is human, animate, physical, or abstract is a matter of its intrinsic character, with little leeway for construal. By contrast, the third topicality factor—definiteness—is mostly subjective, for it does not pertain to the inherent nature of a participant, but rather to the highly extrinsic property of whether the speaker and hearer have succeeded in establishing mental contact with it (3.1). There is a well-known tendency for subjects to be definite (cf.

[16] I claimed earlier (7.2.2) that a prototypical clause has a third-person subject, in accordance with the canonical event model. A third-person subject is *typical* in the sense that most entities one has occasion to talk about are distinct from the speaker and hearer; it is unmarked with respect to the **optimal viewing arrangement**, in which the viewer has an offstage vantage point. At the same time, a first-person subject is *natural* in the sense that we are most directly concerned with ourselves, and is quite *frequent* as a consequence. A first-person subject is unmarked with respect to the **egocentric viewing arrangement**, in which the onstage region (objective scene) is expanded to include the viewer and his immediate circumstances. (For discussion of these notions, see Langacker 1985.)

Givón 1979, pp. 26–28). An indefinite subject often seems awkward and is commonly avoided by means of a special construction:

(21)(a) ??*A lake is in that valley.* (a′) *There is a lake in that valley.*
(b) ?*Migraine headaches plague Sally.* (b′) *Sally is plagued by migraine headaches.*

A natural path is thus defined by the hierarchy *definite > specific indefinite > non-specific indefinite*, whose starting point implies that the speaker and hearer direct their attention to a particular instance t_i of the type in question. Finer distinctions can of course be made. For example, a proper name (such as *George Lakoff*) represents a higher degree of definiteness than a nominal based on a common noun (e.g. *the cunning linguist*); because the relevant category has only a single member, the conception of t_i is more narrowly focused than in cases where it has to be located within a reference mass comprising an open-ended set of instances. A more focused conception also results to the extent that an instance is bounded, compact, and well-delimited. Objectively motivated contrasts such as count vs. mass, singular vs. plural, concrete vs. abstract, and pointlike vs. extended are therefore not unreasonably regarded as establishing finer degrees of definiteness.

The final topicality factor, figure/ground organization, is almost wholly subjective. Although an entity's selection as the figure within a scene is encouraged by certain objective properties (e.g. compactness; being in motion; contrast with surroundings), in the final analysis figure/ground alignment is not inherent in a situation but a matter of construal. The linguistic relevance of figure/ground organization is shown by the semantic contrast between such pairs as *before* vs. *after*, *above* vs. *below*, and *in front of* vs. *in back of*, which are not distinguished by either conceptual content or profiling (cf. Talmy 1978, 1983; Wallace 1982). I have argued that most relational predications confer special prominence on one of the participating entities, and that this entity—the trajector—is plausibly analyzed as the figure within the profiled relationship (Vol. 1, 6.3). I have further suggested that some other entity is capable of standing out from the background as a kind of secondary figure; this is referred to as the landmark (or the *primary* landmark if there are other entities of note). Trajector/landmark alignment is observable at any level of structural complexity, including the clause level; it thus establishes a partial ordering, based on one kind of prominence, among the clausal participants. The trajector (relational figure) is the starting point with respect to this natural path.

To summarize, a prototypical subject ranks highly with respect to all four topicality factors: it is agentive, human, definite, and the figure within the profiled relationship. The cognitive salience implied by this high degree of topicality makes a subject easily accessible for participation in grammatical constructions. As a consequence, in any given language a certain array of grammatical behaviors comes to be associated with subjects; it is on this basis that the subject relation is posited and its instantiations are identified. However, these behaviors need not be associated with the subject exclusively, nor is their inventory precisely the same from one language to the next. In short, they are symptomatic of the special prominence of subjects but do not per se constitute a characterization of subjecthood, which is claimed instead to be conceptual in nature. Some further questions concerning that claim must now be addressed. Assuming that the prototype has been correctly described, can we also posit a *schematic* characterization of subjects valid for all instances? What is the relationship between a subject and a topic? Can it be maintained that the subject relation is universal?

7.3.1.2. *A Schematic Definition.* If there is something that all subjects have in common, it cannot pertain to either empathy or definiteness. It is natural for the subject to be human (especially a speech-act participant), but examples are readily found of subjects occupying any position along the empathy hierarchy. In many languages, a subject can also rank extremely low on the definiteness scale (e.g. *Workable strategies are being sought by corporate management*). Thus, while empathy and definiteness are components of topicality, they could not be included in a universally valid schematic characterization of subjecthood. What about agentivity? It is obvious that not every subject is an agent; in fact, a subject can represent any semantic role. One might however entertain the weaker position that the subject of a *transitive* clause, if not an agent, is always *agent-like* in some significant respect. Perhaps we can find a more schematic notion that is applicable to all transitive subjects and captures what they have in common with the agent prototype.

It might be suggested, for example, that a transitive subject is always the head with respect to the profiled portion of an action chain. In addition to prototypical agents, this definition would accommodate inanimate energy sources, like those in (22), and also instruments, as in (23).[17]

(22)(a) *An earthquake destroyed the village.*
(b) *A meteor made that crater.*
(c) *This locomotive can pull 100 loaded boxcars.*

(23)(a) *The sledge hammer easily crushed even the largest snails.*
(b) *His dull knife wouldn't cut the frozen meat.*
(c) *A 9-iron lofts the ball more than any lower-numbered iron.*

Another large class of examples falls within the purview of the definition if we generalize the notion of an action chain to allow its metaphorical extension to

[17] Observe that the profile in (23) is limited to the interaction between the instrument and the theme. Thus, while the scope of predication may include the conception of an agent, the *profiled* portion of the action chain is headed by the instrument.

non-physical domains. For instance, Talmy (1985, 1988a) applies his conception of force dynamics to the realm of social interactions:

(24)(a) *They urged me to change my vote.*
(b) *The outraged faculty finally forced the chancellor to resign.*
(c) *The blackmail note should persuade him to keep quiet.*

Also conceived in force-dynamic terms is the initiation of a transfer, even one that does not involve any physical motion:

(25)(a) *The bank transferred the deed to the buyer.*
(b) *Phelps told his story to anyone who would listen.*
(c) *The chief assigned three detectives to the case.*

The sentences in (25) portray the object as moving abstractly into the dominion of the recipient, and the subject is construed as supplying the energy that induces the transfer.

The notion *action-chain head* cannot however serve as a universally valid characterization of transitive subjects, for there are many examples that do not involve the transfer of energy, even in an abstract or metaphorical sense. Among them are clauses of the type *EXPER---->ZERO*, in which the subject is an experiencer who merely establishes mental or perceptual contact with the object:

(26)(a) *I remember my childhood very well.*
(b) *The nurse noticed a tear in the oxygen tent.*
(c) *We can't see Mars tonight because of the haze.*

Now it may well be that our conception of these processes invokes some kind of perceptual or ideational subject-to-object path (e.g. the experiencer may be conceived as mentally "reaching out and touching" the other participant). But while such a path is analogous to an action chain in terms of its abstract configuration, there is no transmission of energy to the object, which is completely unaffected by the mental contact; hence the object's semantic role is zero. Needed, then, is a schematic definition of transitive subjects that will handle such expressions in addition to those based on an action chain. Let me offer *active participant in an asymmetrical relationship* as a plausible candidate. In an action chain (e.g. *AG===>PAT*), the interaction is asymmetrical because the energy flows in one direction, and the subject is the active participant in the sense of being the energy source. The relationship *EXPER ---->ZERO* is asymmetrical both in the directionality of the mental path and also because only the subject's involvement is in any way energetic. As the locus of the mental experience and the source of the energy required to sustain it, the subject is clearly the active participant.

Yet even this highly schematic definition fails to accommodate many transitive subjects. There are transitive clauses that describe static situations in which neither participant is active, even in the sense of undergoing a change or having a mental experience. In such examples the semantic role of both the subject and the object is zero (as indicated by the formula *ZERO---->ZERO*):

(27)(a) *A fence surrounds his property.*
(b) *Sharon's apartment faces the courtyard.*
(c) *This nicely-wrapped package contains nothing but crumpled newspapers.*

Moreover, the relationship is sometimes symmetrical (formulaically, *ZERO ----ZERO*):

(28)(a) *Line A intersects line B.*
(b) *The railroad tracks parallel the highway.*
(c) *Joshua resembles Jonathan.*

The symmetry of the profiled relationship rules out any objective basis for choosing one participant as the subject in preference to the other. It therefore seems quite doubtful that all transitive subjects (let alone subjects in general) instantiate any semantic role describable with reference to such notions as activity or asymmetry.

Nevertheless, the relationships in (28) must in some way be asymmetrical, for the corresponding sentences in (29)—with the opposite choices of subject and object—are not precisely synonymous.

(29)(a) *Line B intersects line A.*
(b) *The highway parallels the railroad tracks.*
(c) *Jonathan resembles Joshua.*

Note, for instance, that (28)(c) is a natural response to the question *What does Joshua look like?*, while (29)(c) is not. One might therefore propose that such clauses involve some kind of *subjective* asymmetry: lacking an objective basis, this asymmetry would reside in the very manner in which the situation is conceptualized. It might further be suggested that there is some respect in which the subject is subjectively "active" in both *ZERO---->ZERO* and *ZERO----ZERO* clauses. One specific and quite reasonable hypothesis is that the subject is subjectively active in the sense of standing out from other participants as a focus of interest, and that this itself constitutes an asymmetry in the conception of the profiled relationship. It could then be argued that a transitive subject is always the *subjectively active participant*. While the subject is usually also *objectively* active (which makes it the natural focus of interest), in extreme cases a non-active participant is focused on simply because the speaker opts to construe the situation in that fashion.

This is the kind of description one is led to in trying to find a schematic semantic role instantiated by all transitive subjects. From the perspective of cognitive grammar, the proposal is neither mysterious nor implausible: notions like "focus of interest" are perfectly legitimate, and some such construct is needed to characterize the subtle but real semantic contrast exhibited in examples like (28)–(29). One might however question whether "focus of interest" is properly regarded as a semantic role, since it does not pertain to the nature of an entity's participation in the profiled relationship. While basically accepting the description, I will therefore advance a rather different interpretation of it. I suggest that the rather vague notion "focus of interest" reduces to the well-established phenomenon of figure/ground organization. What all transitive subjects have in common is not a particular semantic role, but rather the status of *figure* within the clausal profile. Of course, this characterization is not inherently tied to transitivity—it is equally applicable to intransitive subjects.

Let us take stock. A prototypical subject is salient by virtue of ranking highly in regard to all four topicality factors. Empathy and definiteness appear to be the most weakly correlated with subjecthood, as a participant with a high value on those parameters is capable of representing any grammatical relation. A subject's semantic role is prototypically that of an agent. Subjects can however manifest a broad variety of semantic roles, and while many of these are subsumed by more schematic definitions such as *action-chain head* and *active participant in an asymmetrical relationship*, there is no apparent role characterization valid even for all transitive subjects. If all subjects do have something in common, it must be subjective in nature (i.e. a matter of construal rather than conceptual content). Since figure/ground organization is basic to cognition and important to the semantics of relational predications in general, it is natural to identify subjects as clause-level trajectors. A clausal subject is thus hypothesized to be the figure within the profiled relationship.

One can legitimately ask whether an all-embracing schematic characterization is really necessary. Cognitive grammar certainly admits that there are complex categories which lack a schema compatible with all class members. It is further recognized that such a category has the capacity for coherent interaction with other elements (Vol. 1, 10.3.4), and that prototype structure is consistent with class membership being categorical rather than a matter of degree (Lakoff 1987, pp. 148–51). Hence the theory does not stand or fall with the possibility of finding a universally applicable schematic definition of subjecthood. Several considerations nevertheless encourage the effort. First, because subjects are so disparate in character, and overlap so extensively with other grammatical relations in terms of the topicality factors, it is not entirely obvious that similarity to the prototype is sufficient to explain the coherence of the subject category in regard to various grammatical behaviors.[18] Also, I

[18] If only subjects participate in a certain construction, schematic reference to the category may be required—a constructional schema referring only to the prototype might not provide adequate basis for extending the pattern to all subjects but no non-subjects. However, I must leave this question open pending a fuller understanding of category coherence.

consider it highly probable that notions like *subject, noun, verb, possessive, count* vs. *mass*, etc. are fundamental to grammar precisely because they are grounded in very basic aspects of cognition, which are directly reflected in their proposed schematic values. Lastly, there does appear to be a viable candidate: *relational figure* nicely captures both the salience of subjects and the great flexibility in their selection.

7.3.1.3. *Subject and Topic.* It is widely agreed that the notions *subject* and *topic* are related in some fashion. There is, however, no consensus regarding the nature of that relationship, partly because of vagueness or disagreement about what a topic is supposed to be. For instance, the rather vague definition of a topic as "what the sentence is about" is fairly common, as is the claim that a subject is usually a topic in that sense (e.g. Keenan 1976, p. 318; Bates and MacWhinney 1982). On the other hand, Chafe (1976, p. 43)—following long tradition—accepts that same definition as roughly valid for *subjects* but offers a different characterization of topics. Only by adopting a limited and reasonably explicit characterization of the notion *topic* can we resolve such discrepancies and properly assess the subject-topic relationship.

Whereas *subject* is a clause-level construct, topics are clearly a discourse phenomenon. We can distinguish two phases in a topic's career. At some point in the flow of discourse, an entity is first *established* as a topic, often by a special marking or grammatical construction. English has several devices for this purpose:

(30)(a) *As for* ***weddings****, they always bore me.*
(b) ***Weddings****, they really leave me cold.*
(c) ***Weddings*** *I just don't care for.*

It may however be sufficient simply to mention the intended topic:

(31) *I've been thinking about* ***the wedding****. I only want to invite the immediate relatives. The back yard would be a good place. We don't need flowers . . .*

Once established, a topic holds sway over a certain stretch of discourse (perhaps until another one replaces it). There may be little need to mention the topic explicitly during this phase of its career. Reference to an established topic is therefore often pronominal, as in (30)(a)–(b), or even omitted altogether; the wedding is not mentioned at all after the initial clause in (31), but the remainder presupposes its topic status.

What precisely is this status? As a first approximation, it is useful to think of a topic as the address to which the content of a clause is supposed to be delivered. Within the mental world of the speech-act participants (and more narrowly, within the current discourse space (3.1.1)), it represents the specific conceptual realm with respect to which the clause is meant to be interpreted and into which its content is integrated. In (31), for example, the back yard is understood to be a good place for the wedding in particular, though it is no doubt suitable for many other things as well. Similarly, the speaker of (31) may have a dire need of flowers (e.g. for an imminent funeral), but the last sentence is nonetheless appropriate provided that flowers are considered superfluous for the wedding.

We can describe a topic more technically as a kind of **subjective reference point**. It is a *reference point* in the sense of being used to establish mental contact with another entity (4.3.2.1). Consider (31) once more. While there are many things for which flowers are unnecessary, i.e. many instances of the process type *We don't need flowers (for X)*, the topic enables the hearer to direct his attention to the specific instance in which *X* is identified as the wedding. This reference point is *subjective* in two respects. For one thing, it remains offstage and often unmentioned. Rather than being explicitly discussed, an established topic is presupposed as part of the common background that the speaker and hearer rely on for making sense of the material presented overtly. A topic is also subjective in that the basis for its reference-point function resides in speaker/hearer knowledge per se. In contrast to possessive expressions, where the possessor serves as reference point by virtue of some objective relationship it bears to the possessed (ownership, part/whole, kinship, etc.), it may be the organization of knowledge itself—even a relationship of class membership—that allows a topic to serve this function. For instance, the topic in (32) names the general class ('fish') of which the subject is a subclass ('red snapper'):[19]

(32) *sakana wa tai ga oisii* [Japanese]
fish TOP red:snapper SUBJ delicious
'(As for) fish, red snapper is delicious.'

By evoking the relevant superordinate category, the topic takes the hearer one step along a path through conceptual space, at the end of which he establishes mental contact with the subject and the profiled relationship.

Fig. 7.4 diagrams the relationship between an established topic and a stretch of discourse that presupposes it. The topic is some entity in the conceptual universe of the speech-act participants. The topic's dominion (D_{TOP}) is the set of conceptions that it tends to activate and for which it can therefore function as a reference point. Ranging along the speech-time axis (T) is the pertinent discourse, which comprises a series of clauses each of which profiles a relationship involving a certain number of participants. While the topic

[19] TOP indicates a topic marker, and SUBJ, a subject marker. Examples (32)–(33) are from Li and Thompson 1976.

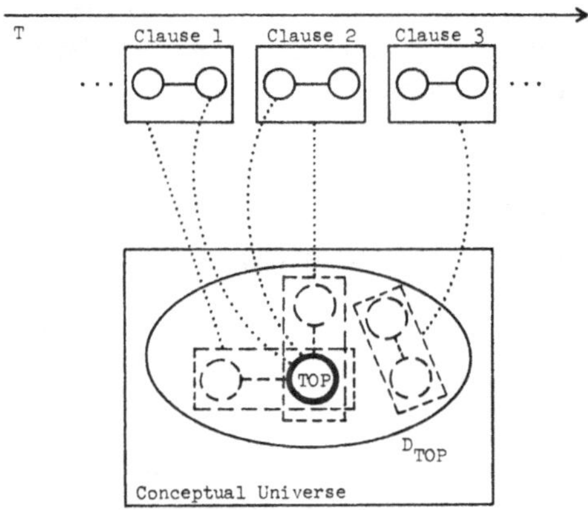

Fig. 7.4

is typically identified with one of the clausal participants (as shown for clauses 1 and 2), this is by no means always the case (clause 3); the only universal requirement is that there be some overlap between the topic's dominion and some facet of the clausal predication. This overlap is what enables the predication to be interpreted with reference to the dominion (as indicated by the dashed-line boxes).

If something along these lines is what people have in mind when they say that a topic is "what the sentence is about," then it is clear that subjects are not invariably topics, or conversely. A topic can in principle correspond to any facet of a clause (though a particular topic construction may define the relationship more narrowly). Often the topic does indeed correspond to the subject, as in (30)(a)–(b), but in (30)(c) it represents an object, and in (31) its participant role is peripheral to the designated process. The topic need not be a participant at all; for example, in (33) it constitutes the setting:

(33) *nèi kuài tián dàozi zhǎngde hěn dà* [Mandarin]
that piece land rice grow very big
'That piece of land, rice grows very big (on it).'

And sometimes, as we saw in (32), the topic merely specifies a realm of knowledge into which the clausal process is somehow supposed to fit. It is of course natural for the subject, as the most prominent clausal element, to be the one through which the connection with the topic is established; identity with the topic may in fact motivate a particular choice of subject. Nevertheless, we can only say that the role of discourse topic is *overlaid* on that of clausal subject—it cannot be invoked as a general *characterization* of subjects.

Pointing to the same conclusion is the incisive discussion of Lambrecht 1987, which concerns a contrast observed in many languages between two types of simple declarative sentences:

(34) *What's the matter?*
(a) *My NECK hurts.*
(b) *Mi fa male il COLLO.* [Italian]
(c) *KUBI ga itai.* [Japanese]

(35) *How's your neck?*
(a) *My neck HURTS.*
(b) *Il collo mi fa MALE.* [Italian]
(c) *Kubi wa ITAI.* [Japanese]

The contrast resides in the discourse status of the subject and is signaled by differences in accent, word order, and/or grammatical markers (e.g. *wa* vs. *ga* in Japanese).[20] According to Lambrecht, the normal situation is the one in (35), where the subject is the topic, about which the remainder of the sentence makes some assertion. However, this "aboutness relation" requires that the subject have a certain degree of "cognitive and pragmatic *accessibility* . . . in the discourse" (p. 375). The constructions in (34) convey that the subject lacks such accessibility—instead of being presupposed as a reference point, the subject is part of what the speaker is presenting to the listener as new (or as newly relevant) material. To properly describe the distinction between these sentence types, we must therefore take the subject-topic association as being prototypical rather than definitional.

But although the subject is not an established discourse topic in (34), it might still be argued that there is some sense in which these sentences are "about" their subjects. Likewise, one might argue that (30)(c) is in some sense about the speaker (despite the topicalization of *weddings*), and that *dàozi* 'rice' is the topic of (33). Can we then find some other, less stringent characterization of the notion *topic*, one to which every subject might conform? Perhaps so. I suggest, however, that the only explicit characterization with any chance of proving viable is the one offered earlier as the schematic definition of subjects: *figure within the profiled relationship*. If the contrast exemplified in (28)–(29) is correctly described as one of figure/ground organization, it seems most likely that the same phenomenon is responsible for the "aboutness" relation in examples like (34)—these latter sentences are

[20] This contrast corresponds to the "thetic"/"categorical" distinction examined by Kuroda in various publications (1972, 1976, 1979). Lambrecht speaks instead of "sentence focus" vs. "predicate focus" structures. Neither sentence type represents a special construction serving to establish a discourse topic (as in previous examples); the function of the contrast is rather to indicate whether or not the subject's status as a local topic is presupposed as having already been established. (Note that Japanese *wa* marks both presupposed topics and those being established—cf. (35)(c) and (32).)

"about" their subjects in the same sense that *Joshua resembles Jonathan* is about Joshua (whereas *Jonathan resembles Joshua* is about Jonathan). I thus conclude once more that a universally applicable definition of subjecthood can only be a matter of construal (not of content), and that *relational figure* is by far the most plausible candidate.

In summary, a subject is not definable as a discourse topic, even though a subject's cognitive salience makes it the unmarked choice to function in that capacity. This salience has a number of ingredients (topicality factors). The one ingredient that is arguably characteristic of all subjects—namely, the status of relational figure—offers a reasonable basis for the weak sense in which a sentence is "about" its subject regardless of discourse considerations. While I am not aware of anyone else advancing *relational figure* as a schematic characterization of subjects, the overall analysis does appear compatible with proposals made by certain other scholars. It is very much in line with how Chafe (1976) describes the subject/topic distinction. Fillmore (1977, pp. 74–75) acknowledges the grammatical relevance of something akin to figure/ground organization and states that a "particular expression . . . presents in the foreground—in perspective—only a particular aspect" of a scene. Moreover, in the same spirit that I speak of *focal participants* (7.2.2), he refers "to the elements . . . brought into perspective—the elements that appear as subjects and objects—as *nuclear elements* in the sentence." Shibatani (1985, p. 832) states that subjects, followed by direct objects, have the highest "degrees of focus" among the clausal participants, being "highlighted against the background of . . . other entities . . . in the consciousness" of the speaker and hearer; they are "more prominent" than other elements, "most salient in the speaker's mind, and call for more attention on the part of the listener." Finally, though Givón regards subjects as topics (1976), his statement that "the subject . . . tends to code [not that it invariably *does* code] the most important, recurrent, continuous topic" (1984, p. 138) implies that the subject and the major discourse topic do not always coincide. His description of a subject and direct object as the "primary" and "secondary clausal topics" resonates with my own account in two respects: the term *clausal* topic suggests a lesser topic status that is perhaps equatable with the weaker kind of "aboutness" relation; also, the reference to *primary* and *secondary* topics recalls my schematic definition of a subject as the most prominent clausal participant (in terms of figure/ground organization), and an object as the second-most prominent participant.

7.3.1.4. *Universality.* While the subject relation is undoubtedly a language universal, the specific nature of its universality remains an unsettled issue. Does it represent an **absolute universal**, found in every language without exception, or just a strong **universal tendency** (Vol. 1, 1.2.6.2)? Are subjects the same in all languages for which they are posited, or would it be more accurate to speak of distinct grammatical relations showing at best a family resemblance? The answers to such questions obviously depend on the type of characterization envisaged. The usual approach, which is to concentrate on the grammatical behavior of subjects, has the effect of highlighting cross-linguistic variation and lessening one's assessment of their universality (cf. Foley and Van Valin 1977). A rather different picture emerges if one adopts a semantic approach in which the grammatical accessibility of subjects is viewed as merely symptomatic of their conceptual prominence.

The question of universality has naturally arisen in regard to ergative languages, where case marking supports a grouping of participants that cross-cuts the classic subject/object distinction: there is one marking for a transitive subject, and another for both a transitive object and the single nominal (the subject?) of an intransitive clause. Moreover, because such languages display a tendency—sometimes quite pronounced—for other grammatical behaviors to pattern in the same way (cf. Dixon 1972, 1979a, 1979b; Heath 1979), it might be suggested that subject and object are inappropriate constructs, and that ergative languages employ an alternate set of grammatical relations. However, ergativity and subject/object organization need not be considered mutually exclusive. Each way of grouping the clausal participants has its own rationale (see 9.1), and every language probably uses both groupings for one purpose or another. Anderson (1976) has argued that the subject relation is motivated by syntactic phenomena in languages classed as ergative on morphological grounds. Moreover, subjects and objects have been attributed to ergative languages on a principled basis by scholars of different theoretical persuasions (e.g. Aissen 1983; Cook 1988a).

A more serious challenge to the universality of subjects was posed by Schachter (1976, 1977) in regard to Tagalog and other Philippine languages. Schachter noted that Tagalog lacks the kind of subject familiar from European languages, in which topic status, agentivity, and a particular array of grammatical behaviors all tend to be associated with the same participant. In fact, from the European perspective the situation is problematic in several respects. First, the roles of topic and agent appear to be completely independent. With the proper marking on the verb, a nominal representing any semantic role can be chosen as the topic, as illustrated in (36). Observe from the glosses that the topic is always interpreted as being definite.[21]

(36)(a) ***Mag**-bibigay* ***ang babae*** *ng bigas sa bata.*
AT-will:give T woman G rice D child
'The woman will give some rice to {a/the} child.'

[21] The markers labeled A, G, and D indicate the respective semantic roles Schachter calls "actor," "goal," and "direction." Which of these is construed as the "topic" or "trigger" (T) is signaled by the verbal affixes glossed AT, GT, and DT. Also, *ang* marks the following nominal as the topic, regardless of semantic role.

(b) ***I**-bibigay ng babae **ang bigas** sa bata.*
GT-will:give A woman T rice D child
'{A/The} woman will give the rice to {a/the} child.'

(c) *Bibigay-**an** ng babae ng bigas **ang bata**.*
will:give-DT A woman G rice T child
'{A/The} woman will give some rice to the child.'

Second, the grammatical behaviors thought to be characteristic of subjects are split, some being associated with the actor (e.g. ability to serve as the subject of an imperative, or as the antecedent of a reflexive), and others with the topic (Quantifier Float; relativizability). Third, the topic does not show the kind of discourse function one would expect. For instance, coming in response to the first sentence in (37), the second sentence has to be "about" the maid, yet *pagkain* 'food' is marked as the topic:

(37) *Nasaan ang katulong? **I**-nihahanda niya **ang pagkain**.*
where T maid GT-prepare A:she T food
'Where's the maid?' 'She's preparing the food.'

Hence there is real doubt whether *topic* is the appropriate term for the *ang*-marked nominal. Because this nominal fits the Eurocentric preconception of neither a subject nor a discourse topic, some scholars now use the neutral term *trigger* to refer to it (Wouk 1986).

Schachter's conclusion that the Philippine languages do not have subjects reflects the still-current view that a subject is an agent and/or a discourse topic, as well as the pivotal element in certain grammatical constructions. But different assumptions lead to different conclusions. For example, using the theory of relational grammar to describe analogous phenomena in Cebuano, Bell (1983) analyzes actors as *initial subjects*, and the "topic" or "trigger" as the *final subject*. A cognitive grammar analysis will also posit subjects but cannot resort to multiple strata.[22] The suggested account is straightforward and easily stated: *subject* = *trigger*. True, the trigger does not precisely match the image of subjects engendered by better-known languages. It does however conform to the proposed characterization, which has a conceptual basis and does not refer to any specific grammatical behavior. Hence it is unproblematic that the grammatical properties commonly linked with subjects are split between the trigger and the actor, for each has a particular kind of cognitive salience that makes it a natural candidate to participate in certain constructions; we should not be surprised that the exact apportionment varies from language to language. Moreover, we have seen that a subject is not invariably a discourse topic (though it is topic-like in the weaker sense of

[22] That is, it cannot invoke two distinct levels of *clausal* organization (such as *deep* vs. *surface structure*, or *initial* vs. *final stratum*). Of course, there may be a difference in grammatical relations (figure/ground alignment) between a simple structure and a complex structure formed on it (e.g. *steal* vs. *stolen*).

being the clause-level figure). In (37), therefore, the response sentence merely exemplifies the common circumstance of the subject (*pagkain* 'food') and the topic (*niya* 'she') failing to coincide. Finally, the inconsistency of the agent-subject (actor-trigger) correlation in Tagalog differs only in degree from that observed in European languages, where the main culprit is the passive construction. Tagalog does have a wider range of voices, only some of which are illustrated in (36); it also requires that the subject be definite. Still, these traits are perfectly consistent with characterizing the trigger schematically as the figure within the profiled relationship.

A broader challenge to the universality of subjects has been issued by Foley and Van Valin (1984, ch. 4). In part their challenge rests on cross-linguistic differences in how subjects behave grammatically. If one actually *defines* the subject relation in terms of such behavior, they are certainly correct in claiming that the construct is language-specific: the nature of a "subject" differs from one language to the next. Foley and Van Valin rely more heavily on the notion "pivot," which they describe as the nominal "crucially involved" in constructions, and as "central to the syntax of the language" in regard to both clause linkage and intraclausal phenomena (p. 110). In some languages the pivot is "semantic," i.e. it is predictable from the semantic roles of the clausal participants. In other languages, the pivot is "pragmatic," which means that the choice is also influenced by discourse factors; for example, the pivot in English is the subject, whose non-predictability on the basis of semantic role alone is demonstrated by the existence of both actives and passives.[23]

What Foley and Van Valin show is that grammatical behaviors often cluster on a particular nominal, and that languages differ as to how that nominal is determined. This observation is not incompatible per se with a semantic characterization of subjects based on conceptual prominence (indeed, some kind of salience must be responsible for a nominal assuming a pivotal syntactic role). If *subject* is defined schematically as *relational figure* (clause-level trajector), it is both coherent and quite reasonable to posit subjects even for a language where the construct appears to have little grammatical significance. They may be largely invisible to the analyst—either because the subject is grammatically inactive, or else because its choice always correlates with some other factor (just as it correlates with definiteness in Tagalog)—but ascribing figure/ground alignment to the clausal participants is plausible nonetheless. Now the subject in English virtually begs the analyst to notice it: not only does it function as the pivot, but its choice as relational figure is often at variance with the other topicality factors. Suppose, however, that the pivot is

[23] These brief comments cannot begin to do justice to Foley and Van Valin's extensive proposals, which I find both interesting and for the most part congenial to the general outlook of cognitive grammar. The two approaches are more alike in their treatment of clause structure than one would surmise from the present discussion, necessarily limited to a single issue.

instead identified as the *theme*, which is salient by virtue of conceptual autonomy. There may be little that subjects do in such a language to attract the linguist's attention, and as a limiting case, there may be nothing at all. The language would then be subjectless by Foley and Van Valin's criteria, whereas I would say that the subject relation's grammatical potential remains latent. They also cite languages where the choice of pivot is consistently determined by semantic role, in accordance with a natural ranking. What this turns out to mean is that the language lacks any construction, such as a passive, which—for discourse purposes—permits one to override the usual ranking. I would rather say that the subject functions as pivot, and that the topicality factors of semantic role and figure/ground alignment are strongly correlated. Because the subject (relational figure) always coincides with the highest-ranked participant, the subject relation does not call attention to itself as a distinct construct. Still, its invisibility does not entail its absence.

7.3.2. *Direct Object*

I have argued that subjects represent a universal category whose semantic characterization includes both a prototype and a highly abstract schema. A comparable claim will be made for direct objects (albeit far more briefly). These notions do however differ in one important respect, namely that the object relation is closely tied to transitivity. Subjects occur in both transitive and intransitive clauses, whereas only the former have direct objects—or to put it another way, a direct object presupposes a subject, but not conversely. Our description of objects should entail this asymmetry.

The subject and object are *focal participants* (7.2.2). As a first approximation, we can describe the subject as the *most prominent clausal participant*, and the object as the *second-most prominent participant*. This characterization does entail the subject/object asymmetry: a participant can rank second in prominence only if another ranks above it. As it stands, however, the description is hardly adequate. For one thing, it offers no insight as to why subjects and objects should align themselves in this fashion. Furthermore, prominence comes in many styles and colors, so merely asserting that something is prominent is rather uninformative—a substantive claim must specify what kind of prominence is supposed to be involved. We did this for subjects by noting that a prototypical subject is highly ranked with respect to each of four topicality factors (7.3.1.1). Can we do likewise for objects? Let me suggest a natural hypothesis: a prototypical object is also salient by virtue of its high ranking on these parameters, but in each case it ranks below a prototypical subject.

The four topicality factors are semantic role, empathy, definiteness, and figure/ground organization. The respective semantic roles of the subject and object prototypes are of course agent and patient, whose archetypal status and cognitive salience have already been discussed. Besides introspection, there is definite psychological evidence for believing that agent surpasses patient in this regard. Through semantic rating experiments, Osgood, Suci, and Tannenbaum (1957) demonstrated the conceptual primacy of 'activity' and 'potency', both agent-related notions. Also, agent and patient function as the head and tail of an action chain, and while it is well known that special prominence attaches to both the initial and final elements in an ordered sequence, the distinct importance of starting points has been shown for a variety of cognitive behaviors (MacWhinney 1977).

Turning now to empathy, the respective prototypes of the subject and object categories are a person and an inanimate physical object. These are not, however, the highest-ranking elements on the empathy hierarchy, as formulated in (19). The source of the difficulty is that a single linear ranking does not capture all the pertinent relationships, particularly those involving higher-order groupings. For instance, while the speaker, the hearer, and other humans have to be distinguished for certain purposes, it is often sufficient to treat them as a single class. The result of so grouping them is to leave the inclusive *human* class, corresponding to the subject prototype, at the top of the hierarchy. Of course, we still face a problem in that the object prototype does not rank directly below it—between *human* and *physical object* intervenes the class of *animals*. But we have yet to consider a basic distinction of substantial cognitive significance; let us superimpose on the hierarchy a further grouping into the higher-order classes of animate (AN) vs. inanimate (INAN) entities:

(38) [$_{AN}$ ***human*** > *animal* $_{AN}$] > [$_{INAN}$ ***physical object*** > *abstract entity* $_{INAN}$]

Since animacy is strongly correlated with ability to serve as an energy source, there is a natural association between subjects and the upper portion of the hierarchy. And since energy is typically directed at inanimate entities, objects are naturally associated with the lower portion. We can now observe that the prototypical value of each grammatical relation is the highest-ranked element within its own sector. Thus, when higher-order groupings are properly taken into account, a clear sense emerges in which *human* and *physical object* stand out as especially salient classes.

A subject is prototypically definite and hence a starting point with respect to the hierarchy *definite > specific indefinite > non-specific indefinite*. This is evident not only on the basis of frequency, but also because an indefinite subject is sometimes awkward or impermissible (cf. (21)). Now an object too is often definite (e.g. *Floyd broke the glass*), and its definiteness (as a kind of subjective individuation) heightens a clause's transitivity. Nevertheless, definiteness is not something that is required or even typical of an object—indefinite objects are both natural and of frequent occurrence. In fact, they serve an important discourse function by allowing the introduction of a new participant (*Floyd was so angry that he picked up* ***a glass*** *and smashed it*). We can further note that most indefinite objects are specific (3.1.2); they are interpretable as being non-specific only after certain verbs (*I need a wrench—any wrench!*) or in special constructions (*He hopes to date a rich and beautiful divorcée—if he can only find one*). From a discourse perspective, one can therefore argue that the unmarked arrangement is for a transitive clause to have a definite subject and a specific indefinite object.

The first three topicality factors reveal a consistent pattern: on each parameter, the values associated with the subject and object prototypes have rankings that respectively imply a primary and a secondary degree of salience. Thus it is not unreasonable to suppose that this pattern might carry over to the fourth factor, figure/ground organization. We have analyzed a subject as the relational figure, which clearly makes it the highest-ranked participant. What can we identify as the second-most prominent element with respect to this parameter? It would have to be an especially salient facet of the ground, i.e. some entity that stands out from the remainder of the ground as a kind of *secondary figure* when attention is focused on the primary figure. It is in this abstract sense that the term *landmark* should be understood, just as *trajector* is understood abstractly as *(primary) figure*. The claim, then, is that the subject and object rank first and second on the hierarchy *primary figure > secondary figure > ground* (or *trajector > landmark > other*).[24] This is not inconsistent with Givón's characterization in terms of *primary* and *secondary clausal topic* (1984, p. 138), or even with the use of *1* and *2* as labels for subject and object in relational grammar (which nonetheless regards them as purely syntactic constructs).

A prototypical direct object is thus the second-most prominent clausal participant, ranking behind the subject in regard to all four topicality factors: whereas a subject is prototypically an *agent*, *human*, *definite*, and the *primary figure*, an object is a *patient*, a *physical object*, *specific indefinite*, and the *secondary figure*. A sentence such as *Floyd ate a pear* exhibits all these properties. But as we saw for subjects, objects are capable of diverging quite drastically from the prototype, so that a value compatible with every instance of the category will have to be highly abstract. Here too it is evident that empathy and definiteness are factors of lesser significance, and that semantic role does not provide the basis for a universally-valid characterization. If there is anything that all direct objects have in common, it can only be their status as secondary figure.

In the case of subjects, we adopted progressively more schematic role descriptions to encompass ever-wider arrays of data: *agent*; then *action-chain*

[24] Recall that trajector/landmark alignment, defined in terms of figure/ground organization, is inherent in relational predications at every level of structure. Peculiar to the clause level is their correlation with the other topicality factors to define the subject and object prototypes.

head (in both the physical and the abstract realm); then *active participant in an asymmetrical relationship*; and finally *subjectively active participant*, which is really just equivalent to *relational figure* (7.3.1.2). We can posit an analogous series of schematic values for the object category. First, by generalizing the notion *patient* to *action-chain tail*, we accommodate interactions (both physical and abstract) in which the object is a mover, as in (39), or an experiencer, as in (40):

(39)(a) *The boys were pushing a heavily-laden wagon up the hill.*
(b) *Our tactics forced him into admitting his complicity in the scandalous affair.*

(40)(a) *Zelda tickled her nephew until he begged her to stop.*
(b) *Zack's hard work pleased his teachers enormously.*

Examples like (41) require a further generalization, for there is no transmission of energy (even in an abstract sense) and the object's role is zero. *Non-active participant in an asymmetrical relationship* approximates the requisite value.

(41)(a) *I don't recognize the name.*
(b) *We counted the craters in that photograph of Io.*

(42)(a) *A well-trimmed hedge encloses their yard.*
(b) *The square of the hypotenuse equals the sum of the squares of the other two sides.*

Finally, exemplified in (42) are sentences describing static situations in which, objectively, the subject and object are both inactive. In (42)(b), moreover, their relationship is symmetrical. Here we observe the limiting case, in which subject/object alignment—normally motivated by objective factors—is solely due to the speaker imposing a particular choice of figure/ground organization. A schematic and fully general characterization of subject vs. object can only be provided by a subjective distinction such as *primary* vs. *secondary clausal figure*.

7.3.3. *Indirect Object*

The term **indirect object** is standardly used for verbal complements that are object-like in some respects yet grammatically distinct from direct objects. The specific behavior that calls attention to their special status varies from language to language. In German, for example, indirect objects occur in the dative case rather than the accusative, as marked in (43) by the feminine definite articles *der* (DAT) vs. *die* (ACC).

(43)(a) *Ich habe **der Frau** geholfen.* 'I helped the woman.'
(b) *Ich habe **die Frau** gesehen.* 'I saw the woman.'

Indirect objects in French contrast with direct objects by taking the preposition *à* 'to'; with pronominal objects, the third-person forms are *lui/leur* instead of *l(e)/l(a)/les*:

(44)(a) *J'ai parlé à **la femme**.* 'I talked to the woman.'
(b) *J'ai regardé **la femme**.* 'I looked at the woman.'

(45)(a) *Je **lui** ai parlé.* 'I talked to her.'
(b) *Je **l'**ai regardée.* 'I looked at her.'

Commonly identified as indirect objects in English are nominals that participate in the so-called Dative Shift alternation, whereby an object of *to* "moves" to immediate post-verbal position and "loses" the preposition. By this criterion, *Zelda* is an indirect object in (46), while in (47) *the wall* is merely a prepositional object.

(46)(a) *I mailed the notice to **Zelda**.*
(b) *I mailed **Zelda** the notice.*

(47)(a) *I nailed the notice to **the wall**.*
(b) **I nailed **the wall** the notice.*

There has been some uncertainty as to the relative weight of semantic and grammatical considerations in the characterization of indirect objects. On the one hand, indirect-objecthood is known to be closely associated with particular semantic roles, such as the recipient with verbs of transfer, and the addressee with verbs of communication. On the other hand, the nominals that instantiate these roles often provide no clear or consistent indication that they represent a distinct grammatical relation. Consider (46). If we examine these sentences individually, we have no reason not to simply analyze *Zelda* as a prepositional object in (a) and the direct object in (b); only their comparison—the fact that both patterns are permissible—offers a grammatical basis for positing a separate relation. Even this rather tenuous motivation is often lacking:

(48)(a) *I delivered the notice to Zelda.*
(b) **I delivered Zelda the notice.*

While (48)(a) is semantically parallel to (46)(a), so that *Zelda* is regarded as an indirect object, the impermissibility of (48)(b) leaves this analysis without grammatical support. Cross-linguistic study reveals a comparable situation (cf. Chung 1976; Comrie 1982; Aissen 1983; Dryer 1986). There are languages in which a "notional indirect object" is always oblique, others where it consistently behaves like a direct object, and still others (like English) that allow either option. It is therefore not uncommon for apparent direct objects to have semantic roles thought to be characteristic of indirect objects. Rules like Dative Shift, which supposedly derives a direct object from an underlying indirect object, are often proposed to handle these discrepancies.

Such analyses are doubly mistaken, first because they distinguish between underlying and surface structure (thus violating the content requirement (Vol. 1, 1.2.6.2)), and second because they presuppose an incorrect view of indirect objects. I suggest that *indirect object* ought not to be considered a grammatical relation of the same type as *subject* and *direct object*. Subject and object are characterized as the most and second-most prominent clausal participants, and the one constant ingredient of their prominence is their status as primary and secondary clausal figures. As a consequence, there is a certain amount of flexibility in the choice of these focal participants—the two spotlights can be directed at elements representing a variety of semantic roles. The flexibility is naturally greatest in the case of the primary figure (we will see in Ch. 8 that there is no inherent restriction on what can be a subject), but even for the secondary figure it is hardly negligible.[25] Hence the alternation in (46) is simply a matter of co-existing constructions involving different selections of secondary figure (mover vs. recipient); it does not point to any discrepancy between surface and underlying grammatical relations or motivate a rule deriving (b) from (a). *Zelda* is thus the true direct object in (46)(b), not an indirect object masquerading as one (cf. Vol. 1, p. 39–40, 51).

An extension of this prominence-based analysis to indirect objects does not appear promising. The characterization "tertiary clausal figure" is hardly plausible, especially since an indirect object does not always presuppose a direct object (e.g. (43)(a)). Such an analysis would also fail to account for the semantic coherence of the elements traditionally regarded as indirect objects, as well as the occasional incoherence of their grammatical manifestation.[26] I thus propose that indirect objects are best characterized in terms of semantic role. To appreciate the nature of their semantic coherence, let us first consider Fig. 7.5, which does not represent any particular class of expressions but is rather a composite diagram depicting some typical connections among the basic role archetypes. With the thematic participant identified as patient, mover, or experiencer, the sequence *AG===>INSTR===>TH* constitutes a canonical action chain. With the thematic role identified as zero, *EXPER---->TH* corresponds to a simple perceptual or conceptual relationship in which the experiencer establishes mental contact with the theme. Of course, a single event may incorporate both an action chain and an experiential relationship. For example, if I throw a ball, either I or someone else can watch

[25] Consider, for example, the alternate choices possible with a verb like *teach*: *Zelda teaches {mathematics/handicapped students/elementary school/seventh grade/one course per semester}*.

[26] For instance, we see from (46)–(47) that not every object of *to* is an indirect object, nor does an indirect object invariably follow *to*.

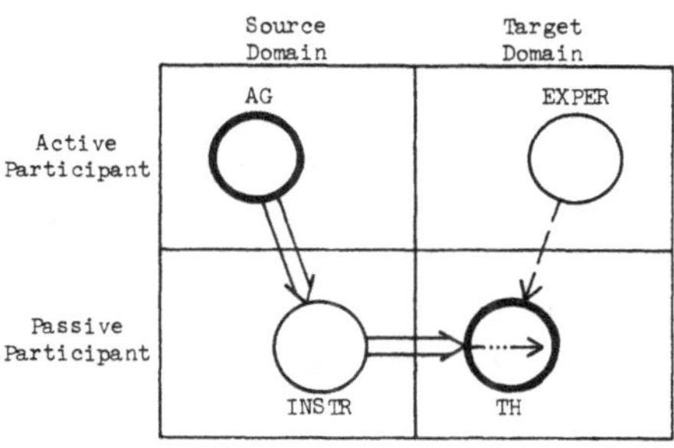

Fig. 7.5

its flight. Or if someone breaks my arm, I am both the patient with respect to the action and an experiencer with respect to the resultant change of state.

Superimposed on this scheme is a grid that groups the role archetypes into natural classes.[27] With respect to the flow of energy, a basic division is made between the **source domain**, comprising agent and instrument, and the **target domain**, subsuming both the theme and an extra-thematic experiencer. An agent and an instrument are alike—and unlike a theme or experiencer—in that each transfers energy to another participant. Cross-cutting this division is the distinction between **active** and **passive participants**, where an active participant is one that functions as an original source of energy and thereby *initiates* an interaction. Within the source domain, the agent is clearly the active participant, for an instrument merely transmits the energy supplied by an agent. In the target domain, the experiencer is initiative in the sense of generating the cognitive activity through which an internal representation is produced or mental contact is otherwise established. Finally, the agent and theme are depicted with heavy lines to suggest their inherent cognitive salience, which makes them the unmarked choices to be coded as focal participants (7.1.3).

What, then, is an indirect object? It is usefully characterized as an **active experiencer in the target domain**. Properly understood, this schematic definition handles most central cases and provides a reasonable basis for extension to other senses. Supporting the prototypicality of the *experiencer* role is the frequent occurrence of indirect objects with verbs of perception, judgment, sensation, emotion, or mental experience generally (e.g. 'tell', 'show', 'seem', 'please', 'be hungry', 'be cold', 'frighten', 'bother', 'satisfy'). Another serious candidate for prototype status is the role of *recipient* (or more broadly, *possessor*), which indirect objects assume with 'give' and many

[27] This grid is quite analogous to a vowel chart, which specifies the natural groupings of vocalic segments in regard to the front-back and high-low dimensions. To carry the analogy one step farther, these role archetypes are analogous to the cardinal vowels.

other verbs of transfer. There is little point in arguing that either role is more basic than the other, for in any case they are closely associated and often hard to distinguish. With a verb like 'say' or 'tell', for example, the indirect object is an experiencer by virtue of perceiving the utterance and understanding its meaning, but can also be regarded as the recipient and subsequent possessor of the information conveyed. Even in cases of physical transfer ('give', 'hand', 'deliver', etc.), the recipient typically perceives the transferred entity coming into his dominion, has knowledge of the resulting possessive relationship, and enjoys its benefits. Possession can also be the reason for an action giving rise to a mental experience, as witnessed by a French expression like *Je lui ai cassé le bras* 'I broke his arm' (literally: 'I to him broke the arm'). While the indirect object is usually thought of as identifying the possessor, it can just as well be taken as coding the experiencer—the breaking of an arm induces a sensation registered specifically by the person who possesses it.

The specification that the experiencer occupies the *target* domain effects the traditional exclusion of subjects from the indirect object category. As the name implies, an indirect object must be object-like, in the sense that it lies downstream from the subject along an action chain or with respect to some abstract analog of energy flow. Hence the experiential relationship characteristic of an indirect object cannot itself be the "backbone" of the clause's processual profile (i.e. the source-to-target path connecting the focal participants). Instead, as shown in Fig. 7.5, it must join obliquely to the action chain or its analog, as a kind of "side chain" in the target domain. The perceiver is thus an indirect object in *I showed the picture to my wife*, for the agent, theme, and experiencer are aligned in precisely that fashion. But in *My wife saw the picture*, the subject is not considered an indirect object, though it is likewise the perceiver in an *EXPER---->ZERO* relationship. With *see*, this relationship stands alone as the processual profile of the transitive clause and thereby constitutes an extension from the transitive-clause prototype, *AG===>TH*. By the terms of this extension, the experiencer corresponds to the agent, and the perceptual path is construed as being analogous to the flow of energy. The perceiver's position with respect to this action-chain analog is therefore upstream, at its head, rather downstream as required for an object.

The import of defining an indirect object as an *active* experiencer in the target domain is that its role cannot be purely thematic: there must be some respect in which its initiative capacity is called into play, or in which it is distinguished from a thematic direct object. With verbs of transfer, as in (46)(a), the direct object is a mover whose role is essentially passive, whereas the recipient role of the indirect object is initiative in various ways already described. In a sentence such as *Je lui ai cassé le bras* 'I broke his arm', distinct facets of the victim's participation are separately coded by the direct and indirect objects—the arm's passive change of state by the former, and the victim's awareness and proprietary interest by the latter. On the other hand, an experiencer tends to be coded by a *direct* object to the extent that the mental experience per se constitutes the thematic relationship, especially when it is construed as being driven by an external force that overwhelms or supplants the experiencer's initiative role. Sentences like *She tickled me* and *Her behavior shocked me* thus highlight the passive nature of the object's participation.[28]

It is of course possible for a target-domain experiencer to be attributed an active role even in the absence of a direct object. There is none in (45)(a), for example, but it is quite evident that the indirect object is viewed as the perceiver and recipient of a verbal message, which simply remains uncoded. Providing a different kind of example are German verbs such as *dienen* 'serve', *folgen* 'follow', *trauen* 'trust', *gehorchen* 'obey', and *helfen* 'help' (cf. (43)(a)). Smith (1985b, 1987) has argued that these verbs take indirect rather than direct objects because the non-subject participant has an initiative role with respect to a salient (albeit implicit) process, e.g. the process of giving an order (for 'obey') or leading the way (for 'follow'). Although this participant is not solely or even primarily an experiencer, it is nevertheless an active participant in the target domain, hence its expression as an indirect object constitutes a natural extension of that category. It is unproblematic that the corresponding verbs take direct objects in English and many other languages. A role of this kind being prototypical of neither a direct nor an indirect object, its coding as one or the other is a matter of language-specific convention.

[28] By contrast, *I'm tickled at her progress* and *To me her behavior was most shocking* portray the experiencer as *exercising judgment*. It thus has an active, initiative role not limited to the passive registration of an externally induced sensation.

CHAPTER 8

Marked Clause Structure

WE HAVE THUS FAR focused on unmarked coding, in which a notion approximating a conceptual archetype is coded linguistically by a structure taking that archetype for its prototypical value. Such expressions reveal most clearly the meaningfulness of grammatical constructs and are thus a natural place to initiate a semantically based description. But languages cannot limit themselves to this ideal arrangement; they need the versatility to express any situation imaginable, under any conceivable set of discourse conditions. Consequently, every language deploys a large inventory of lexico-grammatical devices that effect the coding of non-canonical situations and allow a given situation to be portrayed in alternate ways. This chapter examines such devices, first discussing variability in the choice of clausal subject, then in the choice of direct object. Also considered are phenomena that bear on the number and the distinctness of clausal participants.

8.1. Choice of Subject

Our working hypothesis is that a subject is properly characterized as the *primary clausal figure*. Contributing to the plausibility of that analysis are some general similarities between subject choice and the imposition of figure/ground organization (see also Vol. 1, 6.3.1). Both follow well-pronounced natural tendencies, which in language are based on such factors as semantic role, empathy, and definiteness, while in perception they pertain to size, mobility, contrast, etc. Moreover, in both instances these tendencies are often overridden—given proper motivation, the choice of either perceptual figure or grammatical subject manifests substantial flexibility. For example, when a small white spot is surrounded by a field of black it is normally perceived as the figure; with little effort, however, we can reverse the alignment, so that what we perceive is a large dark surface with a hole in it, seen against a white background. The constructions examined in the present section can be regarded as rough grammatical analogs of this phenomenon. First to be considered is the effect of profiling on subject choice. We will then discuss voice (active vs. passive), followed by constructions in which the subject is not a participant, but rather some kind of setting.

8.1.1. *The Effect of Profiling*

A finite clause designates a process construed as constituting a single event or a single situation. Within the processual profile, the subject and object are twin foci, salient participants whose own prominence enhances that of the interconnections involving them directly. It is crucial to realize that the focal status of the subject and object, as well as the basis for choosing them, pertain specifically to the *profiled* relationship. For example, in *The corporal obeyed the sergeant*, the corporal is coded by the subject even though the sergeant initiates and controls the overall train of events; while the sergeant's actions are an important part of the base, the clausal profile is limited to what the corporal does in response, and within that process the corporal is the active participant. As a general point, the objective properties of a complex occurrence do not themselves determine the subject/object alignment of a clause describing it. There is no secure basis for predictions or even strong expectations concerning that alignment until various aspects of construal have been decided, most importantly the selection of a profile (7.2.1).

When proper allowance is made for profiling, subject choice proves less idiosyncratic than is generally thought. Consider *receive*, the stock example of a verb that chooses the "wrong" participant for its subject. Why does the recipient supposedly represent an inappropriate, or at least highly marked, choice of subject? Because its role is seemingly passive—the donor is agentive, and the object's role is dynamic (it moves from the donor's dominion to the recipient's), but the recipient does not necessarily do anything at all. Thus, if we accept this standard way of looking at things, the expected subject/object alignment is that of *give*, sketched in Fig. 8.1(a): the donor is coded as the subject (S), and the mover as the object (O), leaving the recipient to assume its natural role as indirect object.

We can certainly admit that *give* represents the unmarked coding of a canonical act of transfer. I suggest, however, that the markedness of *receive* is limited to the fact that it designates only a portion of the overall happening; as shown in Fig. 8.1(b), the profile subsumes the recipient's involvement and the mover's transition into its dominion, but does not include the exertions of the agent. In terms of that profiling, one can argue that the choice of subject and object conforms to the unmarked alignment. We noted in 7.3.3 that the recipient's role is not in actuality a passive one. Besides engaging in unspecified physical activity to take possession of the mover (the complete absence of such activity being a special, limiting case), the recipient typically perceives the transfer, establishes mental contact with the mover, exercises sub-

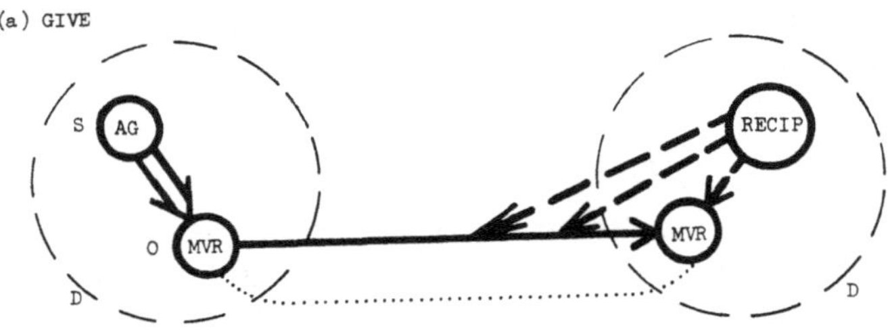

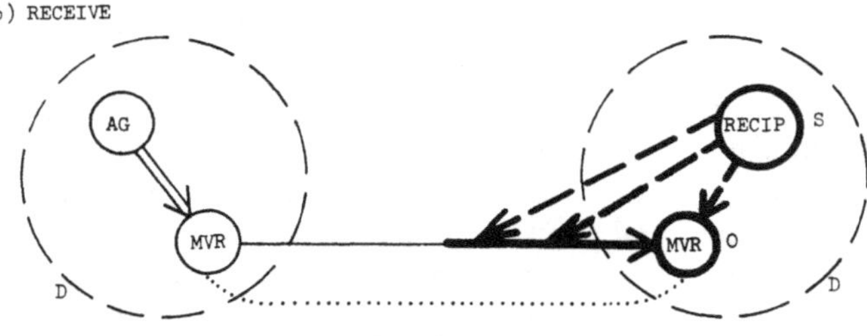

Fig. 8.1

sequent control over it, and is cognizant of the full occurrence and its consequences. Hence the recipient is active and initiative in much the same way as the subject of verbs like *have*, *see*, and *know*. On the other hand, the mover *is* essentially passive, for it does not initiate its motion (the donor does that), and it lies downstream from the recipient with respect to several abstract analogs of energy flow. The subject and object are therefore chosen in a normal fashion, so long as we confine our attention to the profiled interaction: the subject is describable as the *active participant in an asymmetrical relationship*, and the object—despite its motion—as the *non-active participant*.

The effect of profiling on subject choice can also be observed in sets of expressions like the following:

(1)(a) *Sharon dried her hair with the blower.*
(b) *The blower dried her hair.*
(c) *Her hair dried.*

(2)(a) *The thief opened the window with a crowbar.*
(b) *A crowbar opened the window.*
(c) *The window opened.*

(3)(a) *My daughter woke me up with an explosion.*
(b) *An explosion woke me up.*
(c) *I woke up.*

Many English verbs allow as their subject either an agent, an instrument, or a thematic participant, as respectively illustrated in the (a), (b), and (c) examples. Once profiling is taken into account, the choice of subject is quite regular and easily stated. The respective profiles of the (a), (b), and (c) examples are depicted in Fig. 8.2. Profiled in (a) is a complete action chain

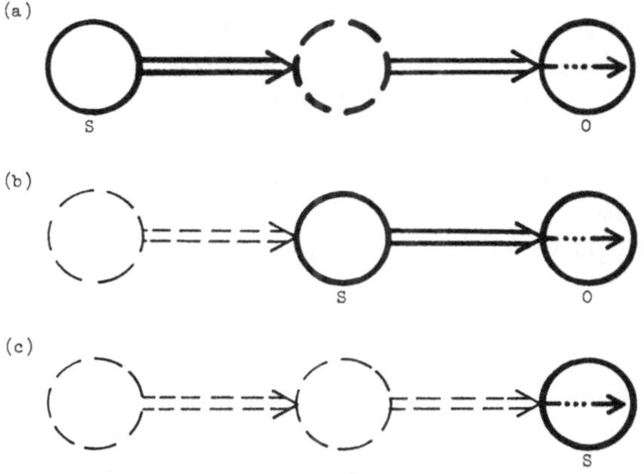

Fig. 8.2

leading from an agent to the theme.[1] By contrast, the profile is limited in (b) to the instrument-theme interaction, and in (c) to the thematic process itself. The generalization is obvious: the subject is in each case the *head* with respect to the *profiled portion of the action chain*. Similarly, the object is the action-chain tail, provided that the head and tail are distinct. The (c) examples represent the degenerate case in which the head and tail coincide, and since an object presupposes a subject (but not conversely), the single profiled participant functions in the latter capacity.

To account for data like (1)–(3), Fillmore (1968, p. 33) posited a hierarchy determining subject choice in unmarked instances. For our purposes his hierarchy can be restated as follows: *AG* > *INSTR* > *TH*. That is, if an agent is present, it is selected as the subject; if not, and if an instrument is present, the instrument becomes the subject; otherwise, the theme is chosen as subject. Fillmore merely stipulated this hierarchy, but in our approach it falls out as a consequence of basic constructs and definitions. The sequence *AG* > *INSTR* > *TH* corresponds to the flow of energy along an action chain, different portions of which can function as the clausal profile. Therefore, characterizing a prototypical subject as the head with respect to the profiled portion of an action chain entails that its choice will conform to Fillmore's hierarchy. These precedence relations do not represent an autonomous or unmotivated gram-

[1] Note that the theme is a patient in (1), a mover in (2), and an experiencer in (3); the notation for the last participant in the action chain represents the schema subsuming all three possibilities (Fig. 7.3). Dashed-line circles are used for participants whose inclusion is optional (for a given choice of subject).

matical fact—rather they reflect the inherent conceptual content of certain idealized cognitive models with archetypal status.

One can reasonably ask whether the unmarked subject is indeed the head of the *profiled* portion of the action chain, or whether it might instead be characterized as the head of that portion falling within the *scope of predication*. Figs. 8.2(b)–(c) show the optional presence of unprofiled participants upstream from the subject, and if such participants are in fact included in the scope of predication, then profiling must be the relevant factor. One might however argue that the scope of the (b) and (c) examples is limited to the profiled relationship, so that any reference to an agent in (b), or to a source-domain participant in (c), is extrinsic to the linguistic meaning of these expressions. Imposing such boundaries is of course counter to the spirit of cognitive grammar. I consider it far more natural to suppose that these unprofiled participants are evoked (and figure in an expression's meaning) to varying degrees, depending on the example and the circumstances. For instance, it is easy to construe (3)(b) without invoking an agent, but not so easy in the case of (2)(b), since crowbars do not open windows all by themselves.

There is however a class of thematic-subject sentences for which an analysis that did not postulate an unprofiled agent would be highly implausible:

(4)(a) *The window opened only with great difficulty.*
(b) *This ice cream scoops out quite easily.*
(c) *The dried mud scraped off effortlessly.*
(d) *A good tent puts up in less than five minutes.*
(e) *With the rebate, these cars are selling quickly.*

This construction has been analyzed in depth by van Oosten (1977, 1986), who claims that it portrays the subject as being in some sense responsible for the profiled action, and is used when the role of an agent is considered irrelevant to the discourse. I would amend this description only by saying instead that *identifying* the agent is considered irrelevant. Certainly an agent is implied—we do not, for example, envisage the ice cream wielding a scoop and lifting itself out of the container. And while the ease or difficulty of carrying out the action is attributed to inherent properties of the subject, it can only be assessed as easy or hard in relation to the capability of an actual or potential agent. We must therefore adopt the analysis diagrammed in Fig. 8.3. The profile is limited to the thematic process, together with the hindrance (<) or

Fig. 8.3

facilitation (>) offered to its occurrence by inherent characteristics of the theme; by virtue of being the only profiled participant, the theme is chosen as subject. Although the agent is non-salient and left unspecified (△), it is nevertheless incorporated as an unprofiled facet of the base (scope of predication).

8.1.2. *Voice*

In the departures from unmarked coding just examined, something other than a full, canonical action chain was selected for profiling; however, within the chosen profile, subject/object alignment in each case conformed to natural tendencies. We will now consider phenomena representing the opposite situation, namely **voice** alternations, which pertain to the choice of clausal subject. The markedness of a passive or passive-like construction does not derive from profiling (indeed, a passive is most felicitous when it designates a canonical event). Rather, it resides in the fact that the participant otherwise expected to be the subject is bypassed in favor of a less qualified candidate. It is hardly surprising that subject status is usually conferred instead on what would normally be the second-most prominent participant, namely the direct object. Thus passivization is often described in generative grammar as the "promotion" of a direct object to the rank of subject.

To contrast a true passive with the constructions discussed in 8.1.1, let us consider the sentences in (5), which could all be used to describe the same event.

(5)(a) *He opened the door.*
(b) *The door opened very easily.*
(c) *The door suddenly opened.*
(d) *The door was opened.*

Of course, each portrays the event in a different fashion, as indicated by the respective diagrams of Fig. 8.4. Sentence (a) is a prototypical active clause; it profiles an action chain involving an agent and a mover, which are coded by the subject and direct-object nominals. Examples (b) and (c) are also in the active voice, but they designate only the mover's participation, so the mover is the subject by virtue of being the sole profiled participant. The

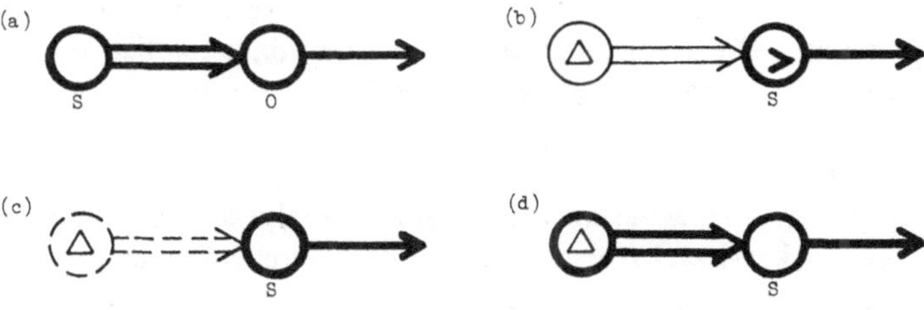

Fig. 8.4

adverbs *very easily* and *suddenly* bring out the difference between these constructions (which may be just a matter of degree): in (b), the efforts of an unspecified agent are definitely implied and are portrayed as being (in this case) facilitated by inherent characteristics of the thematic subject; whereas in (c), the implicit reference to an agent is non-salient and may be absent altogether (i.e. the construal of the profiled thematic process may be *absolute*). Observe, now, that the passive in (d) is like a canonical active in that the full action chain stands in profile. At the same time, it resembles the constructions of (b) and (c) in leaving the agent unspecified and choosing the theme for its subject.

A comparison of actives and passives reveals an additional aspect of the subject/object asymmetry discussed in 7.3.2. The active example is of course transitive, its non-subject participant being the direct object. In the passive, however, the non-subject participant (i.e. the unspecified agent) is not a direct object and the clause is consequently intransitive. But why is it not an object? Despite its unspecificity, is it not the second-most prominent clausal participant? There are at least two reasons. It must first be remembered that *second-most prominent participant* is only a shorthand way of referring to the more precise and elaborate description of 7.3.2, in which an object was characterized schematically as the *secondary clausal figure*. Hence the mere presence of two profiled participants does not guarantee that one of them will be a direct object: a particular kind of salience is required for that status (it is not enough just to be the second-most prominent element by default), and since the main function of a passive construction is to "defocus" the agent (Shibatani 1985), that kind of salience is simply not accorded to it. Furthermore, direct-objecthood is closely tied to transitivity and the notion of energy transmission along an action chain. A prototypical direct object lies *downstream* from the subject in the flow of energy. Likewise, in most extensions from the prototype the object is downstream from the subject with respect to some abstract analog of energy flow; when no such relationship is discernible, the non-subject nominal is at best a peripheral member of the direct-object class. Now the agent in a passive not only fails to manifest this relationship, but as shown in Fig. 8.4(d), it actually lies *upstream* from the subject, in direct violation of the category prototype. Thus a passive agent could hardly be categorized as a direct object. In contrast to the subject, which is capable of manifesting any semantic role or occupying any position along an action chain, an object can only belong to the target domain, never the source domain (Fig. 7.5).

Let us quickly review the cognitive grammar analysis of the English passive (5.2.1; Langacker 1982b). Each grammatical morpheme that appears in the passive construction has a precisely-characterized meaning closely related to the meanings it displays in other uses. Starting from a transitive verb stem (such as *open*), the perfect participial morpheme ($PERF_3$) derives a passive participle (*opened*); it does so by suspending sequential scanning and according trajector status to the participant functioning as the primary landmark of the stem (Fig. 5.1). The resulting participle is a complex atemporal relation, i.e. it profiles all the component states of the original process but views them holistically (by means of summary scanning). The passive *be* (BE_2) is a fully schematic process. When its component states are elaborated by those of the participle (Fig. 5.4(c)), the result is a higher-level verb (*be opened*) capable of serving as a clausal head. From that point on the assembly of the clause proceeds as it would with any intransitive verb: minimally, a grounding predication must be supplied (*was opened*), and the trajector is elaborated by a nominal which thereby constitutes the clausal subject (*The door was opened*). The fact that the subject corresponds to the landmark of the verb stem reflects the semantic contribution of $PERF_3$. And since (for reasons just explained) the verb stem's trajector does not conform to the characterization of a direct object, it cannot be elaborated through the direct-object construction and usually remains unspecified.

Even though the actor is implicit and unidentified, the expressions so derived are complete sentences well suited for use in particular discourse situations (e.g. when the actor is either unknown or else apparent from the context). In cases where the actor has to be overtly indicated, there may still be good reason for conferring subject status on the thematic participant (e.g. for clause-linkage purposes, or because the theme outranks the actor in regard to empathy or definiteness (7.3.1.1)). English resolves this conflict through an augmented passive construction that specifies the actor periphrastically as the object of the preposition *by*.[2] This *by*-periphrasis is quite similar to that described earlier for nominalizations (1.2.2, especially Figs. 1.9–11). Although the passive *by* is related semantically to other senses (cf. *a play by Molière*; *She did it by herself*), it has naturally been adapted to the specific requirements of its periphrastic function. Thus it profiles a stative relation whose trajector is a schematic passive participle and whose landmark is the unspecified actor (i.e. the trajector of the verb stem on which the participle is formed). *By*'s landmark is elaborated by a nominal in accordance with the usual prepositional-object construction, producing a prepositional phrase (e.g. *by a butler*) whose schematic trajector is instantiated by a passive participle (*opened by a butler*). A finite clause is then derived just as before:

[2] Such periphrasis is infrequent in speech, and many languages have no comparable device (cf. Langacker and Munro 1975). Inherently suspect, therefore, are analyses like the original transformational account of Chomsky 1957, which treat the *by*-phrase or its analog as a central feature of passives per se. For careful examination of the factors motivating the inclusion or omission of *by*-phrases, see van Oosten 1986. By "actor," I simply mean the participant that would be the transitive subject were a passive not employed; it can thus have a variety of semantic roles and need not be an agent or even animate.

through combination with *be* to form a clausal head (*be opened by a butler*), followed by grounding (*was opened by a butler*) and elaboration of the clause-level trajector (*The door was opened by a butler*).

It may prove helpful to compare this analysis with the description of passivization in relational grammar (Perlmutter and Postal 1983). Relational grammar views syntax as being autonomous vis-à-vis semantics; treats grammatical relations as syntactic "primitives" (see Rosen 1984); claims the necessity for a "multistratal" account of syntactic structure (i.e. one that posits both "initial" and "final" strata, which are functionally equivalent to deep and surface structure in transformational grammar); and describes grammatical structure independently of discourse and functional considerations. Passive is regarded as a universal rule that promotes a direct object to the rank of subject (more technically, a nominal bearing a 2-relation on one stratum instead bears a 1-relation on the next). Since two nominals cannot bear the same grammatical relation on the same stratum, the original subject is demoted to the status of "chômeur" (it is 'out of work' in the sense of no longer being a subject or object). The final subject and the chômeur are marked in accordance with the usual patterns of the language, *by* marking the chômeur in English. Special passive morphology, such as *be* and the participial inflection, are language-specific "side effects" of the universal rule.

There are points on which the two analyses agree. For one thing, they agree that identifying the functional and discourse factors that motivate the passive construction does not eliminate the need to describe it explicitly in grammatical terms. Next, they both recognize that the "demoted" participant is neither a subject nor a direct object. A further similarity is that regular, language-specific patterns account for the manifestation of the subject and the other participant, once passive alignment has been imposed. Finally, they both invoke multiple levels of organization that differ in the status accorded the relational participants.

The major points of divergence reflect fundamental differences between the two theoretical frameworks. In contrast to relational grammar's acceptance of the autonomy thesis, the present theory claims that grammatical structure reduces to patterns for the structuring and symbolization of conceptual content, and that all valid grammatical constructs have some kind of conceptual import. The basic grammatical relations are therefore attributed semantic values (7.3) rather than being regarded as syntactic primitives. Likewise, whereas relational grammar makes no attempt to analyze *by*, *be*, and the participial morpheme as meaningful elements, ascertaining their semantic import constitutes the initial and critical step in a cognitive grammar description. In particular, the "2-to-1 advancement" characteristic of passives is analyzed as one facet of the meaning of the participial inflection (which is not a mere "side effect"). A second fundamental contrast pertains to levels of organization. Cognitive grammar is not a "multistratal" theory in the sense of positing multiple sets of grammatical relations at the clausal level. It does however posit multiple levels defined by successive steps in the assembly of a complex symbolic structure out of simpler components. And just as profiling often differs from one step to the next along a compositional path, so is it possible for the grammatical relations (figure/ground alignment) of the verb stem to be overridden at a higher level of organization in the construction of a finite clause. In English, this happens within the clausal head when $PERF_3$ combines with the verb stem to form the passive participle. Hence cognitive grammar can be thought of as a multistratal theory provided that the strata—unlike those of relational grammar—are equated with *different levels of structural complexity*.[3]

A further issue is whether "2-to-1 advancement" constitutes an autonomous rule that captures what is essential and universal to passives. Now it is certainly true that most languages have devices whereby subject status is conferred on a thematic participant that would otherwise be coded as a direct object. But this may simply reflect the salience of primary landmarks and the flexibility of figure/ground alignment—it does not establish that an advancement rule per se has independent cognitive status as a "purely syntactic" entity. On that view, passive alignment could hardly be analyzed as representing one meaning of a specific, polysemous element such as the participial morpheme (5.2.1). Nor does that view accommodate the functional, systemic, and ecological aspects of passives. By abstracting away from "side effects" and language-specific details, it obscures the fact that "advancement" is an integral (if not indissociable) facet of complex grammatical constructions, which are well designed to serve particular discourse functions and are related in various ways and degrees to other constructions. Thus it affords no basis for either anticipating or illuminating the empirical finding that many languages have two or more distinct passive constructions (cf. Chung 1976). Furthermore, a number of scholars have argued that the promotion of the direct object is less essential to a passive than the "demotion" or "defocusing" of the actor (Keenan 1976; Comrie 1977; Shibatani 1985; van Oosten 1986). In particular, Shibatani has shown how this conception better accounts for the relation of passives to other constructions, and for the fact that the morphology characteristic of passives is often used as well for such things as plural subjects, honorifics, spontaneous events, and reflexive/reciprocal expressions.

[3]Obviously, these brief remarks (even when combined with others scattered about in Vols. 1 and 2) do not constitute an adequate critique of relational grammar or a demonstration that cognitive grammar can successfully accommodate all the phenomena it deals with. Such a demonstration will require numerous studies comparable to Cook 1988a, a detailed cognitive grammar description of Samoan clause structure, which Cook had previously analyzed in relational terms (1987). (For other critiques and restatements of relational descriptions from kindred perspectives, see Schwartz 1986 and Shannon 1987.)

We will return to these matters in 8.3. For now, let us briefly note some further options displayed by passive constructions and consider how they might be described in cognitive grammar, starting with alternate ways of coding the actor. If defocusing the actor really is the primary function of passive constructions, it is not surprising that many languages provide no means for expressing it within the passive clause. For those which do allow its expression, the most common device is a periphrastic construction employing an adposition or inflection with a basic meaning such as 'with', 'from', or 'through'. In the passive, this marker designates the relationship between the actor and the clausal process, and as a vestige of its basic sense, it may further describe the nature of that relationship. For instance, 'from' portrays the actor as the *source* of the action (or of the energy that drives it), whereas 'through' construes it as the means (or "conduit") leading to its accomplishment. How saliently this conception is evoked is an index of how far grammaticization has proceeded; at the extreme, it fades away entirely, leaving—as the unadorned meaning of the periphrastic element—only the inherent whole-part relation between a process and one of its participants (cf. Fig. 1.9).

In principle, it should also be possible to make the actor explicit non-periphrastically. Since the actor is a profiled participant (Fig. 8.4(d)), one can perfectly well envisage a language-specific pattern in which it serves as e-site for direct elaboration by a nominal, just as a trajector and primary landmark are directly elaborated by nominals thereby identified as the subject and direct object. Providing an apparent example is a passive construction of Bahasa Indonesia, a Western Austronesian language. As described by Chung (1976), voice is marked on the verb by the contrast between the transitive prefix *mem-* and the passive prefix *di-*; hence *buku itu* 'the book' is the object in (6)(a) but the subject in (b), where it precedes the verb in accordance with regular word order.

(6)(a) *Ali mem-batja buku itu.*
Ali TRANS-read book the
'Ali read the book.'

(b) *Buku itu di-batja (oleh) Ali.*
book the PASV-read by Ali
'The book was read by Ali.'

Parentheses indicate that the preposition *oleh* 'by' is optional. When it is present, the *oleh*-phrase presumably specifies the actor periphrastically in much the same way as a *by*-phrase in English. What concerns us, though, is its absence, i.e. expressions such as *Buku itu di-batja Ali* 'The book was read [by] Ali'. The passive verb *di-batja* profiles a relation of the abstract form *EXPER---->ZERO* and takes as its trajector the thematic (zero) participant; *buku itu* is the subject because it elaborates that trajector. What about *Ali*, which elaborates the experiencer? It is not the subject, and it cannot be the direct object, for it lies *upstream* from the subject with respect to the analog of energy flow. In relational grammar it is called a chômeur, being analyzed as an underlying (or initial) subject demoted as a consequence of 2-to-1 advancement. In cognitive grammar it is simply a **direct participant** that qualifies as neither subject nor direct object. By direct participant, I mean one that is specified directly by a nominal, rather than through a relational predication such as a prepositional phrase. Nothing in principle precludes the existence of a special construction allowing the direct (non-periphrastic) elaboration, by a nominal, of a participant that does not have the status of either primary or secondary clause-level figure.

Let us now shift our attention from specification of the actor to the marking of passive alignment itself. For English, imposition of the marked figure/ground organization characteristic of passives was imputed to the meaning of the participial morpheme (PERF$_3$), and though details may differ, passives in most languages have some kind of morphological element for which a comparable analysis might be contemplated. But not all languages. For instance, Cook (1988a) has argued convincingly that Samoan has an active/passive contrast signalled only by word order:

(7)(a) *Na opo e le tama le teine.* 'The boy hugged the girl.'
PAST hug ERG the boy the girl
(b) *Na opo le teine e le tama.* 'The girl was hugged by the boy.'
PAST hug the girl ERG the boy

Both sentences conform to the regular word order of Samoan, in which the subject follows the verb and precedes a direct object and any other sort of complement. Hence *e le tama* 'the boy' and *le teine* 'the girl' function respectively as the subject and direct object in (a); on the other hand, *le teine* is the passive subject in (b), while *e le tama* specifies the actor but is neither a subject nor an object.[4]

What we need to say in cases of this sort is that the passive variant of the verb has the same form as the active variant. We must therefore postulate a regular pattern that has the semantic effect of deriving passive verbs from active ones but is phonologically null.[5] There are three possible ways to describe such a pattern: (1) We can posit a *phonologically zero derivational morpheme*. The semantic pole of this dependent morpheme consists of the standard-to-target mapping [[***AG***= = =>TH]---->[AG= = =>***TH***]], where boldface indicates the trajector. At the phonological pole, its standard and target are the same (i.e. it amounts to an identity function): [[. . .] ---->[. . .]]. (2) We can speak in terms of a productive *pattern of semantic*

[4] It is thus a direct but non-focal participant, just like *Ali* in the previous example. See Ch. 9 for discussion of the case marking, which Cook has shown to be indicative of semantic role in Samoan, irrespective of grammatical relations.

[5] An analysis of this kind is not at all problematic or mysterious, for zero derivation is a well-attested linguistic phenomenon. Note, for example, that essentially any noun in English can be used as a verb with no change in form (cf. Clark and Clark 1979).

extension, whereby any verb with an appropriate meaning is allowed to assume a semantic value that differs in figure/ground alignment but is otherwise unaltered. The equivalent of a "lexical rule" in other theories, for us this pattern is simply a schematized categorizing relationship that abstracts away from the specifics of individual active-to-passive extensions: [[***AG***= = = > TH/. . .] ---->[AG= = = >***TH***/. . .]]. (3) The two variants of the verb can be regarded as constituting a *defective grammatical construction*, defective in the sense of having only one component structure rather than two. Describing this construction is a schema in which the single component structure is characterized as an active verb ([***AG***= = = = >TH/. . .]), and the composite structure as the corresponding passive verb ([AG= = = = > ***TH***/. . .]). Which of these options should we choose? It turns out not to matter—from the standpoint of cognitive grammar, (1)–(3) are exactly equivalent, nothing more than different ways of interpreting precisely the same configuration of symbolic units (see Vol. 1, 12.2). It is thus a virtue of the theory that it allows us to describe the phenomenon without being forced to make artificial distinctions.

A final point is that voice alternations are not always limited to a simple active/passive contrast. Occasionally one encounters a passive-like construction where subject status is granted to a non-thematic element that is not the direct object in the corresponding active expression. For example, Malagasy has three voices: an active, a passive, and a "circumstantial" voice in which the subject is either an instrument or else a spatial or temporal setting (Thyme 1989). Recall as well (from 7.3.1.4) that certain Philippine languages have elaborate voice systems in which the subject (or "trigger") can represent any one of a number of semantic roles, including agent, theme, instrument, beneficiary, and location. Chosen as the trigger in (8)(a)–(b), from Tagalog, are an instrument and a location:[6]

(8)(a) ***Ipinan**bili ng lalake ng isda **ang pera** sa tindahan.*
bought AG man TH fish T money LOC store
'The man bought fish in the store with the money.'

(b) *Binil**han** ng lalake ng isda ng pera **ang tindahan**.*
bought AG man TH fish INSTR money T store
'The man bought fish in the store with money.'

Shibatani (1985, pp. 834–36) has suggested that the function of non-active voice in such a system is not the negative one of defocusing the agent (as in a passive), but rather the positive one of highlighting some other element; the agent therefore tends to be explicitly coded in the usual way (non-periphrastically). In a cognitive grammar analysis, this highlighting function reflects

[6]The sentences are from Foley and Van Valin 1984 (p. 135). Voice is indicated by the portions of the verb given in boldface, and the subject/trigger (also in boldface) takes *ang* in lieu of its usual case marker. For further illustration, see examples (36)–(37) of Ch. 7.

the meaning of the voice-marking inflection on the verb. Sketched in Figs. 8.5(a)–(b) are the semantic poles of the respective voice markers in (8). Each profiles a schematic process and identifies its trajector (relational figure) as

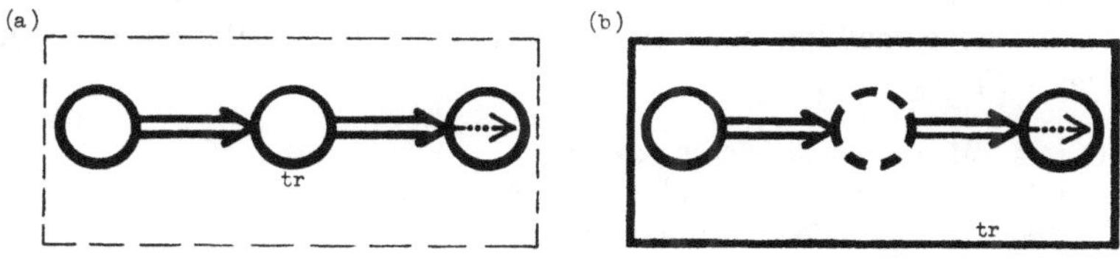

Fig. 8.5

the element bearing a particular semantic role: instrument in (a), and location/setting in (b). When the voice predication is elaborated by a verb stem, it imposes this figure/ground organization on the specific process that the stem introduces and designates.

8.1.3. *Setting vs. Participant*

An important aspect of the canonical event model is the distinction between a stable, inclusive *setting* and the smaller, more mobile *participants* who interact within it (7.1.1). In unmarked coding, the setting/participant distinction is reflected in clause structure by the grammatical opposition between clause-level adverbs of time and place, on the one hand, and nominal complements of the verb, on the other (7.2.2). The subject and object nominals are conceptually autonomous and central to the structure of a clause, for they elaborate the trajector and primary landmark of the clausal head. By contrast, the adverbs are optional and quite peripheral; being conceptually dependent vis-à-vis the remainder of the clause, they are modifiers representing the outermost layer of clausal organization.[7] However, clause structure and the setting/participant contrast do not always dovetail quite so neatly: not every complement to the verb that takes the form of a nominal is construed semantically as a participant. We have just noted, for example, that some languages have a non-active voice in which subjecthood is conferred on a setting or a location (i.e. a setting fragment). Also encountered are cases where a non-subject nominal fails to be accorded participant status.

8.1.3.1. *Relevance to Transitivity.* Either of these circumstances represents a departure from the transitive-clause prototype, in which the subject and object are distinct and well-delimited participants. The result is diminished transitivity and less likelihood of a non-subject nominal being cate-

[7]Consider *Sean fixed his bicycle in the garage*. *Sean* and *his bicycle* are complements to *fixed*, the clausal head, by virtue of the elaborative relationship they bear to its salient substructures. At a higher level of organization, *in the garage* modifies *Sean fixed his bicycle* because the latter elaborates its schematic trajector and is also the profile determinant.

gorized as the direct object. Hence a clause is not necessarily transitive just because it has two non-oblique nominals, nor is the non-subject nominal necessarily a direct object. For instance, the well-known failure of the verbs in (9) to passivize is commonly taken as evidence that their non-subject complements are something other than direct objects (cf. Allerton 1982; Rice 1987a, 5.6).

(9)(a) *My cat weighs eleven pounds.*
(a′) **Eleven pounds {is/are} weighed by my cat.*
(b) *This candy bar costs a dollar.*
(b′) **A dollar is cost by this candy bar.*
(c) *The temperature reached ninety degrees.*
(c′) **Ninety degrees was reached by the temperature.*

We can reasonably suppose that these "metric" verbs are intransitive because their landmarks are not construed as participants. Rather than interacting with the trajector, the landmark is simply a point along an abstract scale used to measure one of its properties. Hence their relationship does not at all resemble a prototypical participant-participant interaction involving energy transfer; if anything, it is more like a canonical participant-setting relation, in which the participant merely *occupies* some location.

A different kind of example is found in Mixtec (a language of Mexico), where intransitives with two non-oblique nominals represent a major pattern. For the most part, Mixtec expresses location by means of noun-noun compounds based on body-part terms (Brugman and Macaulay 1986):

(10)(a) *bílu wã̌ã hižaa nuù-žuu* 'The cat is on the mat.'
cat that be:located face-mat
(b) *ni-ndečé ɨ̄ɨ̄ saà žata-žúnu* 'A bird flew behind the tree.'
PERF-fly one bird back-tree

Though body parts are usually participants, their construal as locations is natural because their position within the body as a whole is a crucial and salient facet of their characterization. A noun like *žata* '(human) back' receives a locational construal to the extent that the notions of position and spatial extension are highlighted at the expense of material substance. This is the first in a regular series of semantic extensions that lead systematically to compounds such as *žata-žúnu*. The next step involves using the body-part term for the analogous location with respect to a non-human object (such as a tree). And finally, it comes to designate the spatial region contiguous to that location. The resulting compound is nominal rather than relational (see Brugman 1983 for arguments that it is *not* a prepositional phrase), and it elaborates a salient landmark within the verbal predication.[8] It is thus a nomi-

[8] Clearly, 'be located' evokes in schematic terms the conception of a location, which can thus serve as an e-site. The locational e-site of 'fly' is either the final location resulting from the trajector's motion or else the path it traverses (a series of locations).

nal complement of the verb, but since it lacks participant status, it does not qualify as a direct object.

The extensive grammatical significance of the setting/participant distinction is starting to become apparent (Langacker 1986c, 1987a; see also Denny 1984). Evident as well is the close connection between transitivity and the prototypical configuration sketched in diagram (a) of Fig. 8.6. Two essential

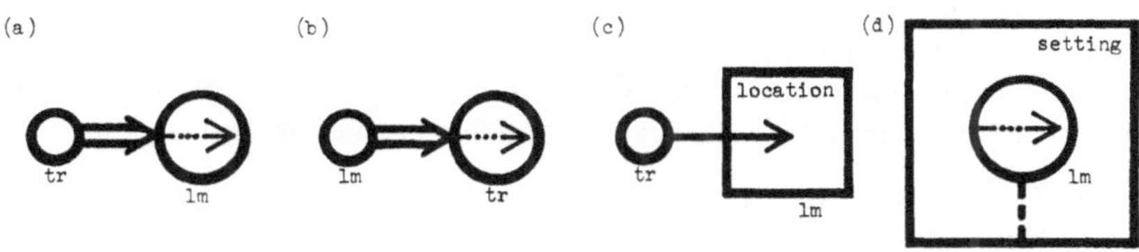

Fig. 8.6

aspects of this configuration are, first, that the trajector and landmark are both construed as participants, and second, that the landmark lies downstream from the trajector in terms of either the transmission of energy or some conceived analog of energy flow. If a clause substantially departs from this prototype in either respect, it is low in transitivity and a non-subject nominal is at best a marginal member of the direct-object category. We noted the non-transitivity of configuration (b) in our discussion of passives (8.1.2); even when the upstream participant is accorded sufficient prominence to be considered a landmark, and is coded non-periphrastically by an overt nominal (as in (6)(b)), it is never considered a direct object. It is equally uncontroversial that the locational complements in Mixtec are not direct objects, even in expressions like (10)(b), where—as shown in (c)—the location lies downstream in regard to the path traversed by the subject. We will now examine a variety of constructions representing configuration (d), in which the setting is chosen as trajector. These expressions also prove intransitive, despite the coding of the landmark by a non-oblique nominal that is clearly a participant.

8.1.3.2. *Setting-Subject Constructions*. We have been referring to the subject and direct object as *focal participants* and have described the subject informally as *the most prominent clausal participant*. Though apt in most instances, that terminology is inappropriate for constructions in which the subject is not a participant but a setting. When speaking strictly rather than loosely, we must therefore describe the subject more inclusively as the most prominent clausal *element*. We must likewise use the term *focal elements* for the nominals that elaborate the trajector and the most salient landmark, either of which may be a non-participant. These elements can in any case be characterized as the *primary* and *secondary clausal figures*. They serve as foci within the processual profile, and their own prominence heightens that of any interconnections which involve them directly. This focusing effect has subtle but important semantic repercussions, one of which is especially relevant here. Namely, conferring trajector status on the setting in which a process unfolds has the inherent result of heightening the prominence of the setting-process relationship itself. Indicated by the dashed line in Fig. 8.6(d), this "container-content" relation between the setting and what happens within it automatically becomes a central facet of the processual profile when the "container" is made the primary figure.

Let us adopt the term **setting-subject construction** for expressions of this sort. The sentences in (11) represent one such construction:

(11)(a) *Thursday saw yet another startling development.*
(b) *Independence Hall has witnessed many historic events.*

These sentences give the appearance of being transitive, for a nominal directly follows the verb. However, their well-known failure to passivize suggests otherwise:

(12)(a) **Yet another startling development was seen by Thursday.*
(b) **Many historic events have been witnessed by Independence Hall.*

It is in fact a consequence of our analysis that the post-verbal nominal is not a direct object. The subject in (11) is the spatial or temporal setting for some occurrence that is expressed by the other nominal. Since these nominals respectively elaborate the trajector and primary landmark of the verb, we must attribute to *see* or *witness* a semantic value that constitutes a semantic extension from its basic sense, which profiles an *EXPER---->ZERO* relationship with canonical trajector/landmark alignment. In this construction, the verb instead designates the more abstract configuration [*(EXPER---->)ZERO*], in which the experiential relationship is defocused (though not altogether absent) and the setting (represented by the brackets) functions as trajector. That is, *see* or *witness* assumes a value that we can gloss (quite roughly) as 'be the setting for ({seeing/witnessing})'. With this meaning the verbs are intransitive, for the trajector is not a participant and is not connected to the landmark via an action-chain analog, but rather through a container-content relation. Their non-passivizability is therefore predictable.

It is worth noting that the verb *contain* itself is intransitive provided that the profile is limited to a static container-content relation, i.e. [*ZERO*], as in (13).

(13)(a) *The dam contains 2000 acre feet of water.*
(b) **2000 acre feet of water {is/are} contained by the dam.*

(14)(a) *So far the dam is containing the surging floodwaters.*
(b) *So far the surging floodwaters are being contained by the dam.*

But in (14), we observe the transitivity of the force-dynamic construal [= = = = >*MVR*], which highlights the container's resistance to the tendency on the part of the contents to escape its confines.[9] This suggests that there is in fact a connection between the setting/participant distinction and the container-content relationship, which is one of the **image schemas** that Johnson (1987) and Lakoff (1987, ch. 17) propose as being fundamental to human cognition. The notions *setting/participant* and *action chain* should perhaps be regarded as particular manifestations of the respective image schemas *container-content* and *source-path-goal*—specifically, as their embodiment in the conception of canonical events. Nevertheless, they have substantial cognitive salience and experiential motivation in their own right, being grounded in the archetypal stage and billiard-ball models.

Although the prototypical setting is a spatial or temporal expanse, other kinds of entities can also be so construed. A film, for example, is naturally regarded as a setting for the actors who appear in it. By analyzing (15)(a) as a setting-subject construction we can thus explain the ill-formedness of its passive counterpart:

(15)(a) *Stallone's latest movie stars Woody Allen.*
(b) **Woody Allen is starred by Stallone's latest movie.*

Moreover, the verb *feature* has two semantic variants used in reference to films. One variant accords trajector status to the film's creator, and the other to the film itself, as respectively shown in (16)(a)–(b).

(16)(a) *Fellini features Olympia Dukakis in his new film.*
(b) *Fellini's new film features Olympia Dukakis.*

(17)(a) *Olympia Dukakis is featured by Fellini in his new film.*
(b) **Olympia Dukakis is featured by Fellini's new film.*

Our analysis therefore predicts the judgments in (17), under the reasonable assumption that the film is construed as a setting whereas the director is a participant.

The construction in (18) permits a variety of entities to be construed as settings and coded as subjects:

(18)(a) *My cat is crawling with fleas.*
(b) *The sidewalk is bustling with shoppers.*
(c) *The garden is swarming with bees.*
(d) *The flowers are glistening with dew.*

[9]The progressive aspect in (14) tells us that adding this force-dynamic component to *contain* also renders it perfective. Unless one is specifically describing some facet of the world's structure (e.g. *This column supports the main crossbeam*), the exertion of energy is normally conceived as occurring in bounded episodes.

In (18)(a), it is the fleas who actually do the crawling (the cat may be quite sedentary). It is likewise the shoppers that bustle, the bees that swarm, and the dew that glistens. The import of this construction is that the subject hosts a certain type of activity by the components of a mass that is essentially coextensive with it, so that instances of that activity also extend to its boundaries. We saw in Ch. 3 that a verb in English can be used, without any special marking, to designate a *replicate process* consisting of indefinitely many instances of the basic process type. In the present construction, the verb assumes a value representing one further semantic adjustment: trajector status is not assigned to the *replicate trajector* (i.e. the mass comprising the trajectors of the individual process instances), but rather to the coextensive host or setting. Thus *crawl*, for example, takes on a meaning something like 'be the {host/setting} for pervasive crawling activity'. This particular construction is overtly intransitive, for instead of being specified directly by a bare nominal, the mass that carries out the activity is introduced periphrastically as the object of the preposition *with*.[10] Of course, a Verb + Preposition sequence in English is often categorized as a complex transitive verb eligible for passivization, as illustrated in (19)(a)–(b).

(19)(a) *Tommy was often yelled at by his mother.*
(b) *George is always being fought with by his co-workers.*
(c) **Fleas are being crawled with by my cat.*

But as we see from (19)(c), which is not only ill-formed but quite uninterpretable, the V + *with* sequence of this setting-subject construction cannot be so categorized. This is further evidence for the non-transitivity of such constructions.

8.1.3.3. *Double-Subject Constructions*. Examples like (18)(a) suggest the naturalness of construing a person or an animal as the setting for a process that occurs within it. At the same time, the creature as a whole has a greater measure of intrinsic cognitive salience than its parts and is thus a natural candidate to be construed as the figure within a scene. The interaction of these two factors results in a special type of construction found in numerous languages, as exemplified by the following Luiseño expressions:[11]

(20)(a)	*noo=p*	*no-te?*	*tiiwu-q*	'I have a stomach ache.'
	I=3s	my-stomach	hurt-TNS	

[10] *With* has basically the same meaning as in expressions like *a cat with fleas* and *flowers with dew on them*. In this [V [with NML]] construction, *with*'s trajector corresponds to the host, and its landmark (the prepositional object) to the coextensive mass.

[11] The suffix *-q* marks tense (TNS), and '=' indicates cliticization (as opposed to suffixation). The clitics =*p* and =*n* attach to the first word or constituent of a finite clause and normally indicate that the subject is third-person singular (3s) or first-person singular (1s), respectively. Either clitic is possible in either sentence.

(b) *noo = n no-puuš konokniš* 'I have green eyes.'
I = 1s my-eye green

This is usually called a "double-subject construction" because both nominals appear to have a valid claim to subject status (Steele 1977). Whereas *noo* 'I' is the subject form of the first-person singular pronoun, it is also true that the last two words of each expression constitute a well-formed sentence in which the body-part term functions as subject: *no-teʔ tiiwu-q* 'My stomach hurts'; *no-puuš konokniš* 'My eyes are green'. Moreover, the clitic can either be third person, suggesting that the body-part term is the subject, or (less commonly) first person, which argues that the speaker enjoys that status.

Cognitive grammar affords an unproblematic description of this construction that requires no concepts or constructs not already motivated for other purposes. It is in fact a double-subject construction, but the two subjects pertain to different levels of structural complexity, the higher level representing a setting-subject construction. The first level, a simple clause such as *no-teʔ tiiwu-q* 'My stomach hurts', is the component structure shown on the right in Fig. 8.7. The subject at this level is a body-part expression, and the profile is a relationship in which the body part participates. Included as an unprofiled facet of the base is the possessive relation between the part and the person as a whole; indicated by a dashed line, it can also be thought of as a container-content relation between the body and the process that occurs within it. A comparable relation is latent in the other component structure, depicted at the left, which is simply a nominal that designates a person (e.g. *noo* 'I'). The

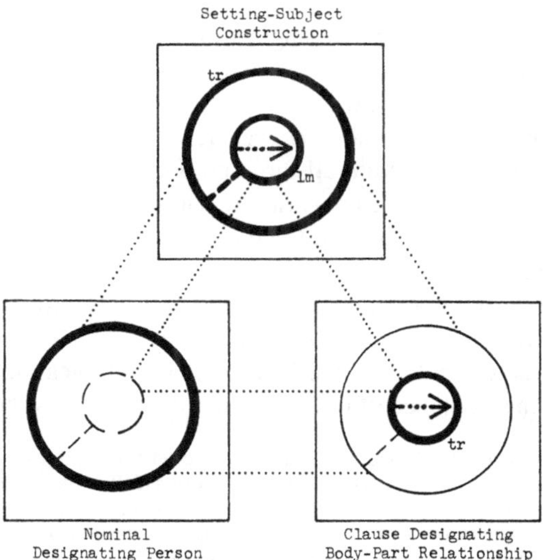

Fig. 8.7

pivotal correspondence equates that person with the possessor evoked by the clausal predication (shown as well is a correspondence between the relevant body parts). Now each component structure contributes something to the composite expression, represented at the top: from the clausal component, the composite structure inherits the conception of a process involving a body part; inherited from the nominal component is the special prominence accorded the person as a whole, which functions as trajector at the higher level of clausal organization.[12] An automatic consequence of choosing the person as trajector is to augment the salience of the interconnections that it anchors, notably those that constitute the possessive or container-content relationship. The result is a setting-subject construction that is of course intransitive despite the presence of two nominals. And because the possessive relationship serves as the focus within the processual profile, these sentences translate naturally into English with 'have' (e.g. 'I have a stomach ache'), even though the Luiseño expressions do not include a verb of possession.

What about the clitics that attach to the first nominal? Since each nominal is the subject of a structure categorizable as a finite clause, it is not surprising that a clitic specifying the person of a finite-clause subject might be able to reflect either option. Things may be just that simple. Let us suppose, however, that the clitic combines with the remainder of the clause at the highest level of constituency, and that it is only sensitive to grammatical relations at that level (e.g. those of *noo no-teʔ tiiwu-q* as a whole). How, then, is it possible for the clitic to indicate the person of either nominal (and most frequently the second, which is not the subject at that level)? I suspect that the clitics are being used with special values induced by the atypical nature of the double-subject construction. In a typical single-subject clause, the nominal that the clitic "agrees" with combines three properties: (1) it is construed as a participant; (2) it corresponds to the trajector of the verb; and (3) it is the subject at the clausal level of organization. However, in sentences like those in (20) there is no single nominal with all three properties, hence the clitics cannot be used with precisely the same import. Thus, by a process of **semantic accommodation** (Vol. 1, 10.4.2), the clitics systematically assume either of two extended values in the context of this construction: their specification of person pertains to the nominal characterized either by properties (1) and (2) (as in example (a)) or by property (3) (as in (b)).[13]

While the structure in Fig. 8.7 appears to be prototypical for double-subject constructions, the existence of other variants should at least be noted in pass-

[12] Neither component structure can be identified as a profile determinant, since the composite structure profile is not precisely the same as that of either one. The existence of a profile determinant is prototypical but by no means a universal trait of valence relations (see Vol. 1, 8.2.1).

[13] A parallel rationale can be offered for the possibility in Japanese of the subject marker *ga* following both nominals in the double-subject construction: *Taroo ga hana ga hikui* 'Taro has a flat nose'. See Shibatani 1986; Langacker 1986c, 1987a.

ing. In one variant, the body-part nominal is a non-subject at the lower level of organization. Steele (1977) cites examples like (21)(a), where *ʔexval* 'sand' corresponds to the verbal trajector and *no-puuš* 'my eye' is oblique.[14]

(21)(a) *noo=p no-puuš-ŋa ʔexval ŋo-q* 'I have sand in my eye.'
I=3s my-eye-in sand be:inside-TNS
(b) *noo=n no-toonav yawaywiš qala* 'I have a beautiful basket.'
I=1s my-basket beautiful is

Steele also cites expressions such as (21)(b), in which the possessive relation does not pertain to a body part. What these suggest (though we will not pursue the matter here) is that the notion *setting-subject* might be generalized to that of *reference-point-subject*, a setting or container being just one kind of reference point. Lastly, there are double-subject constructions where the clause at the lower level of organization makes no reference at all to possession. The following examples are from Newari, a Tibeto-Burman language spoken in Nepal (Hung 1988; Cook 1988b):

(22)(a) *wa khicaa-yaake bhugin du* 'The dog has flies.'
the dog-COM fly exist
(b) *ji-ta wa baanlaa* 'I think she's beautiful.'
I-DAT she beautiful

In (22)(a), the dog is construed as the setting for the process *bhugin du* 'flies exist'; signalling a relationship between the dog and that process is *-yaake*, the marker for comitative case, which is regularly used for animate sources and possessors. The dative case marker *-ta* in (22)(b) represents the subject as an experiencer (see Ch. 9), and thus as a *mental* setting rather than a physical one. The relationship *wa baanlaa* 'she is beautiful' is portrayed as occurring in the mind of the subject, which is a natural way to indicate that it represents the subject's opinion.

8.1.3.4. *Abstract Settings.* Even our limited sample should make it apparent that setting-subject constructions represent a common, if not ubiquitous, linguistic phenomenon. In form and behavior, they are reminiscent of another large class of constructions, which are characterized by subjects usually regarded as "syntactic dummies"—meaningless "placeholders" inserted for purely grammatical purposes. The German pronoun *es* 'it' is often attributed such a role:

(23)(a) *Es steht eine Vase auf dem Tisch.* 'There stands a vase on the table.'
(b) *Es spielt ein Kind im Garten.* 'There's a child playing in the garden.'

[14]Comparable examples from modern Irish are found in McCloskey and Sells 1988 (which analyzes them from a radically different theoretical perspective).

In this and other constructions, *es* appears to lack the definite reference it displays in its basic pronominal use (e.g. *Es steht auf dem Tisch* 'It is standing on the table'). Still, *es* is clearly the subject grammatically, even though—notionally—it is the vase that does the standing, and the child the playing. A standard transformational account would thus derive these sentences by means of a rule replacing the underlying subject (*eine Vase*; *ein Kind*) with the "dummy" *es*.

What is pertinent for us is that these sentences have two non-oblique nominals but are nevertheless intransitive (they do not passivize), and that the post-verbal nominal is not a direct object (the case marking is nominative rather than accusative). We have seen that these properties are typical of setting-subject constructions and follow from our characterization of transitivity and other notions. Strongly indicated for constructions like (23), therefore, is an analysis wherein *es* or its counterpart designates some kind of **abstract setting** (see Smith 1985a). So analyzed, the construction proves quite comparable to others previously described, its special character hinging on the integration of the subject with the verb (e.g. *es* with *steh* 'stand'). Their integration is parallel in major respects to Fig. 8.7: the composite structure (*es steh*) inherits the verb's processual profile but takes the setting for its trajector; this entails a shift in focus to the setting-process (container-content) relationship itself.

The English glosses in (23) represent a very similar construction, for which transformational grammarians posited the rule of *There*-Insertion: *A vase is on the table* ====> *There is a vase on the table*. One problem with this analysis is that some *there*-sentences have no apparent source, e.g. *Suddenly there was a loud commotion* (cf. **Suddenly a loud commotion was*). The problem does not arise in cognitive grammar, for a *there*-clause is not derived from a *there*-less underlying structure; though assembled from mostly the same pieces (linked by analogous sets of correspondences), the two types of clauses are separate and parallel. The pivotal step in assembling a *there*-clause is the integration of *there* and *be*, as shown in Fig. 8.8. *There* designates an abstract setting construed as hosting some relationship. This is put in correspondence with the relationship profiled by *be*, namely the continuation through time of a stable situation (characterized only schematically). The composite structure *there be* is an imperfective process equivalent to *be* apart from the (by now familiar) shift in focus that results from trajector status being conferred on the setting. The trajector of *be* remains a salient participant at this higher level of organization; it is thus a landmark (lm_1) and is elaborated by a nominal complement (*there be* ***a vase***). Also serving as landmark (lm_2) and as e-site is the schematic situation invoked by *be*, which is instantiated by an appropriate relational complement (*there be a vase* ***on***

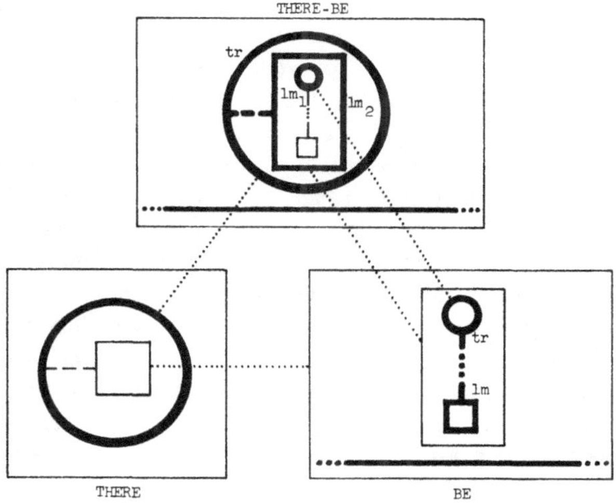

Fig. 8.8

the table). Grounding then yields a finite clause (*There is a vase on the table*).[15]

I am by no means the first to suggest that the "dummy" *there* in fact refers to an abstract setting. In his important study of the many kinds of *there*-constructions in English (1987, case study 3), Lakoff describes it as referring to a mental space (but does little to clarify the nature of that space). Bolinger (1977, p. 93) speaks of an abstract location that he identifies as the mental "awareness" of the speech-act participants. Despite the overall insight of his discussion, I feel he is wrong in this particular.[16] Still, he is certainly correct that a *there*-clause brings an element into awareness and thus serves a *presentational* function. Kirsner (1979b) offers a revealing analysis of presentational sentences in Dutch, e.g. *Er blaft een hond* 'There barks a dog', which exhibit a wider range of verbs than English *there*-clauses but are otherwise comparable. He emphasizes *er*'s opposition to the other deictic adverbs *hier* 'here' and *daar* 'there'; of this set, *er* conveys the lowest degree of "situational deixis," i.e. it is the weakest in terms of urging the hearer to seek out the

[15] While the imperfective *be* is prototypical, this construction is extended to certain other verbs (*stand, lie, exist, appear*, etc.) and to *be* used perfectively (*There was another bicycle stolen last night*). The description of these variants requires only minor adjustments in the basic pattern. Examples like *There was a loud commotion* result from leaving lm_2 unelaborated, probably because it is identified with the very same relationship of *occurrence within a setting* that constitutes the focus of the processual profile. (For discussion of lm_1, see Rando and Napoli 1978.)

[16] Bolinger's characterization fails with a sentence like *Susan believes there to be several flaws in the new design*, for the belief does not pertain to the speaker's or the hearer's awareness. (Cf. Ch. 10.)

intended setting. Though *er* can be interpreted spatially, the linguistic and situational context often favors a more abstract construal, whereby it indicates "general presence or availability," or what Kirsner calls "mere sceneness": while an entity is in some sense "on the scene," the identity of that scene is immaterial (p. 81). The effect of putting an element like *er* or *there* in clause-initial position (and in our analysis, of making it the relational figure) is to background the participant (e.g. *een hond* 'a dog') without foregrounding anything else of real substance. This enables the construction to introduce a *new* participant while observing the usual pattern of beginning a clause with an element that is *given* (i.e. accessible from the current discourse space).

The notion of an abstract setting awaits further elucidation (a beginning is made in 8.3), but I would at least maintain that it is natural and coherent in the context of our overall approach, and that it affords an analysis of certain constructions which in large measure predicts and explains their special grammatical properties. For now, let us note just one additional feature of *there*-clauses, which is not at all typical of setting-subject constructions and is seemingly problematic. *There* apparently takes on the number of the "logical subject," i.e. the post-verbal nominal that elaborates lm_1. When that nominal is plural, the subject *there* is also plural, as witnessed by number inflection on the verb:

(24)(a) *There are people dancing in the streets.*
(b) *There are said to be people dancing in the streets.*

One cannot simply say that verb agreement is exceptional in a *there*-clause, reflecting the number of the logical (rather than the grammatical) subject. That analysis fails to handle sentences like (24)(b), in which *there* appears in a clause that does not itself describe the event for which it serves as the setting (i.e. in "raising" constructions, discussed in Ch. 10). Observe that *people* is not the logical subject of *say* in this example, but only of *dance*, yet the main-clause verb is plural.

What is happening, I suspect, is that *there* is in fact construed as being plural in an extended sense of that term. Plurality represents a complex category. Prototypically, it indicates a mass comprising discrete entities that are instances of the same type and can also be referred to individually. With both nouns and verbs, however, plural morphology may have other values: many nouns (*scissors*, *bleachers*, etc.) deviate from the prototype in regard to discreteness and individuality, so that the plural ending merely signals some kind of internal multiplicity (2.3.1); in the case of verbs, the component entities need not even instantiate the same type (e.g. *A man and a woman were sitting here*). It is crucial to realize that the conception of a replicate mass is quite abstract—whereas *table* designates a physical object, *tables* profiles an *abstract region* established as such only because its constituent entities share a type specification. Hence there is nothing far-fetched about a semantic extension through which *there* comes to be categorized as a special sort of plural in examples like (24). The basis for this extension is a perceived similarity between a replicate mass and an abstract setting in which multiple participants are involved in a common type of process. Indeed, a replicate mass is a kind of set, and metaphorically we think of sets as containers for their members, just as settings are viewed as containers for events and participants.

8.2. Choice of Object

Within a verb's processual profile, the most prominent element (in the sense of being the primary figure) is called the *trajector*. The trajector may be either a setting or a participant, but in the case of processual predications it is apparently always a thing.[17] A nominal that elaborates a clause-level trajector is a *subject*. The subject is a *nominal complement* to the clausal head: a *complement* (rather than a modifier) because it elaborates a salient substructure of the head; and *nominal* (as opposed to relational) because it profiles a thing.

A prominent element other than the trajector is referred to as a *landmark*. Either a thing or a relation can function as landmark (cf. Fig. 8.8), and a nominal landmark can either be a participant or some kind of setting or location. Often there are multiple landmarks, which vary in the degree of prominence accorded them; a *primary landmark* is one that stands out as being especially salient (a secondary figure). Depending on its nature, a landmark is elaborated by either a nominal or a relational complement. When specified non-periphrastically by a nominal complement, an element with participant status is termed a *direct participant*. A *direct object* can then be characterized schematically as a nominal with the following properties: (1) it elaborates a primary landmark; (2) it represents a direct participant; and (3) this participant lies downstream from the trajector (also a participant) with respect to the transmission of energy or some analogous asymmetry.[18]

In an event of any complexity, there are likely to be a number of entities susceptible to being coded as direct object, even for a particular choice of

[17] By contrast, the trajector of an atemporal predication may be either nominal or relational. A relational trajector is characteristic of adverbs.

[18] This characterization reflects the traditional practice of using the term direct object fairly narrowly, thereby excluding many non-subject nominal complements (e.g. the ones in (9)). It can of course be weakened in various ways to accommodate a broader range of cases—at the extreme, a direct object could simply be described as a *secondary clausal figure* (parallel to *primary clausal figure* for subjects), with no qualification as to participant status or relational asymmetry. Any line we draw for terminological purposes is bound to be arbitrary to some degree. The essential point is to recognize that properties (1)–(3) all characterize central members of a fundamental grammatical category. A particular grammatical phenomenon (e.g. passivizability), or even the same phenomenon in different languages, may be sensitive to direct-objecthood under either a broad or a restrictive construal.

trajector and processual profile. Alternate selections of primary landmark may then constitute the major semantic contrast between different verbs or variants of the same verb. Consider, for example, the distinct senses of *tie* illustrated in (25).

(25) *He tied {his shoe/his shoelace/a bow with his shoelace}.*

Even assuming that all three expressions describe a canonical act of shoe-tying (and thus evoke the same conceptual content), the very fact that different elements are chosen as primary landmark and coded by the direct object assures their semantic non-equivalence. The chosen element is a focal participant whose status as the secondary clausal figure enhances the salience of the interconnections and component relationships that immediately involve it. For instance, the first option (*his shoe*) brings into focus those relations involving the shoe as a whole (notably the snugness of its attachment to the foot), whereas the second (*his shoelace*) highlights relationships pertaining to the lace in particular (e.g. that the ends no longer drag along the ground). Thus one might well say *He tied his shoe to keep from getting a blister* [from the foot rubbing against the inside of the shoe], or *He tied his shoelace to keep from tripping* [by stepping on the loose ends], but *He tied his shoelace to keep from getting a blister* is somewhat less natural.[19]

Affecting the choice of direct object in a rather different manner is variation as to what portion of a clause functions as its *content verb* (5.1). Observe in this regard that certain conventional expressions, e.g. *take advantage of*, passivize in either of two ways:

(26)(a) *An unscrupulous lawyer took advantage of the helpless widow.*
(b) *Advantage was taken of the helpless widow by an unscrupulous lawyer.*
(c) *The helpless widow was taken advantage of by an unscrupulous lawyer.*

It is generally assumed that a passive subject is the direct object of the corresponding active. Thus (26)(b) implies an analysis of (26)(a) in which *advantage* is the object, and this in turn implies that *take* is the content verb. But by the same token, (26)(c) shows that (26)(a) can also be analyzed with *the helpless widow* as direct object, which means that the content verb must be the full sequence *take advantage of*. This type of phenomenon poses no particular descriptive problem in cognitive grammar (Vol. 1, 11.2.3). An expression's structural description resides in its categorization by an assembly

[19] It is pointless (unless, of course, one has a special fondness for chicken-and-egg-type conundra) to ask whether the choice of direct object results from "prior" identification of the primary landmark, or whether explicit mention by the direct object is itself responsible for this focal prominence. The very question belies a construction's essential *systemic* nature: its components are mutually accommodating, and important aspects of their value derive from their role within the system as a unified, coherent whole.

of class and constructional schemas. It is quite possible for the same expression to straightforwardly instantiate alternate sets of schemas, and for the same class schema to categorize expressions that differ in size and grammatical organization. Thus, to the extent that a sequence like *take advantage of* is construed as conforming semantically to the characterization of a transitive verb, it may be so categorized despite its internal complexity. Its integration with the following nominal then instantiates the constructional schema describing the verb-object relationship of a transitive clause.

Rice (1987a, ch. 3) has carefully examined the analogous categorization of Verb + Preposition sequences as complex transitive verbs. She has found that the likelihood of this analysis is influenced by numerous factors relating to prototypical transitivity, as reflected in the canonical event model. For instance, when the preposition describes a path that leads to a goal, a V + P sequence is more likely to coalesce as a complex verb than when it describes a path leading away from a source; the reason is that the former configuration bears an abstract resemblance to the flow of energy along an action chain to the patient. Other things being equal, therefore, *rush to* is more readily categorized as a transitive verb than *flee from*, as we see in (27)–(28) on the basis of passivizability.

(27)(a) *George rushed to Marsha, because he needed advice.*
(b) *Marsha was rushed to by George, because he needed advice.*

(28)(a) *George fled from Marsha, because she intimidated him.*
(b) **Marsha was fled from by George, because she intimidated him.*

(29)(a) *George rushed to the countryside, because he needed a rest.*
(b) **The countryside was rushed to by George, because he needed a rest.*

Likewise, the contrast between (27) and (29) shows the relevance of the setting/participant distinction. *Marsha* and *the countryside* are of course prototypical of participants and settings, respectively. And since a direct object must have participant status, *Marsha* facilitates the transitive construal of *rush to*, whereas *the countryside* hinders it.

The question of whether a particular nominal functions as direct object is more difficult to resolve in clauses with multiple target-domain participants. Both descriptive and theoretical problems thus arise in regard to verbs such as *give*, *sell*, *send*, *hand*, *lend*, *tell*, *show*, etc., which take as complements both a thematic participant (typically a mover) and a recipient or experiencer (see Figs. 7.5 and 8.1(a)). On the basis of marking or other grammatical behavior, it is sometimes obvious—as in (30)(a)—that the former is a direct object and the latter is not.

(30)(a) *Ruth gave a candy bar to the baby.*
(b) *Ruth gave the baby a candy bar.*

But things are not always so clear-cut. In (30)(b), both the recipient and the theme are direct participants (neither is marked oblique by a preposition), and each in some sense lies downstream from the subject, whose action affects the theme directly and physically, the recipient more abstractly and indirectly (by virtue of the theme moving into its dominion). Can we then say that (30)(b) has *two* direct objects? If there is only one, which nominal is it? Though details vary, verbs of this sort pose comparable problems in many languages.

In sorting these matters out, it is important to bear in mind the distinction between *grammatical relations* and *semantic roles*. The basic grammatical relations, *subject* and *direct object*, are characterized primarily in terms of prominence. Hence they are to some degree independent of semantic role, which pertains instead to conceptual content, specifically to the structure of an event and the nature of an element's involvement. The notion *theme* is schematic for the various roles (zero, mover, patient, etc.) associated with a conceived event's conceptually autonomous core (7.1.2). Crucially, we have found that *indirect object* (of which *recipient* is a special case), though traditionally regarded as a grammatical relation, is more coherently analyzed as a semantic role (7.3.3). An indirect object is *an active experiencer in the target domain* (Fig. 7.5); by *active* is meant that it is distinguished from a purely thematic participant, usually by being attributed some kind of initiative capacity (if only as a locus of awareness). Granted this characterization, direct and indirect objects need not be mutually exclusive. For instance, *the baby* manifests the semantic role of indirect object in both sentences of (30), even though in (30)(b) it is also the direct object (secondary clausal figure).

In a prototypical transitive clause, the focal prominence characteristic of subject and object status is conferred on elements whose semantic role also lends them a measure of special salience. Thus the subject in *Floyd broke the glass* is simultaneously the primary figure, the agent, and the starting point with respect to energy flow. Likewise, *the glass* is both the secondary figure and the theme, i.e. the starting point with respect to conceptual autonomy/dependence (7.1.2–3). But suppose a clause has two participants in the target domain, as in (30). Each lies downstream from the subject, so either one could in principle be made the secondary figure and hence the direct object. Moreover, each has a particular kind of role-based salience that makes it a natural candidate for selection as a focal participant. The theme is favored not only on grounds of conceptual autonomy, but also because it quite closely approximates the direct-object prototype: it is the action-chain tail (energy sink), and its role is purely passive. At the same time, the indirect object is salient because it is human or sentient, and its role is to some degree active and initiative—it interacts with the theme (and is thus affected by the subject) partly by virtue of its own activity in the mental sphere. In view of these competing rationales, it is hardly surprising that languages vary as to which target-domain participant is accorded focal prominence.[20] Some languages consistently choose the theme as direct object, just as in a prototypical transitive clause. Other languages consistently choose the indirect object, thereby achieving the co-alignment of two natural paths: the most and second-most *prominent* participants coincide with the two most *active* participants from the standpoint of initiative capacity (the most active overall, and the most active within the target domain). And in some languages, including English, alternate constructions allow both kinds of naturalness to be accommodated.

Let us briefly summarize these two constructions. In a sentence like (30)(a), the agent and theme respectively function as subject and direct object, as shown in Fig. 8.1(a). The indirect object is introduced periphrastically, as the object of the preposition *to*. The *to*-phrase is a relational complement: it specifies the theme's path, which the verb saliently evokes but characterizes only schematically. What about the "Dative Shift" construction of (30)(b)? It is essentially the same in regard to conceptual content and profiling. The basic difference is that the recipient rather than the mover (or more generally, the indirect object rather than the theme) is the secondary figure and thus serves as e-site for the direct-object nominal. Conferring focal prominence on the recipient has the inherent consequence of heightening the salience of the interconnections it anchors, notably those involving its initiative role. The English construction requires in particular that the theme's movement result in a possessive relationship whereby the recipient in some sense controls or has access to it. The specification of the theme can be described in either of two ways. The most straightforward analysis is to regard the thematic participant as a secondary landmark and e-site; the elaborating nominal then represents a direct participant but does not qualify as either a subject or a direct object. Alternatively, the possessive relationship can be taken as a landmark elaborated by a relational complement formed by zero derivation from a nominal; in (30)(b), for example, *a candy bar* would actually represent a relational predication semantically equivalent to *have a candy bar* apart from being construed atemporally.[21] Since the two analyses yield the same composite structure from the same ultimate components, choosing between them is not an issue of any great moment. I suspect, in fact, that the matter is indeterminate both analytically and cognitively.

Be that as it may, sentence pairs like (30)(a)–(b) are claimed to be seman-

[20] See Dryer 1986 for a comprehensive survey. Despite a difference in theoretical orientation, Dryer's account of this variation is largely compatible with the one offered here.

[21] This analysis is less suspicious than it sounds, for possession is often marked by zero (4.3.2), and the relational use of nominals is attested for English by predicate-nominative constructions (2.2.4). With the theme construed relationally, *give the baby a candy bar* is structurally parallel to *elect Sally treasurer*, *provide the students with supplies*, or even *give a candy bar to the baby*, in that the verb is followed by a nominal and then a relational complement.

tically distinct, if only because one highlights the mover and the path it traverses, whereas the other accords greater prominence to the recipient and the resultant possessive relationship. This imagic contrast has empirical consequences (cf. Goldsmith 1980; Ikegami 1985, p. 286; Langacker 1986b, pp. 14–16). For example, since a verb like *send* does not necessarily imply a change of possession, an expression with *to* may receive a purely spatial construal. And since either a participant or a setting can serve as the endpoint of a spatial path, both sentences in (31) are acceptable.

(31)(a) *I sent the walrus to Harvey.*
(b) *I sent the walrus to Antarctica.*

(32)(a) *I sent Harvey the walrus.*
(b) **I sent Antarctica the walrus.*

The facts in (32) are predictably different, for only a participant can be a recipient of the sort required by the Dative Shift construction, which itself imposes a possessive construal and characterizes the direct object as the recipient/possessor. The analysis further explains why sentences representing this construction are available as counterparts to some but not all expressions with *for*:

(33)(a) *I drew a picture for him.* (a′) *I drew him a picture.*
(b) *I washed the windows for him.* (b′) **I washed him the windows.*

(34)(a) *I cleared the floor for him.*
(b) **I cleared him the floor.*
(c) *I cleared him a place to sleep on the floor.*

While drawing a picture for someone provides him with access to something that was previously unavailable, washing windows does not entail a change of possession under normal circumstances. The examples in (34) are especially interesting because the differential acceptability of (b) and (c) cannot be attributed to the verb. Like washing windows, clearing a floor does not per se have any possessive implications. However, clearing someone *a place to sleep on the floor* makes him a possessor in the sense of having that place at his disposal for a particular purpose.

Of the non-thematic participants capable of assuming direct-object status, indirect objects do so the most commonly and often without any special marking on the verb. With appropriate marking, however, it is not unusual for a language to permit some other option, and occasionally a number of different non-thematic elements can be chosen. This phenomenon is best known from certain African languages of the Bantu family (Kisseberth and Abasheikh 1977; Givón 1979, ch. 4; Kimenyi 1980; Dryer 1983). In Kinyarwanda, for example, the object may be (*inter alia*) an instrument, a location, a beneficiary, or someone who accompanies the subject in carrying out the profiled activity.[22] The first two possibilities are exemplified in (35) and (36), respectively (the endings glossed ASP are aspect markers):

(35)(a) *umugabo y-a-tem-eje igiti n-umupaanga*
man he-PAST-cut-ASP tree with-saw
'The man cut the tree with a saw.'

(b) *umugabo y-a-tem-ej-**eesha** umupaanga igiti*
man he-PAST-cut-ASP-INSTR:OBJ saw tree

(36)(a) *umwaana y-a-taa-ye igitabo mu maazi*
child he-PAST-throw-ASP book in water
'The child has thrown the book into the water.'

(b) *umwaana y-a-taa-ye-**mo** amaazi igitabo*
child he-PAST-throw-ASP-LOC:OBJ water book

Sentence (35)(a) is a prototypical transitive clause in which the direct object is thematic (a patient) and the instrument is oblique. In (35)(b), on the other hand, the instrument is coded as a direct participant, and the verbal suffix *-eesha* indicates that it is also the direct object. Although the two sentences describe the same relationship, the difference in their choice of secondary figure renders them semantically non-equivalent. The contrast in (36) is analogous, the suffix *-mo* indicating that direct-object status is accorded to the location rather than the mover.

This variation is reminiscent of subject choice in Tagalog (7.3.1.4; 8.1.2), and a parallel analysis will be proposed. Almost any clausal element can assume the status of subject (or "trigger") in Tagalog, with the form of the verb indicating its semantic role. We analyzed these verbal inflections as schematic processes in which an element with the appropriate semantic role is identified as the *trajector* (Fig. 8.5). In similar fashion, a suffix like *-eesha* in (35)(b), or *-mo* in (36)(b), represents a schematic processual predication that attributes to a particular role (instrument, location, or whatever) the status of *primary landmark*. The semantic pole of *-eesha*, for instance, is sketched in Fig. 8.9. When the schematic process profiled by the suffix is elaborated

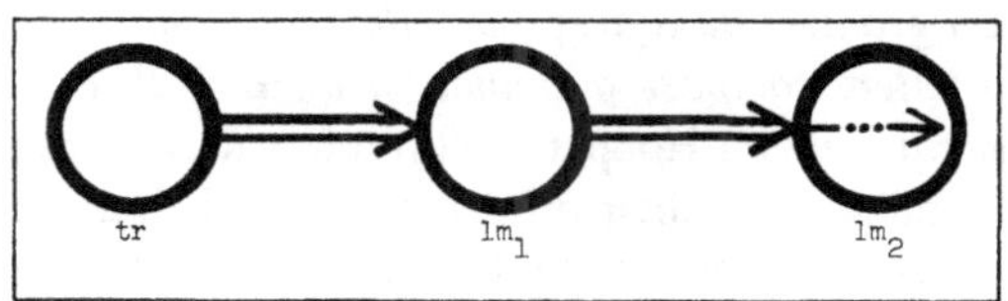

Fig. 8.9

by a verb stem, the composite structure designates a specific process in which an instrument is accorded the focal prominence characteristic of direct objects.

[22] These imply a very broad construal of the direct-object category, as described in fn. 18.

8.3. Non-Distinct Argument Phenomena

The nominal complements of a relational predication are often referred to as its **arguments**. The arguments of a prototypical transitive clause represent distinct, clearly delimited participants that are sharply differentiated from each other, from the profiled event, and from the countless other entities that could conceivably participate in their stead. Found in all languages, however, are grammatical devices that accommodate departures from this canon. Such devices permit the efficient coding of events in which the participants are not in fact distinct, or where the speaker is either unable or uninclined to specify an argument with any precision. The resulting expressions usually have diminished transitivity, even to the point of being fully intransitive.

8.3.1. *Process vs. Participant*

The billiard-ball model makes a fundamental and clear-cut distinction between *objects* and the *interactions* in which they participate. Whereas an object consists of material substance and has indefinite temporal extension, an interaction is transient and resides primarily in the transfer of energy. And whereas an interaction cannot occur without its participants, the converse fails to hold: in the course of an object's existence, a particular interaction is but a brief and generally inessential episode. The conception of two participants thusly interacting is a central feature of the canonical event model, the prototype for transitive clauses. The participants of a prototypical clause are therefore separate and discrete physical objects that exist both prior to the profiled event and independently of its occurrence.

Obviously, not every clause conforms to this archetype—human experience is far too rich and varied. Our immediate interest lies with the broad class of non-conforming expressions in which a participant is not wholly independent of the designated process. A minimal lack of independence is exhibited by participants that have no prior existence but are rather created by the event itself: *build a cabin*; *knit a sweater*; *carve a figure*; *paint a masterpiece*; *draw a diagram*; *light a fire*; *make dessert*; *cause a traffic jam*; *devise a plan*; *write a letter*; *compose a sonnet*; *strike a deal*; *create a consensus*; *invent a new technique*; etc. Hopper (1985) refers to such participants as "effected" objects and surveys their properties in English and other languages. He finds that effected objects are seldom distinguished from "affected" objects by any special marking; they may however show behavior symptomatic of lesser transitivity. Observe, for instance, that *He cut a slice of cake* permits an effected-object interpretation whereby the cutting brings the slice into existence. However, adding the particle *up* imposes the affected-object construal: *He cut up a slice of cake* can only mean that a pre-existing slice was dismembered. Hopper notes that *cut up* represents a higher degree of transitivity than *cut* alone, for it generally indicates that the action affects the object in its entirety (e.g. *He cut up the meat* vs. *He cut the meat*—cf. Lindner 1981).

Once created, the effected objects listed above may continue to exist indefinitely; in that sense they are independent of the processes that spawn them. The same is not true of expressions representing the "cognate-object" construction: *sing a song*; *dance another dance*; *fight a good fight*; *scream a blood-curdling scream*; *live a hard life*; *die a terrible death*; *breathe a deep breath*; *jump the longest jump in history*; and so on. The special feature of this construction is that the object's head noun is a nominalization of the verb stem (or is at least morphologically related) and designates a single episode of the process type in question—in fact, that episode is identified with the specific process instance profiled by the verb. The object thus constitutes a reification of the process itself, so its existence is limited to the timespan of the verb's temporal profile. Rice (1987a, 5.3) has examined cognate-object constructions in a number of languages and documented their diminished transitivity. In English, for example, they show a certain reluctance to passivize:

(37)(a) *One of the campers heard a blood-curdling scream.*
(b) *A blood-curdling scream was heard by one of the campers.*

(38)(a) ?*One of the campers screamed a blood-curdling scream.*
(b) ?**A blood-curdling scream was screamed by one of the campers.*

However, the following sentences sound quite natural:

(39)(a) *The blood-curdling scream that they had all heard in countless horror movies was screamed by one of the campers.*
(b) *That precise scream was screamed by the murder victim.*

The reason for the difference is that the scream referred to in (39) transcends the specific event profiled by the verb. It represents a particular, recognizable *type* of scream whose existence is therefore independent of any single instantiation.

In cognitive grammar, the description of a cognate-object construction is completely straightforward. The expressions are of course redundant, since the verb and object each describe the same event and may invoke essentially the same conceptual content; however, every construction manifests some overlap between its component structures—full overlap is merely a special case. Recall, now, that the component states of a process constitute a set of interconnected entities and thus implicitly define an abstract region. Though usually latent, this region can be recognized as such and even profiled, the result then being an episodic nominalization (1.2.1.1; Fig. 1.3). In a cognate-object construction, sketched in Fig. 8.10, this abstract region is salient in both the verb and its object: it is profiled by the object, and the verb accords it the status of primary landmark. A correspondence between the verbal land-

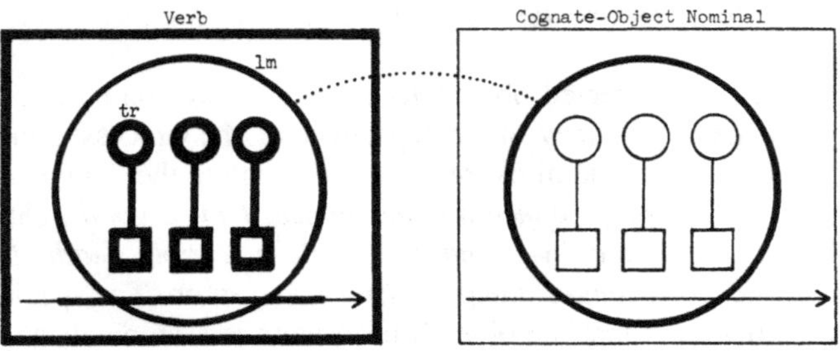

Fig. 8.10

mark and nominal profile effects the integration of the two component structures, in full conformity with the direct-object construction. Still, the nominal is rather peripheral to the direct-object category owing to the difficulty of construing the reified event as a participant lying downstream from the trajector.

The cognate-object construction reinforces the observations made in 7.2.1 concerning the flexibility of coding and construal and the indirectness of the relationship between an event's objective nature and the grammatical structure of an expression describing it. We can agree that an act of yawning is most naturally coded by a verb (*Alice yawned*), and that such a verb is unlikely to be transitive (**Alice yawned Metathesis*). Yet we can perfectly well describe such an act by means of a marginally transitive expression in which the event is coded by the object noun (*Alice yawned a big yawn*). This discrepancy between the "expected" grammatical structure and the actual structure stems from two factors: our capacity for conceptual reification, which allows an event to be coded in nominal form; and the tolerance of redundancy, up to and including full overlap between the components of a complex expression. Such discrepancies do not entail that grammar is autonomous in the sense of requiring anything other than symbolic units for its characterization. They merely show that grammatical organization is not subject to absolute predictability on the basis of conceptual content (let alone objective circumstances), as there are different ways to construe the same content and distribute it over the clausal constituents.

Expressions such as *do a dance*, *let out a scream*, *take a breath*, *make a turn*, and *crack a smile* distribute the content in still another way. We will not concern ourselves with the differences among the verbs (the most common being *take*, *do*, and *make*), nor with the motivation for using this construction instead of a cognate object or a simple verb (e.g. *do a dance* vs. *dance a dance* vs. *dance*). What is relevant here is the concentration of conceptual content in the object noun, the verb being quite schematic. Consider the following set of examples: *take a {breath/look/peek/glance/rest/nap/snooze/bow/shot/swing/walk/stroll/hike/swim/drink/sip/bite/nip/sniff/leak/fall/ride/drive}*.

Clearly, the verb itself does very little to identify the profiled event; it tells us only that the subject does something and that the event constitutes a discrete, bounded occurrence. It is the object noun, representing a reification of this event, that contributes all the specific information about its character.

This kind of flexibility in the distribution of conceptual content is an important factor in the analysis of expressions describing meteorological conditions. In the eyes of linguists, such expressions are nearly as problematic and ill-behaved as the weather itself: they not only have many special properties, but from one language to the next the same phenomenon is coded linguistically in ways that are lexically or grammatically quite distinct (Ruwet 1986). For example, it rains differently in different languages—attested pluvial expressions (translated literally) include *Rains*, *It rains*, *Rain falls*, *It falls rain*, *Rain is*, *Rain goes*, and *Rain rains*. Linguists have also puzzled over the *it* that does the raining in English and many other languages. Some regard it as a meaningless "dummy" inserted just for grammatical purposes (in languages which require that a finite clause have an overt subject). Those otherwise inclined have not found it easy to say what *it* does in fact mean.

The most serious effort has been made by Bolinger (1977, ch. 4), who speaks of "ambience" or an "all-encompassing environment." Importantly, his notion of ambience is not limited to the atmosphere or the physical surroundings, and meteorological expressions are seen as forming a gradation with other *it*-constructions. He posits an abstract meaning shared by all uses of *it*: ". . . It is a 'definite' nominal with almost the greatest possible generality of meaning, limited only in the sense that it is 'neuter'. . . . It embraces weather, time, circumstance, whatever is obvious by the nature of reality or the implications of context" (pp. 84–85). Bearing in mind the inherent difficulty of describing a conception characterized by maximal generality (a word like *zebra* is much easier to define in a way that sounds convincing), I feel that Bolinger's analysis is very much on the right track. The one refinement I will offer at this juncture is to suggest that the "ambient" sense of *it* designates an *abstract setting* (cf. 8.1.3.4). As a consequence of the subject's non-participant status, sentences of the type *It falls rain* are intransitive. Note, for instance, that the French expression cannot be passivized:

(40)(a) *Il tombe de la pluie.* 'It falls (some) rain.'
(b) **De la pluie est tombée par lui.* '(Some) rain is fallen by it.'

Similarly intransitive are sentences like *It's raining cats and dogs* and *It's raining big drops*. Their failure to passivize (e.g. **Big drops are being rained by it*) argues that the post-verbal nominal is not a direct object (at least in any narrow sense).

The variability of meteorological expressions has been attributed by Ruwet (1986, pp. 202–3) to an incongruence between the global character of the occurrences they describe and the analytical nature of the syntactic structures available to code them. We normally experience rain, snow, heat, cold, fog, etc. as all-encompassing phenomena; they lack the clear-cut division into setting, process, and discrete participants that would dictate their coding by clauses with a particular type of lexico-grammatical organization. The lexeme *rain*, for instance, is subject to alternate construals that determine its grammatical class and the kinds of constructions in which it is likely to appear. It may designate the process of water falling from the sky; under this processual construal, it belongs to the class of verbs. As a noun, it can profile either the water itself (e.g. *Some rain came through the window*) or an abstract region representing a reification of the process (*The rain continued*; *We had a good rain*). When *rain* profiles the physical substance, *Rain falls* is a perfectly natural way to describe the meteorological phenomenon, and *It falls rain* is simply the setting-subject variant (8.1.3; Fig. 8.6). In locutions of the type *Rain is* or *Rain goes*, the verb merely predicates the occurrence or existence of its subject (cf. Langacker 1981, 1986a); *rain* conveys the essential semantic content, with either of its nominal senses yielding a coherent conception.

The other locution types all employ *rain* as a processual predication. They differ as to which facet of the designated process is accorded the status of primary figure and coded as the clausal subject. One option, diagrammed in Fig. 8.11(a), is to confer this status on the setting, as in English.[23] A second

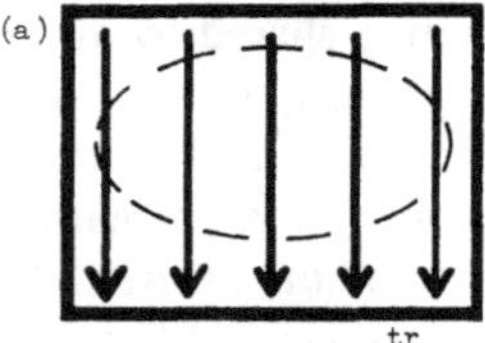

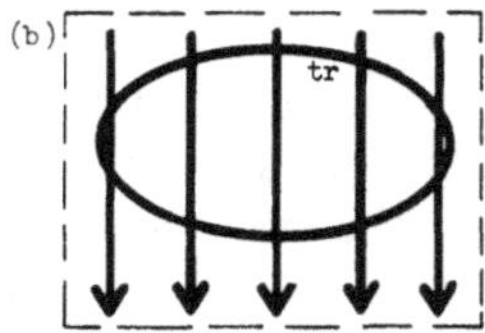

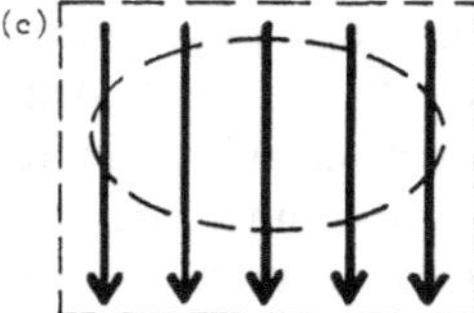

Fig. 8.11

possibility, shown in diagram (b), is for the entity that lends itself most readily to construal as a participant—namely the water—to be chosen as the subject. The result is a "cognate-subject" expression (*Rain rains*) in which the subject and verb redundantly convey the same conceptual content. Finally, the verb may occur alone, without an overt subject (e.g. Spanish *llueve*, Latin *pluit*, Hopi *yooyoki*). The most straightforward analysis of such expressions is the

[23] Interestingly, the subject of 'rain' in Palestinian Arabic is literally 'the world' (Givón 1984, p. 90). The *it* of *It's raining* does not necessarily receive a physical or spatial construal, however; its value may be more akin to Kirsner's notion of "sceneness" or "general presence/availability" (8.1.3.4; Kirsner 1979b). Also, there is no intrinsic conflict between this sort of analysis and one that attributes the occurrence of *it* to a syntactic constraint (the requirement that a finite clause have an overt subject). In Bolinger's words: "Saying that *it* is meaningful is not to deny that there are syntactic problems connected with its use, but only to say that syntax should not be the exclusive focus. There is a gradient at one extreme of which *it* is a relatively independent lexical item, and at the other approaches a rather tightly controlled element of syntax" (1977, p. 85).

traditional one, which regards the verbs as inherently subjectless (zero-place predicates). If we opt for this approach in cognitive grammar, we must recognize that a processual predication may sometimes lack a trajector, as in diagram (c). The notion of a trajectorless process is perfectly coherent in the context of the theory. The essential feature of a relational predication is the profiling of interconnections—in the case at hand, changes through time in the position of drops of water along the vertical axis. For such a conception to lack a trajector would simply mean that no particular entity was singled out as the figure within the scene (it would not entail that nothing moved or that entities were not being situated in relation to one another).

8.3.2. *Reflexivization*

In the unmarked situation, clausal participants are not only distinct from the setting and the designated process, but also from one another. The profiled interaction involves separate and discrete entities, each of which instantiates a single role archetype and is coded individually by an overt nominal. There are, however, many events in which the same participant plays more than one role; in particular, a person (unlike a billiard ball) is capable of acting on himself in much the same way as on another individual. Constructions that accommodate this type of circumstance are traditionally labeled **reflexive**, especially when the same individual fills the roles normally coded by the clausal subject and direct object. Our treatment of reflexives will largely be confined to such cases (for a fuller survey, see Faltz 1977 and Kemmer 1988).

Identity of the subject and object participants can be dealt with in several basic ways. One strategy, not uncommon in the first and second persons, is to code the participant twice, by means of the usual subject and object pronouns. For example, in a French reflexive such as *Je me regarde* 'I look at myself', the subject pronoun has the same form as in the non-reflexive *Je le regarde* 'I look at him', and the object pronoun matches that of *Il me regarde* 'He looks at me'. However, this strategy is seldom used in third-person reflexives, for in the context of the speech event there may be numerous possible referents for a third-person pronoun. Thus, if French *le* had reflexive use, an expression like *Il le regarde* would fail to distinguish the reflexive and non-reflexive meanings (i.e. 'He looks at himself' vs. 'He looks at him'). The language avoids this problem by employing the special form *se* to mark the identity of third-person participants: *Il se regarde* 'He looks at himself'.

Special reflexive markings divide into two broad categories: *nominal* and *relational*. Markers of the first type profile things and are therefore nouns (in the broadest sense). In fact, as illustrated by the English reflexive pronouns (*myself, himself, yourselves*, etc.), they tend to stand alone as independent words or phrases and often constitute full, epistemically grounded nominals. Nominal reflexive markers may either be unanalyzable (e.g. German *sich*) or morphemically complex. We will not concern ourselves with their internal structure except to note in passing that they are commonly formed on nouns such as *self*, *person*, *body*, or *spirit*, and that they frequently incorporate a possessor pronoun (e.g. Luiseño *no-taax* 'myself' [literally: my person]). With respect to all these properties, *relational* reflexive markers show the opposite tendencies. They are verbs rather than nouns, being analyzed as schematic processual predications deriving reflexive verbs from non-reflexive stems. Accordingly, they are generally manifested as verbal affixes rather than separate words, and are usually either invariant in form or at least not segmentable into discrete component morphemes. An example is the Hopi prefix *naa-*, the same in all persons: *nɨʔ naa-tɨwa* 'I saw myself'; *ʔɨm naa-tɨwa* 'You saw yourself'; *pam naa-tɨwa* 'He saw himself'.

A *nominal* reflexive marker has the semantic value sketched in Fig. 8.12(a). It profiles a thing, which may be epistemically grounded (often via possession), and construes the designatum as participating in a schematically

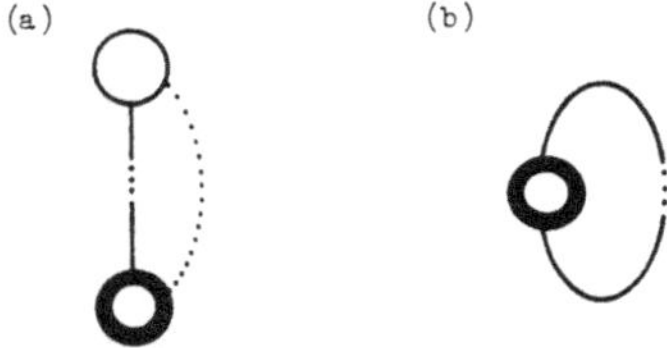

Fig. 8.12

characterized relationship. Its crucial specification, namely the identity of the two relational participants, is indicated by the dotted correspondence line. Fig. 8.12(b) is merely a notational variant, in which participant identity is shown directly by means of superposition. Diagrammed in Fig. 8.13 is a reflexive construction employing such a marker. When the reflexive nominal (labeled SELF) functions as direct object, it evokes as its base the schematic conception of a process and profiles the processual landmark. Its integration with the verb represents a special case of the direct-object construction, which pivots on a correspondence between the verbal landmark and the nominal profile; additional correspondences equate the schematic process evoked by SELF with the specific process designated by V. Of course, the elaboration afforded by SELF does not pertain to the intrinsic properties of V's landmark (V itself is generally more detailed in that regard), but rather to its dual processual role. The composite structure is thus equivalent to V apart from trajector-landmark identity and any other specifications it might inherit from SELF (e.g. person and gender, in the case of the English reflexive pronouns).[24]

[24] Other reflexive constructions—where identity holds between participants manifesting other roles or grammatical relations—are handled analogously. Each permitted relationship between the identical participants implies a variant of the reflexive nominal which takes as its base a schematic relation of the proper type. Moreover, each such variant figures in a grammatical

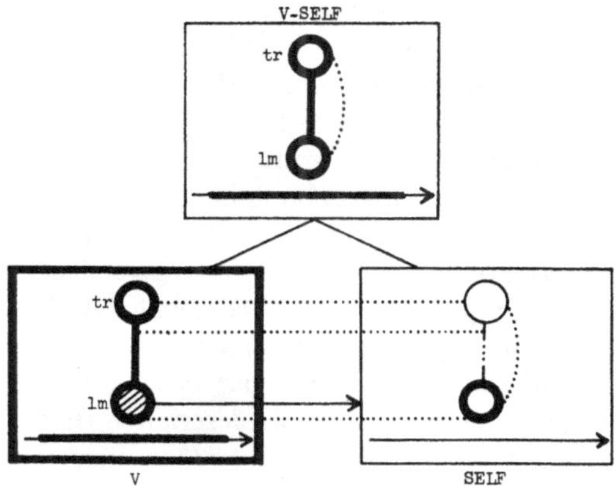

Fig. 8.13

A *relational* reflexive marker is commonly described as a derivational morpheme that converts a verb taking *n* arguments into one that instead takes only *n-1* arguments. In cognitive grammar, a derivational element constitutes a dependent predication whose standard and target (i.e. "input" and "output") are respectively schematic for the basic and derived structures. Fig. 8.14 thus

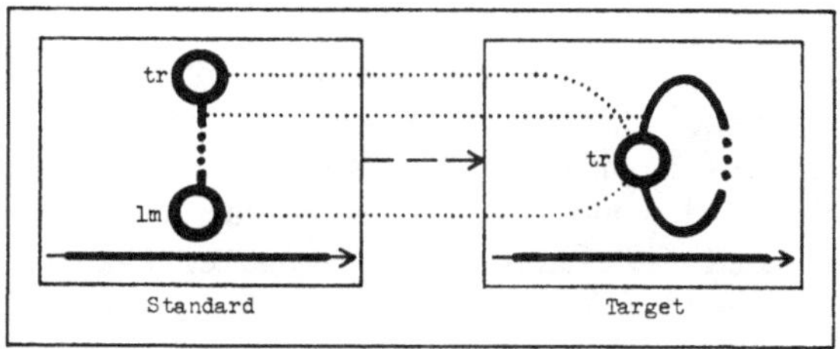

Fig. 8.14

depicts the semantic pole of a marker specifying the identity of two participants that would otherwise be coded as the subject and object of a transitive verb. The standard represents a schematic transitive process and serves as e-site for the verb stem. The target is the same except that a single participant (its trajector) corresponds to both the trajector and the landmark of the standard. Since the target determines the nature of the composite structure, the derived verb is intransitive and behaves as such at higher levels of grammatical organization.

A noteworthy feature of this account is that nominal and relational reflexive markers are semantically quite similar. Comparison of SELF in Fig. 8.13 with

construction that equates this schematic relation with the specific relation introduced by other elements.

the target in Fig. 8.14 reveals no essential contrast apart from profiling: each specifies the identity of two processual participants that would otherwise be taken as distinct (recall that the diagrams in Fig. 8.12 are notational variants). The choice of profile—a participant in the first instance, the overall process in the second—determines the grammatical category of the reflexive marker and hence the nature of the construction through which it combines with the verb. Yet the composite semantic structure is the same whether arrived at via one compositional path or the other. Moreover, a given language may happen to offer no firm basis for preferring either the nominal or the relational analysis; it is not immediately apparent, for example, whether French *se* should be analyzed as a special kind of object pronoun or as a detransitivizing verbal clitic, for either option allows a workable description. In the present framework, one can contemplate the possibility that the matter may actually be indeterminate, that the two analyses co-exist as competing or complementary alternatives. The common historical process whereby a nominal reflexive marker evolves into a relational marker is readily understood from this perspective, as is the concomitant loss of phonological independence that is frequently observed. The tendency for a nominal marker to be phonologically autonomous vis-à-vis the verb, and a relational marker to be phonologically dependent, iconically reflects the contrast between the conceptual autonomy of a nominal complement and the conceptual dependence of a derivational morpheme.

Reflexive markers—particularly of the relational variety—have a well-known tendency to be extended to other kinds of departures from the canon for transitive clauses. Kemmer (1988) has meticulously documented the attested paths of extension and elucidated the abstract semantic similarities on which they are based. For example, the same marker is very commonly used for both reflexive and **reciprocal** expressions; thus French *Ils se regardent* can be glossed as either 'They look at themselves' or 'They look at each other'. What motivates *se*'s extension from reflexive to reciprocal use is the shared conception of the same participant (necessarily plural in the case of reciprocals) functioning as both the head and the tail of an action chain or its analog. Each extension of this sort involves a new node being added to the network of conventionally established senses representing the marker's semantic value. Possibly added as well is a schema expressing the commonality of the basic and extended meanings.

Kemmer points out that the verb from which a "true" (or prototypical) reflexive is derived carries with it the default-case expectation that the processual participants will be referentially distinct and thus coded by separate nominals; the reflexive marking has the specific import of overriding this expectation (Fig. 8.14). With many verbs, however, the situation is basically the opposite: although the designated process involves multiple semantic roles, the normal expectation is that these roles will be filled by a single participant.

Typical examples include verbs of grooming (such as *wash* and *shave*), posture (*stand, sit, lie*), and non-translational motion (*stretch, turn, bow*), in which the same participant generally functions as both the agent and the theme. Since events of this sort are intermediate between canonical transitives (two roles, two participants) and the most elementary kind of intransitive (one role, one participant), languages have different ways of coding them. English uses simple intransitives (*He {washed/stood/stretched}*). But in a great many languages, the verb assumes a special form—traditionally called the **middle**—that is either identical to that of a true reflexive (e.g. French *se laver* 'wash', *se lever* 'stand up', *s'étirer* 'stretch') or else derives historically from reflexive marking. Either synchronically or diachronically, therefore, the middle represents a semantic extension from the reflexive's prototypical value. In contrast to a true reflexive, it does not indicate that the subject acts on itself in just the same way that it would act on another individual (note, for instance, that standing up or stretching is a very different activity depending on whether it is manifested in one's own body or applied to another object—cf. Tuggy 1981, 5.3). Its import is rather that the profiled event has a certain role complexity but nevertheless deviates from canonical transitivity by not invoking the conception of distinct participants.[25]

Hence a true reflexive and a middle represent successive degrees of departure from the archetypal conception of distinct objects interacting asymmetrically—they share the property of conflating dual roles in a single participant, but the middle goes farther by lacking even the expectation of distinct participants. Moreover, the middle can itself be a rather complex category. The middle marker (which may also be the reflexive marker) is often extended from the kinds of processes noted above to a variety of other types. In her comprehensive survey (1988), Kemmer observes that an overarching similarity uniting the many classes of middle verbs is the "low degree of elaboration of events," of which the identity of relational participants constitutes a special case.[26] An event may also be relatively unelaborated in the sense that a participant remains unprofiled or even unspecified. As a consequence, middle and reflexive marking is frequently extended to various kinds of passive and impersonal constructions, whose basic feature is the unspecificity of the action-chain head (e.g. French *Le livre se vend bien* 'The book sells well').

[25] The middle is related to the true reflexive in much the same way as the plural inflection on nouns like *binoculars, trousers*, and *stairs* is related to prototypical plurality. The former in each case signals a kind of internal complexity that nonetheless lacks the differentiation into discrete subparts implied by the latter. Furthermore, it is common for both the middle and the extended sense of the plural to occur with stems that cannot be used independently.

[26] Another feature typical of middle verbs, particularly verbs of perception and cognition, is "initiator as affected entity." While Kemmer treats this separately, it can also be subsumed under the overarching generalization, for in a fully elaborated event (a canonical transitive) the initiator and the affected entity are separate participants coded as the subject and object.

8.3.3. *Unspecificity*

Like other aspects of meaning, transitivity is in large measure determined by construal (Rice 1987a). An event is not coded by a transitive clause just because, objectively, it comprises the asymmetrical interaction of separate and discrete participants—the crucial matter is whether the speaker chooses to conceive and portray it in that fashion. Since transitivity depends on the *conception* of distinct, well-differentiated participants, it is potentially influenced by the extent of their differentiation along not only the *objective* but also the *subjective* axis. That is, a clause's transitivity is affected not only by the distinctness from one another of the actual event participants, but also by whether the conceptualizer manages to bring these participants into clear, sharp focus and distinguish them mentally from other entities that might conceivably participate instead. It is for this reason that grammatical behavior symptomatic of transitivity often correlates with factors such as definiteness.[27]

The subjective component of participant distinctness has several parameters, one being the precision and detail of its type specification. In contrast to *object*, *entity*, and *thing*, which are quite schematic, a noun like *onion*, *scalpel*, or *diamond-backed rattlesnake* evokes a well-articulated image and achieves a greater measure of differentiation from other potential kinds of participants. A second parameter is degree of definiteness, which pertains to whether the speaker and hearer have succeeded in making mental contact with a particular instance of the type in question. A definite nominal such as *the scalpel* implies that a unique instance has been singled out, whereas *a scalpel* carries no such implication, and *scalpel* by itself (ungrounded, as in *scalpel designer*) merely names a type—it neither refers to a specific instance nor even necessarily invokes the conception of distinct instantiations. A third parameter involves the profile's *extension*, in one or another sense of that term. The designatum more readily stands out conceptually as a focused, well-delimited entity when, with respect to any of several oppositions falling under the general rubric *compact* vs. *extended/diffuse*, it represents the former pole. Among these oppositions are the following: spatially compact vs. spatially extended; participant vs. setting; singular vs. plural; count vs. mass; concrete vs. abstract; and restricted portion of a reference mass vs. the mass as a whole.

In a typical clause like *Floyd broke the glass*, the subject and object show a high degree of subjective participant distinctness. However, owing to either limited knowledge or the nature of the profiled event, the speaker cannot always be that specific concerning the clausal elements. Languages therefore display a variety of lexico-grammatical devices that accommodate exceptionally low degrees of differentiation and specificity in regard to one or more of

[27] In Russian, for example, a definite object is more likely than an indefinite one to be marked for accusative case (with verbs that afford an option).

the above parameters. For instance, maximally schematic nouns such as *thing* and *one* allow the speaker to finesse the issue of a type specification (e.g. *something*, *this one*). Also, special constructions like the passive enable the speaker to direct the spotlight of focal prominence away from a major participant, which may consequently remain unelaborated and wholly unspecified (*The glass was broken*). Let us now briefly examine some additional phenomena pertaining to participant non-distinctness along the subjective axis. They involve a certain "fuzziness" in the conception of clausal elements (even if, objectively, those elements are distinct and well-delimited) and hence contribute to what Kemmer calls the "low degree of elaboration of events."

One such phenomenon, prevalent in languages of the Uto-Aztecan family, is for the verb to bear a marking which explicitly signals the unspecificity of one of its arguments. Compare the following expressions from Northern Paiute:[28]

(41)(a)	*usu tɨhɨǰa hoawaʔi*	(b)	*usu tɨ-hoawaʔi*
	he deer hunting		he UNSPEC-hunting
	'He is hunting deer.'		'He is hunting.'

Whereas (41)(a) is a transitive clause with an overt object, the prefix *tɨ-* in (41)(b) indicates that the verb's landmark remains unspecified (UNSPEC). This prefix is describable as a noun that is ungrounded and fully schematic; it is maximally unspecific in regard to the parameters of definiteness and type. Semantically, *tɨ-* is thus comparable to the *thing* of *something*, except that it also portrays its profile as a processual landmark. Its integration with the verb is analogous to that of V and SELF in Fig. 8.13, with the important difference that *tɨ-* does not stipulate trajector-landmark identity, but rather that **the landmark's description proceeds no further than its characterization as a thing**. Since *tɨ-* is ungrounded, it is only a noun (not a nominal), so grammatically it fails to qualify as direct object even though it (vacuously) elaborates the verb's primary landmark. In fact, because its meaning is incompatible with further elaboration (including grounding), its actual effect is to render the composite verb intransitive.

There are variations on this theme. For instance, Shoshoni has markers for both an unspecified landmark and an unspecified trajector (Miller 1972):

(42)(a)	*nɨ tɨ-pe'ka-'nu*	(b)	*ta-ka^{h}ni-pai*
	I UNSPEC-kill-PERF		UNSPEC-house-have
	LM		TR
	'I killed.'		'[One] has a house.'

[28]The data is from Snapp, Anderson, and Anderson (1982, p. 19). For the relation between reflexive/middle markings and unspecified argument phenomena, see Langacker 1976; Langacker and Munro 1975; Anderson, Anderson, and Langacker 1976; Langacker and Bascom 1986; and Kemmer 1988, *in press*.

The cognate prefixes in Classical Nahuatl, *tee-* and *ƛa-*, both mark unspecificity of the landmark, but they do characterize it as human vs. non-human; hence *ƛa-k^{w}a* 'eat [something]' contrasts with *tee-k^{w}a* 'eat [someone]' (as in *tee-k^{w}aa-ni* 'jaguar [man eater]'). We see, then, that a noun with a type description somewhat more specific than just 'thing' can function as an unspecified-argument marker—the import of *tee-*, for instance, is that the processual landmark is 'human' but that its characterization proceeds no further, in terms of either type or grounding. In actuality, there is no inherent limit to the specificity of an ungrounded noun that elaborates a verbal landmark or trajector; observe that *ka^{h}ni* 'house' corresponds to the landmark of *pai* 'have' in (42)(b), just as *ta-* represents its trajector. Of course, the greater the specificity of such a noun, the less felicitous it becomes to speak of an unspecified-argument marker. A noun like *ka^{h}ni* in (42)(b) is usually referred to instead as an **incorporated object**.

Object incorporation has generated considerable interest in recent years (see, for instance, Mardirussian 1975; Woodbury 1975; Merlan 1976; Sadock 1980, 1986; Allen, Gardiner, and Frantz 1984; Mithun 1984, 1986; Miner 1986; Myhill 1988; Baker 1988). As one would expect where linguists are involved, there is some disagreement as to what object incorporation is supposed to be and what sorts of phenomena are properly subsumed by the term. Examples that most everyone would accept as incorporation, e.g. Shoshoni *ka^{h}ni-pai* 'have house' or Nahuatl *naka-k^{w}a* 'eat meat', share a number of properties: morphologically, the noun and verb form a single word or stem; grammatically, the noun occurs in lieu of a direct-object nominal; and semantically, the noun is non-referential (hence it does not pluralize or take an article or demonstrative). Little interest attaches to the issue of what to call expressions that diverge from this prototype. More important than terminology is the recognition that the properties are largely independent, and that this basic type of incorporation represents the intersection of several classes of phenomena, each of which is considerably more inclusive.

The incorporated element does not invariably represent a participant that would otherwise be coded by a direct object. For instance, Tuggy (1986) cites Tetelcingo Nahuatl expressions in which it codes the trajector (e.g. *toonal-kiisa* [sun-emerge] 'sun come out'), an instrument (*laapis-k^{w}ilowa* [pencil-write] 'write with pencil'), or the direct object's **active zone** (Vol. 1, 7.3.4), i.e. the subpart directly affected by the profiled action (*kama-teriksa* [mouth-kick] 'kick in mouth'). Object incorporation is thus a special case of **noun incorporation**, which in turn instantiates the broader phenomenon of compounding or complex-stem formation. At the same time, not every non-referential noun that occurs in lieu of a direct object is incorporated in the verb stem morphologically. Consider these Turkish examples (Mithun 1984, pp. 872–73):

(43)(a) *Ahmet pipo-sun-u ič-iyor.*
Ahmet pipe-his-ACC drink-TNS
'Ahmet is smoking his pipe.'

(b) *Ahmet pipo ič-iyor.*
Ahmet pipe drink-TNS
'Ahmet is pipe-smoking.'

While (43)(a) is straightforwardly transitive, the landmark in (43)(b) is elaborated by a noun, *pipo* 'pipe', that lacks both a grounding predication (such as *-sun* 'his') and the marking for accusative case (ACC) that would signal direct-object status. Some linguists would thus describe *pipo* as an incorporated object even though it stands alone as a separate word. In my terms, it is simply an ungrounded noun that provides a type specification for the verbal landmark but does not itself designate a particular instance of that type. It is neither a nominal nor a direct object, hence it is not inflected for accusative case.

If the term *incorporation* is taken to mean that the noun and verb are morphologically joined, then it is not inherently limited to nouns representing ungrounded type specifications. In particular, there are many languages in which the verb regularly incorporates a marker that specifies the person of the trajector and/or the landmark, as in Nahuatl *ni-k-iˀta* (I-it-see) 'I see it'. The central descriptive and theoretical issue posed by such constructions is whether the marker is a nominal element or whether it is simply a verbal inflection that agrees with the subject or object. Although the distinction may not always be clear-cut, it does appear that two basic kinds of constructions must be posited (cf. Bresnan and Mchombo 1987). On the one hand, the marker may actually be an incorporated personal pronoun. The person-marking prefixes of Classical Nahuatl are susceptible to such an analysis, whereby *ni-* and *k-* are treated as the actual subject and object of *ni-k-iˀta* 'I see it' (Andrews 1975). So analyzed, they are not only nouns (quite schematic in regard to type) but full, grounded nominals by virtue of their specifications for person and definiteness. On the other hand, it is possible for a verbal marking to specify the person, number, or gender of the trajector or landmark without itself being categorized as a noun (examples include the person/number inflections of English and the other Indo-European languages). As described in cognitive grammar, a marker of this sort designates a process whose characterization is schematic apart from what it indicates about the participant in question; it is manifested morphologically on a verb stem that generally characterizes the process in greater detail. But despite its schematicity and phonological dependence, the marker is categorized as a verb on the basis of its processual profile.

Although personal pronouns are uniformly definite (as a matter of definition), the subjective distinctness of their referents varies considerably. First- and second-person pronouns imply the property 'human' under normal circumstances, but the type specification of a third-person form can be fully schematic ('thing'). With respect to extension (i.e. oppositions roughly describable as *compact* vs. *extended/diffuse*), pronominal systems usually offer at least a singular vs. plural contrast. Moreover, a plural pronoun is quite flexible in terms of both the number of individuals comprising its referent and what proportion they represent of the pertinent reference mass. Consider *we*, for example. While this pronoun consistently designates a set of individuals that includes the speaker, the extension of that set (and hence its subjective distinctness) is determined by the context and exhibits a broad range of variation. The designatum may be limited to the speaker and the addressee, in which case it is compact and well-delimited conceptually. However, *we* can also profile a larger set that is not so readily delineated or brought into clear mental focus (e.g. *We have a lot of coyotes around here*; *We never should have given women the right to vote*). And at the extreme, *we*'s profile is coextensive with the reference mass, i.e. it designates mankind as an undifferentiated whole (*We did NOT descend from apes!*; *We do not yet know how life originated*). The construal of *they* is equally flexible as to extension and even more so in regard to type. When used in reference to people, *they* excludes the speaker and hearer but may otherwise have indefinite extension; one well-established meaning is roughly '[other] people in general' (*They'll never discover how life originated*; *They say you can't have too much life insurance*). A pronoun interpreted in this generic fashion can still be considered definite: it designates an instance that coincides with the relevant reference mass, and since there is only one such instance, contextual uniqueness arises by default. However, the maximal extension of the referent also results in a vague, unfocused conception comparable to that of an unspecified-argument marker.[29]

We can now be somewhat more precise about the nature of "dummy" subjects, particularly the *it* that occurs in meteorological expressions. Evidence that a pronoun of this sort designates an abstract setting was presented earlier (8.1.3.4; 8.3.1), as was Bolinger's notion of "ambience" and his claim that *it* is "a 'definite' nominal with almost the greatest possible generality of meaning" (1977, p. 84). We have just observed that definiteness is not per se incompatible with either generality or subjective non-distinctness. The sole import of *it* being definite is that mental contact with a unique instance is presupposed (i.e. the intended referent need not be sought among other instances of the same type), and maximal generality can itself be the source of such uniqueness. Otherwise, *it*'s referent is essentially unconstrained.[30] It can thus be identified with any facet of the linguistic or situational context—even with something as diffuse or abstract as the setting, a topic, the discourse itself, or "general circumstances"—and is not necessarily either explicit,

[29] This is the same ambivalence that leads to generic mass nouns being marked definite in some languages but not in others, e.g. French *le vin* vs. English *wine* (3.1.1).

[30] It must be neuter and singular, but these are themselves symptoms of minimal differentiation (cf. Zubin and Köpcke 1986).

well delineated, or fully determinate (see Gensler 1977). The "dummy" or "ambient" *it* pushes this unspecificity to the limit; its referent is the polar opposite of a well-articulated, clearly focused participant, being characterized instead by maximal extension and minimal differentiation. In fact, even asking what *it* refers to is somewhat misleading, since the question presupposes a range of differentiated alternatives.[31] We can therefore acknowledge the rationale for calling *it* a "dummy": its meaning is too unspecific to articulate, and speakers have no clear conception of its referent. But that precisely is its crucial semantic property, and from the perspective of cognitive semantics, it is both coherent and natural to regard such an element as meaningful.

[31] If *it* neutralizes the setting/participant distinction, the statement that it designates an abstract setting will have to be adjusted, but not in any way that affects the earlier discussion of transitivity. We are of course describing the most extreme value of *it*, the limiting case of non-differentiation and subjective non-distinctness. Presumably the value it assumes in particular constructions, expressions, and contexts approximates that limit to varying degrees. It is not precluded, for example, that speakers might sometimes accord it a more specific interpretation (e.g. as designating the spatial setting or the atmosphere).

CHAPTER 9

Ergativity and Case

CASE MARKING is one device (others being agreement and word order) for distinguishing clausal participants by signalling their semantic roles or grammatical relations. This chapter focuses on the nature of case markers themselves, and of the two basic types of case-marking systems: **nominative/accusative** and **ergative/absolutive**. Contrary to received wisdom, it is claimed that case markers are invariably meaningful. It is further argued that their value pertains primarily to semantic role, their correlation with grammatical relations being secondary, non-universal, and incomplete.

9.1. Ergative vs. Accusative

Reduced to a thumbnail sketch, the standard view of case runs more or less as follows. Case markers are semantically empty formatives that occur with nominals. They have the purely syntactic purpose of indicating a nominal's grammatical relation within the clause—whether it functions as the subject, the direct object, or in some other capacity. Two major types of case-marking systems are distinguished on the basis of how the marking of an intransitive clause compares to that of a transitive. In a **nominative/accusative** system, intransitive and transitive subjects have the same form, and the direct object is marked differently; a subject is said to bear **nominative** case (NOM), and an object, **accusative** case (ACC). The Luiseño examples in (1) are typical in that the nominative case is marked by zero, while the accusative is morphologically overt.[1]

(1)(a) *nawitmal puraara-q* 'The girl is cold.'
girl(NOM) be:cold-TNS

(b) *ʔawaal ʔiswut-i xaari-q* 'The dog is growling at a wolf.'
dog(NOM) wolf-ACC growl:at-TNS

[1] Both nominative and accusative are sometimes marked overtly (e.g. in Latin). Less common is the pattern (attested in the Yuman languages) of marking the subject but not the object. From the standpoint of cognitive grammar, it is immaterial whether the unmarked form is thought of as bearing a zero-marked case or as simply being caseless.

The hallmark of an **ergative/absolutive** system is that a transitive subject is specially marked, whereas an intransitive subject has the same form as a transitive object; the two cases are respectively called **ergative** (ERG) and **absolutive** (ABS). Absolutive case is virtually always zero, as in Samoan:

(2)(a) *'ua oti le teine.* 'The girl has died.'
PERF die the girl(ABS)

(b) *Na fufulu e le tama le ta'avale.* 'The boy washed the car.'
PAST wash ERG the boy the car(ABS)

A non-zero case marker is typically an affix or inflection (e.g. Luiseño *-i*) but can also be a separate particle (Samoan *e*).

This standard conception is problematic in certain respects, one being the notion that case markers are semantically empty elements whose function is strictly grammatical. Granted traditional assumptions, there are indeed several reasons for regarding them as meaningless: (1) They signal grammatical relations (notably subject and object) that are themselves denied semantic import. (2) Case is often *governed* by a verb, preposition, or construction (i.e. a particular case is required, with no option in its selection). (3) Case marking is sometimes induced by *agreement* (e.g. a modifier agreeing in case with a noun), where by definition it fails to contribute "independent" semantic content. (4) It has generally not proved possible to isolate any single meaning that is clearly appropriate for a particular case in all its occurrences. However, when the same issues are examined from the standpoint of cognitive grammar, all these reasons are seen to be invalid: (1) A marker indicating subject or object status can perfectly well be regarded as meaningful if these grammatical relations are themselves attributed conceptual import. (2) It is erroneous to assume that a governed morpheme is *ipso facto* devoid of meaning—being obligatory is not the same as being meaningless, and linguistic convention often specifies the co-occurrence of particular meaningful elements. (3) A morpheme's failure to contribute independent semantic content does not imply that it is semantically empty, but only that its contribution is redundant; all composition involves semantic overlap, and full overlap is an expected limiting case. (4) Polysemy represents the normal situation for both lexical and grammatical morphemes; in neither instance does the absence of a single semantic value accounting directly for all of a morpheme's uses entail that it has no meaning at all.

Consequently, the potential meaningfulness of case markings is no more doubtful than that of other grammatical constructs whose conceptual import has already been described. The matter is even clearer when we expand our concern to encompass not only the "central" cases identifying subjects and objects, but also those that mark obliques: dative, instrumental, locative, ablative, etc. It is quite evident that the oblique cases make a definite semantic contribution in many (if not all) of their uses (9.3)—only through extraordinary theoretical gymnastics could one analyze them as being consistently meaningless. Semantically, the oblique cases are typical complex categories, comprising networks of related senses each centered on a prototype. If the subject- and object-marking cases depart somewhat from this model, it is only by virtue of the abstract nature of their meanings.

A second problem with the standard conception lies in the very assumption that the primary function of the ergative and absolutive cases is to mark the subject and object relations. If that is their central purpose, it must be admitted that they are poorly designed to accomplish it: one case (ERG) is used for some subjects but not all, while the other (ABS) occurs not only on objects but also certain subjects. Moreover, although a description based on grammatical relations yields the coherent value 'transitive subject' for the ergative, the best one can do for the absolutive is the disjunctive characterization 'transitive object *or* intransitive subject.' This suggests that the marking of subjects and objects is not per se the prime objective of an ERG/ABS system. We should explore the possibility that such a system has some other rationale, and that the correlation with grammatical relations is secondary or even incidental. Perhaps there is some respect in which the grouping of transitive objects and intransitive subjects (to the exclusion of transitive subjects) is sufficiently natural in cognitive terms to be reflected in the nominal morphology of many languages.

Supporting this idea is the fact that the same grouping has frequent linguistic manifestation outside the domain of case, even in languages whose case marking follows the nominative/accusative pattern. Illustration from English is provided by periphrastic constructions that specify the participants of nominalized verbs (1.2.2). Consider first *the chanting of the demonstrators*, in which the verb stem receives an intransitive construal (as in *The demonstrators chanted all morning*); here *of* introduces the participant corresponding to the verb's trajector ("inner subject"). Next, *the chanting of the slogans* shows that *of* can also introduce the participant corresponding to the verb stem's landmark ("inner object"). And lastly, we see from *the chanting of the slogans by the demonstrators* that when the landmark and trajector are both specified periphrastically, the latter occurs with *by* rather than *of*. Hence *by* is used for a transitive subject, and *of* for either an intransitive subject or a transitive object—in short, the periphrasis manifests ergative/absolutive organization (cf. Williams 1987).

Further exemplification is afforded by verb-stem suppletion in Luiseño. A fair number of Luiseño verbs have completely different stems depending on whether a certain participant is singular or plural (Hyde 1971, pp. 163–65). As in many languages, the relevant participant—the one whose number controls the choice of stem—is determined on an ERG/ABS basis. An intransitive stem reflects the number of its single focal participant, the trajector, which is coded by the clausal subject:

(3)(a) *ʔawaal pok^{w}a-q*
dog run:SG-TNS:SG
'The dog is running.'

(b) *ʔawaal-um ŋoora-an*
dog-PL run:PL-TNS:PL
'The dogs are running.'

Observe that number is registered not only by the verb stem (*pok^{w}a* vs. *ŋoora*) but also by the tense suffix (*-q* vs. *-an*). On the other hand, a transitive stem indicates the number of its landmark, coded by the clausal direct object:

(4)(a) *ʔiswut ʔawaal-i moqna-q* 'The wolf is killing the dog.'
wolf dog-ACC kill:SG-TNS:SG

(b) *ʔiswut-um ʔawaal-i moqna-wun* 'The wolves are killing the dog.'
wolf-PL dog-ACC kill:SG-TNS:PL

(c) *ʔiswut ʔawaal-um-i qeʔee-q* 'The wolf is killing the dogs.'
wolf dog-PL-ACC kill:PL-TNS:SG

(d) *ʔiswut-um ʔawaal-um-i qeʔee-wun* 'The wolves are killing the dogs.'
wolf-PL dog-PL-ACC kill:PL-TNS:PL

Thus *moqna* 'kill SG' is used in both (4)(a) and (4)(b), since the object ('dog') is in each case singular, whereas *qeʔee* 'kill PL' occurs in (c) and (d) because the object ('dogs') is plural. Comparison of (a) with (b), or (c) with (d), demonstrates that the number of a transitive subject is irrelevant to the choice of verb stem. It does however control the form of the tense suffix (*-q* SG vs. *-wun* PL), just as for intransitives. We see, then, that stem suppletion conforms to the ERG/ABS pattern, even though both tense and case marking (ø NOM vs. *-i* ACC) show NOM/ACC organization.

The situation is not unusual. Languages regularly confront us with two competing organizational schemes: one in which transitive and intransitive subjects pattern together in opposition to direct objects; and one in which transitive subjects stand opposed to both objects and intransitive subjects. Because these groupings are most frequent and visible in the realm of case marking, it is common to speak of **nominative/accusative** vs. **ergative/absolutive organization**—or more simply, of **accusativity** vs. **ergativity**. Nevertheless, these patterns have numerous other linguistic manifestations. In fact, every language probably uses both patterns in one fashion or another, though the mixture varies and a particular pattern is often predominant. It is thus a reasonable supposition that accusativity and ergativity are both quite natural, albeit in different ways, each having a particular kind of cognitive or conceptual motivation. Presumably the cognitive basis of accusativity is in some sense stronger, for nominative/accusative organization is generally observed in a wider range of phenomena and predominates in a higher proportion of languages.

What might be proposed as the conceptual basis for NOM/ACC and for ERG/ABS organization? Case marking offers a clue. Recall that it is very common for one member of each case opposition to have zero marking, the other being phonologically overt. Moreover, the distribution is heavily biased:

the zero-marked case is usually the nominative in a NOM/ACC system, and invariably the absolutive in an ERG/ABS system. We can plausibly attribute this formal distribution to NOM and ABS being in some way conceptually more basic than ACC and ERG. How might the nominative be considered more basic than the accusative? In a strict NOM/ACC system, the respective cases consistently mark the subject and direct object, which we have characterized schematically as the primary and secondary clausal figures. Now it should be evident that the former notion has a certain autonomy or priority vis-à-vis the second: if only one participant is accorded the status of figure, that participant is the primary figure by default; on the other hand, a secondary figure can qualify as such only if there is also a primary figure (for precisely this reason, single-participant clauses have subjects rather than direct objects). We can make the same point in reference to the prominence hierarchy *primary figure > secondary figure > ground*, which constitutes a *natural path*. To the extent that NOM and ACC indicate subject and object status, NOM is more basic in the sense that the subject represents the *starting point* of that path, the object lying one step beyond the subject (7.3.2).

Is there some comparable respect in which the absolutive is more basic than the ergative? Indeed there is: ABS represents the starting point of a natural path defined in terms of conceptual autonomy/dependence. Recall that the A/D layering inherent in a complex event conception defines a path running counter to the flow of energy along an action chain (7.1.3). Comprising this path are the participants encountered through the expansion of a thematic relationship—by incrementation of conceptually dependent event components involving causation or energy input—into autonomous event conceptions of progressively greater complexity: $(T) > (E_1(T)) > (E_2(E_1(T))) > (E_3(E_2(E_1(T))))$. Each successive layer of causation introduces a participant construed as the immediate source of energy for the structure already assembled. The participants sequentially accessed in this fashion form a natural path whose starting point is the *theme*, i.e. the participant evoked as part of a processual predication's conceptually autonomous core. For a specific example, consider *Floyd broke the glass with a hammer*. Its A/D layering subsumes the progressively more complex autonomous conceptions of the glass breaking, the hammer breaking the glass, and Floyd causing the hammer to break the glass: *(glass break) > (hammer= = =>(glass break)) > (Floyd= = =>(hammer= = =>(glass break)))*. Hence *glass > hammer > Floyd* constitutes a natural path representing the order in which the participants are encountered in assembling the complex structure, and its starting point is the thematic participant, namely the glass.

The property shared by the nominals taking absolutive case—transitive objects and intransitive subjects—is that they code the theme, the initial participant encountered along this A/D path. By contrast, ergative case occurs on a transitive subject, which codes the participant lying at the end of the path (the head of the action chain or its analog). Nominative and absolutive case are thus alike in that each marks a participant serving as the origin of a natural path along a parameter known to be both cognitively and linguistically significant (figure/ground organization; A/D alignment). They are conceptually more basic than accusative and ergative case in the sense that these latter indicate participants lying *beyond the origin* along the respective paths (hence their own characterization makes reference to the starting point). That the more basic member of each opposition should typically be marked by zero is both natural and predictable. What is responsible for the greater prevalence of NOM/ACC systems? One factor is the substantial cognitive salience of figure/ground organization. Additionally, the natural path associated with the ERG/ABS pattern runs counter to the direction of energy flow, which is highly salient even at the level of conscious awareness.

On this account, an ERG/ABS system does not specifically or primarily mark grammatical relations, but pertains instead to the structure of conceived events. It indicates whether a participant is *central* or *peripheral* to the profiled event in terms of A/D layering, i.e. whether it undergoes the thematic process that constitutes its conceptually autonomous core, or whether it occupies the outermost layer by virtue of being the ultimate energy source. There is of course a correlation between ERG/ABS case and grammatical relations, since a theme and an energy source are respectively prototypical for the object and subject categories. And to the extent that this correlation is consistent, it has the potential to be exploited—ERG, for example, might in fact come to signal a transitive subject. Nevertheless, the factors cited previously argue that the characterization based on A/D organization is fundamental, with any relation-marking function of ERG and ABS representing a secondary overlay.

Reinforcing that conclusion are the many instances where ERG/ABS case marking fails to show the expected correlation with the subject and object relations. In Samoan passives, for example, the agent takes *e* 'ERG' even though it is neither the subject nor an object (see Ch. 8, ex. (7)). More generally, Cook (1988a) has demonstrated that Samoan case consistently reflects semantic roles and is independent of grammatical relations. In Newari, ERG marks the subject of certain verbs that are grammatically intransitive (so that ABS would be anticipated); semantically, however, they imply a second, thematic participant (Hung 1988):

(5) *raam-an* *tona* 'Raam smoked.'
Raam-ERG smoke

It appears to be a general tendency of ergative languages for case and grammatical relations to be rather loosely correlated, and for semantic role to exert a substantial influence on case marking. Moreover, the correlation between case and grammatical relations is less than perfect even in NOM/ACC languages. Subjects and objects are sometimes marked by cases other than NOM and ACC (e.g. dative subjects; genitive objects). By the same token, the use of NOM and ACC is seldom confined to clausal subjects and objects. The German accusative, for instance, also occurs on adverbs and the objects of certain prepositions. Smith (1987) has argued that it is meaningful in all its uses, and that the value it assumes with direct objects belongs to a network of related senses (9.3).

There is probably no language in which case and grammatical relations are perfectly correlated, such that one case consistently and exclusively marks subjects, and another, direct objects. And even if there were such a language, it could still be argued that these cases were meaningful and associated with semantic roles, since the subject and object relations have both schematic semantic import (based on figure/ground organization) and prototypical values defined by particular role archetypes. If one further acknowledges that the marking of grammatical relations is at best a secondary function of ERG and ABS, and that the oblique cases serve mainly to indicate semantic role, it becomes apparent that the standard view of case approaches it from the wrong direction. To maintain that case is primarily a device for marking grammatical relations, and that any semantic correlations are merely subsidiary, is to fixate on just one end of a broad spectrum. A more comprehensive and fundamentally accurate description of case is that it specifies the *semantic role* of clausal participants. The marking of grammatical relations constitutes a natural extension from this basic function.

A brief characterization of case as viewed in cognitive grammar is thus as follows. Case markers are meaningful elements that combine with nominals to specify the nature of their involvement in a clausal process. A case is usually polysemous: it comprises a network of related senses pertaining primarily to semantic role, and takes some role archetype (experiencer, instrument, agent, goal, etc.) as its prototypical value. Even when their use is grammatically determined, most cases retain this basic character; for instance, a case governed by a verb or preposition may nevertheless have a role-type meaning (e.g. the German dative, as discussed in 7.3.3). However, correlating strongly with semantic role are other significant aspects of clausal organization, namely figure/ground alignment and centrality with respect to A/D layering. It is therefore quite natural for certain cases to be interpreted as directly signalling these other factors, with the consequence that their association with particular roles becomes subsidiary and often inessential. Commonly (if not typically), a case-marking system dedicates one or two of its members to such "grammatical" functions. Of course, they are not regarded in cognitive grammar as being sharply distinct from the other cases, or as strictly syntactic elements devoid of meaning—it is simply that their semantic value is somewhat more abstract than a role specification.

Because A/D layering reflects the structure of event conceptions, the "grammatical" cases of an ERG/ABS system bear a close relation to semantic roles. The basic value of absolutive case, "theme," is itself a schematic role specification subsuming zero, patient, mover, experiencer, etc., whose common denominator is their capacity to serve as the sole participant of an autonomous event component (thematic relationship). Ergative case takes the agent role for its prototype (and in some languages is largely confined to agents); more abstract values—such as "action-chain head," "energy source," or "peripheral participant with respect to A/D structure"—arise when ERG is extended to other sorts of transitive subjects. By comparison, the grammatical cases of a NOM/ACC system have greater flexibility in regard to semantic role, as there is no intrinsic connection between an event conception's structure and the figure/ground organization imposed on it. Nominative and accusative case are identified as such to the extent that they specifically signal "subject" and "object," so that their own meanings are assimilated to those of the subject and object categories. Thus, while NOM and ACC have "agent" and "patient" as their prototypical values, they can only be characterized schematically as marking the primary and secondary clausal figures.

The contrast between NOM/ACC and ERG/ABS systems is often said to reside in whether an intransitive subject receives the same marking as a transitive subject (NOM) or a transitive object (ABS). Though correct so far as it goes, this description conceals the fact that each alignment has its own rationale: like a transitive subject, an intransitive subject has the status of primary figure; and like a transitive object, it represents the theme. Additionally, there are languages in which the subject of an intransitive clause can be marked the same as either the subject or the object of a transitive. This type of system also has a coherent rationale: the case of a subject or object is determined by semantic role, roughly on an agent/patient basis (cf. Dahlstrom 1983). The examples in (6)–(7) are from Eastern Pomo, a Hokan language of northern California (McLendon 1978).

(6)(a) *háa míip-al šáak'a*
I:AG he-PAT kill
'I killed him.'

(b) *xáas-uulàa wí kook^{h}óya*
rattlesnake-AG I:PAT bite
'Rattlesnake bit me.'

(7)(a) *háa wáduukìya*
I:AG go
'I'm going.'

(b) *wí ˀéčkiya*
I:PAT sneeze
'I sneezed.'

The AG/PAT contrast is marked either suffixally (*-uulàa* vs. *-al*) or by alternate forms of certain pronouns. From (6) alone, it might appear that *háa* and *wí* are the subject and object forms of the first-person singular pronoun ('I' vs. 'me'). That cannot be correct, however, for in (7) we observe that *háa* and *wí* can each occur as an intransitive subject. Instead, the choice depends on whether the speaker's role is construed as being agent-like or patient-like, in terms of volitionality and other factors. With verbs allowing either construal, both the agent and the patient forms are possible, the difference signaling a semantic contrast, e.g. *háa c'eexélka* 'I'm sliding' vs. *wí c'eexélka* 'I'm slipping'.

9.2. Ergativity

We can speak of ergative/absolutive organization whenever intransitive subjects pattern with transitive objects (to the exclusion of transitive subjects). So defined, ergativity is independent of case marking and has many linguistic manifestations, some being observable in any given language. At the same time, ergativity competes with accusativity even in languages where it represents the predominant pattern. It is common, in fact, for a phenomenon that mostly follows an ergative pattern to display accusative organization under particular circumstances. The question thus arises whether the characterization of ergativity might not shed some light on its distribution.

9.2.1. *Correlates of Autonomy*

Our characterization of ergativity rests on a fundamental aspect of linguistic organization, namely A/D layering, wherein an autonomous component, A, elaborates a dependent component, D, to form a higher-order autonomous structure, (D(A)). In such a configuration, there is a strong tendency for component A to be "heavier" than component D, in the sense that its semantic and/or phonological content is more extensive, specific, and concrete. Moreover, since D requires the support of A for its full implementation (but not conversely), it is much less likely than A to occur independently. A vowel, for example, is both the nucleus and the sonority peak of a syllable; it can stand alone as a syllable in many languages and outweighs its tautosyllabic consonants in terms of phonic substance. Likewise, stems are usually capable of independent occurrence and are generally heavier than affixes, both semantically and phonologically (Vol. 1, p. 361).

Of present concern is the A/D layering inherent in the structure of conceived events. Hence A (at the innermost layer) can be identified as a thematic relationship, and D (at any layer) as an event component involving causation or the input of energy. In the simplest case, an intransitive clause comprises A alone, while a transitive has the form (D(A)), i.e. it includes just one layer of energy input; since event component D contributes the participant coded by a transitive subject, whereas A introduces either an intransitive subject or a transitive object, we find in this organization the basis for ergativity.[2] The issue before us, then, is whether—in this realm also—the autonomous and dependent components differ in "weight" and the potential for independent occurrence, and whether the distribution of ergativity can somehow be related to these factors.

On the face of it, the answer appears to be affirmative. Consider the many verbs in English that can be used either transitively or intransitively without any difference in form: *open*, *close*, *roll*, *crack*, *cook*, *roast*, *boil*, *fry*, *burn*, *tear*, *rip*, *break*, *snap*, *drop*, *sink*, *lock*, *melt*, *freeze*, *thaw*, *smear*, *ignite*, *start*, *stop*, *turn*, etc. These verbs display an ergative pattern in which the semantic role of the intransitive subject matches that of the transitive object. More precisely, Y is the theme in both an intransitive clause, $Y\ V_i$, and the corresponding transitive, $X\ V_t\ Y$, whereas X is the action-chain head and thus supplies the energy that drives the thematic process; the door, for example, has the same thematic role in *The door opened* and *Sam opened the door*, Sam being the agent who causes it to move. And since V_t represents a full structure of the form (D(A)), while V_i corresponds just to A, we see that the autonomous event component, A, does indeed occur independently (in contrast to D, which cannot).

One can argue, moreover, that A is heavier than D. That is certainly true at the phonological pole, where A and (D(A)) are formally identical; all the phonic "substance" is thus provided by A, with D being phonologically vacuous (an identity function). At the semantic pole, A describes a fairly specific thematic process and often provides substantial information about the theme: only certain kinds of entities are capable of cracking, tearing, snapping, locking, boiling, melting, or igniting. D is abstract and schematic by comparison; its essential content is limited to the notion of causation, and the participant it introduces is characterized only as a source of energy. An expression such as *X melted Y* therefore tells us more about Y than it does about X—whereas Y must at least be a physical solid capable of liquefication, the possible instantiations of X are so diverse that a characterization covering all of them would be equivalent to the noun-class schema.[3] Thus A, but hardly D, is rich enough

[2] Of course, an intransitive clause may also have the structure (D(A)), where the same participant figures in both event components (i.e. as both an energy source and the theme, as in *He jumped*); it is then the thematic role that motivates absolutive case and other manifestations of ergativity. When a transitive clause involves multiple layers of causation, e.g. (D(D(D(A)))), the transitive subject is the participant associated with the outermost layer.

[3] X need only be conceived as having some association with heat. It may be physical or abstract, and a physical entity can be solid, liquid, or gaseous: *The {oven/candle/sun/fire/heat/high temperature/de-icing fluid/steam} melted the ice*. If X is a person, his involvement may or may not be agentive, and what he actually does to effect the melting is highly variable: *Fred melted the ice by {putting it in the oven/aiming a flamethrower at it/accidentally dropping it into the fire/sitting on it/holding it in his mouth/failing to block the sun}*. It is not even necessary that an association with heat be intrinsic to X's characterization: *The hammer melted the ice when we heated it and put the two in contact*.

in semantic content to be profitably used independently. It is informative and potentially quite useful to learn that something has cracked, torn, snapped, locked, boiled, melted, or ignited. By itself, however, the information that something has engaged in causation seems unlikely to affect one's course of action.

This characterization affords some insight into various manifestations of ergativity noted by Keenan (1984). He observes, for example, that certain semantic roles are far more commonly associated with intransitive subjects and transitive objects than with transitive subjects. In our terminology, these roles include patient (e.g. *It broke*; *He broke it*), mover (*It rolled*; *He rolled it*), and zero (*It exists*; *He created it*).[4] These are all thematic roles, and the present analysis reveals their association with intransitive subjects and transitive objects to be a consequence of conceptual autonomy. Other correlations pointed out by Keenan reflect the semantic weight of the autonomous event component (A) and the fact that A's precise configuration is determined primarily by the theme (since non-thematic participants belong to outer layers). For one thing, the choice of theme is more likely than the choice of transitive subject to give rise to meaning differences substantial enough to be regarded as distinct senses. *Run*, for instance, has noticeably different meanings when predicated of a horse, a motor, or a faucet, whether this functions as an intransitive subject (*The {horse/motor/faucet} is running*) or a transitive object (*He is running the {horse/motor/faucet}*). Similarly, a verb often imposes highly specific "selectional restrictions" on the thematic participant (cf. Vol. 1, p. 282). Thus *peel* requires that its theme have a skin-like covering (*It peeled easily*; *He peeled it easily*), and *shatter* that it be brittle and crystalline (*It shattered*; *He shattered it*), but seldom if ever does a transitive verb attribute properties of comparable specificity to its subject. Keenan further notes that noun incorporation tends to follow an ergative pattern; the resulting verb stems are of course highly specific as to the nature of their theme, e.g. Tetelcingo Nahuatl *meec-toona* (moon-shine:brightly) 'it be a bright night' and *aa-saka* (water-cart) 'cart water' (Tuggy 1979, pp. 47–49). It might be added that the theme commonly governs verb-stem suppletion (recall the Luiseño examples in (3)–(4)). Evidently, a theme's plurality affects the overall configu-

[4]The experiencer role is equally likely to be associated with transitive subjects. This reflects the experiencer's initiative capacity in regard to establishing mental contact with other entities and the categorization of *EXPER---->ZERO* relationships as extensions from *AG===>PAT*, the transitive-clause prototype (7.3.3). With some transitive verbs (e.g. *follow, chase, carry, take, bring*), both the subject and the object are movers. However, the subject's movement is often secondary to its agentivity and may even be suspended (e.g. *They brought the anchor to the surface by hauling in the line*), whereas the object tends to be a mover exclusively. Keenan notes that a source locative specifies the *path* of an object but the *location* of a transitive subject: *Tom pushed Bill from the bus* indicates either that Tom was *on* the bus (and possibly stationary) when he pushed Bill or that Bill was *removed* from the bus by Tom's action.

ration of the designated process more saliently than does the plurality of a transitive subject.

9.2.2. *Absolute Construal*

By virtue of semantic weight and conceptual autonomy, a thematic process can often stand alone as a clausal head (*It melted*; *It sank*; *It exists*). However, an intransitive verb's scope of predication is not always limited to a thematic relationship. We have noted, for instance, that thematic-subject sentences such as *It broke easily* and *It opened only with great difficulty* invoke the efforts of an unspecified agent as an unprofiled facet of their base (Fig. 8.3). Even within the processual profile, many intransitive verbs have one or more layers of causation. These are verbs in which the same participant both undergoes the thematic process and supplies the energy that brings it about; for example, the subject of *walk*, *crawl*, *jump*, *swim*, or *dive* not only moves through space but carries out a pattern of muscular exertion to propel itself along this path. Moreover, a single verb may have alternate senses that incorporate causal chains of different lengths, e.g. A, (D(A)), and (D(D(A))). A case in point is *fall*: although it usually designates a bare thematic relationship (as in *Some rain is falling*), *fall*'s profile can also be expanded to encompass a physical action that induces the thematic process (*By carelessly leaning over too far, he fell off the ladder*) as well as the exercise of volitional control (*Following the script perfectly, she fell right on cue*).

To the extent that the autonomous event component is evoked or profiled independently, its construal is said to be *absolute* (7.1.2). The notion of absolute construal has substantial linguistic significance, but properly assessing it requires that certain subtleties be taken into account. First, there need not be any overt indication of whether a verb's construal is absolute or energetic; in *He fell*, for instance, *fall* can have any of the senses just described. Another subtlety is that the conception of causation is not simply present or absent—it may instead be invoked with varying degrees of salience (e.g. *He broke it* vs. *It broke easily* vs. *It broke*). Finally, one must recognize that the absolute/energetic contrast is indeed a matter of construal and is thus to some degree independent of objective reality. Either convention or personal choice may lead a speaker to focus just on the final segment of an action chain, effectively portraying it as an autonomous occurrence. Furthermore, experiential and cultural expectations weigh heavily in determining what does or does not count as energetic. Relevant here is the distinction drawn in 7.1.2 between *intrinsic* and *experiential* A/D alignment, the latter reflecting the actual clusterings of event components that occur in our experience and coalesce to form established concepts. Since we know, for example, that objects fall due to the force of gravity, falling decomposes into downward spatial movement (A) and the gravitational attraction that induces it (D) when analyzed in terms of intrinsic A/D alignment. These two event components are nevertheless so closely and consistently associated in our everyday experience that they form a cognitively fundamental conceptual gestalt. Experientially, therefore, this entire gestalt functions as an autonomous thematic relationship that constitutes the basic sense of *fall*. Only when expanded to incorporate an additional layer of causation does *fall* count as being energetic.

A likely example of absolute construal is provided by those (non-reflexive) verbs in French that take the auxiliary *être* 'be' (rather than *avoir* 'have') in the perfect: *aller* 'go', *venir* 'come', *monter* 'ascend', *descendre* 'descend', *arriver* 'arrive', *partir* 'leave', *naître* 'be born', *mourir* 'die', etc. These are basic intransitive verbs describing either the direction of spatial movement, or more abstractly, some notion of coming onto the scene or departing therefrom.[5] Conspicuously absent from this set are any verbs describing either the rate or the manner of motion (*courir* 'run', *voler* 'fly', *nager* 'swim', etc.); such verbs consistently take *avoir*, as do *monter* and *descendre* when used as transitives or causatives (e.g. *Elle a monté les valises* 'She brought the suitcases up'). Clearly, energy figures prominently in the conception of either rapidity or the method of locomotion. It is therefore highly plausible to suppose that the *être*-verbs impose an absolute construal on the movement they designate. This does not imply that the motion is conceived as being inherently non-energetic, but rather that only the thematic process itself (i.e. the movement per se) is saliently evoked and placed in profile.

In recent work on Mexican Spanish (1988), Maldonado has shown that the "reflexive" clitics, when they occur with intransitive verbs, distinguish between an absolute and a force-dynamic construal of the designated process. A true reflexive use of these clitics is of course limited to transitive verb stems (e.g. *Juan se miró* 'Juan looked at himself'). From transitive stems, *se* also derives intransitive verbs in which the theme assumes trajector status, the efforts of any non-thematic participant being non-salient and unspecified:

(8)(a) *Juan rompió la taza.* 'Juan broke the cup.'
(b) *La taza se rompió.* 'The cup broke.'

This latter value is quite similar to the one *se* displays when it combines with inherently intransitive verb stems. With intransitives, *se* not only indicates a thematic trajector (which the stem has in any case), but further signals that the profiled event has a force-dynamic character. Hence *se* derives an energetic, thematic-subject verb in either of two ways: from a transitive stem, by

[5] The centrality of this latter notion was called to my attention by Andrew Meisel. In relational grammar, these verbs would probably be analyzed as "unaccusative," i.e. as having an object but no subject at the initial stratum (cf. Perlmutter 1978). Though I have not explored the matter systematically, I suspect that verbs regarded as unaccusative in relational grammar are always reasonably viewed in the present framework as single-participant thematic processes whose construal is absolute.

defocusing the initial portions of an action chain; or from an intransitive stem, by imposing a force-dynamic interpretation on an event whose construal would otherwise be absolute.

The clearest illustration is afforded by *caer* 'fall', which occurs with *se* so frequently that it is sometimes considered inherently reflexive:

(9)(a) *Juan se cayó.* 'Juan fell down.'
(b) *La pelota se cayó de la mesa.* 'The ball fell off the table.'

There are, however, circumstances, in which the stem occurs unadorned:

(10)(a) *La lluvia está cayendo.* 'The rain is falling.'
(b) *En el otoño, las hojas caen de los árboles.* 'In autumn, the leaves fall from the trees.'
(c) *La pelota cayó de la canasta.* 'The ball fell from the basket.' [in a basketball game]

The contrast between (9) and (10) is describable on two different levels, each essential to an overall account of *se*'s distribution. At the purely physical level, the expressions in (10) depict events in which the trajector's descent does not encounter significant resistance or obstruction. It is energetic only in the sense of being induced by gravity, so from the standpoint of experiential A/D alignment the motion counts as absolute. On the other hand, the events in (9) receive a force-dynamic construal, wherein a steady-state situation maintained by a balance of forces undergoes disruption resulting in downward motion. Normally, a person maintains the balance and muscular control needed to keep himself upright despite the pull of gravity, and a table is strong enough to counterbalance the gravitational force acting on an object placed on its upper surface. Falling occurs when the resistance to gravity is effectively cancelled or overcome (e.g. the person loses his balance, or the ball rolls beyond the table's edge).

The contrast between (9) and (10) can also be described at a more abstract level. The events in (10) conform to natural expectations, given what we know about the physical world and cultural practices. It is natural for rain to fall—that is what rain does, essentially by definition. It is likewise expected for leaves to fall in the autumn. Should they do so in the spring, this departure from the usual course of events is marked by *se*:

(11) *En la primavera, las hojas se cayeron de los árboles.* 'In the spring, the leaves fell from the trees.'

And after a score in basketball, we fully expect the ball to come down (it is by design that the net is open at the bottom). However, the events described in (9) represent accidental or unanticipated occurrences: a person falls down when he is unsuccessful at maintaining his canonical upright posture, and we put things on a table because we intend for them to stay there. Of course, special circumstances may engender different expectations. The behavior of *se* varies accordingly:

(12)(a) *La pelota se cayó de la mesa inesperadamente.* 'The ball fell off the table, unexpectedly.'
(b) *La pelota cayó de la mesa como era esperado.* 'The ball fell off the table, as was expected.'

These limited observations merely hint at the subtle intricacies of Spanish *se* that Maldonado has begun to unravel. Yet several conclusions do seem warranted. First, instead of being arbitrary the distribution of *se* is motivated by discernible semantic considerations. Moreover, the presence vs. the absence of *se* with certain intransitive verbs iconically signals the contrast between an energetic and an absolute construal of the designated process. Lastly, the objective level of physical energy is only one factor involved in determining whether a process receives an absolute or a force-dynamic construal. An occurrence that is energetic in actuality may nevertheless be portrayed as absolute, either because its force-dynamic character is experientially non-salient, or simply because the speaker opts to present it in that fashion. Also, either a physical or an abstract conception of energy may be relevant for linguistic purposes. Whatever its physical basis, an event can sometimes be construed as absolute because it conforms to expectations, desires, or the "normal course of events," or as energetic because it diverges from this flow or even runs counter to it.

Further illustration of this last point is offered by Cupeño, a Uto-Aztecan language (recently extinct) of southern California. As reported by Hill (1969), Cupeño verb stems divide into three morphological classes, marked by *-in*, by *-yax*, and by zero. Stems representing two or all three classes can often be formed on the same verb root, e.g. *huč-in* 'take off', *huč-yax* 'be undone/untied', and *huč* 'skin'. Though partially obscured by lexical idiosyncrasies, the system has a definite semantic basis. By and large, the stems with *-in* are transitive and involve either causation or volition, whereas those with *-yax* tend to be intransitive, indicating a non-volitional event or something that happens to the subject. Hill characterizes the zero-class stems as referring to processes that are in some sense "natural" occurrences. Included are most verbs for states of mind (e.g. 'be angry', 'be embarrassed', 'want/like'); most verbs designating natural bodily processes ('eat', 'drink', 'see', 'urinate', 'menstruate', 'grow old'); many verbs involving the behavior of plants, animals, inanimate objects, and the weather ('grow', 'rot', 'bloom', 'dig' [gophers], 'snow', 'rain'); and verbs for "natural, culturally required acts" or "good, solid Cupeño cultural behavior" ('make acorn mush', 'make a basket', 'shoot arrows', 'hunt', 'gamble', 'make image dolls for the burning ceremony', 'relate tribal history'). My own interpretation is that the zero verbs are non-energetic in the abstract sense described above: because the designated process flows with the "normal course of events," it is construed as absolute.

9.2.3. *Discourse Function*

Although ergativity is defined in terms of clause structure, recent studies have shown that it also has substantial relevance at the discourse level. We will examine two facets of this relevance: for the introduction of new discourse participants; and for a type of construction called **antipassive**.

9.2.3.1. *Introducing Discourse Participants.* Examination of actual discourse (as opposed to the isolated example sentences typically constructed by linguists) reveals a significant tendency for at most a single focal participant within each clause to be coded by a full, "lexical" nominal. That is, sentences such as *He saw a bear* or *He saw it* are frequent in comparison to those like *The hunter saw a bear*, where both the subject and object are overt and non-pronominal. And since a full nominal is generally required to introduce a new participant into the discourse, the introduction of such participants also tends to be restricted to one per clause. Du Bois (1987) found these tendencies to be especially strong in Sacapultec Maya (a language of Guatemala). He further noted an overwhelming bias in favor of either a transitive object or an intransitive subject as the vehicle for introducing a new discourse participant—hardly ever does a transitive subject serve this function. Though often less pronounced, the same bias is observed in other languages.[6] There appears to be a cross-linguistic tendency for new participants to enter the discourse as themes, and not as transitive subjects.

Why should the introduction of new participants conform to this ergative/absolutive alignment? Du Bois takes this to be a consequence of other discourse factors. Because human protagonists are the central participants in most narrative discourse, they tend to be maintained as topics over long sequences of clauses. An established topic is unlikely to be coded lexically by a full nominal—some kind of pronominal reference (including verbal inflection or even zero) can generally be expected. Thus, since transitive subjects are typically human and usually correspond to the discourse topic, they are seldom used to introduce a new, lexically specified participant. By contrast, transitive objects often are inanimate patients that rarely persist in the discourse for more than a few successive clauses. The steady shifting of patient referents makes object position a frequent locus for new, lexical mentions. What about intransitive subjects? These commonly do introduce human participants, often with a semantically unexciting verb such as 'come', 'arrive',

[6] In English, for example, *Suddenly, he saw a bear* is considerably more natural than *Suddenly, a bear saw him* (assuming that bears have not previously been under discussion).

'appear', 'exist', or 'there be'. By devoting a clause of this sort to putting a protagonist onstage, the speaker delays for one clause the specification of a transitive event, which can then be coded in a clause with only a single new participant (e.g. *A hunter came by; he was tracking a bear*, rather than *A hunter was tracking a bear*).

While I accept the basic thrust of Du Bois's account, I also believe that a consideration of A/D layering will add another dimension to our understanding. We have already noted a strong correlation, observable in diverse facets of linguistic structure, between *autonomy* and *richness of content*: in a layered structure (D(A)), component A is generally "heavier" than D and hence more likely to occur independently (9.2.1). In the case of verbs, A represents a thematic process; its participant (the theme) is generally specified in more detail than the one invoked by D, and contributes more saliently to the perceived configuration of the overall event (as evidenced by the theme's control of stem suppletion). The ergativity observed in the introduction of new discourse participants can be seen as reflecting this same asymmetry at a higher level of organization, namely the clausal level. Discourse conforming to this tendency features clauses in which only the thematic participant is elaborated by a full, lexical nominal: *The butter finally melted*; *He melted the butter*. Like the verb itself, such clauses are more specific concerning the theme than about a possible energy source; effected by a pronominal element, the latter's characterization is quite schematic by comparison. Recall, moreover, that mere existence or being in some place constitutes the most fundamental kind of thematic relationship (7.1.2). It is therefore natural that a theme should be the vehicle for placing a new participant onstage and establishing its existence within the current discourse space. This is an abstract analog of the objective existence or spatial location conveyed by verbs like 'come', 'exist', and 'appear'.

9.2.3.2. *Antipassives.* Further indicating the discourse relevance of ergativity is the prevalence in ergative languages of a construction type called the **antipassive**. The contrast between an active clause and an antipassive can be illustrated by the following sentences from Greenlandic Eskimo (Woodbury 1977):

(13)(a)	*arna-p*	*niqi*	*niri-vaa*	'The woman ate the meat.'
	woman-ERG	meat(ABS)	eat-INDIC	
(b)	*arnaq*	*niqi-mik*	*niri-nnig-puq*	'The woman ate (some of)
	woman(ABS)	meat-INSTR	eat-ANTIPASV-INDIC	the meat.'

The active example, (13)(a), is a typical transitive clause in which the subject takes ergative case and the object is absolutive (zero). Although its antipassive counterpart, (13)(b), conveys virtually the same conceptual content, it is nevertheless quite different in grammatical organization. Antipassive voice is signalled by the verbal suffix *-nnig*, which precedes the third-person indicative ending (the grounding predication). Crucially, the derived verb *niri-nnig* is intransitive: *niqi* 'meat' is not a direct object, but instead is marked as oblique by the instrumental suffix *-mik*. And because the clause is intransitive, the subject *arnaq* 'woman' is absolutive rather than ergative.

As the term suggests, antipassive constructions are very similar to passives despite a significant point of contrast. The two construction types are alike in the following respects: (1) each allows the formation of an intransitive clause based on a verb that would otherwise be transitive; (2) this detransitivization is in each case motivated by discourse considerations; (3) both passives and antipassives are commonly marked by verbal affixes; (4) both involve the defocusing of a central clausal participant; and (5) the defocused participant can often be specified periphrastically as an oblique. The pivotal difference is that a passive construction defocuses the participant corresponding to the transitive subject, whereas an antipassive defocuses the transitive object. In each instance the remaining focal participant assumes the status of primary figure and is coded by the clausal subject. A passive subject therefore corresponds to the transitive object, while an antipassive clause has the same subject as the corresponding active.[7]

Although both passive and antipassive constructions can be found in any kind of language, there is a notable tendency for the former to be associated with nominative/accusative systems, and the latter with ergative/absolutive systems. Hence the two construction types are often regarded as manifestations of the same basic phenomenon, their difference stemming from the very nature of accusativity vs. ergativity. How might this insight be captured in terms of our overall analysis? Recall that accusativity and ergativity reflect distinct natural paths, which run in opposite directions with respect to energy flow. We speak of accusativity to the extent that grammatical phenomena invoke the natural path based on figure/ground organization, whose starting point (the subject, or primary figure) is prototypically an agent. Likewise, we speak of ergativity to the extent that grammatical phenomena invoke the natural path based on A/D layering, whose starting point is the thematic participant. In either type of system, the starting point (subject or theme) generally takes precedence in regard to such matters as zero case marking, control of

[7]In some languages a passive-like construction defocuses the subject without affecting the direct-object status of the remaining focal participant. An example from Hopi is *taaqa-t niina-ya* (man-ACC kill-PL:SUBJ) 'He was killed/They (i.e. someone) killed him', where the accusative suffix *-t* and the plural-subject suffix *-ya* indicate that *taaqa* 'man' is the object and not the subject. I analyze such constructions as involving a lesser degree of defocusing, wherein the trajector is left unspecified (being characterized in only the vaguest terms, if at all) but nonetheless retains its standing as the primary figure.

agreement, and serving as the "pivot" (i.e. the shared element) in the linkage of clauses. For example, it is not uncommon for an ergative language to specify that only a theme can act as pivot (cf. Dixon 1979b; Foley and Van Valin 1984, ch. 4; Fox 1987).

These notions enable us to describe passive and antipassive constructions as having a common semantic function: **each defocuses the participant that would otherwise be the starting point of the relevant natural path, thereby conferring on the other focal participant the salience and accessibility that comes with starting-point status**. By defocusing the agent (or more generally, the head of an action chain or its analog), a passive allows the theme to emerge by default as the primary clausal figure and thus enjoy the privileges of subjecthood; the more extensive these privileges, the greater the motivation for such a device—hence the correlation of passives with accusativity. Similarly, when an antipassive defocuses the theme, the agent (or action-chain head) emerges by default as the most theme-like focal participant—though peripheral in terms of A/D layering, it is still the first focal participant encountered in tracing outward from the conceptually autonomous core. An antipassive subject may thereby assume the grammatical behavior characteristic of a theme; and since this option takes on greater significance the more such properties there are, antipassives are closely associated with ergativity.

9.2.4. *Split Ergativity*

In ergative languages, it is quite common for ERG/ABS organization to be manifested in some but not all circumstances, a phenomenon known as **split ergativity**. Investigation reveals that such splits are far from being random—split ergative systems show considerable regularity in the factors determining the distribution of ergativity (see Dixon 1979b; DeLancey 1981; Tasaku 1981). Our characterization of ergativity suggests a particular way of interpreting these factors.

One kind of split is based on location along the *empathy hierarchy* (7.3.1.1), in which the speaker and hearer outrank third-person participants, humans outrank non-humans, animates outrank inanimates, and so on. Depending on the language, there is a particular point along this hierarchy at which ergative case marking "kicks in" for transitive subjects; such a split most commonly divides the speech-act participants from all other entities, so that the only transitive subjects to occur without ergative marking are the first- and second-person pronouns. The usual explanation for this phenomenon is that high-ranking entities are inherently agentive: only for elements lower on the hierarchy is agentivity sufficiently "newsworthy" to be signaled overtly by ergative case. So far as it goes, this account seems quite plausible. Yet I doubt that it tells the whole story. Why, for instance, should third-person humans be considered inherently less agentive than the speech-act participants?

Let me offer an alternate (or complementary) interpretation. The empathy hierarchy reflects the speaker's assessment of his relationship to other sorts of entities, which lie at different "distances" in regard to such matters as likeness and common interests. While the speaker is the ultimate starting point for assessing these distances, in the context of the speech event the speaker and hearer (as co-participants) can further be construed as constituting a joint, higher-order starting point established by the immediacy and implicit solidarity of the communicative act.[8] This notion permits a coherent description of the type of split in question: in a language of this sort, ergative case signals that a nominal lies beyond the starting point not only along the natural path based on A/D layering (which is characteristic of ergative case in general), but along the empathy hierarchy as well. That is, ergative case assumes a meaning based on the co-alignment of two natural paths (each a *cognitive domain* in the sense of Vol. 1, Ch. 4) and specifies that the ERG-marked nominal is non-initial with respect to both parameters.

I propose a similar analysis for a second, less common type of split attested in Newari (Hung 1988; Givón 1984, p. 154), where one factor determining whether a transitive subject takes ergative case is degree of focus. For example, sentence (14)(a)—with an ERG-marked subject—is appropriate in response to the question 'Who's cooking the rice?', whereas (14)(b) answers the question 'What's the man doing?'.

(14)(a) *wa manu-nan jaa thuyaa cona* 'THE MAN is cooking the rice.'
the man-ERG rice cooking be

(b) *wa manu jaa thuyaa cona* 'The man IS COOKING THE RICE.'
the man rice cooking be

The focused element represents the novel or informative part of an utterance, i.e. that portion of its semantic content which surpasses what has already been established in the discourse. At any given moment, the content already established provides a baseline for evaluating the following utterance, whose focus comprises whatever information extends beyond this starting point. The ERG case in (14)(a) can thus be interpreted as indicating that the subject is non-initial (lies beyond the starting point) on each of two natural paths, one defined in terms of A/D layering and the other by the introduction of semantic content in the flow of discourse.

[8] Observe that *here* sometimes refers to the speaker's location as distinct from the hearer's (e.g. *Bring it over here!*) but also has a more inclusive construal that takes the speech-act participants as a joint reference point (*Get ready—here comes another wave!*).

An additional and very common type of split is the restriction of ergativity to clauses marked for either past tense or perfective aspect. This is often explained by the observation that non-past tense and imperfectivity diminish a clause's transitivity, in that they lessen the extent to which the object is seen as being affected by the action of the verb. We might add that such non-completion amounts to the absence of a fully instantiated thematic relationship capable of lending itself unproblematically to construal as a complex event's conceptually autonomous core. Now according to our analysis, the very basis for ergativity resides in well-differentiated A/D layering, with a clear distinction between core and periphery. Consequently, any factor that detracts from the salience of an object or its role in a clear-cut thematic relationship reduces its likelihood of being invoked as the starting point for a natural path based on A/D alignment. To state it in positive terms, past tense and perfectivity contribute significantly to event conceptions involving clearly discernible A/D layering and full instantiation of the autonomous thematic relationship. Since these are the very factors that give rise to ergativity, it is hardly surprising that some languages limit its manifestation to these optimal conditions.

9.3. Case Marking

Case markers are phonologically dependent formatives (affixes, inflections, clitics, or unstressed particles) that occur with nominals and indicate their grammatical relation or semantic role within a clause. That I regard them as meaningful elements should come as no surprise to anyone who has read this far. Offered here is a brief sketch of their semantic characterization and of certain case-marking constructions.

9.3.1. *Meaningfulness*

Despite such notable exceptions as Jakobson 1936, linguistic theorists in the modern era have generally regarded case markers as purely grammatical elements essentially devoid of semantic content. Among the reasons for this attitude (discussed in 9.1) have been the difficulty of finding any single meaning that would account directly for all uses of a given case, as well as the focus on cases that identify a nominal as subject or direct object (these *grammatical* relations supposedly being unsusceptible to semantic characterization). Such considerations lose most of their force when it is recognized that polysemy represents the norm for both "lexical" and "grammatical" expressions, and when the subject and object relations are themselves attributed conceptual import. Case semantics is thus viewed in cognitive linguistics as a viable and important topic of investigation.

The first extensive study of case from the cognitive grammar perspective was by Smith (1985b, 1987), who examined the contrast between dative and accusative case in modern German. For two reasons this problem poses a significant challenge to a semantically-based description. First, the association of direct objects with accusative case is quite regular—in one basic use, ACC is properly described as signaling direct-object status. Second, DAT and ACC mark both central clausal participants and the objects of prepositions; moreover, certain prepositions consistently govern either DAT case or else ACC, whereas others allow both options. Smith demonstrated the coherence and insight of an analysis in which each case is considered meaningful in all its uses. Although the specific nature of the DAT/ACC opposition is different in the clausal and the prepositional realms, each case is describable semantically as a complex category whose various senses display a clear family resemblance. (The following summary is limited to the major patterns and hence greatly oversimplifies Smith's analysis.)

With respect to central clausal participants, the choice between accusative and dative case indicates whether a nominal functions as a direct or an indirect object (cf. 7.3.3). Accusative case can thus be considered meaningful to the same extent, and in the same way, as the direct object relation itself (7.3.2). Prototypically, therefore, ACC marks a thematic participant (with the status of secondary figure) that lies downstream from a participant subject (primary figure) in regard to the flow of energy along an action chain. By extension, it further marks the downstream participant in comparable configurations involving some abstract analog of energy flow. Smith takes these configurations to be instantiations of the structure diagrammed in Fig. 9.1. This is an **image**

Fig. 9.1

schema in the sense of Johnson 1987 and Lakoff 1987, i.e. a schematic yet cognitively fundamental conception that emerges from multitudinous aspects of everyday bodily experience and is projected metaphorically onto other cognitive domains. Among the image schemas that Johnson and Lakoff enumerate are *container-content*, *part-whole*, *source-path-goal*, *center-periphery*, *link*, *up-down*, *front-back*, *balance*, and *force*. Image schemas play an important role in structuring cognitive domains (such as the canonical event model) that support the characterization of basic grammatical constructs. For example, the *force* schema merges with *source-path-goal* in the conception of an action chain. Also, the setting/participant distinction can be seen as one manifestation of the *container-content* schema (8.1.3.2).

Fig. 9.1 represents a portion of the *source-path-goal* schema. Smith observes that two essential features of this schema—the path's *directionality* and the fact that it *reaches* the goal—can be regarded as special manifestations of the more general notions *asymmetry* and *completion*. These factors thus contribute to the likelihood of a clause being construed as transitive and taking an ACC-marked direct object (cf. Rice 1987a). Of course, many verbs conform so closely to prototypical transitivity that the direct-object status of the downstream participant is essentially predictable; in such instances accusative case merely reinforces the obvious construal. Likewise, dative case will almost certainly (and somewhat redundantly) mark a participant that clearly and exclusively instantiates the indirect-object prototype (experiencer and/or recipient). There are, however, many verbs for which either a direct- or an indirect-object construal would be quite plausible. In such instances the choice of DAT vs. ACC is not predictable in any absolute sense. Yet Smith argues that it virtually always has a discernible *motivation*: rather than being arbitrary, the selection is invariably appropriate in some way given the basic meanings of the cases and prominent aspects of the situation being coded. Some verbs allow both options, i.e. the non-subject complement appears as either dative or accusative. Through its own semantic contribution, case inflection then provides the basis for determining how the verb itself should be interpreted. In (15), for example, the contrast between *mir* 'me:DAT' and *mich* 'me:ACC' signals whether *klopfen* refers to light physical contact, in which the transmission of energy is negligible, or whether the contact is forceful and the action complete in the sense of having a real effect on the downstream participant.

(15) *Er klopfte {mir/mich} auf die Schulter.* 'He {patted/hit} me on the shoulder.'

To state it another way, ACC reflects the object's construal as a patient, whereas DAT highlights its role as possessor of the body part specified in the locative complement (and also as experiencer, to the extent that the touching is conceived as having communicative intent).

For those verbs that permit no option, case marking may be considered uninformative, but it is nevertheless motivated by semantic factors. These emerge most clearly from the comparison of verbs that govern different cases despite being quite similar in meaning. For instance, even though *treffen* and *begegnen* can each be glossed as 'meet', we see from (16) that the former governs accusative case, the latter dative (case is marked on the definite article: *den* 'the:MASC:ACC' vs. *dem* 'the:MASC:DAT').

(16)(a) *Ich habe den Mann auf der Brücke getroffen.* 'I met the man on the bridge.'

(b) *Ich bin dem Mann auf der Brücke begegnet.* "

What is the difference? *Treffen* encompasses the possibility of a planned meeting, where the subject goes to see somebody; hence the subject and object roles are potentially asymmetrical in terms of motion and/or volition. By contrast, *begegnen* suggests a chance encounter in which the interaction is basically symmetrical (e.g. the two participants simultaneously appear from opposite directions). On grounds of asymmetry, therefore, *treffen* offers a closer approximation to the accusative configuration of Fig. 9.1. Let us take just one more example. *Jagen* 'chase' and *folgen* 'follow' respectively govern accusative and dative case even though they might describe precisely the same physical activity. With *jagen* the subject controls the action: the object's motion is triggered by its desire to avoid the subject's pursuit. On the other hand, *folgen* conveys less intensity and less asymmetry in the roles of the two participants. The subject does pursue the other participant, but not necessarily with the intent of reaching it—it may be sufficient that they traverse the same spatial path. Moreover, the subject's movement and choice of path are determined by those of the other participant, which thus has a certain measure of *initiative capacity*, as is characteristic of indirect objects (7.3.3).

In sum, the use of accusative case to mark direct objects is always motivated in some way by the image schema sketched in Fig. 9.1, whether this takes the form of an action chain (its prototypical clause-level instantiation) or is manifested more abstractly. Similarly, dative case indicates that a target-domain participant approximates the prototype for indirect objects, or more generally, that the profiled relationship significantly deviates from the accusative schema (e.g. in terms of asymmetry, contact, or completion). The case inflection is coherently regarded as meaningful even when its meaning is wholly subsumed by that of the verb, and the choice of case consistently has a semantic basis, even when it is conventionally determined and not subject to full semantic predictability. An important virtue of this analysis is that it extends in natural fashion to the case marking of prepositional objects. Smith argues that the ACC schema (Fig. 9.1) is regularly discernible in the conception coded by prepositional phrases taking ACC case, whereas DAT signals a substantial departure from that configuration. He further establishes an interesting difference in how this contrast is implemented by the "1-way prepositions" (i.e. those that govern a particular case) and the "2-way prepositions" (those that allow both DAT and ACC).

The 1-way prepositions that govern accusative case include *bis* 'until', *gegen* 'against', *für* 'for', *durch* 'through', *um* 'around', and *ohne* 'without'. The notion of a path that reaches a goal is clearly central to the meaning of *bis*, *gegen*, and *für* (although with *für* the traversal of this path may only be potential). *Durch* represents the special situation in which the path extends through the landmark itself; traversing the landmark completely, the path takes as its goal that extremity of the landmark lying opposite its point of entry. Why *um* should govern ACC is less obvious, since the path is not directed at the landmark and is circular instead of straight. But despite its non-preservation of basic image-schematic properties, the extension can be seen as motivated: *um* resembles *durch* in that the path traverses the landmark itself (albeit on the perimeter rather than through the interior); moreover, *um*'s prototypical sense involves a complete circuit of the landmark (indeed, a circle is emblematic of completion—cf. *come full circle*). The last of these prepositions (and also the most problematic) is *ohne*, for which Smith suggests that ACC is motivated by the notion of completeness.[9]

The 1-way prepositions that govern dative case are *aus* 'out of', *von* 'from', *seit* 'since', *nach* 'toward', *bei* 'by', *mit* 'with', *zu* 'at', and *ausser* 'besides, except'. It is striking that all of these conflict with the ACC image schema in some basic respect. *Aus*, *von*, and *seit* describe paths that lead away from the landmark (i.e. the prepositional object), thus taking it as their source rather than their goal. *Nach* does invoke a path directed at a goal but specifically focuses on its incompleteness. *Bei* and *mit* do not imply a path or even contact, merely some kind of proximity or accompaniment. Although *zu* is often glossed 'to', in fact it has a variety of senses, and Smith argues that it virtually always deviates in some way from the ACC configuration. For example, it often describes a static location (e.g. *die Universität zu Berlin* 'the university at/of Berlin'), and when it does refer to a goal the mover may simply enter the landmark's vicinity instead of making contact with the landmark itself (*Er fährt zu seinem Eltern* 'He travels to his parents'). Finally, *ausser* is more abstract but clearly indicates separation from the landmark (a trait observable in central values of all the 1-way dative prepositions).

From the perspective of cognitive grammar, therefore, the case markings governed by the 1-way prepositions are consistently meaningful despite the absence of any option. Although their occurrence is mandated by linguistic convention (which might well be different and has to be learned), they nevertheless reflect and reinforce certain aspects of the prepositional meanings. The meaningfulness of DAT and ACC is perhaps more evident (though by no means universally accepted) with the 2-way prepositions: *an* 'at, to', *auf* 'on', *hinter* 'behind', *in* 'in', *neben* 'near', *über* 'over', *unter* 'under', *vor* 'in front of', and *zwischen* 'between'. Here case marking may represent the only overt distinction between two sentences with very different meanings. In (17), for example, the contrast between *der* 'the:FEM:DAT' and *die* 'the:FEM:ACC' provides the only indication whether the plane remains above the city (as in a holding pattern) or whether it passes through the airspace above the city as part of a longer trajectory.

(17) *Das Flugzeug fliegt über {der/die} Stadt.* 'The plane is flying over the city.'

[9] At worst one could just say that, with *ohne*, case selection is arbitrary and ACC semantically vacuous (i.e. an identity function). In cognitive grammar this would be seen as merely representing the extreme, limiting case in regard to degree of meaningfulness and semantic motivation. By contrast, ACC is traditionally regarded as totally meaningless and arbitrary with *all* the 1-way prepositions.

Of course, the case inflections do not refer to the city's airspace per se, but rather to a more abstract construct called the **search domain** (Hawkins 1984). A search domain is the space to which a locative predication confines its trajector: *in* tells us that the trajector is somewhere within the landmark's interior, *near* takes the landmark's vicinity for its search domain, and so on. The search domain for *über* 'over' is the space above the landmark, which in (17) is naturally equated with the city's airspace.

For the 2-way prepositions in German, Smith draws the generalization that DAT signals motion (or static location) wholly within the preposition's search domain (Fig. 9.2(a)), whereas ACC indicates a trajectory that takes the search

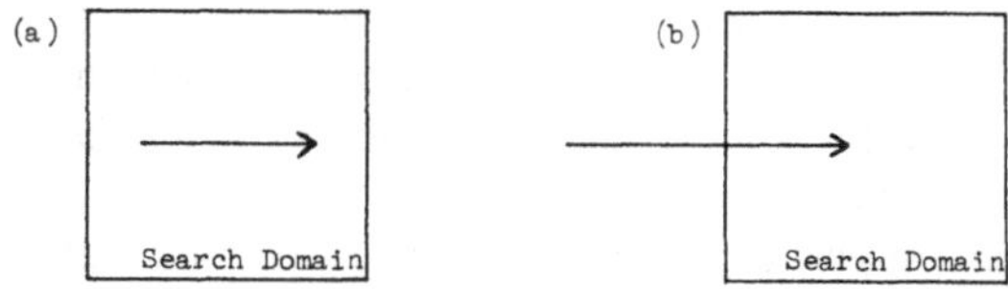

Fig. 9.2

domain as its goal and penetrates its boundary (Fig. 9.2(b)). Clearly, only this latter configuration instantiates the *path-goal* image schema, which is therefore pivotal to the DAT/ACC opposition just as it is in the clausal and 1-way prepositional realms. We see, then, that this opposition—when viewed schematically—is essentially the same in all three realms, which nevertheless interpret it in very different ways. For clauses the goal-directed path motivating ACC is prototypically identified as the transmission of energy, while with prepositions it most basically pertains to spatial motion. Moreover, the 1-way prepositions identify the goal as the *landmark itself*, while the relevant goal for the 2-way prepositions is the *search domain* associated with the landmark.

Even if one accepts the meaningfulness of dative and accusative case in German, it does not follow that case markings are invariably meaningful in all languages. That thesis nevertheless represents the natural expectation in the context of cognitive grammar and has the virtue of allowing a unified account of lexico-grammatical structure as an inherently symbolic phenomenon. Further supporting the thesis is a small but growing body of cognitively oriented research dealing with case in diverse languages (e.g. Janda 1990, *to appear*; Cook 1988a, 1988b; Hung 1988; Langacker 1990a, ch. 9; Wierzbicka 1981, 1988). The more traditional, contrary view of case markers—that they are usually (if not always) semantically empty—stems primarily from an inappropriate conception of linguistic semantics. The basis for regarding case markings as meaningless formatives largely evaporates once it is recognized that an element may be meaningful despite such factors as abstractness, polysemy, predictability, and full semantic overlap.

9.3.2. *Case-Marking Constructions*

Assuming that case markers are indeed meaningful, it remains to determine the precise nature of their characterization and of the grammatical constructions in which they occur. The basic generalization is that case marking on a nominal evokes in schematic terms the conception of a relationship in which the nominal referent participates; that relationship is subsequently rendered specific in a higher-order construction taking the case-marked nominal as one component structure.

Thus a case marker's scope of predication comprises a schematic relation of the appropriate sort, one of whose participants the case-marking construction puts in correspondence with the nominal profile. In its prototypical value, for example, instrumental case evokes as its base the schematic conception of an action chain involving an agent, an instrument, and a theme. What does it profile? The answer depends on the array of elements we choose to identify as case markers, in particular whether formatives comparable to the English prepositions are subsumed under that rubric. We have analyzed English prepositions as atemporal relations, and there is no apparent reason to depart from that analysis even for the instrumental *with* (e.g. *Floyd broke the glass with a hammer*), whose counterpart in many other languages would be a case inflection. Sketched in Fig. 9.3(a), the instrumental *with* profiles the relationship between an agentive process overall (its trajector) and an instrument (its

Fig. 9.3

landmark) which figures in that process. The instrumental landmark of *with* is elaborated by a nominal via the regular prepositional-object construction (e.g. *with a hammer*). At a higher level of organization, the processual trajector of the prepositional phrase is then elaborated by a constituent consisting of the verb and its complements (*Floyd broke the glass*).[10]

Yet not all case-like elements are plausibly analyzed as relational predications. For example, on the usual assumption that prepositional objects are nominal rather than relational, the case marking that accompanies such an object (as in (17)) cannot alter its nominal character. Similarly, nominative

[10] Whether these complements include the subject depends on one's assumptions concerning clausal constituency; these have no bearing on the issue at hand. The box in Fig. 9.3(a) does not represent the setting (as in certain previous diagrams). The intent is rather to indicate that the event as a whole (i.e. the full agent-to-theme action chain) functions as trajector in the profiled relationship.

and accusative case are never seen as affecting the nominal status of subjects and direct objects. At least some case markers are therefore best analyzed as themselves being nominal in character, since the effect of combining them with a nominal is to derive a higher-order nominal. Let us reserve the term *case* for predications of this sort. The instrumental *with* is not a case marker by this definition, but its inflectional counterpart in other languages may very well be.[11] In its prototypical sense a marker of instrumental case thus has the structure depicted in Fig. 9.3(b): the schematic conception of an action chain serves as its base, and within that base it designates a participant characterized in terms of the *instrument* role archetype. At the semantic pole, the integration of such a marker with a nominal is effected by a correspondence between their profiles.

A construction of this sort is sketched in Fig. 9.4. The first level of constituency represents the inflection of a nominal for instrumental case. The nominal of course designates a thing; its various semantic specifications are abbreviated as X. The nominal profile corresponds to that of the case predication, whose characterization is limited to its instrumental function. The case-marked nominal (NML-INSTR) thus designates a thing with certain properties (X) that is further portrayed as an instrument in a schematically characterized process. At the second level of constituency, NML-INSTR combines with a verb that profiles a specific process, though it may be neutral as to whether an instrument figures in the action chain (hence the dashed-line circle). A global correspondence identifies V's profile with the schematic process evoked by NML-INSTR; also shown is the local correspondence equating the two instrumental participants (merely potential within V, but profiled by NML-INSTR). The resulting composite expression designates a specific process that definitely involves an instrument with particular properties.

What about case agreement? Suppose, for example, that instrumental case is marked not only on a noun but also on a modifying adjective. Though multiple case marking of this sort does imply a certain amount of redundancy (motivated by functional/communicative factors beyond the scope of our present concern), it does not follow that either occurrence of the marker is meaningless or that anything other than symbolic units are necessary to describe the construction. A number of analyses are actually possible, some representing distinct construction types. For instance, the noun and the apparent adjective may in fact constitute separate, coreferential nominals standing in an appositional relationship (e.g. [*He cut it*] *with (a) knife, with (a) sharp one*). Such an analysis suggests itself for languages in which nouns and modifying

[11] Although the distinction between relational elements and true (nominal) case markers presumably correlates with that between separate words and inflections, the correlation is at best imperfect. It is even possible for the same marker to have both relational and nominal variants (e.g. Spanish *a* as a preposition and as a case marker for human direct objects).

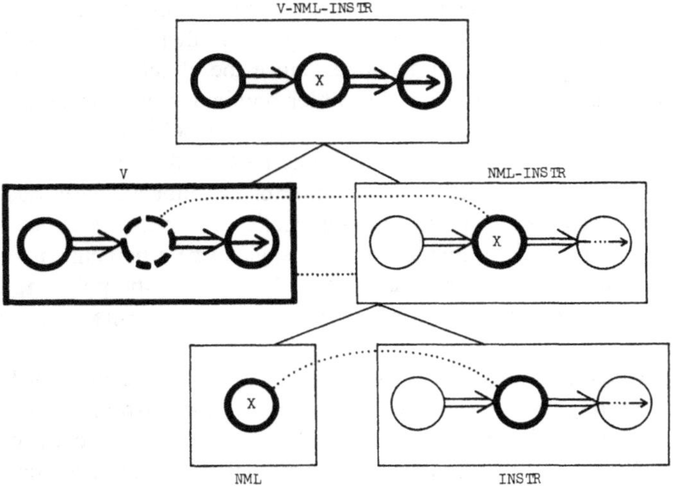

Fig. 9.4

adjectives need not be contiguous, or where they are morphologically indistinguishable. Let us assume, however, that the case-marked noun and adjective are part of a single nominal and that the adjective is indeed relational rather than pronominal. Let us further assume that each element is individually marked for case prior to their integration.[12]

Fig. 9.5 diagrams one implementation of such an analysis. Shown on the left, the formation of the case-marked noun is directly analogous to that of the case-marked nominal in Fig. 9.4: through a correspondence between their profiles, N and INSTR merge to form a composite structure (N-INSTR) that profiles a thing; the designatum inherits from N a particular set of semantic specifications (X), and from INSTR the further specification of its instrumental role in a schematically characterized event. The formation of the case-marked adjective is shown on the right. Although the adjective profiles a stative relation, its case inflection can be attributed the same semantic value it has with nouns. Their integration is effected by a correspondence between the adjectival trajector and the instrument profiled by INSTR, and since ADJ is the profile determinant, the composite structure ADJ-INSTR designates a stative relation whose trajector is further specified as having instrumental function. Finally, at the highest level of constituency, N-INSTR and ADJ-INSTR combine in accordance with the usual pattern for a noun-modifier

[12]This implies that case marking affects individual nominal constituents rather than the grounded nominal as a whole. Alternatively, one could posit a single case predication that does combine with the full nominal but whose phonological manifestation is potentially complex and discontinuous, a separate copy appearing on each word of the nominal.

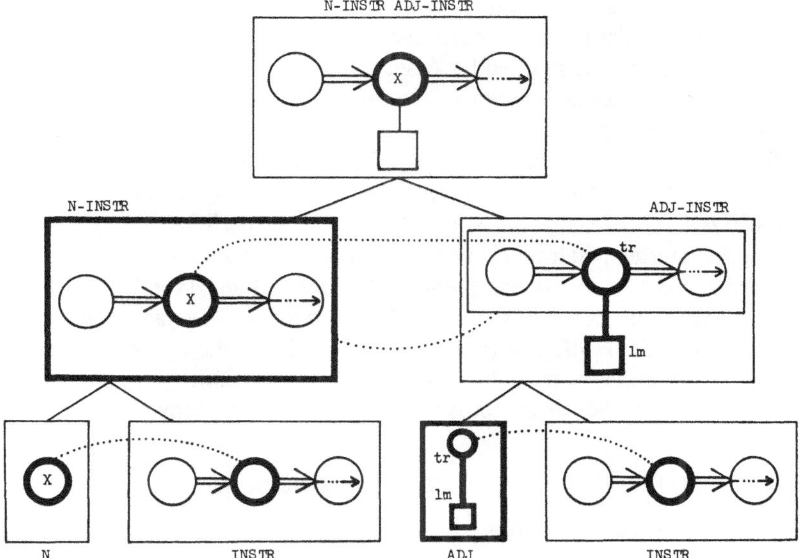

Fig. 9.5

construction, whereby the noun's profile corresponds to the adjective's trajector. Observe that a second correspondence equates the two events introduced by the case predications, so that only a single event figures in the overall composite structure. Since the noun is the head, the composite expression designates a thing with certain properties (X) that is further characterized as the trajector of a specific stative relation (contributed by the adjective), and also as the instrument within a schematic event (which may subsequently be specified by a verb as part of a higher-order construction (cf. Fig. 9.4)).

Expressions of this sort are licensed by a complex constructional schema that we can abbreviate as [[N-INSTR][ADJ-INSTR]]. We can readily envisage comparable schemas for other cases and other types of noun modifiers, as well as more abstract schemas representing higher-level generalizations supported by such patterns. Likewise included in a full, usage-based description will be subschemas describing local regularities, and even specific combinations learned as units (whether regular or idiosyncratic). Now a constructional schema like [[N-INSTR][ADJ-INSTR]] merely specifies the conventionality of double case marking, i.e. that such "agreement" is *possible*. Suppose, however, that the double marking is *obligatory*. We can then assume that [[N-INSTR][ADJ-INSTR]] is the only schema available to sanction the integration of an instrumental noun and adjective. In the absence of any competing constructional schema (such as [[N-INSTR][ADJ]], [[N][ADJ-INSTR]], or [[N][ADJ]]), [[N-INSTR][ADJ-INSTR]] is necessarily selected as the *active structure* used to categorize a target expression. Measured against that standard, a noun-adjective combination is judged ill-formed unless both elements are marked for case.

Case government is handled in similar fashion. Recall, for instance, that German *gegen* 'against' governs accusative case, and *von* 'from' governs dative, whereas the object of *über* 'over' can occur with either case. Accordingly, we can posit the constructional schemas [[gegen][ACC-NML]], [[von][DAT-NML]], [[über][ACC-NML]], and [[über][DAT-NML]] to represent the attested patterns. Conventional usage affords no basis, however, for extracting such schemas as [[gegen][DAT-NML]] or [[von][ACC-NML]]. An expression of this sort is therefore categorized as a deviant manifestation of [[gegen][ACC-NML]] or [[von][DAT-NML]]. On the other hand, a well-entrenched schema is available to license a prepositional phrase with *über* regardless of whether its object is marked dative or accusative.

9.4. Causative Constructions

The term **causative** applies to constructions that serve to code the energy input responsible for the occurrence of a process. With respect to A/D layering, a causative construction expands an autonomous event conception (thematic or complex) to encompass the instigating force and the participant from which it emanates. Equivalently, we can see it as adding a link at the beginning of an action chain, thereby extending the scope of predication to include the original energy source. A viable account of case and grammatical relations must obviously be able to handle such constructions.

There are of course many verbs—such as *kill*, *throw*, and *chop*—in which the notion of causation is inherent yet *sublexical*, in the sense of not being coded individually. Though still implicit, that notion is somewhat more "visible" to the analyst with verbs like *break*, *open*, and *cook*, for it constitutes the only semantic difference between their intransitive and transitive variants (e.g. *It broke* vs. *He broke it*). Explicit causatives commonly involve a verbal affix or inflection, as in the following Luiseño example:

(18) *noo poy ʔowoʔa-**ni**-n* 'I will make him work.'
I him work-CAUS-FUT

Causation can also be expressed by a separate verb, such as *make*, *cause*, or *have*. Whether verbal or affixal, the causative predication imposes its profile on the verb stem or infinitive describing the instigated process: it is the act of causation (not that of working) that is profiled and grounded in both (18) and its English translation. This construction represents a head-complement relation in which 'work' elaborates the instigated process that 'make' characterizes only schematically.

9.4.1. *Grammatical Relations*

Recent investigations of causative expressions have tended to focus on either of two main issues. The first is a putative distinction, on grounds of productivity and semantic regularity, between "lexical" causatives and those constructed by syntactic rule (Shibatani 1976). We shall leave this matter aside, except to note that cognitive grammar is comfortable with patterns of any degree of productivity and regularity, and encourages the expectation that causative constructions might vary continuously along these parameters rather than falling into sharply dichotomous groups. The second issue is whether the grammatical relations of a causative sentence are predictable. Given that a verb, V, assigns grammatical relations to its participants in a particular way, what relations will these participants bear to the complex clausal head, (CAUS(V)), derived from V by a causative predication?

A well-known proposal (from unpublished work by Perlmutter and Postal) is as follows: the subject of V is always the object of (CAUS(V)) in cases where V is intransitive; but when V is transitive, it is rather V's object that becomes the object of (CAUS(V)), V's subject being manifested by an oblique complement (typically an indirect object). Consider these examples from French:

(19)(a) *Je ferai pleurer le témoin.* 'I will make the witness cry.'
(b) *Je ferai interroger le témoin à l'avocat.* 'I will make the lawyer question the witness.'

In (19)(a), *le témoin* 'the witness' is understood as the "logical subject" of the intransitive *pleurer* 'cry' and is uncontroversially the direct object of the causative verb group *faire pleurer*. On the other hand, in (19)(b) *le témoin* is the direct object of both *interroger* 'question' and *faire interroger*, while *l'avocat* 'the lawyer' is the subject of *interroger* but the indirect object of the overall expression. This pattern does appear to be prototypical, yet subsequent work has revealed a greater variety of possibilities (cf. Cole and Sridhar 1977; Rosen 1983; Gibson and Raposo 1986). For one thing, an intransitive subject is sometimes manifested not as the direct object of a causative but as an indirect object. There are also languages in which the subject rather than the object of a transitive verb corresponds to the causative direct object.

The grammatical relations of causative expressions must therefore be specified by the constructional schemas describing their formation. In fact, the choice of focal participants is attributable to the causative predication itself, which imposes its own figure/ground organization on (CAUS(V)) as one aspect of its profile determinance. CAUS may, for example, have the semantic structure depicted in Fig. 9.6: its trajector is the energy source; its primary landmark is the trajector of the instigated process (represented by the squiggly

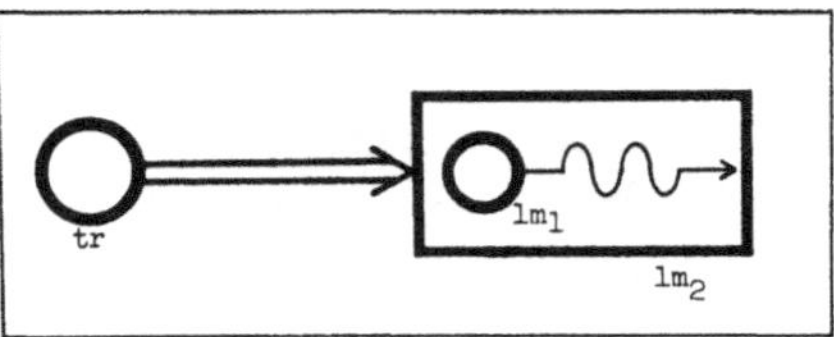

Fig. 9.6

arrow); and that process—taken as a whole—functions as a secondary, relational landmark. Another type of causative predication takes as its primary landmark the participant corresponding to the theme (rather than the trajector) of the instigated process. In either case, the trajector and the primary landmark of (CAUS(V)) serve as the respective e-sites for nominals which are thus identified as the subject and direct object. The secondary landmark is likewise an e-site, being elaborated by a verb stem or an infinitival complement. A participant not selected as subject or direct object may be specified either periphrastically or as one instantiation of the indirect-object construction (cf. (19)(b)).

Of course, causative constructions do not assign grammatical relations randomly but in accordance with strong universal tendencies. A comprehensive linguistic theory will specify the basic patterns in the form of schematic constructions ranked for prototypicality (Vol. 1, 1.2.6.2) and will also attempt to explain the basis for their apparent naturalness. These patterns are in fact natural consequences of using a single clause to code a complex event. Most obvious is the basis for the instigator (i.e. the energy source) invariably being selected as the causative subject: this participant is an agent or at least the action-chain head, which is prototypical for the subject category. What about the causative object? Suppose first that V is intransitive, so that it has just a single focal participant, usually a theme. (CAUS(V)) then profiles a two-participant action chain whose head is chosen as trajector and whose tail (corresponding to V's trajector) has a thematic role. This latter participant is virtually always accorded direct object status for the simple reason that it instantiates the direct-object category prototype (a thematic participant downstream in the flow of energy from a participant subject).

When V is transitive, the action chain profiled by (CAUS(V)) has three major participants: $[AG_1 = = = > [AG_2 = = = > TH]]$, where AG_1 is the agent of causation, AG_2 corresponds to V's subject, and TH to its object. Now given that a single clause can have just two focal participants, what is the most natural assignment of grammatical relations? The unmarked selections are AG_1 as subject and TH as direct object, since these represent the prototypical values of the subject and object categories—AG_1 is both agentive and the action-chain head, while TH is both thematic and the action-chain tail.

Though it is also agentive, AG_2 is neither the head nor the tail of the profiled action chain; its role is thus analogous to that of an instrument in a canonical action chain (*AG= = =>INSTR= = =>TH*), and like an instrument the nominal that codes it is typically oblique.

There is however a competing rationale, which motivates a pattern of lesser prevalence wherein AG_2 is chosen as direct object. Recall that an object is characterized schematically as the second-most prominent clausal participant (secondary figure). It is not unnatural, therefore, that the most salient of V's participants—namely its trajector, AG_2—should be accorded that special status (AG_1 being the primary figure), even though the object thus selected is non-prototypical in regard to semantic role. Hence the alternate patterns reflect a conflict between prominence and thematicity, the two major components of objecthood.[13]

9.4.2. *Case*

The subject and direct object of a causative sentence are typically marked for case in the same way as any other subject or object. Thus the subject and object pronouns in (18), *noo poy ʔowoʔa-ni-n* (I him work-CAUS-FUT) 'I will make him work', have the same forms as they would in any Luiseño transitive clause (cf. *noo poy čuŋi-n* 'I will kiss him'). Even in such instances case marking is regarded as meaningful, since conceptual import is imputed to the subject and object relations themselves. We have seen, however, that case markers function primarily to indicate semantic role. Causative constructions provide some instructive examples.

Consider this oft-cited contrast in Japanese:

(20) *taroo ga* *ziroo* {***o*/*ni***} *ik-ase-ta* 'Taro caused Jiro to go.'
Taro NOM Jiro {ACC/DAT} go-CAUS-PAST

The only overt difference between the two variants resides in the object nominal being marked for accusative vs. dative case. We can leave to Japanese specialists the issue of whether *ziroo* is the direct object in both sentences, or whether *o* and *ni* function in the usual way to mark it as a direct vs. an indirect object. Our concern is rather with the fact that *o* is appropriate when Taro 'is indifferent to whether [Jiro] consents to go', whereas *ni* indicates that Jiro 'willingly carries out the action in question' (Cole 1983, p. 125). That is, case marking signals a subtle yet important distinction in the construal of the object's semantic role: *o* highlights its thematic role as a mover driven by exter-

[13] The two patterns for the choice of causative direct object can also be seen as manifestations of ergativity vs. accusativity. The first pattern is ergative because—with respect to V itself—the participant chosen is always thematic (the subject when V is intransitive, the object when V is transitive). The second pattern is accusative because the causative object is always V's subject (regardless of its transitivity).

nal forces, whereas *ni* emphasizes its capacity to undertake or control the thematic process (even when externally induced).

The example is not unusual. Cole notes that many languages allow the "causee" to be marked with different cases depending on the specific nature of its semantic role. He further makes the insightful observation that degree of agentivity is the primary determining factor; the typical pattern is for dative or instrumental case to mark a causee whose role is to some degree agentive, while accusative indicates that its involvement is totally passive. Why not the opposite pattern? Indeed, why should there be any correlation at all between case and semantic role? This is actually somewhat mysterious from Cole's perspective, since—in accordance with the standard assumptions of autonomous syntax—he apparently attributes no meaning to either case markers or the grammatical relations he takes them as signalling. On the other hand, it represents a natural expectation in the context of our overall analysis and the general claim that all grammatical elements are meaningful.

The meanings ascribed to these cases in their causative use constitute straightforward semantic extensions from their prototypical semantic values. It is natural that ACC should be used when the causee is passive and non-volitional, for these properties are characteristic of canonical direct objects. Of course, this passivity is only relative. The ACC-marked mover in (20) may control his actions physically—he simply has no option but to carry them out. Moreover, the caused event may itself be transitive, as in the following example from Quechua, described by Cole as expressing direct, coercive causation:

(21)	*nuqa*	*fan-ta*	*rumi-ta*	*apa-či-ni*	'I make Juan carry the rock.'
	I	Juan-ACC	rock-ACC	carry-CAUS-I	

Here the causee (Juan) definitely exerts a force on the rock; it is however non-agentive in that it lacks volition, and theme-like in the sense of being a target of coercion (thus absorbing either physical or abstract energy). The meaning assumed by ACC in such uses is in some respects quite far from its prototypical value. At the same time, the two meanings have discernible similarities, which stand out yet more clearly when comparison is made with other case-marking options.

In contrast to the direct or coercive causation implied by accusative case, dative or instrumental case is usually indicative of indirect or non-coercive causation, where the causee still exercises some measure of volition or initiative.[14] We can thus describe it in shorthand fashion as a *secondary agent*: secondary in the sense of being downstream from the original energy source,

[14]That is, it does so when the language allows an option. If the same case is used in all circumstances, its meaning is neutral in regard to agentivity and directness of causation.

yet agentive in the sense of having some initiative role. It is apparent that this meaning represents a plausible semantic extension with respect to the prototypical values of both instrumental and dative case. Quite obviously, a secondary agent is directly analogous to an instrument by virtue of being an intermediary in the flow of energy from the (primary) agent to the theme. Recall now that dative case centers on the notion of *mental experience*, one facet of which is volitionality. And while the experiencer role may be purely thematic, an *initiative* construal (in which the experiencer establishes mental contact with another entity) is equally likely. It might even be observed that our characterization of a dative or indirect object as an *active experiencer in the target domain* (7.3.3) applies quite well to a secondary agent.

Quechua offers interesting corroboration of this account. Cole reports that both dative and instrumental case can mark the causee in instances of indirect, non-coercive causation:

(22)(a) *nuqa runa-man rikʰu-či-ni* 'I showed it to the man.'
I man-DAT see-CAUS-I

(b) *nuqa fan-wan rumi-ta apa-či-ni* 'I had Juan carry the rock.'
I Juan-INSTR rock-ACC carry-CAUS-I

He observes that DAT occurs with verbs like 'see', 'know', 'eat', and 'remember', i.e. with precisely those verbs that Quechua classifies as "verbs of experience."

Lastly, Cole notes a pattern (attested in Kannada) whereby an agentive causee is marked with instrumental case, and a non-agentive causee with dative case. Since INSTR and DAT are each readily extended to causative intermediaries, it is not surprising that both developments might occur in a single language; the formal difference between the cases would then be exploited to signal a contrast in agentivity. INSTR is a natural choice to code a higher degree of agentivity because—in terms of role archetypes and their systemic relationships—an instrument is conceived as an extension of the agent and belongs to the source domain, whereas an experiencer belongs to the target domain (Fig. 7.5). One can, however, offer a perfectly good rationale for the opposite alignment: because the relevant contrast in agentivity largely pertains to the mental sphere, it is natural for a secondary agent to be marked by DAT, with INSTR reserved for a non-volitional intermediary. The possibility of such a system is therefore predicted by our analysis.

Part III
BEYOND THE CLAUSE

PARTS I AND II respectively examined the structure of nominals and of finite clauses. Remaining to be considered are some important grammatical phenomena whose scope extends beyond a single clause's confines. Multiclausal sentences are the specific concern of Chapter 10, which discusses them in general terms before focusing on *complementation*, a type of subordination accorded great prominence in modern linguistic theory. Chapter 11 offers brief, exploratory treatments of several basic topics: coordination, anaphora, speech acts, and the interaction of "syntactic rules." Dealt with in Chapter 12 are a variety of fundamental theoretical issues, including the assumptions and goals of linguistic investigation, the autonomy thesis, the nature of rules and representations, and the affinity of cognitive grammar to *connectionist* models of mental processing.

CHAPTER 10

Complex Sentences

ALTHOUGH A SENTENCE may consist of just a single finite clause, every language also provides an array of constructions permitting the assembly of **complex**—i.e. multiclausal—expressions. Our initial concern in this chapter is to describe the intersecting factors responsible for the great variety of such constructions. We will then take a closer look at complement clauses, which have been a focus of theoretical discussion throughout the history of generative grammar.

10.1. General Discussion

Traditionally, a fairly sharp distinction is drawn between *coordination*, illustrated in (1), and various kinds of *subordination*, as in (2).

(1) *Janet weeded the garden, and Phil mowed the lawn.*

(2)(a) *The person* ***who picked out that tie*** *must be color blind.*
(b) *We all expected* ***that Jerry would eventually finish college.***
(c) *Put those magazines away* ***before your mother gets home!***

Relative, **complement**, and **adverbial clauses** are considered to be the basic types of subordinate structures. A relative clause modifies a head noun; e.g. *who picked out that tie* modifies *person* in (2)(a). A complement clause functions as a clausal participant; thus in (2)(b), *that Jerry would eventually finish college* is the direct object of *expect*. An adverbial clause is analogous to other adverbs in that it modifies a relational expression; in (2)(c), *before your mother gets home* modifies the main clause *put those magazines away*.

Though useful so far as it goes, this taxonomy proves simplistic when measured against the actual complexities of multiclausal constructions, which do not in fact divide themselves naturally into a small number of discrete classes with uniquely characteristic properties. Even the seemingly fundamental distinction between coordination and subordination is very often problematic. Not only is it common for coordinate and subordinate structures to share certain markings, but sometimes they are formally indistinguishable (cf. Norwood 1981; Langacker *to appear*). When both formal and semantic factors are taken into account, a construction may still be intermediate or of indeterminate classification. For instance, (3) is formally parallel to (1) except that *while* replaces *and*, yet *while*-clauses are usually considered adverbial.[1]

(3) *Janet weeded the garden, while Phil mowed the lawn.*

Note further that *while* has a non-temporal, "concessive" reading (roughly, 'but on the other hand') that is not unlike the meanings of certain conjunctions. Indeed, *while* belongs to a set of clause-introducing elements (including *since, because, if, unless, when, so that*, etc.) traditionally referred to as *subordinating conjunctions*—a term that would have to be considered contradictory if coordination and subordination were really sharply distinct.

Subordinate clauses show even less inclination to sort themselves neatly into discrete, well-differentiated classes. The general rubrics *relative, complement*, and *adverbial clause* each subsume an extensive and heterogeneous array of construction types. Cross-cutting this division are alternative groupings whose basis seems no less significant. For example, relative, complement, and adverbial clauses can all be finite, as in (2), but a subjectless, infinitival clause marked by *to* can also serve in all three capacities:

(4)(a) *The person* ***to discuss the matter with*** *is the manager.*
(b) *We all expected* ***to finish college eventually****.*
(c) *He put the magazines away* ***to impress his mother with his neatness****.*

Form is generally a treacherous guide at best to membership in the traditional classes. Subordinate clauses with question words are usually complements, as in (5)(a), yet the formally identical structure in (5)(b) is considered a relative clause despite the absence of a head noun:

(5)(a) ***What he stole*** *is a mystery.*
(b) ***What he stole*** *is worth a fortune.*

(6) *The fact* ***that she forgot*** *is unimportant.*

Likewise, the subordinate structure in (6) has a relative clause interpretation (in which *fact* is understood as the object of *forgot*), but it can also be taken as standing in apposition to the head (i.e. that she forgot *constitutes* the fact in question), in which case it is more akin to a complement. The constructions in (7) are even more problematic for the basic taxonomy:

[1]To be sure, *while-* and *and*-clauses differ in grammatical behavior, notably in terms of preposability (*{While/*And} Phil mowed the lawn, Janet weeded the garden*) and observation of the "coordinate structure constraint" (*the garden that Janet weeded {while/*and} Phil mowed the lawn*). There is good reason to believe, however, that such behavior is determined by semantic rather than structural factors (cf. Lakoff 1986).

(7)(a) *She told a funny story* ***which greatly amused me.***
(b) *She told a funny story,* ***which greatly amused me.***

The *which*-clause in (7)(a) is a normal, *restrictive* relative. Set off by a pause, however, as in (b), it is semantically *non-restrictive* or *appositional* (i.e. it fails to restrict the head noun's type specification); in terms of both intonation and meaning, it resembles a coordinate structure (cf. *She told a funny story, (and) it greatly amused me*). Moreover, (7)(b) has another interpretation, whereby *which* does not refer to the story but rather to the fact that she told it. This latter construction defies traditional classification.

Despite their familiarity, therefore, such standard terms as *coordination, subordination, relative clause*, etc. do not necessarily refer to notions that are clearly defined or thoroughly understood, nor can they be accepted as representing an optimal, revelatory, or even adequate classificatory system. Indeed, it is doubtful that any single classification could accommodate the actual diversity of multiclausal constructions together with the many kinds and degrees of similarity displayed by overlapping subgroups. A better strategy is to examine individually the various factors that figure in a full characterization of such constructions; a particular construction is then defined by a constellation of properties, each of which is shared by certain others. The factors to be considered are (1) how closely a structure approximates a full, finite clause; (2) markers of interclausal connections (e.g. subordinators); (3) correspondences involving clauses or clausal elements; and (4) aspects of global organization (such as profile determinance).

10.1.1. *Internal Elaboration*

Although the term *subordinate clause* is well entrenched in both traditional grammar and modern linguistics, there is no explicit, universal agreement as to precisely what it implies and what it subsumes. We shall postpone the issue of what it means for a clause to be *subordinate*. Let us start instead by asking what it means for a subordinate structure to be a *clause*. Of course, the terminological issue holds little interest per se—it is merely a vehicle for exploring a certain range of structural variation.

At one extreme, exemplified by the complements in (8), are subordinate structures whose clausal status is utterly impeccable: full, finite clauses that could stand alone as independent sentences with no appreciable difference in form or meaning.

(8)(a) *Everyone thought* ***he was a very handsome young man.***
(b) *I wonder* ***which surgeon is better at that procedure.***

Nor does anyone question the clausehood of the subordinate structures in (2), which differ from sentences only by the addition of a subordinator (*that*; *be-*

fore) or by having a relative pronoun (*who*) as subject.[2] If fully articulated finite clauses are therefore regarded as prototypical, the issue is that of determining how far and in what ways a structure can deviate from this prototype and still be considered a subordinate clause. Departures from the prototype are of two basic sorts: the absence of clausal elements; and having a non-processual profile. The farther a structure strays from the prototype along either or both parameters, the more reluctant grammarians are to call it a *clause*. However, drawing an absolute boundary at any particular location would seem to be gratuitous.

Frequently "absent" from a subordinate clause is some nominal required in a full, independent clause to code a participant. Compare *She bought a skirt* with *The skirt* ***she bought*** *was too tight*. Although *buy* normally takes a direct object, there is no overt object in the relative clause *she bought*. It is nevertheless understood that she bought something, namely the skirt—a fact that transformational grammarians typically accounted for by positing an underlying object that fails to surface (though it may leave behind a phonologically invisible "trace"). The devices of cognitive grammar permit a more straightforward description. Internally, *buy* makes schematic reference to both a trajector and a primary landmark (as well as certain non-focal participants), which in a full clause are respectively elaborated by the subject and object nominals. A relative clause like *she bought* is not obtained by deforming such a structure; it merely represents an alternate construction in which only the trajector is elaborated (cf. Vol. 1, 8.4.2). The schematic landmark is however specified indirectly as part of a higher-order construction: effecting the integration of the relative clause with the head noun is a correspondence that equates the former's landmark with the latter's profile. In *the skirt* ***she bought***, the thing bought is thus identified as the skirt.

The absence of an elaborating nominal does not per se affect a structure's clausal status. Even when several nominals are "missing"—as in *a fork* ***to eat with*** (where the trajector and landmark of *eat* remain unspecified and *fork* corresponds to the landmark of *with*)—qualms about the clausehood of *to eat with* stem primarily from its infinitival nature. That is, the essential feature of a clause is considered to be its verbal character, which is largely independent of whether participants receive explicit coding. But what does this "verbal character" consist of? Presumably it finds optimal manifestation in a finite clause, which designates a grounded instance of a process type (Chs. 5–6). A structure is therefore not clause-like just because it contains a

[2] Actually, the subordinate clause in (2)(c) comprises just *your mother gets home*, a relational complement of *before*; taken as a whole, *before your mother gets home* is a stative relation with adverbial function (cf. *before noon*). Comparable remarks hold for numerous other examples, but I will generally follow standard usage (and thus speak of *before*-clauses, *while*-clauses, *that*-clauses, etc.) when that aspect of the analysis is not in focus.

verb: also essential are semantic function and profiling at the highest level of organization.

Intrinsic to semantic function is a kind of A/D layering, wherein a type specification is conceptually autonomous, instantiation presupposes a type, quantification pertains to instances, and grounding represents the outermost layer. Starting from a verb stem, which supplies a type specification (T), functionally autonomous expressions incorporating any number of layers can be assembled: (T) > (I(T)) > (Q(I(T))) > (G(Q(I(T)))). How clause-like an expression is considered to be correlates with how many layers it incorporates; by definition, a finite clause is fully elaborated in this respect, subsuming all four functions. A structure with any lesser degree of functional elaboration can nevertheless be used in a subordinate capacity.[3]

The difference in semantic function between a finite clause and an infinitival or participial clause is the presence vs. the absence of a grounding predication: (G(Q(I(T)))) vs. (Q(I(T))). Thus tense and modals occur in finite-clause relatives, as illustrated in (9)(a)–(b), whereas (c) and (d) show that neither is permitted in an infinitival or participial modifier.

(9)(a) *the girl* ***who was sitting on that bench***
(b) *the girl* ***who should have sat on that bench***
(c)* *the first girl* ***to was sitting on that bench***
(d)* *any girl* ***shoulding have sat on that bench***
(e) *the first girl* ***to {sit/be sitting/have sat} on that bench***
(f) *any girl* ***{sitting/having sat} on that bench***
(g) *the girl* ***on that bench***

We see from (e) and (f) that non-finite modifiers can however incorporate progressive or perfect aspect, which serve a quantifying function with respect to a verb's processual profile. While infinitival and participial modifiers are generally considered clausal, the same cannot be said for a prepositional-phrase modifier, such as *on that bench* in (g): lacking a verb, it does not fulfill even the minimal clausal function of specifying a process type.

If formula (Q(I(T))) characterizes infinitival and participial constructions allowing perfect and progressive aspect, then (I(T)) must describe an otherwise comparable construction that precludes them. Well-known examples are the complements of certain verbs of perception, notably *see* and *hear*. There are two semantically contrasting variants (cf. 10.2.1.2), distinguished by whether the complement is marked by *-ing* or by zero:

(10)(a) We saw the sun ***slowly sinking in the western sky***.
(b) I heard George Bush ***recite the Pledge of Allegiance with great emotion***.

[3]Cf. Foley and Van Valin 1984, chs. 5–6. Their classificatory scheme for clause linkage is similar in spirit to that presented here; I see no fundamental incompatibility.

Although the complement has a clause-like internal structure in regard to such elements as objects and adverbs, neither variant tolerates the aspectual auxiliaries:

(11)(a) **She saw him {**being writing/having written**} **his paper**.*
(b) **They heard me {**be smashing/have smashed**} **the windows**.*

At least with *-ing*, however, the complement may be passive (e.g. *I heard it being discussed*), since voice per se does not effect temporal quantification.

Subordinate structures comprising only a type specification (T) are common in the realm of verbal morphology. Many languages allow the formation of complex verb stems through successive layers of affixation, each imposing its own processual profile on the autonomous structure it attaches to. Consider this Luiseño example (for detailed analysis, see Langacker 1988a):

(12) *noo poy ˀowoˀa-ni-viču-q* 'I want to make him work.'
I him work-make-want-TNS

The tense marker *-q* is a grounding predication. Within the complex stem *ˀowoˀa-ni-viču* 'want to make work', *ˀowoˀa* is a complement of *-ni*, and *ˀowoˀa-ni* a complement of *-viču*. Neither complement is considered to be a clause even though it designates a process (and could stand alone as a clausal head). We can instead describe *ˀowoˀa*, *ˀowoˀa-ni*, and *ˀowoˀa-ni-viču* as representing progressively more elaborate type specifications. It is only the complex stem *ˀowoˀa-ni-viču*, taken as a whole, that undergoes instantiation, is capable of being grounded, and has its focal participants specified by subject and object nominals.

If complements like *ˀowoˀa* and *ˀowoˀa-ni* are only minimally clause-like from the standpoint of structural elaboration and semantic function, they do resemble full clauses in having a processual profile. They contrast in this regard with a complement formed by nominalization, as in *The powder causes **itching***, which profiles a thing despite its verbal source.[4] To be sure, even nominal structures are clause-like to varying degrees. Thus *itching* is clausal at least in comparison to a noun like *acne*, which does not derive from a verb at all. More strikingly, the subject complements in (13) are progressively more clause-like owing to the functional and structural elaboration of the structure that undergoes the nominalization (1.2.1.2).

(13)(a) ***Zelda's reluctant [$_N$signing$_N$] of the contract** surprised the entire crew.*
(b) ***Zelda's [$_N$reluctantly signing the contract$_N$]** surprised the entire crew.*
(c) ***[$_N$That Zelda reluctantly signed the contract$_N$]** surprised the entire crew.*

[4] Any such assessment pertains to a particular level of organization: whereas at one level *itch* is a verbal complement of *-ing*, at a higher level *cause* takes *itching* as a nominal complement. (Cf. fn. 2.)

In (a) the verb stem *sign* alone undergoes the nominalization; as with *itching*, the nominalized structure subsumes only a type specification. One can argue that the complement in (a) is more clause-like than *itching*, in the sense that *Zelda's*, *reluctant*, and *of the contract* make explicit the same notions that a full clause would specify by means of a subject, adverb, and direct object (1.2.2). These are nevertheless noun modifiers, the subject in (a) being structurally parallel to an ordinary nominal (cf. *Sally's cozy cabin in Colorado*). By contrast, (b)'s subject has for its head noun the gerundive nominalization *reluctantly signing the contract*. Here the structure that undergoes the nominalization (*reluctantly sign the contract*) is semi-clausal, lacking only a subject (specified periphrastically by *Zelda's*) and a grounding predication. Finally, the subject in (c) represents the nominalization of a complete finite clause. Janus-faced, it is fully clausal internally while offering the visage of an abstract noun for purposes of elaborating the main-clause trajector.

In terms of profiling, nominalization represents the greatest departure from the processual nature of a verb or a clause. There are intermediate possibilities, the full sequence being *process* > *complex atemporal relation* > *simple atemporal relation* > *thing*. The minimal deviation from a process, namely a complex atemporal relation, is non-processual only in mode of scanning (summary as opposed to sequential); a simple atemporal relation further restricts the profile to a single component state; whereas a nominalization does not profile any kind of relationship but rather a thing. Holding all other factors constant, a subordinate structure is therefore less clause-like the farther it lies along this path. In some of their uses, for example, *to* and *-ing* suspend sequential scanning to derive a complex atemporal relation:

(14)(a) *I would like him* ***to receive another prestigious award.***
(b) *I can see him* ***receiving another prestigious award.***

But in (15) the possessive form *his* indicates that the following structure is nominalized, hence a bit less clause-like:

(15) *I really resent* ***his receiving another prestigious award.***

Consider also the contrast between ***burning*** *logs* and ***burnt*** *toast*. The active participle *burning* is a complex relation, hence verb-like to some degree, while *burnt* is considered adjectival because it profiles only a single, resultant state.

10.1.2. *Connectors*

A second factor figuring in the characterization of multiclausal constructions is the occurrence of special markings that indicate the nature of the interclausal connections. The elements in question are those traditionally referred to by such terms as *subordinator*, *conjunction*, and *subordinating con-*

junction. So as not to prejudge their analysis (which is very much at issue), let us adopt for them the neutral term **connector**.

The formation of a complex sentence does not invariably require a connector. There are relative and complement clauses in English that have no special marking (*the bench* ***she painted***; *I know* ***she painted it***). It is also not uncommon across languages for coordination to be effected by simple juxtaposition (in the style of *I came, I saw, I conquered*). When a connector does occur, it is typically either clause-initial (e.g. *and*; *while*; *because*; *that*) or attached to the verb (*-ing*). Our main concern here is to distinguish two broad classes of connectors on the basis of their meanings.

The following examples raise the central issue:

(16)(a) ***Working in the garden,*** *Janet found a lizard.*
(b) ***While she was working in the garden,*** *Janet found a lizard.*
(c) ***While working in the garden,*** *Janet found a lizard.*

Each is a complex sentence with a preposed adverbial clause. In (16)(a), the participial morpheme *-ing* is generally attributed a subordinating function. On the other hand, *while* is clearly the connector in (b); the *-ing* that occurs on *work* is part of the progressive auxiliary construction (*be . . . -ing*). How do we then describe the construction in (c)? In particular, is *-ing* a connector, as in (a), or a progressive marker, as in (b)? Either option seems problematic. The first implies the co-occurrence of two connectors, *while* and *-ing*. Is that possible? The second option requires that *-ing* be analyzed as progressive despite the absence of *be*. But if that is reasonable, why should the *-ing* in (a) not also be analyzed as progressive?

The key to the matter lies in the semantic characterization of the elements concerned. *While* instantiates a class of connectors that saliently and specifically make internal reference to two clause-like structures as an essential aspect of their meaning. *While* itself profiles a relationship of temporal inclusion between two schematic events or situations, one (its landmark) being elaborated by a finite or participial subordinate clause, and the other (its trajector) by the main clause. Like other connectors in this class (*when, before, after, because, since, if,* etc.), it is a stative relation that designates the very nature of the connection between the clauses it associates. By contrast, *-ing* instantiates a class of elements (also including *to, that,* and the past participial morpheme) that make salient reference only to a single schematic process as part of their own internal structure. Their basic effect is to atemporalize or nominalize the processual predication that elaborates them. They do not specifically refer to an interclausal relationship. Though usually regarded as subordinators, the sense in which they serve as connectors is weak and indirect: because the elaborating structure is rendered non-processual, it cannot be grounded to form an independent finite clause; for non-elliptic use it must

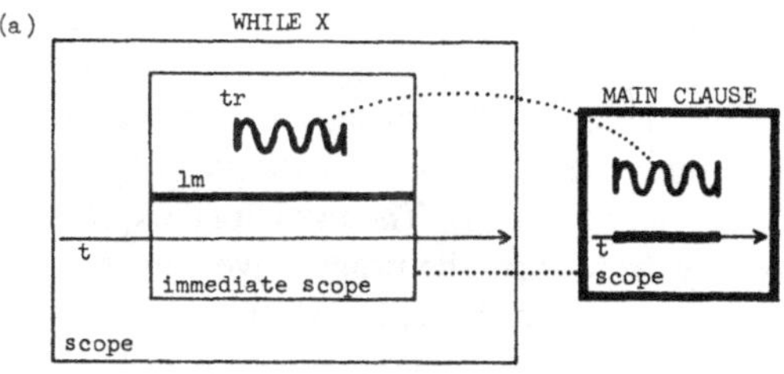

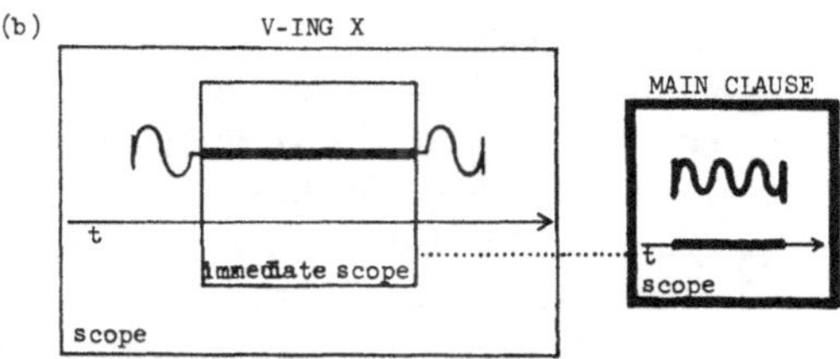

Fig. 10.1

therefore be incorporated in a larger structure for which such grounding is possible.

While is thus a true, explicit connector, whereas *-ing* is basically an atemporalizer deriving non-processual structures suitable for subordinate use. There is no conflict in these functions, hence the two kinds of connectors can co-occur if they are otherwise semantically compatible. The meanings of *while* and *-ing* are not only compatible but dovetail rather neatly. *While* is a stative relation that designates the temporal inclusion of its trajector (a process) within its landmark (a complex relation, either processual or atemporal). As shown on the left in Fig. 10.1(a), the landmark's projection in the domain of conceived time can be thought of as imposing on the trajector an *immediate scope of predication* that must include the trajector's temporal profile.[5] Diagram (a) represents the integration of the main and adverbial clauses in sentences following the pattern of (16)(b). The adverb is actually a stative relation in which a finite clause instantiates the landmark of *while* (cf. fn. 2). At the level of organization that concerns us, the main clause elaborates the adverb's trajector, as indicated by the upper correspondence line. The other correspondence is the construction-level manifestation of *while*'s essential property, namely that the landmark's extension defines the trajector's temporal scope.

Our descriptive and theoretical framework has the virtue of letting us attribute precisely the same meaning to all three occurrences of *-ing* in (16). The

[5]This need not be *proper* inclusion: the temporal profile of an imperfective trajector coincides with that of the landmark (e.g. *Janet was happy* ***while she worked in the garden***).

progressive *-ing* of (16)(b) was previously described as having the value depicted on the left in Fig. 10.1(b): taking a perfective process as its base, it suspends sequential scanning and imposes an immediate scope of predication comprising a representative series of internal states construed as homogeneous (see 5.2.2, especially Fig. 5.5). The participial expression so derived may be retemporalized by *be* to form the progressive construction, but it can also stand alone as a temporal adverb, as in (16)(a). Unlike *while*, the participialized clause does not profile a stative relation, nor does the main clause elaborate its trajector. Instead, as seen in diagram (b), its integration with the main clause hinges on a correspondence that equates the latter's overall temporal scope with its own immediate scope.[6]

Comparison of diagrams (a) and (b) reveals the similarity between the two constructions: *while* and *-ing* each impose an immediate temporal scope of predication that comes to be identified with the main-clause scope. To be sure, this immediate scope is delimited by the *landmark* of *while*, and by the *profile* of *-ing*, but that difference does not amount to an incompatibility, as we see from the co-occurrence of *while* and *-ing* in (16)(c). This last construction is quite straightforward: it is simply a matter of using a participial clause to elaborate *while*'s landmark. Since the landmark of *while* and the profile of *-ing* are thus identified, they define the same immediate scope, which is subsequently equated with the main-clause scope at the highest level of organization (just as in the other two constructions).

Even considered as general types, connectors show substantial diversity. The classes illustrated by *while* and *-ing* are but two of the types encountered cross-linguistically, and actually lie at opposite extremes with respect to the full array of options. *While*-type connectors render their connecting function maximally salient and explicit: they go so far as to *profile* the interclausal relationship (e.g. temporal inclusion) and thereby specify its nature periphrastically. Consequently they are best suited for adverbial clauses (since by definition a complement or relative clause relates to the main clause in a particular way—i.e. as an argument or noun modifier). By contrast, the connecting function of *-ing* is at best an indirect reflection of its meaning. Though *-ing* does figure in certain multiclausal constructions (e.g. Fig. 10.1(b)), internally it refers to just one clause-like entity, namely the process it atemporalizes. It is thus free to occur in many different kinds of subordinate structures, and can even combine with *be* to form a clausal head.

Connectors of another sort are intermediate in the salience accorded their connecting function. These can be exemplified from Hopi, where they appear as suffixes on the subordinate-clause verb (Kalectaca 1978):

(17)(a)	***ni***ˀ ***paki-t***	*pi*ˀ	*qatɨvtɨ*	'After entering, I sat down.'
	I enter-after	then	sit:down	

[6] A second correspondence (not shown) equates the two trajectors.

(b) ***pam nanan-kʸaŋ*** *coˀomti* 'While laughing, he jumped.'
he laugh:DUR-while jump

(c) ***niˀ pɨt tɨw-eˀniˀ*** *waaya-ni* 'If I see him, I'll run away.'
I him see-if I run:away-FUT

Despite their translational equivalence, one cannot assume that Hopi *-t*, *-kʸaŋ*, and *-eˀ* are precisely the same as English *after*, *while*, and *if*. The fact that the Hopi connectors attach directly to the verb, and more significantly, that they preclude its grounding, suggests that they might better be analyzed as atemporalizing predications (similar in that respect to *-ing* and *to*).[7] At the same time, they clearly resemble their English counterparts in referring specifically to the relationship between two events or situations as a central aspect of their meaning. The most promising analysis is thus to describe them as atemporalizing elements that nonetheless specify the connection between two processes as a salient though unprofiled facet of their base.

On this account, Hopi *-t* evokes as its base the conception of two events occurring in temporal sequence, and profiles the first of these events under an atemporal construal (i.e. with summary scanning), as shown on the left in Fig. 10.2. The overall diagram represents a higher level of organization, at

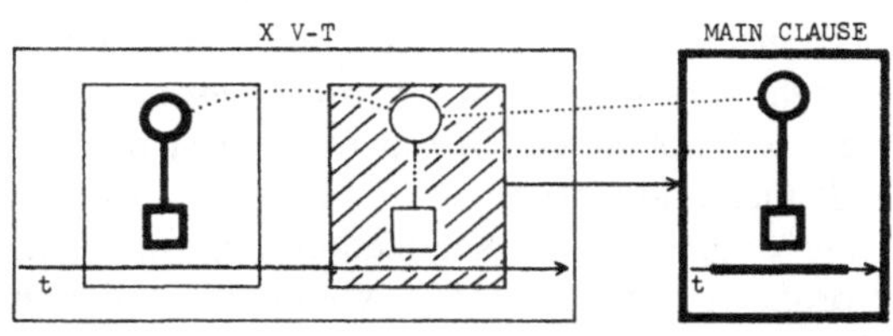

Fig. 10.2

which the adverbial clause marked by *-t* is integrated with the main clause. This is primarily a matter of the main clause elaborating the schematic, unprofiled process evoked by *-t*.

The construction does however have another essential facet to it: all the connectors in (17) specify that the two associated processes have the same trajector. This identity is indicated in Fig. 10.2 by the correspondence line internal to the first component structure, and is reflected at the construction level by the upper of the two correspondences shown. Compare the respective examples in (17) to those in (18), where the two clauses in each case have different subjects:

(18)(a) ***niˀ paki-q*** *pɨˀ pam qatɨvtɨ* 'After I entered, he sat down.'
I enter-DS then he sit:down

[7] Some of the periphrastic connectors of English also function as prepositions (e.g. *I'll work on it **after** lunch*), which reinforces their analysis as preposition-like stative relations. The Hopi endings in question are unrelated to any of the postpositions in that language.

(b) ***nɨʔ nanan-q*** *pam coʔomti* 'While I was laughing, he jumped.'
I laugh:DUR-DS he jump

(c) ***pam nɨy tɨwa-q*** *piʔ nɨʔ waaya-ni* 'If he sees me, I'll run away.'
he me see-DS then I run:away-FUT

Hopi uses the suffix *-q* as an alternative to all the "same-subject" adverbial connectors. It specifically indicates that the two clausal trajectors are *not* the same (hence the gloss DS, for "different subject"). Like its same-subject counterparts, *-q* can be analyzed as referring internally to two events or situations and profiling one of them under an atemporal construal. Yet, because it alternates with them all, *-q* differs from *-t*, *-kʸaŋ*, *-eʔ*, etc. in that the nature of the interclausal relationship is left schematic—it specifies only that the two processes have different trajectors, and is neutral as to whether they are simultaneous, occur in sequence, or are related in some other fashion. Connectors like these which indicate the sameness or difference of clausal subjects are not at all unusual in the world's languages (cf. Haiman and Munro 1983).

To summarize, we have seen that some connectors actually profile the interclausal relationship, whereas others evoke it (in either specific or schematic terms) as an unprofiled facet of their base, and still others make salient internal reference to just a single event or situation. Since we have focused thus far on elements traditionally considered either subordinators or subordinating conjunctions, one might very well ask where true, *coordinating* conjunctions fit into this scheme. I will not pretend that there is any sharp distinction between conjunctions and other kinds of connectors. Rather, I suggest that the elements regarded as "true" or prototypical conjunctions represent a limiting case with respect to both profiling and the nature of the interclausal relationship.

Connectors like *after*, *while*, and *if* are depicted abstractly in Fig. 10.3(a). Within these predications, the interclausal relationship is not only highly prominent (being profiled) but also fairly contentful, involving such objectively construed notions as temporal anteriority, temporal inclusion, and conditionality. Represented in diagram (b) are elements like Hopi *-t*, *-kʸaŋ*, and

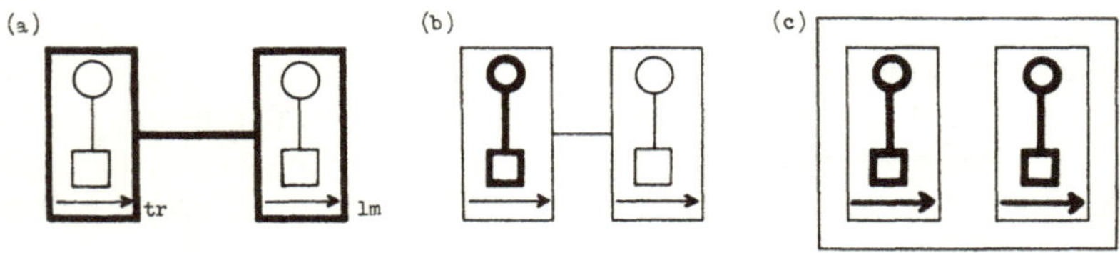

Fig. 10.3

-eʔ. Although they include a comparable connecting relationship in their base, it is one of the events or situations participating in this relationship that is rendered salient by profiling. A connector of this sort thus confers less prominence on the connecting relationship itself than on one of its partici-

pants. We can view a prototypical conjunction as carrying this difference to the extreme: as shown in diagram (c), any semblance of an objective connecting relationship fades from the picture entirely, and each component process is separately profiled as such.

Even among subordinators, connecting relationships vary considerably in their contentfulness and objectivity. The temporal relations expressed by *after* and *while* have a firmer objective basis than *if*, *although*, and *whereas*, which are more dependent on how the speaker assesses contingencies. We have noted that *while* not only has a temporal reading expressing the objective simultaneity of two events, but also a "concessive" value in which the speaker, subjectively, is simultaneously willing to entertain each of two attitudes or propositions (e.g. *While he's rich, he's also quite obnoxious*). A "pure" conjunction can be characterized as one that retains no vestige of any objective connecting relationship and at best a minimal subjective relationship.[8] Stripped to the bare minimum, an *and*-type conjunction merely indicates the mental juxtaposition of two co-equal conceptions (their co-equality reflecting the *absence* of any conceived relationship that would impose an asymmetry). More subtle (and less common cross-linguistically) are *or*-type conjunctions: these also involve the co-equality of two conceptions, but the conceptualizer does a mental flip-flop, alternating between them rather than merging them into a single gestalt.

This co-equality is reflected in the dual, "separate-but-equal" profiles of a coordinate expression (Fig. 10.3(c)). In the context of a larger construction, the two profiles participate in parallel sets of correspondences and relationships with other elements—i.e. for some portion of the overall conception, the conceptualizer establishes parallel structures as either co-existing or alternative options. There is no inherent reason why mental juxtaposition or alternation of this sort should be limited to clauses, so it comes as no surprise that coordination occurs at virtually any level of organization. Furthermore, in the absence of any contentful connecting relationship there is no intrinsic reason why the number of parallel structures should be restricted to just two: three or more co-equal structures can perfectly well be juxtaposed or considered alternatively. Accordingly, a single conjunction often associates a potentially unlimited number of conjuncts (e.g. *the law firm of Graves, Tombs, Pitts, Paul, . . . , Flowers, Stone, and Coffin*).

10.1.3. *Referential Linkage*

We have thus far considered two factors in the characterization of multiclausal constructions: how closely the components approximate full, finite

[8]This ideal may seldom be realized, for in actual usage even the "purest" of conjunctions tends to pick up pragmatically induced interpretations involving temporal sequence, causation, etc.

clauses; and the connectors that indicate the nature of their association. Let us turn now to a third factor, namely correspondences involving the component clauses or their substructures. Correspondences establish *referential linkages*, in the sense that they indicate which entities within the component conceptions are construed as being identical. It is through the superimposition of such entities that the components merge to form a coherent overall conception.

In many constructions the pivotal correspondence involves the clausal profile, i.e. the process designated by the clause as a whole (often under an atemporal or even a nominal construal). One such example is that of a main clause elaborating the schematic trajector of a *while*-adverbial (e.g. *She whistled* ***while I worked***). As shown in Fig. 10.1(a), their integration depends on a correspondence between the adverb's trajector and the main-clause processual profile. Providing further illustration is a coordinate structure such as ***The Cubs won*** *and* ***the Padres lost***. Recall that *and* evokes—and separately profiles—two or more schematic conjuncts, in this case processes (Fig. 10.3(c)). Each clause elaborates one such conjunct by virtue of a correspondence between its own processual profile and that of its e-site. With complement clauses, moreover, a correspondence involving the clausal profile is present as a matter of definition. Thus, in *She hopes* ***to graduate next June***, the landmark of *hope* is equated with the atemporally construed process designated by the infinitival clause.

Referential linkage can also be established through entities other than the clausal profile; often these are salient participants in the profiled relationship. We find exemplification in a typical relative clause construction, such as *The skirt* ***she bought*** *was too tight*. Here the integration pivots on a correspondence between the primary landmark of *bought* and the profile of *skirt*, itself identified (at a higher level of organization) with the main-clause trajector. It is not essential, however, that the corresponding entities be prominent or singled out for individual mention. Consider the sentence ***Alarms ringing,*** *the burglar fled*, which instantiates the construction diagrammed in Fig. 10.1(b). The only correspondence of note is between two stretches of conceived time: the immediate scope of *ringing* (i.e. the temporal projection of its profile); and the overall scope of *fled* (which includes its temporal profile). When two clauses are integrated by means of just a single correspondence between abstract, non-salient entities, they are naturally felt to be only loosely associated.[9]

Clause linkage can either be direct or mediated by a pronominal element.

[9]Because neither clause elaborates a salient substructure of the other, they do not (strictly speaking) participate in either a *complement* or a *modifier* relationship. The term **adjunct** is commonly applied in such cases.

Instructive in this regard is the following example from Classical Nahuatl (Andrews 1975, p. 317), to be compared with its English translation:[10]

(19) *a^{ʔ}moo ƛaakateek^{w}ƛi onkaan kiisa* ***ii-pampa in a^{ʔ}moo senka^{ʔ} k^{w}alli***
NEG lord there leave it-on:behalf ART NEG very good
in iin-nemilis teelpoopoočtin
ART their-life youths
'No lord comes out of there, because the way of life of the youths is not very good.'

In both the Nahuatl and the English expressions, the connector (*pampa*; *because*) is a relational predication whose trajector is directly elaborated by the main clause (just as in the case of *while*—cf. Fig. 10.1(a)). The two languages however employ rather different constructions to elaborate the connector's landmark. With *because*, the landmark undergoes direct elaboration by a finite clause (*the way of life of the youths is not very good*). By contrast, *pampa* takes a pronominal object: *ii-pampa* is capable of standing alone as an adverbial modifier roughly translatable as 'on his behalf' or 'because of it'. The interclausal relationship is then established indirectly, through a correspondence equating the profile of the pronoun *ii* with that of the finite clause *in a^{ʔ}moo senka^{ʔ} k^{w}alli iinnemilis teelpoopoočtin* (perhaps under a nominal construal).

The distinction between direct and indirect elaboration can also be observed in cases where clause linkage is established via relational participants. Linkage mediated by a pronoun is especially prevalent in relative clause constructions, sometimes involving a special, **relative pronoun** such as *who* or *which*. We have seen that English has a number of constructions in which the head noun directly elaborates a salient participant of either a finite or a nonfinite relative clause (*the skirt* ***she bought***; *the girl* ***sitting on that bench***; *the first girl* ***to sit on that bench***; *the person* ***to discuss the matter with***). Relative pronouns, on the other hand, are limited to finite clauses: *the skirt* ***which she bought***; *the girl* ***who sat on that bench***; *the bench* ***which she sat on***; *the woman* ***whose friend's doctor told me to quit smoking***. Whatever its role within the clause—subject, direct object, prepositional object, possessor—the pronoun instantiates a relational participant at some level of organization. Its correspondence with the head noun thus establishes a link between the relative clause and the clause in which the head itself participates.

Certain contrasts noted earlier are describable in terms of referential linkage. Consider first the examples in (7), *She told a funny story(,)* ***which greatly amused me***. Depending on the presence or absence of a pause (indi-

[10]The sound [ƛ] is a voiceless lateral affricate. Except for pronominal prefixes, word-internal morpheme boundaries are ignored. It is not essential for the point at issue whether *pampa* is analyzed as a postposition or as a relational noun; the former is assumed for expository purposes.

cated orthographically by the comma), there are three possible interpretations. In all three constructions the second clause has precisely the same internal structure; in particular, the pronoun *which* instantiates the clausal trajector. The constructions are further alike in that *which* in each case corresponds to the profile of the constituent that the *which*-clause combines with. What distinguishes the three constructions is the nature of that constituent.

When (7) is uttered without a pause, the *which*-clause is interpreted as a restrictive relative, i.e. one that restricts the head noun's type specification. The clause combines with *funny story* to derive the complex noun *funny story which greatly amused me*. This noun is then grounded by *a*, yielding a nominal that elaborates the landmark of *tell* at a higher level of organization. When uttered with a pause, (7) has two possible interpretations. The second clause may represent a non-restrictive relative, in which case it does not combine with just *funny story*, but with the full, grounded nominal *a funny story*. The *which*-clause is thus external to the nominal and does not contribute to its type specification. However, since *funny story* and *a funny story* have the same profile, *which* corresponds to the same entity on both the restrictive and non-restrictive readings. The other interpretation results when the *which*-clause combines with the main clause as a whole (instead of with a nominal element). The referent of *which* is therefore not the story, but the full, grounded event conception coded by the initial finite clause.[11]

The ambiguity of (6), *The fact **that she forgot** is unimportant*, can also be explicated in terms of referential linkage. On the relative clause interpretation, the head noun *fact* directly elaborates *that she forgot* by virtue of a correspondence between the former's profile and the latter's primary landmark. On the other interpretation the object of *forget* remains unspecified—she did not forget the fact, but something else, and that she forgot is what *constitutes* the fact. Central to this second construction is a correspondence between the profiles of two full nominals, *the fact* and *that she forgot* (the nominalization of a finite clause). The construction thus represents a kind of apposition: two nominals that designate the same conceived entity but describe it in different ways combine to form a higher-order, doubly-grounded nominal with the same profile. Despite the formal similarity, this is not a relative clause construction, because *the fact* corresponds to the following clause as a whole (a reified proposition) rather than just a processual participant. And despite the formal *dis*similarity, it resembles an ordinary complement clause construction in that a process (with nominal construal) functions as a participant of the main clause (cf. ***That she forgot** is unimportant*).

[11] The main clause has a processual profile, but for purposes of clause linkage the subject pronoun *which* imposes a nominal construal on the same event. This type of discrepancy between a pronoun and its linguistic antecedent is attested in other kinds of anaphoric reference (e.g. *She has nobody to care for her—it's very tragic*). See Gensler 1977 for examples and discussion.

Such examples make it apparent that form per se is less essential to characterizing the traditional categories than are certain conceptual factors, such as profiling, correspondences, and semantic function. We have seen, for instance, that both relative and complement clauses can occur either with a head, as in (6), or without one (e.g. ***What he stole** is worth a fortune* vs. ***What he stole** is a mystery*). The common feature of relative and complement clause constructions is that a main-clause participant is in each case coded by a constituent which either consists of or prominently includes a clause-like structure. The ultimate basis for distinguishing between relative and complement clauses is a semantic factor, namely correspondence: whether the main-clause element in question corresponds to a *participant* of the subordinate clause, or to the *overall process* designated by that clause.[12]

From this perspective, there is nothing strange or problematic about the phenomenon referred to as "headless" or "internally headed" relative clauses (Gorbet 1976, 1977; Cole 1987). Consider the following Diegueño example:[13]

(20) ***tənay ˀwaa ˀ-wuuw**-pu-L^y ˀ-čiyaw-x*
yesterday house I-see-DEM-in I-sing-IRR
'I'll sing in the house I saw yesterday.'

The construction is at first quite puzzling to the Eurocentric analyst: it is clearly the house that is understood to be the landmark of the postposition -L^y and the entity grounded by the demonstrative *-pu*; formally, though, it appears that the sequence *-pu-*L^y does not combine with the noun *ˀwaa* 'house', but rather with the entire subordinate clause (attaching as suffixes to the final word of that clause—cf. Vol. 1, 9.3.2). The absence of a head noun external to the clause makes it look like an instance of complementation instead of relativization.

There is however another way to look at it. The essential feature of relativization is not an external head noun but a particular kind of clause linkage based on correspondence: the same conceived entity (in the case of (20), the house) figures simultaneously in the situations described by both component clauses. Now if either clause were to occur independently, that entity would be coded by an overt noun: *tənay ˀwaa ˀ-wuu* 'I saw the house yesterday'; *ˀwaa-pu-*L^y *ˀ-čiyaw-x* 'I'll sing in the house'. Consequently there are two basic options for avoiding redundancy when component clauses describing these situations combine to form a complex sentence. On the one hand, the pivotal entity can be coded by a main-clause noun and left unexpressed (or

[12]This process may of course undergo nominalization or atemporalization in either type of construction, as described in 10.1.1.

[13]Diegueño is a Yuman language spoken in southern and Baja California (data from Gorbet 1977, p. 270). The symbol [L^y] represents a palatalized voiceless lateral, and futurity is one interpretation of the irrealis marker (IRR).

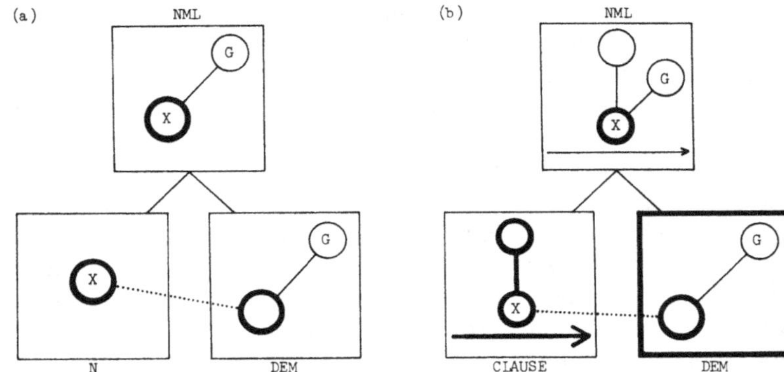

Fig. 10.4

expressed by just a pronoun) in the subordinate clause. In English, for example, the main clause has the same form as a full, independent sentence (*I'll sing in the house*), whereas the subordinate clause lacks an overt object (*I saw yesterday*). On the other hand, the pivot might receive overt expression in the subordinate clause and remain implicit in the main clause. The Diegueño construction embraces this second option. It is thus the subordinate clause (*tənay ʔwaa ʔ-wuu*) that enjoys the full elaboration characteristic of an independent sentence.

How does this work, precisely? How does the integration of a finite clause with a demonstrative add up to a relative clause construction? Consider first the usual N + DEM pattern, diagrammed in Fig. 10.4(a). The noun designates a thing and evokes specific conceptual content (abbreviated X). The demonstrative also profiles a thing, but apart from the relation it bears to the ground (G) its characterization is schematic (recall that a grounding predication profiles the *grounded entity* rather than the *grounding relationship*). The two profiles correspond, so the composite structure designates a grounded thing with specific properties. An example is *ʔwaa-pu* 'the house'.

How, then, can a demonstrative combine with a finite clause such as *tənay ʔwaa ʔ-wuu* 'I saw the house yesterday' to form a nominal that designates the house? There are two possibilities.[14] We might analyze the clause as undergoing an extension or zero derivation whereby the profile is shifted from the process itself to one of its participants (the house in our example); in that case

[14] The difference between them is more apparent than real in the present framework. It comes down to whether the shift from a processual to a nominal profile *allows* integration with the demonstrative or is *induced* by it. The point may be moot, for the shift depends on the clause occurring in this particular construction, which involves the same basic structures and correspondences under either analysis.

the noun so derived combines with the demonstrative in accordance with the regular pattern. Alternatively, we can posit a variant construction in which the demonstrative itself functions as a nominalizing predication. On this analysis the demonstrative combines directly with a clause by virtue of a correspondence between its profile and one of the clausal participants, as shown in Fig. 10.4(b). The demonstrative serves as profile determinant, hence the composite expression designates a grounded thing characterized both by intrinsic properties ('house') and its role in the clausal process. In cognitive grammar the description of this construction is straightforward and requires no special theoretical apparatus.

10.1.4. *Global Organization*

Let us now address a basic question postponed earlier: precisely what does it mean to say that a clause is *subordinate*? In neither traditional grammar nor in linguistics is there any clear understanding or general agreement as to what the term implies and subsumes. The reason, I believe, is that several distinct factors figure in grammarians' intuitive understanding of the notion. These factors delimit very different ranges of phenomena, but no one of them has emerged in the field's collective consciousness as the obvious candidate for a standard definition. Why not? Perhaps because the best candidate is based on an aspect of construal—profiling—that has been specifically recognized only in cognitive grammar.

One aspect of subordination is morphological: the use of non-finite verb morphology, in contrast to the finite (i.e. grounded) character of a main clause. The problem with defining subordination in this manner is that various kinds of clauses normally considered subordinate are finite nonetheless. Indeed, relative, complement, and adverbial clauses can all be grounded (cf. (2)). Understanding *subordinate* to mean *non-finite* or *ungrounded* thus fails to reflect the traditional breadth of the notion and is pointless given the availability of the latter terms. An alternative morphological approach might focus on the occurrence of a subordinator, such as *that*, *to*, or *while*. We have seen, however, that not every subordinate clause contains such an element (*the skirt* ***she bought***; *I know* ***she left***). This approach would also face the charge of circularity. How does one know which elements count as subordinators without a prior definition of subordination? For instance, what about *while*, traditionally called a *subordinating conjunction*?

A second aspect of our intuitive understanding of subordination is that one clause is "contained" inside another. Here the problem is to specify just what this notion of containment consists of. It cannot, for example, reside in one clause being flanked on both sides by phonological material representing another. Instead one clause must be an element of the other in some grammatical or semantic sense, irrespective of phonological placement.[15] The most obvious way to state this in cognitive grammar makes reference to *conceptual dependence*: D is conceptually dependent on A to the extent that A elaborates a salient substructure of D. In the case of two clauses, A could then be defined as *subordinate* to D. On this account complement clauses are prototypical instances of subordination; in *I know* ***she left***, for example, *she left* elaborates the landmark of *know*. For a relative clause to count as subordinate, the definition can be extended to encompass a clause functioning as one component of a larger structure that elaborates a main-clause element. Thus, in *The skirt* ***she bought*** *was too tight*, the relative is one component of the nominal *the skirt* ***she bought***, and this nominal—as a whole—elaborates the main-clause trajector. Adverbial clauses would not be considered subordinate by this definition, for if anything it is the main clause that serves an elaborative function: in *She whistled* ***while I worked***, for instance, *she whistled* elaborates the trajector of *while*.[16] Also, a characterization of this sort would not apply in the case of *adjuncts*, as in ***Alarms ringing***, *the burglar fled*, where neither clause elaborates a salient substructure of the other (Fig. 10.1(b)).

Although this characterization does correspond to one standard use of the term, a *subordinate clause* can also be understood more broadly as one that is not a main clause; adverbial clauses and adjuncts are thus included. Is there, then, something that all such clauses have in common that sets them apart from main clauses? I suggest that there is, and that the distinction rests on profiling. Specifically, a **main clause** is the *head* at a particular level of organization, i.e. the clause that lends its profile to the composite structure of a multiclausal expression. A **subordinate clause** is then describable as one whose profile is overridden by that of a main clause. This way of characterizing the traditional notions is flexible (as it has to be) by virtue of not being tied to any particular structural configuration. At the same time, it captures the intuition that one clause is somehow *subordinated* to the other.

Let us see how this works. In a typical complement clause construction, the two clauses combine directly and the main clause is clearly the profile determinant: *I know* ***she left*** designates the process of knowing, not of leaving. The main clause is likewise the head in its combination with an adjunct; at the composite structure level, ***Alarms ringing***, *the burglar fled* profiles the act of fleeing. In the case of relatives, e.g. *The skirt* ***she bought*** *was too tight*, integration with the main clause is usually indirect—*she bought* first combines with the head noun *skirt*, and the full subject nominal elaborates

[15] In generative grammar, it is a matter of one S-node dominating another in a syntactic phrase tree. However, phrase trees as such are artifactual (Vol. 1, 9.1.2), and the basis for positing a particular tree configuration is often obscure (especially in regard to adverbial clauses).

[16] The consequence of *she whistled* being classed as subordinate can be avoided by recognizing that *while* is external to the clause *I worked*. (See fn. 2.)

the main-clause trajector at a higher level of organization. Still, the relative clause's processual profile is overridden even at the lowest level (*skirt* ***she bought*** designates the skirt), and that of the main clause prevails for the sentence overall. The connection may also be indirect in the case of adverbial clauses, as in *She whistled* ***while I worked***. At the first level that concerns us, *while* is the head and imposes its profile when *I worked* elaborates its landmark (hence *I worked* is a complement of *while*). The composite structure is thus a stative relation, whose trajector is then elaborated by *she whistled* at the next level of constituency. Since the elaborating structure functions as profile determinant at this level, the sentence as a whole designates an act of whistling, and *while I worked* is an adverbial modifier.

Besides accommodating the diverse constructions considered instances of subordination (broadly construed), the proposed characterization correctly excludes prototypical cases of coordination, e.g. ***The Cubs won*** *and* ***the Padres lost***. The reason, quite simply, is that neither clausal profile overrides the other; the distinguishing feature of "pure" coordination is the separate and equal profiling of each conjunct (Fig. 10.3(c)). Thus, instead of standing in a main-clause/subordinate-clause relationship, the conjuncts each have legitimate claim to main-clause status. Bear in mind, however, that profiling—as one kind of prominence—is potentially a matter of degree. Strict coordination can therefore be seen as a limiting case, where disparity in the prominence accorded the component clauses dwindles to zero. We can thus envisage expressions with intermediate or indeterminate status. Intuitively, for example, a *while*-clause feels less like a subordinate structure and more like a conjunct to the extent that *while* sheds its temporal value in favor of its more abstract, "concessive" interpretation (cf. (1) and (3)).

The main-clause/subordinate-clause distinction can be made on either a local or a global basis. In local terms, it holds between two clauses within the minimal structure that subsumes them both. What is locally a main clause at one level of constituency may of course be subordinate at a higher level; for instance, *I know* is the main clause within *I know* ***she left***, yet this entire structure is subordinate to *they believe* in the more complex expression *They believe* ***I know she left***. In global terms, a main clause can be characterized as one whose profile prevails at the level of an entire sentence. Barring coordination, there is generally only one such clause in any sentence of English.[17] Consider (21), for example.

(21) ***Even before she tried it on to see if it would fit,*** *she knew* ***that the skirt she bought was too tight.***

[17] Possible exceptions include cases of direct quotation (e.g. *Fred replied: "That's a lie!"*) and parenthetical insertion (*Her husband decided—you'll never believe this—that he was going to have a sex-change operation!*).

Locally, there are several main clauses: *to see* (in relation to *if it would fit*); *she tried it on* (vis-à-vis *to see if it would fit*); *the skirt was too tight* (in relation to *she bought*); and *she knew* (with respect to *that the skirt she bought was too tight*). Globally, however, only the last is a main clause—as a whole, sentence (21) designates a process of knowing.

At the risk of caricature, we can say that English makes extensive use of complex sentences, often involving multiple levels of subordination; that the component clauses are readily delimited, each containing a single content verb; that locally the components of a multiclausal construction show a pronounced main-/subordinate-clause asymmetry (based on profile determinance); and that globally a single clause stands out as having main-clause status. This is not the only possible scheme (even for English), and in other languages alternate patterns predominate. For instance, what English says in several clauses, another language might code in just one clause headed by a polymorphemic content verb whose internal organization mirrors that of a complex sentence. Recall example (12): Luiseño *noo poy ʔowoʔa-ni-viču-q* (I him work-make-want-TNS) 'I want to make him work'. Another option, called **parataxis**, is the avoidance of complex sentences in favor of single-clause expressions loosely strung together, none obviously subordinate to any other (cf. Givón 1979; Du Bois 1987). Finally, many languages make extensive use of **serial verb constructions**, whose instantiation in English is limited to such expressions as *go eat* and *come look*. Although serial verb constructions constitute a heterogeneous class, a recurrent feature is the inclusion within a single clause of two or more content verbs seemingly of equal status. In the English construction, the two verbs represent successive temporal phases of what is construed to be one overall event. They join to form a composite verb that functions as a clausal head (5.1).[18]

10.2. Complementation

Complement clause constructions have been a prominent topic of concern in generative grammar since the publication of Rosenbaum 1967. The large number of descriptive and theoretical issues that arise, together with the vastness of the literature thus engendered, make it necessary that our own treatment be highly selective. Let us therefore concentrate on two central problems: the markings that occur with complement clauses; and the phenomena that in classic transformational analyses were handled by means of "raising" rules.

[18] Thus *go eat* profiles a single process comprising two separately-coded phases, whereas the coordinate expression *go and eat* has two processual profiles (Fig. 10.3(c)). (The distinction can however be blurred—see 11.2.3.) In *go to eat*, only *go* is profiled, *to eat* being subordinate.

10.2.1. *Complementizers*

Although they are not limited to complement clauses, the markers that accompany such clauses are generally referred to as **complementizers**. The term is due to Rosenbaum, who—in the spirit of the times—analyzed them as semantically empty formatives inserted transformationally. The subsequent trend has been toward recognizing, if not their meaningfulness, at least the relevance of semantic factors in determining their distribution (e.g. Bresnan 1970; Kiparsky and Kiparsky 1970; Spears 1973; Kirsner and Thompson 1976; Dirven 1989). The most extensive effort at actually describing their meanings explicitly has been made by Wierzbicka (1988, ch. 1). Despite a rather different approach to semantic description, her analyses are roughly compatible with the ones sketched below. We will focus on basic meanings and representative uses of the complementizers, not attempting a broad survey comparable to Wierzbicka's of the values they assume across a wide variety of constructions and subconstructions.

The markings to be considered are *that*, *to*, *-ing*, and zero.[19] All are possible with object-complement clauses (i.e. those which elaborate a main-clause landmark), and all but zero are possible with subject-complement clauses (which elaborate the main-clause trajector):

(22)(a) *We realize* ***that you have to make a profit.***
(b) *His wife only pretended* ***to believe his implausible story.***
(c) *Portia really enjoys* ***walking along the beach.***
(d) *Numerous witnesses heard the bomb* ***explode.***

(23)(a) ***That prices will rise sharply*** *is all but certain.*
(b) ***To acknowledge her failure*** *was very difficult for Gwendolyn.*
(c) ***Having worked for the newspaper*** *gives Evelyn a great deal of pride.*

Each element occurs in other constructions (e.g. *that*, *to*, and *-ing* mark relative clauses), and each has multiple, related senses that in large measure determine its distribution. Factors that must figure in a full characterization of their meanings include semantic function, scanning, profiling, aspect, and perspective.

10.2.1.1. *Conceptual Subordination.*

A fully articulated finite clause subsumes the layered semantic functions of grounding, quantification, instantiation, and type specification: (G(Q(I(T)))). We saw previously that a subordi-

[19] We will not examine devices allowing periphrastic specification of the clausal subject (e.g. ***Zelda's leaving*** *was inexplicable*; ***For that to happen*** *would be catastrophic*); the *POSSESSIVE . . . -ing* combination was treated in 1.2.2, and Wierzbicka discusses the contrast between *to* and *for . . . to*. Also ignored are "subjunctive" *that*-clauses (*It's imperative* ***that you be here by noon***).

nate clause can represent an autonomous structure of any size with respect to this conceptual A/D layering (10.1.1). We may now observe that each complementizer combines with structures at a particular level of functional organization and thus makes schematic reference to such a structure as part of its own semantic characterization. Specifically, *that* requires the full configuration (G(Q(I(T)))); *to* and *-ing* attach to structures that are maximal apart from grounding, i.e. (Q(I(T))); while the zero-marked complements that concern us (as in (22)(d)) are limited to (I(T)). This itself has consequences for the occurrence of the complementizers in higher-order constructions. Because grounding locates an event in relation to the speaker's conception of reality, it is natural for *that*-clauses to occur with verbs of propositional attitude, such as *know, believe, think*, and *realize*. It is also natural that zero-marked complements occur with perception verbs like *see, hear*, and *feel*, for an instance of a physical process is something that can be perceived (whereas grounding per se cannot). When these latter verbs do take a *that*-clause complement, they are no longer understood as being strictly perceptual.[20]

By the very nature of a complement clause, the process it describes undergoes a kind of *conceptual subordination*: rather than being viewed in its own terms as an independent object of thought, it is primarily considered for the role it plays within the superordinate relationship expressed by the main clause. Viewing the subordinate process as a main-clause participant implies a conceptual distancing whereby this process is construed holistically and manipulated as a unitary entity. It therefore encourages *summary scanning* of the component states (*sequential*, state-by-state scanning being more compatible with a "close-up" view) if not their reification as an abstract region. For this reason complementizers are plausibly analyzed as imposing an atemporal, perhaps even a nominal construal on the structures they combine with. Whether they are merely atemporalizing predications or actual nominalizers is unclear (and may well be indeterminate).[21] However, we can at least say that each complementizer takes a clause some distance along the path leading from a processual to a nominal profile.

The atemporalizing character of *to*, *-ing*, and zero can also be seen as a consequence of the fact that they combine with ungrounded structures and are not themselves grounding predications. This follows from a general proposal concerning grounding and processual profiles. A grounding predication situates a profiled thing or process with reference to the ground, which of course

[20]That is, a sentence like *I {see/hear/feel}* ***that the situation is becoming difficult*** pertains primarily to cognition, communication, or judgment, and only secondarily (if at all) to sensory perception. See Newman 1981 for extensive discussion of related phenomena.

[21]Certainly *-ing* has nominalizing uses (cf. 1.2.1 and Fig. 1.4), and the demonstrative origin of *that* lends credence to its analysis as a nominalizer. I believe that a clausal subject always profiles a thing, but the nominalization of a subject-complement clause is not necessarily attributable to the complementizer itself.

is centered on the speech-act participants. I suggest that one should take quite seriously the notion of the ground being—in some real sense—the vantage point from which a linguistically coded scene is viewed. In particular, the circumstances of the speech event, together with the nature of the grounding relationship, can be thought of as defining a kind of **viewing frame** representing what is immediately accessible for focused observation. As the locus of viewing attention, this frame constitutes the *onstage region* (or *immediate scope of predication*) for the grounded structure. In the default-case situation the viewing frame is temporally delimited by the time of speaking, although the grounding predication may put it in some other location, e.g. past reality (cf. Fig. 6.3). The frame is likewise confined to known reality (Fig. 6.2(a)) unless some special factor (such as a modal) overrides this default to shift it elsewhere. But wherever it might be located, the viewing frame serves as a window on the situation described by a finite clause, and the clause's processual profile is by definition the focal point within the immediate scope thus defined.

Now suppose we make the reasonable assumption that this focal-point status is necessary for the state-by-state, sequential scanning characteristic of a process. Thus, although a number of verbs may figure in the composition of a finite clause, only the *grounded* process—the one designated by the clause as a whole—is scanned sequentially and retains its full processual nature. When a process that is profiled at one level of organization is superseded by another at a higher level, it receives an atemporal construal by the very fact of being pushed into the background and viewed at a greater conceptual distance in the shadow of the higher-level profile. In a multiverb clause such as *It had been being discussed*, it is therefore only *have*, which is grounded and profiled at the composite structure level, that fully manifests its verbal character. It so happens that backgrounding of the other verbs is explicitly marked in English by means of participial inflections, which also make semantic contributions pertaining to voice and aspect (5.2). However, atemporalization is inherent in the multiverb constructions and would not necessarily have to be signaled overtly or effected by special predications.

What is true for a single clause holds as well for the component clauses of a complex sentence. If just one of these clauses is grounded (hence finite), it is that one which functions as the main clause and imposes its processual profile on the overall expression. Because a complement clause marked by *to*, *-ing*, or zero is ungrounded, it supplies no viewing frame through which the speech-act participants can directly observe the described process in the close-up, focused manner required for sequential scanning. The subordinate process is backgrounded to the main-clause profile and viewed holistically both for that reason and also by virtue of being construed as a main-clause participant.

There is an additional way in which the notion of a viewing frame is relevant to the semantics of complementizers. In certain ways the relationship between a main clause and a complement clause is analogous to the one between the ground and the grounded structure. The analogy is strongest when the subject (or another main-clause participant) functions as conceptualizer with respect to the contents of the subordinate clause, e.g. with verbs like *say, believe, imagine, see, want, enjoy*, and *realize*. The subject's conceptualizing role vis-à-vis the subordinate structure is then comparable to that of the speech-act participants in conceptualizing an expression's meaning (the *construal relationship*). The semantics of a multiclause construction may therefore specify the subject's *vantage* on the subordinate structure, perhaps including some counterpart to the speaker/hearer's viewing frame. Or to phrase it more accurately, the speaker/hearer frame is a *subjective* counterpart to that inherent in the *objective* viewing relationship coded in certain complex sentences.

10.2.1.2. *Temporal Coincidence*. The most obvious examples of objective viewing relationships are found in complex sentences involving physical perception: *We saw the ship* {***sink/sinking***}; *I heard him* {***call/calling***}; *She felt the earth* {***shake/shaking***}. An episode of direct, physical perception has a limited duration that can be thought of as a temporal viewing frame; if based on perception alone, apprehension is restricted to that portion of an event which temporally coincides with the frame (cf. Vol. 1, p. 193). The viewing frame is also delimited spatially by the field of perception (corresponding to the overall scope of predication), and can be identified more narrowly as the locus of attention (immediate scope). Because attention enhances both perceptual acuity and a perceived entity's salience, it is natural to assume that the viewing frame implied by a verb like *see* contains and limits the profile of a complement clause describing the object of perception.

The semantic structure of such a verb is diagrammed in Fig. 10.5. The dashed arrows represent a perceptual relationship between the trajector and

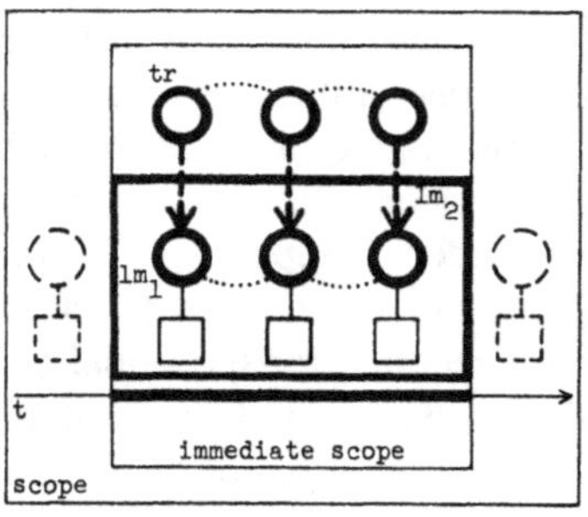

Fig. 10.5

the primary landmark; in *We saw the ship* ***sinking***, the former is elaborated by the subject *we*, and the latter by the direct object *the ship*. Employed in the construction, of course, is a semantic variant of the verb in which the object of perception is not merely a thing (lm_1) but further includes some process in which that thing participates (as its trajector). The perceptual relationship does not necessarily encompass this process as a whole: as noted above, the duration of perceptual contact delimits a temporal viewing frame that constitutes the immediate scope of predication for its characterization. Hence just those portions of the overall process that fall within this frame achieve the prominence of a major verbal participant and function collectively (under atemporal construal) as a secondary, relational landmark. In construction, this landmark (lm_2) serves as e-site for the complement clause (e.g. *sinking*).

That brings us to the semantic contributions of the complementizers. It is generally recognized that the zero form (as in *We saw the ship* ***sink***) indicates that the entire subordinate event is perceived, whereas *-ing* (*We saw the ship* ***sinking***) conveys that only part of it is. The notion of a viewing frame allows us to describe this contrast with reference to independently established values of *-ing* and zero. We can attribute to *-ing* precisely the same value that it has in the progressive construction (Fig. 5.5) and in certain adverbial clauses (Fig. 10.1(b)): on the process designated by the verb stem it imposes an immediate scope of predication comprising a representative series of internal states; the profile is necessarily confined to these states, which it construes holistically and as being effectively homogeneous. The participial clause formed by *-ing* combines straightforwardly with a perceptual verb such as *see* (or with a higher-order expression obtained by elaborating lm_1, e.g. *see the ship*). Specifically, the clause elaborates the verb's relational landmark (lm_2), the immediate scopes of the two component structures being put in correspondence. That is, the perceptual verb's viewing frame is identified as being responsible for the restricted, "internal perspective" imposed by *-ing* on the subordinate process.

What about a zero-marked complement, as in *We saw the ship* ***sink***? Here too the complement elaborates the perceptual verb's relational landmark, and here too I suggest that the viewing frame implied by the verb is identified with an immediate scope of predication imposed on the subordinate process by the complementizer. The contrast between zero and *-ing* resides in the relationship between the immediate scope they impose and the overall profile of the subordinate verb: in the case of *-ing*, the immediate scope falls *within* the boundaries of the verb stem's processual profile, whereas with zero the immediate scope *coincides* with those boundaries. Apart from this semantic difference inhering in the complementizers, the two complement clause constructions are quite comparable.

But why posit a zero complementizer at all? Why not analyze the perceptual verb as combining directly with the subordinate verb under the condition of temporal coincidence? While that would certainly work, two considerations incline me towards the analysis proposed.[22] For one thing, postulating a zero complementizer makes the complement clause construction exactly parallel to the one with *-ing*. Moreover, the zero predicate turns out to be quite analogous to the grounding predication, also generally zero, that situates the grounded process in *immediate reality* (Ch. 6). Recall that this "present tense" morpheme (PRES) was described as imposing an immediate temporal scope that precisely coincides with the time of speaking (Fig. 6.3). That scope is, of course, what we are now interpreting as a viewing frame. The zero grounding predication and the zero complementizer can therefore be regarded as semantic variants. They share the basic conception of a process being observed through a viewing frame whose temporal expanse is coextensive with its own. The primary difference is that, with the grounding predication, the frame is specifically characterized with reference to the ground and delimited by the time of speaking, whereas the complementizer is either unspecific concerning the frame or perhaps relates it to an objectively construed perceptual event. The parallelism between the grounding and complement clause constructions—immediacy and temporal coincidence in each case being signaled iconically by zero—reinforces an important notion: that the construal relationship between the ground and the grounded structure is the subjective counterpart of the perceptual and conceptual relationships portrayed objectively in certain complex sentences (typically holding between the main-clause subject and a complement clause).

Temporal coincidence of the main- and subordinate-clause events represents the consistent value of zero complementation with perception verbs and should probably be considered prototypical. Zero marking may however assume an extended value with causative verbs, as in *I {made/let/had} him* ***clean the garage***, since an event's occurrence seldom exactly coincides with its instigation. But even here zero signals a kind of immediacy that is lacking, say, with the *to*-marked complement of *cause*: in contrast to the direct, volitional causation of *I made him* ***clean the garage***, the relationship between causing and cleaning in *I caused him* ***to clean the garage*** may well be interpreted as indirect, non-volitional, and temporally distant (cf. Fodor 1970; Wierzbicka 1975). Temporal coincidence is also the hallmark of *-ing*, which occurs with many more types of main-clause predicates than does zero. In the case of *-ing*, though, a distinction has to be made between the overall subordinate event and the profiled segment of that event, i.e. the portion subtended by *-ing*'s immediate scope. With perception verbs there is full temporal co-

[22] *Mutatis mutandis*, the comments in fn. 14 are perfectly applicable here as well.

incidence of the main-clause process and the *profiled segment* of the subordinate event (not the event overall). When we cast our nets more widely and consider other main-clause predicates taking complements marked by *-ing*, we find that any fully general characterization will have to be somewhat weaker. The most one might hope to say for the entire class of such constructions is that there is always *some kind of overlap* between the main- and subordinate-clause profiles.

Whether even this weaker generalization can be maintained is problematic. Certainly it captures an essential feature of many *-ing* constructions, as witnessed, for example, by the contrast between *She tried* ***to move her legs*** and *She tried* ***moving her legs***. The former is non-committal as to whether any movement actually took place; the trying is aimed at effecting—and thus precedes—the subordinate event. The latter sentence does however imply that the movement occurred: the trying is not aimed at effecting it, but at ascertaining its consequences once initiated. Similarly, verbs such as *want, hope, wish, desire, expect, prepare, seek, plan, coax, ask, persuade,* and *promise* take *to*-complements that refer to future events, whereas *enjoy, experience, tolerate, love, hate, like, dislike, detest, resent, keep, go on,* and *continue* govern *-ing* in constructions clearly involving temporal overlap between the main and subordinate processes.

There are nevertheless many apparent exceptions to the characterization of *-ing* in terms of temporal overlap. Wierzbicka (1988, ch. 1) makes a valiant attempt to explain them away with reference to her analysis of the governing predicates. For instance, her decomposition of *I remember* ***dancing with the Prince of Wales*** runs as follows: "I can see in my mind this: 'I am dancing with the Prince of Wales'; I can see this not because it is happening to me now; I can see this because some time before now I thought of the same thing: it is happening to me now" (p. 71). She advances comparable analyses for verbs like *imagine, consider, think about, dread, dream of, recommend, suggest,* and *propose*, claiming that in each case the conception of something "happening now" is properly included somewhere within the overall description. While acknowledging the insight of Wierzbicka's characterizations, one may still consider it unsettled whether all uses of the complementizer *-ing* involve temporal overlap. The issue, however, is merely a matter of whether that value is universal to the category or only prototypical.

10.2.1.3. *Objectivity.* In contrast to the "happening now" value attributed to *-ing*, Wierzbicka ascribes a future orientation ("this will happen") to most and perhaps all *to*-complement constructions. As for the many apparent counterexamples, one must realize that in her system futurity is not per se claimed to be the meaning of *to*, but need only appear as one component in her natural-language paraphrase of a *to*-construction. It is clearly present in sentences like *X remembered* ***to lock the door***, where the locking is subsequent to the remembering: "X thought this: I want this: I will lock the door; X did it because of that; X thought this because some time before that time X thought this of the same thing: 'I should do this' " (p. 71). By Wierzbicka's analysis futurity is no less present in an example such as *It ceased* ***to rain***, where the raining obviously does not follow the ceasing. The crucial observation is that *cease* "suggests an ongoing process . . . which at a certain point can be expected to come to an end" (whereas *stop* implies abruptness and unpredictability). Hence the following decomposition: "Before [time] *t*, it was raining; one could think then: more of it will happen after now; at *t*, one could think this: more of it will not happen after now; after *t*, more of it didn't happen" (p. 81).

At the very least, Wierzbicka has persuaded me that there is more to the meaning of the infinitival *to* than I have previously claimed (1987b): that it merely suspends sequential scanning, thus deriving a complex atemporal relation that profiles all the component states of the verb it combines with. I would still propose this as a schematic characterization valid for all class members, while recognizing that its prototypical value further incorporates some notion of futurity. It is not hard to see a connection between projection into the future and the fulfillment of an expectation (even for an already initiated process, as in the case of *cease*). Also, attributing such a value to the complementizer *to* itself renders more transparent the nature of its relationship to the variant that occurs in purpose clauses (e.g. *He did it* ***just to annoy her***) as well as the path preposition (*They walked to the store*). Inherent in all these notions is the *path-goal* image schema (cf. 9.1), which is even discernible in the proposed schematic characterization: the component states of a process are construable as a path leading to its completion, and—in contrast to *-ing* and some senses of the perfect participial morpheme—the infinitival *to* profiles that entire path.

Wierzbicka has also anticipated the basic distinction I wish to draw between the complementizers *to* and *that*. She claims that, whereas *to*-complements are "associated with a personal, subjective, first-person mode: 'I want', 'I think', or 'I know'," *that*-complements "introduce an 'objective', impersonal, 'one can know' perspective" (pp. 164–65). Accordingly, her decomposition of *She was delighted* ***to have won*** contains the components "I know this now: this happened to me," while *She was delighted* ***that he had won*** instead contains "one can know this: this happened" (p. 165). Note that in this formulation the viewer is identified as the main-clause subject: it is to the subject, acting as a *surrogate speaker* (3.1.2), that the words 'I', 'me', and 'now' are attributed. Wierzbicka thus acknowledges the parallelism between the speaker's role as conceptualizer vis-à-vis a grounded expression, and the subject's with respect to a complement clause.[23] I would add that each relationship involves a viewing frame, as previously described, and that in each case the notions of *subjectivity/objectivity*—as these terms are understood in cognitive grammar—are relevant to the description of grammatical phenomena.

I propose that the complementizer *that*, in addition to imposing an atemporal (and possibly nominal) construal on the clause it combines with, serves to objectify the conception of the proposition expressed. A subtle semantic contrast is thus imputed to sentence pairs such as *She knows* ***he likes her*** vs. *She knows* ***that he likes her***. In both expressions the proposition 'he likes her' is subordinated to the main-clause process (by virtue of being a processual participant) and hence construed holistically as a unitary entity. Since *that* itself refers to the subordinate process as a unitary entity (its e-site), including it has a further distancing effect, reflected iconically in the phonological distance it introduces between the two clauses (cf. Haiman 1983, 1985). To the extent that the subordinate structure represents a conceptualization attributed to the subject (or some other main-clause participant), this enhanced objectivity is manifested in the viewing relationship along the main-clause/subordinate-clause axis. *That* also renders more objective the conception of the subordinate process by the speaker and hearer, who may be the only apparent conceptualizers (e.g. ***That the project has been cancelled*** *is false*).

Some corroboration of *that*'s distancing effect is afforded by expressions where the main-clause subject is also understood to be the subordinate-clause trajector. In such cases there are two basic options for the complement clause: the participant in question can either be coded overtly by means of a subject pronoun, as in (24)(a), or else left implicit, as in (b).

(24)(a) *Phil definitely expects* ***that he will reach the summit by noon.***
(b) *Phil definitely expects* ***to reach the summit by noon.***
(c) **Phil definitely expects* ***that will reach the summit by noon.***

However, (c) shows that this latter option is impermissible with *that*, since a finite clause in English has to have an overt subject.[24] Now I have argued on

[23] Also reflecting that parallelism are the *logophoric pronouns* found in many languages. Such pronouns tend to occur in complements to verbs of mental experience or communication, and their antecedent is the individual whose conceptualization is being reported (cf. Kuno 1986, 1987; Sells 1987).

[24] *That* itself is not responsible for this restriction (which also holds for main clauses and unmarked finite-clause complements). The point is rather that the objectivity inherent in finite clauses is fully consonant with the value attributed to *that*, which may be limited to such clauses precisely because it signals and reinforces that objectivity. Rejected, of course, is the classic transformational account that derives (b) from roughly the same underlying structure as (a) by the rule of Equi-NP Deletion.

independent grounds (1985) that overt mention correlates with objective construal, and that entities tend to remain implicit when construed subjectively. The constructions in (a) and (b) are therefore plausibly analyzed as contrasting semantically in regard to how the main-clause subject views his role in the subordinate process: whether Phil construes himself objectively, viewing his own activity in the same way that he would anybody else's; or whether he views himself subjectively, in which case he conceptualizes the subordinate process more from the vantage of one engaged in actually carrying it out.

Ruwet (1984) adduces considerable evidence that a distinction of this sort holds between the corresponding constructions of French. For example, *vouloir* 'want' normally requires an infinitival complement when the main- and subordinate-clause trajectors are the same; the French analog of a *that*-clause is infelicitous:

(25)(a) *Je veux **partir**.* 'I want to leave.'
(b) **Je veux **que je parte**.* 'I want that I leave.'

Ruwet observes, however, that anything suggesting greater distance between the subject's desire and ultimate achievement of the action makes the second type of sentence more acceptable. Such factors include passivization, the modal verb *pouvoir* 'be able to', perfect aspect, and intervening conditions or events:

(26)(a) ?*Je veux **que je sois autorisé à partir demain**.* 'I want that I be authorized to leave tomorrow.'
(b) ?*Je veux **que je puisse partir dès demain**.* 'I want that I be able to leave as of tomorrow.'
(c) *Je voudrais bien **que je puisse être autorisé à partir**.* 'I would really like that I could be authorized to leave.'
(d) *Je veux absolument **que je sois parti dans dix minutes**.* 'I absolutely want that I be gone in ten minutes.'
(e) *Je veux **que j'aie le temps de me préparer à partir**.* 'I want that I have the time to prepare myself to leave.'

The data argue strongly that distance and objectivity, specifically in regard to the subject's construal of the subordinate process, are central to the semantics of this construction.

Finally, a word is in order concerning the notion that *that* imposes an atemporal or even a nominal construal on a finite clause. This might seem contradictory, since by definition a finite clause designates a process. But there are multiple levels of organization to consider, and multiple paths through which the contents of a *that*-clause are accessible from the ground. Internally—that is, at the level of constituency where *that* has not yet been appended—a finite clause does indeed have a processual profile. Furthermore, because this structure incorporates a grounding predication, the speech-act participants have direct access to the designated process, which is scanned sequentially within the associated viewing frame and thus retains its full processual character. When it functions as a complement, however, a finite clause also participates in external relationships that entail another way of viewing it and provide an additional path of access from the ground. Objectification, atemporalization, and nominalization are concomitants of the clause as a whole (including its grounding predication) being embedded within a more elaborate conceptualization and subordinated to a process that has its own grounding and imposes its own perspective; it is from this latter perspective that the finite-clause complement is construed holistically as a unitary entity. This dual perspective and simultaneous accessibility via two viewing frames is responsible for the special character of finite subordinate clauses.

10.2.2. *Raising*

Some of the strongest motivation for adopting a transformational description of English syntax was provided by the apparent existence of syntactic rules whose effect is to "raise" a subject or object nominal from a complement clause into the main clause. The raised nominal "replaces" the complement clause out of which it ascends, in the sense that it assumes the main-clause grammatical relation borne by the complement in underlying structure. This analysis accounted for the supposed synonymy of sentence pairs that differ quite significantly in their surface grammatical structure.

For example, the rule of Subject-to-Object Raising derives (27)(b) from the same structure that underlies (27)(a):

(27)(a) *I want* ***for you to have a successful career.***
(b) *I want you* ***to have a successful career.***

In (a), *want* takes as its object a complement clause marked by *for . . . to*, and *you* is generally analyzed as the subject of that clause. In (b), on the other hand, it is *you* that functions as the main-clause object; the remainder of the complement clause is a separate constituent that no longer has direct-object status (a *chômeur* in the terminology of relational grammar). By positing such a derivation one can account for the fact that *you* is "understood" as the subject of *have* in (b), and the complement clause as the object of *want*, even though the superficial grammatical relations are very different. Comparable derivations have been proposed to relate the sentence pairs in (28) and (29):

(28)(a) ***For Sheila to win Saturday's 10K race*** *is likely.*
(b) *Sheila is likely* ***to win Saturday's 10K race.***

(29)(a) ***To find a good housekeeper*** *is very difficult.*
(b) *A good housekeeper is very difficult* ***to find.***

Thus (28)(b) supposedly derives from the same underlying structure as (28)(a) by the rule of Subject-to-Subject Raising, and (29)(b) from that of (29)(a) by Object-to-Subject Raising.

10.2.2.1. *Critique*. Even within the transformational tradition it was noted that sentences claimed to be related by raising are often semantically non-equivalent (e.g. Borkin 1973; Postal 1974, ch. 11). Particularly clear are examples with *find*:

(30)(a) *Susan found* ***that the bed was uncomfortable***.
(b) *Susan found the bed* ***to be uncomfortable***.
(c) *Susan found the bed* ***uncomfortable***.

As Borkin described it, (a) might be used if Susan had searched through her files to learn the results of consumer reaction tests, whereas (b)—supposedly derived by Subject-to-Object Raising—would be more appropriate if Susan herself had conducted such tests. Additionally, sentence (c)—thought at the time to be derived by a further rule deleting *to be*—implies that Susan tried the bed herself and directly experienced the discomfort. Such contrasts were unexpected and problematic in the context of generative theory and were dealt with (if at all) by ad hoc means. On the other hand, cognitive grammar necessarily treats the three sentence types as representing distinct constructions each with its own conceptual import.

In large measure the semantic contrasts reflect the presence or absence of particular "grammatical" elements. The indirectness of the relation between Susan and the experience of discomfort in (30)(a) is partly ascribable to the conceptual distance conveyed by the complementizer *that*. A more important factor is the characterization of the complement clauses in terms of semantic function. Because the *that*-clause in (a) shows full functional elaboration and incorporates a grounding predication, the conception imputed to Susan is abstract and propositional: it includes not only an assessment of the bed being uncomfortable, but also its epistemic status as embodied in the grounding relationship (i.e. its location in time and reality with respect to the current speech situation). The other two examples, with ungrounded complements, attribute to Susan a simpler, less abstract conceptualization. In (30)(b), the occurrence of the verb *be* in the complement clause implies that she conceives of the bed's uncomfortableness as extending through some span of time, and with *to* there is no specification of temporal coincidence. The sentence thus suggests an overall judgment that goes beyond immediate experience. By the same token, the absence of *be* in the complement of (30)(c) means that Susan's conception is not specifically portrayed as embracing any period other than the moment at which she makes her judgment. An assessment of uncomfortableness *tout court* (as opposed to uncomfortableness extending through time) is naturally interpreted as being induced by direct perceptual experience (cf. Newman 1981).

If we do not posit raising rules, and instead treat these sentence types as separate, parallel constructions, how can we accommodate the considerations that originally motivated the raising analysis? How, for example, can we account for the fact that the "logical object" of (27)(b), *I want you* ***to have a successful career***, is not its "surface" object *you*, but rather the clause *(for) you (to) have a successful career*, as in (27)(a)? The short answer is that these considerations were spurious to begin with. In particular, the notions "logical subject" and "logical object" have been invoked and applied in an a priori manner without any clear understanding of their basis and in the absence of a well-articulated, strongly supported, or cognitively realistic conception of linguistic semantics (i.e. they are **non-substantive** in the sense of Vol. 1, 1.1.5). The issue, then, is whether there is any valid basis for going beyond a sentence's overt form and positing a set of "deep," "underlying," "logical," "initial," or "true" grammatical relations distinct from those actually observed. Though usually left implicit, several kinds of considerations appear to have motivated the postulation of such relations in the generative tradition; they pertain to semantic roles, logic, and uniformity in the characterization of governing predicates. I believe, however, that they are all subject to challenge.[25]

One possible reason for hypothesizing a level of deep or underlying structure is that it yields a more consistent correlation between grammatical relations and semantic roles than is evident at the surface level. For example, if a passive such as *The glass was broken by Floyd* is derived from an underlying active, the subject and object relations maintain their respective associations with the agent and patient roles despite the surface discrepancy. This motivation is exceedingly weak, since the subject and object relations are in any case associated with a variety of semantic roles even in sentences for which there is no question of any derivation by relation-changing rules (7.3). Semantic roles and grammatical relations are generally recognized as different kinds of constructs whose correlation is only partial even in underlying structure (for those who posit it).

The reference to *logical* grammatical relations suggests an appeal to logic as possible justification for underlying representations. Consider (28)(b), *Sheila is likely* ***to win Saturday's 10K race***. One might argue that, logically, the subject of *likely* can only be an event or proposition (not a person), so that

[25] An additional type of argument, prevalent in relational grammar, is that differences in grammatical behavior are predictable on the basis of distinct configurations of grammatical relations on the initial stratum (e.g. Perlmutter 1978). In cognitive grammar, the behavior in question is not attributed to initial grammatical relations, but is seen instead as depending directly on the semantic factors that make their postulation seem plausible (cf. 9.2.2, especially fn. 5).

(28)(b) has to be analyzed as the surface manifestation of an underlying structure comparable to (28)(a), ***For Sheila to win Saturday's 10K race** is likely*. The problem with this argument is its aprioristic character. Logics are man-made objects that come in many shapes, sizes, and colors. Which particular logic is one appealing to? More importantly, why should we expect a given logical system to be an accurate reflection of natural-language semantics (or conversely)? But let us suppose—just for the sake of argument—that the world (or human cognition) implicitly defines a "true" logic waiting to be discovered and formulated, and that a *likely*-type predicate figures in this logic. Even then, it does not follow that English *likely* necessarily conforms to this predicate in all particulars, nor that grammatical relations directly and consistently manifest any specific features of the logic.

A similar kind of argument proceeds as follows: "The overt subject of *likely* in (28)(b) is *Sheila*. However, this sentence does not mean that Sheila is likely (whatever that would involve)—it is rather her winning of the race that is understood as being likely. We can capture this by deriving (28)(b) from an underlying structure like (28)(a), which represents the grammatical relations that actually figure in the expression's semantic interpretation." Because it relies on linguistic factors (instead of logic), this argument has a certain intuitive appeal, and I have often used it (with some success) in teaching transformational syntax. Nevertheless, in retrospect I consider it fallacious. The reason is that it tacitly and erroneously prejudges both the meaning of the governing predicate and the nature of grammatical relations.

The argument assumes that the governing predicate has precisely the same meaning in raising and non-raising constructions. The meaning it has in the latter, i.e. in (28)(a) or in sentences such as *Another eruption is likely*, presumably represents its prototypical value; it refers to the potential occurrence of an event and confers on that event the status of trajector (figure within the profiled relationship). Now in making the foregoing argument, I was tacitly interpreting *likely* in just that way: Sheila is not an event, and (28)(b) certainly does not mean that Sheila herself is likely—taking that word in its prototypical sense. Thereby ignored, however, is the possibility that *likely* might have another, related sense in the context of the raising construction. This alternate meaning has the same conceptual content as the prototype, evoking the same objectively conceived relationships (and thus having the same logical properties). The difference resides in an aspect of construal: rather than the potential event, it is the event's central participant that is accorded trajector status and is thus elaborated by the subject nominal (the event itself is specified by a relational complement). By this analysis, there is nothing anomalous about the surface grammatical relations of (28)(b). Sheila is indeed *likely*—not in the basic sense of being an event ready to occur, but in the extended sense of being the central figure in such an event.

10.2.2.2. *The Active-Zone Analysis.* The two senses of *likely* are sketched in Fig. 10.6. They evoke the same conceptual content: each takes as landmark a certain region on a scale of probability and specifies that a process falls

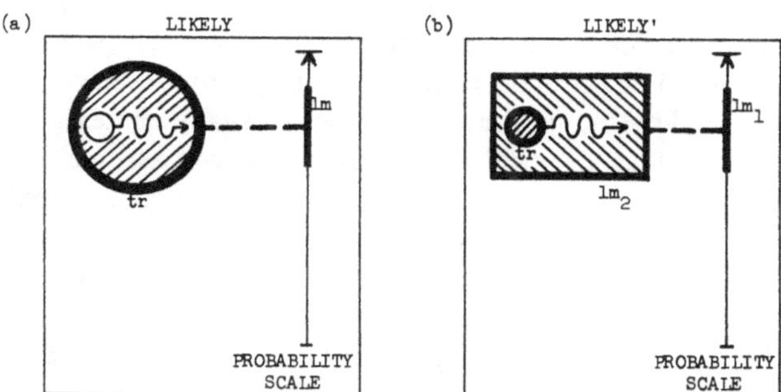

Fig. 10.6

within the landmark region. As shown in diagram (a), the basic sense of *likely* accords trajector status to the process itself (under a nominal construal). The cross-hatching has been added just to remind us that this trajector functions as an e-site; its elaboration by the subject nominal results in sentences such as (28)(a).[26] Diagram (b) represents the extended sense of *likely* that occurs in the "raising" construction. Here it is not the situated process but the central processual participant that stands out as the primary figure within the scene. Cross-hatching once more indicates that this trajector serves as e-site for the subject nominal. Additionally, the situated process can be regarded as a secondary landmark and is elaborated by an infinitival complement. Thus in (28)(b), *Sheila is likely* ***to win Saturday's 10K race***, *Sheila* elaborates the trajector, while *to win Saturday's 10K race* specifies lm_2. Observe that this analysis accounts automatically for the fact that Sheila is understood as the subject of *win* (which was one motivation for the raising rule): it is a direct consequence of *tr* being a substructure of lm_2 (specifically, its trajector).

Comparable descriptions are proposed for each raising construction and each of the governing predicates.[27] It should be pointed out that this analysis emerges naturally from a number of independently motivated claims of cognitive grammar. First, meaning is a function of both the conceptual content

[26] This elaboration takes place at a higher level of organization: the subject does not directly elaborate the trajector of *likely*, but of the composite expression *be likely*. The two trajectors correspond in any case, since *be* merely gives temporal extension to the relationship profiled by the adjective.

[27] All valid generalizations are captured: constructional schemas describe the various sentence types; and regularities in the sets of lexical items that participate in each construction are expressed by constructional subschemas, as well as by schemas reflecting patterns of semantic extension (Vol. 1, p. 444).

evoked and how that content is construed, including the relative prominence conferred on various substructures. Second, polysemy represents the normal situation for frequently occurring lexical items. Third, the same content often gives rise to distinct meanings differing only in construal; in particular, it is not unusual for a relational expression to have alternate senses that differ primarily in the figure/ground organization they impose on a common base (Vol. 1, 7.3.3). Fourth, semantic extension is usually context-induced, with the consequence that a lexical item might very well assume a specific extended value only when it occurs in a certain construction. Finally, despite their correlation with semantic roles, the notions *subject* and *direct object* are characterized most fundamentally in terms of prominence: primary and secondary clause-level figure. Hence there is nothing problematic about these relations being alternatively assigned to different entities within the same scene, even if some are less directly involved than others in pivotal aspects of the profiled relationship.

This last factor is no doubt what has led certain linguists to speak of *logical* grammatical relations. Consider once more the two semantic variants of *likely*, as diagrammed in Fig. 10.6. The crucial aspect of the profiled relationship is the location of a process with respect to a probability scale. Now let us grant that a person per se cannot be situated on such a scale—a person's interaction with the scale is *indirect*, being mediated by some process in which he participates. Of the entities that figure in the meaning of *likely*, we can therefore say that the process is directly involved in the key facet of the profiled relation, and a processual participant, only indirectly. It is this contrast that renders intuitively plausible the claim that the "logical" subject of *likely* in (28)(b) is not Sheila but the proposition *(for) Sheila (to) win Saturday's 10K race*. However, I do not regard this to be a matter of logic, nor is there any reason to think that grammatical relations—or any other aspect of linguistic structure—specifically or consistently mirror logical relationships. It is more appropriate to think of the subject and object relations as spotlights of focal prominence that can be aimed at different facets of an integrated conception. An expression's logical properties inhere in the structure of that conception, regardless of where the spotlights are directed.

Hence the distinctive character of raising constructions and their governing predicates does not stem from any logical deficiency. What seemingly makes them "special" is rather that **an entity accorded focal prominence does not precisely coincide with the one that participates most directly and crucially in the profiled relation**. However, I have argued elsewhere (1984) that in this regard they are really not special at all. Those facets of an entity which participate most directly in a relation are referred to as its **active zone** with respect to that relation (Vol. 1, 7.3.4). "Raising" thus amounts to a discrepancy between the entity profiled as a focal relational participant and the active zone of that entity for the relation in question. Now it turns out that such discrepancies between profiled participant and active zone are not at all unusual for relational predications—to the contrary, they represent *the normal situation*. Raising constructions are therefore just a particular manifestation of an ordinary, run-of-the-mill phenomenon.

Discrepancies between profiled participant and active zone are so ubiquitous and natural that they usually escape the linguist's attention. Consider *Eve ate an apple*, a perfectly normal sentence on almost any account. The profiled participants are Eve and the apple, which the subject and object nominals refer to as unitary wholes. Yet only certain facets of these entities figure directly and crucially in the profiled relationship. Presumably involved are Eve's hands, mouth, teeth, tongue, and the upper parts of her alimentary canal, but not her hair, knees, or ovaries. Likewise, only certain portions of the apple are probably consumed (not the stem, core, or seeds), although the term *apple* designates the entire fruit. It is readily seen that most verbs lend themselves to comparable observations—seldom does the profiled relation involve the focal participants as undifferentiated wholes. Why not be more precise? Why, for example, do we use a noun like *Eve* as the subject of *eat, think, hear, lick, breathe, walk, nod, wink, smile, whistle*, or *digest* even though each activity is primarily localized to different parts of her body? Several reasons are evident. There is no real need for anatomical accuracy, since each verb evokes a cognitive domain (the conception of a familiar process) that intrinsically specifies the nature of the subject's involvement. Full precision would hardly be practical in any case, for numerous body parts may figure in the action, and to varying degrees.[28] Finally, we think of the world as being populated by people and objects, not by their parts; and when we do focus on a part, the person or object as a whole is generally invoked as a reference point for its characterization. In this sense the whole has special cognitive salience that makes it a preferred candidate for explicit linguistic coding.

The greater the discrepancy between profiled participant and active zone, the more likely it is to catch our attention and strike us as being "special." It is considerably more striking (once noticed) in the case of *Eve blinked* than for *Eve walked*, since blinking is localized to the eyes whereas walking involves the whole person (albeit some parts more saliently than others).[29] Importantly, the active zone is not invariably a subpart of the profiled participant—there need only be an evident *association* between them. In *I heard a*

[28] It is much easier to say *Eve ate the apple* than *Eve's hands, mouth, teeth, tongue, and the upper parts of her alimentary canal ate all portions of the apple except the stem, core, and seeds*. Moreover, any attempt to be fully precise is destined to failure, as greater precision can always be demanded. (How many teeth did Eve actually use? Which teeth did what to which parts of the apple?)

[29] One linguistic consequence is the possibility of saying *She blinked her eyes*, but hardly **She walked her {legs/body}*.

rifle, for instance, the rifle's active zone with respect to *hear* is the sound it emits when fired. Similarly, *The kettle is boiling* fails to evoke the conception of a pool of molten metal, as we take the water inside to be the kettle's active zone with respect to *boil*. And *I'm in the phone book* does not imply that I am personally sandwiched in the white or yellow pages; it is rather a graphic representation of my name, address, and phone number that participates most directly in the locative relationship. Observe that in all these examples the discrepancy allows an entity with substantial cognitive salience to be mentioned explicitly, the less salient active zone remaining covert: a whole is salient relative to its parts; an observable container relative to its hidden contents; and a physical object (especially a person) relative to an abstract entity.[30]

The final step is to recognize that one kind of entity associated with a profiled participant, and capable of serving as its active zone, is a process in which it has a central role. For example, when I say *This barber is fast*, I do not imply that the barber himself—*qua* person or physical object—falls within a certain region on a scale of rapidity. It is rather a characteristic activity in which the barber engages, such as shaving, cutting hair, or even running (the default for people in general), that directly interacts with the scale and is thus the subject's active zone with respect to *fast*. Likewise, *She began a novel* refers to the initiation of a process involving the novel (e.g. reading, writing, or editing it) that remains covert but is nonetheless its active zone with respect to *begin* (cf. Newmeyer 1970). We can therefore analyze the complement clause in a raising construction as a means of specifying the "raised" nominal's active zone in regard to the main-clause relationship; in (28)(b), for instance, *to win Saturday's 10K race* is Sheila's active zone in regard to *likely*. Because a processual participant is conceptually autonomous and usually less abstract than the process itself, the discrepancy between active zone and profiled participant once again enables the spotlight of main-clause focal prominence to fall on an entity of greater cognitive salience.

The complement clause in raising constructions can thus be seen as allowing the expression of an active zone in cases where it fails to coincide with the entity accorded the prominence of a focal participant. Languages have a variety of devices that serve this function. To specify the barber's active zone with respect to *fast*, we could say either *This barber is fast* ***at giving a shave***, or else ***When it comes to giving a shave,*** *this barber is fast*. Prepositional phrases are often employed for this purpose. For example, whereas *It bit me* has a naturally salient direct object, and *It bit my ankle* is specific concerning

[30]These discrepancies might also be seen as cases of **metonymy**, where a term is applied to some entity associated with its usual referent (cf. Fauconnier 1985; Lakoff 1987). If the shift is limited to a particular expression or construction, it may be indeterminate whether it affects the noun (so that *kettle*, for instance, means 'water in kettle') or the relational predication (so that *boil* means something like 'be a container in which boiling occurs').

the locus of the biting, *It bit me on the ankle* combines both advantages by using a prepositional phrase to code the object's active zone. Yet another device for coding a focal participant's active zone is compounding or noun incorporation, as in *She is breastfeeding her new baby* (8.3.3; Tuggy 1986).

One prediction of this analysis is that the complement clause might sometimes be omitted from what otherwise appears to be a raising-type construction when the process serving as active zone either represents a default or is apparent from the context. An obvious candidate for default-case status is mere existence or coming onto the scene. Thus (31)(b) can be regarded as analogous to (31)(a) (supposedly derived by Subject-to-Object Raising) except that the active zone remains implicit.

(31)(a) *We're expecting another guest* ***to arrive****.*
(b) *We're expecting another guest.*

(32)(a) *Jo is certain* ***to come to the party****, and George is likely* ***to come****.*
(b) *Jo is certain, and George is likely.*

More striking are the examples in (32). The standard account of (32)(a) posits Subject-to-Subject Raising in each conjunct, and without a complement clause we usually cannot refer to a person as being *likely*, or even as being *certain* (on a parallel interpretation). Yet (32)(b) is perfectly acceptable given an appropriate context, e.g. in response to the question *Who's coming to the party?*. Furthermore, if (33)(a) derives by Object-to-Subject Raising, the same rule cannot be responsible for (33)(b):

(33)(a) *Volkswagens are easy* ***to fix****.*
(b) ***When it comes to fixing them****, Volkswagens are easy.*

In the active-zone analysis the (b) examples are unproblematic and even expected, but it is not evident what a raising analysis would say about them.

10.2.2.3. *Raising vs. Equi.* The classic transformational account distinguished the rules of Subject-to-Object and Subject-to-Subject Raising from another rule called Equi-NP Deletion. Applying to different underlying structures, Raising and Equi derive expressions whose surface forms are precisely analogous. Two contrasting properties appear to support the claim that distinct constructions are involved despite their superficial identity, and thus to motivate the postulation of underlying representations. One property pertains to syntactic "dummies," the other to the result of passivizing the complement clause.

A standard example is the contrast between *expect*, a raising verb, and *persuade*, which governs Equi. On first examination the expressions in (34) appear to be quite parallel:

(34)(a) *I expected a reporter* ***to interview my boss.***
(b) *I persuaded a reporter* ***to interview my boss.***

However, the usual analysis posits distinct underlying structures:

(35)(a) *I expected* ***(for) a reporter to interview my boss.***
(b) *I persuaded a reporter (of)* ***(for) a reporter to interview my boss.***

The crucial difference is that *a reporter* is the underlying direct object of *persuade* but not of *expect*. It becomes the superficial object of *expect* by virtue of Subject-to-Object Raising. On the other hand, *a reporter* is the object of *persuade* in both surface and underlying structure, as well as the underlying subject of the complement. Its failure to surface in this latter role is due to Equi, which deletes it under coreference to the main-clause object.[31]

Why posit these different types of underlying structure? Consider first what happens when the complement clause is passivized:

(36)(a) *I expected my boss* ***to be interviewed by a reporter.***
(b) *I persuaded my boss* ***to be interviewed by a reporter.***

The important observation is that (34)(a) and (36)(a) are roughly synonymous, whereas (34)(b) and (36)(b) are semantically distinct. More precisely, (34)(a) and (36)(a) are applicable to the same set of situations, for with either expression the speaker entertains the same expectation (that the reporter will interview the boss). By contrast, (34)(b) and (36)(b) are properly used in different circumstances, depending on whether the target of persuasion (the person whose intention was swayed) was the reporter or the boss. The underlying structures in (35) account for this difference. Since the "logical" object of *expect* is propositional, and passivization does not alter the proposition expressed, (35)(a) is semantically appropriate as the source of both (34)(a) and (36)(a); the complement clause can either remain active or be passivized, but in both cases its subject (*a reporter* in the active, *my boss* in the passive) is raised to become the main-clause object. With *persuade*, however, the surface object—the target of persuasion—is also the "logical" object. The underlying structures of the two examples must therefore be distinct: (34)(b) derives from (35)(b), while (36)(b) derives from (37).

(37) *I persuaded my boss (of)* ***(for) a reporter to interview my boss.***

Whether underlyingly or through passivization, the subject of the complement clause must be coreferential to the main-clause object and as a consequence undergoes deletion by Equi.

[31] For present purposes it does not matter whether the complement subject is a full, lexical nominal that undergoes deletion, or whether it is some kind of pro element even at the deep-structure level. We need also not concern ourselves about the possible inclusion of *for* and *of* and why they are not overtly manifested.

A second reason for distinguishing the constructions in (34) has to do with supposedly meaningless nominal elements such as the presentational *there*, the meteorological *it*, and "chunks" of idioms, e.g. the *tabs* of *keep tabs on*. All of these occur as subjects (in the case of *tabs*, under passivization):

(38)(a) *There is an alligator in the basement.*
(b) *It will rain all morning.*
(c) *Tabs were kept on several prominent activists.*

Moreover, they are all licensed by specific clause-internal factors: the presentational *there be* construction, the meteorological verb *rain*, and the idiom. They cannot occur freely in the absence of these factors. In particular, they are impermissible as the object of *expect:*[32]

(39) **I expect {there/it/tabs}.*

Observe, however, that they do appear as the object of *expect* in the context of the raising construction:

(40)(a) *I expect there* ***to be an alligator in the basement.***
(b) *I expect it* ***to rain all morning.***
(c) *I expect tabs* ***to be kept on several prominent activists.***

The raising analysis accounts for the fact that what is superficially the main-clause object is able to occur at all only by virtue of its role as complement clause subject. On the other hand, *persuade* governs Equi instead of Raising, and its surface object is also its underlying object. The ill-formedness of the following sentences is therefore correctly predicted:

(41)(a) **I persuaded there* ***to be an alligator in the basement.***
(b) **I persuaded it* ***to rain all morning.***
(c) **I persuaded tabs* ***to be kept on several prominent activists.***

There are very good arguments, then, for distinguishing the constructions in (34) despite their superficial parallelism. The issue we now face is whether these differences can be accommodated without positing transformational derivations from distinct underlying structures. From the standpoint of cognitive grammar, the contrasting properties of the two construction types are most naturally seen as consequences of the meanings of the governing predicates. No underlying structures are posited, and the sentences in (34) are grammatically parallel in the sense that the "superficial" direct object of *expect* and *persuade* is in each case its "true" (and its only) direct object.

A preliminary point is that *there*, *it*, and idiom chunks are considered meaningful elements (see 8.1.3.4, 8.3, and Vol. 1, pp. 93–94). That they

[32]It is true but irrelevant that (39) is well-formed when *it* and *tabs* are given other interpretations.

should function semantically as a subject or direct object is in no way intrinsically anomalous, therefore.[33] Also relevant is a general observation concerning idioms that is readily extended to other fixed collocations, including such combinations as *there be* and *it rain*. A collocation need not have a single, invariant form, nor do its components have to constitute a contiguous linear sequence (e.g. *keep tabs on* has the discontinuous variant *tabs . . . kep(t) on* in (38)(c)). It has further been established that a collocation's variants cannot in general be derived transformationally from a single variant inserted as a contiguous expression in underlying structure (Vol. 1, 1.1.5; Bresnan and Grimshaw 1978). As viewed in cognitive grammar, the essential aspect of a collocation is not a fixed linear sequence, but rather an assembly of symbolic relationships and correspondences that may be manifested (and susceptible to schematic characterization) in a variety of structural configurations (Vol. 1, 12.2.3). Consequently, the fact that *there*, *it*, and *tabs* are licensed in (40) by factors internal to the complement clause does not imply that they have to originate there.

If one assumes that the surface direct object of *expect* or *persuade* is in each case a "real" direct object by virtue of elaborating its primary landmark, to what can we attribute the contrasting properties just described? Is there some difference in meaning from which these properties follow as a natural consequence? Even in the absence of a detailed semantic investigation, I believe that such a difference is discernible. In fact, the same characteristic responsible for the seemingly "special" nature of raising constructions also proves pivotal to the issue at hand.

Recall that in a raising construction the entity accorded focal prominence is not the one that participates most directly and crucially in the profiled relationship—instead, its active zone with respect to that relationship is a process in which this entity is a central participant. In the case of *expect*, for example, sentences like (34)(a), *I expected a reporter* ***to interview my boss***, alternate with semantically very similar expressions that take a clausal direct object:

(42) *I expected* ***that a reporter would interview my boss***.

This latter type of sentence directly reflects the "logical" feature that an expectation pertains to some kind of proposition or event. It does so by according this event the status of primary landmark, as sketched in Fig. 10.7(a),

[33] If *there* and *it* are properly analyzed as abstract settings, they will not satisfy the narrow definition of a direct object (a participant downstream from a participant subject with respect to the flow of energy or some analog thereof). They can however be accommodated under the broadest, most schematic characterization, i.e. *secondary clausal figure* (8.2). There is independent evidence that the raised nominal can indeed be a setting: *Thursday is likely* ***to see yet another startling development***; *I expect my cat* ***to be crawling with fleas*** (8.1.3.2). It is referred to throughout as a participant merely for expository convenience.

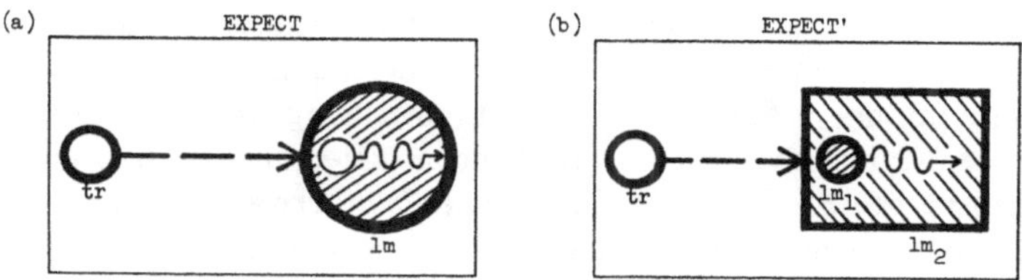

Fig. 10.7

where the dashed arrow indicates mental contact and other pivotal aspects of the *expect* relationship. That same relationship is invoked and profiled in Fig. 10.7(b), which represents the meaning *expect* assumes in the raising construction. Here, of course, we find a discrepancy between the projected event and the entity singled out as primary landmark and coded by the direct-object nominal. The event itself, a secondary landmark elaborated by the infinitival complement, mediates the interaction between the subject and direct object—it is the object's active zone with respect to the profiled relationship.

The essential point is that, with *expect*, there is no other relation of any consequence between the subject and the "raised" nominal. To be sure, the subject in (34)(a) makes mental contact with the object, but that per se imposes no constraints on the object's nature, since mental contact can be established with any sort of entity. Otherwise, the object interacts with the subject solely by virtue of its role within the landmark event coded by the infinitival clause, and attracts the spotlight of focal prominence solely by virtue of its status as trajector of that event. That the raised nominal appears to "replace" the complement clause out of which it ascends (in the sense of assuming the same main-clause grammatical relation) follows automatically on this account. The *transparency* of raising, whereby any sort of nominal—including *there*, *it*, and idiom chunks—can be "raised," is thus attributable to the fact that each is capable of serving as subordinate-clause trajector, and that no other demands are made on it by the main-clause relationship. Moreover, passivizing the subordinate clause entails that a different nominal is accorded the special salience of a main-clause focal participant, but owing once more to the absence of any direct interaction between the main-clause subject and object, the resulting semantic contrast (e.g. between (34)(a) and (36)(a)) is limited to figure/ground organization.

On the other hand, an Equi verb like *persuade* fails to display the same transparency and synonymy under passivization precisely because its subject and object participate directly in a substantial interaction not mediated by the event described in the complement clause. In (34)(b), *I persuaded a reporter **to interview my boss***, not only do the subject and object both envisage the projected event (i.e. the interview), but they also take part in a verbal interaction in which the subject exerts pressure that induces the object to adopt the projected event as an intention. The object must therefore be an entity which (unlike *there*, *it*, or *tabs*) is capable of participating in such an interaction. Furthermore, alternate choices of object (correlating with whether the subordinate clause is active or passive) result in non-equivalent meanings. Thus (34)(b) and (36)(b), *I persuaded my boss* ***to be interviewed by a reporter***, are distinct in terms of conceptual content (not just construal) because different individuals function as the target of persuasion.

Preliminary investigation suggests that the distinction between constructions derived by Raising and by Equi consistently has this character. These constructions are alike in that the subject or object of the main clause functions simultaneously as a focal participant (typically the trajector) of a complement clause that also has a central role in the main-clause relationship. The basic difference resides in the nature of the participant's main-clause role. Traditionally analyzed as raising constructions are those in which its participation in the profiled relationship is wholly mediated by the subordinate-clause event or situation—its active zone with respect to the profiled process (see Figs. 10.6(b) and 10.7(b)). Equi is posited instead for those constructions in which some facet of the profiled relationship involves the participant directly. For example, *She is certain* ***to win the lottery*** is analyzed as a raising construction because the subject interacts with the probability scale evoked by *certain* only indirectly, by participating in an event situated at one extremity of the scale. On the other hand, *She is certain of* ***winning the lottery*** is seen as being derived by Equi because in this case the subject, in addition to participating in such an event, is portrayed as a conceptualizer who assesses the event's location on the scale.

Let us take just one more example, namely "the two verbs *begin*" described in Perlmutter 1970. A variety of evidence leads Perlmutter to claim that *begin* has two incarnations: one as a raising verb analogous to *seem*, *appear*, and *happen*; and the other as an equi verb analogous to *try*, *condescend*, and *refuse*. Accordingly, a sentence like *Zeke began* ***to think*** would be structurally ambiguous, either deriving by Raising from an underlying tree structure of roughly the form [[*Zeke think*] *began*], or by Equi from the underlying structure [*Zeke began* [*Zeke think*]]. By contrast, the cognitive grammar analysis posits a single verb *begin* that has two semantic variants. It does not appeal to any notion of underlying structure, and *Zeke began* ***to think*** is attributed the same constituency and grammatical relations under either interpretation.

Both variants of *begin* profile the initiation of a process (i.e. the transition from its non-occurrence to the occurrence of an initial series of component states). The full process is in each case a kind of relational landmark; it is construed atemporally and coded by the infinitival complement. With either variant, moreover, the trajector of the landmark process is also singled out as the trajector of the process that *begin* designates (that of initiation). By virtue of elaborating this trajector, *Zeke* is the true (and only) subject of *Zeke began **to think*** on both readings. The contrast between the two senses of *begin* is a matter of whether the profiled relationship is limited to the process of initiation as a purely temporal/aspectual phenomenon, or whether it further incorporates the force-dynamic notion of effort being expended to induce it. The first variant is the one that supposedly governs Raising. It clearly conforms to the proposed characterization of raising constructions, as the subject has nothing to do with the profiled event (initiation) except by virtue of participating in the initiated process (thinking). We have seen that transparency (i.e. lack of restrictions on the subject, as witnessed in *There began **to be problems*** or *It began **to rain***) is a consequence of this property. It is equally apparent that the second variant, which supposedly governs Equi, involves the subject in a more substantial way: besides participating in the landmark process, the subject supplies the energy that induces its initiation. In short, the distinction between the two interpretations of *Zeke began **to think*** does not reside in (underlying) syntactic form but rather in the structure of the alternate conceptions it is capable of coding.

CHAPTER 11

Further Issues

PREVIOUS CHAPTERS have dealt with essential aspects of nominal structure, clause structure, and complex sentences. For the most part they have left untouched a number of basic grammatical phenomena that do not fit neatly under any one of these rubrics. Nor have these topics—including rule interactions, coordination, anaphora, and speech acts—as yet been the focus of intensive, far-reaching research in cognitive grammar. Their treatment in this chapter is therefore both brief and exploratory. Rather than presenting carefully developed analyses, the discussion should be thought of as suggesting possible strategies and lines of attack.

11.1. Rule Interactions

In its classic form (e.g. as formulated in Chomsky 1965a), transformational grammar envisaged the step-by-step derivation of "surface" syntactic structures from hypothesized "deep" or "underlying" structures by a substantial number of syntactic rules (transformations). Granted this conception, how these rules *interact* with one another becomes a fundamental issue. The standard view in generative theory was that syntactic rules must apply in *sequence* (rather than simultaneously), that an *ordering* has to be imposed on their application, and that a certain series of ordered rules can reapply in *cyclic* fashion (working from "bottom to top," clause by clause, through a syntactic tree structure).

Cognitive grammar does not postulate underlying structures and thus has no direct analog of transformational derivations. More in line with the current Zeitgeist, it sees an expression's well-formedness as depending on the simultaneous satisfaction of multiple constraints. The imposition of these constraints takes the form of categorization by conventional units of the grammar, including constructional schemas representing established grammatical patterns (Vol. 1, Ch. 11). How, then, does this framework accommodate the phenomena that appeared, from the transformational perspective, to demand the sequenced, ordered, and cyclic application of syntactic rules? A prior question is, where have all the transformations gone? That is, what devices does cognitive grammar invoke to express the relationships and regularities that transformations were designed to capture? There is no single or simple answer to that question (if there were, the theories might well be mere notational variants). And since transformations derive surface structures from substantially different underlying representations—in direct violation of the content requirement and the what-you-see-is-what-you-get spirit of cognitive grammar—one should not expect the correspondences to be very close.

Even for the class of "relation-changing" transformations (i.e. those that affect the assignment of grammatical relations) there is no single corresponding device in cognitive grammar. In the case of Passive and *There*-Insertion, the apparent "change" in grammatical relations is seen instead as a discrepancy between simpler and more complex structures, i.e. between distinct levels of organization arrived at in the assembly of a clause through the successive integration of symbolic components. Thus passivization is not a rule that modifies a full clause by reassigning its grammatical relations, but reflects instead the meaning of the past-participial morpheme, which imposes its own figure/ground organization on the content supplied by the verb stem it attaches to (Vol. 1, Fig. 9.11). And in lieu of a rule deriving one clause from another by inserting *there* as the subject (e.g. *A frog is in the bathtub* = = => *There is a frog in the bathtub*), we have posited a construction in which focal prominence is differently assigned by the component *be* and by the composite structure *there be* (Fig. 8.8; cf. Lakoff 1987, case study 3). On the other hand, the alternation attributed to the rule of Dative Shift (e.g. *Jack gave a bracelet to Jill* = = => *Jack gave Jill a bracelet*) is handled by positing two semantic variants of the governing verb, which differ in their choice of primary landmark and consequently in the nature of the construction that serves to elaborate their non-focal participant (8.2). Likewise, the various kinds of Raising are described with reference to semantic variants of the governing predicates in which a profiled participant fails to coincide with its active zone (Figs. 10.6–7).[1]

Other phenomena handled by classic rules of transformational syntax are dealt with in a variety of ways. Instead of "movement rules," cognitive grammar posits alternate constructions involving differences in constituency and linear order, but where the same entities are nevertheless put in correspondence (Vol. 1: 8.4.2, 12.2.3). Hence there is no rule of WH Movement that advances a relative pronoun in the formation of a relative clause: *the skirt she*

[1]The relationship between lexical variants need not be idiosyncratic. Any systematicity, whereby lexical items that share a semantic property undergo parallel semantic extensions, is captured by a schema describing an established pattern of extension. Such schemas, which may be capable of sanctioning novel instances, are comparable to "lexical rules."

bought which = = = > *the skirt* ***which she bought***. Rather, the clause is assembled directly via the integration of *which* and *she bought*, and *which* is the object of *bought* by virtue of elaborating its primary landmark (not because it originates in "object position" after the verb). The effect of "deletion rules" can also be accomplished in other ways. For instance, *the skirt* ***she bought*** is not derived from *the skirt* ***which she bought*** by deletion of the relative pronoun; it represents a distinct construction in which the head noun corresponds directly to the primary landmark of the relative clause (10.1.3). Equi-NP Deletion is simply a matter of the governing predicate attributing multiple roles to the same participant, which can thus be specified by a single (main-clause) nominal; for example, *She expects* ***to win the race*** involves a semantic variant of *expect* that is just the same as the raising variant (sketched in Fig. 10.7(b)) except that the trajector and primary landmark coincide. Moreover, instead of invoking a rule of Reflexivization (e.g. *Sam likes Sam* = = = > *Sam likes himself*), cognitive grammar attributes participant identity to the meaning of the reflexive morpheme (Figs. 8.12–14). Subject-Verb Agreement comes down to whether the semantic properties ascribed to the clausal trajector by the grounding predication are compatible with those independently supplied by the subject nominal (6.1).

The problem of rule interaction arises for sentences whose derivation requires *multiple rule applications*, involving either distinct rules or more than one occurrence of the same rule. In the simplest case, there is no interaction at all: one rule application is wholly unaffected by another, in terms of whether the rule applies, and what it applies to. For example, Subject-Verb Agreement applies independently within each finite clause of a complex sentence. Within a single clause, Subject-Verb Agreement does not interact with Particle Shift (e.g. *She put out the cat* = = = > *She put the cat out*) because the two rules pertain to distinct aspects of clausal structure. Situations like these pose no conceptual problems for a system based on the simultaneous satisfaction of multiple constraints. Even in a derivational framework the rules could perfectly well be allowed to apply simultaneously.

The matter may seem less obvious for derivations requiring that rules apply in a certain *sequence*. The usual reason for invoking sequenced rule application is that one rule creates (gives as "output") the structure to which the other rule applies (takes as "input"). For example, in the derivation that follows, Dative Shift applies before Passive: *Jack gave a bracelet to Jill* = = = > *Jack gave Jill a bracelet* = = = > *Jill was given a bracelet by Jack*. Only through Dative Shift does *Jill* become the direct object of *give*, and only direct objects become subjects through passivization. While this sequencing is indeed required if the relationships in question are handled by transformational derivation from an underlying structure, a comparable effect can also be achieved in a very different manner. A cognitive grammar analysis posits two semantic variants of *give*, one taking the mover as its primary landmark, the other taking the recipient.[2] Either variant is capable of combining with the passive participial morpheme, which imposes an atemporal construal on the process designated by the verb stem and assigns trajector status to its primary landmark (irrespective of semantic role). Hence the passive participle *given* also has two semantic variants: complex atemporal relations in which either the mover or the recipient functions as trajector. From the latter variant, a sentence like *Jill was given a bracelet by Jack* is assembled as described in 5.2.1 and 8.1.2.

Or consider the following derivation: *Floyd expects* ***for Floyd to be considerate*** = = => *Floyd expects Floyd* ***to be considerate*** = = => *Floyd expects himself* ***to be considerate***. Here Subject-to-Object Raising "feeds" Reflexivization by creating the structure needed for its application. Reflexivization takes as input a structure having two coreferential nominals in the same clause, and reduces the second of those nominals to a reflexive pronoun. It is only by virtue of Raising that both occurrences of *Floyd* wind up in the main clause, hence only subsequent to Raising is Reflexivization applicable. In lieu of Raising, however, we have posited semantic variants of the governing predicates in which a schematic process (specified by the infinitival complement) serves as a focal participant's active zone with respect to the profiled relationship. The raising variant of *expect* was diagrammed in Fig. 10.7(b): the trajector entertains a certain propositional attitude in regard to a process (the secondary landmark), and selected as primary landmark is the trajector of that process. In the present example, the primary landmark of *expect* is elaborated by *himself*, and its secondary landmark by *to be considerate*. *Himself* profiles a thing characterized as third-person masculine singular, and further indicates that its designatum corresponds to another clausal participant (prototypically the trajector). In the composite structure *expect himself* ***to be considerate***, the same individual is thus identified as the main-clause trajector and primary landmark, as well as the trajector of the infinitival complement. A well-formed sentence results provided that the semantic characterizations of that individual supplied by the subject nominal (e.g. *Floyd*) and by the grounding predication (*-s*) are each compatible with the third-person masculine singular specification of the reflexive pronoun.

Syntactic transformations were thought to be *ordered*: the grammar lists them in a fixed sequence, and in the course of a derivation they are checked in that sequence for possible application. In most instances the ordering proves to be *intrinsic*, which means that the rules in question could only apply in a particular order even in the absence of an explicit ordering statement.

[2]These variants are related by a pattern of semantic extension (fn. 1) that in some respects is functionally analogous to Dative Shift. For some essential differences between patterns of extension and the rules of a derivation (as normally conceived), see Vol. 1, 11.3.3 (especially p. 444).

This is so for the ordering Dative Shift > Passive in the derivation of *Jill was given a bracelet by Jack*, and for Raising > Reflexivization in *Floyd expects himself* ***to be considerate***—in each case the first rule creates the conditions needed for the second to apply. Ordering is *extrinsic* (i.e. it has to be stipulated by the analyst) when two rules could in principle apply to a structure in either order, but in fact only one sequence yields a well-formed output. A typical example is Passive > Subject-Verb Agreement. Suppose these rules were left unordered, hence free to apply in any sequence. In that case, the verb in a passive clause should be able to agree with either the underlying or the surface subject, depending on whether Agreement happens to apply prior to passivization or subsequently. But in fact the verb must agree with the surface subject: *Sam {is/*are} admired by elderly women*. To impose this restriction it can be stipulated that Agreement follows Passive.

That may not be the best solution, however. Observe that Agreement would also have to be ordered extrinsically to follow both Subject-to-Subject Raising (*The thieves {*is/are} likely* ***to be caught***) and Object-to-Subject Raising (*Competent thieves {*is/are} tough* ***to catch***). With this approach it is purely coincidental that Agreement consistently follows any rule deriving new subjects; nothing captures the generalization that the verb always agrees with the *surface* subject whenever the surface and underlying subjects are distinct.[3] By contrast, the generalization falls out as an automatic consequence of the cognitive grammar account. Recall that a verb's "agreement" with the subject in English is analyzed as an inherent aspect of grounding: certain grounding predications not only situate the grounded process with respect to time and reality, but further include a schematic characterization of its trajector (for person and number). Now by definition, the grounded process is the one profiled at the highest level of organization within a finite clause—it corresponds to the schematic process profiled by the grounding predication itself, which represents the outermost layer in terms of semantic function. Therefore, if there is any discrepancy in the choice of trajector at different levels of organization (i.e. at different levels of complexity in the assembly of a clause out of simpler components), it is the choice that prevails at the highest level which counts for "agreement" purposes. The clause is well-formed in this regard unless there is some incompatibility between the semantic specifications attributed to the highest-level trajector by the subject nominal (which elaborates it) and by the grounding predication.

Extrinsic ordering also appears necessary for derivations such as this: *Jack expects* ***for Jill to criticize Jill*** *===> Jack expects* ***for Jill to criticize herself*** *===> Jack expects Jill* ***to criticize herself***. Since Reflexivization

[3] Despite well-known difficulties, I believe this generalization holds even for sentences derived by *There*-Insertion (e.g. *There {*is/are} several frogs in the bathtub*). A proposal concerning the apparent plurality of *there* was made at the end of 8.1.3.4.

requires the occurrence of two coreferential nominals within the same clause, it has to apply within the subordinate clause before Subject-to-Object Raising removes the first instance of *Jill*; were the rules allowed to apply in either order, Raising could "bleed" Reflexivization (i.e. destroy the conditions needed for its application), in which case regular pronominalization would yield *Jack expects Jill* ***to criticize her*** (impermissible when *Jill* and *her* are coreferential). This problem does not arise in the cognitive grammar description. Examining the raising variant of *expect* in Fig. 10.7(b), we find that the same participant functions simultaneously as the primary landmark with respect to the profiled (main-clause) relationship, and as the trajector of the process specified by the infinitival complement (lm_2). The fact that the nominal elaborating lm_1 constitutes the main-clause direct object has no effect on the dual role of the participant it designates. In particular, nothing prevents lm_2 from being elaborated by an infinitival clause such as *to criticize herself*, in which *herself* indicates that the trajector and landmark correspond. If we now step back and compare the two analyses, we see that ordering is needed in the transformational account because it confounds *the position of the direct-object nominal* with *the semantic role of the individual it profiles*. But in the present theory, even though the nominal appears in just one place the designated individual can perfectly well have multiple roles within the conceptualization.

The apparent need for *cyclic* rule application can be illustrated by the following derivation: *Jack expects* ***for Sam to criticize Jill*** = = => *Jack expects* ***for Jill to be criticized by Sam*** = = => *Jack expects Jill* ***to be criticized by Sam*** = = => *Jill is expected by Jack* ***to be criticized by Sam***. Since *Jill* is understood as the "logical object" of *criticize* and supposedly has no other grammatical relation in underlying structure, it can surface as the main-clause subject only by dint of several rule applications. First, Passive applies within the subordinate clause to make *Jill* the derived subject at that level. As a complement clause subject, *Jill* is then eligible to undergo Subject-to-Object Raising, whereby it becomes the direct object of the main-clause verb *expect*. Finally, another application of Passive, this time within the superordinate clause, elevates *Jill* to the status of main-clause subject. The necessary sequence of rule applications is thus Passive > Raising > Passive, which is contradictory if one assumes that rules observe a strict, purely linear ordering. A number of such contradictions were resolved by the notion of the cycle: certain rules apply in sequence within a subordinate clause, then reapply in the same sequence within a superordinate clause, and so on clause by clause through all the levels of a complex sentence. In the case at hand, Passive applies on the first pass through this cycle (Raising being inapplicable at the lowest level), and then both Raising and Passive apply on the second pass.

In cognitive grammar, the effect of cyclic rule application stems from the very nature of complex sentences. A subordinate clause represents one level of organization in the assembly of a complex structure out of simpler symbolic components. The profiling and grammatical relations imposed at such a level are overridden by those of main-clause elements in the formation of a higher-order structure that subsumes them both. If that structure is in turn subordinated to another clause, the latter's organization again prevails, and so on, until the entire complex sentence has been assembled. And since many constructions (e.g. those pertaining to passivization) are available for the assembly of a clause at any level, an effect comparable to cyclic rule application is achieved.

Consider, then, the assembly of a complex sentence of the form *X is expected by Y* ***to be criticized by Z***. Essential aspects of its composition are diagrammed in Fig. 11.1. At the lowest level, the verb *criticize* invokes two central participants: the trajector is the source of verbal communication and social/psychological pressure, represented by the double broken arrow; these are directed at the landmark individual, an experiencer (as indicated by the single dashed arrow). From *criticize*, the full subordinate clause *to be criticized by* Z is formed in several steps (not individually shown) in accordance with constructions previously described. Most important for immediate purposes is the integration of *criticize* with the passive participial morpheme ($PERF_3$), which has the effect of elevating the experiencer to trajector status. Additionally, *criticized* combines with the prepositional phrase *by* Z, which specifies the source participant periphrastically; *be* derives a complex verb from the atemporal *criticized by* Z; and *to* reimposes an atemporal construal.

The middle portion of Fig. 11.1 represents the integration of *to be criticized by* Z and the main-clause verb *expect*. This is simply a matter of the infinitival clause elaborating the verb's secondary landmark in conformity with the usual "raising" construction. Recall that the raising variant of *expect* accords the status of primary landmark to the participant serving as the trajector of lm_2, hence it corresponds to the experiencer of the passive complement clause. The resulting composite structure profiles a relationship of expectation whose trajector is the individual entertaining this propositional attitude, and whose primary landmark is the target of criticism. This complex processual structure is in turn susceptible to passivization: $PERF_3$ confers trajector status on its primary landmark (the individual criticized); the prepositional phrase *by Y* specifies periphrastically the person holding the expectation; and *be* retemporalizes the participial structure to form the complex clausal head *be expected by Y to be criticized by Z*.[4] Elaboration of the trajector by the subject

[4] Word order suggests an alternative constituency, wherein *to be criticized by* Z does not combine directly with *expect* but with the already passivized structure *expected by Y*. Under this analysis the infinitival clause elaborates the active zone of the passive subject (rather than the direct object), which makes the construction an analog of Subject-to-Subject (rather than Subject-to-Object) Raising. The difference has no real bearing on the point at hand.

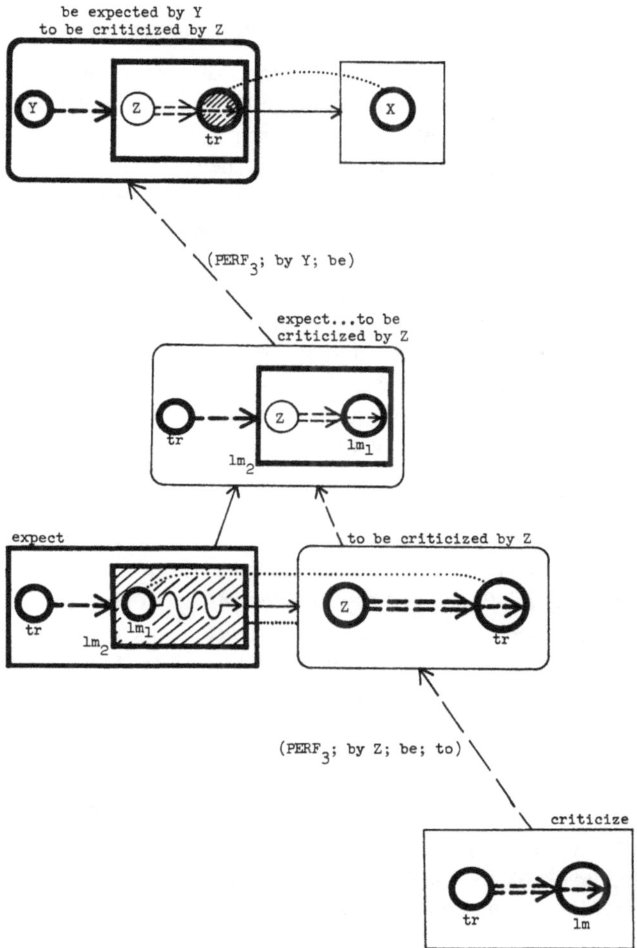

Fig. 11.1

nominal (*X*), together with grounding (not shown), then yields the full sentence: *X is expected by Y to be criticized by Z.*

These few examples hardly afford a full appreciation of how cognitive grammar accommodates the phenomena for which sequenced, ordered, and cyclic rule application were thought necessary. They do however indicate that such phenomena are not *in principle* incompatible with a framework based on the simultaneous satisfaction of multiple constraints, as expressed by configurations of symbolic units. Indeed, classic instances of rule interaction are handled quite straightforwardly given analyses proposed on independent grounds.

11.2. Coordination

Long recognized as posing special problems of description and theory, coordination remains a topic of prime concern for linguists of varied theoretical persuasions (e.g. Goodall 1983, 1984; Hudson 1984, 1988; Sag, Gazdar, Wasow, and Weisler 1985; Steedman 1985). It is special first in terms of constituency, for while constituent structure generally tends rather strongly to be binary, coordinate structures apparently allow an indefinite number of co-equal conjuncts (e.g. *A, B, C, D, . . . , X, Y, and Z*). Moreover, these conjuncts have to be "parallel" in certain respects not yet fully understood; in particular, they must represent the same grammatical class and participate in parallel grammatical relationships with external elements. Additional problems pertain to the interaction between coordination and other aspects of constituent structure (e.g. the conjoining of non-constituents), and to various devices for avoiding repetition across a set of conjuncts.

11.2.1. *Conjunctions*

It was suggested in 10.1.2 that "pure" conjunctions represent the limiting (zero) case for connectors in regard to both the asymmetry and the objectivity of the connecting relationship. They show no vestige of any objective relation (such as causality or temporal precedence) whose very conception would render the coordinated entities different in status. Instead, the connection is wholly subjective: it reduces to the mental juxtaposition of co-equal structures, on either a simultaneous or an alternating basis. Several basic features of coordinate structures can be seen as either consequences or natural concomitants of this characterization. These traits include the parallelism exhibited by the conjuncts; the absence of any intrinsic limit on their number; and the possibility of conjoined structures representing different grammatical classes and levels of organization (not just clauses).

More specifically, a conjunction is analyzed as having not just one profile, but two or more separate and co-equal profiles representing the same basic class. A given conjunction usually has multiple semantic variants, which differ in the number of profiled entities, the class they represent, and their level of specificity in regard to either parameter. For instance, one variant of *and* profiles two nominals (as in *the sausage and the bacon*), another designates three adjectival relations (*red, white, and blue*), and so on. Highly specific variants such as these reflect the occurrence of certain types of expressions with sufficient frequency that the particular interpretations of the conjunction they induce achieve the status of conventional units (this being, of course, a matter of degree). More schematic variants capture broader generalizations and may be called upon to sanction expressions not conforming to any frequent pattern. We can thus envisage a schematic variant of *and* that profiles two relations of any type; one that designates multiple processes but does not specify a particular number; and even a maximally schematic variant that simply profiles 'multiple entities' of any type or number.

Consider first the assembly of a simple conjoined structure of the form *a and b*, assuming (for the sake of illustration) that the conjuncts are nominal structures. Their bipolar representations can be given as [A/a] and [B/b]: *A* and *B* are predications that profile things, while *a* and *b* abbreviate the phonological structures that effect their symbolization. A bipolar sketch of their coordination is offered in Fig. 11.2. As usual, the heavy-line circles enclosing *A* and

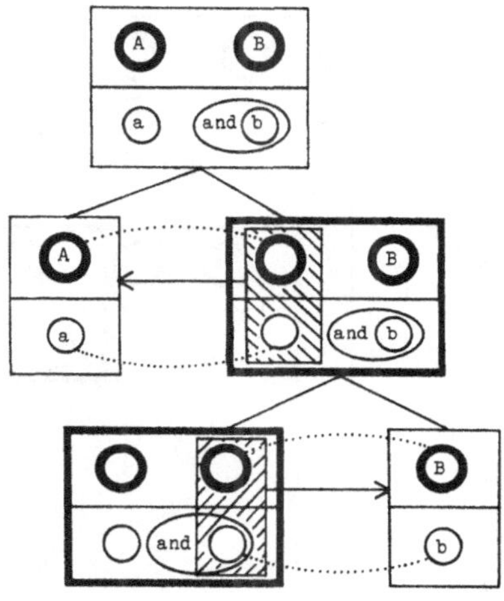

Fig. 11.2

B at the semantic pole stand for their nominal profiles. At the other pole, circles and ellipses enclose structures that are phonologically autonomous (in unipolar terms), such as words or phonological phrases. The notation *(and (b))* indicates that *b* is such a structure, and that the phonologically dependent *and* attaches to it as a rhythmic satellite (cf. Vol. 1, Ch. 9).

The conjunction *and* is schematic for the coordinate structures it derives. The variant in question evokes—as simultaneous and co-equal profiles—the conception of two things, each of which stands in symbolic correspondence to the autonomous phonological structure shown directly below it in the diagram. The conceptual juxtaposition of the two nominal entities is symbolized by the phonological juxtaposition of their phonological correspondents, together with the rhythmic attachment of *and* to the last of these in the temporal sequence. Successive elaboration of the two schematic conjuncts, by [B/b] and then by [A/a], yields the composite expression [A B/a and b]. It is important to observe that conceptual coordination does not necessarily correlate with grammatical constituency; the fact that A and B are conceptually juxtaposed as co-equals does not entail that [A/a] and [B/b] directly combine as co-constituents. Their conceptual juxtaposition represents *an inherent aspect of the semantic pole* at a given level of organization (note the semantic pole of *and*, of *and b*, or of *a and b*). It does not necessarily reflect the order in which the component expressions combine via elaborative relations to derive the composite structure.

What about an expression of the form *a, b, and c*? Because three conjuncts are associated by a single occurrence of *and*, we must assume a variant that profiles three co-equal entities, each symbolized by an autonomous phono-

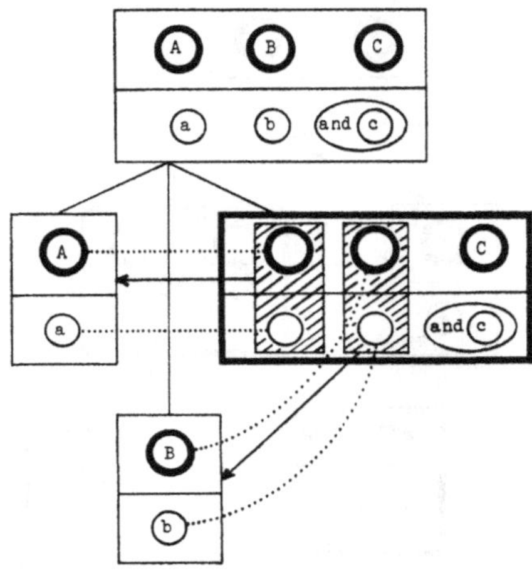

Fig. 11.3

logical structure. The result of [C/c] elaborating the final schematic conjunct is shown on the right in Fig. 11.3. Elaboration of the other two conjuncts by [A/a] and [B/b] then produces the composite structure [A B C /a b and c]. In the absence of contrary evidence, grammatical constituency is presumed to correlate with intonational grouping, hence a construction with three component structures is posited—*a* does not form a subconstituent with *b*, nor *b* with *and c*.[5] Clearly, this description can be generalized to single-conjunction coordinate structures with any number of conjuncts.

Consider next the alternative pattern in which a conjunction appears with every conjunct except the first: *a, and b, and c, and d, and e, ...* On the assumption that each occurrence of the conjunction signals a distinct instance of coordination, I interpret this as a "chaining" construction, where each phrase *and x* adds another link to a coordinate structure already assembled.

[5]This is not a necessary assumption. As just noted, the co-equality of coordinate entities is a matter of conceptual structure, not grammatical constituency per se.

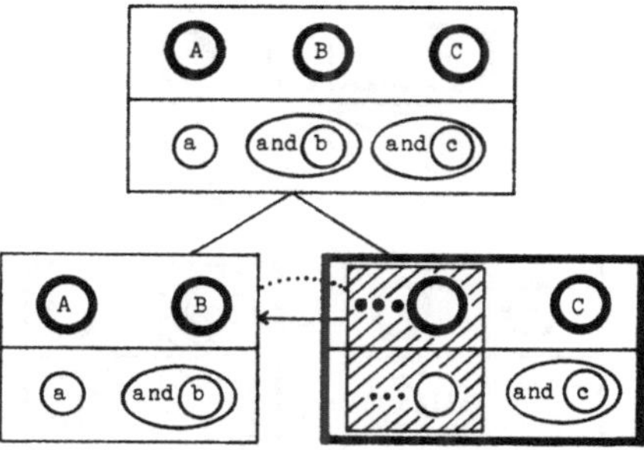

Fig. 11.4

One step in the assembly of such an expression is depicted in Fig. 11.4. The component shown on the left is the minimal coordinate structure *a and b* (the composite structure of Fig. 11.2). On the right is the link to be added: the schematic coordinate structure . . . *and c*, which comprises an indefinite number of conjuncts, the last of which has been elaborated by [C/c]. Note that the elaboration site in 11.4 subsumes the entire sequence of conjuncts preceding the conjunction. There is a global correspondence between this e-site as a whole and the other component, *a and b*, which specifies both the number and the identity of the prior conjuncts. Note further that the composite semantic structure [A B C] is the same as for *a, b, and c* (Fig. 11.3)—despite the grouping *(a and b) and c*, whereby the first two conjuncts form a grammatical constituent, all three profiled entities are separate and co-equal. Why? Because the co-equality of multiple profiles (representing a single level of conceptual coordination) is inherent in the semantic pole of . . . *and c*, the profile determinant in this construction. The fact that all conjuncts but the last are schematic and collectively function as e-site in no way obviates their conceptual parallelism with the final conjunct; the elaborating structure merely effects the finer-grained specification of schematic elements (it does not impose a different conceptual organization on the scene). The situation at the phonological pole is quite analogous. Component . . . *and c* indicates that the respective conjuncts are manifested by a string of autonomous and co-equal phonological structures. Since *a and b* is merely elaborative, the same organization is observed at the composite structure level: *(a) (and (b)) (and (c))*.

There is however an interpretation of the sequence *a and b and c* in which *a and b* (or alternatively, *b and c*) does form both a conceptual and an intonational subgroup.[6] In this case, grammatical constituency (order of symbolic composition) is indeed reflected in (unipolar) hierarchies at both the semantic

[6]This organization is brought out most clearly when the conjunctions differ: *(either) a and b or (else) c*.

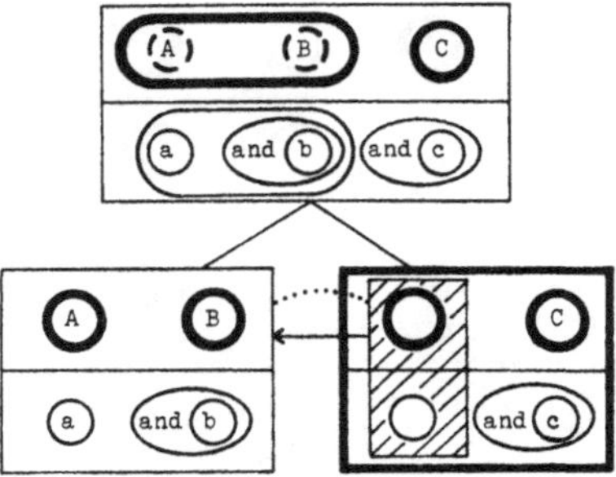

Fig. 11.5

and the phonological poles (cf. Vol. 1, 2.3.1.2). Diagrammed in Fig. 11.5, this construction is only minimally different from the preceding one in terms of its component structures. Comparison of Figs. 11.4 and 11.5 reveals that, in the former, *a and b* elaborates a *series* of schematic conjuncts within . . . *and c*, whereas in the latter it corresponds to a *single* conjunct. In 11.5, therefore, . . . *and c* comprises just two conjuncts, one of which is elaborated by the coordinate structure *a and b*. Hence the composite structure manifests two levels of conceptual coordination: the single entity conceived as being coordinate with C happens to be internally complex, resulting from the coordination of A and B at a lower level of conceptual organization. Likewise, the single autonomous structure coordinate with *and c* at the phonological pole is elaborated by a complex structure that itself consists of two autonomous substructures. The composite phonological structure thus shows the phrasing *((a) (and (b))) / (and (c))*, where *((a) (and (b)))* undergoes a certain amount of temporal compression to make it rhythmically parallel to the simpler *(and (c))* (cf. Vol. 1, p. 363).

11.2.2. *Level of Coordination*

On the face of it, structures representing almost any level of grammatical organization can be conjoined. These range from full, multiclause sentences, as in (1)(a); to finite clauses, as in (b); to "phrasal" constituents of various sizes, (c)–(e); to single words, (f)–(g); and even to loosely bound prefixes, (h).

(1)(a) *When he came home, Carl was exhausted, and because there was nothing to eat, he went straight to bed.*

(b) *I believe that either the market will stabilize or else there will be a severe recession.*

(c) *Zelda sold real estate in Chicago and ran a bar in Detroit.*

(d) *We found dust on the furniture and under the bed.*

(e) *She knitted a blue scarf and a cute green sweater.*

(f) *The new hand groomed and watered the horses.*

(g) *Abernathy hires only young and beautiful secretaries.*
(h) *Your insurance covers both pre- and post-operative care.*

Expressions involving the coordination of elements smaller than clauses are often semantically equivalent (or virtually so) to instances of clausal coordination. For example, (1)(d)–(e) have essentially the same meanings as (2)(a)–(b):

(2)(a) *We found dust on the furniture and we found dust under the bed.*
(b) *She knitted a blue scarf and she knitted a cute green sweater.*

Thus linguists have sometimes analyzed such expressions as reduced forms of underlying multiclausal structures (Chomsky 1957; Gleitman 1965). It was originally thought that rules of "conjunction reduction" might enable one to eliminate all but clausal (or sentential) coordination at the deep-structure level. Of course, the natural bias in cognitive grammar is to describe subclausal coordination directly, in its own terms. We will find that this approach is generally workable and often necessary. And while certain expressions do require something akin to a reduction analysis, the framework provides a way of describing these without resorting to derivations from underlying structures.

It has long been recognized that some instances of subclausal coordination cannot reasonably be derived by conjunction reduction (Smith 1969; Lakoff and Peters 1969). The respective sentences in (3), for example, can hardly be derived from those in (4), which are either ill-formed or different in meaning.

(3)(a) *Harry and Sally met in Chicago.*
(b) *The boy munched on a peanut butter and jelly sandwich.*
(c) *They were bouncing a red and yellow beachball.*

(4)(a) **Harry met in Chicago and Sally met in Chicago.*
(b) *The boy munched on a peanut butter sandwich and the boy munched on a jelly sandwich.*
(c) *They were bouncing a red beachball and they were bouncing a yellow beachball.*

Instead, each coordinate expression in (3) conceptually invokes a complex entity that functions as a unitary whole in its interaction with another clausal element. The conceptual coordination forming this entity must therefore occur at a lower level of organization, so that it will be available for integration with that element in the course of assembling a single clause. For instance, *peanut butter and jelly* is construed as the name of a composite substance comprising intermingled patches of the component substances *peanut butter* and *jelly* (cf. Figs. 1.5(b) and 2.12(c)). A *peanut butter and jelly sandwich* is conceived as being made from this composite substance, hence grammatically it is parallel to *cheese sandwich*—it is only the composite expression (not the individual conjuncts) that is integrated with *sandwich*.[7]

As for (3)(a), *meet* is one of numerous verbs and adjectives describing a roughly symmetrical relationship between two or more participants (e.g. *fight, wrestle, collide, kiss, alike, similar, identical*). Most of these have two semantic variants. One variant chooses a single participant as its trajector, the other participant being specified by a direct or oblique complement (*She fought (with) him*; *She kissed him*; *She is similar to him*). The second variant confers trajector status on the higher-order entity comprising the set of participating individuals, as shown on the right in Fig. 11.6(a). In a sentence like

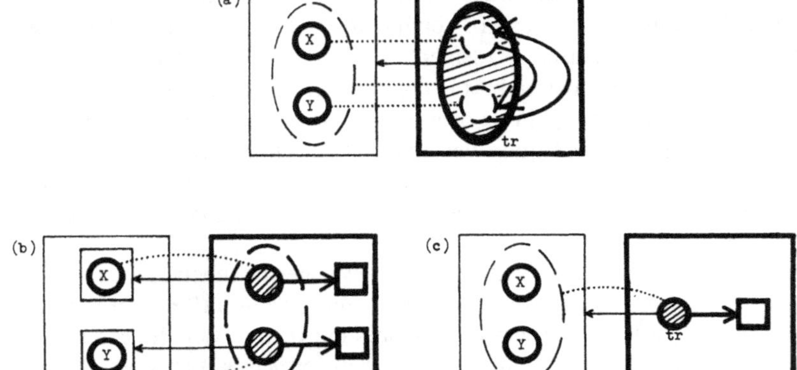

Fig. 11.6

(3)(a), that entity is put in correspondence with the region implicitly defined by the conceptual juxtaposition of nominal profiles within the coordinate expression (recall that mere co-conception is sufficient to establish a set of elements as an abstract region). Thus the semantics of the verb induces a construal of the conjoined nominal that highlights the coherence of its co-equal profiles to form a complex whole at a higher level of conceptual organization. This effect is even stronger with a verb like *arrive*, which may invoke just a

[7] It is irrelevant that the peanut butter and the jelly are separately spread on the bread and are physically intermingled only to a limited extent; they nonetheless do form a composite substance in a more abstract, *functional* sense (e.g. from the standpoint of the taste sensation they induce). Note that verb inflection is sensitive to the conceptual distinction between a single, composite substance and a higher-order entity consisting of two separate substances: *Peanut butter and jelly {is/are} good for making sandwiches*. The same contrast is observable with abstract substances (1.2.1.1): *Reading and writing {is/are} hard work*. The choice of *is* reflects the construal of *reading and writing* as a single, composite activity in which patches (or episodes) of the component activities are interspersed if not simultaneous (cf. *Reading and writing at the same time {is/*are} hard work*).

single participant. A sentence such as *Harry and Sally arrived in Chicago* has two basic interpretations, diagrammed in Figs. 11.6(b) and (c). On the one hand, *arrive* can designate a replicate process comprising two separate instances of the atomic process (see Ch. 3), so that the sentence is roughly equivalent to one involving conjoined clauses (*Harry arrived in Chicago and Sally arrived in Chicago*). In this case the conjuncts can be thought of as individually elaborating the components of the verb's replicate trajector (TR). On the other hand, the sentence may be construed as designating just one instance of arriving in which Harry and Sally participate as a single complex entity (i.e. they arrive as a couple). As shown in diagram (c), this interpretation reflects a correspondence between the verb's non-replicate trajector and the higher-order entity consisting of the subject's twin profiles.[8]

What about *a red and yellow beachball*? A color adjective profiles the relationship between a region in color space (its landmark) and some entity (its trajector) that induces a color sensation which falls within that region. Prototypically, the trajector is an object whose entire outer surface (or most of it) induces the sensation in question. Because we cannot simultaneously perceive two colors at the same location, a compound color term such as *red and yellow*—when applied to a single object—has a composite semantic value that does not preserve intact the prototypical value of either adjective. It specifies that distinct portions of the object's surface project to each landmark region of color space, and while in each case this portion is substantial, in neither case is its coverage complete. When the compound adjective combines with a singular noun, it is the composite color *red and yellow* (not *red* or *yellow* individually) that is attributed to the nominal profile.[9]

11.2.3. *Differentiation of Conjuncts*

The examples just considered make it apparent that not all instances of subclausal coordination are felicitously analyzed as reductions of conjoined clauses. Rather, there appears to be a gradation in the extent to which the entities profiled by conjuncts are conceived as being clearly differentiated and as participating individually in relationships with other clausal elements. Toward one extreme of this spectrum lie expressions such as *a gin and tonic*, *a*

[8] Thus a complex entity is construed holistically for combinatory purposes, just as in Fig. 11.5, representing expressions of the form *a and b and c* (where A and B form a conceptual constituent). Since *Harry and Sally arrived in Chicago* has the same grammatical constituent structure under either interpretation, we have further evidence that grammatical constituency per se is not responsible for the conceptual groupings within a coordinate structure.

[9] With a plural noun, as in *red and yellow beachballs*, the composite color may either be attributed to each beachball individually, or else to the replicate mass as a whole (in which case some beachballs may be entirely red, others entirely yellow). Hence the conceptual coordination of the colors takes place at different levels of organization vis-à-vis the replication involved in conceiving the plural mass, yet there is no apparent difference in grammatical constituency. (This is quite similar to what we observed for quantifier scope (3.3.2).)

peanut butter and jelly sandwich, or *a red and yellow beachball*, in which the conjuncts jointly describe a composite substance or color whose special composite character is crucial to its role in the overall conceptualization. A sentence like *Harry and Sally arrived* is comparable to the extent that it approaches the interpretation sketched in Fig. 11.6(c), where Harry and Sally are construed as a single entity that participates as a unitary whole in just one atomic instance of arrival (e.g. they might—as a couple—be arriving to compete in a tango contest). This type of configuration is depicted abstractly in Fig. 11.7(a).

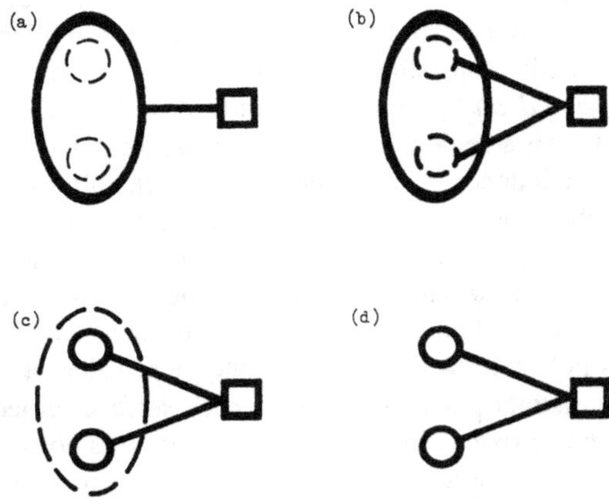

Fig. 11.7

Less extreme, and more likely as an interpretation of *Harry and Sally arrived*, is the configuration shown in Fig. 11.7(b). Here the components of the coordinate entity have somewhat greater salience, because a relationship involving that entity can to some degree be factored into subrelations in which the components participate individually. Viewed in this fashion, the joint arrival of Harry and Sally is construed as a single event that is nonetheless recognized as being complex—a replicate process comprising two instances of the atomic process *arrive*, each associated with a distinct component of the replicate trajector. Predicates describing symmetrical relationships instantiate configuration (b) to the extent that the subrelations running in opposite directions are capable of existing independently. In *Harry and Sally embraced*, for example, each individual carries out an action separately identifiable as an instance of *embrace*; thus Harry can embrace Sally without Sally reciprocating.[10] The sentence *He's wearing shoes and socks* offers a slightly different

[10] By contrast, *Line A and line B intersect* is less decomposable because line A cannot intersect line B unless B also intersects A. Hence it is not a very good exemplar of configuration (b), even though we can impose a figure/ground asymmetry by saying *Line A intersects line B* (or conversely).

kind of example. The component relationships are easily differentiated, for either shoes or socks can perfectly well be worn without the other. And since *wear* normally takes a singular object, the salience of the coordinate entity as a unitary whole is not imposed by the verb (as it is with *meet* or *embrace*—cf. Fig. 11.6(a)). It derives instead from the status of *shoes and socks* as a fixed expression describing an utterly familiar, quotidian assembly of items that collectively serve a basic function.

As we move toward the opposite end of the spectrum, the coordinate entity becomes less salient than its components (the profiles of the individual conjuncts), which participate in separate though parallel relationships with other elements. In configuration (c), the coordinate entity is still invoked, but only incidentally (nothing requires its construal as a unitary whole), whereas (d) represents the limiting case in which the conception of a higher-order entity is absent altogether. Configuration (c) corresponds to typical cases of subclausal coordination generally regarded as equivalent to clausal coordination and thus derivable by conjunction reduction. For example, *She knitted a scarf and a sweater* means roughly the same as *She knitted a scarf and she knitted a sweater*; the scarf and the sweater were presumably knitted independently and are construed as constituting a higher-order entity only by virtue of the nominal coordination itself. Similarly, *Harry and Sally arrived* instantiates configuration (c) when interpreted to mean that the two people arrived in separate, unrelated events.

Configurations (a)–(d) differ primarily in the relative salience of certain substructures. Because this is largely a matter of degree, with no clear lines of demarcation, it seems arbitrary to single out a portion of the spectrum for description in terms of conjunction reduction. Candidates for such description cannot expect any special treatment in cognitive grammar; from this perspective, they are most naturally seen as being assembled directly in the manner suggested by their surface form. When interpreted as an instance of configuration (c), for example, *Harry and Sally arrived* is constructed as diagrammed in Fig. 11.6(b): *arrive* is construed as designating a replicate process, and each component of its complex trajector is elaborated by one conjunct of the coordinate structure *Harry and Sally* (already assembled at a lower level of organization). The essential point is that the sentence's interpretation is basically independent of its grammatical constituency. Interpretations vary as to the number of atomic events, the relative prominence of simple and complex participants, as well as the specific correspondences established between the verb's trajector and the coordinate subject. Yet they can all be accommodated in a grammatical analysis that posits coordination only within the subject nominal.

The type of analysis proposed for expressions instantiating configuration (c) is similar in spirit to recent accounts in other theoretical frameworks. For instance, Goodall (1983, 1984) has suggested that coordination represents a third dimension in phrase trees that are otherwise basically two-dimensional. Whereas Hudson (1984, 1988) for the most part describes grammatical relationships in terms of dependency alone, he employs constituency for the specific case of coordinate structures. The approach adopted here agrees with these in treating coordination as an aspect of grammatical structure that is in some sense orthogonal to the remainder.[11] Specifically, it ascribes multiple, co-equal profiles to both conjunctions and the conjoined structures derived by elaborating their schematic conjuncts (Figs. 11.2–5). The analyses agree, moreover, in claiming that the conjuncts participate simultaneously in parallel grammatical relationships with other clausal elements. Both in Hudson's description and in the present account, these parallel relationships provide an alternative to the *coordinate structure constraint* proposed by Ross (1967 [1986]).

As a universal constraint on movement transformations, Ross stated that no conjunct can be moved out of a coordinate structure, nor can any element be moved out of a conjunct. Exemplifying a movement transformation is the rule that supposedly moves a relative pronoun to clause-initial position, as in (5)(a).

(5)(a) *the scarf* ***she knitted which*** = = => *the scarf* ***which she knitted***
(b) *the scarf* ***she knitted which and a sweater*** = = => **the scarf* ***which she knitted and a sweater***

Note that in (5)(b) the relative pronoun *which* originates as one conjunct of the conjoined nominal functioning as the direct object of *knitted* (cf. *She knitted a scarf and a sweater*). The preposing of *which* therefore violates the coordinate structure constraint, and the resulting relative clause construction is claimed to be ungrammatical for this reason. A similar violation occurs in (6)(a), except that here two clauses are conjoined and the transported relative pronoun is an element of a single conjunct.

(6)(a) *the car* ***Joe washed which and Bill mowed the lawn*** = = => **the car* ***which Joe washed and Bill mowed the lawn***
(b) *the car* ***Joe washed which and Bill polished which*** = = => *the car* ***which Joe washed and Bill polished***

Ross found one systematic exception to the constraint: an element can be moved out of a conjunct provided that the rule applies *across the board*, i.e.

[11] There are of course differences. Despite their appearance on the printed page (e.g. Fig. 5.11), the constituency trees of cognitive grammar are not linearly ordered (temporal order is internal to each node, at the phonological pole), hence they do not have the two-dimensionality of generative phrase trees in the first place. I have also argued that the hierarchy apparent in multilevel coordinate structures (e.g. *a and b or c*) is primarily a matter of *unipolar* (i.e. intrinsic conceptual and phonological) organization and need not correlate with grammatical constituency, which reflects the assembly of progressively more complex *bipolar* structures.

the same element is simultaneously extracted from all the conjuncts. Hence the derivation in (6)(b) yields a well-formed output because *which* is the underlying object in both conjoined clauses.

Hudson does not attribute the deviance of examples like (5)(b) and (6)(a) to the violation of any constraints on movement rules. Rather, he claims that any grammatical dependency which crosses a conjunct boundary must be shared by all the conjuncts. Hudson's dependencies (e.g. between a verb and its direct object) are roughly comparable to the valence links described here in terms of correspondences and elaborative relationships, and his proposal is quite analogous to one that suggests itself (though it has not yet been carefully investigated) in the context of cognitive grammar. The relative clauses in (6)(a)–(b) are respectively diagrammed in Fig. 11.8(a)–(b) (where W, J, B,

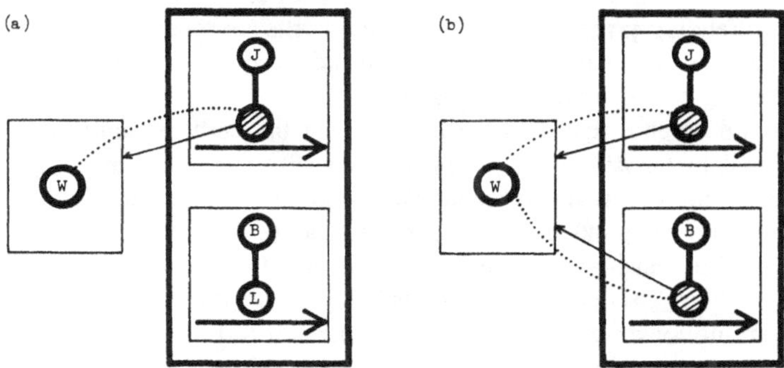

Fig. 11.8

and L abbreviate the semantic specifications of *which*, *Joe*, *Bill*, and *the lawn*). Observe that in (a), *which* elaborates the landmark of one conjunct but is not directly connected with the second, whereas in (b), the relative pronoun elaborates the landmarks of both conjuncts. The ill-formedness of (6)(a) is attributable to the fact that only one conjunct participates in this basic grammatical linkage, according to the following rationale.

The essence of coordination is the conceptual juxtaposition of co-equal structures. Central properties of coordination can be seen as following in a general way from this characterization (even though their implementation is subject to a certain amount of conventional determination as specified in constructional schemas established in particular languages). It is natural, for example, that the conjuncts of a coordinate expression should represent the same basic grammatical class, since that is determined by the most salient aspect of their meanings, namely their profiles. It is further natural that the conjuncts should be co-equal in terms of their function, and thus in terms of their interaction with other elements. One manifestation of this functional co-equality is joint inclusion as essential facets of a unitary whole (e.g. *gin and tonic*;

red and yellow [*beachball*]; *shoes and socks*; *mortar and pestle*). Participation in parallel grammatical relationships, as in diagram (b), can be seen as another manifestation. The problem with structures like the one in diagram (a) is that two conjuncts are evoked as co-equals in the context of a grammatical construction in which only one of them participates. This grammatical asymmetry clashes with the functional parallelism that constitutes the *raison d'être* of coordination and the motivation for using it in a particular structural setting—whereas the coordinate construction itself portrays the conjuncts as being analogous in function, they do not in fact both participate in the most salient structural relationship within the broader grammatical context defining that function. Although such conflicts do not impose an absolute cross-linguistic prohibition on every kind of grammatical asymmetry involving conjoined structures, they do exert a constant pressure against the adoption of clearly offending expressions. The specific results are reflected in the array of constructional schemas detailing the conventionally established usage of coordinate expressions in a given language.

I should emphasize that these conflicts are basically *semantic* in nature: conceptual juxtaposition and co-equality constitute the very meaning of coordination; moreover, the grammatical asymmetries in question involve relationships of correspondence and elaboration between structures at the semantic pole. One can therefore predict that as coordinate constructions deviate from the "pure" semantic value we have been considering, so that the conjuncts are no longer conceived in strictly parallel fashion, certain departures from strict grammatical parallelism might also start to be tolerated. To take just one example, sentences like the following have long been cited as counterexamples to the coordinate structure constraint:

(7)(a) *What should I go to the store and buy?*
(b) *What do they plan to sit around and discuss?*
(c) *What did she fall asleep and dream about?*

The problem is that the question word *what* in each case bears a grammatical relationship to the second conjunct but not to the first; in terms of a movement-rule analysis, the extraction does not take place across the board. It should be apparent, however, that the conjuncts do not represent separate, parallel events. They are instead construed as successive phases in a single overall occurrence that instantiates a coherent, familiar type of scenario (cf. Lakoff 1986). The component processes are not viewed as co-equal alternatives, but as closely related processes one of which creates the conditions in which the other takes place. Under this construal, the question word's association with the second conjunct alone does not give rise to any semantic conflict: the coordinate expression designates a cohesive train of events only the last of which—coded by the final conjunct—evokes as a direct participant the entity that *what* refers to.

11.2.4. *Phonological Coinstantiation*

Up to this point, we have focused on the conjoining of structures that are universally recognized as grammatical constituents. We have also avoided any analysis based on conjunction reduction; even when equivalent to conjoined clauses, expressions involving subclausal coordination were claimed to be directly assembled in the manner suggested by their surface form. Thus *Harry and Sally arrived* has the same constituency under any of the construals represented in diagrams (a)–(c) of Fig. 11.7: coordination affects two nominals (not two clauses), and the complex nominal so formed then combines with *arrive*. By this analysis the assembly of such expressions is in full conformity with normal assumptions about constituent structure.

However, conjoining is by no means limited to sequences standardly recognized as constituents. A case in point is *Joe washed and Bill polished the car*, where each conjunct comprises a subject and verb but excludes the verb's direct object. Now some instances of non-constituent coordination may be only apparent, for as conceived in cognitive grammar constituency is potentially quite variable (Vol. 1, 8.4.2). The present example is susceptible to such analysis. Alongside the canonical (S(VO)) constituent structure of English transitive clauses, there is good reason to posit ((SV)O) as a secondary pattern (e.g. for relative clauses like the one in (6)(b)). Thus *Joe washed* and *Bill polished* are reasonably analyzed as subject-verb constituents that undergo coordination and joint elaboration by the direct-object nominal *the car* (cf. Fig. 11.8(b)).

Still, for many coordinate expressions any such analysis seems implausible. Consider (8)(a).

(8)(a) *You sent a letter to France on Monday, and a package to Zambia on Thursday.*

(b) *You sent a letter to France on Monday, and you sent a package to Zambia on Thursday.*

Each conjunct in (8)(a) comprises a direct object (*a letter*; *a package*), a locative indicating the goal of the object's motion (*to France*; *to Zambia*), and an adverb specifying the temporal setting (*on Monday*; *on Thursday*). Since the first two elements are complements of *send*, and the other a clause-level adverb, they can hardly combine directly with one another to form a constituent that excludes the verb.[12] Moreover, there is no semantic or grammatical evidence (apart from such coordinate expressions themselves) that would lead one to posit a constituent subsuming just these elements. For cases of this sort something akin to conjunction reduction appears to be required. Resistant to

[12] In particular, the temporal adverb's integration with the remainder of the clause hinges on a correspondence between its trajector and the process that the verb introduces and designates.

analysis as a single-clause expression formed by the coordination of subclausal constituents, (8)(a) is perhaps less problematically regarded as elliptic for the biclausal (8)(b).

What form can such ellipsis take in a theoretical framework that does not posit derivations from underlying structures? Recall that certain putative discrepancies between overt and underlying structures are accepted in cognitive grammar as having some basis, but are reinterpreted as differences between component and composite structures in the assembly of a complex expression. Let us therefore consider the possibility that a sentence like (8)(a) might in fact involve the conjoining of two full clauses, but that one of these components receives only partial phonological manifestation at the composite structure level. By this analysis, (8)(a) is assembled by integrating one clausal conjunct (*you sent a letter to France on Monday*) with another (*and you sent a package to Zambia on Thursday*). However, only the first conjunct is reflected intact at the composite structure's phonological pole.[13]

Expressions of this sort represent a special case of a far more general linguistic phenomenon, which we will call **phonological coinstantiation**. As a basic illustration of this phenomenon, consider **haplology**, the occurrence of a single syllable in lieu of two adjacent syllables that are either identical or very similar. Linguists, for example, sometimes shorten *morphophonemics* (or *morphophonology*) to *morphonemics* (*morphonology*). Analyzed in terms of coinstantiation, the *pho* of *morphonemics* is not identified exclusively as that of either *morpho* or *phonemics*—rather it simultaneously manifests them both. Each component motivates the inclusion of one instance of the same syllable type, *pho*, as part of the composite structure's phonological pole. Normally the two instances would be manifested at distinct locations in the domain of instantiation, namely speech time (T). However, since component structures merely *categorize* and thus *motivate* facets of the composite structure (as opposed to being the building blocks used to construct it), the less usual situation diagrammed in Fig. 11.9 is not ruled out in principle. Its special feature is that each instance of the syllable type (S) specified at the component structure level projects to the same instance at the composite structure level. A more elaborate example of phonological coinstantiation is the concisely emphatic (albeit excessively moralistic) statement *A lie is a lie is a lie*

[13] To argue that this is merely a way of disguising a deletion transformation and smuggling it into the description would really be beside the point. I do not claim that every transformationally described relationship is wholly spurious, or that nothing remotely analogous to such relationships can ever be found anywhere within a cognitive grammar analysis. The claim is rather that deep structures and transformations need not be posited as distinct types of entities: to the extent that the relationships in question have any validity, they are interpretable as residing in other, independently established aspects of linguistic organization (cf. Vol. 1, pp. 476–77). In particular, any linguistic theory has to deal with composition and must accommodate phonological discrepancies between component and composite structures (e.g. *break* vs. *broken*; *catch* vs. *caught*).

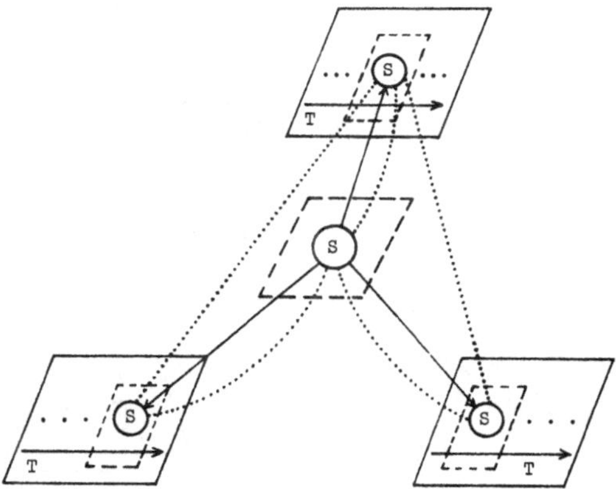

Fig. 11.9

is a lie is a lie. This sentence is assembled by chaining together four occurrences of the clause *a lie is a lie*. As each link is added to the chain, its phonological integration with the structure already assembled involves not only their adjacency in the speech stream but a certain amount of temporal overlap. Each medial occurrence of *a lie* at the composite structure level is doubly motivated: phonologically it manifests both the predicate nominative of one component clause and the subject of the next.[14]

There is no intrinsic reason why phonological coinstantiation should be limited to sequences that would otherwise be temporally contiguous, or to sequences representing grammatical constituents (consider *morphonemics*). Diagrammed in Fig. 11.10 is the phonological pole of a generalized constructional schema that is neutral in these respects. The coinstantiated sequence is given as *(a)(b)(c)*, where *a*, *b*, and *c* are structures of any size (e.g. syllables, words, or phonological phrases); collectively they need not comprise either a phonological or a grammatical constituent.[15] W, X, Y, and Z stand for any phonological sequence whatever, including the null sequence. The import of the diagram is that *(a)(b)(c)*, while motivated by each component structure, is manifested at the composite structure level only in the position associated with the first component (i.e. flanked by W and X). The composite structure therefore reflects only one component structure in its full, undistorted form,

[14] Phonological coinstantiation might also be considered for the description of (non-standard) sentences such as *There was a farmer had a dog*, analyzed in Lambrecht 1988.

[15] Although for illustrative purposes the sequence is shown as consisting of three adjacent elements, a maximally general characterization would not specify any particular number of elements and would even be neutral as to their possible contiguity. (The coinstantiation of non-adjacent elements is exemplified in (11)(c) below.) The actual range of options permitted in a given language is of course specified by an appropriate array of constructional schemas and subschemas.

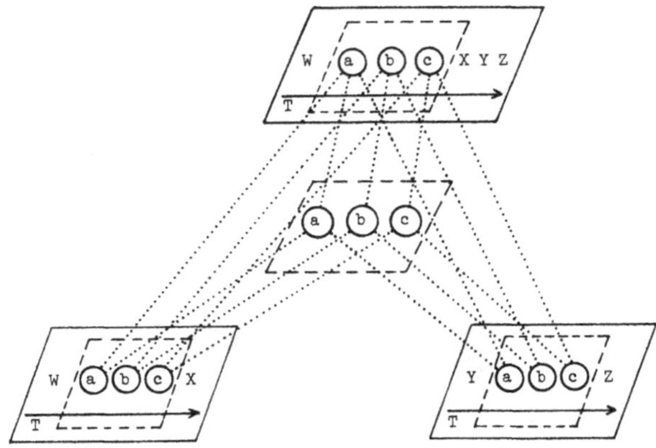

Fig. 11.10

even though the single occurrence of *(a)(b)(c)* instantiates the corresponding sequence of both components. It is readily seen that a sentence like (8)(a) is describable in this fashion: the coinstantiated sequence is *you sent*; W is null; X = *a letter to France on Monday*; Y = *and*; and Z = *a package to Zambia on Thursday*. Semantically and grammatically, each conjunct can thus be thought of as a clause having both a subject and a finite verb. The sentence's elliptic nature is due to portions of the second conjunct being instantiated phonologically at the same position in the speech stream as corresponding portions of the first conjunct.

Though quite reminiscent of Goodall's account of coordination (1983, 1984), in which identical portions of separate sentences are merged syntactically and thus treated as a single entity for purposes of phonological interpretation, the present analysis is different in major respects. For one thing, Goodall proposes this mechanism for all instances of subclausal coordination traditionally analyzed in terms of conjunction reduction; on this view *Harry and Sally arrived* represents the conflation of two full sentences. By contrast, I regard phonological coinstantiation as a secondary, rather special phenomenon—it is by no means rare, but neither is it the primary vehicle for the assembly of coordinate expressions. I have argued that conjunction reduction is unnecessary for the description of conjoined subclausal constituents, and that sentences with such constituents have a variety of possible construals (schematized in Fig. 11.7(a)–(c)) most of which are incompatible with a reduction analysis. Now it may well be that phonological coinstantiation is also a possible source of sentences with conjoined constituents. I suspect, however, that it is then mostly limited to cases where the conjuncts are set off from one another by pauses: *Harry, and Sally, arrived*. This intonational separation correlates with the fact that the apparent conjuncts are related only extrinsically, i.e. as a consequence of the partial coinstantiation of conjoined *clauses*. Because the actual coordination takes place at the clausal level, the elements that appear to be conjoined (on the basis of the overt phonological sequence) are not necessarily directly conceived in relation to one another and need not be construed as forming a higher-order coordinate entity. This corresponds to the configuration diagrammed in Fig. 11.7(d).

A further difference from Goodall's account is that phonological coinstantiation is potentially available for coordination at any level of organization, not just the clause or sentence level. Consider this example:

(9) *A tall and a short man were standing together under a tree.*

This is not plausibly analyzed as an instance of constituent coordination, since other factors point to (ART (ADJ N)) rather than ((ART ADJ) N) as the constituency of nominals comprising an article, an adjective, and a noun (cf. Ch. 4). Moreover, directly conjoining two ART + ADJ constituents would leave unexplained the puzzling fact that the head noun *man* is singular—and indeed, has to be singular (**a tall and a short men*)—even though two men are clearly designated. Nor can (9) be analyzed as a case of phonological coinstantiation involving two component clauses, since neither clause would be internally coherent (**a tall man were standing together under a tree*; **and a short man were standing together under a tree*). However, the sentence is unproblematically described in terms of phonological coinstantiation involving two component *nominals*. The proposal, in other words, is that (9) be considered an elliptic variant of (10), whose subject is formed by directly conjoining two subclausal constituents.

(10) *A tall man and a short man were standing together under a tree.*

The difference between (10) and (9) resides in whether the nominal conjuncts are phonologically integrated by juxtaposition or by the coinstantiation of *man*. But either way the subject is conceptually plural (as reflected in the composite structure's semantic pole), which meets the specifications imposed by *were standing together under a tree* when the two combine at a higher level of organization.

Phonological coinstantiation also bears some resemblance to the notion of "replacement" proposed by Hudson (1989) for **gapping** and other kinds of ellipsis. The term gapping is due to Ross (1970a); it refers to the class of ellipses which leave a "gap" in all but one conjunct of a coordinate structure, as illustrated by the non-initial conjuncts in (11).

(11)(a) *Fred plays the piano, Sharon the tuba, and Myron the cello.*
(b) *Tuesday it rained in Chicago, and Thursday in Milwaukee.*
(c) *Charles prefers sausage with his eggs, and Alex bacon.*

It should be apparent that gapping is readily described in terms of phonological coinstantiation.[16] Generalized to accommodate any number of conjuncts (as well as the non-adjacency of coinstantiated elements), constructional schemas analogous to Fig. 11.10 are capable of representing the conventionally established patterns.

11.3. Anaphora

In modern linguistics, the term **anaphora** is understood as indicating the relationship between two linguistic references to some entity within the same sentence or discourse: one reference, termed the **antecedent**, represents the "full," "normal," or "unreduced" linguistic specification of the entity in question; the other, termed the **anaphor**, is "reduced" or less elaborate by comparison (possibly even zero).[17] A typical example is the relationship between a personal pronoun and its nominal antecedent:

(12) ***Your bookie*** *called and said* ***he*** *wants the money right away.*

Your bookie and *he* stand in an anaphoric relationship provided that they are construed as being **coreferential** (i.e. as referring to the same individual). Once the referent has been introduced and characterized by the antecedent, referring to it subsequently by means of an anaphoric element enhances communicative efficiency by avoiding needless repetition.

From the generative perspective, it seemed natural to derive anaphoric expressions by rules of deletion or reduction from underlying structures containing repeated elements (Lees and Klima 1963). Thus (12) would have two occurrences of *your bookie* in underlying structure, the second reducing to *he* by virtue of being coreferential to the first. Similarly, derivation (13) involves the deletion of a sequence identical in form and meaning to its antecedent:

(13) *Sheila can* ***run a 10K*** *faster than I can* ***run a 10K*** ====> *Sheila can* ***run a 10K*** *faster than I can.*

However, since reduction analyses turned out to be problematic for certain kinds of data,[18] the general trend in generative studies has been for more and

[16] The notion of coinstantiation might even be stretched to handle examples where the coinstantiated sequences are not identical in strictly phonological terms (e.g. *I am a doctor, and my daughter a nurse*). Recall that instantiation is treated as a kind of categorizing relationship (2.2.3), as is the relationship between component and composite structures (Vol. 1, 12.2). In cases of morphologically related forms (such as *am* and *is*), one form might count as the instantiation of the other through categorization by *extension* (rather than elaboration).

[17] For a variety of contemporary perspectives on anaphora, see Chomsky 1981, Reinhart 1983, Kuno 1987, and Givón 1989 (ch. 6). Kuno surveys the basic lines of generative research on this topic.

[18] Most striking were sentences with two pronouns, each contained in the antecedent of the other, such as *The linguist who needed it most failed to get the grant he applied for* (Karttunen

more anaphoric elements to be directly introduced as such in the syntax. This accords with the natural inclination in cognitive grammar, which of course is to accept anaphoric expressions at face value and describe them in their own terms. Anaphoric expressions are seen as occupying various positions along a spectrum of communicatively motivated coding options, which range from silence at one extreme, to phonologically overt, fully articulated objective descriptions at the other. It is actually the latter that require special circumstances and ought to be considered special. Discourse presupposes a common ground, including knowledge of the current discourse space (3.1); at least in spoken language, it generally proceeds by adding only small increments to what has already been introduced (cf. Lambrecht 1984; Du Bois 1987). Full, explicit reference is normally reserved for such increments. Elaborateness of overt coding correlates with the extent of departure from the common ground, and those entities mentioned in explicit detail usually represent merely the tip of the communicative iceberg.

Phenomena that transformational grammarians used to handle by means of reduction or deletion rules receive a variety of treatments in cognitive grammar. The closest analog of deletion transformations is phonological coinstantiation, posited for gapping and other kinds of ellipses (11.2.4). The apparent deletion is analyzed as residing in a discrepancy between the maximal phonological string that component structures might lead one to expect and their actual manifestation at the composite structure's phonological pole. The discrepancy comes about because a single phonological sequence at the composite structure level simultaneously instantiates the sequences motivated by two or more component structures, as sketched in Fig. 11.10; the absence of this sequence in the location(s) where it would otherwise occur is readily attributed to a deletion operation by analysts who think in terms of underlying and surface representations. But in the cognitive grammar analysis the discrepancy is assimilated to the categorizing relationship between component and composite structures.

Other cases of anaphora involve the failure of a schematic element to be elaborated in the usual way. Recall, for example, that an English modal—as a grounding predication—designates a schematic process that is normally elaborated by the clausal head (6.3; Fig. 6.7(c)). Thus *Jerry will complain* is formed when the verb *complain* elaborates the schematic processual profile of *will*, and *Jerry* elaborates its trajector. Now what about a sentence like *Jerry will*, which lacks an overt head? Its apparent simplicity can be accepted at face value. Rather than being derived by reduction from a more fully specified underlying representation, the sentence really does consist of just two

1971). Also problematic (for those concerned with meaning) are semantic contrasts between anaphoric expressions and their putative sources, e.g. between ***Sally** expects* {***Sally/herself***} *to be perfect* and ***Sally** expects to be perfect* (cf. Ruwet 1984; Langacker 1985).

elements: *Jerry* elaborates *will*'s trajector, but the process *will* designates remains unelaborated and is consequently schematic at the composite structure level. Out of context, of course, the sentence is too uninformative to have any real communicative utility. It is however appropriate when a correspondence can be established with a specific process type active within the current discourse space (e.g. when the sentence comes in response to the question *Is anybody likely to complain?*). Examples of this sort abound. All of the English modals and auxiliary verbs behave analogously, as does the infinitival *to* (e.g. *I don't want to*). The schematic things profiled by demonstratives and by quantifiers such as *all*, *some*, and *each* remain unelaborated when these elements stand alone as full nominals. It is also common for relational participants to be left unexpressed when their nature is apparent from the context, general knowledge, or the expression's meaning (*They never drink*; *I'll drive*; *She's reading*; *Scrape harder!*).

Some apparent anaphoric relationships are analyzed instead as instances of a verb attributing multiple semantic roles to a single participant. For example, comparison of *Sharon washed her cat* with *Sharon washed* might suggest an analysis whereby the object of *wash* is deleted when it happens to be coreferential to the subject (similarly for *shave*, *scratch*, *turn*, *twist*, *stretch*, *move*, and so on). An alternative more compatible with general principles of cognitive grammar is to posit two semantic variants of such verbs, one in which the agent and theme are distinct, and one in which the same participant functions in both capacities. Thus *Sharon washed* is not a transitive clause whose direct object is a zero anaphor, but rather an inherently intransitive clause whose single participant is specified by the subject nominal. A comparable analysis was proposed in 11.1 as an alternative to the rule of Equi-NP Deletion (e.g. ***Allan*** *wants for* ***Allan*** *to be rich* = = => ***Allan*** *wants to be rich*). A verb that "governs Equi" is attributed a semantic value in which the same individual has two semantic roles, one of them corresponding to the trajector of the infinitival complement.

Certain other putative instances of anaphora are handled by correspondences inherent in particular constructions. Proposed in lieu of conjunction reduction, for example, are coordinate constructions in which each conjunct participates in parallel correspondences with other elements (see Figs. 11.6(b) and 11.8(b)). Consider also relative clauses that lack a relative pronoun, as in *the skirt she bought*. In the classic transformational account, the subordinate verb has an underlying direct object that reduces to a relative pronoun by virtue of being coreferential to the head; subsequently this pronoun is optionally deleted. By contrast, cognitive grammar describes such expressions directly in terms of their overt form. They represent a relative clause construction that pivots on a correspondence between a clausal landmark and the profile of the head noun. Though normally *buy*'s schematic landmark would be elaborated by a direct-object nominal, in the context of this construction it remains unspecified within the relative clause itself, since the head provides its characterization. Thus *buy* does not have an anaphoric direct object—its landmark is merely specified in an alternate manner.

Of course, many anaphoric relationships do involve explicit pronouns or pro-forms of other kinds (cf. 4.1.2). Although these elements are not derived in cognitive grammar by the reduction of fully specified underlying representations, they can be regarded as anaphors provided that correspondences are established with linguistic antecedents (either in the same sentence or in the preceding discourse). These pro-forms are independently meaningful (albeit quite schematic), and their meanings partially determine their grammatical behavior. In its prototypical value, for example, the reflexive pronoun *herself* not only indicates that its profile is third-person and female, but further identifies it as the landmark of a schematic process whose trajector and landmark correspond; the form thus occurs as a verbal object, elaborating the landmark of a verb that itself elaborates the schematic process that constitutes its base (Fig. 8.13). Likewise, a personal pronoun such as *he* is inherently grounded and thus functions grammatically as a nominal, whereas *one* provides only a schematic type specification and is consequently just a head noun (e.g. *the black one*). Some pro-forms are relational in character. For instance, the combination of non-auxiliary *do*, which designates a schematic action, and *so*, which pertains to manner, participates in anaphoric relationships with a verb and its non-subject complements (e.g. *I asked her to* ***wash the cat****, and she* ***did so*** *immediately*).

Linguistic studies of anaphora have been much concerned with formulating constraints on the relative position of an anaphor and its antecedent (Langacker 1969; Ross 1969b; Reinhart 1983; McCawley 1984; Kuno 1987). It is not the case, for instance, that the antecedent always has to precede the anaphor in terms of linear order, as we see from (14)(a).

(14)(a) *Before* ***she*** *left,* ***your mother*** *said to wash the cat.*
(b) ****She*** *said that* ***your mother*** *really dislikes dirty cats.*

On the other hand, they are not free to occur in any relative positions whatever; thus (14)(b) is ill-formed when *she* and *your mother* are construed as being coreferential. A plausible hypothesis suggested by the present framework is that the antecedent must precede the anaphor along some *natural path* (7.1.3), where the relevant natural paths include not only temporal order but also paths based on the prominence of participants (SUBJECT > OBJECT > OBLIQUE), prominence due to profiling (MAIN CLAUSE > SUBORDINATE CLAUSE), and the elaborative relationship between a head and its complements. How this generalization is implemented in a particular language is of course specified by an inventory of constructional schemas describing conventionalized anaphor-antecedent configurations. I will not pursue the matter any further here except to state that the problem appears to be quite amenable to a cognitive grammar treatment and is currently being investigated in considerable detail (van Hoek *to appear*).

11.4. Speech Acts

To a philosophically inspired tradition of semantic analysis preoccupied with questions of truth and logical inference, the publication of Austin 1962 brought the revelation that making assertions is not the sole purpose of natural-language sentences. In uttering a sentence, a speaker may accomplish many kinds of **speech acts** other than assertion—he can also give an order, ask a question, make a promise, issue a proclamation, convey a warning, effect a christening, offer an invitation, take an oath, confer a title, express congratulations, and so on. Austin further called attention to a special type of sentence called a **performative**, illustrated in (15).

(15)(a) *I tell you that we will have a major earthquake within a decade.*
(b) *I ask you why corporate takeovers continue to be permitted.*
(c) *I order you to shred these documents at once!*
(d) *I promise you that I won't do any more gambling.*
(e) *I hereby christen this ship the USS Ambivalence.*

The distinctive property of a performative is that it explicitly describes a speech act, and that a speaker accomplishes this speech act by uttering the sentence with the proper intent in an appropriate set of circumstances.[19]

Working in the theory of generative semantics, Sadock (1969) and Ross (1970b) proposed that speech acts be represented by performative clauses in underlying structure, even for sentences which lack such clauses overtly. Thus the sentence *We will have a major earthquake within a decade* would derive from an underlying structure analogous to (15)(a): the main clause (which fails to surface) is headed by an abstract communicative verb that specifies a type of speech act, and whose subject and indirect object refer to the speaker and hearer, respectively. Two decades later, this "syntactic" approach to speech acts lies abandoned. The problem of describing a sentence's **illocutionary force** (i.e. what kind of speech act it represents) is nevertheless still with us. More in line with contemporary attitudes is an alternative that Ross considered but found too nebulous to pursue: a "pragmatic analysis," which claims that certain elements are present in the context of the speech

[19]For example, (15)(e) will effect an act of christening, but only if a ship is present and the speaker has the proper authority. To be performative, a sentence must be interpreted as representing a true present tense (e.g. it must not be construed as habitual). *Hereby* generally forces the performative interpretation.

event—are "in the air," so to speak—and may have syntactic consequences. In principle, the constructs of cognitive grammar permit a precise and coherent formulation of the pragmatic analysis. This is not to say, however, that illocutionary force belongs to a separate "pragmatic component." Rather, it is naturally seen in this framework as an inherent aspect of grammatical structure and linguistic semantics.

11.4.1. *Domains and Organization*

Two basic principles of cognitive semantics suggest a straightforward way of approaching the problems posed by speech acts and related phenomena. For one thing, any kind of conceptualization is capable of being invoked as a cognitive domain supporting the semantic characterization of linguistic expressions. Moreover, an expression's semantic value may be encyclopedic in scope, comprising an open-ended set of domains with varying degrees of centrality. Though some domains are far more central to its meaning than others, there is no natural basis for distinguishing sharply between "semantic" and "pragmatic" specifications, or between "linguistic" and "extra-linguistic" knowledge (Vol. 1, 4.2).

The first principle implies that the conception of the *ground*—i.e. the participants and circumstances of the speech event itself—can function as a domain in the characterization of an expression's meaning. It does so most obviously with words like *I*, *you*, *here*, and *now*, which either designate a facet of the ground or invoke it as a central relational participant. Though slightly less apparent, the ground's role is also pivotal in expressions such as *this*, *may*, and *tomorrow*, where it serves as an offstage reference point. The import of the second principle is that the ground is not completely excluded from the meaning of any expression, however peripheral, extrinsic, and tenuous its role might be. It is part of the encyclopedic characterization of *cat*, for example, that English speakers conventionally use this word as the basic term for a particular type of creature (cf. Vol. 1, 2.1.3).[20] This aspect of its meaning is thus instantiated by the ground whenever a speaker does in fact use the term with such intent. In this way the ground can always be thought of as constituting at least a contingent and highly marginal facet of an expression's semantic value. Although it may remain implicit and unnoticed, the ground does figure in the speaker's tacit understanding of the conventional basis of

[20] Distinct levels of conceptual organization must be recognized. The first level comprises our knowledge of the profiled entity per se, irrespective of any linguistic considerations. The next level invokes the domain of symbolic space (Vol. 1, 2.2.1) and includes the correspondence between the expression's phonological pole and the conceptual complex constituting the first level (i.e. the fact that the entity has a particular phonological symbolization can itself be regarded as one aspect of the expression's semantic value). Finally, specifications concerning the sociolinguistic status of this symbolic relationship constitute the highest level, which incorporates cognitive domains pertaining to language use, social relations, and the overall speech community.

his utterance. Pushing things to the extreme, the very fact that a speaker is using an expression can be taken as an aspect of the meaning it assumes in the fleeting context of the usage event.

The ground subsumes not only the physical circumstances of the speech event but also the psychological status of its participants, including such factors as the speaker's desires and communicative intent, the hearer's expectations, their knowledge of the current discourse space, as well as their feelings and social relationship vis-à-vis one another. These factors can therefore be invoked as cognitive domains for the semantic characterization of linguistic elements. For example, feelings of solidarity and assessments of relative social status determine the choice between *tu* and *vous* in French (cf. Brown and Gilman 1960); though both pronouns designate the addressee, they do so against the background provided by contrasting conceptions of the affective and social context. In similar fashion, a conception of how the speaker intends his utterance, and how he expects the hearer to interpret and respond to it, provides a background in terms of which the relationship profiled by a sentence is construed and into which it must somehow fit. These psychological aspects of the ground are the locus of illocutionary force and furnish the cognitive domains required for the characterization of speech acts.

Suppose, for instance, that a speaker makes a statement with the intent that the hearer will interpret the proposition it conveys as being one that the speaker both accepts as being true and also wishes the hearer to accept as being true on the basis of the speaker's authority. Convoluted though it may be, the conception of such an intent is one that we are perfectly capable of entertaining; a conception of roughly this sort serves as the cognitive domain needed to characterize the canonical speech act of *assertion*. Likewise, the speech act of *ordering* invokes the conception of the speaker naming an action with the intent that the hearer will understand that he is thereby obliged to satisfy the speaker by carrying out the action in question. The speech act of *promising* involves a conception whose content includes a number of well-known "felicity conditions": that the speaker has the ability to bring about the event described; that the event would not routinely occur without his efforts; that the hearer wants the event to occur; and so on. In short, speech acts are not "in the air" but are rather part of the ground, residing in the speaker's and hearer's understanding of what is intended in the context of a particular set of communicative circumstances.

Without the proper intent, even the utterance of a sentence with the formal properties of a performative fails to qualify as a valid performance of the speech act it names. Thus (15)(e) does not count as an act of christening—even when uttered by the right person in the presence of the ship—if the speaker is merely rehearsing for the subsequent ceremony. For the utterance of such a sentence to constitute an actual performance of the speech act, that utterance must be identified with the one referred to in the cognitive domain in terms of which the act is characterized. This domain is an idealized cognitive model comprising the full set of social, psychological, and communicative circumstances in which an utterance must be embedded for the speech act in question to be successfully performed. Within the model itself, reference to the utterance is of course schematic and has the status of a type specification. To actually perform the speech act, the speaker not only must utter an appropriate kind of sentence, but must also specifically conceive of his utterance as instantiating that type specification and as conforming to the cognitive model it is based on. The express content of the sentence is thus grounded in the circumstances defining the speech act, and those circumstances are themselves an aspect of its meaning.

The various aspects of a sentence's meaning are not all of equal standing, for they include both "semantic" specifications and those traditionally regarded as "pragmatic." Although cognitive semantics claims that any sharply drawn distinction between these categories is artifactual, the standard division is not entirely lacking in motivation. The "pragmatic" aspects of sentence meaning share with semantic structure the fundamental property of being characterized with respect to conceptual complexes, some of which are fully conventional idealized cognitive models. What makes them special to some extent is that these conceptualizations pertain to the circumstances of the speech event itself, at the level of either a type specification or an actual event that instantiates it. As facets of the ground, they also tend to be coded less fully and less explicitly than notions traditionally thought of as falling within the purview of "semantics." These are, however, matters of degree, since semantic notions are often left implicit (as in *Alice likes tuna more than Metathesis*), while many expressions make reference to the ground as an intrinsic part of their linguistic meaning (e.g. *I*; *hereby*; *yesterday*). There is every reason to assume that we are dealing with a gradation rather than a strict dichotomy.

Within the complex, multifaceted conception that constitutes a sentence's full semantic value, levels of organization can be discerned which vary in their relationship to the ground, the objectivity of their construal, and how explicitly they tend to be coded phonologically. A typical sentence minimally comprises a finite clause that profiles an objectively construed event or situation. In the unmarked case, the designated process is distinct from the speech event; its central participants are third-person (i.e. distinct from the speaker and hearer); and both the process and its participants are coded overtly. In a clause of this sort, the ground's role is merely that of reference point for the nominal and clausal grounding predications, in which its construal is highly subjective (2.4). Now a finite clause does not per se embody a speech act. In particular, uttering a declarative clause does not necessarily amount to an act of assertion. The clause may, for instance, be taken as representing a viewpoint other than the speaker's; thus in uttering (16)(a) the speaker does not assert that a major earthquake is imminent.

(16)(a) *According to some experts, we will have a major earthquake within a decade.*
(b) *It is unlikely that we will have a major earthquake within a decade.*
(c) *Conceivably, we will have a major earthquake within a decade.*

That a finite clause is not being asserted may also be apparent from a main clause to which it is subordinated, as in (16)(b), or from an accompanying adverb, such as *conceivably* in (16)(c). By itself, a grounded clause merely names a proposition, i.e. it describes a process and specifies its location in time and reality taking the ground as point of reference. However, a finite clause does not intrinsically carry with it any commitment from the speaker that he considers the proposition to be true, nor any directive to the hearer that he accept it as such. The proposition is actually asserted only when the speaker utters the clause with the proper intent under an appropriate set of circumstances.

Thus, performing a speech act involves embedding a clause's intrinsic content within a more inclusive conception pertaining to the speech event itself, especially its psychological dimensions. This higher level of conceptual organization generally receives a subjective construal, so it tends to be left implicit. In performing an assertion, for instance, we simply utter a sentence with assertive intent—that intent constituting a subjectively construed aspect of how the expression is understood—without specifically *observing* that we are performing an act of assertion or saying so explicitly. We do of course have considerable flexibility in this regard. We are perfectly capable of focusing attention on the speech act itself, even to the point of putting it onstage as the profile of a finite main clause. When the speech act is construed objectively and coded explicitly in this fashion, the resulting expression is a *performative*, as in (15) (cf. 6.2.1, Fig. 6.3). A performative evokes as part of its base the cognitive model in terms of which a speech act is characterized, equates the speech event with the utterance referred to schematically within that model, and describes the speech act in question by means of a content verb that is directly grounded and functions as the main-clause head.

11.4.2. *Viewing Arrangements*

It was suggested in 10.2.1 that the ground should be thought of, almost literally, as the vantage point from which the speaker and hearer conceptualize the content evoked by a nominal or a finite clause. Vantage point, moreover, is just a single facet of the **viewing arrangement** implicit in any such expression, considered either abstractly (as an expression type) or as a specific usage event (cf. Vol. 1, 11.2.1). Comprising an expression's viewing arrangement are the full circumstances of the speech event (i.e. the ground) together with the relationship between the ground and the situation under description; this relationship involves both content (e.g. whether some portion of the ground itself is being described) and construal (notably subjectivity/objectivity). The specific form an expression takes is in large measure determined by the viewing arrangement it presupposes.

Particular kinds of viewing arrangements are capable of being invoked as cognitive domains for the characterization of linguistic structures (such as basic sentence types—see 11.4.3). One domain invoked by expressions generally regarded as prototypical is an idealized cognitive model representing the **canonical viewing arrangement**. Canonically, the ground consists of a single speaker engaged in face-to-face verbal communication with a single addressee.[21] Also part of the canonical arrangement are psychological aspects of the ground, including those which characterize the speech act of assertion, as well as the speaker's and hearer's commitment to cooperate for communicative purposes (the basis for implicature and Grice's maxims (1957, 1975)). With respect to the relationship between the ground and the situation being described, the canonical viewing arrangement incorporates the *canonical event model* (Fig. 7.2), or at least those portions of it dubbed the *stage model* (7.1.1). This model specifies that the ground is construed subjectively, with the speaker and hearer directing their attention to an external region—the *onstage region*—which is the locus of an event or situation that they construe objectively. To use another metaphor, their directed attention defines a *viewing frame* that delimits the scene immediately available for focused observation. As the viewers' window on the scene described by a finite clause, this frame constitutes the clause's immediate scope of predication, and its focal point is the clause's processual profile.

First- and second-person pronouns represent one fairly minor departure from the canonical viewing arrangement. Because it designates a speech-event participant, a nominal such as *I* or *you* presupposes an alternative, **egocentric viewing arrangement** in which the onstage region is gerrymandered to include the viewer and his immediate surroundings (Vol. 1, 3.3.2.4). Of course, we are sufficiently concerned with ourselves and our own affairs that the egocentric viewing arrangement is not only common but has strong claims to prototypicality; sentences with first- or second-person pronouns are perfectly natural and usual. They do, however, fail to maintain the correlation—equally natural in another way—between distinctness from the ground

[21] Examples of the ground (and hence the viewing arrangement) being non-canonical are circumstances in which there are multiple addressees; where the speaker is talking (or thinking) to himself; and where the speaker and addressee are distant in time or space (e.g. in writing a letter or speaking by telephone).

and objectivity of construal.[22] Explicit reference to the speaker or hearer puts a conceptualizer onstage as a target of focused conception, and thus distorts the canonical alignment wherein notions receive overt linguistic coding just to the extent that they go beyond what is presumed to be already available within the current discourse space. Performative sentences carry this type of distortion to the extreme: in addition to putting the speaker and hearer onstage as central participants, they objectify the speech act itself as the profiled event (the focal point within the viewing frame).

There are many other kinds of departure from the canonical viewing arrangement. One of them relates to the distinction between grounding predications and speech acts, which involve the ground in different ways and usually at different loci in the grammatical structure of a complex sentence. By definition, a grounding predication is part of every finite clause, whether main or subordinate, and specifies the location of the profiled entity in basic *epistemic* domains pertaining to time, reality, and mental contact by the speaker and hearer (2.4). The actual ground serves as the reference point for this purpose, even when the clause describes the contents of someone else's conceptualization. In (17), for example, the gun is proximal to the actual speaker and hearer, and the supposed state of being loaded was prior to the actual time of speaking, even though the proposition so characterized is attributed to Toni.

(17) *Toni believed that this gun was loaded.*

On the other hand, speech acts invoke cognitive domains pertaining to communicative intent and what the speaker hopes to accomplish, and are normally associated only with a sentence's main clause. Thus (17) is readily interpreted as an assertion about Toni's belief, but it is not an assertion about the gun being loaded, nor does the subordinate clause represent any other type of speech act. Canonically, then, a speech act is only associated with the process profiled within the viewing frame at the highest level of grammatical organization. Certain exceptions can however be noted (cf. Hooper and Thompson 1973; Lakoff 1987, pp. 473–80):

(18)(a) *The evidence for a bribery conviction is overwhelming, although the senator is really innocent.*

(b) *You are not going to the movies, because I order you to stay in the barracks.*

(c) *It gives me great pleasure to say that I hereby christen this ship the USS Ambivalence.*

(d) *This car, which I promise to buy you when I can afford it, is a great value for the money.*

[22] Analogously, seeing or hearing *oneself* blurs the fundamental distinction between the *observer* and the *observed*, so in that sense it is "special" compared to the perception of external objects (note that our eyes and ears are directed outward).

Observe that the adverbial clause in (18)(a) can be understood as making an assertion, while the adverbial clause in (b), the complement clause in (c), and the non-restrictive relative clause in (d) are all explicit performatives. Such expressions are not inherently problematic in the present framework. The ground figures in every finite clause, offering a particular vantage on the situation it describes. And while epistemic grounding is typically the extent of its involvement in subordinate clauses, there would seem to be no intrinsic reason why its role should not in some cases be expanded to encompass the psychological and other factors constitutive of speech acts.

Other departures from the canonical viewing arrangement pertain, not to how the ground is manifested at particular levels of grammatical organization, but rather to the special nature of the ground itself and the vantage it affords on the situation being coded. Canonically the ground provides a fixed viewing platform from which the speaker and hearer observe the world around them and the flow of events unfolding through time. From that platform, moreover, they can direct their attention to other times and places, both real and imagined; the viewing frame is thereby shifted to another location, which is usually specified in some fashion (e.g. by a past-tense marker, by a modal, or by a locative or temporal adverb). But despite the flexibility of this orderly arrangement, many expressions presuppose substantially different viewing circumstances. For example, the historical present involves a mental transfer wherein the speaker and hearer assume for discourse purposes a vantage point that they recognize as being distinct from their actual one. Instead of describing a past occurrence from the standpoint of the actual speech event, the speaker portrays it as if he were there observing it unfold as part of immediate reality.[23] Thus the "historical present" does not constitute a special value of the present-tense category. It is better analyzed as residing in the adoption of a non-canonical viewing arrangement that encompasses both the actual and a virtual vantage point. From this latter perspective, an event that actually occurred in the past nonetheless falls within the unshifted, default-case viewing frame associated with the present-tense inflection (or absence of inflection) in its usual semantic value.

The viewing platform afforded by the ground is not invariably fixed or stable. Thus a sentence like (19)(a) presupposes a viewer in motion through the valley who reports on the scene that appears within the immediate viewing frame as the journey progresses (Talmy 1988b).

(19)(a) *There's a house every now and then through the valley.*
(b) *The mountain is coming toward me at 200 miles per hour.*

Or consider the pilot of a disabled plane, who radios sentence (19)(b). While

[23] That is, instead of portraying the occurrence as distal with respect to the actual *deictic center* (the here-and-now of the speech event), the speaker sets up a new deictic center at a location from which the occurrence is viewed as immediate (cf. 6.2.3.2).

it is actually the speaker that is moving, he portrays his unfortunate situation as if he himself were stationary, describing quite literally and accurately what he observes adopting that frame of reference. Note that this complex viewing arrangement involves something comparable to a mental transfer; the speaker assumes for expressive purposes a non-actual arrangement that conforms more closely to the canonical one.[24]

Still more drastic departures from the canonical viewing arrangement are possible. Via mental scanning, for example, the speaker can move abstractly through time, even in a backwards direction, and recount in sequence the events encountered during this subjective journey:

(20) *Professor Muddle died last night at the age of 75. He suffered from an inflamed ego for several years prior to his death. He taught theoretical basketweaving for almost four decades at MIT. He received his Ph.D. from that institution in 1948.*

Once the special viewing arrangement is taken into account, the ordering of the component sentences can be recognized as iconic—they occur in the same order as the events described, not in terms of their actual temporal sequence, but with respect to the order in which they come within the viewing frame as the speaker scans backwards through conceived time.

Let me mention just in passing two other broad classes of departures from the canonical situation. Literary works are well known for the variety and potential complexity of their viewing arrangements. Their full interpretation makes reference to analogs of the ground at two distinct levels of organization: besides the author and the actual or envisaged reader, there is often a narrator, as well as an audience to whom the narration is supposedly directed. The narrator and his audience may be identified with either the author and reader or with characters in the story. Moreover, narrations can be embedded within narrations, and any narrator can adopt any viewing arrangement with respect to the story he tells. The possible variations are clearly endless. The other broad class of departures from the canonical arrangement consists of signs and labels (cf. Sadock 1974): *Beware of dog*; *Shake well before using*; *Danger!*; *No smoking*; *Press here to open*; *Push*; *Mix with two cups of milk*; *Contains no artificial preservatives*. The meanings of such expressions derive in large measure from our knowledge of the entities bearing the labels, and from cognitive models that pertain to labeling conventions. The arrangement is special in that the "speaker" remains anonymous, the message is perma-

[24] Certain examples discussed in Vol. 1 involve special viewing arrangements similar to these. *This road is winding through the mountains* would be uttered by a speaker actually travelling along the road; what counts as the road at any one instant is that segment of it which the speaker can see from his current vantage point (p. 257; see also Langacker 1987b). *The house is above the kite* could be uttered by a speaker standing on his head who describes what he actually sees as if he were viewing it in the canonical upright orientation (p. 123).

nently available rather than evanescent, and the addressee is generic—the message applies to anyone who happens to read it. Observe that both the labeled entity and the addressee are generally unexpressed, since their identity is apparent from the context. This and other aspects of the viewing arrangement are largely responsible for the special grammatical properties of these expressions (e.g. the absence of a subject).

11.4.3. *Basic Sentence Types*

It was mentioned previously that notions coded explicitly usually represent merely the tip of the communicative iceberg. The extent to which a notion undergoes *phonological objectification*—being signaled overtly by means of substantial (primarily segmental) phonological content—correlates fairly robustly with the degree to which it embodies substantial, objectively construed conceptual content not yet established in the current discourse space. Such content is embedded in an open-ended array of background knowledge that tends to be left implicit or coded in more subtle ways (e.g. by inflection, intonation, or word order). Overtly coded elements receive a coherent interpretation only when construed against this background, and any facets of the background thus invoked are part of an expression's meaning.

The notions left implicit typically include the nature of the speech act and of the viewing arrangement overall. Viewing (or conception) is an asymmetrical relationship in which attention is directed outward and focused on the scene being viewed, so canonically it is that scene—and not the viewing itself—which is construed objectively and coded overtly. Explicit performatives are therefore rather infrequent, and a non-performative sentence is capable of expressing distinct speech acts without any difference in overt form. Moreover, markings that do signal speech acts are often subtle and may have other values as well.

The terms **declarative**, **imperative**, and **interrogative** are usually reserved for basic sentence types defined on the basis of their overt form, as respectively exemplified in (21)(a)–(c).

(21)(a) *I will come back tomorrow.*
(b) *Drive slowly.*
(c) *What have they caught?*

Prototypically, a declarative sentence is interpreted as a simple statement or assertion, but in the proper context it might also be construed as a promise, a threat, a warning, a prediction, etc. An English imperative lacks an overt subject, and the verb is uninflected. Although the speech act of ordering represents the default-case value, expressions of this form can also be used with the gentler force of advice or admonition, and even as conditionals. Thus (22)(a) is roughly equivalent to (22)(b).

(22)(a) *Drive slowly and everyone else will pass you.*
(b) *If you drive slowly, everyone else will pass you.*

An interrogative sentence in English is characterized by the occurrence of a question word (*what, who, why, when, how,* etc.) and/or by the positioning of the subject nominal after the first auxiliary in the verb group. Note that each of these devices has non-interrogative uses: most of the question words also function as relative pronouns, and "subject-auxiliary inversion" is found in certain other constructions (e.g. *Seldom had she been so disgusted*).

Thus each of the basic sentence types—as characterized by their overt grammatical form—takes as its prototypical semantic value one of the three fundamental speech acts most plausibly regarded as archetypal: assertion, ordering, and questioning.[25] A particular sentence type (or a marking that contributes to its characterization) can however assume other values that constitute either extensions or elaborations of the prototype. So long as the prototypical value is intended, or the illocutionary force is apparent from the context, the speech act itself can be left uncoded. Should this not be the case, or if the speaker has reason to emphasize the speech act and make it explicit, he can use a performative to objectify it and put it onstage as the profiled relationship.

Aspects of a sentence's form are directly attributable to particular features of the viewing arrangement it presupposes. For example, it follows from the very nature of a performative that its subject is first person, the direct object is usually second person (but not, for instance, with *christen*), and the verb is present tense (i.e. the designated process is part of immediate reality). A declarative sentence has an overt subject and can occur in any tense because an assertion might be made about any conceivable entity in regard to a situation holding at any time relative to the speech event. By contrast, an imperative lacks an overt subject because the cognitive model that characterizes the speech act of ordering specifically identifies the trajector of the mandated process as the addressee; it is spelled out overtly (e.g. *You leave him alone!*) only in cases of emphasis, when the speaker wants to grab the hearer's attention and make his obligation explicit and unmistakable. The imperative verb is uninflected for a similar reason: since the cognitive model of ordering specifies that the mandated action is not yet realized, and is thus subsequent to the time of speaking, there is no need for this to be coded explicitly by a separate grounding predication.

To be sure, the precise form of the basic sentence types is less than fully predictable—despite certain universal tendencies, it is subject to conventional determination as described in language-specific constructional schemas. For

[25] In this respect the basic sentence types are analogous to grammatical relations or case categories, which take archetypal semantic roles as their prototypical values.

instance, sentences like (21)(b) represent a special construction of English. A constructional schema specifies the integration of a non-finite processual expression (e.g. *drive slowly*) with an imperative predication that is phonologically zero (or at best signaled only by intonation). Because it incorporates the cognitive model of ordering, and further makes reference to the actual speech event, this imperative predication combines the semantic functions of grounding and illocutionary force. More precisely, the participants evoked by the cognitive model are equated with the actual speaker and addressee; the utterance referred to in the model is equated with the actual speech event; and the profile of the processual expression is put in correspondence with the mandated event, which the model characterizes only schematically.

The form of interrogative sentences reflects the interaction of various factors that have not yet been analyzed in any depth. One factor is the cognitive model of questioning, in which the speaker lacks but wants certain information, believes that the hearer possesses it, and directs the hearer to supply it. A second factor is the meaning of "WH," the initial element of the question words (***who***, ***what***, ***where***, ***why***, ***when***, etc.). Presumably WH is a kind of deictic, in the sense that it presupposes a range of alternatives and "points to" one of them by putting it in profile. When these forms are used as relative pronouns, they point to the nominal head (i.e. the profile corresponds to that of the head). In subordinate-clause interrogatives, exemplified in (23), the information potentially supplied by the pointing is portrayed as lacking, desired, or pertinent with respect to some viewpoint either indicated or implied by the main clause.

(23)(a) *My landlord wonders* ***who stole his cat.***
(b) ***Why the administration rejected our proposal*** *is important (to all of us).*

(24)(a) *Who stole his cat?*
(b) *Why did the administration reject our proposal?*

Main-clause questions like those in (24) are comparable except that the context for interpreting the interrogative clause is not another, superordinate clause, but rather a subjectively construed viewing arrangement that subsumes both the actual speech event and the cognitive model of questioning. The viewpoint with respect to which the information is lacking is thus the speaker's, and the hearer is directed to provide this information.

Other factors contributing to the characterization of interrogative sentences will be mentioned just in passing. One of these is the semantic import of placing the subject after the first auxiliary. Possible clues to the meaning of this word-order option are the fact that it only occurs in main-clause interrogatives; that in "yes-no" questions (e.g. *Can you hear me?*) it is the only mark of interrogative status; and that the first auxiliary is always the *grounded verb*, whose processual profile is schematic for that of the clause as a whole, and whose inflection specifies its epistemic status. Yet another factor is the conceptual import of clause-initial position, which in interrogatives is occupied either by a question word or by the finite auxiliary. Its value no doubt has something to do with topic status or with the first clausal element establishing a frame in terms of which the remainder is interpreted. The last factor is intonation (cf. Langacker 1970; Bolinger 1982a, 1982b), which is sometimes the sole marker of interrogation (e.g. *You're finished?*). A comprehensive description of English interrogatives will presuppose a clear understanding of each factor taken individually, and must accommodate the complex ecology of their interaction with one another and with related phenomena.

As a final point, let us note that a sentence representing one basic type can often be interpreted as having the illocutionary force normally associated with another (cf. Sadock 1970, 1971, 1972). Thus (25)(a) would more likely be taken as a polite request than as a true question, and (25)(b) can be construed as a negative statement ('I don't have that kind of money').

(25)(a) *Could you open that window?*
(b) *Do I have that kind of money?*

I attribute to such expressions a complex viewing arrangement in which the conceived circumstances defining one speech act are embedded in those defining another. Although a sentence like (25)(a) does involve the cognitive model of questioning, this is part of a more inclusive conception in which an act of questioning is subordinated to another, overriding purpose. The speaker, as it were, pretends to ask a question, with the expectation that the hearer—given normal standards of empathy and communicative cooperation—will deduce that the speaker actually wants him to open the window. Similarly, in (25)(b) the speaker poses a question with the expectation that the hearer, just by considering the matter, will find the negative answer obvious without the speaker having to provide it as a direct statement.[26] Complex viewing arrangements of this sort are capable of being established as conventional linguistic units productively and reliably used to achieve the intended purpose. Though submerged and invisible, the viewing arrangement both shapes and supports the iceberg's visible tip, and is thus an integral facet of an expression's meaning.

[26] This type of analysis does not conflict with accounts based on Gricean implicature. Rather, the tacit reasoning of such implicature is part of the characterization of the complex viewing arrangement.

CHAPTER 12

Theoretical Discussion

IN THE FOREGOING chapters, we have examined a substantial variety of grammatical phenomena from the perspective of cognitive grammar, some in considerable detail. With this background we can now address systematically a number of basic theoretical issues touched on repeatedly in these two volumes. First to be discussed are certain issues pertaining to the nature of linguistic thought and investigation. Considered next are the grounds for rejecting the *autonomy thesis*, a central dogma of generative theory. The final section deals with the status of rules and representations in the context of alternative models of cognitive processing.

12.1. Metaphors, Goals, and Expectations

What one finds in language depends in large measure on what one expects to find.[1] Among the factors that shape these expectations is *metaphor*, whose pervasiveness and formative influence in our mental life have been emphasized in a number of recent studies (Lakoff and Johnson 1980; Lakoff 1987; Turner 1987; Lakoff and Turner 1989). Metaphor plays an important role in virtually all phases of scientific inquiry, and there is perhaps no field where this is more apparent than in linguistics. Of course, the indisputable power of metaphor does not come without certain dangers. In particular, one has no guarantee that a seemingly apt metaphor will actually prove appropriate and helpful when pushed beyond the limited observations that initially inspired it. An investigator who wishes not to be misled must make himself aware of the metaphors he uses and remain alert to both their limitations and the continuous pressure they subtly exert.

[1] For example, if one expects language to be organized into discrete "modules," abundant evidence for modularity will be forthcoming—any phenomenon that might conceivably be interpreted in modular terms will tend to be seized upon as strong support for modularity, with little thought given to alternative explanations. This will happen, moreover, even in the absence of any clear and consistent understanding of precisely what modularity is supposed to be and to entail. (Those familiar with the current theoretical scene may realize that the example is not entirely hypothetical.)

Linguistic thought in the modern era has been much influenced by a largely coherent, mutually supportive group of metaphors some of which are so basic to our thinking that we are hardly aware of them. The most fundamental of these is the **container metaphor**, corresponding to one of the image schemas described in Johnson 1987 and Lakoff 1987. The concept of a discrete container, whose rigid sides define a sharp boundary between an inside and an outside, underlies both set theory and formal logic, as well as the classic criterial-attribute model of categorization. Beyond formal semantics and the traditional view of linguistic categories, its influence is manifested in myriad ways. These include the postulation of many standard dichotomies (e.g. synchrony vs. diachrony, competence vs. performance, semantics vs. pragmatics, literal vs. figurative language), the general expectation of absolute predictability (Vol. 1, 1.2.6.1), and the assumption that the internal grammar of a language is a discrete entity divisible into distinct components. Over the course of Vols. 1 and 2, all of these have been called into question.

The container metaphor figures prominently in the **conduit metaphor**, which Reddy (1979) has shown to be a basic, deeply entrenched folk model that has a profound influence in shaping how we think and talk about language. According to this model, linguistic expressions are vehicles for transporting ideas along a conduit leading from the speaker's mind into the hearer's. These vehicles are strings of words each of which contains a finite amount of a substance called "meaning." The speaker assembles and loads the vehicle, and then sends it along the conduit; the hearer unloads it to determine what idea the speaker *has in mind* and wants to *get across* by *putting it into words*. The conduit metaphor dovetails with the **dictionary view** of lexical semantics, which holds that a word's linguistic meaning is strictly limited and distinct from general knowledge, and also with the **building-block metaphor**, wherein the meaning of a complex expression is constructed just by stacking together the meanings of its parts in accordance with general combinatory rules. This way of thinking and talking is so ingrained that there is no point trying to avoid it.[2] We will be well advised, however, to remember that it represents a blatantly inaccurate folk model capable of leading us into serious error to the extent that we tacitly adopt it for theoretical purposes. Only sound waves actually travel from the speaker to the hearer. Words are not containers for meaning but serve instead to elicit knowledge systems of indefinite expanse, in a flexible and open-ended manner. Moreover, the components of a complex expression should not be thought of as providing the material used to construct it—their function is rather to categorize and motivate facets of the composite structure, which often displays emergent or contextually induced properties that no individual component is capable of evoking.

[2] I therefore speak of "meaning" as an abstract substance, of meanings being *conveyed*, of complex expressions being assembled out of smaller parts, and so on.

To the container, conduit, and building-block metaphors the generative tradition has added a number of others that reflect and help maintain its formalistic bent. A grammar was first likened to a machine (or assembly line) that builds structures and then modifies them step by step, giving "all and only the grammatical sentences of the language" as its "output." Electronic devices have inspired a number of metaphors used by generative theorists: the internal grammar is a "black box"; it consists of separate "components" hooked together; it is learned by a "language acquisition device"; and more recently, it is seen as having a highly "modular" organization (even within a single component). Other metaphors have a mathematical origin: the grammar of a language is like an algorithm, a computer program, or a formal deductive system. These three classes of metaphors—based on machines, electronics, and mathematics—all manifest an overarching metaphor that construes the mind as being analogous to a serial digital computer. Needless to say, the computer metaphor has been enormously influential in recent decades, both in linguistics and in many other disciplines (not to mention popular culture).

The power of such a metaphorical system should not be underestimated. Far from being merely heuristic, it can be recognized as the source of tacit but nonetheless pervasive attitudes, working assumptions, and methodological stances. Although perhaps nobody would defend it as being fully appropriate, still it offers conceptual coherence for views explicitly held, biases research towards certain kinds of approaches and subject matter, and determines whether an idea will be adopted by default or accepted only reluctantly even when supported by overwhelming evidence. Let us note just a few examples. The attitude that a linguistic description ought to be as brief and economical as possible (consistent with generating the right forms) coheres with the standard conception of optimality for machines (which are supposed to be efficient), computer programs (quick-running), and mathematical proofs (sparse and elegant). The analogy to formal logic and digital computers engenders the expectation that linguistic expressions should be describable in terms of well-defined operations on strings of discrete symbols (or other discrete representations, such as phrase trees and feature bundles). Also, the fundamental notion that a phenomenon has a single "right" analysis, and that the proper description of languages must conform to a specific kind of formal theory, is reinforced by the knowledge that a mechanical or electronic device operates in a particular way, and that a computer does what it does because a specific program tells it to.

In addition to their metaphorical coherence, such notions resonate with our idealized cognitive model of "hard science."[3] Hence they are generally considered self-evident and uncontroversial, so obvious that they are simply taken for granted. Yet they are all subject to legitimate question, as is the appropri-

[3]It is no doubt incidental that they have the further advantage of defining the task of linguistic investigation in terms that correspond to what most linguistic theorists are best equipped to do.

ateness to natural language of the metaphorical system they reflect. Suppose we were to adopt a different guiding metaphor. In particular, suppose we liken a linguistic system to a *biological organism*. This alternative metaphor is not at all far-fetched; indeed, since language is manifested in biological organisms, it has great inherent plausibility. This analogy naturally has its limitations, and how far we can usefully push it remains to be determined. Nevertheless, fundamental issues appear to us in a new light as soon as we start thinking about language in this way.

One does not expect the comprehensive description of a biological organism to be algorithmic in character or to take the form of well-defined operations on strings of discrete symbols. One does not expect the characterization of all facets of an organism—anatomical, physiological, biochemical, molecular, cellular, genetic, developmental, behavioral, ecological—to be embraced by a single formal theory, nor is the description of a particular facet necessarily limited to specified types of statements and representations. Furthermore, multiple descriptions of the same phenomenon can be accepted as equally valid and revelatory, each contributing in its way to the overall scientific enterprise. For instance, no one anatomical drawing reveals everything there is to know about the structure of an organism or even a single cell; the same entity can be validly and usefully described by means of any number of drawings done from different perspectives and at varying levels of detail. And since a given drawing can always be superseded by one of greater detail and resolution, no drawing is ever "correct" and definitive to the exclusion of all others. In this situation achieving the briefest possible description hardly seems a relevant concern. Faced with the daunting, multifaceted complexity of an organism, biologists seeking to characterize it are unlikely to waste much time with simplistic notions of economy based on symbol-counting.

Cognitive grammar is not in fact based in any strict or systematic way on the metaphor equating a language with a biological organism. I do however suggest that this metaphor is more nearly appropriate to natural language than the others cited, and offers an alternative perspective on the goals and expectations of linguistic investigation. Consider, for example, the many diagrams that appear in Vols. 1 and 2 and in other works on cognitive grammar. Linguistic theorists tend either to interpret these diagrams as formal representations (in which case they are hopelessly inadequate), or else to dismiss them precisely because they fail to constitute a formal representational system. Both reactions stem from the supposition that a linguistic description has to instantiate such a system to be rigorous or even viable—the "pictures" of cognitive grammar bear little resemblance to the discrete, formulaic representations that theorists tacitly expect. However, the appropriateness of these expectations is very much at issue; if linguistic description is seen as analogous to the task of describing a biological organism, an algorithmic characterization comprising strings of discrete symbols does not loom as a realistic objective. The diagrams employed in cognitive grammar are reasonably compared instead to anatomical drawings. While they are not formal representations (relying as they do on the viewer's ability to interpret them in accordance with implicit pictorial and diagrammatic conventions), they nevertheless capture many of the elements and relationships that figure in the structure of concern. Moreover, no single diagram is considered definitive or is intended to represent everything that would in principle be said in a truly comprehensive description; multiple diagrams—corresponding to different "sections" through the structure or to views at different levels of magnification—can all be simultaneously valid, each revelatory in its own way. Of course, to the extent that we actually understand a phenomenon, suitable notations of any desired degree of precision (either diagrammatic or formulaic) can be devised to represent it. In short, algorithmic formalization is not the only conceivable mode of scientific description (nor is it *ipso facto* a guarantee of validity or scientific interest).

Let us now attempt a more comprehensive statement of the goals and expectations of linguistic investigation as conceived in cognitive grammar. We must first be clear about what a language is supposed to be and where it is supposed to be located. *Cognitive grammar* is so called because it makes a serious attempt to deal with language in realistic terms as an integral facet of human cognition. A language is thus a psychological entity residing in the minds of individual speakers. It does not reduce to the sounds speakers make, to a corpus of attested utterances, or to externally observable linguistic behavior. A language is not an infinite set of well-formed sentences, nor any other kind of platonic ideal. It does not reside in the "collective consciousness" of a speech community. It is rather an aspect of cognitive processing that can ultimately be characterized in terms of recurrent patterns of neural activation. Although for purposes of analysis and exposition we can hardly avoid the reification of linguistic structures, they must eventually be interpreted not as static entities but as organized mental activity.

I am engaging in reification when, in the fashion of generative theory, I speak of "the grammar of a language." On one interpretation, this expression refers to the internal representation of linguistic structure, the psychological entity that cognitive grammar takes as the object of investigation. This *internal* grammar was characterized in Vol. 1 (2.1) as a **structured inventory of conventional linguistic units**, a **unit** being defined in processing terms as a *cognitive routine*. It was emphasized that such a grammar cannot be sharply or precisely delimited, for it is matter of degree whether a structure is sufficiently entrenched to be considered a unit, whether it is conventionally established throughout the speech community, and even whether it can be regarded as linguistic. In view of these gradations, it is misleading to conceptualize the grammar of a language as a discrete container—it is more accurately described as an assembly of cognitive structures (recurrent patterns of neural activation) extending in various directions from a central core comprising structures that are thoroughly entrenched, fully conventional, and indisputably linguistic. The *center-periphery* image schema offers a more appropriate metaphor than does the *container-content* schema.

One also speaks of "the grammar of a language" with reference to an actual or hypothetical linguistic description. These *external* grammars are of various sorts, distinguished by different goals and expectations. Pedagogical and reference grammars are actually written and published; not at all concerned with cognitive processing, they have the more practical aim of enabling an intelligent user to figure out how things might be said in the language described. By contrast, the classic conception of a generative grammar represented a platonic ideal that could never be realized in practice. It was envisaged as a completely formal mathematical system that would exhaustively enumerate and characterize the well-formed sentences of a language without relying in any way on the knowledge of a user. And although a generative grammar was intended to be a model of linguistic "competence," i.e. the internal grammar of an ideal speaker, both idealization and the competence/performance distinction insulated the enterprise from any direct concern with cognitive processing. What about "the cognitive grammar of a language"? Taken as an ideal objective, it can be conceived as **the most complete description possible of those aspects of cognitive processing which constitute the mental representation of a linguistic system.**[4] Even ideally, we cannot expect a description to be utterly complete and definitive, if only because the linguistic system lacks precise delimitation and shades into other aspects of cognition (for reasons cited above, and also since no a priori distinction is made between competence and performance). Recall as well the suggestion that a linguistic system is better likened to a biological organism than to a computer program: as in the case of an organism, no characterization ever achieves such fine-grained comprehensiveness that it cannot in principle be surpassed by another of even greater scope and resolution. Moreover, we cannot demand that the description be algorithmic in nature or that it be limited to statements representing a particular type of formalism. Even a single phenomenon may be revealingly described in different formats and from multiple perspectives, each contributing to our overall understanding.

A speech sound, for example, can be characterized with equal validity as a complex articulatory gesture, as an image (articulatory, auditory, or kines-

[4]This is not a practical objective—one cannot imagine actually writing a comprehensive cognitive grammar, and if one could, it would not necessarily be any more readable than a generative grammar. This is not to say, of course, that particular facets of a language's structure cannot be analyzed in terms of the framework and presented via useful and readable descriptions. It is important to distinguish the question of what linguists actually produce from the theoretical issue of what kind of characterization could in principle be envisaged as an ideal goal.

thetic), or in terms of the cognitive events responsible for these at any level of processing or neurological organization (Vol. 1, p. 78). We can similarly characterize a semantic structure at either the phenomenological level—by describing essential aspects of a conceptualization in any way that proves revelatory—or else with respect to the neurological processing whose occurrence constitutes the mental experience in question. Any type of unit can further be examined from a number of other perspectives: diachronic, acquisitional, psychological, communicative, discourse, sociolinguistic, and "ecological" (i.e. the system of oppositions it enters into, as well as the variant forms it assumes in adapting to different contexts). These "functional" considerations do not eliminate the need to explicitly characterize the semantic, phonological, and symbolic units that constitute the grammar of a language; they do however allow us to make sense of these units, to see the linguistic system as one viable response to a diverse array of constraints and formative pressures. The grammar is thus analogous to the anatomical structure of an organism, which may likewise seem strange or arbitrary until we consider it from the evolutionary, developmental, physiological, behavioral, and ecological perspectives. An explicit anatomical description is nevertheless not only possible but essential to working out these other facets of the organism's characterization.

Ideally, therefore, a comprehensive linguistic description will encompass both the grammar of a language as well as extensive accounts of the varied functional considerations that have shaped it. A comparable arrangement holds at the level of linguistic theory. One facet of a comprehensive theory will be a list of the constructs available for the characterization of semantic, phonological, and symbolic structures (e.g. profiling, scope of predication, conceived time, subjectivity/objectivity, basic domains, autonomy/dependence, correspondence, categorizing relationships, noun, verb, nominal, finite clause, trajector, primary landmark, type/instance, domain of instantiation, consonant, vowel, syllable, root, word, component and composite structures, constructional schema, and so on). In and of itself, this inventory will not be highly restrictive, for it must accommodate the full range of structures attested in natural language and will no doubt project to many others we would never actually expect to encounter. How, then, will the theory achieve restrictiveness? Not by means of explicit prohibitions or categorical statements about what every language must have, but rather through a positive characterization of prototypicality and the factors that determine it (Vol. 1, 1.2.6.2).[5] The theory will thus incorporate substantive descriptions of the

[5] Although I have stated it negatively for expository purposes ("The *only* units ascribable to a linguistic system . . ."), the content requirement can formulated in positive terms ("Possible linguistic units include semantic, phonological, and symbolic structures that occur overtly, schematizations of linguistic structures, and categorizing relationships between linguistic structures"). It amounts to a statement of the kinds of structures capable of arising given a reasonable conception of cognitive processing and language acquisition (cf. 12.3).

various kinds of linguistic structures with the status of prototypes (e.g. an inventory of typical vowel systems, case categories, or grammatical constructions), together with an indication of their degree of prototypicality (hence the likelihood of their being instantiated in a given language). These structures will further be characterized in terms of how they resolve the various functional constraints and pressures alluded to above. The descriptive constructs of cognitive grammar define a broad space of structural possibilities, but within that space certain regions are favored owing to their *functionality*: the options they comprise are natural and common cross-linguistically because they successfully accommodate the varied types of optimality that compete and cooperate to shape language structure (cf. Langacker 1977). It is this functional "warping" of the space of possibilities—rather than any specific stipulations or prohibitions—that is responsible for certain kinds of structures being universal and others non-occurrent.

12.2. The Autonomy Issue

The central claim of cognitive grammar is that language is fully describable in terms of semantic structures, phonological structures, and symbolic links between the two. Only symbolic structures need be posited for the characterization of lexicon, morphology, and syntax, which form a gradation that can be divided only arbitrarily into discrete components. It is further claimed that a linguistic system comprises nothing more than semantic, phonological, and symbolic structures that are part of overtly occurring expressions, schematizations of such structures, and categorizing relationships. If workable, this view of linguistic structure is intrinsically desirable on grounds of naturalness, conceptual unification, and theoretical austerity. Linguists thus ought to be concerned with making it work if at all possible—only with extreme reluctance should they be willing to abandon it in favor of theories that are less constrained and fail to achieve the reduction of grammar to symbolic relationships.

Of course, this is not currently the prevailing attitude among linguistic theoreticians. Generative theorists in particular incline toward a highly modular view of language, and it is widely believed that the autonomy of grammatical structure—and more specifically, of syntax—has been established beyond all reasonable doubt. Naturally, I consider this belief to be mistaken; in these two volumes I have tried to demonstrate that an account of grammar which treats it as inherently meaningful (hence non-autonomous vis-à-vis semantics) shows every likelihood of proving both viable and revelatory. Because of its pivotal nature, the autonomy issue demands careful consideration. If the autonomy of grammar has not been proved, why is it accepted by so many able scholars? And is cognitive grammar indeed capable of accommodating all aspects of grammatical structure?

12.2.1. *Defining the Issue*

A variety of factors contribute to the widespread acceptance of the autonomy thesis. Some are "human" considerations that had best be left aside (e.g. vested interest; sociological pressures; insufficient exposure to cognitive linguistics). Another important factor is the power of the metaphorical system described in 12.1, together with the natural analytical preference for discreteness and precise delimitation. Still other reasons, the focus of our present interest, pertain to how the issue has been conceived and formulated. I suggest that certain erroneous conceptions, as well as a lack of conceptual clarity in its formulation, have kept the autonomy issue from being properly considered.

A fundamental question is whether grammatical elements are meaningful. For example, do such categories as noun and verb have a semantic basis? These problems have traditionally been examined from an *objectivist* perspective assuming truth-conditional semantics and the classical model of categorization. If the issue is posed in objectivist terms, the answer is bound to be negative—certainly there are no objective properties shared by the referents of all and only the members of either the noun or the verb class. Each class is however susceptible to semantic characterization based on its *prototype*. Moreover, if one adopts a *conceptualist* view of meaning that properly accommodates construal, then semantic descriptions applicable to all class members are possible at least in principle (irrespective of whether the proposals advanced here are correct in all particulars). By viewing meaning as a conceptual phenomenon, one can further arrive at plausible semantic characterizations of other basic classes, of grammatical markers, and of such constructs as subject, direct object, head, modifier, and subordinate clause. We have repeatedly observed that the semantic import of grammatical structure is primarily a matter of construal (as opposed to specific conceptual content), and it is precisely this aspect of meaning that objectivist semantics fails to countenance.

Needless to say, proper examination of the autonomy thesis requires a reasonably precise statement of that thesis and a clear understanding of what it would take to establish it against conceivable alternatives. Its consideration has, I think, been clouded by the confounding of distinct issues and by a simplistic view of what the alternatives might be. For our purposes, it can be stated as in (1).

(1) **Autonomy Thesis:** Grammar constitutes a separate, irreducible level of linguistic structure (one with its own constructs, representations, primitives, etc.) that is properly described without essential reference to meaning.[6]

[6] I believe this formulation captures the most central and fundamental of the issues involved. The thesis is usually adopted for syntax specifically ("the autonomous syntax hypothesis"), but

So formulated, the autonomy thesis stands directly opposed to a pivotal claim of cognitive grammar, given in (2).

(2) **Symbolic Alternative:** Grammar is inherently symbolic; only units with both semantic and phonological import are required for its proper characterization.

The pertinent issue is therefore whether grammar reduces to assemblies of symbolic structures, or whether the elements needed to describe it are separate and *sui generis*.

That issue has to be distinguished from certain others with which it tends to be conflated. We may first note a possible equivocation in how the term *modularity* has come to be used and understood. It may refer to the organization of a linguistic system into such large-scale "modules" or "components" as syntax, morphology, and lexicon; the kind of autonomy described in (1) would motivate the postulation of a syntactic or grammatical component of this sort. The term is also used to indicate that a complex phenomenon with apparent idiosyncrasies is best analyzed as the regular intersection of other, more basic phenomena each of which proves quite regular when independently described; a "modular" account of this sort is obviously preferable to one that simply states the idiosyncrasies in ad-hoc fashion (cf. Hale, Jeanne, and Platero 1977). The essential observation is that this second kind of modularity does not entail the first. From the fact that multiple, independently describable factors intersect to shape a phenomenon it does not at all follow that language is organized into autonomous large-scale components such as syntax, lexicon, and semantics, nor that the grammatical factors involved require anything other than symbolic units for their characterization. Indeed, this second kind of modularity is fully compatible with both the letter and the spirit of cognitive grammar, in which an expression's structural description resides in simultaneous categorization by numerous schematic units each pertaining to a particular aspect of its organization.

The autonomy issue, as defined in (1)–(2), must also be distinguished from questions of *predictability*. It is commonly assumed (explicitly in Newmeyer 1983) that the autonomy of grammar is established if any aspect of grammatical structure is less than fully predictable on the basis of meaning or other independent factors. Grammar is autonomous, in other words, unless all grammatical patterns and restrictions fall out as automatic consequences of something more basic (so that they need not be stated explicitly). Now if that is all one means by the term, then grammar is indeed autonomous—it is certainly *not* the case that all grammatical structure is subject to *absolute*

since I reject any strict dichotomy between syntax and morphology (or between either of these and lexicon), I have stated it in terms of grammar overall. This does not affect the structure of the argument.

predictability on semantic or functional grounds (although much of it is strongly *motivated* by such considerations). From there, however, one cannot legitimately proceed to the further conclusion that grammar is autonomous in the sense under discussion. Taking that further step constitutes the **type/predictability fallacy**: it confuses the distinct issues of (1) what *kinds* of structures there are, and (2) the *predictability* of their behavior. In particular, it fails to anticipate the perfectly coherent alternative represented by cognitive grammar, which recognizes that grammatical structure is less than fully predictable, but denies that it is separate and irreducible. Although grammatical patterns and restrictions do require full, explicit statement, only symbolic units figure in their proper formulation.

The point is so fundamental (and so often misapprehended) that it merits reiteration: cognitive grammar does not claim that grammar is *predictable* from meaning, but rather that it is *meaningful* because it embodies and symbolizes a particular way of construing conceptual content. Moreover, contrary to how the issue is usually posed, questions of predictability do not in fact have any bearing on the autonomy thesis as formulated in (1). The pattern of thought which leads to such misconceptions is part of the objectivist legacy. In discussing the relationship between meaning and grammar, theorists tend to presuppose that the former—reducing to conditions on objective truth—is known or at least straightforwardly determinable; hence they conceive the issue as being whether aspects of grammar can be characterized or predicted on that basis. Crucially, however, cognitive grammar conceives the inherent logic of the situation as being quite different. Meaning is a conceptual phenomenon, and by virtue of construal a given objective situation can be coded by any number of expressions all of which are semantically distinct. Furthermore, construal is generally as invisible to us as a pair of glasses or contact lenses—despite its formative influence on how we view a scene, our awareness is focused on the scene itself. There is consequently no sense in which an expression's semantic characterization is known prior to linguistic analysis or available as an independent basis for prediction.

The task we therefore face is to develop *simultaneously* an account of semantic structure as well as an account of grammatical structure, each informed and supported by how it articulates with the other.[7] Although this would seem to be more difficult than describing either meaning or grammar independently, in fact each facet of the analysis both constrains and illuminates the other. The analyst cannot, for instance, assume that grammatical markers are semantically empty, or claim that substantially different constructions are the same in meaning and related by transformational derivation. Nor can he assume that he knows what something means from a gloss, a transla-

[7]For example, the notion of *profiling* was adopted as a construct indispensable to semantic description, but it also proves essential for the characterization of grammatical structure.

tion, or even a full characterization of the objective situation it describes: he must also accommodate construal, essential aspects of which are embodied and symbolized by grammatical structure. Hence grammar yields essential clues about conceptual structuring that we cannot afford to overlook. Rather than striving (vainly) to predict grammar from meaning, we must learn to interpret those clues and thus determine what the grammatical structure of a language is trying to tell us about its semantic structure. It is then the adequacy, coherence, and insight of this overall description—embracing both meaning and grammar—that must taken as the basis for evaluation.

To some, a conceptualist semantics is inherently mysterious and thus an unacceptable foundation for the characterization of grammatical structure.[8] Contributing to this attitude is the apparent belief that imagery is unsusceptible to empirical verification (possibly just a figment of the cognitive grammarian's imagination) and that the basis for ascribing conceptual import to linguistic elements is ad hoc and unprincipled. This is not the case, however. Without denying that particular descriptions may be provisional and even speculative, I would argue that cognitive semantics is indeed a viable empirical enterprise in which descriptions and basic constructs are arrived at non-arbitrarily and are often capable of explicit justification. In fact, I would not at all concede that these semantic analyses are any less believable or securely grounded than the abstract syntactic and phonological descriptions that linguistic theoreticians are accustomed to.

Various kinds of considerations can be advanced to justify the semantic descriptions proposed in cognitive grammar. The first is intuition (for whatever it may be worth). Although a workable description requires careful analysis (not just introspection), for speakers to regard it as natural and revealing can at least be taken as a point in its favor. And while intuition alone will not tell us how to describe a meaning or provide the requisite constructs, a speaker may well be able to ascertain that a proposed characterization captures something that he dimly felt but was unable to articulate.[9] A second consideration is that the analyses presuppose only obvious, well-established cognitive phenomena (e.g. figure/ground organization; the focusing of attention; metaphor; construal at various levels of specificity; cognitive models; the

[8] One might counter that it is far less mysterious than the notion of an autonomous grammatical component grounded in neither meaning nor sound, the two essential "content" domains of language. Unconstrained by semantic considerations, autonomous accounts of grammar vary greatly and frequently posit descriptive constructs of dubious psychological validity that are connected only in the most tenuous way to any kind of observable reality.

[9] An excellent example is Lindner's (1981, 1982) analysis of English verb-particle combinations (e.g. *turn out, black out, fill out, start out; write up, start up, board up, clean up*). Few who read her description fail to appreciate that the particles (traditionally regarded as meaningless) make systematic contributions to the meanings of these expressions. It seems to me that such intuitions are at least as trustworthy as the grammaticality judgments that figure so prominently in generative grammar.

ability to mentally assume different vantage points; and so on). They therefore have an inherent psychological plausibility that other semantic theories cannot necessarily claim. Furthermore, a limited set of basic descriptive constructs are posited, which prove to be systematically applicable to an extremely broad array of diverse data. Profiling figures in the characterization of every expression at every level of grammatical organization, for example, and trajector/landmark asymmetry in virtually every relational predication. While a full, definitive set of constructs has yet to be established, it is decidedly not the case that basic descriptive elements are made up on the spot to accommodate each new array of data that comes along.[10]

A further source of justification resides in the predictions that an element's semantic characterization allows us to make concerning its behavior. These predictions may be less than absolute, for they often hinge on such graded factors as prototypicality, relative prominence, and the compatibility of images; but when properly formulated (in some cases referring to degrees of likelihood or naturalness), they nevertheless afford a substantial measure of empirical control. Let me call attention to a few of the many examples contained in these two volumes.

□ The semantic characterization of the "Dative Shift" construction, namely that it highlights a resultant possessive relationship between the two post-verbal nominals (Vol. 1, pp. 39–40), predicts the contrast in acceptability between sentence pairs like the following:

(3)(a) **I cleared him the floor.*
(b) *I cleared him a place to sleep on the floor.*

□ The proposed distinction between *few* and *a few*—that the former indicates a negative departure from an expected quantity, the latter a positive departure from zero (2.3.2)—correctly predicts that only *few* should govern a negative-polarity item, such as *any*:

(4)(a) *Few blondes actually have any fun.*
(b)**A few blondes actually have any fun.*

□ The characterization of (5)(a) as a setting-subject construction entails that the post-verbal nominal is at best a highly peripheral member of the direct-object category, and thus predicts its failure to passivize (8.1.3.2):

(5)(a) *January witnessed another rash of daring robberies.*
(b)**Another rash of daring robberies was witnessed by January.*

□ The description of grounding predications—in particular, the claim that they profile the *grounded entity* rather than the *grounding relation-*

[10] A distinction has to be made here between fundamental descriptive notions (e.g. profile, trajector, scope, vantage point, schematicity, correspondence, image schemas, etc.) and the cognitive domains in which they are manifested. The latter (i.e. the conceptualizations, cognitive models, and knowledge systems that furnish the actual content of linguistic predications) constitute an open-ended class, and to describe a particular expression we must often invoke a unique domain or one not previously encountered.

ship—predicts their possible use as pro-forms for nominals and finite clauses (e.g. *Most will*), as well as their failure to behave analogously to stative relations that appear to be semantically similar (2.3.2; 2.4):

(6)(a) *His enemies are {many/*most}.*

(b) *Their departure is {in the future/*will}.*

□ The meaning proposed for the "true" or "simple" present tense (i.e. exact coincidence of the profiled process with the time of speaking) predicts its general incompatibility with perfective verbs, and further predicts the exceptionality of performatives in this regard (6.2.1).

Two additional considerations help to justify the semantic descriptions adopted in this framework. One can argue, first, that the constructs it makes available are quite successful at representing crucial aspects of linguistic meaning. Time and time again, they have enabled us to state explicitly the precise ways in which semantically similar expressions (or senses of the same expression) differ in meaning, as well as the nature of their commonality. One can further argue that the proposed semantic characterizations do indeed prove adequate as the basis for a coherent and revealing account of grammatical structure, as this volume has attempted to show in some detail for a broad range of representative phenomena. I maintain, therefore, that the conceptualist semantics being developed in cognitive grammar derives strong empirical support from its not inconsiderable descriptive success.

12.2.2. *Assessing the Symbolic Alternative*

If workable, the symbolic view of grammar ought to be preferred by linguistic theorists on grounds of naturalness, conceptual unification, and theoretical austerity. A fundamental goal of these volumes has been to show that it is indeed workable, that it can in principle accommodate even those kinds of phenomena generally regarded as *prima facie* evidence for the autonomy thesis. By way of summary, let us briefly consider how cognitive grammar proposes to deal with these matters, which include the following: (1) grammatical classes; (2) grammatical rules and constructions; (3) supposed representations and primitives that are specific to grammar; (4) "semantically empty" grammatical markers; (5) the semantically arbitrary fact that expressions often have to take a certain form, even though another form could perfectly well express the same meaning; (6) non-predictability of the class of elements that participate in a given morphological or syntactic construction; (7) our apparent ability to judge grammaticality independently of meaning; and (8) restrictions that seemingly have to be stated in purely formal terms. These topics will be discussed in the order listed.

(1) Classes are established on the basis of either intrinsic or extrinsic properties. I have argued that *intrinsic*, semantic properties (pertaining primarily to the nature of the profile) permit the characterization of classes that

are fundamentally important to grammatical description (such as noun, verb, count noun, imperfective verb, atemporal relation, nominal, and finite clause). Each class represents a complex category centered on a prototype that reflects a basic aspect of our everyday experience. More controversially, I have also proposed highly schematic descriptions—applicable to all class members—whose origin presumably lies in basic cognitive abilities (e.g. the ability to construe a set of entities as a unitary region, or to conceptualize an event either sequentially or in summary fashion). Elements are categorized *extrinsically* by their occurrence in particular structural frames; since an element tends to activate the frames in which it frequently occurs, those frames can be thought of as part of its characterization. An essential claim of cognitive grammar is that the constructional schemas defining these frames are reducible to assemblies of symbolic structures.

(2) No distinction is made between grammatical rules and constructions, nor (apart from level of specificity) between rules/constructions and instantiating expressions. Patterns and regularities are embodied in *constructional schemas*, which are simply schematized expressions—by abstracting away from points of divergence, each reveals some commonality observable across an array of data. A constructional schema is thus a complex symbolic structure whose internal organization mirrors that of the expressions it is extracted from. Any generalization supported by the data is representable by an appropriate schema, which can then be used as a template for assembling new expressions on the same pattern. A given expression is simultaneously categorized by many class and constructional schemas, each pertaining to a different facet of its structure. The full set of categorizing relationships in which an expression participates constitutes its *structural description*.

(3) Grammatical structure is traditionally described with reference to such notions as *subject*, *object*, *head*, *modifier*, *complement*, *coordination*, and *subordination*, which are usually thought of as being specific to grammar and primitive at least in the sense of being unsusceptible to semantic characterization.[11] Reasonable and (I believe) viable conceptual definitions have nonetheless been proposed for all of these, invoking such basic semantic constructs as profiling, figure/ground alignment, and conceptual autonomy/dependence.[12] Also specific to grammar are the *syntactic phrase trees* of transformational theory; although they play a role in semantic and phonological inter-

[11] Views differ as to whether they are primitive within grammar as well or reducible to more fundamental grammatical notions. For instance, relational grammar departed from transformational grammar by claiming that the subject and object relations are primitive rather than being definable in terms of tree configuration.

[12] A subject and direct object are characterized schematically as primary and secondary clause-level figure. A head is the profile determinant at a particular level of organization, a main clause being the head with respect to a subordinate clause. At a given level, a modifier is conceptually dependent vis-à-vis the head, whereas a complement is conceptually autonomous. Coordination is defined in terms of separate and co-equal profiles.

pretation, the trees themselves (as distinct from the lexical items inserted into them) are not seen as semantic or phonological objects. Cognitive grammar does not employ such representations. To be sure, it recognizes and accommodates the kinds of information they convey: *constituency* is merely the order in which simpler symbolic structures combine to form successively more complex ones; *constituent type* (corresponding to node labels) is given by categorizing relationships between class schemas and symbolic structures of any size; *linear order* is actually temporal order, one aspect of phonological structure, hence its specification is part of every symbolic structure's phonological pole. Because all the requisite information is provided by configurations of symbolic structures (including categorizing relationships, as well as compositional paths, which reduce to categorizing relationships (Vol. 1, 12.2)), it would be superfluous to posit syntactic tree structures as a separate type of entity.

(4) I believe that every grammatical marker is properly attributed some kind of meaning, however tenuous it might be. Specific semantic descriptions have been proposed here for a considerable variety of markers, including *of*, *-er*, *-ee*, the passive *by*, the possessive ending, articles, case markers, gender inflections, and all the elements of the English auxiliary (*be*, *have*, *do*, *-ing*, tense inflections, the past participial morpheme, and the modals). Why are such elements often considered meaningless? In part because the kinds of meanings they represent are neither anticipated nor readily accommodated by objectivist semantics: they tend to be highly schematic (thus imposing no truth conditions); to invoke abstract, seemingly "mysterious" conceptions (e.g. mental contact); and to have a particular type of construal as their primary (if not their sole) semantic value. Moreover, grammatical markers incline toward semantic invisibility because their meanings are largely or wholly included by those of the elements they combine with. Hence their semantic contribution is sometimes essentially vacuous, at least in terms of informational content. But even in such instances, they are more coherently viewed as limiting cases on the scale of contentfulness or informativeness than as having no semantic value whatever.

(5) By definition, a language constrains its speakers to say things in certain ways rather than others. Let us accept the fact that many grammatical constraints (classic examples include agreement, case government, and word-order conventions) are semantically arbitrary, in the sense that relaxing or changing them would have no substantial effect on the meanings of the expressions in which they figure.[13] This observation establishes the *convention-*

[13] It would necessarily have some semantic effect, but this might be limited to minor aspects of construal and thus be invisible from the standpoint of truth conditions or translational equivalence. Recall that one facet of an expression's semantic value is the compositional path leading to its composite semantic structure; hence even a slight difference in grammatical composition constitutes a meaning difference (which may of course be negligible for all practical purposes).

ality and *non-predictability* of grammatical structure. However, it does not at all establish the *autonomy* of grammar as defined in (1), i.e. it does not show that grammar represents a separate, irreducible level of linguistic structure properly described without essential reference to meaning. While grammar must indeed be learned and explicitly described, I have argued that it reduces to configurations of symbolic structures. It is therefore indissociable from semantics and forms a gradation with lexicon, whose generally more contentful form-meaning pairings likewise constrain speakers to say things in particular ways.

(6) One aspect of grammatical non-predictability pertains to the classes of elements allowed to participate in certain morphological and syntactic constructions. While the elements that occur in a given construction may be more or less amenable to semantic or phonological characterization, the precise inventory cannot invariably be predicted on the basis of intrinsic properties. The participating elements therefore have to be listed. This does not, however, support the autonomy thesis: provided that such listing is effected by means of symbolic units, it is quite compatible with the symbolic alternative. In cognitive grammar, the information that a lexical item conventionally occurs in a particular construction takes the form of a *constructional subschema* which incorporates that specific item. This subschema can be viewed from either of two perspectives. With respect to the lexical item, it constitutes a structural frame that is part of the item's characterization. At the same time, it belongs to the complex category defining the construction overall, i.e. the network of schemas and subschemas that embody the regularities discernible at varying levels of abstraction. Distributional privileges and limitations follow from the structure of such networks (including the salience or entrenchment of each node) when these are implemented in a reasonable model of cognitive processing based on competition and interactive activation.

(7) A standard argument for the autonomy thesis, dating from Chomsky 1957, is our putative ability to make judgments of grammaticality independently from judgments of meaning. Chomsky's prime example was *Colorless green ideas sleep furiously*, which was held to be grammatically well-formed despite its semantic anomaly. Conversely, a sentence that is semantically impeccable and easily understood may nevertheless be judged ungrammatical (e.g. because of incorrect word order or omission of required agreement). Although Chomsky's portrayal of the situation is hardly unassailable, for the sake of discussion let us simply accept it at face value. Let us stipulate, in other words, that a language does indeed contain a set of patterns and restrictions properly considered "grammatical," and that the possibility of judging whether a sentence conforms to them does not depend on its semantic coherence or anomaly (as determined by its "lexical" content). Does this entail the autonomy thesis? No, for once again the observation is perfectly compatible

with the symbolic alternative. Cognitive grammar specifically recognizes the existence of grammatical structures that have to be learned and explicitly described—it merely claims that their characterization is reducible to configurations of symbolic units, including a vast array of constructional schemas. Thus an expression can perfectly well be grammatical yet semantically anomalous. This comes about when the component lexical items are integrated in the fashion specified by constructional schemas, but where such integration (via the superimposition of corresponding entities) results in the same entity being attributed conflicting specifications (see Langacker 1988b, pp. 43–46). Likewise, a semantically coherent expression can nevertheless be ungrammatical because it violates the specifications of a categorizing schema.[14]

(8) Finally, the symbolic alternative must be able to handle various kinds of restrictions that are generally thought to be statable only in formal terms. Examples include restrictions on the relative position of a pronoun and its antecedent (thus ***Tom*** *knows* ***he*** *is lucky*, but not *****He*** *knows* ***Tom*** *is lucky*) and conditions on "extraction," such as the coordinate structure constraint (**What did she buy a skirt and?*). Constraints of this sort are usually formulated with reference to syntactic phrase trees. How, then, can they be accommodated in cognitive grammar, which specifically rejects this type of representation? Let us first put things in proper perspective: it is well known (though often conveniently forgotten) that purely syntactic accounts of these phenomena are highly problematic if not downright unworkable (cf. McCawley 1984; Kuno 1987; Lakoff 1986). There is good reason to believe that the relationships in question pertain to *conceptual* configurations whose manifestation through particular kinds of grammatical structures is typical but not necessarily exclusive or invariable (11.3; 11.2.3). We have further seen that assemblies of symbolic structures can represent all the kinds of information depicted by syntactic phrase trees, and that such a description is capable of restrictiveness despite the absence of explicit prohibitions. In principle, therefore, a symbolic account of grammar makes possible just the combination of semantic and formal specifications that the phenomena seem to demand.

I consequently see no reason whatever to accept the autonomy thesis or to doubt the workability of the symbolic alternative. Grammar does exist and

[14] Consider the English ADJ + N schema that sanctions such expressions as *good idea*, *green cup*, *stupid cat*, etc. Semantically, it establishes a correspondence between the adjective's trajector and the noun's profile. Phonologically, it specifies that the adjective directly precedes the noun along the temporal axis. Now if the adjective *green* and the noun *idea* are combined in accordance with this schema, the resulting expression *green idea* is semantically anomalous: because the trajector of *green* is a physical entity, whereas the profile of *idea* is abstract, the schema demands the superimposition of two entities with conflicting specifications. On the other hand, **cup green* is semantically coherent but ungrammatical, because its integration violates the temporal ordering prescribed by the schema at its phonological pole.

does require explicit characterization in its own terms, but it is not irreducible and does not constitute a separate or self-contained "component" of the linguistic system. Because the function of language is to establish correspondences between meanings and strings of sounds, theorists should welcome the prospect of reducing grammar to symbolic relationships. Lexical items provide a basic set of symbolic links between semantic and phonological structures, which are grounded in conceptual and phonetic capabilities that are to some degree independent of language. Grammar has no comparable pre- or extra-linguistic grounding, i.e. there is no separately apprehensible "grammatical content" analogous to the conceptual and phonetic content of linguistic expressions. It therefore seems implausible that grammar would constitute a distinct or autonomous cognitive entity. Far more natural and believable is the notion that grammatical structures are simply schematized expressions; on this account they are themselves symbolic in nature, and form a gradation with lexicon along the parameters of specificity and symbolic complexity. Hence the content of grammatical structures is indistinguishable from that of the expressions they schematize: it reduces to the commonality of such expressions, which is generally too rarified to be manifested independently. Grammar is thus conceived as being immanent in its instantiating expressions, from which it emerges—organically and straightforwardly—by the mutual reinforcement of their common organizational features. I suggest that one ought to prefer the simplicity, naturalness, and conceptual unification of this scheme to one that views grammar as being separate, autonomous, and seemingly unmotivated with respect to the symbolic function of language.

12.3. Processing, Rules, and Representations

The metaphors that guide linguistic research reflect broader metaphorical systems pertaining to human cognition in general. Preeminent in our era has been the metaphor likening mind to the operation of a digital computer. This conception has of course been enormously influential in such disciplines as psychology, linguistics, artificial intelligence, and cognitive science, so much so that its metaphorical nature tends to be overlooked. Nevertheless, a metaphor's institutional success does not guarantee its appropriateness, and recent years have witnessed the emergence of a very different view of cognitive processing. Variously called **parallel distributed processing** (PDP), **connectionism**, and **neural network modeling** (terms that I will use interchangeably), this alternate conception draws its metaphorical inspiration, not from the digital computer, but from the brain itself. Despite its short history, PDP is widely recognized as a credible rival to more traditional processing models. It has forced a fundamental reexamination of the nature of mental representations and consequently has serious implications for linguistic theory. In particular, the status of the notion *linguistic rule* has become a point of considerable controversy. I suggest that cognitive grammar affords a useful perspective on this issue.

12.3.1. *The Connectionist Alternative*

For our purposes, the important aspect of a standard digital computer is that it represents a particular *style of computation*, which is characterized by several well-known properties. The first, naturally, is that the computational device operates in *digital* fashion (though analog processes can of course be simulated); at the most basic level, computation consists of discrete operations performed on sequences of numbers each of which is either *0* or *1*. Second, the computation proceeds in accordance with an explicit *program* that specifies precisely what the machine will do at every step as a function of the immediate input and its current state. The third property is *seriality*: the program is executed one step at a time by a central processing unit. The fourth is *local memory*, by which I mean that each memory item is stored at a particular "address" and is the only item stored at that location. Finally, a clear distinction is maintained between *rules* and *representations*, i.e. between the program directing the computation and the data being operated on.

Connectionism represents an alternative style of computation that differs with respect to all the foregoing properties and is said to be "neurally inspired."[15] The processing device comprises a large array of *units*, which are thought of as being analogous to neurons. Like neurons, each unit bears *connections* to many other units, receiving input from some and providing input to others. A connection is either *excitatory* or *inhibitory*, and at a given moment it has a certain *weight*, i.e. a numerical value representing "connection strength." Moreover, associated with each unit is a numerical value representing its current level of *activation*; at any given moment, this value is a function of the previous value together with the activation received from other units. A unit's own level of activation determines the nature of the input it provides to others. When its value reaches a certain threshold, for instance, it may "fire" and thereby tend to either excite or inhibit those units to which it bears a connection. The amount of excitation or inhibition it imparts to each such unit depends on the magnitude of its output and the strength of the connection between them.

A network of this sort includes a set of *input units* and a set of *output units* that allow communication with elements outside the system; all other units are said to be *hidden*. A computational step is initiated when a particular

[15] For a comprehensive introduction to PDP, see the seminal and foundational *Parallel Distributed Processing: Explorations in the Microstructure of Cognition* (Rumelhart and McClelland 1986b; McClelland and Rumelhart 1986). An opposing view is offered in Pinker and Mehler 1988.

pattern of activation is applied to the bank of input units (i.e. some are activated, others not). The effects of this pattern spread through the system as each unit exerts its influence on those it is connected to. The result of the computation—identified as the pattern of activation displayed by the bank of output units—is thus a function of original activation levels, the input pattern, and the network's configuration (including connection weights). The system is "trained" by providing it with appropriate feedback. This is accomplished by comparing the output pattern at each step with the correct or desired output, and then adjusting the connection weights in accordance with some *learning algorithm* (for instance, each weight might be changed by an amount proportionate to the magnitude of the error and the weight's degree of influence in determining the output). Training consists of successively presenting the system with a set of different inputs and supplying the appropriate feedback after each trial; the full cycle of inputs is repeated many times (typically thousands). At any stage, the system can be tested by presenting it with an input—possibly one it has never seen before—and observing what output it produces. In this manner the experimenter ascertains whether the network has "learned" the generalizations inherent in the data and is capable of extending them to new instances.

Consider how this style of computation differs from that of a standard computer. First, although they are capable of responding in discrete fashion to digitized inputs, PDP models have important *analog* properties, in that both connection weights and levels of activation can vary over a continuous range of values. Second, there is no central processing unit, and no program telling the system what to do. Each unit autonomously performs a strictly *local computation*: it sums its inputs to determine its own level of activation, and hence the degree of activation it passes on to other units (depending on connection weights and whether the connections are excitatory or inhibitory). Third, a computation does not proceed serially, one operation at a time, but instead shows massive *parallelism*, as all units simultaneously perform their local computations in mutually interactive fashion. Fourth, the system's memory resides in connection weights, which are the only things modified by training. Memory is therefore *distributed* rather than local, since an item of memory is not inherent in any single weight, but in a configuration of weights that collectively give rise to a particular computational result. It turns out, moreover, that the same assembly of connection weights is capable of "storing" numerous memory items, yielding distinct results for different input patterns. Finally, no distinction is drawn between rules and representations, for there are no explicit rules at all—the system merely learns to respond in certain ways to particular kinds of input. Rather than being distinct and independent entities, the generalizations it extracts are implicit in the similarity of its responses to similar input patterns.

Connectionist models do in fact prove quite effective at extracting generalizations from their input. With sufficient training, they come to behave in a structured manner that is in some way reflective of the regularities inherent in the data.[16] Moreover, they are especially plausible as realistic models of cognitive processing by virtue of certain computational properties. One such property is speed: owing to their massive parallelism, PDP models can quickly compute a function that a serial processor could not implement in real time if the steps were carried out at a pace consistent with the firing rate of neurons. Another desirable property is "graceful degradation." Whereas a computer program can be rendered inoperative by a single coding error, a neural network model continues to operate tolerably well even when a substantial number of units are removed. Reminiscent of human impairment, this feature is a consequence of knowledge being distributed over a large array of connection weights (so that no single unit or connection is critical). A third property is "content-addressable memory." A problem that arises with digital computers is having to search through a vast set of memory locations to find a particular item. By contrast, the distributed memory of a PDP system is such that an input pattern inherently tends to activate any pattern that substantially overlaps it. A further desirable property is context dependency: the response pattern associated with a particular input segment adjusts to accommodate the context in which it is presented. Finally, PDP models are realistic from the standpoint of categorization, being capable, for example, of giving rise to prototype effects.

12.3.2. *The Representation of Linguistic Structure*

Because PDP systems are highly successful at "extracting generalizations," the question inevitably arises as to whether they are adequate for natural language. Can such a system accommodate the many kinds of regularities that linguists capture by positing *rules*? If so, what is their status in a model of cognitive processing where explicit rules are specifically abjured? These issues have been the subject of spirited debate between connectionists and proponents of more traditional processing models (cf. Rumelhart and McClelland 1986a; Pinker and Prince 1988). Our purpose in this final section is to examine the dispute from the standpoint of cognitive grammar, and to suggest that the equation of rules with *schemas* points the way to a possible resolution.

12.3.2.1. *A Spectrum of Positions.* To put the debate in proper perspective, let us first sketch two extreme positions concerning the mental represen-

[16] Often, in fact, certain hidden units develop into "feature detectors," each responding to a particular facet of the input patterns.

tation of linguistic structure. It is likely that no serious scholar actually subscribes to either; they are best conceived as caricatures corresponding to the most simplistic view that proponents on each side of the debate might possibly entertain in regard to what those on the other side believe. At one extreme lies a conception of language processing that an ill-informed connectionist might attribute to a proponent of autonomous syntax working in the generative tradition. The connectionist would probably describe it as "empty symbol pushing."[17] Situated at the other extreme is a conception of mental processing that a mean-spirited generativist might ascribe to PDP modelers. The generativist would no doubt offer the pithy characterization "mind as mush."

On a strict empty-symbol-pushing account, the structure of a language is fully describable by means of a mathematical device—an automaton or (equivalently) a set of rewriting rules—quite comparable to those provided for simple artificial languages in Chomsky's early writings (1957, 1965b; Chomsky and Miller 1963). Consider, for instance, a language which has just two vocabulary items, *a* and *b*, and in which a sentence is grammatical if and only if it consists of a string of *a*'s followed by a string of *b*'s exactly equal in length (thus *ab*, *aabb*, *aaabbb*, *aaaabbbb*, etc. are grammatical, but not **a*, **abb*, **aaab*, or **aaaabbbbb*). This language is generated by a grammar comprising just two rules, namely *S→aSb* and *S→ab*.[18] Grammars of this sort have several basic properties relevant to our discussion: (1) They provide an *explicit representation* of linguistic structure. In particular, a grammar is *generative*, in the sense of constituting a full and precise mathematical characterization of all and only the grammatical sentences of a language. (2) They are *constructive*, i.e. they consist of instructions for assembling grammatical expressions. These instructions are formally distinct from the expressions they characterize (e.g. *S→aSb* is not per se structurally parallel to *aaabbb*). (3) Rules have the property of *full generality*. Each rule applies in the derivation of an open-ended set of expressions and is applicable without exception to any structure that meets its specifications. (4) The rules manipulate *contentless symbols*. A non-vocabulary symbol (such as *S*) is attributed neither semantic nor phonological content. Vocabulary symbols (such as *a* and *b*) are thought of primarily as phonological elements; any meaning they might have is irrelevant to the derivation of a sentence or in assessing its well-formedness

[17] The traditional style of processing is often described as *symbolic*, but the term is then used in a crucially different sense than in cognitive grammar, where it refers to structures having both phonological and semantic import. Instead, *symbolic processing* involves the manipulation of explicit representations consisting of discrete "symbols," which are usually thought of as markers having no intrinsic content. In claiming that all grammatical elements are symbolic, hence meaningful, cognitive grammar specifically rejects the postulation of such markers.

[18] *S* stands for "sentence," while *X→Y* is an instruction to "rewrite" *X* as *Y*. The derivation of a sentence starts with *S* and continues until the derived string contains no symbol capable of being rewritten.

(e.g. I can determine whether a string is grammatical from its form alone, simply by counting the number of *a*'s and *b*'s).

Though it is doubtful that any generativist currently harbors this view of natural-language grammars, it does enjoy the status of an archetype from which more realistic accounts can be seen as having evolved, and which continues to strongly influence how theorists tend to think about linguistic structure. One can therefore imagine the reaction of a generative theorist when first exposed to a conception of cognitive processing that disavows the very notion of explicit rules. From his perspective, connectionists are cavalierly abandoning the only conceivable basis for linguistic regularity. The generativist may acknowledge that "toy" PDP models manage to function halfway decently on extremely simple, artificially designed linguistic tasks, but is confident that connectionist systems are too amorphous to capture the crisp generalizations of generative syntax and are bound to fail miserably for data that even begin to approximate the actual complexity of natural-language expressions.[19] The problem, as he sees it, is that a PDP system has no way of representing or referring to the descriptive and theoretical constructs that linguists posit—it is merely an array of faceless units behaving in a squishy fashion. So to the extent that such a system actually works, a connectionist researcher has no way to explain just *how* it works and no apparent interest in so doing. By eschewing the linguistic constructs needed for discrete, explicit representations, the connectionist commits himself to an unstructured view of mental processing for which the appellation "mind as mush" strikes the generativist as being quite appropriate.

The first step toward a resolution is to recognize that the empty-symbol-pushing and mind-as-mush conceptions are in fact unfair caricatures: the actual dispute involves more elaborate, less extreme positions which have more in common than one might think. The simple rewriting systems of the empty-symbol-pushing caricature bear little resemblance to the kinds of grammars currently envisaged by generative theorists. Indeed, with respect to all four properties described above, developments within the generative tradition itself have led to notions more nearly compatible with the PDP world view. (1) While explicit rules and representations remain the *sine qua non* of generative theory, the strict conception of a grammar as a generative, algorithmic device is no longer universally entertained. It now happens that theories are propounded and extensively applied without any serious attempt at comprehensive formalization (government-binding theory being the most notable example). (2) Theorists are less and less inclined to speak of rewriting rules, or to conceive of grammars as constructive devices. Increasingly prevalent are

[19] A generative grammarian, one supposes, would never restrict the complexity of the data considered, or investigate the capabilities of a formal model by applying it to simple artificial examples.

"unification-based" approaches, where structures are characterized in terms of the simultaneous satisfaction of multiple constraints. There is less reliance on derivations from underlying structures, and a greater tendency for surface constructions (as distinct from the rules that supposedly derive them) to be regarded as important entities in their own right. (3) Generativists are fully cognizant that a linguistic description requires statements at all levels of generality, and have proposed a variety of formal devices to accommodate exceptions, irregularity, and patterns of limited productivity. As these are usually consigned to "the lexicon," the role of this component within the overall linguistic system has steadily increased (to the point that it threatens to overshadow the remainder). (4) Slowly but surely, the intimate relationship of meaning and grammar is coming to be appreciated. Grammaticality judgments are not thought of as being based on strings of words per se, but are relative to particular structural descriptions and (possibly) particular interpretations. It is now commonly recognized that differences in grammatical behavior correlate with differences in meaning, and that the choice among alternate grammatical constructions may have semantic (or at least "pragmatic") consequences.

Likewise, "mind as mush" is not at all descriptive of how connectionists actually conceive of mental processing. Because they seek a viable account of linguistic (and other) behavior, they want their systems to function in a realistic manner that accommodates all degrees of observed regularity, ranging from the exceptionless to the idiosyncratic. PDP systems are in fact capable of highly structured behavior, in which specific patterns of activation are crisply and reliably produced in response to certain kinds of input. Moreover, connectionists are quite concerned with finding out precisely how their systems manage to accomplish what they do. They thus explore, for example, the effect on performance of adopting different learning algorithms or varying the architecture of the connections (e.g. by incorporating a feedback loop). They monitor the activation levels of hidden units across a set of input patterns to ascertain whether certain units have developed into detectors for particular features (input configurations). By measuring the similarity of the response patterns evoked by various inputs, they determine whatever implicit categorization the system may have imposed on the data. In short, connectionists regard the functioning of their models as organized, structured activity that is quite amenable to being studied and understood. And to the extent that a system realistically models an array of data, it is quite conceivable that certain linguistic constructs might be identified with specific aspects of its functioning.

Armed with more accurate sketches of the opposing positions, we can now assess the actual nature of their divergence. The gap remains substantial—although their continued development may very well bring the generative and connectionist approaches closer together, full convergence would seem to be precluded by basic differences in their underlying philosophies.[20] It is at this point that cognitive grammar enters the picture, for in a certain sense it bridges the gap. On the one hand, it accepts the basic tenet of generative theory that a linguistic system comprises a large number of regularities reasonably called "rules" (using that term quite broadly). At the same time, it conceives of these rules in such a way—as *schemas*—that a plausible connectionist interpretation is readily envisaged.

While cognitive grammar is radically different from generative grammar in its archetypal form, the contrast with contemporary generative theory is in some respects less stark. In fact, though its basic framework was established well over a decade ago, cognitive grammar is not unreasonably viewed as the kind of theory that would result if all the aforementioned trends within the generative tradition were brought to their full culmination, and if certain fundamental but erroneous assumptions (e.g. the autonomy thesis) were abandoned to allow the emergence of a restrictive and unified conception of linguistic structure. Let us consider these trends in turn: (1) A grammar is specifically *not* conceived as being generative; indeed, the recursive enumeration of "all and only the grammatical sentences (form-meaning pairings) of a language" is held to be impossible, since this is not a well-defined set.[21] (2) A grammar is not a constructive device, but simply an inventory of conventional units available for the categorization of usage events. Because an expression's structural description resides in simultaneous categorization by numerous schematic units, each interpretable as a constraint pertaining to some aspect of its organization, cognitive grammar is a "unification-based" model *par excellence*. (3) It is also a *usage-based* model in which rules are simply schematizations of expressions. Rules at all levels of generality are embodied as schemas, which compete for activation on the basis of specificity as well as entrenchment. Schemas expressing low-level generalizations are frequently invoked for the primary categorization of usage events and are thus essential to linguistic structure (if anything, it is the status of higher-level generalizations that is in doubt). (4) In this theory, meaning and grammar are not just intimately associated but *indissociable*, since grammar reduces to the structuring and symbolization of conceptual content. There are no contentless structures: all linguistic units have semantic and/or phonological import.

In short, the non-generative, non-constructive nature of cognitive grammar

[20] I speak here of a true *rapprochement*, to be distinguished from such tactics as implementing a standard generative analysis in a PDP system, or offering rule-based and connectionist accounts for different facets of linguistic ability (e.g. syntax vs. lexicon, or competence vs. performance).

[21] In saying earlier that grammatical patterns and restrictions require explicit formulation, I was referring to their lack of predictability on semantic or functional grounds, not to the nature of their cognitive representation. A connectionist interpretation of the latter will be presented shortly.

should no longer seem exotic to generative theorists, and its greater emphasis on low-level regularities is primarily a matter of degree. More likely to be resisted is the limitation of rules to schematized expressions, yet this too is based on notions also encountered in the generative tradition (structural templates; multiple constraint satisfaction). By contrast, the idea that grammar might reduce to symbolic relationships is totally foreign to the generative outlook, so tightly does it embrace the autonomy thesis. However, this thesis affords no basis for anticipating or explaining the intimate association of meaning and grammar, which is intrinsic to the symbolic alternative. Adopting this central tenet of cognitive grammar makes possible a conceptual unification that reveals a basic compatibility, if not a natural affinity, with the connectionist scheme of mental processing. This affinity has several facets. For one thing, the acquisition of grammar (as of lexicon) becomes a matter of establishing form-meaning mappings, which PDP systems handle straightforwardly as associations between input and output patterns. Moreover, the conception of rules as schematized expressions accords with the absence in PDP of any qualitative distinction between specific and general knowledge. An additional resemblance between cognitive grammar and connectionism is the importance that each attributes to specific knowledge and low-level regularities. Finally, since connection weights amount to constraints on the activation levels of associated units, the simultaneous satisfaction of multiple constraints represents the inherent problem-solving mode of PDP systems.

12.3.2.2. *The Nature of Linguistic Rules.* We can now focus specifically on the issue of explicit rules, with respect to which I have taken two positions that might appear to be contradictory. On the one hand, I have accepted the generative view that grammatical patterns and restrictions require full, explicit statement (though arguing that only symbolic units are needed for this purpose). On the other hand, I have said that cognitive grammar has a natural affinity to connectionism, which makes no use of explicit rules and claims that they are unnecessary for a viable account of mental processing. The inconsistency is only apparent, for the positions were set forth in different contexts in response to different concerns. By way of clarification, I will now indicate how the conception of linguistic rules proposed in cognitive grammar both acknowledges a valid aspect of the generative conception and also has a reasonable PDP interpretation.

Recall first the distinction between an *internal* and an *external* grammar, i.e. between the cognitive representation of linguistic structure and a linguist's attempt to describe it. In the generative tradition, explicit rules are usually regarded as characteristic of both kinds of grammars: the rules that linguists write to describe a language are interpreted as hypotheses concerning its mental representation, and in some form or other, rules that comprise and manipulate discrete symbols are thought to figure as distinct entities in a speaker's mental grammar. As for connectionists, their disavowal of explicit rules pertains primarily to the internal grammar—their interest lies specifically in cognitive processing, and *qua* connectionists they are not concerned with writing linguistic descriptions. What about cognitive grammar? Its outlook has something in common with each of these perspectives, hence the apparent inconsistency noted above. It shares with generative grammar the concern for systematically describing language structure, and at this level—i.e. with respect to an external grammar—it acknowledges that grammatical patterns and restrictions require explicit characterization. At the same time, it conceives of this knowledge in such a way that a connectionist account of its internal representation is quite imaginable.

Grammatical patterns and restrictions require explicit characterization because their specific detail is not predictable on the basis of meaning or functional considerations—a speaker has to learn the grammatical conventions of his language, and a linguist has to describe them as entities in their own right, whatever the extent of their functional motivation. Various formats may be adopted for this purpose, each in some way revelatory, but there is no supposition in cognitive grammar that the formal properties of any particular notation or descriptive technique translate directly into claims about the basic nature of cognitive representation.[22] Linguistic descriptions are instead attributed the more limited role of elucidating certain organizational features that we would expect to be discernible—were we omniscient—somewhere within the cognitive processing constitutive of linguistic ability. Presumably these features are *emergent* rather than fundamental; they reside at higher levels of organization that emerge in processing activity whose basic character is roughly as envisaged in neural network modeling. In the final analysis, therefore, linguistic knowledge is stored in connection weights, and no direct analog of linguistic rules is discernible at that level.

It does not follow, however, that no analog of linguistic rules can be discerned at any level of cognitive organization. I suggest that constructs which prove essential to linguistic description are reasonably hypothesized to have some kind of cognitive validity. Though such constructs are unlikely to be directly and individually represented at the level of weighted neural connections, they might well correspond to certain aspects of the processing supported by these connections. Thus, given a strongly motivated and psychologically plausible linguistic description, as well as a successful PDP model of the same phenomena, it would be both natural and perhaps quite profitable to search for points of contact between the two. The linguistic analysis offers

[22] Thus a formulaic representation does not imply that cognitive processing involves formulas or the manipulation of discrete symbols, nor does a pictorial representation imply that the brain stores information in the form of pictures.

the connectionist a way to interpret the performance of his model and to determine the phenomenological value of specific patterns of activation (or any other aspects of its functioning). At the same time, the PDP implementation offers the linguist a potential source of validation for the constructs he postulates.

The constructs that concern us are linguistic rules. At the descriptive level, cognitive grammar does posit rules and attempt to describe them explicitly. But in so doing, it merely recognizes that a language comprises conventionally sanctioned regularities (at all levels of generality) which speakers have to learn and which have some role in language processing. Crucial to assessing their cognitive status is the further claim that rules are nothing more than schematizations of expressions. As such, they are not conceived as being distinct entities observable independently of their instantiating expressions (although we can hardly avoid discussing them as if they were, for analytical and descriptive purposes). Rather, they are conceived as being *immanent* in their instantiations (Vol. 1, 11.3.1), i.e. as inherent in (and shared by) the patterns of cognitive activity in whose occurrence their instantiations reside. The cognitive analog of a rule is thus not be found in any static configuration (such as a neural circuit), but in recurrent aspects of processing activity.

Conceived in this fashion, linguistic rules have a straightforward connectionist interpretation that invokes the standard notion of a *state space*.[23] A PDP system with *n* units defines an *n*-dimensional state space, in which each dimension comprises a range of values that correspond to a particular unit's possible levels of activation. Each location in this space represents a possible state of the system, i.e. an instantaneous pattern given by the current activation levels of all the units. As the system operates, it changes state from one instant to the next (as activation levels fluctuate) and thus traverses a path through state space. Now if mental experience reduces to patterns of neural activation (however complex they may be), then any particular experience—such as entertaining a concept, or invoking a linguistic structure—can be identified either with a location in state space or a path (a series of locations). A location, however, can be characterized with varying degrees of precision; it can be point-like or diffuse, depending on whether activation levels are specified quite narrowly or only as falling within a certain band of values. Here we find a natural basis for describing the relationship between a schema and its instantiations. In relative terms, a schema corresponds to a diffuse location (or series of locations) in state space, and each instantiation to a more nearly point-like location within it. A schema is immanent in its instantiations for the simple reason that being located in a point-like region of state space

[23] I owe this interpretation to Steve Poteet. For an example of connectionist research in a similar vein, see Elman 1990.

entails being located in a diffuse region that encompasses it.[24] Equally non-mysterious is the "extraction" of a schema from its instantiations: to the extent that patterns of activation corresponding to specific structures cluster within a certain region of state space, they induce adjustments in connection weights which facilitate the occurrence of activation patterns falling anywhere in that region.

Despite its alluring promise, connectionism is very much in its infancy. Connectionist research in language processing has thus far been limited to small-scale demonstrations of its feasibility with respect to specific tasks; whether and how it might be scaled up to accommodate linguistic structure in all its multifaceted complexity has yet to be determined. Though also in its infancy, cognitive grammar has developed to the point of suggesting certain conditions on the adequacy of any PDP system as a realistic model of human cognition. Let me mention just three. First, a linguistically viable PDP model must handle *structured conceptualizations* of extraordinary intricacy. Consider, for instance, the conceptual embedding characteristic of complex sentences (Ch. 10) or of quantifier scope (3.3.2). Next, such a model must allow distinct structures to be co-activated and linked by *correspondences* while to some degree retaining their separate identity. Examples include analyzability (Vol. 1, 12.1), metaphorical structuring (Lakoff and Johnson 1980), and the elaborate correspondences between elements of different mental spaces of the sort described in Fauconnier 1985. Finally, an adequate model must accommodate the many dimensions of *conventional imagery* (or *construal*), including such factors as profiling, trajector/landmark asymmetry, vantage point, and subjectivity.

[24] Likewise, confinement to a narrow range of activation levels entails confinement to a broader range that encompasses it.

Conclusion and Prospectus

WE HAVE COME to the end of two long volumes that can hardly have been much easier to read and assimilate than to compose. The objectives were (1) to reexamine the conceptual foundations of linguistic thought; (2) to erect on new foundations the framework of a theory having reasonable claim to naturalness and cognitive plausibility; and (3) to show the viability of that theory by applying it—at least in preliminary fashion—to a respectably broad and diverse collection of phenomena. I consider these objectives to have been accomplished. Vol. 1 challenged basic methodological and theoretical assumptions of modern linguistics, articulated a coherent alternative outlook, and detailed a comprehensive model of linguistic organization that offers a unified and revelatory account of the varied aspects of language structure. Vol. 2 has applied this model to a wide spectrum of classic grammatical problems in the nominal, clausal, and extraclausal realms. In each case it has yielded a cogent and perspicuous analysis, managing both to accommodate the valid insights of previous descriptions and to overcome some apparent deficiencies. Although more can always be demanded of a theory by way of initial justification, numerous theoretical ships have been launched on the basis of much less.

The point I wish to emphasize in conclusion is the intrinsic desirability of a model that incorporates the central feature of cognitive grammar: the reduction of grammar to symbolic relationships between semantic and phonological structures. Such a model directly and straightforwardly manifests the basic semiological function of language, namely to permit the symbolization of conceptualizations by means of phonological sequences. If it can be accomplished, this reduction is so advantageous for developing an account of acquisition and language processing, as well as from the standpoint of scientific method, that linguistic theorists might reasonably be expected to embrace it as the default-case option—they should want the symbolic view of grammar to prove viable, and should be willing to make every effort to sustain it. Considering the complications engendered by treating grammar as a separate and autonomous entity (not to mention its inherent strangeness from the semiological perspective), I see no reason why an informed and open-minded scholar would not prefer the conceptual unification and theoretical austerity achieved by the symbolic alternative.

Naturally, all this assumes that a symbolic account of grammar can in fact be made to work. I have no personal doubt that it can, and believe that these two volumes—when combined with earlier papers (assembled in Langacker 1990a)—go a long way toward showing just how. Further demonstration of its workability is afforded by a substantial and steadily growing body of literature that applies cognitive grammar, in depth and in detail, to a variety of difficult problems in diverse languages. Examples include English verb-particle combinations (Lindner 1981, 1982); Samoan clause structure (Cook 1988a); Russian aspectual verb prefixes (Janda 1984); transitivity and passivizability (Rice 1987a, 1987b, 1988); Spanish reflexives (Maldonado 1988, *to appear*); locatives in French, English, and Cora (Vandeloise 1984, 1985a, 1985b, 1986, 1987, 1988; Hawkins 1984, 1988; Casad 1982); case semantics in German and Slavic (Smith 1987; Janda *to appear*); Nahuatl verb morphology (Tuggy 1981, 1986, 1988); Chinese coverbs (Poteet 1987); and English pronominal anaphora (van Hoek *to appear*). There is consequently no dearth of resources for scholars wishing to assess the descriptive adequacy and insight of the model.

Of course, a great deal remains to be done. Yet to be undertaken is an extensive and systematic examination of phonology in terms suggested by the overall framework. The potential for further grammatical investigation, with respect to both languages and specific problems, is essentially unlimited. Especially useful will be works analogous to Cook 1988a and van Hoek *to appear*, in that they carefully survey the account worked out for a particular domain in the context of another theory, and show in precise detail how a cognitive grammar description preserves its apparent advantages while insightfully handling a more inclusive range of data. Together with the far broader spectrum of research conducted under the general rubric of cognitive-functional linguistics, such studies will advance us toward the goal of a substantive, comprehensive, and empirically-grounded linguistic theory. As sketched in 12.1, such a theory will have three facets: (1) an inventory of the constructs available for the description of semantic, phonological, and symbolic structures; (2) a catalog of the structures having reasonable claim to the status of prototypes, ranked by their degree of prototypicality and universality; and (3) a functional characterization that explains, in terms of optimality and the resolution of competing formative pressures, why these particular structures are prototypical.

The beginning of my own attempts to devise a workable and cognitively natural linguistic theory coincided with the American bicentennial. Now, as we enter the last decade of the twentieth century, one can see emerging in many disciplines—linguistics, psychology, cognitive science, semiotics, anthropology, computer science, artificial intelligence, philosophy, neuroscience, and others—a constellation of ideas, outlooks, methods, and empirical findings that seem on the verge of coalescing to form a coherent, comprehensive, and biologically natural conception of language and mind. Our challenge in this decade is to develop a linguistic theory that will not only be compatible with this emergent synthesis, but perhaps even serve as its focal point. Creating a new linguistics of this sort would be a fitting way to initiate the next century and the third millennium.

Reference Matter

Glossary

THIS GLOSSARY is based on that contained in Vol. 1 (originally prepared by Larry Gorbet). It has, however, been extensively revised to make it suitable for Vol. 2, while retaining its utility as a general glossary for the work as a whole and for other writings in cognitive grammar. Thus certain entries relevant primarily to Vol. 1 have been eliminated, many other entries have of course been added, and others have been reformulated for reasons of style, coherence, or consistency. The listing is selective, being restricted for the most part to recurrent terms that are either novel to cognitive grammar or assume a special value in this context; no attempt is made to list every technical term employed (hence not every term given in boldface type in the text is included here). Each entry concludes by citing those sections of the two-volume text that introduce the notion in question, substantially elucidate its properties, or describe its significance within the framework; references to Vol. 1 are given in angled brackets, and those to Vol. 2 in square brackets. Intended as a convenience, the glossary is not a surrogate for either the text discussion or the index.

absolute construal The construal of a relationship (especially a conceptually autonomous thematic relationship) without any salient reference to causation or the energy that drives or sustains it. [7.1.2; 9.2.2]

abstract domain A non-basic domain. Any concept or conceptual complex invoked for the characterization of a predication. <4.1.1>

accommodation The adjustment a component structure undergoes when integrated with another to form a composite structure. <2.1.5; 10.4.2>

action chain A chain of interactions, such that each "link" involves one participant transmitting energy to a second, which is thus induced to interact energetically with the next, and so on. The initial energy source is the *head* of the chain, and the ultimate energy "sink" is its *tail*. [7.1.1; 7.3.1.2; 9.4]

active node From the network representing a complex category, that node which is activated to categorize some facet of the target in a specific usage event. <10.2.2; 11.1.2.2; 11.2; 12.2.1> [4.2.3]

active participant A participant capable of serving as an original source of energy and thereby initiating an interaction. (Contrasts with **passive participant**.) [7.3.3] (Cf. **indirect object**; **initiative capacity**.)

active zone Those facets of an entity that most directly interact with a given domain, or participate in a given relationship. <7.3.4> [8.3.3; 10.2.2.2]

actualization The realization of a structure that is in some sense fully prefigured but has not been previously exploited. <11.3.1> [3.1.1]

A/D asymmetry An asymmetry between two component structures wherein, on balance, one of them (A) is autonomous, and the other (D) dependent on it. <8.3; 9.1> [7.1.2] (See **autonomous structure**; **dependent structure**.)

adjective An expression that profiles an atemporal relation with a thing as trajector. (So defined, the class includes more than just traditional adjectives, e.g. prepositions.) <6.0; 6.1.2; 6.3.3>

adverb An expression that profiles an atemporal relation with a relation as trajector. <6.0; 6.1.2; 6.3.3>

analyzability The extent to which a composite structure is construed in relation to its components (so that they are active and their contribution is recognized or in some way consequential). <8.2.2; 12.1>

arbitrary instance With respect to some type, an instance that is "conjured up" for a limited special purpose—e.g. to elucidate some aspect of how the world is structured (how things typically work)—and has no status outside the mental space thereby created. [2.2.4; 3.1.2; 3.2.2]

atemporal relation A relation processed by summary (as opposed to sequential) scanning, thus lacking a temporal profile. <5.0; 6.0; 6.3.3> (See **complex atemporal relation**; **simple atemporal relation**.)

autonomous structure A structure that does not presuppose another for its full manifestation; e.g. vowels are autonomous vis-à-vis consonants. (The opposite is **dependent structure**.) <8.3; 10.4.2> [7.1.2; 9.2.1]

auxiliary verb A verb whose objectively construed conceptual content is limited to a fully schematic process. (Valid for the verbs traditionally considered auxiliaries in English, but not intended as a universal definition for all elements to which the term might be applied.) [5.3.4]

base Those portions of active cognitive domains that a predication specifically invokes, providing the background against which some entity stands out as the profile. <5.1> (Cf. **profile**; **scope of predication**.)

basic conceptual relation One of a small set of fundamental relational conceptions (including identity, separation, association, and inclusion) that form the basis for more complex relationships. <6.0; 6.2.1>

basic domain A cognitive domain (such as time, three-dimensional space, the pitch scale, or color space) that is primitive in the sense of not being characterizable in terms of other domains still more basic. <4.1.1>

basic epistemic model A fundamental cognitive model pertaining to the evolution of *reality*, which can be visualized as a cylinder that "grows" as new situations are overlaid on those defined by its previous history. The face (or leading edge) of the cylinder constitutes *immediate reality* for the conceptualizer. [6.1; 6.3.2] (See **reality**.)

billiard-ball model A fundamental cognitive model that conceives the world as being populated by discrete physical objects that move about and interact energetically when they come into contact. [1.1.1]

bipolar Involving the relationship between two poles, specifically the semantic and the phonological. <2.2.1>

bipolar componentiality Componentiality (i.e. resolution into components) involving structures defined on the basis of symbolic relationships rather than on the basis of semantic or phonological considerations alone. An example is morphology (as opposed to syllabic organization). (Contrasts with **unipolar componentiality**.) <2.3.1> [5.3.3]

bounding The existence of a limit (internal to the scope of predication) to the set of interconnected entities that constitute a region, or the set of component states that constitute a process. <4.1.2; 5.2; 5.3> [1.1.2; 1.2.1.1]

canonical event model A fundamental cognitive model representing the normal observation of a prototypical action. It comprises the energetic interaction of an agent and a patient, which constitutes a single event observed from a vantage point external to its setting. [7.1.1]

canonical viewing arrangement An arrangement involving a single speaker engaged in face-to-face verbal communication with a single addressee, both committed to cooperating for this purpose. Interpreted narrowly, it incorporates the *canonical event model* as well as the conditions required for the speech act of assertion. [11.4.2]

coding The relationship between linguistic units and usage events. Coding is *unmarked* when a notion approximating a conceptual archetype is manifested linguistically by a category taking that conception as its prototype. <2.1.4; 2.2.1; 5.1> [7.2]

cognitive event A cognitive occurrence of any degree of complexity, from the firing of a single neuron to the massive train of neurological activity involved in processing a complicated expression. <3.1.1>

complement In a construction showing notable A/D asymmetry, a complement is an autonomous component structure that elaborates the (dependent) head. <8.3.4> [10.2] (Cf. **modifier**.)

complex atemporal relation An atemporal relation that does not reduce to a single configuration, but consists of a series of component states scanned in summary fashion. <6.1.3>

complex category A category whose characterization does not reduce to any single structure, but requires multiple structures linked by a network of relationships. <Ch. 10> (Cf. **network model**.)

complex scene A scene that does not reduce to a single, consistent configuration. <3.4.2; 6.1.3; 7.1.2> [3.3.3]

component structure A structure that is integrated with one or more other structures to form a composite structure (particularly in a grammatical construction). <8.0>

composite structure A structure formed from two or more component structures through the superimposition of corresponding entities. Within a construction, the composite structure is the target of categorization by its components, and is "active" in the sense of being available for coding or further composition. <2.1.5; 8.0>

composition The relationship between component and composite structures in a construction. Strictly speaking, the components *categorize* and *motivate* the composite structure; they cannot in general be conceived as providing the "building blocks" for its assembly. <Ch. 12>

compositional path An ordered sequence of structures defined by the successive integration of component structures to form composite structures at progressively higher levels of organization. [3.3.2]

compositionality The degree to which composite structures can be thought of as being assembled from their components in accordance with regular compositional principles (as embodied in constructional schemas). In general, only *partial* compositionality can be assumed (as opposed to the *full* compositionality implied by the metaphorical view of component structures as building blocks). <12.1>

conceived time Time as an object of conceptualization. The component states of a process are distributed along this axis. (Contrasted with **processing time**.) <4.3.1>

constituency The order in which component structures are integrated to yield progressively more elaborate composite structures. Each composite structure along a compositional path defines a constituent. <8.4>

construal relationship The relationship between a conceptualizer (the speaker or addressee in particular) and the conceptualization he entertains (the meaning of a linguistic expression). <3.3.2.4> [2.4; 5.2.3.2]

constructional schema A schema that characterizes a grammatical construction. A symbolically complex structure representing the commonality observable across a set of specific complex expressions whose formation follows a discernible pattern. <2.2.2> [Review and Introduction; 4.2.2; 5.3; 9.3.2; 12.2.2] (See **grammatical construction**; **symbolic complexity**.)

content requirement A restriction that rules out arbitrary formal devices. The only structures ascribable to a linguistic system are (1) semantic, phonological, and symbolic structures that occur overtly as (parts of) expressions, (2) schematizations of permitted structures, and (3) categorizing relationships between permitted structures. <1.2.6.2>

conventional Widely shared (and known to be shared) by members of the relevant speech community. <2.1.3; 4.2.2>

conventional expression A multiword expression that is conventionally established and learned as a fixed unit (even though it may be regular in its composition). As such it is one type of *lexical item*. <1.2.2> (Cf. **lexicon**.)

conventionality The degree to which an expression is "well-formed," in the sense of conforming to the established conventions of a language. <2.1.4.2>

current discourse space The mental space comprising those elements and relations construed as being shared by the speaker and hearer as a basis for communication at a given moment in the flow of discourse. [3.1.1]

dependence The degree to which one structure presupposes another for its manifestation. One structure, D, is dependent on another, A, to the extent that A elaborates a salient substructure of D. <8.3; 10.4.2> [10.1.4]

dependent morpheme A morpheme that makes salient internal reference to a schematically characterized stem (particularly at the phonological pole) and is thus describable as a function mapping one stem onto another. <9.1.2; 9.1.3> [5.3.3]

dependent structure A structure that presupposes another for its full manifestation. E.g. a consonant is dependent with respect to a vocalic nucleus, and an affix (or more obviously, a process morpheme) with respect to a stem. (The opposite is **autonomous structure**.) <6.1.1; 8.3> [5.2.1]

direct object A nominal that elaborates the primary landmark of a process profiled at the clausal level of organization. Its profile is thus a *secondary clausal figure* (that of the subject being the primary figure). <7.3.3> [7.3.2; 8.2; 9.3.1]

domain Any coherent area of conceptualization relative to which semantic structures can be characterized (including any kind of experience, concept, or knowledge system). <2.1.3; 3.2.2; Ch. 4> (Cf. **abstract domain**; **basic domain**.)

domain of instantiation The domain in which the instances of a type are primarily thought of as being located and are distinguished from one another on the basis of their locations. It is also the domain of quantification, and the one in which the presence vs. the absence of bounding determines categorization as a count vs. a mass noun, or a perfective vs. an imperfective process. [1.1.1; 1.2.1.1; 2.2; 2.3.1]

dominion The set of entities (or the region comprising them) that a particular reference point allows one to establish mental contact with. (See **reference-point model**.) [4.3.2]

dynamic evolutionary model A fundamental cognitive model which conceives the world as being structured in a particular way, and reality as having a certain *evolutionary momentum* that constrains its future development (certain future paths constituting *potential reality*, and others *projected reality*). [6.3.2] (Cf. **basic epistemic model**; **reality**; **structured world model**.)

egocentric viewing arrangement An arrangement in which the objective scene is expanded beyond the region of perceptual optimality to include the observer (or analogously, the conceptualizer) and his immediate surroundings. <3.3.2.4> [11.4.2] (See **objective scene**.)

elaborated epistemic model The basic epistemic model augmented with the understanding that those facets of reality known to the conceptualizer are not exhaustive of the world and its evolutionary history. [6.1; 6.3.2] (See **basic epistemic model**; **reality**.)

elaboration The relationship borne to a schema by another structure that characterizes the same entity with greater specificity (i.e. finer precision and detail). <2.1.4.3> [2.2.3]

elaboration site In a construction, those facets of one component structure that the other component serves to elaborate. (Called *e-site* for short.) <8.3.3>

encyclopedic Refers to the open-ended nature of meanings and the lack of any specific boundary between linguistic and extra-linguistic knowledge. Hence the meanings of linguistic expressions cannot be characterized by means of short, dictionary-type definitions. <2.1.3; 4.2>

entity A maximally general term: anything one might conceive of or refer to for analytical purposes. An entity need not be discrete, separately recognized, or cognitively salient. <5.3.1> [1.1.2]

epistemic predication A predication that locates a thing or process with respect to the ground in fundamental "epistemic" domains pertaining to reality and speaker/hearer knowledge. Such grounding is prerequisite to the formation of a nominal or a finite clause. <3.3.2.3> [2.4] (See **ground**; **grounding**.)

expression The pairing of a conceptualization with a vocalization, conceived at any level of abstraction. Linguistic expressions form a continuum, varying in degree of specificity and contextual inclusiveness, that subsumes the traditional "sentences" and "utterances" as special cases. <1.1.1; 11.2.1>

extension A categorizing relationship involving some conflict in specifications between the standard and the target. <10.1; 10.2>

finite clause An expression that designates an epistemically-grounded process that is further construed as being *unitary* (i.e. a single event or a single situation). [5.1; Ch. 6]

focal participant A participant with the status of primary or secondary relational figure. At the clause level, the focal participants are coded by the subject and direct-object nominals. [7.2.2; 7.3.2] (Cf. **trajector**; **primary landmark**.)

grammar The grammar of a language, characterized as a *structured inventory of conventional linguistic units*, comprises those aspects of cognitive organization in which resides a speaker's grasp of established linguistic convention. More narrowly, grammar consists of patterns for the integration of symbolic structures to form progressively more elaborate expressions. <2.1> [4.2; 12.1; 12.2.2; 12.3.2.1]

grammatical construction An array of symbolic structures linked by correspondences and categorizing relationships, including component structures and the composite structure formed by their integration. More broadly, the pattern describing such arrays, as embodied in a *constructional schema*. Still more broadly, a family of constructional variants described by a network in which constructional schemas function as nodes linked by categorizing relationships. <2.2.2; 8.0; 11.1> [4.2; 5.3.1]

ground The speech event, its participants, and its immediate circumstances. <3.3.2.3> [11.4]

grounding A semantic function that constitutes the final step in the formation of a nominal or a finite clause. With respect to fundamental "epistemic" notions (e.g. definiteness for nominals, tense/modality for clauses), it establishes the location vis-à-vis the ground of the thing or process serving as the nominal or clausal profile. [2.4; Ch. 3; Ch. 6]

head Locally, at any given level of constituency, the head is that component structure whose profile corresponds to that of the composite structure. Globally, within a nominal or a finite clause, the head is the lowest-level noun or verb which profiles the thing or process instance designated by the nominal or the clause overall. <8.3.4> [4.1.1; 5.1; 5.3.3; 10.1.4]

imagery The ability to construe a situation in alternate ways for purposes of thought or expression. Meaning is a function of both conceptual content and the "image" imposed on it. <1.2.2; 3.2.1>

immanent One structure is immanent in another when those cognitive events responsible for the former are subsumed by those responsible for the latter. <4.3.4; 11.3.1> [2.2.3; 12.2.2; 12.3.2.2]

immediate scope When scopes are nested one within another, the immediate scope is the innermost layer, the one immediately relevant at a given level of organization. A predication's profile is a kind of focal point within its immediate scope. (Equivalent to **objective scene**.) <3.3.1> [10.1.2; 10.2.1.1]

imperfective A process is imperfective when it is unbounded within the temporal scope of predication and its component states are construed as being effectively identical. (The opposite of **perfective**.) <7.0; 7.2> [5.2.2; 6.2.1]

indirect object An active experiencer (or recipient/possessor) in the target domain. (Characterized as a semantic role, not as a grammatical relation analogous to subject and direct object.) [7.3.3] (See **active participant**; **target domain**.)

initiative capacity The capacity to serve as an initial energy source and thus initiate an interaction. [7.3.3]

instantiation Elaboration. In a more specific use, conceiving of a profiled entity as having a certain location in the domain of instantiation, thus constituting an instance distinct from other instances of the same type. <2.1.4.3> [2.2; 2.3.1] (See **elaboration**; **domain of instantiation**.)

integration The combination of component structures to form a composite structure, effected by correspondences established between their subparts. <2.1.5; 8.1>

interconnection Conceived entities are interconnected when the cognitive events constituting their conception are coordinated as components of a higher-order cognitive event. <5.3.1> [1.1.2]

landmark A salient substructure other than the trajector of a relational predication or the profile of a nominal predication. <6.1.2> [7.3.1.1; 8.2]

lexicon The set of fixed expressions in a language. [1.2.3; 4.1.1]

location Any portion or "fragment" of the setting (especially the portion occupied by a participant). [7.2.2] (See **setting**.)

matrix The full set of domains relative to which a predication is characterized. <4.0> [1.2.1.1]

mental contact A conceptualizer establishes mental contact with an entity when he singles it out for individual conscious awareness. [2.4]

mental transfer A speaker's ability to conceptualize a situation as it would appear from different vantage points and to portray it accordingly for linguistic purposes, irrespective of his actual vantage point. <3.3.2.4; 3.4.1> [6.2.3.2]

modifier In a construction showing notable A/D asymmetry, a modifier is a dependent component structure that is elaborated by the (autonomous) head. <8.3.4> (Cf. **complement**.)

morpheme An expression of minimal symbolic complexity, i.e. one not analyzable into smaller symbolic components. <II.0; 12.1.4> (See **analyzability**; **symbolic complexity**.)

natural path Any cognitively natural ordering of the elements of a complex structure (e.g. based on energy flow, participant prominence, conceptual autonomy, or temporal sequencing). [7.1.3; 11.3] (Cf. **starting point**.)

network model The description of a complex category as a network consisting of structures ("nodes") linked by categorizing relationships (including relationships of schematicity and extension). A network subsumes both specific and schematic structures; there need not be any node that is schematic with respect to all the others (a "superschema"). The structures and categorizing relationships vary in their degree of entrenchment and cognitive salience. In particular, one node often stands out as the category prototype, from which all the others arise by (chains of) extensions. (The "radial model" of complex categories pertains to this special case of the network model.) <Ch. 10>

nominal An expression that designates an epistemically-grounded thing. (Equivalent to "noun phrase".) <3.3.2.3> [Chs. 2–4]

nominal predication A predication that profiles a thing. <5.0>

noun An expression that profiles a thing. (So defined, the class includes more than just traditional nouns, e.g. pronouns and nominals.) <5.0> [Ch. 1]

objective An entity is construed objectively to the extent that it functions asymmetrically as the object (as opposed to the subject) of conception in an optimal viewing arrangement. <3.3.2.4> [2.4; 5.2.3.2; 10.2.1.3; 11.4.3]

objective scene The "onstage region," or general locus of viewing attention. In the optimal viewing arrangement, it coincides with the region of maximal perceptual acuity. (Equivalent to **immediate scope**.) <3.3.2.4> [2.4; 6.2.1]

optimal viewing arrangement A situation in which the roles of the observer and the observed are fully distinct, the latter being sharply differentiated from its surroundings and situated in a region of maximal perceptual acuity. <3.3.2.4>

participant An entity thought of as participating in a relationship, as opposed to merely providing the *setting* for its occurrence. Participants tend to be small and mobile, whereas a setting is global, inclusive, and stable. Moreover, participants *interact* with one another but *occupy* portions of a setting (locations). [7.1.1; 8.1.3] (Cf. **stage model**.)

passive participant A participant that does not serve as an original source of energy (or exhibit initiative capacity). (Contrasts with **active participant**.) [7.3.3]

perfective A process is perfective when it is bounded within the temporal scope of predication. (The opposite of **imperfective**.) <7.0; 7.2> [5.2.2; 6.2.1]

perspective An aspect of construal that subsumes such factors as vantage point, orientation, and subjectivity/objectivity. <3.3.2>

phonological pole A phonological structure in relation to a semantic structure that it symbolizes. <2.2.1>

predicate The semantic pole of a morpheme. <II.0>

predication The semantic pole of any expression, regardless of size or type. <II.0>

primary domain Within a matrix, a domain that is particularly prominent and likely to be activated. <4.2.3>

primary landmark The most salient landmark in a relational predication, especially a thing with the status of secondary figure. <7.3.3> [7.3.1.1; 8.2] (See **direct object**.)

process A relation comprising a series of component states distributed through a continuous span of conceived time and scanned sequentially. <5.0; 7.0; 7.1>

processing time Time as a medium of conceptualization, an axis along which cognitive activity takes place. (Contrasted with **conceived time**.) <4.3.1>

profile The entity that an expression designates. A substructure within its base that is obligatorily accessed, accorded special prominence, and functions as the focal point within the immediate scope of predication. <5.0; 5.1>

profile determinant A component structure whose profile corresponds to that of the composite structure (and which is thus schematic for the composite structure). <6.3.1; 8.2.1> (See **head**.)

proposition An epistemically-grounded process (the semantic pole of a finite clause). [1.2.1.2; 11.4.1]

quality space A set of domains supporting the qualitative characterization of a physical or abstract substance. [1.1.2; 1.2.1.1]

reality All those circumstances a conceptualizer accepts as presently obtaining (*immediate* reality) or having obtained at some point in the past (*non-immediate* reality). For a given conceptualizer, a distinction can be drawn between *known* and *unknown reality*. The complement of known reality is called *irreality*, whereas *non-reality* is the complement of reality overall (both known and unknown). [6.1] (See **basic epistemic model; elaborated epistemic model**.)

reference mass The maximal extension of a category (or its maximal extension in the current discourse space). A hypothetical mass with respect to which a profiled mass is assessed as constituting some proportion. [2.3.2; 3.2]

reference-point model A fundamental cognitive model based on our capacity to invoke one conceived entity (a *reference point*) for purposes of establishing mental contact with another (the *target*). [1.2.2; 4.3.2.1] (Cf. **dominion**.)

region A set of interconnected entities. <5.2; 5.3> [1.1.2; 1.2.1.1] (Cf. **thing**.)

relation A set of interconnections among conceived entities. <6.1.1>

relational predication A predication that profiles a relation (either an atemporal relation or a process). <5.0; 6.0; 6.1.1>

replicate mass A mass that comprises indefinitely many instantiations of the same type specification (and can thus be thought of as being formed by the replication—in type—of a discrete entity we are accustomed to dealing with individually). A plural noun profiles a replicate mass. [2.3.1]

replicate process A complex process comprising indefinitely many instantiations of the same process type. [3.2.2; 3.3]

role archetype A role conception (such as agent, instrument, patient, or mover) which is so fundamental and ubiquitous in our experience that it is relevant to the characterization of every language. Role archetypes are appropriated as the prototypes of basic linguistic categories (e.g. agent, patient, and experiencer for subject, direct object, and indirect object, respectively). [7.1.1]

root A phonologically autonomous morpheme. <8.3.4> (Cf. **dependent morpheme**.)

sanction The motivation afforded a novel structure by the conventional units of a grammar. Sanction is *full* or *partial* depending on whether a categorizing relationship is one of elaboration or extension. This determines whether the structure is judged conventional or ill-formed. <2.1.4; 10.1.1; 11.2.2> (Cf. **conventionality**; **schematicity**.)

schema A semantic, phonological, or symbolic structure that, relative to another representation of the same entity, is characterized with lesser specificity and detail. A "coarse-grained" (as opposed to a fine-grained) representation. (Equivalent to the relation between a superordinate and a subordinate category in a taxonomic hierarchy.) <2.1.4.3; 3.3.3; 10.1.1> [12.3.2]

schematicity Relative precision of specification along one or more parameters. Also, the relation between a schema and its instantiation; such schematicity is *full* or *partial* depending on whether there is any conflict in their specifications. <2.1.4.3; 2.1.4.4; 3.3.3> (Cf. **elaboration**; **extension**.)

scope of predication Those portions of active domains that a predication specifically invokes and relies upon for its characterization. <3.3> [7.2.1] (Cf. **immediate scope**.)

search domain The region to which a locative predication restricts its trajector. <8.1.2> [4.3.2.3; 9.3.1]

selection The process of choosing which aspects of a conceived situation to specifically portray or render salient in formulating a linguistic expression. <3.3.1> [7.2.1]

semantic function Used here in reference to four kinds cf semantic requirements—type specification, instantiation, quantification, and grounding—fulfilled in some manner by every nominal and finite clause. [Ch. 2; 4.2.2; 10.1.1]

semantic pole A semantic structure in relation to a phonological structure that symbolizes it. <2.2.1>

semantic scope One expression, E_1, is in the semantic scope of another, E_2, when E_1 is identified with a substructure of E_2 and thereby functions as part of the conceptual configuration subject to E_2's central semantic specifications. Scope relations are thus analyzed as residing in the structure of complex conceptualizations. [3.3]

semantic structure The meaning of any linguistic expression (the conceptualization functioning as its semantic pole). <II.0>

sequential scanning A mode of processing in which a series of component states are activated successively in non-cumulative fashion (i.e. a situation is followed in its evolution through conceived time, as in watching a film). (The opposite of **summary scanning**.) <3.4.2; 7.1.3> [10.2.1.1]

setting A global, inclusive region within which an event unfolds or a situation obtains. (Contrasts with **participant**.) [7.1.1; 7.2.2; 8.1.3] (Cf. **stage model**.)

simple atemporal relation A relation that reduces to a single consistent configuration (or *state*). The same as a **stative relation**. <6.1.3; 7.1.3>

source domain With respect to the semantic roles associated with action chains, refers to "upstream" elements, in particular agent and instrument (which transmit energy to elements farther "downstream"). With respect to metaphor, refers to a domain that provides the basis for metaphorically structuring another. (In either sense, contrasts with **target domain**.) [7.3.3]

stage model A cognitive model which idealizes a fundamental aspect of our moment-to-moment experience, namely the observation of external events, each involving the interaction of *participants* within a *setting*. [7.1.1]

standard A baseline relative to which some target is evaluated. A basis for comparison or categorization. In a dependent structure seen as a "function," the function's "input," which serves as elaboration site for the autonomous component. <3.1.2>

starting point The origin of a natural path (e.g. the agent in terms of energy flow, the subject in terms of participant prominence, the thematic relationship in terms of conceptual A/D layering, or the first word in terms of temporal sequencing). [7.1.3; 9.2.3.2]

stative relation A simple atemporal relation, one that reduces to a single configuration (rather than comprising a series of component states). <6.1.3; 7.1.3>

structured world model A basic cognitive model that views the world as being structured in such a way that certain (kinds of) events are possible while others are precluded. Within the former class, some events are merely *incidental*, whereas others are direct manifestations of the world's structure, being expected to occur whenever the appropriate conditions arise (they represent the *normal course of events*). [6.2.3.1]

subject A nominal that elaborates the trajector of a process profiled at the clausal level of organization. Its profile is thus the primary clausal figure. <6.3.1> [7.3.1; 8.1]

subjectification A semantic extension in which an entity originally construed objectively comes to receive a more subjective construal. [5.2.3.2; 6.3.1]

subjective An entity is construed subjectively to the extent that it functions asymmetrically as the subject (as opposed to the object) of conception. <3.3.2.4> [2.4; 5.2.3.2]

summary scanning A mode of processing in which a set of specifications or a series of component states are activated successively yet cumulatively; thus, after a *build-up phase*, all facets of a complex structure are coactivated and simultaneously accessible. (The opposite of **sequential scanning**.) <3.4.2; 7.1.3> [10.2.1.1]

surrogate ground The circumstances of a speech event being described (as opposed to the actual speech event). [6.2.2.1]

surrogate speaker An individual other than the actual speaker whose conscious awareness is being described, so that his relationship to the content of a clause is to some degree analogous to the construal relationship that the speaker bears to the content of the sentence as a whole. [3.1.2; 6.2.2.1]

symbolic complexity The property of being decomposable into smaller symbolic units. [4.2.1] (Cf. **analyzability**.)

symbolization A relationship holding between a semantic and a phonological structure whereby either one "calls the other to mind." <1.1.1; 2.1.2; 2.2.1; 5.1>

target domain With respect to the semantic roles associated with action chains, refers to "downstream" elements, i.e. those affected (directly or indirectly) by energy transmitted from elements farther "upstream." With respect to metaphor, refers to a domain that is metaphorically structured by another. (In either sense, contrasts with **source domain**.) [7.3.3]

target structure The structure evaluated relative to the standard in an act of comparison or categorization. In a dependent structure seen as a "function," the function's "output," which corresponds to the composite structure and determines its organization. <2.1.4; 3.1.2; 9.1.3; 9.2; 12.2.1>

temporal profile In a processual predication, the span of conceived time during which the evolving relationship is profiled and scanned sequentially. <7.1>

thematic relationship A comparatively simple, conceptually autonomous relationship involving just a single participant (a *theme*). With respect to the conceptual A/D layering of a finite clause, it is the innermost layer, i.e. the minimal autonomous "core" serving as *starting point* for the assembly of more elaborate processual notions. [7.1.2; 9.2.1]

theme The participant in a thematic relationship. The notion is schematic with respect to a number of role archetypes, including patient, mover, (non-initiative) experiencer, and zero. [7.1.2; 9.1; 9.2.3.1]

thing A region in some domain. <5.0; 5.2> [1.1.2]

time-line model A cognitive model that incorporates the basic epistemic model and further invokes the conception of the ground as a reference point and of time as the axis along which reality evolves. (The notions past, present, and future thus arise.) [6.1]

trajector The (primary) figure within a profiled relation. <6.1.2; 6.3.1> [7.3.1.1]

type space For a given type specification, the range of possible subtypes. (Analogous to **quality space** for substances.) [2.2.3]

type specification The conception of an entity abstractly, as a kind, rather than as a specific instance. (Cf. **domain of instantiation**; **instantiation**.) [2.2.1; 3.3.1]

type/predictability fallacy Failure to distinguish between the distinct issues of what *kinds* of structures there are, on the one hand, and the *predictability* of their behavior, on the other. It is by virtue of this confusion that the non-predictability of grammatical structure is erroneously taken as establishing its *autonomy* (in the sense of constituting a separate level or component of linguistic structure properly describable without essential reference to meaning). [12.2.1]

unipolar componentiality Componentiality (i.e. resolution into components) involving structures defined on the basis of semantic or phonological considerations alone, without regard for symbolic relationships. An example is syllabic organization (as opposed to morphology). (Contrasts with **bipolar componentiality**.) <2.3.1> [5.3.3]

unit A structure mastered by a speaker to the point that it can be employed in largely automatic fashion, without requiring attention to its individual parts or their arrangement. (It is said to have *unit status*.) <2.1.1; 3.1.1>

usage event A symbolic expression as employed by a speaker in a particular circumstance for a particular purpose; the pairing of a rich, context-dependent conceptualization with an actual vocalization in all its phonetic detail. <2.1.4.2>

usage-based approach A non-reductive approach to linguistic structure which holds that rules are simply schematizations of expressions; that specific expressions are capable of being learned as units, hence included in the grammar, even when they conform to such rules; that high-level schemas expressing global generalizations coexist in the grammar with low-level schemas spelling out how these generalizations are implemented in actual conventional usage; and that low-level schemas expressing only local generalizations may be activated preferentially for the categorization of usage events. <1.2.5; 11.1.2; 11.2.2> [1.2.3; 12.3.2.1] (Cf. **active node**.)

valence relation The combinatory relationship between component structures in a grammatical construction, effected by correspondences between their subparts. <8.0> (Cf. **integration**.)

verb An expression that profiles a process. (So defined, the class includes more than just traditional verbs, e.g. modals and finite clauses.) <7.0> [1.1]

viewing arrangement The full circumstances of a speech event together with the relationship between the ground and the situation under description, including both content (e.g. whether some facet of the ground is itself being described) and construal (in particular vantage point and subjectivity/objectivity). [11.4.2; 11.4.3] (See **canonical viewing arrangement**; **egocentric viewing arrangement**; **optimal viewing arrangement**.)

zero The semantic role of a participant that merely occupies a location or exhibits a static property. Among the thematic roles, zero is minimal and non-distinctive; it can be thought of as lacking the special properties characteristic of a patient, mover, or experiencer. [7.1.2]

References

The following abbreviations are used in the References:

BLS = *Proceedings of the Annual Meeting of the Berkeley Linguistics Society*
CLS = *Papers from the Regional Meeting of the Chicago Linguistic Society*
IJAL = *International Journal of American Linguistics*
JL = *Journal of Linguistics*
Lg. = *Language*
LI = *Linguistic Inquiry*

Aissen, Judith L. 1983. "Indirect Object Advancement in Tzotzil." In David M. Perlmutter, ed., *Studies in Relational Grammar 1*, 272–302. Chicago: University of Chicago Press.

Akmajian, Adrian, Richard A. Demers, and Robert M. Harnish. 1984. *Linguistics: An Introduction to Language and Communication*. Second edition. Cambridge, Mass.: MIT Press.

Akmajian, Adrian, Susan M. Steele, and Thomas Wasow. 1979. "The Category AUX in Universal Grammar." *LI* 10: 1–64.

Allan, Keith. 1977. "Classifiers." *Lg.* 53: 285–311.

Allen, Barbara J., Donna B. Gardiner, and Donald G. Frantz. 1984. "Noun Incorporation in Southern Tiwa." *IJAL* 50: 292–311.

Allerton, D. J. 1982. *Valency and the English Verb*. London: Academic Press.

Anderson, John, Joy Anderson, and Ronald W. Langacker. 1976. "Non-Distinct Subjects and Objects in Northern Paiute." *Revista de Letras* 18: 11–21.

Anderson, Stephen R. 1976. "On the Notion of Subject in Ergative Languages." In Charles N. Li, ed., *Subject and Topic*, 1–23. New York: Academic Press.

———. 1982. "Where's Morphology?" *LI* 13: 571–612.

Andrews, J. Richard. 1975. *Introduction to Classical Nahuatl*. Austin: University of Texas Press.

Antinucci, Francesco, and Domenico Parisi. 1971. "On English Modal Verbs." *CLS* 7: 28–39.

Aronoff, Mark. 1976. *Word Formation in Generative Grammar*. Cambridge, Mass.: MIT Press.

Austin, J. L. 1962. *How to Do Things with Words*. Cambridge, Mass.: Harvard University Press.

Bach, Emmon. 1967. "*Have* and *be* in English Syntax." *Lg.* 43: 462–85.

Baker, C. L. 1966. "Definiteness and Indefiniteness in English." Masters thesis. Urbana: University of Illinois.

Baker, Mark C. 1988. *Incorporation: A Theory of Grammatical Function Changing.* Chicago: University of Chicago Press.

Bates, Elizabeth, and Brian MacWhinney. 1982. "Functionalist Approaches to Grammar." In Lila Gleitman and Eric Wanner, eds., *Language Acquisition: The State of the Art*, 173–218. Cambridge: Cambridge University Press.

Bell, Sarah J. 1983. "Advancements and Ascensions in Cebuano." In David M. Perlmutter, ed., *Studies in Relational Grammar 1*, 143–218. Chicago: University of Chicago Press.

Bolinger, Dwight. 1977. *Meaning and Form.* London: Longman.

———. 1982a. "Intonation and its Parts." *Lg.* 58: 505–33.

———. 1982b. "Nondeclaratives from an Intonational Standpoint." In Robert Chametzky, Robinson Schneider, and Kevin Tuite, eds., *Papers from the Parasession on Nondeclaratives*, 1–22. Chicago: Chicago Linguistic Society.

Borkin, Ann. 1973. "*To be* and not *to be*." *CLS* 9: 44–56.

Boyd, Julian, and J. P. Thorne. 1969. "The Semantics of Modal Verbs." *JL* 5: 57–74.

Bresnan, Joan. 1970. "On Complementizers: Toward a Syntactic Theory of Complement Types." *Foundations of Language* 6: 297–321.

———, ed. 1982. *The Mental Representation of Grammatical Relations.* Cambridge, Mass.: MIT Press.

Bresnan, Joan, and Jane Grimshaw. 1978. "The Syntax of Free Relatives in English." *LI* 9: 331–91.

Bresnan, Joan, and Sam A. Mchombo. 1987. "Topic, Pronoun, and Agreement in Chicheŵa." *Lg.* 63: 741–82.

Brown, Roger, and A. Gilman. 1960. "The Pronouns of Power and Solidarity." In Thomas A. Sebeok, ed., *Style in Language*, 253–76. Cambridge, Mass.: MIT Press.

Brugman, Claudia. 1983. "The Use of Body-Part Terms as Locatives in Chalcatongo Mixtec." *Survey of California and Other Indian Languages* 4: 235–90.

———. 1988. *The Syntax and Semantics of HAVE and its Complements.* Ph.D. dissertation. Berkeley: University of California.

———. 1989. *The Story of 'Over': Polysemy, Semantics, and the Structure of the Lexicon.* New York: Garland.

Brugman, Claudia, and Monica Macaulay. 1986. "Interacting Semantic Systems: Mixtec Expressions of Location." *BLS* 12: 315–27.

Bybee, Joan. 1985. *Morphology: A Study of the Relation Between Meaning and Form.* Amsterdam: John Benjamins.

Casad, Eugene H. 1982. *Cora Locationals and Structured Imagery.* Ph.D. dissertation. San Diego: University of California.

Chafe, Wallace L. 1974. "Language and Consciousness." *Lg.* 50: 111–33.

———. 1976. "Givenness, Contrastiveness, Definiteness, Subjects, Topics, and Point of View." In Charles N. Li, ed., *Subject and Topic*, 25–55. New York: Academic Press.

Chomsky, Noam. 1957. *Syntactic Structures*. The Hague: Mouton.

———. 1965a. *Aspects of the Theory of Syntax*. Cambridge, Mass.: MIT Press.

———. 1965b. "Three Models for the Description of Language." In R. Duncan Luce, Robert R. Bush, and Eugene Galanter, eds., *Readings in Mathematical Psychology*, vol. 2, 105–24. New York: Wiley.

———. 1970. "Remarks on Nominalization." In Roderick A. Jacobs and Peter S. Rosenbaum, eds., *Readings in English Transformational Grammar*, 184–221. Waltham, Mass.: Ginn.

———. 1981. *Lectures on Binding and Government*. Dordrecht: Foris.

Chomsky, Noam, and Howard Lasnik. 1977. "Filters and Control." *LI* 8: 425–504.

Chomsky, Noam, and George A. Miller. 1963. "Introduction to the Formal Analysis of Natural Languages." In R. Duncan Luce, Robert R. Bush, and Eugene Galanter, eds., *Handbook of Mathematical Psychology*, vol. 2, 269–321. New York: Wiley.

Chung, Sandra. 1976. "An Object-Creating Rule in Bahasa Indonesia." *LI* 7: 41–87.

Clark, Eve V., and Herbert H. Clark. 1979. "When Nouns Surface as Verbs." *Lg.* 55: 767–811.

Coates, Jennifer. 1983. *The Semantics of the Modal Auxiliaries*. London: Croom Helm.

Cole, Peter. 1983. "The Grammatical Role of the Causee in Universal Grammar." *IJAL* 49: 115–33.

———. 1987. "The Structure of Internally Headed Relative Clauses." *Natural Language and Linguistic Theory* 5: 277–302.

Cole, Peter, and S. N. Sridhar. 1977. "Clause Union and Relational Grammar: Evidence from Hebrew and Kannada." *LI* 8: 700–713.

Comrie, Bernard. 1977. "In Defense of Spontaneous Demotion: The Impersonal Passive." In Peter Cole and Jerrold M. Sadock, eds., *Syntax and Semantics*, vol. 8, *Grammatical Relations*, 47–58. New York: Academic Press.

———. 1982. "Grammatical Relations in Huichol." In Paul J. Hopper and Sandra A. Thompson, eds., *Syntax and Semantics*, vol. 15, *Studies in Transitivity*, 95–115. New York: Academic Press.

Cook, Kenneth W. 1987. "A New Relational Account of Samoan Quantifier Float, Case Marking and Word Order." *BLS* 13: 53–64.

———. 1988a. *A Cognitive Analysis of Grammatical Relations, Case, and Transitivity in Samoan*. Ph.D. dissertation. San Diego: University of California.

———. 1988b. "The Semantics of Newari Case-Marking Distinctions." *Linguistic Notes from La Jolla* 14: 42–56.

Craig, Colette, ed. 1986. *Noun Classes and Categorization*. Amsterdam: John Benjamins.

Croft, William A. 1986. *Categories and Relations in Syntax: The Clause-Level Organization of Information*. Ph.D. dissertation. Stanford: Stanford University.

———. 1990. *Syntactic Categories and Grammatical Relations: The Cognitive Organization of Information*. Chicago: University of Chicago Press.

Dahlstrom, Amy. 1983. "Agent-Patient Languages and Split Case Marking Systems." *BLS* 9: 37–46.

Deane, Paul. 1987. "English Possessives, Topicality, and the Silverstein Hierarchy." *BLS* 13: 65–76.

DeLancey, Scott. 1981. "An Interpretation of Split Ergativity and Related Phenomena." *Lg.* 57: 626–57.

———. 1984. "Categories of Non-Volitional Actor in Lhasa Tibetan." In Arlene R. K. Zide, David Magier, and Eric Schiller, eds., *Proceedings of the Conference on Participant Roles: South Asia and Adjacent Areas*, 58–70. Bloomington: Indiana University Linguistics Club.

———. 1985. "Agentivity and Syntax." In William H. Eilfort, Paul D. Kroeber, and Karen L. Peterson, eds., *Papers from the Parasession on Causatives and Agentivity*, 1–12. Chicago: Chicago Linguistic Society.

Denny, J. Peter. 1976. "What are Noun Classifiers Good for?" *CLS* 12: 122–44.

———. 1984. "Lexical Semantics and Logical Form: Locatives, Event Arguments and Conditionals." In David Testen, Veena Mishra, and Joseph Drago, eds., *Papers from the Parasession on Lexical Semantics*, 107–16. Chicago: Chicago Linguistic Society.

Dirven, René. 1989. "A Cognitive Perspective on Complementation." In Danny Jaspers *et al.*, eds., *Sentential Complementation and the Lexicon: Studies in Honor of Wim de Geest*, 113–39. Dordrecht: Foris.

Dixon, R. M. W. 1972. *The Dyirbal Language of North Queensland.* Cambridge: Cambridge University Press.

———. 1979a. "Corrections and Comments Concerning Heath's 'Is Dyirbal Ergative?'." *Linguistics* 17: 1003–15.

———. 1979b. "Ergativity." *Lg.* 55: 59–138.

Donnellan, Keith S. 1966. "Reference and Definite Descriptions." *Philosophical Review* 75: 281–304.

Downing, Pamela. 1977. "On the Creation and Use of English Compound Nouns." *Lg.* 53: 810–42.

———. 1984. *Japanese Numeral Classifiers: A Syntactic, Semantic, and Functional Profile*. Ph.D. dissertation. Berkeley: University of California.

Dryer, Matthew S. 1983. "Indirect Objects in Kinyarwanda Revisited." In David M. Perlmutter, ed., *Studies in Relational Grammar 1*, 129–40. Chicago: University of Chicago Press.

———. 1986. "Primary Objects, Secondary Objects, and Antidative." *Lg.* 62: 808–45.

Du Bois, John W. 1987. "The Discourse Basis of Ergativity." *Lg.* 63: 805–55.

Elman, Jeffrey L. 1985. "An Architecture for Parallel Processing in Speech Recognition: The TRACE Model." *Bibliotheca Phonetica* 12: 6–35.

———. 1990. "Finding Structure in Time." *Cognitive Science* 14: 179–211.

Elman, Jeffrey L., and James L. McClelland. 1984. "Speech Recognition as a Cognitive Process: The Interactive Activation Model." In Norman Lass, ed., *Speech and Language*, vol. 10, 337–74. New York: Academic Press.

Faltz, Leonard. 1977. *Reflexivization: A Study in Universal Syntax*. Ph.D. dissertation. Berkeley: University of California.

Fauconnier, Gilles. 1975. "Pragmatic Scales and Logical Structure." *LI* 6: 353–75.

———. 1977. "Polarité Syntaxique et Sémantique." *Lingvisticae Investigationes* 1: 1–37.

———. 1985. *Mental Spaces: Aspects of Meaning Construction in Natural Language*. Cambridge, Mass.: MIT Press/Bradford.

Fillmore, Charles J. 1968. "The Case for Case." In Emmon Bach and Robert T. Harms, eds., *Universals in Linguistic Theory*, 1–88. New York: Holt.

———. 1977. "The Case for Case Reopened." In Peter Cole and Jerrold M. Sadock, eds., *Syntax and Semantics*, vol. 8, *Grammatical Relations*, 59–81. New York: Academic Press.

———. 1985. "Syntactic Intrusions and the Notion of Grammatical Construction." *BLS* 11: 73–86.

———. 1988. "The Mechanisms of 'Construction Grammar'." *BLS* 14: 35–55.

Fillmore, Charles J., Paul Kay, and Mary Catherine O'Connor. 1988. "Regularity and Idiomaticity in Grammatical Constructions: The Case of *Let Alone*." *Lg.* 64: 501–38.

Fodor, Jerry A. 1970. "Three Reasons for Not Deriving 'Kill' from 'Cause to Die'." *LI* 1: 429–38.

Foley, William A., and Robert D. Van Valin, Jr. 1977. "On the Viability of the Notion of 'Subject' in Universal Grammar." *BLS* 3: 293–320.

———. 1984. *Functional Syntax and Universal Grammar*. Cambridge: Cambridge University Press.

Fong, Heatherbell. 1988. *The Stony Idiom of the Brain: A Study in the Syntax and Semantics of Metaphors*. Ph.D. dissertation. San Diego: University of California.

Fox, Barbara A. 1987. "The Noun Phrase Accessibility Hierarchy Reinterpreted: Subject Primacy or the Absolutive Hypothesis?" *Lg.* 63: 856–70.

Fraser, Bruce. 1970. "Some Remarks on the Action Nominalization in English." In Roderick A. Jacobs and Peter S. Rosenbaum, eds., *Readings in English Transformational Grammar*, 83–98. Waltham, Mass.: Ginn.

Gazdar, Gerald, Geoffrey K. Pullum, and Ivan A. Sag. 1982. "Auxiliaries and Related Phenomena in a Restrictive Theory of Grammar." *Lg.* 58: 591–638.

Gensler, Orin D. 1977. "Non-Syntactic Antecedents and Frame Semantics." *BLS* 3: 321–34.

Gibson, Jeanne, and Eduardo Raposo. 1986. "Clause Union, the Stratal Uniqueness Law and the Chômeur Relation." *Natural Language and Linguistic Theory* 4: 295–331.

Givón, Talmy. 1973. "The Time-Axis Phenomenon." *Lg.* 49: 890–925.

———. 1976. "Topic, Pronoun and Grammatical Agreement." In Charles N. Li, ed., *Subject and Topic*, 149–88. New York: Academic Press.

———. 1978. "Definiteness and Referentiality." In Joseph H. Greenberg, ed., *Universals of Human Language*, vol. 1, *Syntax*, 291–330. Stanford: Stanford University Press.

———. 1979. *On Understanding Grammar*. New York: Academic Press.

———, ed. 1983. *Topic Continuity in Discourse: A Quantitative Cross-Language Study*. Amsterdam: John Benjamins.

———. 1984. *Syntax: A Functional-Typological Introduction*, vol. 1. Amsterdam: John Benjamins.

———. 1989. *Mind, Code and Context: Essays in Pragmatics*. Hillsdale, N. J.: Erlbaum.

Gleitman, Lila R. 1965. "Coordinating Conjunctions in English." *Lg.* 41: 260–93.

Goldsmith, John. 1980. "Meaning and Mechanism in Grammar." *Harvard Studies in Syntax and Semantics* 2: 423–49.

Goldsmith, John, and Erich Woisetschlaeger. 1982. "The Logic of the English Progressive." *LI* 13: 79–89.

Goodall, Grant. 1983. "A Three-Dimensional Analysis of Coordination." *CLS* 19: 146–54.

———. 1984. *Parallel Structures in Syntax*. Ph.D. dissertation. San Diego: University of California.

Gorbet, Larry. 1976. *A Grammar of Diegueño Nominals*. New York: Garland.

———. 1977. "Headless Relatives in the Southwest: Are They Related?" *BLS* 3: 270–78.

Greenberg, Joseph H. 1978. "How Does a Language Acquire Gender Markers?" In Joseph H. Greenberg, ed., *Universals of Human Language*, vol. 3, *Word Structure*, 47–82. Stanford: Stanford University Press.

Grice, H. P. 1957. "Meaning." *Philosophical Review* 66: 377–88.

———. 1975. "Logic and Conversation." In Peter Cole and Jerry L. Morgan, eds., *Syntax and Semantics*, vol. 3, *Speech Acts*, 41–58. New York: Academic Press.

Gruber, Jeffrey. 1965. *Studies in Lexical Relations*. Ph.D. dissertation. Cambridge, Mass.: MIT.

Haiman, John. 1980. "Dictionaries and Encyclopedias." *Lingua* 50: 329–57.

———. 1983. "Iconic and Economic Motivation." *Lg.* 59: 781–819.

———. 1985. *Natural Syntax: Iconicity and Erosion*. Cambridge: Cambridge University Press.

Haiman, John, and Pamela Munro, eds. 1983. *Switch-Reference and Universal Grammar*. Amsterdam: John Benjamins.

Hale, Kenneth. 1973. "A Note on Subject-Object Inversion in Navajo." In Braj B. Kachru, Robert B. Lees, Yakov Malkiel, Angelina Pietrangeli, and Sol Saporta, eds., *Issues in Linguistics: Papers in Honor of Henry and Renée Kahane*, 300–309. Urbana: University of Illinois Press.

Hale, Kenneth, LaVerne Masayesva Jeanne, and Paul Platero. 1977. "Three Cases of Overgeneration." In Peter W. Culicover, Thomas Wasow, and Adrian Akmajian, eds., *Formal Syntax*, 379–416. New York: Academic Press.

Hawkins, Bruce W. 1984. *The Semantics of English Spatial Prepositions*. Ph.D. dissertation. San Diego: University of California.

———. 1988. "The Natural Category MEDIUM: An Alternative to Selection Restrictions and Similar Constructs." In Brygida Rudzka-Ostyn, ed., *Topics in Cognitive Linguistics*, 231–70. Amsterdam: John Benjamins.

Hawkins, John A. 1978. *Definiteness and Indefiniteness: A Study in Reference and Grammaticality Prediction*. London: Croom Helm. [Atlantic Highlands, N. J.: Humanities Press.]

Heath, Jeffrey. 1979. "Is Dyirbal Ergative?" *Linguistics* 17: 401–63.

Hill, Jane H. 1969. "Volitional and Non-Volitional Verbs in Cupeño." *CLS* 5: 348–56.

Hirtle, W. H. 1970. "-Ed Adjectives like 'Verandahed' and 'Blue-Eyed'." *JL* 6: 19–36.

Hockett, Charles F. 1966. "What Algonquian is Really Like." *IJAL* 32: 59–73.

Hooper, Joan B., and Sandra A. Thompson. 1973. "On the Applicability of Root Transformations." *LI* 4: 465–97.

Hopper, Paul J. 1985. "Causes and Affects." In William H. Eilfort, Paul D. Kroeber, and Karel L. Peterson, eds., *Papers from the Parasession on Causatives and Agentivity*, 67–88. Chicago: Chicago Linguistic Society.

Hopper, Paul J., and Sandra A. Thompson. 1980. "Transitivity in Grammar and Discourse." *Lg.* 56: 251–99.

———, eds. 1982. *Syntax and Semantics*, vol. 15, *Studies in Transitivity*. New York: Academic Press.

Huddleston, Rodney. 1969. "Some Observations on Tense and Deixis in English." *Lg.* 45: 777–806.

Hudson, Richard A. 1984. *Word Grammar*. Oxford: Basil Blackwell.

———. 1987. "Zwicky on Heads." *JL* 23: 109–32.

———. 1988. "Coordination and Grammatical Relations." *JL* 24: 303–42.

———. 1989. "Gapping and Grammatical Relations." *JL* 25: 57–94.

Hung, Tony. 1988. "Case and Role in Newari: A Cognitive Grammar Approach." *Linguistic Notes from La Jolla* 14: 95–107.

Hyde, Villiana. 1971. *An Introduction to the Luiseño Language*. Banning, California: Malki Museum Press.

Ikegami, Yoshihiko. 1985. "'Activity'-'Accomplishment'-'Achievement'—A Language that Can't Say 'I burned it, but it didn't burn' and One that Can." In Adam Makkai and Alan K. Melby, eds., *Linguistics and Philosophy: Essays in Honor of Rulon S. Wells*, 265–304. Amsterdam: John Benjamins.

Jackendoff, Ray. 1968. "Quantifiers in English." *Foundations of Language* 4: 422–42.

———. 1975. "Morphological and Semantic Regularities in the Lexicon." *Lg.* 51: 639–71.

———. 1977. *$\bar{X}$-Syntax: A Study of Phrase Structure*. Cambridge, Mass.: MIT Press.

Jakobson, Roman. 1936. "Beitrag zur Allgemeinen Kasuslehre: Gesamtbedeutungen der Russischen Kasus." *Travaux du Cercle Linguistique de Prague* 6: 240–88. [Reprinted in Eric P. Hamp, Fred. W. Householder, and Robert Austerlitz, eds. 1966. *Readings in Linguistics II*, 51–89. Chicago: University of Chicago Press.]

Janda, Laura A. 1984. *A Semantic Analysis of the Russian Verbal Prefixes ZA-, PERE-, DO-, and OT-*. Ph.D. dissertation. Los Angeles: University of California.

———. 1990. "The Radial Network of a Grammatical Category—Its Genesis and Dynamic Structure." *Cognitive Linguistics* 1: 269–88.

———. To appear. *A Geography of Case Semantics: The Czech Dative and the Russian Instrumental*. Berlin: Mouton de Gruyter.

Jelinek, Eloise, and Richard A. Demers. 1983. "The Agent Hierarchy and Voice in Some Coast Salish Languages." *IJAL* 49: 167–85.

Johnson, Mark. 1987. *The Body in the Mind: The Bodily Basis of Meaning, Imagination, and Reason*. Chicago: University of Chicago Press.

Johnson-Laird, Philip N. 1983. *Mental Models*. Cambridge, Mass.: Harvard University Press.

Joos, Martin. 1968. *The English Verb: Form and Meanings*. Second edition. Madison: University of Wisconsin Press.

Kalectaca, Milo. 1978. *Lessons in Hopi*. Tucson: University of Arizona Press.

Karttunen, Lauri. 1971. "Definite Descriptions with Crossing Coreference." *Foundations of Language* 7: 157–82.

Katz, Jerrold J., and Paul M. Postal. 1964. *An Integrated Theory of Linguistic Descriptions*. Cambridge, Mass.: MIT Press.

Kayne, Richard S. 1975. *French Syntax: The Transformational Cycle*. Cambridge, Mass.: MIT Press.

Keenan, Edward L. 1976. "Towards a Universal Definition of 'Subject'." In Charles N. Li, ed., *Subject and Topic*, 303–33. New York: Academic Press.

———. 1984. "Semantic Correlates of the Ergative/Absolutive Distinction." *Linguistics* 22: 197–223.

Kemmer, Suzanne E. 1988. *The Middle Voice: A Typological and Diachronic Study*. Ph.D. dissertation. Stanford: Stanford University.

———. In press. *The Middle Voice*. Amsterdam: John Benjamins.

Kimenyi, Alexandre. 1980. *A Relational Grammar of Kinyarwanda*. Berkeley: University of California Press.

Kiparsky, Paul, and Carol Kiparsky. 1970. "Fact." In Manfred Bierwisch and Karl Erich Heidolph, eds., *Progress in Linguistics*, 143–73. The Hague: Mouton.

Kirsner, Robert S. 1979a. "Deixis in Discourse: An Exploratory Quantitative Study of the Modern Dutch Demonstrative Adjectives." In Talmy Givón, ed., *Syntax and Semantics*, vol. 12, *Discourse and Syntax*, 355–75. New York: Academic Press.

———. 1979b. *The Problem of Presentative Sentences in Modern Dutch*. Amsterdam: North-Holland.

———. 1987. "What It Takes to Show Whether an Analysis 'Fits'." In Hermann Bluhme and Göran Hammarström, eds., *Descriptio Linguistica: Proceedings of the First Conference on Descriptive and Structural Linguistics*, 76–113. Tübingen: Gunter Narr Verlag.

Kirsner, Robert S., and Sandra A. Thompson. 1976. "The Role of Pragmatic Inference in Semantics: A Study of Sensory Verb Complements in English." *Glossa* 10: 200–240.

Kisseberth, Charles W., and Mohammad Imam Abasheikh. 1977. "The Object Relationship in Chi-Mwi:ni, A Bantu Language." In Peter Cole and Jerrold M. Sadock, eds., *Syntax and Semantics*, vol. 8, *Grammatical Relations*, 179–218. New York: Academic Press.

Klima, Edward S. 1964. "Negation in English." In Jerry A. Fodor and Jerrold J. Katz, eds., *The Structure of Language: Readings in the Philosophy of Language*, 246–323. Englewood Cliffs, N. J.: Prentice-Hall.

Kövecses, Zoltán. 1990. *Emotion Concepts*. New York: Springer-Verlag.

Kuno, Susumu. 1986. "Anaphora in Japanese." In S.-Y. Kuroda, ed., *Working Papers from the First SDF Workshop in Japanese Syntax*, 11–70. San Diego: UCSD Department of Linguistics.

———. 1987. *Functional Syntax: Anaphora, Discourse and Empathy*. Chicago: University of Chicago Press.

Kuno, Susumu, and Etsuko Kaburaki. 1977. "Empathy and Syntax." *LI* 8: 627–72.

Kuroda, S.-Y. 1972. "The Categorical and the Thetic Judgment: Evidence from Japanese Syntax." *Foundations of Language* 9: 153–85.

———. 1976. "Subject." In Masayoshi Shibatani, ed., *Syntax and Semantics*, vol. 5, *Japanese Generative Grammar*, 1–16. New York: Academic Press.

———. 1979. "The Semantics of the Japanese Topic Marker *wa*." *Lingvisticae Investigationes* 3: 75–85.

Lakoff, George. 1969. "On Derivational Constraints." *CLS* 5: 117–39.

———. 1970. *Irregularity in Syntax*. New York: Holt.

———. 1986. "Frame Semantic Control of the Coordinate Structure Constraint." In Anne M. Farley, Peter T. Farley, and Karl-Erik McCullough, eds., *Papers from the Parasession on Pragmatics and Grammatical Theory*, 152–67. Chicago: Chicago Linguistic Society.

———. 1987. *Women, Fire, and Dangerous Things: What Categories Reveal About the Mind*. Chicago: University of Chicago Press.

Lakoff, George, and Mark Johnson. 1980. *Metaphors We Live By*. Chicago: University of Chicago Press.

Lakoff, George, and Stanley Peters. 1969. "Phrasal Conjunction and Symmetric Predicates." In David A. Reibel and Sanford A. Schane, eds., *Modern Studies in English*, 113–42. Englewood Cliffs, N. J.: Prentice-Hall.

Lakoff, George, and Mark Turner. 1989. *More than Cool Reason: A Field Guide to Poetic Metaphor*. Chicago: University of Chicago Press.

Lakoff, Robin. 1974. "Remarks on *This* and *That*." *CLS* 10: 345–56.

Lambrecht, Knud. 1984. "On the Status of SVO Sentences in French Discourse." In Russell S. Tomlin, ed., *Coherence and Grounding in Discourse*, 217–61. Amsterdam: John Benjamins.

———. 1987. "Sentence Focus, Information Structure, and the Thetic-Categorical Distinction." *BLS* 13: 366–82.

———. 1988. "There was a Farmer Had a Dog: Syntactic Amalgams Revisited." *BLS* 14: 319–39.

———. In press. *Information Structure and Sentence Form: The Pragmatics of Syntax in Spoken French*. Cambridge: Cambridge University Press.

Langacker, Ronald W. 1968. "Observations on French Possessives." *Lg*. 44: 51–75.

———. 1969. "On Pronominalization and the Chain of Command." In David A. Reibel and Sanford A. Schane, eds., *Modern Studies in English*, 160–86. Englewood Cliffs, N. J.: Prentice-Hall.

———. 1970. "English Question Intonation." In Anthony L. Vanek and Jerrold M. Sadock, eds., *Studies Presented to Robert B. Lees by his Students*, 139–61. Edmonton, Alberta and Champaign, Ill.: Linguistic Research.

———. 1975. "Functional Stratigraphy." In Robin E. Grossman, L. James San, and Timothy J. Vance, eds., *Papers from the Parasession on Functionalism*, 351–97. Chicago: Chicago Linguistic Society.

———. 1976. *Non-Distinct Arguments in Uto-Aztecan*. Berkeley: University of California Press.

———. 1977. "Syntactic Reanalysis." In Charles N. Li, ed., *Mechanisms of Syntactic Change*, 57–139. Austin: University of Texas Press.

———. 1978. "The Form and Meaning of the English Auxiliary." *Lg*. 54: 853–82.

———. 1981. "The Integration of Grammar and Grammatical Change." *Indian Linguistics* 42: 82–135.
———. 1982a. "Remarks on English Aspect." In Paul J. Hopper, ed., *Tense-Aspect: Between Semantics & Pragmatics*, 265–304. Amsterdam: John Benjamins.
———. 1982b. "Space Grammar, Analysability, and the English Passive." *Lg.* 58: 22–80.
———. 1984. "Active Zones." *BLS* 10: 172–88.
———. 1985. "Observations and Speculations on Subjectivity." In John Haiman, ed., *Iconicity in Syntax*, 109–50. Amsterdam: John Benjamins.
———. 1986a. "Abstract Motion." *BLS* 12: 455–71.
———. 1986b. "An Introduction to Cognitive Grammar." *Cognitive Science* 10: 1–40.
———. 1986c. "Settings, Participants, and Grammatical Relations." *Proceedings of the Annual Meeting of the Pacific Linguistics Conference* 2: 1–31.
———. 1987a. "Grammatical Ramifications of the Setting/Participant Distinction." *BLS* 13: 383–94.
———. 1987b. "Nouns and Verbs." *Lg.* 63: 53–94.
———. 1988a. "The Nature of Grammatical Valence." In Brygida Rudzka-Ostyn, ed., *Topics in Cognitive Linguistics*, 91–125. Amsterdam: John Benjamins.
———. 1988b. "An Overview of Cognitive Grammar." In Brygida Rudzka-Ostyn, ed., *Topics in Cognitive Linguistics*, 3–48. Amsterdam: John Benjamins.
———. 1988c. "A Usage-Based Model." In Brygida Rudzka-Ostyn, ed., *Topics in Cognitive Linguistics*, 127–161. Amsterdam: John Benjamins.
———. 1988d. "A View of Linguistic Semantics." In Brygida Rudzka-Ostyn, ed., *Topics in Cognitive Linguistics*, 49–90. Amsterdam: John Benjamins.
———. 1990a. *Concept, Image, and Symbol: The Cognitive Basis of Grammar*. Berlin: Mouton de Gruyter.
———. 1990b. "Subjectification." *Cognitive Linguistics* 1: 5–38.
———. To appear. "Cognitive Grammar Meets the Yuman Auxiliary."
Langacker, Ronald W., and Burton W. Bascom. 1986. "The Syntax and Origin of *ga-* in Northern Tepehuan." In Benjamin F. Elson, ed., *Language in Global Perspective: Papers in Honor of the 50th Anniversary of the Summer Institute of Linguistics, 1935–1985*, 439–50. Dallas: Summer Institute of Linguistics.
Langacker, Ronald W., and Pamela Munro. 1975. "Passives and their Meaning." *Lg.* 51: 789–830.
Lee, Michael. 1987. "The Cognitive Basis of Classifier Systems." *BLS* 13: 395–407.
Lees, Robert B. 1960. *The Grammar of English Nominalizations*. Bloomington: Indiana University Research Center in Anthropology, Folklore, and Linguistics, Publication 12. [*IJAL* 26: 3, Part II.]
Lees, Robert B., and Edward S. Klima. 1963. "Rules for English Pronominalization." *Lg.* 39: 17–28.
LeGrand, Jean E. 1974. "AND and OR: Some SOMEs and All ANYs." *CLS* 10: 390–401.
Levi, Judith N. 1978. *The Syntax and Semantics of Complex Nominals*. New York: Academic Press.

Li, Charles N., and Sandra A. Thompson. 1976. "Subject and Topic: A New Typology of Language." In Charles N. Li, ed., *Subject and Topic*, 457–89. New York: Academic Press.

Lieber, Rochelle. 1981. *On the Organization of the Lexicon*. Bloomington: Indiana University Linguistics Club.

Lindner, Susan. 1981. *A Lexico-Semantic Analysis of English Verb-Particle Constructions with UP and OUT*. Ph.D. dissertation. San Diego: University of California.

———. 1982. "What Goes Up doesn't Necessarily Come Down: The Ins and Outs of Opposites." *CLS* 18: 305–23.

Löbner, Sebastian. 1985. "Definites." *Journal of Semantics* 4: 279–326.

MacWhinney, Brian. 1977. "Starting Points." *Lg*. 53: 152–68.

Maldonado, Ricardo. 1988. "Energetic Reflexives in Spanish." *BLS* 14: 153–65.

———. To appear. *Middle Voice: The Case of Spanish 'se'*. Ph.D. dissertation. San Diego: University of California.

Mardirussian, Galust. 1975. "Noun-Incorporation in Universal Grammar." *CLS* 11: 383–89.

McCawley, James D. 1971. "Tense and Time Reference in English." In Charles J. Fillmore and D. Terence Langendoen, eds., *Studies in Linguistic Semantics*, 96–113. New York: Holt.

———. 1975. "Lexicography and the Count-Mass Distinction." *BLS* 1: 314–21.

———. 1981a. *Everything that Linguists have Always Wanted to Know About Logic but were Ashamed to Ask*. Chicago: University of Chicago Press.

———. 1981b. "Notes on the English Present Perfect." *Australian Journal of Linguistics* 1: 81–90.

———. 1984. "Anaphora and Notions of Command." *BLS* 10: 220–32.

McClelland, James L., and Jeffrey L. Elman. 1986. "The TRACE Model of Speech Perception." *Cognitive Psychology* 18: 1–36.

McClelland, James L., and David E. Rumelhart, eds. 1986. *Parallel Distributed Processing: Explorations in the Microstructure of Cognition*, vol. 2, *Psychological and Biological Models*. Cambridge, Mass.: MIT Press/Bradford.

McCloskey, James, and Peter Sells. 1988. "Control and A-Chains in Modern Irish." *Natural Language and Linguistic Theory* 6: 143–189.

McLendon, Sally. 1978. "Ergativity, Case, and Transitivity in Eastern Pomo." *IJAL* 44: 1–9.

Merlan, Francesca. 1976. "Noun Incorporation and Discourse Reference in Modern Nahuatl." *IJAL* 42: 177–91.

Miller, George A. 1956. "The Magical Number Seven, Plus or Minus Two: Some Limits on Our Capacity for Processing Information." *Psychological Review* 63: 81–97.

Miller, Wick R., comp. 1972. *Newe Natekwinappeh: Shoshoni Stories and Dictionary*. Salt Lake City: University of Utah Press.

Miner, Kenneth L. 1986. "Noun Stripping and Loose Incorporation in Zuni." *IJAL* 52: 242–54.

Mithun, Marianne. 1984. "The Evolution of Noun Incorporation." *Lg*. 60: 847–94.

———. 1986. "On the Nature of Noun Incorporation." *Lg*. 62: 32–37.

Moore, Terence, and Christine Carling. 1982. *Language Understanding: Towards a Post-Chomskyan Linguistics*. New York: St. Martin's Press.

Munro, Pamela. 1984. "Floating Quantifiers in Pima." In Eung-Do Cook and Donna B. Gerdts, eds., *Syntax and Semantics*, vol. 16, *The Syntax of Native American Languages*, 269–87. Orlando, Florida: Academic Press.

Myhill, John. 1988. "Nominal Agent Incorporation in Indonesian." *JL* 24: 111–36.

Newman, John. 1981. *The Semantics of Raising Constructions*. Ph.D. dissertation. San Diego: University of California.

Newmeyer, Frederick J. 1970. "On the Alleged Boundary Between Syntax and Semantics." *Foundations of Language* 6: 178–86.

———. 1983. *Grammatical Theory: Its Limits and Its Possibilities*. Chicago: University of Chicago Press.

Nichols, Johanna. 1986. "Head-Marking and Dependent-Marking Grammar." *Lg*. 62: 56–119.

Norwood, Susan. 1981. *Progressives in Yuman and Romance*. Ph.D. dissertation. San Diego: University of California.

Osgood, Charles E., George J. Suci, and Percy H. Tannenbaum. 1957. *The Measurement of Meaning*. Urbana: University of Illinois Press.

Palmer, F. R. 1977. "Modals and Actuality." *JL* 13: 1–23.

———. 1979. *Modality and the English Modals*. London: Longman.

Perkins, Michael R. 1982. "The Core Meanings of the English Modals." *JL* 18: 245–73.

Perlmutter, David M. 1970. "The Two Verbs *Begin*." In Roderick A. Jacobs and Peter S. Rosenbaum, eds., *Readings in English Transformational Grammar*, 107–19. Waltham, Mass.: Ginn.

———. 1971. *Deep and Surface Structure Constraints in Syntax*. New York: Holt.

———. 1978. "Impersonal Passives and the Unaccusative Hypothesis." *BLS* 4: 157–89.

———, ed. 1983. *Studies in Relational Grammar 1*. Chicago: University of Chicago Press.

Perlmutter, David M., and Paul M. Postal. 1983. "Towards a Universal Characterization of Passivization." In David M. Perlmutter, ed., *Studies in Relational Grammar 1*, 3–29. Chicago: University of Chicago Press.

Perlmutter, David M., and Carol G. Rosen, eds. 1984. *Studies in Relational Grammar* 2. Chicago: University of Chicago Press.

Pinker, Steven, and Jacques Mehler, eds. 1988. *Connections and Symbols*. Cambridge, Mass.: MIT Press/Bradford.

Pinker, Steven, and Alan Prince. 1988. "On Language and Connectionism: Analysis of a Parallel Distributed Processing Model of Language Acquisition." In Steven Pinker and Jacques Mehler, eds., *Connections and Symbols*, 73–193. Cambridge, Mass.: MIT Press/Bradford.

Postal, Paul M. 1969. "On So-Called 'Pronouns' in English." In David A. Reibel and Sanford A. Schane, eds., *Modern Studies in English*, 201–24. Englewood Cliffs, N. J.: Prentice-Hall.

———. 1974. *On Raising*. Cambridge, Mass.: MIT Press.

Poteet, Stephen. 1987. "Paths Through Different Domains: A Cognitive Grammar Analysis of Mandarin *Dào*." *BLS* 13: 408–21.

Pullum, Geoffrey, and Deirdre Wilson. 1977. "Autonomous Syntax and the Analysis of Auxiliaries." *Lg.* 53: 741–88.

Rando, Emily, and Donna Jo Napoli. 1978. "Definites in *There*-Sentences." *Lg.* 54: 300–313.

Reddy, Michael J. 1979. "The Conduit Metaphor—A Case of Frame Conflict in Our Language About Language." In Andrew Ortony, ed., *Metaphor and Thought*, 284–324. Cambridge: Cambridge University Press.

Reichenbach, Hans. 1947. *Elements of Symbolic Logic*. New York: Macmillan.

Reinhart, Tanya. 1983. *Anaphora and Semantic Interpretation*. Chicago: University of Chicago Press.

Rice, Sally. 1987a. *Towards a Cognitive Model of Transitivity*. Ph.D. dissertation. San Diego: University of California.

———. 1987b. "Towards a Transitive Prototype: Evidence from Some Atypical English Passives." *BLS* 13: 422–34.

———. 1988. "Unlikely Lexical Entries." *BLS* 14: 202–12.

Rosch, Eleanor. 1977. "Human Categorization." In Neil Warren, ed., *Studies in Cross-Cultural Psychology*, vol. 1, 1–49. London: Academic Press.

———. 1978. "Principles of Categorization." In Eleanor Rosch and Barbara B. Lloyd, eds., *Cognition and Categorization*, 27–47. Hillsdale, N. J.: Erlbaum.

Rosen, Carol G. 1983. "Universals of Causative Union: A Co-Proposal to the Gibson-Raposo Typology." *CLS* 19: 338–52.

———. 1984. "The Interface Between Semantic Roles and Initial Grammatical Relations." In David M. Perlmutter and Carol G. Rosen, eds., *Studies in Relational Grammar* 2, 38–77. Chicago: University of Chicago Press.

Rosenbaum, Peter S. 1967. *The Grammar of English Predicate Complement Constructions*. Cambridge, Mass.: MIT Press.

Ross, John Robert. 1967. *Constraints on Variables in Syntax*. Ph.D. dissertation. Cambridge, Mass.: MIT. [Published as Ross 1986.]

———. 1969a. "Auxiliaries as Main Verbs." In William Todd, ed., *Studies in Philosophical Linguistics 1*, 77–102. Evanston, Ill.: Great Expectations.

———. 1969b. "On the Cyclic Nature of English Pronominalization." In David A. Reibel and Sanford A. Schane, eds., *Modern Studies in English*, 187–200. Englewood Cliffs, N. J.: Prentice-Hall.

———. 1970a. "Gapping and the Order of Constituents." In Manfred Bierwisch and Karl Erich Heidolph, eds., *Progress in Linguistics*, 249–59. The Hague: Mouton.

———. 1970b. "On Declarative Sentences." In Roderick A. Jacobs and Peter S. Rosenbaum, eds., *Readings in English Transformational Grammar*, 222–72. Waltham, Mass.: Ginn.

———. 1972a. "Act." In Donald Davidson and Gilbert Harman, eds., *Semantics of Natural Language*, 70–126. Dordrecht: D. Reidel.

———. 1972b. "The Category Squish: Endstation Hauptwort." *CLS* 8: 316–28.

———. 1972c. "Doubl-ing." *LI* 3: 61–86.

———. 1986. *Infinite Syntax!* Norwood, N. J.: Ablex.

Rudzka-Ostyn, Brygida, ed. 1988. *Topics in Cognitive Linguistics*. Amsterdam: John Benjamins.

Rumelhart, David E. 1979. "Some Problems with the Notion of Literal Meaning." In Andrew Ortony, ed., *Metaphor and Thought*, 78–90. Cambridge: Cambridge University Press.

Rumelhart, David E., and James L. McClelland. 1986a. "On Learning the Past Tenses of English Verbs." In James L. McClelland and David E. Rumelhart, eds., *Parallel Distributed Processing: Explorations in the Microstructure of Cognition*, vol. 2, *Psychological and Biological Models*, 216–71. Cambridge, Mass.: MIT Press/Bradford.

———, eds. 1986b. *Parallel Distributed Processing: Explorations in the Microstructure of Cognition*, vol. 1, *Foundations*. Cambridge, Mass.: MIT Press/Bradford.

Ruwet, Nicolas. 1984. "A Propos de la Distribution des Complétives à Temps Fini et des Compléments à l'Infinitif en Français." *Cahiers de Grammaire* 7: 74–138.

———. 1986. "On Weather Verbs." *CLS* 22: 195–215.

Sadock, Jerrold M. 1969. "Hypersentences." *Papers in Linguistics* 1: 283–370.

———. 1970. "Whimperatives." In Jerrold M. Sadock and Anthony L. Vanek, eds., *Studies Presented to Robert B. Lees by his Students*, 223–38. Edmonton, Alberta and Champaign, Ill.: Linguistic Research.

———. 1971. "Queclaratives." *CLS* 7: 223–31.

———. 1972. "Speech Act Idioms." *CLS* 8: 329–39.

———. 1974. "Read at Your Own Risk: Syntactic and Semantic Horrors You can Find in Your Medicine Chest." *CLS* 10: 599–607.

———. 1980. "Noun Incorporation in Greenlandic: A Case of Syntactic Word Formation." *Lg.* 56: 300–319.

———. 1986. "Some Notes on Noun Incorporation." *Lg.* 62: 19–31.

Sag, Ivan A., Gerald Gazdar, Thomas Wasow, and Steven Weisler. 1985. "Coordination and How to Distinguish Categories." *Natural Language and Linguistic Theory* 3: 117–71.

Schachter, Paul. 1976. "The Subject in Philippine Languages: Topic, Actor, Actor-Topic, or None of the Above?" In Charles N. Li, ed., *Subject and Topic*, 491–518. New York: Academic Press.

———. 1977. "Reference-Related and Role-Related Properties of Subjects." In Peter Cole and Jerrold M. Sadock, eds., *Syntax and Semantics*, vol. 8, *Grammatical Relations*, 279–306. New York: Academic Press.

Schwartz, Linda. 1986. "Levels of Grammatical Relations and Russian Reflexive Controllers." *BLS* 12: 235–45.

Seiler, Hansjakob. 1983. "Possessivity, Subject, and Object." *Studies in Language* 7: 89–117.

Selkirk, Elisabeth. 1977. "Some Remarks on Noun Phrase Structure." In Peter S. Culicover, Thomas Wasow, and Adrian Akmajian, eds., *Formal Syntax*, 285–316. New York: Academic Press.

———. 1982. *The Syntax of Words*. Cambridge, Mass.: MIT Press.

Sells, Peter. 1987. "Aspects of Logophoricity." *LI* 18: 445–79.

Shannon, Thomas F. 1987. "On Some Recent Claims of Relational Grammar." *BLS* 13: 247–62.

Shibatani, Masayoshi, ed. 1976. *Syntax and Semantics*, vol. 6, *The Grammar of Causative Constructions*. New York: Academic Press.

———. 1985. "Passives and Related Constructions." *Lg*. 61: 821–48.

———. 1986. "On the Transitivity of the Stative Predicate Constructions." In S.-Y. Kuroda, ed., *Working Papers from the First SDF Workshop in Japanese Syntax*, 147–68. San Diego: UCSD Department of Linguistics.

Silverstein, Michael. 1976. "Hierarchy of Features and Ergativity." In R. M. W. Dixon, ed., *Grammatical Categories in Australian Languages*, 112–71. Canberra: Australian Institute of Aboriginal Studies. [Atlantic Highlands, N. J.: Humanities Press.]

Smith, Carlota S. 1964. "Determiners and Relative Clauses in a Generative Grammar of English." *Lg*. 40: 37–52.

———. 1969. "Ambiguous Sentences with *And*." In David A. Reibel and Sanford A. Schane, eds., *Modern Studies in English*, 75–79. Englewood Cliffs, N. J.: Prentice-Hall.

Smith, Michael B. 1985a. "An Analysis of German Dummy Subject Constructions." *Proceedings of the Annual Meeting of the Pacific Linguistics Conference* 1: 412–25.

———. 1985b. "Event Chains, Grammatical Relations, and the Semantics of Case in German." *CLS* 21: 388–407.

———. 1987. *The Semantics of Dative and Accusative in German: An Investigation in Cognitive Grammar*. Ph.D. dissertation. San Diego: University of California.

Snapp, Allen, John Anderson, and Joy Anderson. 1982. "Northern Paiute." In Ronald W. Langacker, ed., *Studies in Uto-Aztecan Grammar*, vol. 3, *Uto-Aztecan Grammatical Sketches*, 1–92. Dallas: Summer Institute of Linguistics and University of Texas at Arlington.

Spears, Arthur K. 1973. "Complements of *Significant*-Class Predicates: A Study in the Semantics of Complementation." *CLS* 9: 627–38.

Steedman, Mark. 1985. "Dependency and Coördination in the Grammar of Dutch and English." *Lg*. 61: 523–68.

Steele, Susan M. 1973. *The Positional Tendencies of Modal Elements and Their Theoretical Implications*. Ph.D. dissertation. San Diego: University of California.

———. 1977. "On Being Possessed." *BLS* 3: 114–31.

———. 1978. "The Category AUX as a Language Universal." In Joseph H. Greenberg, ed., *Universals of Human Language*, vol. 3, *Word Structure*, 7–45. Stanford: Stanford University Press.

Steele, Susan M., Adrian Akmajian, Richard Demers, Eloise Jelinek, Chisato Kitagawa, Richard Oehrle, and Thomas Wasow. 1981. *An Encyclopedia of AUX: A Study of Cross-Linguistic Equivalence*. Cambridge, Mass.: MIT Press.

Sweetser, Eve E. 1982. "Root and Epistemic Modals: Causality in Two Worlds." *BLS* 8: 484–507.

———. 1984. *Semantic Structure and Semantic Change: A Cognitive Linguistic Study of Modality, Perception, Speech Acts, and Logical Relations*. Ph.D. dissertation. Berkeley: University of California.

———. 1990. *From Etymology to Pragmatics: Metaphorical and Cultural Aspects of Semantic Structure*. Cambridge: Cambridge University Press.

Tai, James H-Y. 1985. "Temporal Sequence and Chinese Word Order." In John Haiman, ed., *Iconicity and Syntax*, 49–72. Amsterdam: John Benjamins.

Talmy, Leonard. 1978. "Figure and Ground in Complex Sentences." In Joseph H. Greenberg, ed., *Universals of Human Language*, vol. 4, *Syntax*, 625–49. Stanford: Stanford University Press.

———. 1983. "How Language Structures Space." In Herbert Pick and Linda Acredolo, eds., *Spatial Orientation: Theory, Research, and Application*, 225–82. New York: Plenum Press.

———. 1985. "Force Dynamics in Language and Thought." In William H. Eilfort, Paul D. Kroeber, and Karen L. Peterson, eds., *Papers from the Parasession on Causatives and Agentivity*, 293–337. Chicago: Chicago Linguistic Society.

———. 1988a. "Force Dynamics in Language and Cognition." *Cognitive Science* 12: 49–100.

———. 1988b. "The Relation of Grammar to Cognition." In Brygida Rudzka-Ostyn, ed., *Topics in Cognitive Linguistics*, 165–205. Amsterdam: John Benjamins.

———. To appear. *How Language Structures Space: Towards a Cognitive Semantics*. Cambridge, Mass.; MIT Press/Bradford.

Tasaku, Tsunoda. 1981. "Split Case-Marking Patterns in Verb-Types and Tense/Aspect/Mood." *Linguistics* 19: 389–438.

Taylor, John R. 1989. *Linguistic Categorization: Prototypes in Linguistic Theory*. Oxford: Clarendon Press.

Tesnière, Lucien. 1959. *Eléments de Syntaxe Structurale*. Paris: Klincksieck.

Thyme, Ann. 1989. "Nominalization in Malagasy: A Cognitive Analysis." *Linguistic Notes from La Jolla* 15: 105–36.

Tuggy, David. 1979. "Tetelcingo Nahuatl." In Ronald W. Langacker, ed., *Studies in Uto-Aztecan Grammar*, vol. 2, *Modern Aztec Grammatical Sketches*, 1–140. Dallas: Summer Institute of Linguistics and University of Texas at Arlington.

———. 1981. *The Transitivity-Related Morphology of Tetelcingo Nahuatl: An Exploration in Space Grammar*. Ph.D. dissertation. San Diego: University of California.

———. 1986. "Noun Incorporations in Nahuatl." *Proceedings of the Annual Meeting of the Pacific Linguistics Conference* 2: 455–69.

———. 1988. "Náhuatl Causative/Applicatives in Cognitive Grammar." In Brygida Rudzka-Ostyn, ed., *Topics in Cognitive Linguistics*, 587–618. Amsterdam: John Benjamins.

Turewicz, Kamila. 1986. *Modal Predicates in English: A Cognitive Approach*. Ph.D. dissertation. Gdansk: University of Gdansk.

Turner, Mark. 1987. *Death is the Mother of Beauty*. Chicago: University of Chicago Press.

van Hoek, Karen. In press. "The Organization of the Yiddish Gender System."

———. To appear. *Paths Through Conceptual Structure: Constraints on Pronominal Anaphora*. Ph.D. dissertation. San Diego: University of California.

van Oosten, Jeanne. 1977. "Subjects and Agenthood in English." *CLS* 13: 459–71.

———. 1986. *The Nature of Subjects, Topics and Agents: A Cognitive Explanation*. Bloomington: Indiana University Linguistics Club.

Vandeloise, Claude. 1984. *Description of Space in French*. Ph.D. dissertation. San Diego: University of California.

———. 1985a. "Au-delà des Descriptions Géométriques et Logiques de l'Espace: Une Description Fonctionnelle." *Lingvisticae Investigationes* 9: 109–29.

———. 1985b. "Les Prépositions *Sur/Sous* et la Relation *Porteur/Porté*." *Leuvense Bijdragen* 74: 457–81.

———. 1986. *L'Espace en Français*. Paris: Editions du Seuil.

———. 1987. "La Préposition *à* et le Principe d'Anticipation." *Langue Française* 76: 77–111.

———. 1988. "Length, Width, and Potential Passing." In Brygida Rudzka-Ostyn, ed., *Topics in Cognitive Linguistics*, 403–27. Amsterdam: John Benjamins.

Wallace, Stephen. 1982. "Figure and Ground: The Interrelationships of Linguistic Categories." In Paul J. Hopper, ed., *Tense-Aspect: Between Semantics & Pragmatics*, 201–23. Amsterdam: John Benjamins.

Wierzbicka, Anna. 1975. "Why 'Kill' does Not Mean 'Cause to Die': The Semantics of Action Sentences." *Foundations of Language* 13: 491–528.

———. 1981. "Case Marking and Human Nature." *Australian Journal of Linguistics* 1: 43–80.

———. 1985. "Oats and Wheat: The Fallacy of Arbitrariness." In John Haiman, ed., *Iconicity in Syntax*, 311–42. Amsterdam: John Benjamins.

———. 1988. *The Semantics of Grammar*. Amsterdam: John Benjamins.

Williams, Edwin. 1981. "On the Notions 'Lexically Related' and 'Head of a Word'." *LI* 12: 245–74.

———. 1987. "English as an Ergative Language: The Theta Structure of Derived Nouns." *CLS* 23: 366–75.

Witherspoon, Gary. 1980. "Language in Culture and Culture in Language." *IJAL* 46: 1–13.

Wittgenstein, Ludwig. 1922. *Tractatus Logico-Philosophicus*. [C. K. Ogden, trans.] London: Routledge and Kegan Paul.

Woodbury, Anthony C. 1977. "Greenlandic Eskimo, Ergativity, and Relational Grammar." In Peter Cole and Jerrold M. Sadock, eds., *Syntax and Semantics*, vol. 8, *Grammatical Relations*, 307–36. New York: Academic Press.

Woodbury, Hanni. 1975. "Onondaga Noun Incorporation: Some Notes on the Interdependence of Syntax and Semantics." *IJAL* 41: 10–20.

Wouk, Fay. 1986. "Transitivity in Batak and Tagalog." *Studies in Language* 10: 391–424.

Zubin, David A., and Klaus-Michael Köpcke. 1986. "Gender and Folk Taxonomy: The Indexical Relation Between Grammatical and Lexical Categorization." In Colette Craig, ed., *Noun Classes and Categorization*, 139–80. Amsterdam: John Benjamins.

Zwicky, Arnold M. 1985. "Heads." *JL* 21: 1–29.

Index

Library of Congress Cataloging-in-Publication Data
(Revised for volume 2)

Langacker, Ronald W.
Foundations of cognitive grammar.

Includes bibliographical references and index.
Contents: v. 1. Theoretical prerequisites—
v. 2. Descriptive application.
1. Cognitive grammar.
P165.L36 1987 84-51300
ISBN 0-8047-1261-1 (v. 1: cl.) : ISBN 0-8047-3851-3 (pbk.)
ISBN 0-8047-1909-8 (v. 2: cl.) : ISBN 0-8047-3852-1 (pbk.)

∞ This book is printed on acid-free paper.

Original printing 1991

The authorized representative in the EU for product safety and compliance is:
Mare Nostrum Group
B.V Doelen 72
4831 GR Breda
The Netherlands

www.ingramcontent.com/pod-product-compliance
Lightning Source LLC
Chambersburg PA
CBHW021804270326
41932CB00007B/53

9780804738521